HIDDEN
HAWAII

Ray Riegert

FOURTEENTH EDITION

Ulysses Press

EXPLORE THE HIDDEN REALM

From its lush forests and tropical pathways to its white-sand beaches and volcanic trails, Hawaii is a land of staggering beauty. Each island boasts its own unique charm, such as Kauai's misty cliffs and valleys, and Lanai's idyllic trails to remote oases. The key to experiencing the islands at their most authentic is to follow the locals' lead and visit unfrequented destinations worthy of true travelers, not tourists. While *Hidden Hawaii* still covers many well-loved and luxurious spots on the islands, its ultimate goal is to guide you to little-known sunwashed beaches and secluded snorkeling coves—spots most visitors never see. With specialized maps, highlighted listings and easy-to-follow directions, you'll be able to go beyond flashy resorts and umbrella drinks to the real island experience, one of luscious gardens, world-class island cuisine and private stretches of paradise.

Madame Pele spits fire into the Pacific Ocean on the Big Island.

CULTURAL SIGHTS

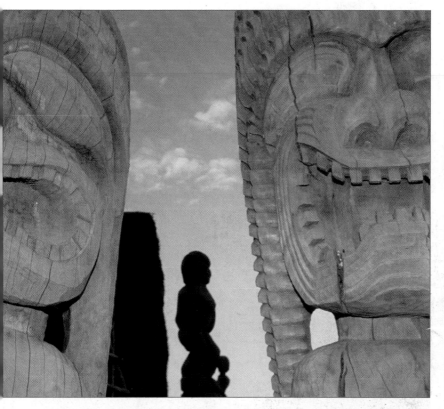

The Big Island's Place of Refuge has long been a sacred locale.

Today, in many Hawaiian neighborhoods, historic traditions are still practiced, continuing to reflect the past in contemporary society. There are also hundreds of sacred *heiau*, ancient temples and mystic ruins scattered throughout the islands, paying tribute to its pre-history. Though these sights are regarded as part of Hawaii's alluring charm, few people venture to them. Many travelers never see native fishermen at work or explore an ancient island shrine. For a truly genuine Hawaiian experience, be sure to stop at these enchanting spots firsthand.

Oahu's **Royal Mausoleum** *(p. 96)* is the burial site of two 19th-century ruling families and is beautifully landscaped with plumerias and ginger. **Iliiliopae Heiau** *(p. 402)* on Molokai, with its rock walls, is an ancient Hawaiian temple. Lanai boasts the **Luahiwa petroglyphs** *(p. 385)*, one of the finest collections of rock carvings in the islands. Kauai's legendary **Menehune Ditch** *(p. 455)* is made of handhewn stones that have long puzzled archaeologists.

BEACHES

In most island communities, the ocean is the focus of daily life and local culture, offering recreation, a way to commune with nature and an important source of food. Catch a taste of authentic island life by lounging on one of the more secluded stretches of sand and watch these activities unfold—or simply bask in your own personal paradise. In the islands you'll find beaches with white, black, green and tan-colored sands, and a few with rocky shores. While some stretch for miles and others frame tiny crescent-shaped coves, the best ones are those you have all to yourself.

Some of the most appealing hidden shorelines include Oahu's **Diamond Head Beach Park** *(p. 110)*, which is physically close to Waikiki but a world away from its crowds. For privacy on Maui, you can't beat the long, narrow strand known as **Black Sands Beach** *(p. 319)*. **Keei Beach** *(p. 219)* offers a nice stretch of sand on what is otherwise a lava-rock shoreline on the Big Island's south Kona Coast. On Kauai, the sand dunes and craggy limestone cliffs add to the dramatic beauty of **Mahaulepu Beach** *(p. 442)*.

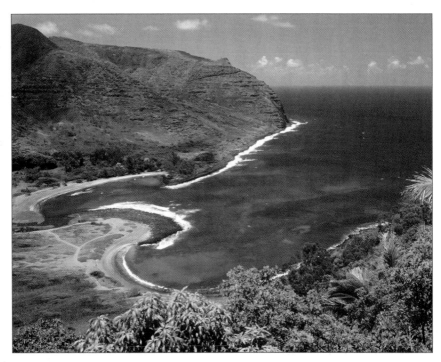

True to its name (Halawa *means curve) is Molokai's Halawa Bay.*

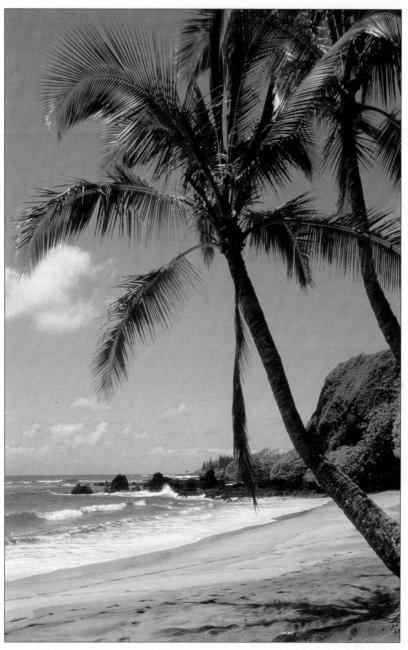

Along the Hana Highway in Maui is powder-soft Hamoa Beach.

BEACHFRONT COTTAGES

Hawaiians formerly lived almost exclusively near the ocean, where it was easy to fish, collect salt, bathe and tend to various crafts, such as preparing the *hala* leaves used in mats and other weavings. They grew crops inland, but most villages were near the sea. While today's comfortable accommodations are a far cry from the simple *pili* grass *hale*, or houses, that Hawaiians once inhabited, staying in a beachfront cottage—instead of a sprawling, impersonal beachfront resort—is still a great way to experience the authentic island lifestyle. You can sit out on your lanai, watch the crashing waves and know that you are doing just what native islanders did a hundred years ago.

On Oahu, the **Ke Iki Beach Bungalows** *(p. 138)* are located right on the beach, between the wintertime big wave breaks of the Banzai Pipeline and Waimea Bay. **The Beach Village** *(p. 417)* on Molokai adds a strong element of luxury to the camping experience with spacious "tenatlows" and queen-sized beds. Lush foliage and swaying coconut palms add to the charm of oceanfront cottages at The **Inn at Mama's Fish House** *(p. 336)* on Maui. For a comfortable throwback to another era, the **Waimea Plantation Cottages** *(p. 458)* is a unique seaside gem on Kauai. If money is no object, pick **Kona Village Resort** *(p. 177)*—a regal retreat set along a white-sand cove on the Big Island.

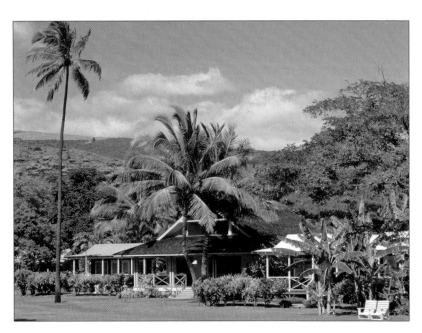

Waimea Plantation Cottages is one of Kauai's most alluring lodgings.

GARDENS

Oahu's Haiku Gardens is revered for its romantic setting.

Much of Hawaii is a natural garden with wild orchids, red-flamed ginger and swaying palms making up the lush landscape. The interior and windward sections of most islands are dense with ferns, flowers and trees that never lose their leaves. In fact, the islands are so conducive to growing that many introduced plants have made it their home. It's surprising that most visitors don't consider a tour of Hawaiian gardens a key stop on their itinerary. Walking amidst dazzling, exotic plants that exist nowhere but the islands is an experience unto itself.

If you're looking for some especially worthwhile gems that are also off the beaten track, start with **Queen Kapiolani Hibiscus Garden** *(p. 64)* on Oahu. With its colorful flowerbeds and shady pavilion, it's an oasis in busy Waikiki. To understand the cultural value of plants, visit the distinctive **Amy B. H. Greenwell Ethnobotanical Garden** *(p. 209)* on the Big Island's Kona Coast. On Kauai, **Kukuiolono Park** *(p. 453)* in Kalaheo offers otherworldly views and a sweet Japanese garden, complete with a stone bridge. For a hidden floral fantasy on Maui, **Enchanting Floral Garden** *(p. 345)* is the place.

HAWAII REGIONAL CUISINE

The blend of Hawaii's cultural diversity and the bountiful fresh fish, game animals, vegetables and tropical fruit of the islands gave rise to a distinct style of cooking known as Hawaii Regional or Pacific Rim cuisine. It's expressed in both true Hawaiian classics, such as *imu*-roasted pig, *laulau*, and *poi*, and creative Asian-influenced menus that combine fresh, local ingredients into palate-pleasing meals. The islands are *the* place to try delicate fish like *opah* paired with mango chutney, cheesecake served with tangy-sweet passionfruit sauce. For a unique cultural experience, indulge in these lush, upscale flavors as they're prepared by chefs who have made a name for themselves around the world.

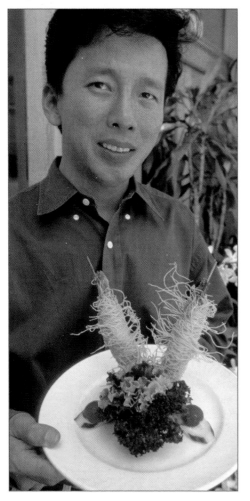

One of the first places to feature Hawaii Regional Cuisine was **Roy's Restaurant** *(p. 115)* on Oahu. The setting is unassuming, but the food is wildly innovative. On Maui, **Haliimaile General Store** *(p. 350)* has converted an old store from the plantation era into a chic eatery with a creative menu based on local ingredients. **Beach House Restaurant** *(p. 448)* on Kauai serves island-inspired taste treats, while offering an ideal sunset view. **Merriman's** *(p. 205)* introduced the Big Island to Pacific Rim cuisine years ago and continues to please the taste buds.

Chai's Island Bistro in Honolulu features dishes such as these Kataifi tiger prawns.

LOCAL-STYLE CUISINE

Food is a big part of life in Hawaii, where eating is both a popular pastime and a way to share cultures. And when it comes to living local, nothing beats a classic plate lunch. These hearty, informal meals are enjoyed any time of the day or night and invariably feature two scoops of rice. The other items may vary from teriyaki beef to fried fish, with various side dishes. They're typically packaged to go and sold from numerous hole-in-the-wall eateries frequented by loyal diners. You can also savor the native island flavors while enjoying a taste of culture at a community-sponsored *luau* where all the classic favorites are available for a cheap, flat price.

For a bite of island flavor go to **Giovanni's Aloha Shrimp Truck** *(p. 139)* on Oahu where they elevate the plate lunch to a higher standard, serving shrimp prepared three ways from the back of a lunch wagon. Visit **Kalena Fish Market** *(p. 434)* for the best plate lunch in Lihue—breaded

Hamura's Saimin diner in Kauai serves island favorites.

mahimahi, *laulau* and *kalua* pig with cabbage, marinated bean sprouts and *kim chee*. **Hamura Saimin** *(p. 433)* has a spectacular *"saimin* special," a combination of noodles, wontons, eggs, meat, onion, vegetables and fish cake in a delicious broth. For a traditional island breakfast hit **Molokai Drive Inn** *(p. 407)*, which serves shrimp omelettes, fried rice, banana pancakes, as well as eggs and spam.

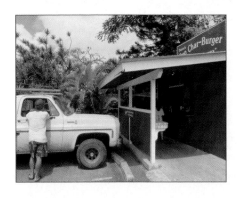

Duane's Ono Char Burger is an Anahola classic.

SHOPPING/
HANDMADE CRAFTS

You can shop everywhere in the islands, from your hotel's boutique to the strands of shops lining popular boulevards, and each place will overflow with bright tropical souvenirs. But instead of perusing the monotonous aisles of mainstream stores, browse the shops stocked with locally made items for a much more authentic island experience. Hawaii boasts numerous products unique to the islands, including the tiny Niihau shells strung into beautiful necklaces, handmade ukuleles, bowls crafted from native woods, as well as clothing and quilts sewn from colorful island prints. Hawaii's ethereal light and laid-back lifestyle attracts many artists and crafters, whose inspired creations can be found at galleries and fairs throughout the islands.

A selection of traditional and contemporary crafts, including carved *koa* wood bowls and Niihau shell leis, can be found at the **Little Hawaiian Crafts Shop** *(p. 76)* on Oahu. At **Kahanahou Hawaiian Foundation** *(p. 218)*, a Big Island apprentice school teaching Hawaiians native arts, you can purchase handwrought hula drums as well as other authentic crafts. The **Maui Crafts Guild** *(p. 341)* showcases a wide range of items, including ceramics, jewelry and baskets. **Kapaia Stitchery** *(p. 436)* on Kauai is an excellent place to purchase Hawaiian quilts, many made by local women.

Beautiful handcrafted leis are sold throughout the islands.

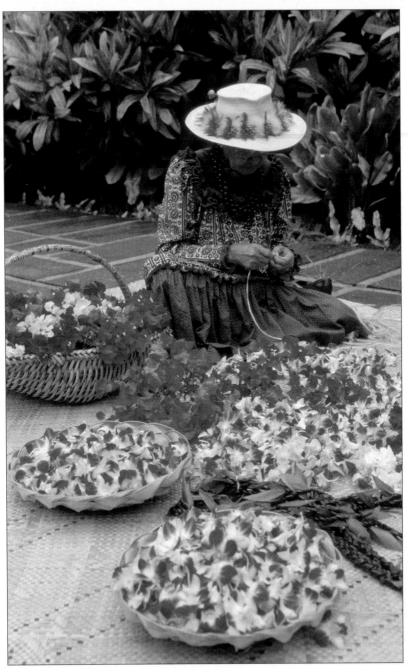

In Honolulu, a woman makes leis by hand.

SURFING

Surfing began as the sport of kings in Hawaii, where the *alii*, or chiefs, rode the legendary waves of these Pacific islands on heavy, hand-carved boards. Today, Hawaii is still famous for its surf spots, which range from small waves for kids and beginners to towering mountains of water that even professional surfers find daunting. With the large number of *hodads* crowding tourist beaches and clamoring for their shot at a wave, it's best to slip away to one of the hidden locales. Mastering your technique at one of these secluded breaks allows you to "hang ten" in your own private corner of paradise.

You'll be most likely to miss the crowds on Oahu at **Hawaiian Electric Beach Park** *(p. 153)*, where "Tracks" is a top break for experienced surfers. On the Big Island, south of Hilo Bay, **Richardson Ocean Park** *(p. 245)* offers good body surfing, boogie boarding and board surfing in the winter. It's a long paddle out to "Infinities," the break at remote **Pakala Beach** *(p. 463)* on Kauai's west side, but the long rides are worth it. The best breaks on Molokai can be found at the secluded beaches on the east end, including **Kumimi Beach** *(p. 409)* and **Poha-kuloa Point** *(p. 409)*, which is the top surf spot on the island.

Lahaina Surfing School students practice their technique.

SNORKELING

Tunnels Beach on Kauai is a spectacular snorkeling spot.

Snorkeling in Hawaiian waters is akin to floating in a teeming aquarium of rare species. The offshore reefs abound with colorful blue and green spectacled parrotfish and rainbow-colored lagoon triggerfish—just to name a few. You can't go anywhere else in the world to see some of these underwater creatures: 25 percent of the fish swimming here can only be found on the reefs in this volcanic paradise. You may be lucky enough to hang out with ancient sea turtles, or skim the waves with a few spinner dolphins. But you can't slip freely through the water if you're caught in a tourist crowd. Escape the masses and glide through open ocean in one of the many tranquil coves dotting the islands. From the Big Island's remote black-sand beaches to Oahu's vast and varied oceanfront strands, secluded inlets are easily found if you know where to look.

Tunnels Beach *(p. 497)*, the favored surfing spot on Kauai's North Shore, offers a technicolor treat when the waters are calm between May and September. Maui's little-known **Honolua Bay** *(p. 302)* along Hono-apilani Highway promises magnificent underwater views, and as part of a marine life preserve, it guarantees great sightings. On the Big Island, you can dip into **Keei Beach** *(p. 219)* and experience what Hawaiians have been viewing for centuries: spectacular schools of fish and exotic coral formations. These are just a few of the hidden underwater treasures awaiting you.

HIKING

Along with the powdery beaches and cool ocean waters, the islands are revered for their lush rainforests, dark volcanic landscapes, abundant tropical flowers and unusual wildlife—parts of nature best enjoyed by hiking through them at a meditative pace. You can trek through bamboo forests and stroll beside a lava barrier in the same day, while catching glimpses of exotic island birds. While eucalyptus branches crack beneath your feet and red honeycreepers soar overhead, you'll be mesmerized by the natural beauty—and by the details you discover miles from the tourist crowds. Few other places in the world afford the opportunity to reach a mountain summit and find a tropical paradise on all sides.

Mauka and *makai*—mountains and ocean—come together at the 5,228-acre paradise known as **Ahupuaa O Kahana State Park** *(p. 130)* on Oahu. On Kauai, you'll find rugged trails, forests and dramatic ocean and canyon views in the cool uplands of **Kokee State Park** *(p. 466)*. **Kepaniwai County Park and Heritage Gardens** *(p. 322)* on Maui offers Japanese gardens, a traditional taro patch and easy hiking trails against a backdrop of sheer cliffs. On the Big Island, taro farms and tropical foliage edge the shoreline of **Waipio Beach** *(p. 253)*. A nice swimming area and rocky coastline, along with shady grove of *kiawe* trees, characterize **Kawakiu Beach** *(p. 419)* on Molokai.

These falls above Hanakapiai Beach are along the Na Pali Coast.

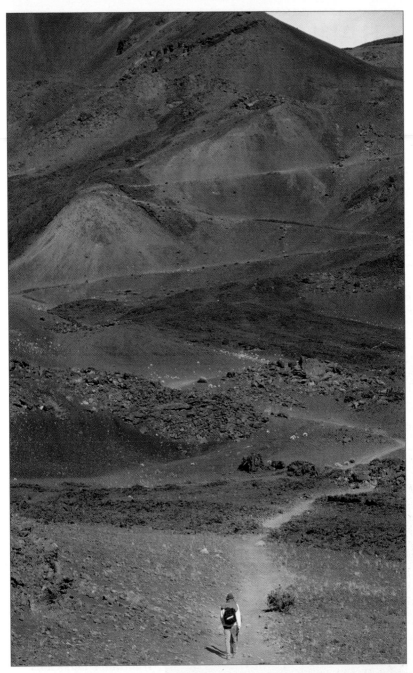

Haleakala Crater is the world's largest dormant volcano.

HAWAIIAN MUSIC

Traditionally, making music in the islands is an informal affair known as *kanikapila*. It works like this: a couple of people start playing music, then other folks stop by and join in, strumming a ukulele or guitar, plucking a washtub bass, adding their voices to the chorus. Today, this tradition remains very much alive, with tropical shirt–clad trios performing at local haunts, encouraging crowds to sing along. Rather than settling for the hotel lounge's radio serenade, stroll down to a hidden spot for a local beer and experience the real thing. While professional performances are more polished, they still retain the casual, low-key feel of a backyard or beach park music session.

On Oahu, the ocean view, tropical décor and nightly Hawaiian music at **Mai Tai Bar** *(p. 78)* make for a classic evening in the islands. A similar waterfront scene can be found at **Kimo's** *(p. 284)* on Maui, where the

sunset view is a special bonus. The best bet for a truly tropical experience and giant mai tais on Kauai can be found at the funky **Tahiti Nui** *(p. 493)*, with a wide porch made just for hanging out. On the Big Island, **Bamboo Restaurant** *(p. 198)* provides tropical drinks and mellow island music to match.

Traditional musicians play ukuleles in Oahu.

HIDDEN
HAWAII

*Including Oahu, Maui, Kauai, Lanai,
Molokai, and the Big Island*

Ray Riegert

FOURTEENTH EDITION

"A bible."
—Honolulu Advertiser

"The perfect choice for the visitor who wants an active
vacation in the islands."
—Travel & Leisure

"Riegert's adventures are crammed with fascinating insider's advice."
—Los Angeles Times

"Unlike many guides that claim to offer inside information,
this one actually delivers."
—Vancouver Sun

"Paints a vivid picture of each island's history, natural wonders
and unique qualities."
—Travel Holiday

Ulysses Press
BERKELEY, CALIFORNIA

Published by: ULYSSES PRESS
                 P.O. Box 3440
                 Berkeley, CA 94703
                 www.ulyssespress.com

ISSN 1097-3222
ISBN-10 1-56975-616-3
ISBN-13 978-156975-616-4

Printed in Canada by Transcontinental Printing

40 39 38 37 36 35 34 33

UPDATE AUTHOR: Joan Conrow
EDITORIAL DIRECTOR: Leslie Henriques
MANAGING EDITOR: Claire Chun
PROJECT DIRECTOR: Elyce Petker
EDITORIAL ASSOCIATES: Lauren Harrison, Emma Silvers, Abigail Reser, Amy Hough, Laurel Shane, Gail Bailey, Ruth Marcus, Emily Reed, Amber Hogue
PRODUCTION: Judith Metzener, Lisa Kester, Steven Schwartz
CARTOGRAPHY: Pease Press
HIDDEN BOOKS DESIGN: what!design @ whatweb.com
INDEXER: Sayre Van Young
COVER PHOTOGRAPHY: Douglas Peebles
COLOR INSERT: Robert Holmes Photography
CONTRIBUTING WRITERS: Leslie Henriques, Elyce Petker

Distributed by Publishers Group West

To Jim Chanin,
for years of friendship

ACKNOWLEDGMENTS

Since this book is now entering its fourteenth edition, there are several generations of people to thank. The person to whom I owe the deepest gratitude has been working on the project since the very beginning. I met my wife Leslie when I first arrived in the islands to write *Hidden Hawaii*. Since then she has contributed to the book as an editor, writer, researcher and innovator. Her energy and spirit have been an inspiration throughout.

The current edition results from the efforts of several people. Claire Chun skillfully shepherded the book through many stages. Elyce Petker worked her magic as the project director. My wife Leslie devoted her talents to the cover design (while I'm at it, Leslie deserves an extra thanks for all her help with the researching and writing of this edition); Douglas Peebles submitted a terrific cover photo; and Robert Holmes provided outstanding interior photos. Bryce Willett, Steven Schwartz, Lee Micheaux, Mark Woodworth, Judith Metzener and Lisa Kester contributed significantly to the project. Lauren Harrison, Emma Silvers, Abigail Reser, Amy Hough, Laurel Shane, Gail Bailey, Ruth Marcus, Emily Reed and Amber Hogue aided and abetted with research and other matters large and small.

Special thanks are also due to those friends from long ago who worked on the very first *Hidden Hawaii*—Sayre Van Young, Peter Beren, Suellen Ethnebuske, John Orfali, Phil Gardner and Carlene Schnabel, Jen-Ann Kirchmeier and Marlyn Amann. To all of them, I want to extend a *mahalo nui loa*—thank you a thousand times for your *kokua*.

CONTENTS

MAPS

OUTDOOR ADVENTURE SYMBOLS

The following symbols accompany national, state and regional park listings, as well as beach descriptions throughout the text.

▲	Camping	🎿	Waterskiing
🏃	Hiking	🏄	Windsurfing
🚲	Biking	🛶	Kayaking/Canoeing
🏊	Swimming	🚤	Boating
🤿	Snorkeling or Scuba Diving	🚤	Boat ramps
🏄	Surfing	🎣	Fishing

HIDDEN LISTINGS

Throughout the book, listings that reveal the hidden realm—spots that are away from tourists or reflect authentic Hawaii—are marked by this icon:

There are also special maps at the start of each section that guide you to some of these hidden listings. Each place is identified with this symbol:

PREFACE

Hawaii. What images does the word bring to mind? Crystal blue waters against a white sand beach. Palm trees swaying in a soft ocean breeze. Volcanic mountains rising in the hazy distance. Bronzed beach boys and luscious Polynesian women. Serenity. Luxury. Paradise.

To many it conjures still another dream—the perfect vacation. There is no more beautiful hideaway than this spectacular chain of tropical islands. For over a century Hawaii has been the meeting place of East and West, a select spot among savvy travelers. These adventurers are attracted not by Hawaii's famed tourist resorts—which are usually crowded and expensive—but by the opportunity to travel naturally and at low cost to an exotic locale.

As you'll find in the following pages, it is possible to tour economically through Hawaii's major sightseeing centers. It's even easier to explore the archipelago's more secluded realms. Few people realize that most of Hawaii's land is either rural or wilderness, and there's no price tag on the countryside. You can flee the multitudes and skip the expense by heading into the islands' endless backcountry. And if you venture far enough, you'll learn the secret that lies at the heart of this book: The less money you spend, the more likely you are to discover paradise.

Quite simply, that's the double-barreled purpose of *Hidden Hawaii*—to save you dollars while leading you to paradise. Whatever you're after, you should be able to find it right here. When you want to relax amid the comforts of civilization, this book will show you good restaurants, comfortable hotels, quaint shops and intriguing nightspots.

When you're ready to depart the beaten track, *Hidden Hawaii* will guide you to untouched beaches, remote campsites, underwater grottoes and legendary fishing holes. It will take you to the Pacific's greatest surfing beaches, on hiking trails across live volcanoes, into flower-choked jungles, through desert canyons and up to the top of the world's most massive mountain.

Hidden Hawaii is a handbook for living both in town and in the wild. The first chapter covers the nuts and bolts—how to get to the islands, what to bring and what to expect when you arrive. Chapter Two prepares you for outdoor life—swimming, hiking, camping and skindiving. The third chapter, covering Hawaii's history and language, will familiarize you with the rich tropical culture.

The last six chapters describe individual islands. Each island is divided geographically. Here you'll find specific information on sightseeing, hotels, restaurants, shops, nightspots and beaches.

This book is not intended for those tourists in plastic leis who plop down on a Waikiki beach, toast for two weeks, then claim they've seen Hawaii when all they've really seen is some bizarre kind of Pacific Disneyland. No, *Hidden Hawaii* is for adventurers: people who view a vacation not as an escape from everyday routine, but rather as an extension of the most exciting aspects of their daily lives. People who travel to faraway places to learn more about their own homes. Folks like you and me who want to sit back and relax, but also seek to experience and explore.

Ray Riegert

No alien land in all the world has any deep, strong charm for me but that one, no other land could so longingly and so beseechingly haunt me, sleeping and waking, through half a lifetime, as that one has done. Other things leave me, but it abides; other things change, but it remains the same. . . . In my nostrils still lives the breath of flowers that perished twenty years ago.

—Mark Twain, 1889

ALOHA STATE

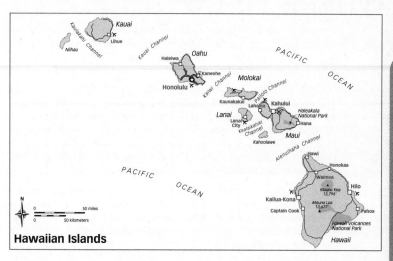

Hawaiian Islands

Hawaii is an archipelago that stretches more than 1500 miles across the North Pacific Ocean. Composed of 132 islands, it has eight major islands, clustered at the southeastern end of the chain. Together these larger islands are about the size of Connecticut and Rhode Island combined.

Each island, in a sense, is a small continent. Volcanic mountains rise in the interior, while the coastline is fringed with coral reefs and white-sand beaches. In the parlance of the Pacific, they are "high islands," very different from the low-lying atolls found elsewhere in Polynesia.

The northeastern face of each island, buffeted by trade winds, is the wet side. The contrast between this side and an island's southwestern sector is sometimes startling. Dense rainforests in the northeast are teeming with exotic tropical plants, while across the island you're liable to see cactus growing in a barren landscape!

Deciding to take a vacation in Hawaii is easy; the hard part comes when you have to choose which islands to visit. All six are remarkably beautiful places, each with unique features to offer the traveler. Eventually, you should try to tour them all, but on a single trip you'll probably choose only one, two or three. Traveling to more in the course of a typical vacation is counterproductive.

To help you decide which to see, I'll briefly describe the key features of each. For more detailed information, you can turn to the introductory notes in each of the island chapters.

My personal favorites are the Big Island and Kauai, the easternmost and westernmost islands in the chain, and I often recommend to friends unfamiliar with Hawaii that they visit these two islands. That way they manage to travel to both ends of the chain, experiencing the youngest and most rugged, and the oldest and most lush, of all the islands. The two offer a startling contrast, one that quickly shatters any illusion that all the islands are alike.

WHERE TO GO

Oahu, Hawaii's most populous island, is dominated by the capital city of Honolulu. Featuring the Waikiki tourist center, this is the most heavily touristed island. It's too crowded for many visitors. But Oahu is a prime place to mix city living with country exploring. It's also rich in history, culture and beautiful beaches.

The island of **Hawaii**, or the Big Island, is true to its nickname. Located at the southeastern end of the Hawaiian chain, and dominated by two 13,000-foot volcanoes, this giant measures more than twice the size of all the other islands combined. It's a great place to mountain climb and explore live volcanoes, to snorkel along the sun-splashed Kona Coast, or to tour orchid farms in the verdant city of Hilo.

Maui, the second largest island, is one of Hawaii's favorite destinations for first-time visitors. Haleakala alone, the extraordinary crater that dominates the island, makes the "Valley Isle" worth touring. The island also sports many of Hawaii's nicest beaches and provides an offshore breeding ground for rare humpback whales.

Directly to the west, lying in Maui's wind shadow, sits the third smallest and most secluded island. **Lanai** is an explorer's paradise, with a network of jeep trails leading to hidden beaches and scenic mountain ridges. There are only 3200 people and about 20 miles of paved road here. If you are seeking an idyllic retreat, this is the place.

Molokai, slightly larger but nearly as remote, provides another extraordinary hideaway. With white-sand beaches, a mountainous interior and a large population of Hawaiians, the "Friendly Isle" retains a unique sense of old Hawaii. Here you can visit a former leper colony on the windswept Kalaupapa Peninsula, a pilgrimage that could prove to be the most inspiring of all your experiences in Hawaii.

The oldest island in the chain, **Kauai** is also the archipelago's prettiest, most luxuriant island. Located at the northwestern end of the chain, it is filled with jewel-like beaches and uninhabited valleys. Along the north shore are misty cliffs that fall precipitously to the sea; from the island's center rises a mountain that receives more rainfall than any place on earth; and along Kauai's southern flank there's a startling desert region reminiscent of the Southwest.

Only seven of the major islands are inhabited: the eighth, Kahoolawe, although sacred to Hawaiians, was used for decades as a bombing range for the U.S. Navy, then was finally turned over to the state of Hawaii in 1994. The seventh island, Niihau, is inhabited but is privately owned and off-limits to the public.

The islands are located 2500 miles southwest of Los Angeles, on the same 20th latitude as Hong Kong and Mexico City. It's two hours earlier

in Hawaii than in Los Angeles, four hours before Chicago and five
hours earlier than New York. Since Hawaii does not practice daylight-
saving, their time difference becomes one hour greater during the
summer months.

3

WHEN TO GO

SEASONS

There are two types of seasons in Hawaii, one keyed to tourists and the
other to the climate. The peak tourist seasons run from mid-December
until Easter, then again from mid-June through Labor Day. Particularly
around the Christmas holidays and in August, the island are crowded.
Prices increase, hotel rooms and rental cars become harder to reserve,
and everything moves a bit more rapidly. Shop around, however; package deals that include discounts on published rates are available.

If you plan to explore Hawaii during these seasons, make reservations
several months in advance; actually, it's a good idea to make advance
reservations whenever you visit. Without doubt, the off-season is the
best time to hit the islands. Not only are hotels more readily available,
but campsites and hiking trails are also less crowded.

Climatologically, the ancient Hawaiians distinguished between two
seasons—*kau*, or summer, and *hooilo*, or winter. Summer extends from
May to October, when the sun is overhead and the temperatures are
slightly higher. Winter brings more variable winds and cooler weather.

The important rule to remember about Hawaii's beautiful weather is
that it changes very little from season to season but varies dramatically
from place to place. The average yearly temperature is about 78°, and
during the coldest weather in January and the warmest in August, the
thermometer rarely moves more than 5° or 6° in either direction.
Similarly, sea water temperatures range comfortably between 74° and
80° year-round.

Seeking a cooler climate? Head up to the mountains; for every thousand
feet in elevation, the temperature drops about 3°F. If you climb high
enough on Maui or the Big Island, you might even encounter snow!

Crucial to this luxurious semitropical environment is the trade wind
that blows with welcome regularity from the northeast, providing a
natural form of air-conditioning. When the trades stop blowing, they
are sometimes replaced by *kona* winds carrying rain and humid
weather from the southwest. These are most frequent in the winter,
when the Hawaiian islands receive their heaviest rainfall.

While summer showers are less frequent and shorter in duration, winter storms are sometimes quite nasty. I've seen it pour for five consecutive days, until hiking trails disappeared and city streets were awash. If
you visit in winter, particularly from December to March, you're risking
the chance of rain.

A wonderful factor to remember through this wet weather is that if it's raining where you are, you can often simply go someplace else. And I don't mean another part of the world, or even a different island. Since the rains generally batter the northeastern sections of each island, you can usually head over to the south or west coast for warm, sunny weather.

Sometimes nasty weather engulfs the entire chain, but there's usually a sunny refuge somewhere. I once spent a strenuous period along the Kona Coast working on a suntan. Across the island near Hilo, flood warnings were up. Twenty-five inches of rain dropped in 24 hours; five feet of water fell in seven days. Toward the end of the week, when my major problem was whether the tan would peel, officials in Hilo declared a state of emergency.

CALENDAR OF EVENTS

Something else to consider in planning a visit to Hawaii is the amazing lineup of annual cultural events. For a thumbnail idea of what's happening when, check the calendar below. You might just find that special occasion to climax an already dynamic vacation. For a comprehensive listing with current updates, check the Hawaii Visitors & Convention Bureau website at www.gohawaii.com.

JANUARY
Early January At **Maui's Annual Festival of Hula** local hula *halaus* compete for Halau of the Year.

During January Occurring at various sites on the Big Island, Kauai and Oahu, the **Sanctuary Ocean Count** is an annual shore-based census of humpback whales during the breeding season.

Mid-January or February The month-long **Narcissus Festival** begins with the Chinese New Year. During the weeks of festivities, there are open houses, street parties and parades in Honolulu's Chinatown.

FEBRUARY
Early February Usher in **Chinese New Year** with Lahaina locals: a colorful lion dance, food booths, Chinese calligraphy and the traditional fireworks are among the festivities.

February through March The Japanese community celebrates its **Cherry Blossom Festival** in Honolulu with tea ceremonies, kabuki theater presentations, martial arts demonstrations and crafts exhibits.

Late February The annual **Whale Day Celebration** on Maui includes food by Maui's top chefs, a Hawaiian craft fair and a carnival for the kids. On Kauai, rodeo events, lei making and ukulele contests, entertainment, food booths and a canoe race are all part of the **Waimea Town Celebration**.

MARCH
During March **Art Maui** is a month-long juried art show featuring new work by local artists.

Mid-March Celebrate the "Mother of Hawaii" with exhibits, entertainment and storytelling at Maui's **Queen Kaahumanu Festival**.

March 26 Major festivities on Kauai mark the **Prince Kuhio Festival**, commemorating the birthdate of Prince Jonah Kuhio Kalanianaole, Hawaii's first delegate to the U.S. Congress.

Late March/Early April The **East Maui Taro Festival** in Hana celebrates taro, the staple of the Hawaiian diet, with exhibits, lectures, music, hula, and, of course, food. For the eco- and creative-minded, the Kaahumanu Center in Kahului, Maui, sponsors the **Trash Art Show**, a glimpse into the wonders of—what else—trash art.

APRIL

The week-long **Merrie Monarch Festival** on the Big Island pays tribute to David Kalakaua, Hawaii's last king. Festivities include musical performances, pageants and a parade. Buddhist temples on all the islands mark **Buddha Day**, the luminary's birthday, with special services. Included among the events are pageants, dances and flower festivals. Maui's annual birthday party for **Lahaina's Banyan** honors the famous tree with cake and exhibits.

MAY

During May **Molokai Ka Hula Piko** marks the birth of hula on Molokai. Hula dancers, local musicians and Hawaiian craftspeople display their many talents. Held for four weekends in May (and sometimes in June), the **50th State Fair** in Oahu features agricultural exhibits, food stalls, dances, music and displays of island arts and crafts. On Maui, the **Maui Classical Music Festival** features chamber music by internationally acclaimed artists.

May 1 **Lei Day** is celebrated in the islands by people wearing flower leis and colorful Hawaiian garb. In Oahu's Kapiolani Park, there are pageants and concerts.

Mid-May Maui's **Mother's Day Orchid Show** presents award-winning orchids. The **Maui Music Festival** fills two days and nights with jazz at the Kaanapali resort.

Late May The Molokai **Ka Hula Piko Festival** honors Maunaloa's art form with hula performances.

JUNE

During June In Honolulu, the music, dance and customs of more than 40 Pacific Rim areas are showcased at the annual **International Festival of the Pacific**. This two-week event features performers from American Samoa, New Zealand, Guam and Hawaii. Also on Oahu, the **Aloha State Games**, featuring Olympic-style events, take place statewide. *Halaus* from around the world participate in Oahu's **Annual King Kamehameha Hula Competition**. Staged at the Eddie Tam Complex in Makawao, the **Upcountry Fair** is where the 4-H crowd swings into action. Enjoy the live entertainment and local delicacies and, if you're an aspiring performer, don't miss the Star Search. On

Kauai, a barbecue and jam session get things rolling at the **Kauai Cowboy Round-up** in Waimea; this week-long celebration of cowboy culture culminates with the **Paniolo Challenge and Mule Races**.

June 10–11 **King Kamehameha Day**, honoring Hawaii's first king, is celebrated on all six islands with parades, chants, hula dances and exhibits.

Mid-June In Lahaina, the annual **Shapers Phoai Na Keiki Nalu** showcases surfers under 12.

June through August On Oahu and the other islands, Buddhists perform colorful **Bon Dances** every weekend to honor the dead.

JULY
During July On the Big Island, the **Hilo Orchid Society Flower Show** is a showy demonstration of tropical colors. On Maui, more than 100 different wines from California, Oregon and Washington, as well as Australia, are sampled at the **Kapalua Wine & Food Symposium**. The **Pineapple Festival**, held in Lanai City, features contemporary Hawaiian music, pineapple cooking contests and arts and crafts.

Early July "Cowboy Town" Makawao, in Maui's ranchland, promotes its **Parade & Rodeo** as a Maui-style Fourth of July.

Late July **Bayfest**, one of Oahu's biggest music festivals, presents three days of nationally known and local artists as well as a midway with rides and games. On Kauai, Poipu celebrates its sugar heritage with **Koloa Plantation Days**, a week-long event featuring a sunset block party, ethnic cooking demonstrations, a rodeo, nature walks, a Polynesian revue and a parade through old Koloa Town. In addition to a raw onion-eating contest, the **Maui Onion Festival** features food booths, live music, a farmers' market and an onion recipe contest.

AUGUST
During August On Oahu, you can see the dramatic **Surf & Sea Cup Haleiwa**, a one-mile ocean swim from Haleiwa Beach Park to Puena Point and back, which draws more than 350 swimmers. In Honolulu, dancers six to twelve years old gather to compete in the **Queen Liliuokalani Keiki Hula Festival**.

Early August The annual **Hawaiian International Billfish Tournament** spans five days in Kona, Hawaii, with teams from throughout the world hunting for the largest Pacific blue marlin in an intense fishing competition.

August 21 Local residents celebrate **Admission Day**, the date in 1959 when Hawaii became the 50th state.

Late August The **Kauai County Fair** runs for four days, offering a garden show, livestock, exhibits, crafts, entertainment and carnival rides.

SEPTEMBER
During September The six-person **Hana Relay**, a 52-mile Maui swim from Kahului to Hana, is one of autumn's more challenging events. The **Haleakala Run to the Sun** is a 36-mile run from the ocean to the 10,023-

foot peak of Haleakala. Molokai's **Bankoh Na Wahine** draws canoers from around the world for a grueling race from Molokai to Oahu.

Early September The **Queen Liliuokalani Canoe Regatta** is staged on Oahu. Everyone keeps their eyes on Maui's **Wilson Kapalua Open Tennis Tournament**; it has Hawaii's largest tennis purse. A six-person relay across the nine-mile channel from Lanai to Kaanapali draws 50 international teams to the **Maui Channel Relay Swim**.

Late September The **Hawaii County Fair** in Hilo on the Big Isle features an orchid show, steer show, lei contest, agricultural displays, plus exhibits of Hawaiian arts and crafts. The **Maui Marathon** is run from the Kaahumanu Shopping Center in Kahului to Kaanapali. Participants vie in hula, song-writing and slack-key guitar competitions during the week-long **Kauai Mokihana Festival**.

Late September and during October The highlight of Hawaii's cultural season is the **Aloha Week Festival**, a series of week-long celebrations featuring parades, street parties and pageants. Each week, a different island stages the festival and the entire sequence ends with a **Molokai-to-Oahu Canoe Race**. The **Maui County Fair** features agricultural exhibits and arts-and-crafts displays at the Wailuku War Memorial Complex.

OCTOBER
During October The **Honolulu Orchid Show** in Honolulu presents thousands of orchids and other tropical plants. The **Kaanapali Classic tournament** on Maui draws top stars from the PGA Tour.

Mid-October The **Ironman Triathlon World Championship** on the Big Island tests the stamina of the world's best-conditioned athletes. The **Emalani Festival** commemorates Queen Emma's historic trek up Kauai's Waimea Canyon and into the Alakai Swamp with a royal procession, authentic hula, traditional Hawaiian music and exhibits at Kokee State Park.

Late October **Halloween in Lahaina** is a memorable street party with a parade, food fair, music and dancing on Front Street.

NOVEMBER
Early November The Big Island's **Kona Coffee Cultural Festival** celebrates the coffee harvest with a parade, international food bazaar and musical entertainment.

During November **Hula O Na Keiki**, a children's hula performance on Maui, gives prizes for top performers in traditional and modern forms of the dance. Surfers and landlubbers alike gather for the **Hawaiian Pro Surfing Championships** on Oahu. The **Aloha Classic Windsurfing** at Hookipa Beach on Maui is a key event during the Pro Boardsailing Association World Tour.

November through December The world's greatest surfers compete on Oahu's north shore in a series of contests including the **Pipeline Masters**, **World Cup of Surfing** and the **Vans Triple Crown of Surfing**.

1 ALOHA STATE CALENDAR OF EVENTS

With 20-foot waves and prize money topping $50,000, these are spectacular events.

DECEMBER

During December **Honolulu City Lights** at Honolulu's City Hall marks the Christmas season. Maui celebrates with arts and crafts, music and dance at the **Na Mele O Maui Festival**. On Molokai, local communities take turns hosting Christmas crafts fairs. Oahu puts on the two-day **Pacific Handcrafters Guild Christmas Festival** at Thomas Square Park featuring over 110 arts and crafts vendors.

Early December Buddha's enlightenment is commemorated on all the islands with **Bodhi Day** ceremonies and religious services. Along Lihue's main drag, **Lights on Rice** is a quaint marching parade of lighted floats, and horses, dogs and bands that culminates in a Christmas-tree lighting at Kauai's historic County Building, which is decked out with an extensive, unique folk-art ornament collection that remains on display throughout the holidays.

Mid-December Runners by the thousands turn out for the **Honolulu Marathon**.

BEFORE YOU GO

VISITORS CENTERS

HAWAII VISITORS & CONVENTION BUREAU ⊠ *State Headquarters, 2270 Kalakaua Avenue, Suite 801, Honolulu* ☎ *808-923-1811, 800-464-2924* ⏴ *www.go hawaii.com, info@hvcb.org* This state-run agency is a valuable resource from which to obtain free information on the islands. With branches on each of the islands, the Bureau can help plan your trip and then offer advice once you reach Hawaii.

Oahu ⊠ *733 Bishop Street, Suite 1520, Honolulu* ☎ *808-524-0722, 877-525-6248* ⏴ *www.visit-oahu.com*

Big Island ⊠ *250 Keawe Street, Hilo* ☎ *808-961-5797; and* ⊠ *250 Waikoloa Beach Drive, Suite B-15, Waikoloa* ☎ *808-886-1655*

Maui ⊠ *1727 Wili Pa Loop, Wailuku* ☎ *808-244-3530* ⏴ *www.visitmaui.com*

Kauai ⊠ *4334 Rice Street, Suite 101, Lihue* ☎ *808-245-3971* ⏴ *www.kauaivisitorsbureau.com*

Molokai ⊠ *P.O. Box 960, Kaunakaki* ☎ *808-553-3876* ⏴ *www.molokai-hawaii.com*

Lanai ⊠ *431 Seventh Street, Suite A, Lanai City* ☎ *808-565-7600* ⏴ *www.visitlanai.com*

PACKING

When I get ready to pack for a trip, I sit down and make a list of everything I'll need. It's a very slow, exact procedure: I look in closets, drawers and shelves, and run through in my mind the activities in which I'll participate, determining which items are required for each. After all the planning is complete and when I have the entire inventory collected in one long list, I sit for a minute or two, basking in my wisdom and forethought.

Then I tear the hell out of the list, cut out the ridiculous items I'll never use, halve the number of spares among the necessary items, and reduce the entire contents of my suitcase to the bare essentials.

Before I developed this packing technique, I once traveled overland from London to New Delhi carrying two suitcases and a knapsack. I lugged those damned bundles onto trains, buses, jitneys, taxis and rickshaws. When I reached Turkey, I started shipping things home, but by then I was buying so many market goods that it was all I could do to keep even.

I ended up carrying so much crap that one day, when I was sardined in a crowd pushing its way onto an Indian train, someone managed to pick my pocket. When I felt the wallet slipping out, not only was I unable to chase the culprit—I was so weighted down with baggage that I couldn't even turn around to see who was robbing me!

I'll never travel that way again, and neither should you. Particularly when visiting Hawaii, where the weather is mild, you should pack very light. The airlines permit two pieces of carry-on luggage; try to take one suitcase and maybe an accessory bag that can double as a beach bag. Dress styles are very informal in the islands, and laundromats are ubiquitous, so you don't need a broad range of clothing items.

Remember, you're packing for a semitropical climate. Take along a sweater or light jacket for the mountains, and a poncho to protect against rain. But otherwise, all that travelers in Hawaii require are shorts, bathing suits, lightweight slacks, short-sleeved shirts and blouses, and summer dresses or muumuus. Rarely do visitors require sport jackets or formal dresses. Wash-and-wear fabrics are the most convenient.

For footwear, I suggest soft, comfortable shoes. Low-cut hiking boots or tennis shoes are preferable for hiking; for beachgoing, there's nothing as good as sandals.

There are several other items to squeeze in the corners of your suitcase—sunscreen, sunglasses, a towel and, of course, your copy of *Hidden Hawaii*. You might also consider packing a mask, fins and snorkel, and possibly a camera. Note that if you're not using a digital camera, you'll want to buy your film in the islands and have it developed before you leave to avoid X-ray damage. Never carry undeveloped film in your checked luggage.

If you plan on camping, you'll need most of the equipment required for mainland overnighting. In Hawaii, you can get along quite comfortably with a lightweight tent and sleeping bag. You'll also need a backpack, canteen, camp stove and fuel, mess kit, first-aid kit (with insect repellent, water purification tablets and Chapstick), toilet kit, a pocket knife, hat, waterproof matches, flashlight and ground cloth.

LODGING

Accommodations in Hawaii range from funky cottages to B&B inns to highrise condos. You will find inexpensive family-run hotels, middle-class tourist facilities and world-class resorts. Generally, the farther a hotel is from the beach, the less it costs.

Whichever you choose, there are a few guidelines to help save money. Try to visit during the off-season, avoiding the high-rate periods during the summer and from Christmas to Easter. (If you do come during high season, book well in advance.) Rooms with mountain views are less expensive than ocean view accommodations. Another way to economize is by reserving a room with a kitchen. In any case, try to reserve far in advance.

To help you decide on a place to stay, I've described the accommodations not only by area but also according to price (prices listed are for double occupancy during the high season; prices may decrease in low season). Budget hotels ($) are generally less than $90 per night for two people; the rooms are clean and comfortable, but lack luxury. The moderately priced hotels ($$) run $90 to $160, and provide larger rooms, plusher furniture and more attractive surroundings. At deluxe-priced accommodations ($$$) you can expect to spend between $160 and $240 for a double in a hotel or resort. You'll check into a spacious, well-appointed room with all modern facilities; downstairs the lobby will be a fashionable affair, and you'll usually see a restaurant, lounge and a cluster of shops. If you want to spend your time (and money) in the island's very finest hotels, try an ultra-deluxe facility ($$$$), which will include all the amenities and cost well above $240.

BED-AND-BREAKFAST INNS

The bed-and-breakfast business in Hawaii becomes more diverse and sophisticated every year. Today there are several referral services that can find you lodging on any of the islands.

Bed and Breakfast Honolulu ⊠*3242 Kaohinani Drive, Honolulu, HI 96817* ✆*808-595-7533, 800-288-4666* ✆*808-595-2030* ✎*www.hawaiibnb.com* Claiming to be the biggest clearinghouse in the state, Bed and Breakfast Honolulu (Statewide) represents over 400 properties.

Bed and Breakfast Hawaii ⊠*P.O. Box 449, Kapaa, HI 96746* ✆*808-822-7771, 800-733-1632* ✆*808-822-2723* ✎*www.bandb-hawaii.com* The original association, this Kauai-based service was founded in 1979 and is well known throughout Hawaii. They claim more than 200 locations.

Hawaiian Islands Bed & Breakfast ✆*808-261-7895, 800-258-7895* ✆*808-262-2181* ✎*www.lanikaibeachrentals.com* For information on lodgings in Oahu call this outfit.

Affordable Accommodations ⊠*2825 Kauhale Street, Kihei, HI 96753* ✆*808-879-7865, 888-333-9747* ✆*808-874-0831* ✎*www.affordablemaui.com* Try this Maui-based service, which offers help finding all types of lodging.

All Islands Bed & Breakfast ✉463 Iliwahi Loop, Kailua, HI 96734 ☎808-263-2342, 800-542-0344 📠808-263-0308 🖱www.all-islands.com This is an Oahu-based reservation service that represents over 700 bed and breakfasts.

Hawaii's Best Bed & Breakfasts ✉P.O. Box 563, Kamuela, HI 96743 ☎808-885-4550, 800-262-9912 📠808-885-0559 🖱www.bestbnb.com While the properties represented by these agencies range widely in price, Hawaii's Best Bed & Breakfasts specializes in small, upscale accommodations on all the islands. With about 100 establishments to choose from, it places guests in a variety of privately owned facilities; most are deluxe priced.

CONDOS

Many people visiting Hawaii, especially those traveling with families, find that condominiums are often cheaper than hotels. While some hotel rooms come with kitchenettes, few provide all the amenities of condominiums. A condo, in essence, is an apartment away from home. Designed as studio, one-, two- or three-bedroom apartments, they come equipped with full kitchens and complete kitchenware collections. Many feature washer/dryers, dishwashers, air-conditioning, color televisions, telephones, lanais and community swimming pools.

Utilizing the kitchen will save considerably on your food bill; by sharing the accommodations among several people, you'll also cut your lodging bill. While the best way to see hidden Hawaii is obviously by hiking and camping, when you're ready to come in from the wilds, consider reserving a place that provides more than a bed and a night table.

VACATION RENTALS

On all the islands, visitors will find numerous private homes in a wide range of sizes that are rented by the day, week or month to vacationers. While these homes offer the same conveniences as condominiums, they are generally stand-alone units and are found in all communities, not just resort areas. But vacationers need to be aware that these rentals are entirely unregulated, and so quality, cleanliness, prices and amenities vary widely. Many do not accept credit cards and require a non-refundable deposit, as well as a cleaning fee. Check the internet, or better yet, a travel agent who will be more familiar with the properties available.

DINING

A few guidelines will help you chart a course through Hawaii's countless dining places. Within a particular chapter, the restaurants are categorized geographically, with each restaurant entry describing the establishment as budget ($), moderate ($$), deluxe ($$$) or ultra-deluxe ($$$$) in price.

To establish a pattern for Hawaii's parade of dining places, I've described not only the cuisine but also the ambience of each establishment. Restaurants listed offer lunch and dinner unless otherwise noted.

Dinner entrées at budget restaurants usually cost $8 or less. The ambience is informal café style and the crowd is often a local one. Moderately priced restaurants range between $8 and $16 at dinner and offer pleasant surroundings, a more varied menu and a slower pace. Deluxe establishments tab their entrées above $16, featuring sophisticated cuisines, plush decor and more personalized service. Ultra-deluxe restaurants generally price entreés above $24.

Breakfast and lunch menus vary less in price from restaurant to restaurant. Even deluxe-priced kitchens usually offer light breakfasts and lunch sandwiches, which place them within a few dollars of their budget-minded competitors. These early meals can be a good time to test expensive restaurants.

TRAVELING WITH CHILDREN

Hawaii is an ideal vacation spot for family holidays. The pace is slow, the atmosphere casual. A few guidelines will help ensure that your trip to the islands brings out the joys rather than the strains of parenting, allowing everyone to get into the *aloha* spirit.

Use a travel agent to help with arrangements; they can reserve bulk-head seats on airlines and determine which flights are least crowded. They can also seek out the best deals on inexpensive condominiums or vacation rentals, saving you money on both room and board.

Planning the trip with your kids stimulates their imagination. Books about travel, airplane rides, beaches, whales, volcanoes and Hawaiiana help prepare even a two-year-old for an adventure. This preparation makes the "getting there" part of the trip more exciting for children of all ages.

And "getting there" means a long-distance flight. Plan to bring everything you need on board the plane—diapers, food, books, toys, and extra clothing for kids and parents alike. I found it helpful to carry a few new toys and books as treats to distract my son and daughter when they got bored. When they were young children, I also packed extra snacks.

Allow extra time to get places. Book reservations in advance and make sure that the hotel or condominium has the extra crib, cot or bed you require. It's smart to ask for a room at the end of the hall to cut down on noise. And when reserving a rental car, inquire to see if they provide car seats and if there is an added charge. Hawaii has a strictly enforced car seat law.

Besides the car seat you may have to bring along, also pack shorts and T-shirts, a sweater, sun hat, sundresses and waterproof sandals. A stroller with sunshade for little ones helps on sightseeing sojourns; a shovel and pail are essential for sandcastle building. Most importantly, remember to bring a good sunblock. The quickest way to ruin a family vacation is with a bad sunburn. Also plan to bring indoor activities such as books and games for evenings and rainy days.

Most towns have stores that carry diapers, food and other essentials. However, prices are much higher in Hawaii. To economize, some people take along an extra suitcase filled with diapers and wipes, baby food, peanut butter and jelly, etc. If you're staying in Honolulu, **ABC Stores** (2432 Koa Avenue, Honolulu; 808-921-2799) carry a limited selection of disposables and baby food. Shopping outside Waikiki in local supermarkets will save you a considerable sum: **Star Market** (2470 South King Street, Honolulu; 808-973-1666) is open 24 hours a day.

A first-aid kit is always a good idea. Also check with your pediatrician for special medicines and dosages for colds and diarrhea. If your child does become sick or injured in the Honolulu area, contact **Kapiolani Medical Center** (808-983-6000). On the Windward Coast of Oahu, call **Castle Medical Center** (808-263-5500); on the North Shore, **Kahuku Hospital** (808-293-9221); and on the leeward side, **Wahiawa General Hospital** (808-621-8411). On the Big Island's east side, there's **Hilo Medical Center** (808-974-4700); in Kona, **Kona Community Hospital** (808-322-9311); Maui, **Maui Memorial Hospital** (808-242-2343); Lanai, **Lanai Community Hospital** (808-565-6411); Molokai, **Molokai General Hospital** (808-553-5331); and Kauai, **Wilcox Memorial Hospital and Health Center** (808-245-1100).

Hotels often provide access to babysitters. On Oahu, **Aloha Baby-sitting Service** (808-732-2029; fax 808-735-1958) is a bonded baby-sitting agency.

If you find yourself in need of a parenting break, check out the summer and holiday programs offered at many of the islands' resorts and large hotels. Hula lessons, lei making, storytelling, sandcastle building and various sports activities keep *keikis* (kids) over six happy while also giving Mom and Dad a break. As an added bonus, these resorts offer family plans, providing discounts for extra rooms or permitting children to share a room with their parents at no extra charge. Check with your travel agent or directly with the facility.

When choosing which island to visit, consider how many diversions it will take to keep your children happy. Oahu offers numerous options, from the Honolulu Zoo to theme parks to museums, while the outer islands have fewer attractions. It might be helpful to read the introductory passages to each of the island chapters before planning your trip.

WOMEN TRAVELING ALONE

Traveling solo grants an independence and freedom different from that of traveling with a partner, but single travelers are more vulnerable to crime and should take additional precautions. An option for those who are alone but prefer not to be is to join a tour group.

It's unwise to hitchhike and probably best to avoid inexpensive accommodations on the outskirts of town; the money saved does not outweigh the risk. Bed and breakfasts, youth hostels and YWCAs are generally your safest bet for lodging, and they also foster an environment ideal for bonding with fellow travelers.

Keep all valuables well-hidden and hold on to cameras and purses. Avoid late-night treks or strolls along beaches or through undesirable parts of town, but if you find yourself in this situation, continue walking with a confident air until you reach a safe haven. A fierce scowl never hurts.

These hints should by no means deter you from seeking out adventure. Wherever you go, stay alert, use your common sense and trust your instincts.

Throughout the islands there are many organizations that can help you in case of emergency.

SEX ABUSE TREATMENT CENTER ✆808-524-7273 On Oahu, contact the Sex Abuse Treatment Center for help or information.

WOMEN HELPING WOMEN ✆808-579-9581 ✐www.whwmaui.net This is a domestic violence shelter on Maui that can provide referrals.

For more helpful hints, get a copy of *Safety and Security for Women Who Travel* (Traveler's Tales).

GAY & LESBIAN TRAVELERS

ALOHA PRIDE CENTER ✉614 South Street #105, Honolulu ✆808-545-2848 ✆808-545-1243 ✐www.alohapridecenter.org, info@alohapridecenter.org The Aloha Pride Center, serving Hawaii's gay community, offers support, various programs and information, as well as activities throughout the year. Call or stop by for more details.

DA KINE ✉2410 Cleghorn Street #2302, Honolulu, HI 96815 ✆808-923-7378 ✆808-922-6124 ✐www.dakinemagazine.com, dakinemagazine@hawaii.rr.com For monthly updates on the gay and lesbian scene in Hawaii, pick up a copy of *Da Kine* at bars and clubs in Waikiki, the main library and the Academy of Arts Theater. Along with coverage of news and entertainment, it provides a calendar of events and a listing of services.

PACIFIC OCEAN HOLIDAYS ✉P.O. Box 88245, Honolulu, HI 96830 ✆808-944-4700, 800-735-6600 reservations only ✐www.gayhawaii.com Pacific Ocean Holidays is also helpful for gay travelers.

BLACK BAMBOO HAWAII ✉P.O. Box 211, Kealakekua, HI 96750 ✆808-328-9607, 800-527-7789 ✐www.blackbamboohawaii.com Spanning the entire Hawaiian chain, the Big Island–based Black Bamboo Hawaii unearths the best cottages and houses for gay and straight travelers. This service also arranges car rentals, hiking tours, birdwatching trips and other sporting activities for its guests.

BOTH SIDES NOW ✉P.O. Box 10711, Lahaina, HI 96761 ✆808-244-4566 ✐www.mauigayinfo.com For information on the gay and lesbian scene on Maui, contact this group. They can provide details on lodging, upcoming events and social gatherings.

For further information, be sure to look under "gay-friendly travel" in the index at the end of the book.

SENIOR TRAVELERS

Hawaii is a hospitable place for senior citizens to visit. Countless museums, historic sights and even restaurants and hotels offer senior discounts that can cut a substantial chunk off vacation costs. The national park system's Golden Age Passport, which must be applied for in person, allows free admission for anyone 62 and older to the two national parks in the islands.

Be extra careful about health matters. Consider carrying a medical record with you—including your medical history and current medical status as well as your doctor's name, phone number and address. Make sure your insurance covers you while you are away from home.

AMERICAN ASSOCIATION OF RETIRED PERSONS (AARP)
✉ *601 E Street NW, Washington, DC 20049* ☎ *888-687-2277* ✐ *www.aarp.org* AARP offers membership to anyone over 50. AARP's benefits include travel discounts with a number of firms.

ELDERHOSTEL ✉ *11 Avenue de Lafayette, Boston, MA 02111* ☎ *800-454-5768* ✆ *617-426-0701* ✐ *www.elderhostel.org* Elderhostel offers reasonably priced, all-inclusive educational programs in a variety of locations throughout the year.

DISABLED TRAVELERS

DISABILITY AND COMMUNICATION ACCESS BOARD ✉ *919 Ala Moana Boulevard, Room 101, Honolulu, HI 96814* ☎ *808-586-8121* ✆ *808-586-8129* ✐ *www.hawaii.gov/health/dcab/home, dcab@doh.hawaii.gov* The Disability and Communication Access Board publishes a survey of the city, county, state and federal parks in Hawaii that are accessible to travelers with disabilities. They also provide "Hawaii Traveler Tips Guides," which cover Oahu, Maui, Kauai and the Big Island, and give information on airports, various hotels, shopping centers, and restaurants that are accessible. Guides are available to download from their website.

SOCIETY FOR ACCESSIBLE TRAVEL & HOSPITALITY ✉ *347 5th Avenue, Suite 605, New York, NY 10016* ☎ *212-447-7284* ✆ *212-444-1928* ✐ *www. sath.org* This society offers information for travelers with disabilities.

Be sure to check in advance when making room reservations. Some hotels feature facilities for those in wheelchairs.

FOREIGN TRAVELERS

PASSPORTS AND VISAS Foreign visitors need a passport and tourist visa to enter the United States. Furthermore, tighter U.S. Department of Homeland Security regulations now mandate that all those traveling to the U.S. by air, including U.S. citizens, must show a valid passport to enter or reenter the U.S. This requirement will expand to include those entering by land and sea by January 2008. Contact your nearest U.S. Embassy or Consulate well in advance to obtain a visa and to check on any other entry requirements.

CUSTOMS REQUIREMENTS Foreign travelers are allowed to carry in the following: 200 cigarettes (1 carton), 50 cigars, or 2 kilograms (4.4 pounds) of smoking tobacco; one liter of alcohol restricted to checked luggage for personal use only (you must be 21 years of age to bring in alcohol); and US$100 worth of duty-free gifts that can include an additional quantity of 100 cigars (except Cuban). As of 2006, the maximum amount of liquid permitted in carry-on luggage is 3 oz. All containers with liquids must be enclosed in a 1-quart plastic Ziploc bag. You may bring in any amount of currency, but must fill out a form if you bring in over US$10,000. Carry any 90-day supply of prescription drugs in clearly marked containers. (You may have to produce a written prescription or doctor's statement for the custom's officer.) Meat or meat products, seeds, plants, fruits, and narcotics are not allowed to be brought into the United States.

Be aware that a vigorous agricultural inspection keeps unwanted pests out of Hawaii. If you forgot that apple tucked into your backpack, a sniffing dog inspector may tag you.

United States Customs and Border Protection ✉ *1300 Pennsylvania Avenue NW, Washington, DC 20229* ☏ *202-354-1000* ✦ *www.cbp.gov* Contact the United States Customs and Border Protection for further information.

DRIVING If you plan to rent a car, an international driver's license should be obtained prior to arrival. Some rental car companies require both a foreign license and an international driver's license. Many car rental agencies require that the lessee be at least 25 years of age; all require a major credit card. Seat belts are mandatory for the driver and all passengers. Children under the age of 6 or weighing less than 60 pounds should be in the back seat in approved child safety restraints.

CURRENCY United States money is based on the dollar. Bills come in six denominations: $1, $2, $5, $10, $20, $50 and $100. Every dollar is divided into 100 cents. Coins are the penny (1 cent), nickel (5 cents), dime (10 cents), quarter (25 cents) and dollar (100 cents). The half-dollar, dollar coin and $2 bill are rarely used.

You may not use foreign currency to purchase goods and services in the United States. Consider buying traveler's checks in dollar amounts. You may also use credit cards affiliated with an American company such as Interbank, Barclay Card, VISA, MasterCard and American Express.

ELECTRICITY AND ELECTRONICS Electric outlets use currents of 110 volts, 60 cycles. For appliances made for other electrical systems, you need a transformer or adapter. Travelers who use laptop computers for telecommunication should be aware that modem configurations for U.S. telephone systems may be different from their European counterparts. Similarly, the U.S. format for videotapes is different from that in Europe; U.S. Park Service visitors centers and other stores that sell souvenir videos often have them available in European format.

WEIGHTS AND MEASUREMENTS The United States uses the English system of weights and measures. American units and their metric equivalents are as follows: 1 inch = 2.5 centimeters; 1 foot (12 inches) = 0.3 meter; 1 yard (3 feet) = 0.9 meter; 1 mile (5280 feet) = 1.6 kilometers; 1 ounce = 28 grams; 1 pound (16 ounces) = 0.45 kilogram; 1 quart (liquid) = 0.9 liter.

MAIL

If you're staying in a particular establishment during your visit, you can usually have personal mail sent there. Otherwise, for cardholders, **American Express** will hold letters for no charge at its Honolulu office for 30 days, and will provide forwarding services. If you decide to use their facilities, have mail addressed to American Express, Client Mail, 2424 Kalakaua Avenue, Honolulu, HI 96815; 808-922-4718. If you don't use this service, your only other recourse is to have mail sent to a particular post office in care of general delivery.

LIBRARIES

HAWAII STATE PUBLIC LIBRARY SYSTEM ✑ www.librarieshawaii.org
The Hawaii State Public Library System provides facilities for residents and non-residents alike, with 50 branches scattered throughout the islands. Visitors can check out books by simply applying for a library card with a valid identification card (non-residents must pay $10 for a three-month membership). The following cities and towns are among many where you can borrow light beach-reading material as well as books on Hawaii: Honolulu, Kailua and Waimanalo on Oahu; Hilo, Kailua-Kona and Pahala on the Big Island; Kahului, Wailuku and Hana on Maui; Lanai City on Lanai; Kaunakakai on Molokai; and Waimea, Lihue and Princeville on Kauai. Most books do not have to be returned to the same branch where they are originally checked out. For a complete list of libraries, check the state library system's website.

TRANSPORTATION

GETTING TO THE ISLANDS

During the 19th century, sleek clipper ships sailed from the West Coast to Hawaii in about 11 days. Today, you'll be traveling by a less romantic but far swifter conveyance—the jet plane. Rather than days at sea, it will be about five hours in the air from the West Coast, nine hours from Chicago, or around 11 hours if you're coming from the East Coast.

American, ATA, Continental, Delta, Hawaiian, Northwest and United fly regular schedules to Honolulu. American, Delta and United also offer flights to Maui, American and United to the Big Island, and United serves Kauai. This nonstop service is particularly convenient for travelers who are interested in visiting the outer islands while by-passing Honolulu.

Foreign carriers include Air Canada, Air New Zealand, All Nippon Airways, China Airlines, Japan Airlines, Korean Airlines, Philippine Airlines and Qantas Airlines.

Whichever carrier you choose, ask for the economy or excursion fare, and try to fly during the week; weekend flights are generally higher in price. To qualify for the lower price fares, it is sometimes necessary to book your flight two weeks in advance and to stay in the islands at least one week. Generally, however, the restrictions are minimal. Children under two years of age can fly for free, but they will not have a seat of their own. Each passenger is permitted two large pieces of luggage plus a carry-on bag. Shipping a bike or surfboard will cost extra.

In planning a Hawaiian sojourn, one potential moneysaver is the package tour, which combines air transportation with a hotel room and other amenities. Generally, it is a style of travel that I avoid. However, if you can find a package that provides air transportation, a hotel or condominium accommodation and a rental car, all at one low price—it is worth considering. Two experienced Hawaii packagers are **Suntrips** (800-514-5194; www.suntrips.com) and **Pleasant Hawaiian Holidays** (866-867-4567; www.hawaii-hawaii.com). Prices are often low, but be forewarned: Some packages will preplan your entire visit, dragging you around on air-conditioned tour buses. Look for the package that provides only the bare necessities while allowing you the greatest freedom.

GETTING BETWEEN ISLANDS

BY AIR

Most inter-island transportation is by plane. **Hawaiian Airlines**, the state's major carrier, provides frequent inter-island jet service. If you're looking for smooth, rapid, comfortable service, this is certainly it. You'll be buckled into your seat, offered a low-cost cocktail and whisked to your destination within 20 to 40 minutes.

go!, a subsidiary of Mesa Airlines, also offers inter-island service on smaller jets than its competitors and frequently at lower prices.

Now that you know how to fly quickly and comfortably, let me tell you about a more exciting way to get between islands. Several carriers, including **Island Air**, **Molokai Air Shuttle**, **Pacific Wings** and **Paragon Air**, fly twin-engine propeller planes. These small airplanes travel at lower altitudes and moderate speeds over the islands. Next to chartering a helicopter, they are one of the best ways to see Hawaii from the air.

BY FERRY

Hawaii Superferry ✉One Waterfront Plaza, 500 Ala Moana Boulevard, Suite 300, Honolulu ☎808-531-7400, 877-443-3779 📠808-531-7410 🖥www.hawaiisuperferry.com Since its inception, this inter-island ferry has been met with equal enthusiasm and concern. While it continues to sail between Oahu and Maui six days a week, it does so under environmental protection surveys intended to ease the controversy. Rides last three-hours (one-way) and include movies, food and shopping. Still a burgeoning endeavor (operation began in December 2007), it is a good idea to check travel policies prior to boarding or making reservations.

Expeditions Inc. ☎*808-661-3756 or 877-464-6284* This company offers inter-island ferry services between Lahaina, Maui, and the islands of Molokai and Lanai (Manele Harbor) five times a day.

Molokai Ferry ✉*658 Front Street, Suite 10, Lahaina* ☎*808-667-6165 or 800-275-6969* ⌨*www.molokaiferry.com* The Molokai ferry runs between Lahaina, Maui, and Kaunakakai, Molokai, twice a day.

CAR RENTALS

Renting a car is as easy in Hawaii as anywhere. Every island supports several rental agencies, which compete fiercely with one another in price and quality of service. So before renting, shop around: check the listings in this book, and also look for special temporary offers that many rental companies sometimes feature.

There are several facts to remember when renting a car. First of all, a major credit card is essential. Also, many agencies don't rent at all to people under 25.

Regardless of your age, many companies charge several dollars a day extra for insurance. The insurance is optional and expensive, and in many cases, unnecessary. (Many credit cards provide the same coverage when a rental is charged to the card. Find out if you credit card company offers this coverage.) Your personal insurance policy may also provide for rental cars and, if necessary, have a clause added that will include rental car protection. Check on this before you leave home. But remember, whether you have insurance or not, you are liable for the first several thousand dollars in accident damage.

Rates fluctuate with the season; slack tourist seasons are great times for good deals. Also, three-day, weekly and monthly rates are almost always cheaper than daily rentals.

Other than on the island of Lanai, I don't recommend renting a jeep. They're more expensive and less comfortable than automobiles, and won't get you to very many more interesting spots. In addition, the rental car collision insurance provided by most credit cards does not cover jeeps. Except in extremely wet weather when roads are muddy, all the places mentioned in this book, including the hidden locales, can be reached by car.

THE LAND & OUTDOOR ADVENTURES

GEOLOGY More than 25 million years ago a fissure opened along the Pacific floor. Beneath tons of sea water molten lava poured from the rift. This liquid basalt, oozing from a hot spot in the earth's center, created a crater along the ocean bottom. As the tectonic plate that comprises the ocean floor drifted over the earth's hot spot, numerous other craters appeared. Slowly, in the seemingly endless procession of geologic time, a chain of volcanic islands, now stretching almost 2000 miles, has emerged from the sea.

On the continents it was also a period of terrible upheaval. The Himalayas, Alps and Andes were rising, but these great chains would reach their peaks long before the Pacific mountains even touched sea level. Not until about 25 million years ago did the first of these underwater volcanoes, today's Kure and Midway atolls, break the surface and become islands. It was not until about five million years ago that the first of the main islands of the archipelago, Niihau and Kauai, broke the surface to become high islands.

For a couple of million more years, the mountains continued to grow. The forces of erosion cut into them, creating knife-edged cliffs and deep valleys. Then plants began germinating: mosses and ferns, springing from windblown spores, were probably first, followed by seed plants carried by migrating birds and on ocean currents. The steep-walled valleys provided natural greenhouses in which unique species evolved, while transoceanic winds swept insects and other life from the continents.

Some islands never survived this birth process: the ocean simply washed them away. The first islands that did endure, at the northwestern end of the Hawaiian chain, proved to be the smallest. Today these islands, with the exception of Midway, are barren uninhabited atolls. The volcanoes that rose last, far to the southeast, became the mountainous archipelago generally known as the Hawaiian Islands.

With several distinct biological regions, there's much more to the islands than lush tropics. Rainforests give way to dry forests, and to coastal habitats where the vegetation is specially suited to withstand wind and salt. Higher in altitude are the bogs, pools of standing water containing rare life forms that have been forced to adapt to a difficult environment. Highest in altitude is the alpine zone, consisting of bare volcanic surfaces scattered with clumps of low-growing herbs and shrubs. Subzero temperatures, frost and even snow help keep this region desolate.

Hawaii's luxurious parks, mountain retreats and deserted beaches make it a paradise for campers and backpackers. Because of the varied terrain and the islands' microenvironments, it's possible to experience all kinds of outdoor adventures. One day you can hike through a steaming rainforest filled with tropical flowers; the next night you can camp atop a volcanic crater in a stark, windblown area that resembles the moon's surface; then you'll descend to a curving white-sand beach populated only by shorebirds and tropical fish.

Paradise means more than physical beauty, however. It also involves an easy life and a bountiful food supply. The easy living is up to you; just slow down from the frantic pace of mainland life and you'll discover that island existence can be relaxing.

As for wild food—you'll find it hanging from trees, swimming in the ocean and clinging to coral reefs. Just be sure to use the proper techniques in taking from the environment and always keep Hawaii's delicate ecosystem in mind.

In this chapter I'll pass along a few facts I've learned while exploring Hawaii. I don't advise that you plan to live off the land. Hawaii's environment is too fragile to support you. Anyway, living that way is a hell of a lot of work! I'll just give a few hints on how to supplement your provisions with a newly caught fish or a fresh fruit salad. That way you'll get a full taste of the islands.

Obviously, none of these techniques were developed by me personally. In fact, most of them date back centuries to the early days, when Polynesian explorers applied the survival skills they had learned in Tahiti and the Marquesas to the newly discovered islands of Hawaii. So as you set out to fish along a coral reef, hunt for shellfish in tidepools or gather seaweed at low tide, give a prayerful thanks to the generations of savvy islanders who have come before you.

FLORA AND FAUNA

FLORA

Many of the plants you'll see in Hawaii are not indigenous. In fact, much of the lush vegetation of this tropical island found its way here from locations all over the world. Sea winds, birds and seafaring settlers brought many of the seeds, plants, flowers and trees from the islands of the South Pacific, as well as from other, more distant regions. Over time, some plants adapted to Hawaii's unique ecosystem and climate, creating strange new lineages and evolving into a completely new ecosystem. This process has long interested scientists, who call the Hawaiian Islands one of the best natural labs for studies of plant and bird evolution.

Sugar cane arrived in Hawaii with the first Polynesian settlers, who appreciated its sweet juices. By the late 1800s, it was well established as a lucrative crop. The pineapple was first planted during the same century. A member of the bromeliad family, this spiky plant is actually a collection of beautiful pink, blue and purple flowers, each of which develops into a fruitlet. The pineapple is a collection of these fruitlets, grown together into a single fruit that takes 14 to 17 months to mature.

Sugar cane and pineapple were once important crops in Hawaii, but competition from other countries and environmental problems caused by pesticides have taken their toll. More recently, coffee, corn and banana have also become key components of Hawaii's agriculture.

Visitors to Hawaii will find the islands a perpetual flower show. Sweetly scented plumeria, deep red, shiny anthurium, exotic ginger, showy birds of paradise, small lavender crown flowers, highly fragrant gardenias and the brightly hued hibiscus run riot on the islands and add color and fragrance to the surrounding area. Scarlet and purple bougainvillea vines, and the aromatic lantana, with its dense clusters of flowers, are also found in abundance.

Each of the main islands has designated a specific bloom as its island flower. Oahu has the *ilima*, a small golden blossom, and the Big Island has the red *lehua*, a furry flower with needle petals resembling a bottlebrush plant. Maui spotlights the *lokelani*, or pink cottage rose while Kauai's pick is the *mokihana*, which is actually a light green berry. Molokai's flower of choice is the small, white *kukui* blossom and Lanai's is the vibrant orange *kaunaoa*.

The beautiful, delicate orchid thrives in Hawaii's tropical heat and humidity. Cultivated primarily on the Big Island, the most popular orchids are the *dendrobium*, which can come in white, purple, lavender, or yellow; the *vanda* (bamboo orchid), which is lavender with white lavender and often used for making leis; and the popcorn, which has small, yellow flowers. The wild *vanda*, with its white and lavender petals, can be spotted along the side of the road year-round.

Hawaii's most unusual plant is the silversword. Delicate looking, this silvery green plant is actually very hardy. It thrives on the moonscape of Haleakala, 6000 to 10,000 feet above sea level on Maui. Very adaptable, it can survive in extreme hot and cold temperatures with little moisture. Its silvery hairs reflect the sun and its leaves curl inward, protecting the stalk and creating a sort of bowl where rain is collected and stored. The plant lives from five to thirty years, waiting until the right moment before sprouting a three- to nine-foot stalk composed of hundreds of small, reddish flowers—and then it dies. In the same family as the sunflower, this particular type of silversword lives only on Haleakala and has been close to extinction for many years. Now protected, it is currently making a comeback.

Another curious specimen found on the leeward slopes of Haleakala and on the Big Island is the protea. With 1500 varieties, this remarkable plant comes in a myriad of shapes, sizes and colors. Some look like pin cushions, others resemble corn cobs. Originally from South Africa and Australia, the Hawaiian plant is a hybrid.

Although many people equate the tropics with the swaying palm tree, Hawaii is home to a variety of exotic trees. The famed banyan tree, known for pillarlike aerial roots that grow vertically downward from the branches, spreads to form a natural canopy. When the roots touch the ground, they thicken, providing support for the tree's branches to continue expanding. The candlenut, or *kukui*, tree, originally brought to Hawaii from the South Pacific islands, is big, bushy and prized for its nuts, which can be polished and strung together to make leis. The state tree, it provided early Hawaiians with oil, light and natural remedies. Covered with tiny pink blossoms, the canopied monkeypod tree has fernlike leaves that close up at night. With its cascades of bright yellow or pink flowers, the cassia tree earns its moniker—the shower tree.

Found in a variety of shapes and sizes, the ubiquitous palm does indeed sway to the breezes on white-sand beaches, but it also comes in a short, stubby form, the Samoan coconut, featuring more frond than trunk. The fruit, or nuts, of these trees are prized for their oil, which can be utilized for making everything from margarine to soap. The wood (rattan for example) is often used for making furniture.

FRUITS AND VEGETABLES

There's a lot more to Hawaii's tropical wonderland than gorgeous flowers and overgrown rainforests. The islands are also teeming with edible plants. Roots, fruits, vegetables, herbs and spices grow like weeds from the shoreline to the mountains. Following is a list of some of the more commonly found edibles.

Avocado: Covered with either a tough green or purple skin, this pear-shaped fruit sometimes weighs as much as three pounds. It grows on ten- to forty-foot-high trees, and ripens from June through November.

Bamboo: The bamboo plant is actually a grass with a sweet root that is edible and a long stem frequently used for making furniture. Often exceeding eight feet in height, the most common bamboo is green until picked, when it turns a golden brown.

Banana: Polynesians use banana trees, which are not trees at all but a *pseudostem* (or false stem) not only for food but also for clothing, medicines, dyes and even alcohol; culturally, it represents man. The fruit, which grows upside down on broad-leaved trees, can be harvested as soon as the first banana in the bunch turns yellow.

Breadfruit: This large round fruit grows on trees that reach up to 60 feet in height. Breadfruit must be boiled, baked or fried.

Coconut: The coconut tree is probably the most important plant in the entire Pacific. Every part of the towering palm is used. The fronds were combined with *pili* grass to thatch roofs, the hollowed trunks are made into *pahu*, or drums, and the fiber can be dried for fuel. It was also fashioned into ropey sandals that allowed Hawaiians to walk across razor-sharp lava. Nutritionally, the water inside is sterile and full of healthful enzymes, and the meat can be eaten or pressed into cream and oil. Most importantly, coconuts grow well close to the ocean, offering welcome shade from the harsh tropical sun. Most people are concerned only with the hard brown nut, which yields delicious water as well as a tasty meat. If the coconut is still green, the meat is a succulent jellylike substance. Otherwise, it's a hard but delicious white rind.

Guava: A roundish yellow fruit that grows on a small shrub or tree, guavas are extremely abundant in the wild. They ripen between June and October.

Lychee: Found hanging in bunches from the lychee tree, this popular summer fruit is encased in red, prickly skin that peels off to reveal the sweet-tasting, translucent flesh.

Mango: Known as the king of fruits, the mango grows on tall shade trees. There are hundreds of varieties that come in varying colors and shapes; the most common in Hawaii are Haden, but I love the Ah Pin. The fruit ripens in the spring and summer.

Maui onion: Resembling an ordinary yellow onion in size and color, these bulbs are uncommonly mild. They are grown on the south side of Haleakala in rich volcanic soil, and enjoy enough sun and altitude to make them very sweet. A member of the lily family, the Maui onion is best eaten raw.

Mountain apple: This sweet fruit grows in damp, shaded valleys at an elevation of about 1800 feet. The flowers resemble fluffy crimson balls; the fruit, which ripens from July to December, is also a rich red color.

Papaya: This delicious fruit, which is picked as it begins to turn yellow, grows on unbranched trees. The sweet flesh can be bright orange or coral pink in color. Summer is the peak harvesting season.

Passion fruit: Known as *lilikoi* on the islands, this tasty yellow fruit is oval in shape and grows to a length of about two or three inches. It's produced on a vine and ripens in summer or fall.

Taro: The tuberous root of this Hawaiian staple is pounded into a gray-ish purple paste known as *poi*. One of the most nutritious foods, it has a rather bland taste. The plant has wide, shiny, thick leaves with reddish stems; the root is white with purple veins. Taro is also served in other forms, such as chips and bread.

FAUNA

In Hawaii, it seems there is more wildlife in the water and air than on land. A scuba diver's paradise, the ocean is also a promised land for many other creatures. Coral, colorful fish and migrating whales are only part of this underwater community. Sadly, many of Hawaii's coral reefs have been dying mysteriously in the last several years. No one is sure why, but many believe this is partially due to runoff from pesticides used in agriculture.

For adventure lovers, Maui, and to a lesser extent the Big Island, offer excellent opportunities for whale watching. Every year, humpback whales converge in the warm waters off the islands to give birth to their calves. Beginning their migration in Alaska, they can be spotted in Hawaiian waters from November through May. The humpback, named for its practice of showing its dorsal fin when diving, is quite easy to spy. They feed in shallow waters, usually diving for periods of no longer than

15 minutes. They often sleep on the surface and breathe fairly frequently. Unlike other whales, humpbacks have the ability to sing. Loud and powerful, their songs carry above and below the water for miles. The songs change every year, yet, incredibly, all the whales always seem to know the current one. Quite playful, they can be seen leaping, splashing and flapping their 15-foot tails over their backs.

Spinner dolphins are also favorites among visitors. Named for their "spinning" habit, they can revolve as many as six times during one leap. They resemble the spotted dolphin, another frequenter of Hawaiian waters, but are more likely to venture closer to the shore. Dolphins have clocked in with speeds ranging from 9 to 25 mph, a feat they often achieve by propelling themselves out of the water (or even riding the bow wave of a ship). Their thick, glandless skin also contributes to this agility. The skin is kept smooth by constant renewal and sloughing (bottlenoses replace their epidermis every two hours). Playful and intelligent, dolphins are a joy to watch. Many research centers are investigating the mammals' ability to imitate, learn and communicate; some believe that dolphin intelligence may be comparable to that of humans.

One of the few mammals to live in the Hawaiian islands before the Polynesians' arrival, the Hawaiian monk seal has been hunted nearly to the point of extinction. Now protected as an endangered species, this tropical seal is found mostly on the outer islands, although it is frequently spotted on Kauai, and more rarely, on Oahu. Closely related to the elephant seal, the monk seal is not as agile or as fond of land as other seals. If you see one basking on the beach, keep your distance, as it's a federal offense to disturb the seals in any way. And never approach a mother seal with a pup, as they can be aggressively protective.

Green sea turtles are common on all of the Hawaiian islands, although this was not always the case. Due to the popularity of their shells and meat, they spent many years on the endangered species list, but are now making a comeback. Measuring three to four feet in diameter, these large reptiles frolic in saltwater only, and are often visible from the shore.

Offshore the coral reefs abound in tropical fish too numerous to describe. Angelfish, fangblenny, butterflyfish, cardinal fish, anthias, grouper, parrotfish—each with many variations and colors—call the Hawaiian waters home. Red, yellow, orange, blue, green—all combinations of the rainbow—dart around reefs, which hide ominous looking eels, swaying anemones, and harmless reef sharks. The multi-finned lionfish and the red-and-white turkey fish or the male psychedelic wrasse with its orange head and luminous spotted body are a few of the more exotic creatures around. Then there is Boreham's sole, which blends in with the rocky sand, not to be noticed by anyone. The reefs themselves are relatively young and are primarily made up of such corals as cauliflower, lobe and finger. Sea urchins and sea cucumbers as well as christmas tree worms also live here. Many of the species in these waters live nowhere else on the planet. Take care not to damage the coral, their source of life.

Hawaii is also home to many rare and endangered birds. Like the flora, the birds on the islands are highly specialized. The state bird, the *nene*, is a distant relative of the Canadian goose and once was found on all the islands. But hunting nearly drove the birds to extinction until a captive-breeding program was implemented to help restore the species. Now *nene* can be seen on the Big Island, Molokai, Maui and Kauai, which has the state's largest population. The birds frequent both uplands and coastal areas, as well as golf courses and other areas with short, green grass. If you see one on the road, be sure to stop, as they do not take flight quickly and cannot get out of your way.

The slopes of Haleakala and Mauna Kea, as well as Kauai's Alakai Swamp, also are home to several extremely rare species, including the Maui parrotbill, the *palila* and the *puaiohi*, all of which are found nowhere else on the planet.

On the endangered species list for many years, the Hawaiian hawk, or *io*, has had its status changed to "threatened." Existing exclusively on the Big Island, the regal *io* is found in a variety of habitats from forest to grassland, but is most often sighted on the slopes of Mauna Kea and Mauna Loa.

There *are* a few birds native to Hawaii that have thus far avoided the endangered species list. Two of the most common birds are the yellow-green *amakihi* and the red *iiwi*.

Known in Hawaiian mythology for its protective powers, the *pueo*, or Hawaiian owl, a brown-and-white-feathered bird, resides on Kauai, the Big Island and in Haleakala crater, as well as pasturelands, where it hunts mice and rats. It is also a threatened species.

The *koae kea*, or "tropic bird," lives on Haleakala, as well as in Kilauea Crater and Kauai's Waimea Canyon. Resembling a seagull in size, it has a long, thin white tail and a striking striping pattern on the back of the wings.

One common seabird is the *iwa*, or frigate, a very large creature measuring three to four feet in length, with a wing span averaging seven feet. The males are solid black, while the females have a large white patch on their chest and tail. A predatory bird, they're easy to spot raiding the nesting colonies of other birds along the offshore rocks. If you see one, you may want to seek cover; legend says they portend a storm.

Other native birds that make the islands their home are the endangered Hawaiian stilt and the Hawaiian coot—both water birds—along with the black noddy, American plover and wedge-tailed shearwater.

Not many wild four-footed creatures roam the islands. Deer, feral goats and pigs were brought here early on and have found a home in the forests. Some good news for people fearful of snakes: There is nary a serpent (or a sea serpent) in Hawaii, although lizards such as skinks and geckos abound.

One can only hope that with the renewed interest in Hawaiian culture, and growing environmental awareness, Hawaii's plants and animals will continue to exist as they have for centuries.

OUTDOOR ADVENTURES

Opportunities for adventuring abound in the islands. In this section you'll find information on popular ocean-based activities, including advice on creative ways to scare up your own supper.

Some, like torchfishing, are part of time-honored Hawaiian traditions. You'll also find some general tips on hiking and camping in the islands (for more specific information, see individual island chapters). For information about other outdoor adventures such as diving, kayaking, surfing, snuba and more, please see individual island chapters.

OCEAN SAFETY

Many water lovers never realize how awesome the sea can be. Particularly in Hawaii, where waves can reach 30-foot heights and currents flow unobstructed for thousands of miles, the ocean is sometimes as treacherous as it is spectacular. Dozens of people drown here every year, many others are dragged from the crushing surf with broken backs, and countless numbers sustain minor cuts and bruises.

These accidents can be entirely avoided if you approach the ocean with a respect for its power as well as an appreciation of its beauty. All you have to do is heed a few simple guidelines. First, never turn your back on the sea. Waves come in sets: one group may be small and quite harmless, but the next set could be large enough to sweep you out to sea. Never swim alone.

Don't try to surf, or even bodysurf, until you're familiar with the sports' techniques and precautionary measures. Be extremely careful when the surf is high.

If you get caught in a rip current, don't swim *against* it: swim *across* it, parallel to the shore. These currents, running from the shore out to sea, can often be spotted by their ragged-looking surface water and foamy edges.

When looking for marine life, swim over the coral, looking in, under and around all the corners, caves and crevices. Many spectacular sea creatures await discovery in these hiding spots. Keep in mind that while coral looks like rock, it is a living creature that can be easily killed. Standing on it, touching it, kicking it with your fin or even kicking sand onto it from the ocean floor can damage the coral. So gently drift over the reef and you will be rewarded with new discoveries and close encounters with beautiful tropical fish. I recommend you buy waterproof fish identification cards. You can take them into the water and use them to identify these magnificently colored creatures.

Around coral reefs, wear something to protect your feet against coral cuts. Particularly good are the inexpensive Japanese *tabis*, or reef slippers. If you do sustain a coral cut, clean it with hydrogen peroxide, then apply an antiseptic or antibiotic substance. This is also a good procedure for octopus bites.

When stung by a Portuguese man-of-war or a jellyfish, rinse the affected area with sea water to remove any tentacles. For jellyfish stings only, you might also try vinegar or isopropyl alcohol. The old Hawaiian remedies, which are reputedly quite effective, involve applying urine or green papaya.

If you step on the sharp, painful spines of a sea urchin, soak the affected area in very hot water for 15 to 90 minutes. Another remedy calls for applying urine or undiluted vinegar. If the pain persists for more than a day, or you notice swelling or other signs of infection, consult a doctor.

Oh, one last thing. The chances of encountering a shark are about as likely as sighting a UFO. But should you meet one of these ominous creatures, stay calm. He'll be no happier to see you than you are to confront him. Simply swim quietly to shore. By the time you make it back to terra firma, you'll have a hell of a story to tell.

FISHING

While you're exploring the islands, the sea will be your prime food source. Fishing in Hawaii is good year-round, and the offshore waters are crowded with many varieties of edible fish. For deep-sea fishing you'll have to charter a boat, and freshwater angling requires a license; so I'll concentrate on surf-casting. It costs nothing to fish this way.

In the individual island chapters within the "Beaches and Parks" listings, you'll find information on the best spots to fish for different species. For information on seasons, licenses and official regulations, check with the Aquatic Resources Division of the State Department of Land and Natural Resources. This agency has offices on most of the major islands.

The easiest, most economical way to fish is with a hand-held line. Just get a 50- to 100-foot line, and attach a hook and a ten-ounce sinker. Wind the line loosely around a smooth block of wood, then remove the wood from the center. If your coil is free from snags, you'll be able to throw-cast it easily. You can either hold the line in your hand, feeling for a strike, or tie it to the frail end of a bamboo pole.

Beaches and rocky points are generally good places to surf-cast; the best times are during the incoming and outgoing tides. Popular baits include octopus, eel, lobster, crab, frozen shrimp and sea worms.

The old Hawaiians also fished at night by torchlight. They fashioned torches by inserting nuts from the *kukui* tree into the hollow end of a bamboo pole, then lighting the flammable nuts. When fish swam like moths to the flame, the Hawaiians speared, clubbed or netted them.

Today, it's easier to use a lantern and spear. (In fact, it's all *too* easy and tempting to take advantage of this willing prey: Take only edible fish and only what you will eat, and follow state rules on size and season limits for some species.) It's also handy to bring a facemask or a glass-bottomed box to aid in seeing underwater. The best time for torchfishing is a dark night when the sea is calm and the tide low.

During daylight hours, the best place to spearfish is along coral reefs and in areas where the bottom is a mixture of sand and rock. Equipped with speargun, mask, fins and snorkel, you can explore underwater grottoes and spectacular coral formations while seeking your evening meal. Spearguns can be purchased inexpensively throughout the islands.

CRABBING

For the hungry adventurer, there are several crab species in Hawaii. The most sought after are the Kona and Samoan varieties. Kona crabs are found in relatively deep water, and can usually be caught only from a boat. Samoan crabs inhabit sandy and muddy areas in bays and near river mouths. All you need to catch them are a boat and a net fastened to a round wire hoop secured by a string. The net is lowered to the bottom; then, after a crab has gone for the bait, the entire contraption is raised to the surface.

SQUIDDING

Between June and December, squidding is another popular sport. Actually, the term is a misnomer: squid inhabit deep water and are not usually hunted. What you'll really be after are octopuses. There are two varieties in Hawaii, both of which are commonly found in water three or four feet deep: the *hee*, a grayish-brown animal that changes color like a chameleon, and the *puloa*, a red-colored mollusk with white stripes on its head.

Both are nocturnal and live in holes along coral reefs. At night by torchlight you can spot them sitting exposed on the bottom. During the day, they crawl inside the holes, covering the entrances with shells and loose coral.

The Hawaiians used to pick the octopus up, letting it cling to their chest and shoulders. When they were ready to bag their prize, they'd dispatch the creature by biting it between the eyes. You'll probably feel more comfortable spearing the beast.

SHELLFISH GATHERING

Other excellent food sources are the shellfish that inhabit coastal waters. The ancient Hawaiians used pearl shells to attract the fish, and hooks, some made from human bones, to snare them. Your friends will probably be quite content to see you angling with store-bought artificial lures. Oysters and clams, which use their muscular feet to burrow into sand and soft mud, can be collected along the bottom of Hawaii's bays. Spiny lobsters, rarely found in Hawaii waters, are illegal to spear, but can be taken in season with short poles to which cable leaders and baited hooks are attached. You can also just grab them with a gloved hand but be careful—spiny lobsters live up to their name! You can also gather limpets, though I don't recommend it. These tiny black shellfish, locally known as *opihi*, cling tenaciously to rocks in the tidal zone. In areas of very rough surf, the Hawaiians gather them by leaping into the water after one set of waves breaks, then jumping out before the next set arrives. Being a coward myself, I simply order them in Hawaiian restaurants.

SEAWEED GATHERING

There are still some people who don't think of seaweed as food, but it's very popular among Japanese, and it once served as an integral part of the Hawaiian diet. It's extremely nutritious, easy to gather and very plentiful.

Rocky shores are the best places to find the edible species of seaweed. Some of them float in to shore and can be picked up; other species cling stubbornly to rocks and must be freed with a knife; still others grow in sand or mud. Low tide is the best time to collect seaweed: more plants are exposed, and some can be taken without even getting wet.

CAMPING

Camping in Hawaii usually means pitching a tent or reserving a cabin. Throughout the islands there are secluded spots and hidden beaches, plus numerous county, state and federal parks. All of these campsites, together with hiking trails, are described in the individual island chapters; it's a good idea to consult those detailed listings when planning your trip. The camping equipment you'll require is listed in the "Packing" section of the preceding chapter. You might also want to obtain some hiking maps; they are available from **Hawaii Geographic Maps & Books** (49 South Hotel Street #215, Honolulu; 808-538-3952, 800-538-3950).

Before you set out on your camping trip, there are a few very important matters that I want to explain more fully. First, bring a campstove: firewood is scarce in most areas and soaking wet in others. It's advisable to wear long pants when hiking in order to protect your legs from rock outcroppings, spiny plants and insects. Also, if you are going to explore the Mauna Kea, Mauna Loa or Haleakala volcanoes, be sure to bring cold-weather gear; temperatures are often significantly lower than at sea level and these peaks occasionally receive snow.

Most trails you'll be hiking are composed of volcanic rock. Since this is a very crumbly substance, be extremely cautious when climbing any rock faces. In fact, you should avoid steep climbs if possible. Stay on the trails: Hawaii's dense undergrowth makes it very easy to get lost. If you get lost at night, stay where you are. Because of the low latitude, night descends rapidly here; there's practically no twilight. Once darkness falls, it can be very dangerous to move around. You should also be careful to purify all of your drinking water. And be extremely cautious near streambeds as flash-flooding sometimes occurs, particularly on the windward coasts. This is particularly true during the winter months, when heavy storms from the northeast lash the islands.

Another problem that you're actually more likely to encounter are those nasty varmints that buzz your ear just as you're falling asleep—mosquitoes. Hawaii contains neither snakes nor poison ivy, but it has plenty of these dive-bombing pests. Like me, you probably consider that it's always open season on the little bastards.

With most of the archipelago's other species, however, you'll have to be a careful conservationist. You'll be sharing the wilderness with pigs, goats, tropical birds, deer and mongooses, as well as a spectacular array of exotic and indigenous plants. All exist in one of the world's most delicate ecological balances. There are more endangered species in Hawaii than in all the rest of the United States. So keep in mind the maxim that the Hawaiians try to follow. *Ua mau ke ea o ka aina i ka pono*: The life of the land is preserved in righteousness.

HIKING

Hiking in Hawaii includes trails through exotic forests, up rugged mountains and past crashing waterfalls. While the Big Island is reputed as a favorite hiking destination for its vast size, high peaks and outstanding views, treks on each island provide unique, up-close encounters with local habitat. Keep your eyes and ears on high alert for the wildlife that shares the lush landscape. You may spot a rarely seen bird such as Kauai's Greater-Necklaced Laughing-Thrush or some unusual vegetation. Be sure to check whether a permit is necessary before heading off on your tropical journey. And don't forget your water!

SIERRA CLUB OUTINGS ✉ *85 2nd Street, 2nd Floor, San Francisco, CA 94105* 📞 *415-977-5522* 📠 *415-977-5795* 🖊 *www.sierraclub.org/outings/national* If you're looking for a fun and fulfilling way to spend ten days, contact this experienced service. Their guided service trips lead you into the islands' most desolate wilderness areas, through lush tropical forests and to coastal waters, restoring natural settings by removing humanmade structures and fencing and conducting research on marine wildlife. Adventurers are able to snorkel, hike and enjoy beautiful views while helping to preserve Hawaii's paradise.

HAWAII ECOTOURISM ASSOCIATION 📞 *877-300-7058* 🖊 *www.hawaii ecotourism.org* This association serves as a clearinghouse for businesses offering tours, activities and adventures that emphasize ecological sustainability and the special attributes of the islands' environment and native culture.

NATURE CONSERVANCY OF HAWAII ☎*808-587-6220 (Maui), 808-553-5236 (Molokai)* ✐*www.nature.org* The Nature Conservancy conducts natural history day hikes of Oahu, Maui and Molokai. Led by expert guides, small groups explore untrammeled beaches, rainforest and an ancient bog. The tours provide a singular insight into the plant and animal life of the Islands. Reservations should be made at least one month in advance.

EARTHVOICE HAWAII ✉*P.O. Box 1433, Honokaa, HI 96727* ☎*888-464-1080* ✐*www.earthmediahawaii.com* An environmentally and culturally active nonprofit that aims to generate respect and responsibility for the natural world and interest in Hawaiian culture and customs. Activities run the gamut from nature walks to volcano watches to stepping through waterfalls.

HISTORY & CULTURE

POLYNESIAN ARRIVAL The island of Hawaii, the Big Island, was the last land mass created in the ongoing dramatic geologic upheaval that formed the Hawaiian islands. But it was most likely the first island to be inhabited by humans. Perhaps as early as the third century, Polynesians sailing from the Marquesas Islands, and then later from Tahiti, landed on Hawaii's southern tip. The boats were formidable structures, catamaran-like vessels with a cabin built on the platform between the wooden hulls. The sails were woven from *hala* (pandanus) leaves. Some of the vessels were a hundred feet long and could do 20 knots, making the trip to Hawaii in a month. Entire families crossed the 2500 miles of untracked ocean with all the provisions they needed for their new home.

The Polynesians had originally come from the coast of Asia about 3000 years before. They had migrated through Indonesia, then pressed inexorably eastward, leapfrogging across archipelagoes until they finally reached the last chain, the most remote—Hawaii. Some Polynesians migrated to the Hawaiian islands due to population pressures that caused famine. The lack of food sources led them to abandon their smaller, less abundant Pacific islands.

These Pacific migrants were undoubtedly the greatest sailors of their day, and stand among the finest in history. When close to land they could smell it, taste it in the seawater, see it in a lagoon's turquoise reflection on the clouds above an island. They knew 150 stars. From the color of the water they determined ocean depths and current directions. They had no charts, no compasses, no sextants; sailing directions were simply recorded in legends and chants. Yet Polynesians discovered the Pacific, from Indonesia to Easter Island, from New Zealand to Hawaii. They made the Vikings and Phoenicians look like landlubbers.

CAPTAIN COOK They were high islands, rising in the northeast as the sun broke across the Pacific. First one, then a second and, finally, as the tall-masted ships drifted west, a third island loomed before them. Landfall! The British crew was ecstatic. It meant fresh water, tropical fruits, solid ground on which to set their boots and a chance to carouse with the native women. For their captain, James Cook, it was another in an amazing career of discoveries. The man whom many call history's greatest explorer was about to land in one of the last spots on earth to be discovered by the West.

He would name the place for his patron, the British earl who became famous by pressing a meal between two crusts of bread. The Sandwich Islands. Later they would be called Owhyhee, and eventually, as the Western tongue glided around the uncharted edges of a foreign language, Hawaii.

It was January 1778, a time when the British Empire was still basking in a sun that never set. The Pacific had been opened to Western powers over two centuries before, when a Portuguese sailor named Magellan crossed it. Since that time, the British, French, Dutch and Spanish had tracked through in search of future colonies.

They happened upon Samoa, Fiji, Tahiti and the other islands that spread across this third of the globe, but somehow they had never sighted Hawaii. Even when Cook finally spied it, he little realized how important a find he had made. Hawaii, quite literally, was a jewel in the ocean, rich in fragrant sandalwood, ripe for agricultural exploitation and crowded with sea life. But it was the archipelago's isolation that would prove to be its greatest resource. Strategically situated between Asia and North America, it was the only place for thousands of miles to which whalers, merchants and bluejackets could repair for provisions and rest.

Cook was 49 years old when he shattered Hawaii's quiescence. The Englishman hadn't expected to find islands north of Tahiti. Quite frankly, he wasn't even trying. It was his third Pacific voyage and Cook was hunting bigger game, the fabled Northwest Passage that would link this ocean with the Atlantic. On January 18, 1778, Captain Cook's HMS *Resolution*, along with the HMS *Discovery*, spotted Oahu.

But these mountainous islands were still an interesting find. He could see by the canoes venturing out to meet his ships that the lands were inhabited; when he finally put ashore on Kauai, on January 20, Cook discovered a Polynesian society. He saw irrigated fields, domestic animals and high-towered temples. The women were bare-breasted, the men wore loincloths. As his crew bartered for pigs, fowls and bananas, he learned that the natives knew about metal and coveted iron like gold.

If iron was gold to these "Indians," then Cook was a god. He soon realized that his arrival had somehow been miraculously timed, coinciding with the Makahiki festival, a months-long celebration highlighted by sporting competitions, feasting, hula and exaltation of the ruling chiefs. Even war ceased during this gala affair. Makahiki honored the roving deity Lono, whose return to Hawaii on "trees that would move over seas" was foretold in ancient legend. Cook was a strange white man sailing tall-masted ships—obviously he was Lono. The Hawaiians gave him gifts, fell in his path and rose only at his insistence.

But even among religious crowds, fame is often fickle. After leaving Hawaii, Cook sailed north to the Arctic Sea, where he failed to discover the Northwest Passage. He returned the next year to Kealakekua Bay on the Big Island, arriving at the tail end of another exhausting Makahiki festival. By then the Hawaiians had tired of his constant demands for provisions and were suffering from a new disease that was obviously carried by Lono's archangelic crew—syphilis. This Lono was proving something of a freeloader.

Tensions ran high. The Hawaiians stole a boat. Cook retaliated with gunfire. A scuffle broke out on the beach and in a sudden violent outburst, which surprised the islanders as much as the interlopers, the Hawaiians discovered that their god could bleed. The world's finest mariner lay face down in foot-deep water, stabbed and bludgeoned to death.

Cook's end marked the beginning of an era. He had put the Pacific on the map, his map, probing its expanses and defining its fringes. In Hawaii he ended a thousand years of solitude. The archipelago's geographic isolation, which has always played a crucial role in Hawaii's development, had finally failed to protect it, and a second theme had come into play—the islands' vulnerability. Together with the region's "backwardness," these conditions would now mold Hawaii's history. All in turn would be shaped by another factor, one which James Cook had added to Hawaii's historic equation: the West.

KAMEHAMEHA AND KAAHUMANU The next man whose star would rise above Hawaii was present at Cook's death. Some say he struck the Englishman, others that he took a lock of the great leader's hair and used its residual power, its *mana*, to become king of all Hawaii.

Kamehameha was a tall, muscular, unattractive man with a furrowed face, a lesser chief on the powerful island of Hawaii. When he began his career of conquest a few years after Cook's death, he was a mere upstart, an ambitious, arrogant young chief. But he fought with a general's skill and a warrior's cunning, often plunging into the midst of a melee. He had an astute sense of technology, an intuition that these new Western metals and firearms could make him a king.

In Kamehameha's early years, the Hawaiian islands were composed of many fiefdoms. Several kings or great chiefs, continually warring among themselves, ruled individual islands. At times, a few kings would carve up one island or a lone king might seize several. Never had one monarch controlled all the islands.

But fresh players had entered the field: Westerners with ample firepower and awesome ships. During the decade following Cook, only a handful had arrived, mostly Englishmen and Americans, and they had not yet won the influence they soon would wield. However, even a few foreigners were enough to upset the balance of power. They sold weapons and hardware to the great chiefs, making several of them more powerful than any of the others had ever been. War was imminent.

Kamehameha stood in the center of the hurricane. Like any leader suddenly caught up in the terrible momentum of history, he never quite realized where he was going or how fast he was moving. And he cared little that he was being carried in part by Westerners who would eventually want something for the ride. Kamehameha was no fool. If political expedience meant Western intrusion, then so be it. He had enemies among chiefs on the other islands; he needed the guns.

When two white men came into his camp in 1790, he had the military advisers to complement a fast expanding arsenal. Within months he cannonaded Maui. In 1792, Kamehameha seized the Big Island by inviting his main rival to a peaceful parley, then slaying the hapless chief. By 1795, he had consolidated his control of Maui, grasped Molokai and Lanai, and begun reaching greedily toward Oahu. He struck rapidly, landing near Waikiki and sweeping inland, forcing his enemies to their deaths over the precipitous cliffs of the Nuuanu Pali.

The warrior had become a conqueror, controlling all the islands except Kauai, which he finally gained in 1810 by peaceful negotiation. Kamehameha proved to be as able a bureaucrat as he had been a general. He became a benevolent despot who, with the aid of an ever-increasing number of Western advisers, expanded Hawaii's commerce, brought peace to the islands and moved his people inexorably toward the modern age.

He came to be called Kamehameha the Great, and history first cast him as the George Washington of Hawaii, a wise and resolute leader who gathered a wartorn archipelago into a kingdom, Kamehameha I. But with the revisionist history of the 1960s and 1970s, as Third World people questioned both the Western version of events and the virtues of progress, Kamehameha began to resemble Benedict Arnold. He was seen as an opportunist, a megalomaniac who permitted the Western powers their initial foothold in Hawaii. He used their technology and then, in the manner of great men who depend on stronger allies, was eventually used by them.

As long a shadow as Kamehameha cast across the islands, the event that most dramatically transformed Hawaiian society occurred after his death in 1819. The kingdom had passed to Kamehameha's son Liholiho, but Kamehameha's favorite wife, Kaahumanu, usurped the power. Liholiho was a prodigal son, dissolute, lacking self-certainty, a drunk. Kaahumanu was a woman for all seasons, a canny politician who combined brilliance with boldness, the feminist of her day. She had infuriated Kamehameha by eating forbidden foods and sleeping with other chiefs, even when he placed a taboo on her body and executed her lovers. She drank liquor, ran away, proved completely uncontrollable and won Kamehameha's love.

It was only natural that when he died, she would take his *mana*, or so she reckoned. Kaahumanu gravitated toward power with the drive of someone whom fate has unwisely denied. She carved her own destiny, announcing that Kamehameha's wish had been to give her a governmental voice. There would be a new post and she would fill it, becoming in a sense Hawaii's first prime minister.

And if the power, then the motion. Kaahumanu immediately marched against Hawaii's belief system, trying to topple the old idols. For years she had bristled under a polytheistic religion regulated by taboos, or *kapus*, which severely restricted women's rights. Now Kaahumanu urged the new king, Liholiho, to break a very strict *kapu* by sharing a meal with women.

Since the act might help consolidate Liholiho's position, it had a certain appeal to the king. Anyway, the *kapus* were weakening: these white men, coming now in ever greater numbers, defied them with impunity. Liholiho vacillated, went on a two-day drunk before gaining courage, then finally sat down to eat. It was a last supper, shattering an ancient creed and opening the way for a radically new divinity. As Kaahumanu had willed, the old order collapsed, taking away a vital part of island life and leaving the Hawaiians more exposed than ever to foreign influence.

Already Western practices were gaining hold. Commerce from Honolulu, Lahaina and other ports was booming. There was a fortune to be made dealing sandalwood to China-bound merchants, and the chiefs were forcing the common people to strip Hawaii's forests. The grueling labor might make the chiefs rich, but it gained the commoners little more than a barren landscape. Western diseases struck virulently. The Polynesians in Hawaii, who numbered 300,000 in Cook's time, were extremely susceptible. By 1866, their population had dwindled to less than 60,000. It was a difficult time for the Hawaiian people.

MISSIONARIES AND MERCHANTS Hawaii was not long without religion. The same year that Kaahumanu shattered tradition, a group of New England missionaries boarded the brig *Thaddeus* for a voyage around Cape Horn. It was a young company—many were in their twenties or thirties—and included a doctor, a printer and several teachers. They were all strict Calvinists, fearful that the second coming was at hand and possessed of a mission. They were bound for a strange land called Hawaii, 18,000 miles away.

Hawaii, of course, was a lost paradise, a hellhole of sin and savagery where men slept with several wives and women neglected to wear dresses. To the missionaries, it mattered little that the Hawaiians had lived this way for centuries. The churchmen would save these heathens from hell's everlasting fire whether they liked it or not.

The delegation arrived in Kailua on the Big Island in 1820 and then spread out, establishing important missions in Honolulu and Lahaina. Soon they were building schools and churches, conducting services in Hawaiian and converting the natives to Christianity.

The missionaries rapidly became an integral part of Hawaii, despite the fact that they were a walking contradiction to everything Hawaiian. They were a contentious, self-righteous, fanatical people whose arrogance toward the Hawaiians blinded them to the beauty and wisdom of island lifestyles. Where the natives lived in thatch homes open to the soothing trade winds, the missionaries built airless clapboard houses with New England–style fireplaces. While the Polynesians swam and surfed frequently, the new arrivals, living near the world's finest beaches, stank from not bathing. In a region where the thermometer rarely drops much below 70 degrees, they wore long-sleeved woolens, ankle-length dresses and claw-hammer coats. At dinner they preferred salt pork to fresh beef, dried meat to fresh fish. They considered coconuts an abomination and were loath to eat bananas.

And yet the missionaries were a brave people, selfless and God-fearing. Their dangerous voyage from the Atlantic had brought them into a very alien land. Many would die from disease and overwork; most would never see their homeland again. Bigoted though they were, the Calvinists committed their lives to the Hawaiian people. They developed the Hawaiian alphabet, rendered Hawaiian into a written language and, of course, translated the Bible. Theirs was the first printing press west of the Rockies. They introduced Western medicine throughout the islands and created such an effective school system that, by the mid-19th century, 80 percent of the Hawaiian population was literate. Unlike almost all the other white people who came to Hawaii, they not only took from the islanders, they also gave.

But to these missionaries, *giving* meant ripping away everything repugnant to God and substituting it with Christianity. They would have to destroy Hawaiian culture in order to save it. Though instructed by their church elders not to meddle in island politics, the missionaries soon realized that heavenly wars had to be fought on earthly battlefields. Politics it would be. After all, wasn't government just another expression of God's bounty?

They allied with Kaahumanu and found it increasingly difficult to separate church from state. Kaahumanu converted to Christianity, while the missionaries became government advisers and helped pass laws protecting the sanctity of the Sabbath. Disgusting practices such as hula dancing were prohibited.

Politics can be a dangerous world for a man of the cloth. The missionaries were soon pitted against other foreigners who were quite willing to let the clerics sing hymns, but were damned opposed to permitting them a voice in government. Hawaii in the 1820s had become a favorite way station for the whaling fleet. As the sandalwood forests were decimated, the island merchants began looking for other industries. By the 1840s, when over 500 ships a year anchored in Hawaiian ports, whaling had become the islands' economic lifeblood. More American whaling ships visited Hawaii than any other port in the world.

Like the missionaries, the whalers were Yankees, shipping out from bustling New England ports. But they were a hell of a different cut of Yankee. These were rough, crude, boisterous men who loved rum and music, and thought a lot more of fornicating with island women than saving them. After the churchmen forced the passage of laws prohibiting prostitution, the sailors rioted along the waterfront and fired cannons at the mission homes. When the smoke cleared, the whalers still had their women.

Religion simply could not compete with commerce, and other Westerners were continuously stimulating more business in the islands. By the 1840s, as Hawaii adopted a parliamentary form of government, American and British fortune hunters were replacing missionaries as government advisers. It was a time when anyone, regardless of ability or morality, could travel to the islands and become a political powerhouse literally overnight. A consumptive American, fleeing the mainland for reasons of health, became chief justice of the Hawaiian Supreme Court while still in his twenties. Another lawyer, shadowed from the East Coast by a checkered past, became attorney general two weeks after arriving.

The situation was no different internationally. Hawaii was subject to the whims and terrors of gunboat diplomacy. The archipelago was solitary and exposed, and Western powers were beginning to eye it covetously. In 1843, a maverick British naval officer actually annexed Hawaii to the

Crown, but the London government later countermanded his actions. Then, in the early 1850s, the threat of American annexation arose. Restless Californians, fresh from the gold fields and hungry for revolution, plotted unsuccessfully in Honolulu. Even the French periodically sent gunboats in to protect their small Catholic minority.

Finally, the three powers officially stated that they wanted to maintain Hawaii's national integrity. But independence seemed increasingly unlikely. European countries had already begun claiming other Pacific islands, and with the influx of Yankee missionaries and whalers, Hawaii was being steadily drawn into the American orbit.

THE SUGAR PLANTERS There is an old Hawaiian saying that describes the 19th century: The missionaries came to do good, and they did very well. Actually the early evangelists, few of whom profited from their work, lived out only half the maxim. Their sons would give the saying its full meaning.

This second generation, quite willing to sacrifice glory for gain, fit neatly into the commercial society that had rendered their fathers irrelevant. They were shrewd, farsighted young Christians who had grown up in Hawaii and knew both the islands' pitfalls and potentials. They realized that the missionaries had never quite found Hawaii's pulse, and they watched uneasily as whaling became the lifeblood of the islands. Certainly it brought wealth, but whaling was too tenuous—there was always a threat that it might dry up entirely. A one-industry economy would never do; the mission boys wanted more. Agriculture was the obvious answer; and eventually they determined to bind their providence to a plant that grew wild in the islands—sugar cane.

The first sugar plantation was started on Kauai in 1835, but not until the 1870s did the new industry blossom. By then, the Civil War had wreaked havoc with the whaling fleet, and a devastating winter in the Arctic whaling grounds practically destroyed it. The mission boys, who had prophesied the storm, weathered it quite comfortably. They had already begun fomenting an agricultural revolution.

THE GREAT MAHELE Agriculture, of course, means land, and until the 19th century all Hawaii's acreage was held by chiefs. So in 1848, the mission sons, together with other white entrepreneurs, pushed through the Great Mahele, one of the slickest real estate laws in history. Rationalizing that it would grant chiefs the liberty to sell land to Hawaiian commoners and white men, the mission sons established a Western system of private property.

The Hawaiians, who had shared their chiefs' lands communally for centuries, had absolutely no concept of deeds and leases. What resulted was the old $24-worth-of-beads story. The benevolent Westerners wound up with the land, while the lucky Hawaiians got practically nothing. Large tracts were purchased for cases of whiskey; others went for the cost of a hollow promise. The entire island of Niihau, which is still owned by the same family, sold for $10,000. It was a bloodless coup, staged more than 40 years before the revolution that would topple Hawaii's monarchy. In a sense it made the 1893 uprising anticlimactic. By then Hawaii's future would already be determined: white interlopers would own four times as much land as Hawaiian commoners.

Following the Great Mahele, the mission boys, along with other businessmen, were ready to become sugar planters. The *mana* once again was passing into new hands. Obviously, there was money to be made in cane, a lot of it, and now that they had land, all they needed was labor. The Hawaiians would never do. Cook might have recognized them as industrious, hardworking people, but the sugar planters considered them shiftless. Disease was killing them off anyway, and the Hawaiians who survived seemed to lose the will to live. Many made appointments with death, stating that in a week they would die; seven days later they were dead.

Foreign labor was the only answer. In 1850, the Masters and Servants Act was passed, establishing an immigration board to import plantation workers. Cheap Asian labor would be brought over. It was a crucial decision, one that would ramify forever through Hawaiian history and change the very substance of island society. Eventually these Asian workers transformed Hawaii from a chain of Polynesian islands into one of the world's most varied and dynamic locales, a meeting place of East and West.

The Chinese were the first to come, arriving in 1852 and soon outnumbering the white population. Initially, with their long pigtails and uncommon habits, the Chinese were a joke around the islands. They were poor people from southern China whose lives were directed by clan loyalty. They built schools and worked hard so that one day they could return to their native villages in glory. They were ambitious, industrious and—ultimately—successful.

Too successful, according to the sugar planters, who found it almost impossible to keep the coolies down on the farm. The Chinese came to Hawaii under labor contracts, which forced them to work for five years. After their indentureship, rather than reenlisting as the sugar bosses had planned, the Chinese moved to the city and became merchants. Worse yet, they married Hawaiian women and were assimilated into the society.

These coolies, the planters decided, were too uppity, too ready to fill social roles that were really the business of white men. So in the 1880s, they began importing Portuguese, over 20,000 of them. But the Portuguese thought they already *were* white men, while any self-respecting American or Englishman of the time knew they weren't.

The Portuguese spelled trouble, and in 1886 the sugar planters turned to Japan, with its restricted land mass and burgeoning population. The new immigrants were peasants from Japan's southern islands, raised in an authoritarian, hierarchical culture in which the father was a family dictator and the family was strictly defined by its social status. Like the Chinese, they built schools to protect their heritage and dreamed of returning home someday; but unlike their Asian neighbors, they only married other Japanese. They sent home for "picture brides," worshipped their ancestors and Emperor and paid ultimate loyalty to Japan, not Hawaii.

The Japanese, it soon became evident, were too proud to work long hours for low pay. Plantation conditions were atrocious; workers were housed in hovels and frequently beaten. The Japanese simply did not adapt. Worst of all, they not only bitched, they organized, striking in 1909.

So in 1910, the sugar planters turned to the Philippines for labor. For two decades the Filipinos arrived, seeking their fortunes and leaving their wives behind. They worked not only with sugar cane but also with pineapples, which were becoming a big business in the 20th century. They were a boisterous, fun-loving people, hated by the immigrants who preceded them and used by the whites who hired them. The Filipinos were given the most menial jobs, the worst working conditions and the shoddiest housing. In time, another side of their character began to show—a despondency, a hopeless sense of their own plight, their inability to raise passage money back home. They became the untouchables of Hawaii.

REVOLUTIONARIES AND ROYALISTS Sugar, by the late 19th century, was king. It had become the center of island economy, the principal fact of life for most islanders. Like the earlier whaling industry, it was drawing Hawaii ever closer to the American sphere. The sugar planters were selling the bulk of their crops in California; having already signed several tariff treaties to protect their American market, they were eager to further strengthen mainland ties. Besides, many sugar planters were second-, third- and fourth-generation descendants of the New England missionaries; they had a natural affinity for the United States.

There was, however, one group that shared neither their love for sugar nor their ties to America. To the Hawaiian people, David Kalakaua was king, and America was the nemesis that had long threatened their independence. The whites might own the land, but the Hawaiians, through their monarch, still held substantial political power. During Kalakaua's rule in the 1870s and 1880s, anticolonialism was rampant.

The sugar planters were growing impatient. Kalakaua was proving very antagonistic; his nationalist drumbeating was becoming louder in their ears. How could the sugar merchants convince the United States to annex Hawaii when all these silly Hawaiian royalists were running around pretending to be the Pacific's answer to the British Isles? They had tolerated this long enough. The Hawaiians were obviously unfit to rule, and the planters soon joined with other businessmen to form a secret revolutionary organization. Backed by a force of well-armed followers, they pushed through the "Bayonet Constitution" of 1887, a self-serving document that weakened the king and strengthened the white landowners. If Hawaii was to remain a monarchy, it would have a Magna Carta.

But Hawaii would not be a monarchy long. Once revolution is in the air, it's often difficult to clear the smoke. By 1891, Kalakaua was dead and his sister, Liliuokalani, had succeeded to the throne. She was an audacious leader, proud of her heritage, quick to defend it and prone to let immediate passions carry her onto dangerous ground. At a time when she should have hung fire, she charged, proclaiming publicly that she would abrogate the new constitution and reestablish a strong monarchy. The revolutionaries had the excuse they needed. They struck in January 1895, seized government buildings and, with four boatloads of American marines and the support of the American minister, secured Honolulu. Liliuokalani surrendered to avoid bloodshed and was imprisoned in Iolani Palace. Sanford Dole, a missionary's son whose name eventually became synonymous with pineapples, became Hawaii's first president.

It was a highly illegal coup; legitimate government had been stolen from the Hawaiian people. But given an island chain as isolated and vulnerable as Hawaii, the revolutionaries reasoned, how much did it really matter? It would be weeks before word reached Washington of what a few Americans had done without official sanction, then several more months before a new American president, Grover Cleveland, denounced the renegade action. By then the revolutionaries would already be forming a republic.

Not even revolution could rock Hawaii into the modern age. For years, an unstable monarchy had reigned; now an oligarchy composed of the revolution's leaders would rule. Officially, Hawaii was a democracy; in truth, the Chinese and Japanese were hindered from voting, and the Hawaiians were encouraged not to bother. Hawaii, reckoned its new leaders, was simply not ready for democracy. Even when the islands were finally annexed by the United States in 1898 and granted territorial status, they remained a colony.

More than ever before, the sugar planters, alias revolutionaries, held sway. By the early 20th century, they had linked their plantations into a cartel, the Big Five. It was a tidy monopoly composed of five companies that owned not only the sugar and pineapple industries, but the docks, shipping companies and many of the stores, as well. Most of these holdings, happily, were the property of a few interlocking, intermarrying mission families—the Doles, Thurstons, Alexanders, Baldwins, Castles, Cookes and others—who had found heaven right here on earth. They golfed together and dined together, sent their daughters to Wellesley and their sons to Yale. All were proud of their roots, and as blindly paternalistic as their forefathers. It was their destiny to control Hawaii, and they made very certain, by refusing to sell land or provide services, that mainland firms did not gain a foothold in their domain.

What was good for the Big Five was good for Hawaii. Competition was obviously not good for Hawaii. Although the Chinese and Japanese were establishing successful businesses in Honolulu and some Chinese were even growing rich, they posed no immediate threat to the Big Five. And the Hawaiians had never been good at capitalism. By the early 20th century, they had become one of the world's most urbanized groups. But rather than competing with white businessmen in Honolulu, unemployed Hawaiians were forced to live in hovels and packing crates, cooking their poi on stoves fashioned from empty oil cans.

Political competition was also unhealthy. Hawaii was ruled by the Big Five, so naturally it should be run by the Republican Party. After all, the mission families were Republicans. Back on the mainland, the Democrats had always been cool to the sugar planters, and it was a Republican president, William McKinley, who eventually annexed Hawaii. The Republicans, quite simply, were good for business.

The Big Five set out very deliberately to overwhelm any political opposition. When the Hawaiians created a home-rule party around the turn of the century, the Big Five shrewdly co-opted it by running a beloved descendant of Hawaii's royal family as the Republican candidate. On the plantations they pitted one ethnic group against another to prevent the Asian workers from organizing. Then, when labor unions finally formed, the Big Five attacked them savagely. In 1924, police killed 16 strikers on Kauai. Fourteen years later, in an incident known as the "Hilo massacre," the police wounded 50 picketers.

The Big Five crushed the Democratic Party by intimidation. Polling booths were rigged. It was dangerous to vote Democratic—workers could lose their jobs, and if they were plantation workers, that meant losing their houses as well. Conducting Democratic meetings on the plantations was about as easy as holding a hula dance in an old missionary church. The Democrats went underground.

Those were halcyon days for both the Big Five and the Republican Party. In 1900, only five percent of Hawaii's population was white. The rest was composed of races that rarely benefitted from Republican policies. But for the next several decades, even during the Depression, the Big Five kept the Republicans in power.

While the New Deal swept the mainland, Hawaii clung to its colonial heritage. The islands were still a generation behind the rest of the United States—the Big Five enjoyed it that way. There was nothing like the status quo when you were already in power. Other factors that had long shaped Hawaii's history also played into the hands of the Big Five. The islands' vulnerability, which had always favored the rule of a small elite, permitted the Big Five to establish an awesome cartel. Hawaii's isolation, its distance from the mainland, helped protect their monopoly.

THE JAPANESE AND THE MODERN WORLD All that ended on December 7, 1941. On what would afterwards be known as the "Day of Infamy," a flotilla of six aircraft carriers carrying over 400 planes unleashed a devastating assault on Pearl Harbor. Attacking the Pacific Fleet on a Sunday morning, when most of the American ships were unwisely anchored side by side, the Japanese sank or badly damaged six battleships, three destroyers and several other vessels. Over 2400 Americans were killed.

The Japanese bombers that attacked Pearl Harbor sent shock waves through Hawaii that are still rumbling today. World War II changed all the rules of the game, upsetting the conditions that had determined island history for centuries.

Ironically, no group in Hawaii would feel the shift more thoroughly than the Japanese. On the mainland, Japanese-Americans were rounded up and herded into relocation camps. But in Hawaii that was impossible; there were simply too many (160,000—fully one-third of the island's population), and they comprised too large a part of the labor force. Instead, the community's business, religious and civic leaders were sent to internment camps in Hawaii and on the mainland.

Many were second-generation Japanese, *nisei*, who had been educated in American schools and assimilated into Western society. Unlike their immigrant parents, the *issei*, they felt few ties to Japan. Their loyalties lay with America, and when war broke out they determined to prove it. They joined the U.S. armed forces and formed a regiment, the 442nd, which became the most frequently decorated outfit of the war. The Japanese were heroes, and when the war ended many heroes came home to the United States and ran for political office. Men like Daniel Inouye and Spark Matsunaga began winning elections and would eventually become United States senators.

By the time the 442nd returned to the home front, Hawaii was changing dramatically. The Democrats were coming to power. Leftist labor unions won crucial strikes in 1941 and 1946. Jack Burns, an ex-cop who dressed in tattered clothes and drove around Honolulu in a beat-up car, was creating a new Democratic coalition.

Burns, who would eventually become governor, recognized the potential power of Hawaii's ethnic groups. Money was flowing into the islands—first military expenditures and then tourist dollars, and non-whites were rapidly becoming a new middle class. The Filipinos still constituted a large part of the plantation force, and the Hawaiians remained disenchanted, but the Japanese and Chinese were moving up fast. Together they formed a majority of Hawaii's voters.

Burns organized them, creating a multiracial movement and thrusting the Japanese forward as candidates. By 1954, the Democrats controlled the legislature, with the Japanese filling one out of every two seats in the capital. Then, when Hawaii attained statehood five years later, the voters elected the first Japanese ever to serve in Congress. Today one of the state's U.S. senators and a congresswoman are Japanese. On every level of government, from municipal to federal, the Japanese predominated. They had arrived. The *mana*, that legendary power coveted by the Hawaiian chiefs and then lost to the sugar barons, had passed once again—to a people who came as immigrant farm-workers and stayed to become the leaders of the 50th state.

The Japanese and the Democrats were on the move, but in the period from World War II until the present day, everything was in motion. Hawaii was in upheaval. Jet travel and a population boom shattered the islands' solitude. While in 1939 about 500 people flew to Hawaii, now about seven million visitors land every year. The military population escalated as Oahu became a key base not only during World War II but throughout the Cold War and the Vietnam War, as well. Hawaii's overall population exploded from about a half-million just after World War II to over one million at the present time.

No longer did the islands lag behind the mainland; they rapidly acquired the dubious quality of modernity. Hawaii became America's 50th state in 1959, Honolulu grew into a bustling highrise city, and hotels and condominiums mushroomed along the beaches of Maui, a neighboring island. Outside investors swallowed up two of the Big Five corporations, and several partners in the old monopoly began conducting most of their business outside Hawaii. Everything became too big and moved too fast for Hawaii to be entirely vulnerable to a small interest group. Now, like the rest of the world, it would be prey to multinational corporations.

By the 1980s, it would also be of significant interest to investors from Japan. In a few short years they succeeded in buying up a majority of the state's luxury resorts, including every major beachfront hotel in Waikiki, sending real estate prices into an upward spiral that did not level off until the early 1990s. During the rest of the decade, the economy was stagnant, with real estate prices dropping, agriculture declining and tourism leveling off at seven million visitors annually.

HAWAIIAN SOVEREIGNTY One element that has not plateaued during the last ten years is the Native Hawaiian movement. Nativist sentiments were spurred in January 1993 by the 100th anniversary of the American overthrow of the Hawaiian monarchy. Over 15,000 people turned out to mark the illegal coup. Later that year, President Clinton signed a statement issued by Congress formally apologizing to the Hawaiian people.

In 1994, the United States Navy returned the island of Kahoolawe to the state of Hawaii. Long a rallying symbol for the Native Hawaiian movement, the unoccupied island had been used for decades as a naval bombing target. By 1996, efforts to clean away bomb debris and make the island habitable were well under way, although completion of the clean-up is still years off.

Then in 1998, the issue of Hawaii's monarchy arose again when demonstrators marched around the entire island of Oahu and staged rallies to protest the 100th anniversary of the United States' annexation of Hawaii.

Today, numerous perspectives remain to be reconciled, with grass-roots movements working to secure a degree of autonomy for Hawaii's native people. The most common goal seems to be a status similar to that accorded the American Indians by the federal government, although there are still those who seek a return to an independent Hawaii, either as a restored monarchy or along democratic lines. Also pending resolution is the distribution of land to Native Hawaiians with documented claims, as well as a financial settlement with the state government. It's a complex situation involving the setting right of injustices of a century past.

HAWAIIAN CULTURE

Hawaii, according to Polynesian legend, was discovered by Hawaii-loa, an adventurous sailor who often disappeared on long fishing trips. On one voyage, urged along by his navigator, Hawaii-loa sailed toward the planet Jupiter. He crossed the "many-colored ocean," passed over the "deep-colored sea," and eventually came upon "flaming Hawaii," a mountainous island chain that spewed smoke and lava.

History is less romantic. The Polynesians who found Hawaii were probably driven from their home islands by war, famine or some similar calamity. They traveled in groups, not as lone rangers, and shared their canoes with dogs, pigs and chickens, with which they planned to stock new lands. Agricultural plants such as coconuts, yams, taro, sugar cane, bananas and breadfruit were also stowed on board.

Most important, they transported their culture, an intricate system of beliefs and practices developed in the South Seas. After undergoing the stresses and demands of pioneer life, this traditional lifestyle was transformed into a new and uniquely Hawaiian culture.

It was based on a caste system that placed the *alii* or chiefs at the top and the slaves, *kauwas*, on the bottom. Between these two groups were the priests, *kahunas* and the common people or *makaainanas*. The chiefs, much like feudal lords, controlled all the land and collected taxes from the commoners who farmed it. Each island was divided like a pie into wedge-shaped plots, *ahupuaas*, which extended from the ocean to the mountain peaks. In that way, every chief's domain contained fishing spots, village sites, arable land and everything else necessary for the survival of his subjects.

Life centered around the *kapu*, a complex group of regulations that dictated what was sacred or profane. For example, women were not permitted to eat pork or bananas; commoners had to prostrate themselves in the presence of a chief. These strictures were vital to Hawaiian religion; *kapu* breakers were directly violating the will of the gods and could be executed for their actions. And there were a lot of gods to watch out for, many quite vindictive. The four central gods were *Kane*, the creator; *Lono*, the god of agriculture and peace; *Ku*, the war god; and *Kanaloa*, lord of the underworld. They had been born from the sky father and earth mother, and had in turn created many lesser gods and demigods who controlled various aspects of nature.

It was, in the uncompromising terminology of the West, a stone-age civilization. Though the Hawaiians lacked metal tools, the wheel and a writing system, they managed to include within their inventory of cultural goods everything necessary to sustain a large population on a chain of small islands. They fashioned fish nets from native *olona* fiber, made hooks out of bone, shell and ivory, and raised fish in rock-bound ponds. The men used irrigation in their farming. The women made clothing by pounding mulberry bark into a soft cloth called *tapa*, dyeing elaborate patterns into the fabric. They built peak-roofed thatch huts from native *pili* grass and *hala* leaves. The men fought wars with spears, slings, clubs and daggers. The women used mortars and pestles to pound the roots of the taro plant into poi, the islanders' staple food. Bread, fruit, yams and coconut were other menu standards.

The West labeled these early Hawaiians "noble savages." Actually, they often lacked nobility. The Hawaiians were cannibals who practiced human sacrifice during religious ceremonies and often used human bone to fashion fish hooks. They constantly warred among themselves and would mercilessly pursue a retreating army, murdering as many of the vanquished soldiers as possible.

But they weren't savages either. The Hawaiians developed a rich oral tradition of genealogical chants and created beautiful lilting songs to accompany their hula dancing. Their musicians mastered several instruments including the *ukeke* (a single-stringed device resembling a bow), an *ohe hano ihu* or nose flute, rattles and drums made from gourds, coconut shells or logs. Their craftsmen produced the world's finest featherwork, tying thousands of tiny feathers onto netting to produce golden cloaks and ceremonial helmets. (Conscious of the fragility of their resources, Hawaiians used to trap birds by smearing branches with sticky sap. Once the birds were caught, they would pluck only the choicest feathers, clean the bird's claws and then release them.)

The Hawaiians helped develop the sport of surfing. They also swam, boxed, bowled and devised an intriguing game called *konane*, a cross between checkers and the Japanese game of go. They built networks of trails across lava flows, and created an elemental art form in the images—petroglyphs—that they carved into lava rock along the trails.

They also achieved something far more outstanding than their varied arts and crafts, something that the West, with its awesome knowledge and advanced technology, has never duplicated. The Hawaiians created a balance with nature. They practiced conservation, establishing closed seasons on certain fish species and carefully guarding their plant and animal resources. The Hawaiians sustained themselves by primarily eating vegetables and *poi*, while supplementing their diet with fish and several varieties of seafood or *limu*. Further, they used nature's herbs such as *nani* and *kukui* to treat ailments. But what they took from nature they also gave back.

They led a simple life, without the complexities the outside world would eventually thrust upon them. It was a good life: food was plentiful, people were healthy and the population increased. For a thousand years, the Hawaiians lived in delicate harmony with the elements. It wasn't until the West entered the realm, transforming everything, that the fragile balance was destroyed. But that is another story entirely.

PEOPLE

Because of its unique history and isolated geography, Hawaii is truly a cultural melting pot. It's one of the few states in the union in which caucasians are a minority group. Whites, or *haole* as they're called in the islands, comprise only about 27 percent of Hawaii's 1.2 million population. Asians (including Japanese, Korean, Filipino, Chinese and "other Asian") 41 percent, Hawaiians and part-Hawaiians account for 29 percent, and other racial groups 3 percent. It's a very vital society, with nearly 19 percent of the people born of racially mixed parents.

One trait characterizing many of these people is Hawaii's famous spirit of aloha, a genuine friendliness, an openness to strangers, a willingness to give freely. Undoubtedly, it is one of the finest qualities any people has ever demonstrated. Aloha originated with the Polynesians and played an important role in ancient Hawaiian civilization.

The aloha spirit is alive and well in the islands, although bad attitudes toward *haole*, are not unknown. All parties, however, seem to understand the crucial role tourism has come to play in Hawaii's economy, which means you're not likely to experience unpleasantness from the locals you'll meet—unless you behave unpleasantly. A smile goes a long way.

ECONOMY

For years, sugar was king in Hawaii, the most lucrative part of the island economy. Today, tourism is number one. About four million Americans, and almost seven million travelers worldwide visit the Aloha State every year. It's now a $10 billion business that expanded exponentially during the 1970s and 1980s, leveled off in the 1990s.

The U.S. military is another large industry, with some 17 percent of the state's population either on active duty or retired personnel—Hawaii has a greater percentage of its population in the military than any other state. With 161 installations in the state, the military controls nearly 6 percent of Hawaii's land mass, including 22 percent of Oahu. The armed forces pump more than $3 billion into the local economy annually, and it is pursuing plans to expand and step up its training, research, development and testing activities on all islands.

Sugar, long the agricultural mainstay of the islands, is now produced only on Maui and Kauai due to high production costs and dramatic reductions in federal subsidies. Much of the former cane land has been turned over to developers, where the state's $4.8 billion construction industry is busy building lavish estates and resort-related developments.

Pineapple is another crop that has nearly disappeared in Hawaii, largely because it can be grown and processed more cheaply in Thailand and the Philippines. The state's last pineapple plantation can be found on Maui.

Hawaii is the only place in the United States that grows coffee, with production centered on Kauai and the Kona district of the Big Island. Orchids, anthuriums and other tropical flowers also are important crops. Seed corn is another big industry, although a controversial one, because it involves crops that have been genetically modified. The islands have become a major testing area for genetically modified crops, a trend that has been bitterly opposed by environmentalists and native Hawaiians.

Because it is almost entirely dependent upon tourism and construction, Hawaii's economy is fragile and subject to frequent boom and bust cycles. The cost of living is at least 30 percent higher than the rest of the nation, due to the expense of importing fuel, food and other necessities. Although unemployment is low, most jobs are in the low-paying service industry, requiring many residents to hold more than one job. Meanwhile, housing prices have skyrocketed beyond the reach of most local families, resulting in widespread homelessness, especially on Oahu and among native Hawaiians.

CUISINE

Nowhere is the influence of Hawaii's melting pot population stronger than in the kitchen. While in the islands, you'll probably eat not only with a fork, but with chopsticks and fingers as well. You'll sample a wonderfully varied cuisine. In addition to standard American fare, hundreds of restaurants serve Hawaiian, Japanese, Chinese, Korean, Portuguese and Filipino dishes. There are also fresh fruits aplenty—pineapples, papayas, mangoes, bananas and tangerines—plus local fish such as mahimahi, marlin and snapper.

A quick translation will help you when choosing a seafood platter from Hawaiian waters. Firm-textured with a light taste, the most popular fish is mahimahi, or dolphin fish (no, it's not one of those amazing creatures that do fancy tricks on the waves); its English equivalent is dorado. *Ahi* is yellowfin tuna and is especially delicious as sashimi (raw) or blackened. Opakapaka is pink snapper and is a staple of Pacific Rim cuisine. Other snappers include *uku* (gray snapper), *onaga* (ruby snapper) and *ehu* (red snapper). *Ono* (which means delicious in Hawaiian) is king mackerel or *wahoo*, a white fish that lives up to its name.

The mainstay of the traditional Hawaiian diet is poi, a purplish paste pounded from baked or steamed taro tubers. It's pretty bland fare, but it does make a good side dish with *imu*-cooked pork or tripe stew. You should also try *laulau*, a combination of fish, pork and taro leaves wrapped in a *ti* leaf and steamed. And don't neglect to taste baked *ulu* (breadfruit) and *opihi* (limpets). Among the other Hawaiian culinary traditions are *kalua* pig, a shredded pork dish baked in an *imu* (underground oven); *lomilomi* salmon, which is salted and mixed with onions and tomatoes; and chicken *luau*, prepared in taro leaves and coconut milk.

A good way to try all these dishes at one sitting is to attend a luau. I've always found the tourist luaus too commercial, but you might watch the newspapers for one of the special luaus sponsored by local organizations.

Japanese dishes include sushi, sukiyaki, teriyaki and tempura, plus an island favorite—*sashimi*, or raw fish. On most any menu, including McDonald's, you'll find *saimin*, a noodle soup filled with meat, vegetables and *kamaboko* (fishcake).

You can count on the Koreans for *kim chi*, a spicy salad of pickled cabbage and *kalbi*, barbecued beef short ribs prepared with soy and sesame oil. The Portuguese serve up some delicious sweets including *malasadas* (donuts minus the holes) and *pao doce*, or sweet bread. For Filipino fare, I recommend *adobo*, a pork or chicken dish spiced with garlic and vinegar, and *pochero*, a meat entrée cooked with bananas and several vegetables. In addition to a host of dinner dishes, the Chinese have contributed treats such as *manapua* (a steamed bun filled with barbecued pork) and oxtail soup. They also introduced crack seed to the islands. Made from dried and preserved fruit, it provides a treat as sweet as candy.

As the Hawaiians say, *"Hele mai ai."* Come and eat!

LANGUAGE

The language common to all Hawaii is English, but because of its diverse cultural heritage, the archipelago also supports several other tongues. Foremost among these are Hawaiian and pidgin. Hawaiian, closely related to other Polynesian languages, is one of the most fluid and melodious languages in the world. It's composed of only twelve letters: five vowels—*a, e, i, o, u* and seven consonants—*h, k, l, m, n, p, w.* The glottal stop ('), when used, counts as a thirteenth letter.

At first glance, the language appears formidable: how the hell do you pronounce *humuhumunukunukuapuaa*? But actually it's quite simple. After you've mastered a few rules of pronunciation, you can take on any word in the language.

The first thing to remember is that every syllable ends with a vowel, and the next to last syllable usually receives the accent.

The next rule to keep in mind is that all the letters in Hawaiian are pronounced. Consonants are pronounced the same as in English (except for the *w*, which is pronounced as a *v* when it introduces the last syllable of a word—as in *ewa* or *awa*. Vowels are pronounced the same as in Spanish: *a* as in *among*, *e* as in *they*, *i* as in *machine*, *o* as in *no* and *u* as in *too*. Hawaiian has four vowel combinations or diphthongs: *au*, pronounced *ow*; *ae* and *ai*, which sound like *eye*; and *ei*, pronounced *ay*. As noted above, the glottal stop (') occasionally provides a thirteenth letter.

By now, you're probably wondering what I could possibly have meant when I said Hawaiian was simple. I think the glossary that follows will simplify everything while helping you pronounce common words and place names. Just go through the list, starting with words like aloha and luau that you already know. After you've practiced pronouncing familiar words, the rules will become second nature; you'll no longer be a *malihini* (newcomer).

Just when you start to speak with a swagger, cocky about having learned a new language, some young Hawaiian will start talking at you in a tongue that breaks all the rules you've so carefully mastered. That's pidgin. It started in the 19th century as a lingua franca among Hawaii's many races. Pidgin speakers mix English and Hawaiian with several other tongues to produce a spicy creole. It's a fascinating language with its own vocabulary, a unique syntax and a rising inflection that's hard to mimic.

Pidgin is definitely the hip way to talk in Hawaii. A lot of young Hawaiians use it among themselves as a private language. At times they may start talking pidgin to you, acting as though they don't speak English; then if they decide you're okay, they'll break into English. When that happens, you be one *da kine brah*.

So *brah*, I take *da kine* pidgin words, put 'em together with Hawaiian, make one big list. Savvy?

aa (ah-**ah**)—a type of rough lava

ae (eye)—yes

aikane (eye-**kah**-nay)—friend, close companion

akamai (ah-kah-**my**)—wise

alii (ah-**lee**-ee)—chief

aloha (ah-**lo**-ha)—hello; greetings; love

aole (ah-**oh**-lay)—no

auwe (ow-**way**)—ouch!; oh no!

brah (bra)—friend; brother; bro'

bumby (**bum**-bye)—after a while; by and by

da kine (da kyne)—whatdyacallit; thingamajig; the best

dah makule guys (da mah-**kuh**-lay guys)—senior citizens

diamondhead—in an easterly direction (Oahu only)

duh uddah time (duh **uh**-duh time)—once before

ewa (**eh**-vah)—in a westerly direction (Oahu only)

e komo mai (eh kohmoh mai)—welcome, come in

hale (**hah**-lay)—house

haole (**how**-lee)—Caucasian; white person

hano hou (hah nah hou)—encore

hapa (**hah**-pa)—half

hapa-haole (**hah**-pa **how**-lee)—half-Caucasian

heiau (hey-**yow**)—temple

hele on (**hey**-lay on)—go, move, outta here

hoaloha (ho-ah-**lo**-ha)—friend

holo holo (**ho**-low **ho**-low)—to visit

howzit? (hows-it)—how you doing? what's happening?

huhu (hoo-hoo)—angry

hukilau (**who**-key-lau)—community fishing party

hula (**who**-la)—Hawaiian dance

imu (**ee**-moo)—underground oven

ipo (**ee**-po)—sweetheart

kahuna (kah-**who**-nah)—priest; specialist or expert in any field

kai (kye)—ocean

kaka-roach (**kah**-kah roach)—ripoff; theft

kamaaina (kah-mah-**eye**-nah)—one born and raised in Hawaii; a long-time island resident

kane (**kah**-nay)—man

kapu (**kah**-poo)—taboo; forbidden

kaukau (cow-cow)—food

keiki (**kay**-key)—child

kiawe (key-**ah**-vay)—mesquite tree

kokua (ko-**coo**-ah)—help

kona winds (**ko**-nah winds)—winds that blow against the trades

kuli kuli (koo-lee koo-lee)—be quiet, be still

lanai (lah-**nye**)—porch; also island name

lauhala (lau-**hah**-lah) or *hala* (**hah**-lah)—a pandanus tree whose leaves are used in weaving

lei (lay)—flower garland

lolo (low-low)—stupid

lomilomi (**low**-me-**low**-me)—massage; salted raw salmon

luau (**loo**-ow)—Hawaiian meal

mahalo (mah-**hah**-low)—thank you

mahalo nui loa (mah-**ha**-low **new**-ee **low**-ah)—thank you very much

mahu (**mah**-who)—gay; homosexual

makai (mah-**kye**)—toward the sea

malihini (mah-lee-**hee**-nee)—newcomer; stranger

mauka (**mau**-kah)—toward the mountains

nani (**nah**-nee)—beautiful

ohana (oh-**hah**-nah)—family

okole (oh-**ko**-lay)—rear; ass

okolemaluna (oh-ko-lay-mah-**loo**-nah)—a toast: bottoms up!

ono (**oh**-no)—tastes good

pahoehoe (pah-**hoy**-hoy)—smooth or ropy lava

pakalolo (pah-kah-**low**-low)—marijuana

popakiki (poh-poh-**key**-key)—stubborn; hard head

pali (**pah**-lee)—cliff

paniolo (pah-nee-**oh**-low)—cowboy

pau (pow)—finished; done

pilikia (pee-lee-**key**-ah)—trouble

puka (**poo**-kah)—hole

pupus (**poo**-poos)—hors d'oeuvres

shaka (**shah**-kah)—hand greeting

swell head—"big head"; egotistical

tapa (**tah**-pah)—also *kapa*; fabric made from the beaten bark of mulberry trees

wahine (wah-**hee**-nay)—woman

wikiwiki (**wee**-key-**wee**-key)—quickly; in a hurry

you get stink ear—you don't listen well

MUSIC

Music has long been an integral part of Hawaiian life. Most families keep musical instruments in their homes, gathering to play at impromptu living room or backyard jam sessions. Hawaiian folk tunes are passed down from generation to generation. In the earliest days, it was the sound of rhythm instruments and chants that filled the air. Drums, including the *pahu hula*, were fashioned from hollowed-out gourds, coconut shells or hollowed sections of coconut palm trunks, then covered with sharkskin. Gourds and coconuts, *uliuli*, adorned with tapa cloth and feathers, were also filled with shells or pebbles to produce a rattling sound. Other instruments included the nose flute, or *ohe*, a piece of bamboo similar to a mouth flute, but played by exhaling through the nostril; the bamboo organ; and *puili*, sections of bamboo split into strips, which were struck rhythmically against the body. Stone castanets, *illili*, and *ke laau* sticks are also used as hula musical instruments.

Western musical scales and instruments were introduced by explorers and missionaries. As ancient Hawaiian music involved a radically different musical system, Hawaiians had to completely re-adapt. Actually, Western music caught on quickly, and the hymns brought by missionaries fostered a popular musical style—the *himeni,* or Hawaiian church music.

Hawaii has been the birthplace of several different musical instruments and styles. The ukulele, modeled on a Portuguese guitar, quickly became the most popular Hawaiian instrument. Its small size made it easy to carry, and with just four strings, it was simple to play. Legend has it that the ukulele was introduced to the islands in 1879 when the *Ravenscrag* arrived in Honolulu from the island of Madeira, bringing a boatload of Portuguese to work the sugar cane fields. Known as a *braguinha* by the Portuguese, the Hawaiians named it the ukulele, or "jumping flea," for the way one's fingers dance across the instrument. King David Kalakaua was purported to design and play his own instruments after he was taught by Augusto Dias, whose shop he visited frequently. Other notable Hawaiian royalty ukulele players included Queen Emma, Queen Liliuokalani, Prince Leleiohoku and Princess Likelike.

The slack-key style of guitar playing also comes from Hawaii, where it's called *ki ho'alu.* When the guitar was first brought to Hawaii in the 1830s by Mexican and Spanish cowboys, the Hawaiians adapted the instrument to their own special breed of music. In tuning, the six (or twelve) strings are loosened so that they sound a chord when strummed and match the vocal range of the singer. Slack-key is played in a variety of ways, from plucking or slapping the strings to sliding along them. A number of different tunings exist, and many have been passed down orally through families for generations. Some of the more renowned guitarists playing today include Keola Beamer, Raymond Kane and Cyril Pahinui.

During the late 19th century, *"hapa*-haole" songs became the rage. The ukulele was instrumental in contributing to this Hawaiian fad. Written primarily in English with pseudo-Hawaiian themes, songs like "Tiny Bubbles" and "Lovely Hula Hands" were later introduced to the world via Hollywood. The Hawaiian craze continued on the mainland with radio and television shows such as "Hawaii Calls" and "The Harry Owens Show." In the 1950s, little mainland girls donned plastic hula skirts and danced along with Hilo Hattie and Ray Kinney.

It was not until the 1970s that both the hula and music of old Hawaii made a comeback. Groups such as the Sons of Hawaii and the Makaha Sons of Niihau, along with the late Auntie Genoa Keawe and Gabby Pahinui, became popular. Before long, a new form of Hawaiian music was being heard, a combination of ancient chants and contemporary sounds, performed by such islanders as Henry Kapono, Kalapana,

Olomana, the Beamer Brothers, Bla Pahinui, the Peter Moon Band and the Brothers Cazimero.

Today many of these groups, along with other notables such as Hapa, the Kaau Crater Boys, Brother Noland, Willie K., Del Beazley, Butch Helemano, Obrien Eselu and Jake Shimabukuro, bring both innovation to the Hawaiian music scene and contribute to the preservation of an ancient tradition. The trend continues with hybrid infusions of reggae and rock, dubbed "Jawaiian," while performers like Kealii Reichel and groups like Kapena maintain the soft-edged sounds so well-suited to the islands.

Pro-sovereignty groups like Sudden Rush have taken this trend one step further, laying down their message-imbued rap lyrics on reggae tunes and Hawaiian classics to create a truly unique genre. In addition, now-deceased masters of Hawaiian song like Gabby Pahinui and Israel Kamakawiwoole have gained renewed popularity and respect for the links they created between old and contemporary Hawaiian music.

Tune in to KPOA-FM 93.5 and 102.7 for island sounds and Hawaiian music.

HULA

Along with palm trees, the hula—swaying hips, grass skirts, colorful leis—is linked forever in people's minds with the Hawaiian Islands. This western idea of hula is very different from what the dance has traditionally meant to native Hawaiians.

Hula is an old dance form, its origin shrouded in mystery. The ancient hula, *hula kahiko*, was more concerned with religion and spirituality than entertainment. Originally performed only by men, it was used in rituals to communicate with a deity—a connection to nature and the gods. Accompanied by drums and chants, *hula kahiko* expressed the islands' culture, mythology and history in hand and body movements. It later evolved from a strictly religious rite to a method of communicating stories and legends. Over the years, women were allowed to study the rituals and eventually became the primary dancers.

When westerners arrived, the *hula kahiko* began another transformation. Explorers and sailors were more interested in its erotic element, ignoring the cultural significance. Missionaries simply found it scandalous and set out to destroy the tradition. They dressed Hawaiians in western garb and outlawed the *hula kahiko*.

The hula tradition was resurrected by King David Kalakaua. who said, "Hula is the language of the heart, and therefore the heart beat of the Hawaiian people." Known by the moniker "Merrie Monarch," Kalakaua loved music and dance. For his coronation in 1883, he called together the kingdom's best dancers to perform the chants and hulas once again. He was also instrumental in the development of the contemporary hula, the *hula auwana*, which added new steps and movements and was accompanied by ukuleles and guitars rather than drums.

By the 1920s, modern hula had been popularized by Hollywood, westernized and introduced as kitschy tropicana. Real grass skirts gave way to cellophane versions, plastic leis replaced fragrant island garlands, and exaggerated gyrations supplanted the hypnotic movements of the traditional dance.

Fortunately, with the resurgence of Hawaiian pride in recent decades, Polynesian culture has been reclaimed and *hula kahiko* and traditional chants have made a welcome comeback. Hula *halaus* (schools) are serious business throughout the islands (and even on the mainland). Competitions bring together *halau* throughout the islands, the most well-known being the Big Island's Merrie Monarch Festival.

OAHU

Oahu

Honolulu, Somerset Maugham once remarked, is the meeting place of East and West. Today, with its highrise cityscape and crowded commercial center, Hawaii's capital is more the place where Hong Kong meets Los Angeles. It's the hub of Hawaii—a city that dominates the political, cultural and economic life of the islands.

And it's the focus of Oahu as well. Honolulu has given Oahu more than its nickname, The Capital Island. The city has drawn three-fourths of Hawaii's population to this third-largest island, making Oahu both a military stronghold and a popular tourist spot.

With military installations at Pearl Harbor and outposts seemingly everywhere, the armed forces control about one-quarter of the island. Most bases are off-limits to civilians; and tourists congregate in Honolulu's famed resort area— Waikiki. Both defense and tourism are big business on Oahu, and it's an ironic fact of island life that the staid, uniformly dressed military peacefully coexist here with crowds of sun-loving, scantily clad visitors.

The tourists are attracted by one of the world's most famous beaches, an endless white-sand ribbon that has drawn sun worshippers and water lovers since the days of Hawaiian royalty. In ancient times Waikiki was a swamp; now it's a spectacular region of world-class resorts.

Indeed, Waikiki is at the center of Pacific tourism, just as Honolulu is the capital of the Pacific. Nowhere else in the world will you find a population more varied or an ambience more vital. There are times when Waikiki's Parisian-size boulevards seem ready to explode from the sheer force of the crowds. People in bikinis and wild-colored aloha shirts stroll the streets, while others flash past on mopeds.

During the 1980s this sun-splashed destination became a focal point for millions of wealthy tourists from Japan. As a result, Waikiki has moneychanging shops, restaurants displaying menus in Japanese only, stores where the clerks speak no English and an entire mall filled with duty-free shops.

Today the development that created modern-day Waikiki continues, albeit at a slower pace and on a less intense scale, at the Koolina Resort, along the south central Oahu coast near residential Ewa Beach, with the JW Marriott Ihilani Resort & Spa providing a flagship hotel for the resort. Nearby, work continues on the development of Kapolei as a "second city" for Oahu, planned for as many as 200,000 people and designed to reduce the population concentration on urban Honolulu.

So hurry. Visitors can still discover that just beyond Honolulu's bustling thoroughfares stretches a beautiful island, featuring countless beaches and two incredible mountain ranges. Since most of the tourists (and a vast majority of the island's 863,100 population) congregate in the southern regions around Honolulu, the north is rural. You can experience the color and velocity of the city, then head for the slow and enchanting country.

As you begin to explore for yourself, you'll find Oahu also has something else to offer: history. *Oahu* means "gathering place" in Hawaiian, and for centuries it has been an important commercial area and cultural center. First populated by Marquesans around A.D. 500, the island was later settled by seafaring immigrants from Tahiti. Waikiki, with its white-sand beaches and luxurious coconut groves, became a favored spot among early monarchs.

Warring chiefs long battled for control of the island. Kamehameha I seized power in 1795 after landing troops along the coast just east of Waikiki, proceeding inland and sweeping an opposing army over the cliffs of Nuuanu Pali north of Honolulu. Several years earlier the British had "discovered" Honolulu Harbor, a natural anchorage destined to be one of the Pacific's key seaports. Over the years the harbor proved ideal first for whalers and sandalwood traders and eventually for freighters and ocean liners.

By the 1840s, the city, originally a village called Kou, had grown into a shipping port and the commercial and political capital of the Hawaiian kingdom. Here in 1893 a band of white businessmen illegally overthrew the native monarchy. Almost a half-century later, in an ill-advised but brilliantly executed military maneuver, the Japanese drew the United States into World War II with a devastating air strike against the huge naval base at Pearl Harbor.

There are some fascinating historical monuments to tour throughout Honolulu, but I recommend you also venture outside the city to Oahu's less congested regions. Major highways lead from the capital along the east and west coasts of this 608-square-mile island, and several roads bisect the central plateau en route to

Closest to Honolulu is the east coast, where a spectacular seascape is paralleled by the Koolaus, a jagged and awesomely steep mountain range. This is Oahu's rainswept Windward Coast. Here, traveling up the coast past the bedroom communities of Kailua and Kaneohe, you'll discover beautiful and relatively untouched white-sand beaches. On the North Shore are some of the world's most famous surfing spots—Waimea Bay, Sunset, the Banzai Pipeline—where winter waves as high as 20 to 30 feet roll in with crushing force.

The Waianae Range, rising to 4040 feet, shadows Oahu's western coast. The sands are white here, the beaches as uncrowded, but I've always felt slightly uncomfortable on the Leeward Coast. Theft can be a problem here. Wherever you go on Oahu, never leave valuables unattended, but be particularly watchful around this area.

Between the Koolau and Waianae ranges, remnants of the two volcanoes that created Oahu, spreads the Leilehua Plateau. This fertile region is occupied by sugar and pineapple plantations as well as several large military bases.

Geologically, Oahu is the second-oldest island in the chain; two million years ago it was two individual islands, which eventually were joined by the Leilehua Plateau. Among its geographic features is the *pali*, an awesome wall of sheer cliffs along the windward coastline, and three famous tuff-cone volcanoes—Diamond Head, Punchbowl and Koko Head.

Hosting millions of tourists each year, Oahu has become a favorite location among travel agents. Many people can't even conceive of visiting Hawaii without going to "the gathering place," and some never venture out of Waikiki. But if, like me, you think of a vacation in terms of experiencing the crowds, and then leaving them behind—plan on venturing outside of Waikiki and Honolulu to unspoiled rural Oahu.

WAIKIKI

To understand the geography of Waikiki you need only know about Waikiki Beach. And to understand Waikiki Beach, you must know two things. The first is that major hotels line the beach, practically from one end to the other, and are used as landmarks by visitors and local residents alike. The other fact to remember is that to visitors Waikiki Beach is a single sandy ribbon two miles long, but to local folks it represents many beaches in one. When you park your beach towel here, consider that every few strides will carry you into another realm of Waikiki's culture and history.

Waikiki is where Hawaiian tourism began, and its reputation as a retreat dates back centuries. It is believed that the area was a favorite recreation site for the long-ago kings of Oahu and Maui, and a holy place as well. The site of the Royal Hawaiian Hotel was previously a *heiau pookanaka*, or sacrificial temple, and strictly off limits to the common people.

THE UKULELE HOUSE

PAGE 76

Everything ukulele: children's souvenirs, vintage models, free lessons and even the world's largest one

THE BREAKERS

PAGE 67

Classic 1950s resort with "Asian" ambiance—truly a find

DIAMOND HEAD GRILL

PAGE 73

Hawaii Regional cuisine—innovative and artfully presented

QUEEN KAPIOLANI HIBISCUS GARDEN

PAGE 64

Peaceful and pretty place to stroll among colorful tropical flowers and picnic under shady pavilions

This fabled peninsula extends two miles from the Ala Wai Yacht Harbor to Diamond Head and measures a half-mile in width from the Ala Wai Canal to the Pacific. Kalakaua Avenue, the main drag, is packed elbow to elbow with throngs of visitors. Paralleling the ocean, this broad boulevard is all at once noisy, annoying, exciting, cosmopolitan and fascinating. Today, visitors from Japan, Korea and Australia add to the international atmosphere.

But the main appeal is still the district's white-sand corridor. Dotting the beach are picnic areas, restrooms, showers, concession stands and beach equipment rentals. Most of the beach is protected by coral reefs and sea walls, so the swimming is excellent, the snorkeling fair. This is also a prime area for surfing. Two- to four-foot waves, good for beginners and still challenging to experienced surfers, are common here.

OAHU WAIKIKI SIGHTS

WAIKIKI HISTORIC TRAIL

www.waikikihistorictrail.com With the glut of high-rise resorts and upscale boutiques, it may be hard to believe that Waikiki had a noteworthy history at all. You can explore the hidden past of Hawaii's most popular tourist destination by following this historic walking tour. The pamphlet describes such places as the heiau, where it is purported the last human sacrifice was made by King Kamehameha; the wizard stones of Kapaemahu (placed by four Tahitian soothsayers); the Moana Hotel, the first hotel to make Waikiki a resort destination. Even if you don't take the walk, the historical information is worth reading. Be sure to download the walk from the website before you embark on the tour. If you don't have a computer, you'll need to head to the Hawaii Tourism Authority in Honolulu's Hawaii Convention Center (1801 Kalakaua Avenue; 808-973-2255).

HILTON HAWAIIAN VILLAGE ⊠2005 Kalia Road It's difficult to visit Waikiki and not spot this colorful "village." Even if you're staying somewhere else on the island, be sure to wander through the shops and gardens of the complex; the landscaped grounds include 22 acres of indigenous flora sprinkled with koi ponds, penguin and flamingo habitats, and a number of squawking cockatoos. Two rainbow-patterned mosaics flank both sides of the Rainbow Tower.

BISHOP MUSEUM

⊠Hilton Hawaiian Village, 2005 Kalia Road ℡808-949-4321 📠808-951-5458 *www.hiltonhawaiianvillage.com* In the sweeping Kalia Tower, the Hilton Hawaiian Village has established a satellite branch of the Bishop Museum with material you won't find in the main headquarters. Visitors are met with *oli* (traditional chants) and move through the exhibits to the rhythms of Hawaii's musical heritage. There are vivid life-size scenes of life in Waikiki over the past two centuries, and an impressive collection of art and photographs.

KAHANAMOKU BEACH The western flank of Waikiki Beach sits near the Hilton Hawaiian Village. Here you will find a pretty lagoon fringed by palm trees. The curving strand nearby, fronting the resort, is called Kahanamoku Beach. Named for Hawaii's great surfer, Duke Kahanamoku, it features numerous facilities. Beach stands rent everything from towels, chairs and air mattresses to snorkel sets, surfboards and Hobie-cat sailboats.

62

Waikiki

POINTS OF INTEREST

- Ⓐ Ala Moana Center
- Ⓑ Hilton Hawaiian Village
- Ⓒ International Marketplace
- Ⓓ Kings Village
- Ⓔ Queen Kapiolani Hibiscus Garden
- Ⓕ Rainbow Bazaar
- Ⓖ Royal Hawaiian Shopping Center
- Ⓗ U.S. Army Museum of Hawaii
- Ⓘ Waikiki Aquarium
- Ⓙ Waikiki Shell
- Ⓚ Waikiki Shopping Plaza

FORT DERUSSY BEACH Owned by the military but open to the public, this strand features the area's widest swath of white sand. It is also beautifully backdropped by a grove of palm trees. There are restrooms, picnic tables and barbecues, plus tennis, squash and volleyball courts on the property.

U.S. ARMY MUSEUM OF HAWAII ✉*On the grounds of the Hale Koa Hotel, 2055 Kalia Road, Fort DeRussy* ☏*808-438-2821* 🖷*808-941-3617* ✎*www.hiarmy museumsoc.org, info@hiarmymuseumsoc.org* Showcasing every weapon from Hawaiian shark teeth blades to Vietnam-era instruments of destruction, this museum near Fort DeRussy Beach features a rotating gallery and theater. You can also trace the United States' unending series of military campaigns from the uniforms and equipment (ours and theirs) on exhibit here. Closed Monday.

HIGHRISE HOTELS Past Fort DeRussy Beach stretches a palisade of highrise hotels. Lining the beachfront, they provide numerous facilities for thirsty sunbathers or adventuresome athletes. Continue on and you will pass "the strip," a lengthy stretch of Waikiki Beach fronted entirely by hotels. This section marks Waikiki's center of action. The first hotel is the **Outrigger Reef on the Beach**, followed by the **Halekulani**, a pricey property that many consider Waikiki's finest hotel. Next is the **Sheraton Waikiki**. A highrise structure built with two curving wings, it resembles a giant bird roosting on the beach.

ROYAL-MOANA BEACH The hotels along Waikiki Beach are so famous that the nearby strand is named after them. Stretching between the Royal Hawaiian and Moana hotels, this beach has been a sunsoaked gathering place for decades. That's because these two grand dames are Waikiki's oldest hotels.

ROYAL HAWAIIAN HOTEL ✉*2259 Kalakaua Avenue* ☏*808-923-7311* ✎*www.royal-hawaiian.com* A Spanish Moorish–style caravansary painted a distinctive pink, this historic gem is dubbed the "Pink Palace." Built in 1927, it is a labyrinth of gardens, colonnades and balconies; the place certainly captures Waikiki's bygone era. At one time, the back lawn of the hotel had nearly 10,000 coconut trees. Now you can find 10,000 stores.

MOANA SURFRIDER RESORT ✉*2365 Kalakaua Avenue* ☏*808-922-3111, 866-716-8112* 🖷*808-924-4799* ✎*www.moana-surfrider.com* Built in 1901, the Moana was Waikiki's first resort. Its vaulted ceilings, tree-shaded courtyard and spacious accommodations reflect the days when Hawaii was a retreat for the rich. Further delving into the history of the place can be done in its **Historical Room**, containing interesting photographs and memorabilia dating from the hotel's conception. The **Moana Banyan tree**, planted on the grounds in 1904, stretches 150 feet across and 75 feet high. The Moana's beach is also the site of one of Waikiki's most renowned surfing spots, **Canoe's Surf**.

OUTRIGGER CANOES Along Waikiki Beach, concessions offer rides on outrigger canoes. They are long, sleek fiberglass crafts resembling ancient Polynesian canoes. Each seats four to six passengers, plus a captain. For a fee you can join the crew on a low-key wave-riding excursion that will have you paddling as hard and fast as you can to catch waves and ride them far into the shore.

KUHIO BEACH PARK ✉*Kalakaua Avenue* Just beyond the Moana is this popular park, which runs along Kalakaua Avenue from Kaiulani to Kapahulu avenues. In addition to a broad sandy beach and a creative layout that includes a **banyan tree,** traditional **healing stones** and a cascading fountain, there are numerous facilities here—picnic areas, beach equipment rentals, showers and restrooms, as well as lifeguards. The shady pavilions also attract local folks who come to play cards and chess. Needless to say, it's often quite crowded. Diners like it because of its proximity to many Waikiki budget restaurants; parents favor the beach for its protective sea wall, which provides a secure area where children can swim; and people-watchers find it an ideal place to check out the crowds of tourists and local residents. The park features broad walkways, grassy areas and artificial waterfalls and tidepools.

QUEEN'S SURF

The strand just beyond Kuhio Beach Park is named after Queen Liliuokalani who once had a beach home here. Something of a bohemian quarter, this pretty plot draws gays, local artists and a wide array of intriguing characters. On the weekends, conga drummers may be pounding out rhythms along the beach while others gather to soak in the scene. Several weekends each month, hit films are shown on a 30-foot screen. The "**Sunset on the Beach" festivities** start at 3 p.m. with a craft fair featuring the work of local artisans. Pick up some snacks or a plate lunch at one of the food booths and find a comfy spot on the sand or pier. Live music begins at about 4:30 p.m., followed by the movie at sunset. There also are picnic areas, shady pavilions, restroom facilities and showers.

KAPIOLANI REGIONAL PARK ✉*Kalakaua Avenue* Extending across 140 acres on both sides of Kalakaua Avenue, beautiful Kapiolani Park is just next door to Queen's Surf. Hawaii's oldest park, this tree-studded playland dates back to 1887 when it was dedicated by King Kalakaua in honor of his Queen Kapiolani. Perhaps more than anything else, it has come to serve as a jogger's paradise. From dawn 'til dark, runners of all ages, colors, sizes and shapes beat a path around its perimeter. But Kapiolani offers something to just about anyone. There are tennis courts, softball and soccer fields, an archery area, and much more. To fully explore the park, you must visit each of its features in turn.

QUEEN KAPIOLANI HIBISCUS GARDEN

✉*Monsarrat and Paki avenues* Across from Kapiolani Park, this garden, with its colorful hibiscus flowerbeds and shady pavilion, is a pretty place to stroll and picnic. Despite its proximity to the

Waikiki waterfront and a busy shopping area, the little spot has maintained its peace—I'm almost hesitant to mention it here. Perhaps it has remained a secret because of its relatively small size (tour buses can't stop here). Or perhaps there are more mysterious reasons for it. According to legend, Tahitian *kahunas* (priests) visited the area in the 14th century and left behind more than spiritual healing. The story goes that they also imbued the stones in the garden with their powers, which now protect the park's blossoms against errant pickers.

WAIKIKI SHELL ⌂*Kapiolani Park* ☎808-527-5400, 808-591-2211 (box office) ☎808-527-5433 ⌂*www.blaisdellcenter.com* This is a great place for an evening under the stars with Diamond Head as a backdrop. General admission means lawn seating, which is the perfect way to enjoy the Honolulu Symphony backing up headliners like Jimmy Buffet, local favorites like Kalapana, or megastars like Bob Dylan. Check with the Blaisdell Center box office to see if anything is scheduled for the Shell while you're in town and plan to go.

HONOLULU ZOO ⌂*Kapiolani Park* ☎808-971-7171 ☎808-971-7173 ⌂*www. honoluluzoo.org* Kapiolani Park's grandest feature is its vast zoo, teeming with fascinating species. Like city zoos everywhere, this tropical facility has a resident population of elephants, giraffes, ostriches, zebras, hippos, Sumatran tigers, lions, alligators and so on. But it also includes animals more common to the islands, creatures like the nene (a rare goose), Komodo dragons and Galápagos tortoises. Perhaps most interesting of all, there is an outstanding population of tropical birds. Admission.

WAIKIKI AQUARIUM ⌂*2777 Kalakaua Avenue* ☎808-923-9741 ☎808-923-1771 ⌂*www.waquarium.org, webmaster@waquarium.org* The aquarium is the place where you can finally discover what a *humuhumunukunukua-puaa*, that impossibly named fish, really looks like. (Don't be surprised if the name proves to be longer than the fish.) Within the aquarium's glass walls, you'll see more than 420 different species of aquatic animals and plants originating from Hawaiian and South Pacific waters. Ranging from rainbow-hued tropical fish to staghorn coral, they constitute a broad range of underwater species. Then there are Hawaiian monk seals (an endangered species) and other intriguing wildlife. The new jellyfish gallery features a variety of these mysterious and ethereal creatures. Admission.

SANS SOUCI BEACH Kapiolani Park includes a stretch of beach called Sans Souci, a popular spot where residents and visitors share the sand and reef-sheltered waters. It's also an easy place to set out for a kayak paddle to the marine preserve off Diamond Head or to head toward Waikiki, which stands in highrise silhouette.

NATATORIUM Sans Souci Beach is bordered to the west by this saltwater pool and grandstand built in the 1920s as a monument to the 179 islanders who lost their lives in World War I. Closed in 1979 due to slipshod maintenance and deterioration, there is much debate whether it will ever reopen.

DIAMOND HEAD More than any other place in the islands, Diamond Head is the trademark of Hawaii. A 760-foot crater, it is the work of a volcano that has been dead for about 100,000 years. To the Hawaiians it was known as *Leahi*. They saw in its sloping hillsides the face of an *ahi*, or yellowfin tuna. Then, in the 19th century, sailors mistook its volcanic glass rocks for rare gems and gave the promontory its present name. Formed 350,000 years ago, this natural landmark was a sacred place to the ancient Hawaiians. A *heiau* once graced its slopes and King Kamehameha is said to have worshiped here, offering a human sacrifice to the Polynesian war god.

It is possible to drive into the gaping maw of this old dragon. Just take Kalakaua Avenue until it meets Diamond Head Road, then follow the latter around to the inland site of the crater. From there a tunnel leads inside. Once within, there is a steep three-quarter-mile trail climbing to the rim of the crater. From here you can gaze along Oahu's southeast corner and back across the splendid little quarter called Waikiki.

LODGING

While it may no longer be the simple country retreat it was at the 20th century's turn, Waikiki does have one advantage: believe it or not, it's a great place to find low-rent hotels. A lot of the cozy old hostelries have been torn down and replaced with highrises, but a few have escaped the urban assault. Some of those skyscrapers, too, are cheaper than you might think.

Waikiki is not exactly quiet. Early-morning garbage trucks and late-night party-goers make considerable street noise. Streets on the outskirts are less noisy than those in the heart of things. Ask for rooms off the street or high in the sky!

ISLAND HOSTEL/HOTEL

$ 20 ROOMS ✉1946 Ala Moana Boulevard ☎ 808-942-8748 📠 808-942-8748

What better combination can you ask for than a place that is both a hotel *and* a hostel? At this unusual establishment, located inside the Hawaiian Colony building, you can book a room with private bath (though hard to get since reservations aren't accepted here) or join fellow travelers in a coed dorm room. The dorm includes kitchen privileges.

THE POLYNESIAN BEACH CLUB HOSTEL

$ 69 BEDS ✉2584 Lemon Road ☎808-922-1340, 877-504-2924 📠808-262-2817
🌐www.hostelhawaii.com, reservation@hostelhawaii.com

This hostel offers private, semiprivate and dormitory accommodations in a converted apartment building. Studios have their own refrigerators and all have bathrooms and can sleep up to three people. Laundry facilities and a full kitchen are available for guests, as well as a barbecue and outdoor deck area. It is the closest hostel to the beach, which is one block away.

HOSTELLING INTERNATIONAL—WAIKIKI

$ 50 BEDS ✉2417 Prince Edward Street ☎808-926-8313 📠808-922-3798
🌐www.hostelsaloha.com, ayhaloha@lava.net

Budget travelers might also consider a stay here. This helpful facility features single-sex dormitory-style accommodations and private studio units with private baths. Open to both men and women, the hostel provides bedding and a common kitchen and creates a family-style atmosphere conducive to meeting other travelers. High-speed internet access is available for a fee. Seven-day maximum stay.

WAIKIKI PRINCE HOTEL

$ 24 ROOMS   ✉2431 Prince Edward Street   ☎808-922-1544   📠808-924-3712
🖥www.waikikiprince.com, info@waikikiprince.com

Some of the walls are still cinderblock, but the price is right here. All guest rooms have air conditioning and cable television; many of the units are equipped with kitchenettes (which are outfitted with mini-refrigerators, microwaves, stoves and utensils).

THE BREAKERS

$$-$$$ 64 ROOMS   ✉250 Beach Walk   ☎808-923-3181, 800-426-0494
📠808-923-7174   🖥www.breakers-hawaii.com, breakers@aloha.net

This lowrise hotel tucked away in the shadow of vaulting condominiums is truly a find. Dating to the 1950s, this Waikiki original consists of 64 rooms and 15 suites surrounding a pool and landscaped patio. Shoji doors provide an "Asian" ambiance while kitchenettes in every room and a location one block from the beach round out the features.

ROYAL GROVE HOTEL

$ 87 UNITS   ✉151 Uluniu Avenue   ☎808-923-7691   📠808-922-7508
🖥www.royalgrovehotel.com, rghawaii@hawaiitel.net

Rising higher from the ground, while still keeping costs low, is this six-story establishment. If you can get past the garish pink exterior here, you'll find the rooms more tastefully designed. All accommodations are carpeted and comfortably furnished, and some are decorated in simple but appealing styles. There are TVs and phones in all of the rooms, plus an almond-shaped pool and spacious lobby. Rents vary according to which wing of this sprawling building your bags are parked in. Most rooms even have kitchenettes with microwaves, as well as air conditioning, so it's hard to go wrong here.

KAI ALOHA APARTMENT HOTEL

$ 18 ROOMS   ✉235 Saratoga Road   ☎808-923-6723   📠808-922-7592
🖥www.magickhawaii.com/kaialoha, kai.aloha@gte.net

Offering intimacy combined with modern convenience, each guest room at the Kai Aloha has air conditioning, an all-electric kitchen, radio, telephone with voice mail, cable television and carpeting. Studio apartments feature lovely rattan furniture and are attractively decorated with old drawings and paintings. The one-bedroom apartments will comfortably sleep four people. Daily maid service is provided.

EWA HOTEL

$$-$$$$ 90 ROOMS   ✉2555 Cartwright Road   ☎808-922-1677   ☎800-359-8639
📠808-923-8538   🖥www.ewahotel.com, mail@ewahotel.com

Tucked away on a back street one block from the beach, this pastel-and-rattan establishment has a 1980s aura about it. Close to Kapiolani

Park and offering kitchenettes in many rooms, it is particularly convenient for families.

WAIKIKI HANA HOTEL

$$ 73 ROOMS   ✉2424 Koa Avenue   ✆808-926-8841, 800-695-8284   📠808-924-3770

About the same size as the Ewa Hotel is the Waikiki Hana, a place that offers a restaurant and small lobby. Quiet (for Waikiki), friendly and comfortable, its rooms are brightly decorated and trimly appointed with air conditioning and color televisions. Some have kitchenettes and lanais.

ASTON HONOLULU PRINCE

$$$ 119 ROOMS   ✉415 Nahua Street   ✆808-922-1616   📠808-922-6223
🖱www.honoluluprince.com, res.hop@resortquesthawaii.com

Once a college dormitory, today the Honolulu Prince is a ten-story hotel with a comfortable lobby. The standard rooms are small and blandly decorated. Located about three blocks from the beach, this hotel also has one- and two-bedroom suites available with full kitchens.

HOLIDAY INN WAIKIKI

$$$ 198 ROOMS   ✉1830 Ala Moana Boulevard   ✆808-955-1111, 888-992-4545
📠808-947-1799   🖱www.holiday-inn.com, holinnwk@pixi.com

A good bargain within easy walking distance from both Ala Moana Center and the beach, accommodations at this 17-story caravansary are "Holiday Inn" plush. Each room has air conditioning, television, telephone, decorations, carpeting, a shower-tub combination, as well as a small refrigerator. The room I saw was quite spacious and contained a king-size bed. There's also a fitness center.

WAIKIKI GRAND HOTEL

$$$ 61 ROOMS   ✉134 Kapahulu Avenue   ✆808-923-1511   📠808-923-5003
🖱www.waikikigrand.com, res@waikikigrand.com

Located right across the street from lush Kapiolani Park, the individually named and decorated rooms in this ten-story building are comfortable, pleasant places to park your bags. Downstairs there's a windswept lobby.

CELEBRITY RESORTS WAIKIKI

$$$ 80 ROOMS   ✉431 Nohonani Street   ✆808-923-7336, 866-507-1428
📠808-923-1622   🖱www.celebrityresorts.com

This modern, attractive complex of three low-slung buildings surrounds a garden and swimming pool. The rooms are decorated in a tropical theme with rattan furniture and come with all-electric kitchenette, telephone, TV and air conditioning.

RESORTQUEST COCONUT PLAZA HOTEL

$$ 80 ROOMS   ✉450 Lewers Street   ✆808-923-8828   📠808-923-3473
🖱www.aquaresorts.com, reservations@aquaresorts.com

A ten-story highrise, the Coconut Plaza has accommodations with kitchenettes; all guest rooms have refrigerators and microwaves; standard rooms have a wet bar. Decorated in Mexican tile and furnished with wicker, the rooms are attractively appointed. The lobby adds elements of elegance in the form of an open-air lounge and a small pool. Continental breakfast included.

QUEEN KAPIOLANI HOTEL

$$$ 314 ROOMS   ✉150 Kapahulu Avenue   📞808-922-1941, 800-367-2317
📞808-922-2694   ✑www.queenkapiolani.com, reservations@queenkapiolani.com

Rising 19 stories above nearby Kapiolani Park, this sparkling hotel features a spacious lobby, three floors of public rooms, several shops and a swimming pool. The guest rooms are plainly decorated and modest in size. Located one block from the beach.

HAWAIIANA HOTEL

$$–$$$ 93 ROOMS   ✉260 Beach Walk   📞808-923-3811, 800-367-5122
📞808-926-5728   ✑www.hawaiianahotelatwaikiki.com, hawaiana@lava.net

The Hawaiiana is an intimate, lowrise facility that offers a garden courtyard arrangement with rooms surrounding either of the hotel's two pools. Some rooms have a private lanai; all have wicker armoires, kitchenettes and pastel decor.

RESORTQUEST WAIKIKI CIRCLE HOTEL

$$$$ 104 ROOMS   ✉2464 Kalakaua Avenue   📞808-923-1571   📞808-926-8024
✑www.rqwaikikicircle.com, res.cir@resortquesthawaii.com

If you'd like to stay directly across the street from the beach, book a room here. This 14-story hotel-in-the-round has air-conditioned rooms, many with an ocean view, which is the main advantage.

THE CABANA AT WAIKIKI

$$$ 15 ROOMS   ✉2551 Cartwright Road   📞808-926-5555, 877-921-2121
📞808-926-5566   ✑www.cabana-waikiki.com, jim@cabana-waikiki.com

Catering to gay and lesbian visitors, the Cabana offers a piece of paradise just walking distance from Queen's Surf. The hotel has nicely decorated one-bedroom suites, with queen beds in the bedroom and a full-sized day bed in the living room. Rattan furnishings and Hawaiian prints convey a tropical feel. All suites have TV/VCR/stereos and microwave-equipped kitchenettes, complete with coffeemakers, toasters and blenders. There is an eight-person jacuzzi for guest use. Continental breakfast and cocktails are included.

NEW OTANI KAIMANA BEACH HOTEL

$$$–$$$$ 125 ROOMS   ✉2863 Kalakaua Avenue   📞808-923-1555, 800-356-8264
📞808-922-9404   ✑www.kaimana.com, rooms@kaimana.com

This attractive facility, on the edge of Waikiki, is removed from the crowds and rests beside beautiful Sans Souci Beach in the shadow of Diamond Head. Its two restaurants and oceanside bar lend the feel of a big hotel, but the friendly staff and standard rooms create a family atmosphere.

DIAMOND HEAD BEACH HOTEL

$$$ 50 ROOMS   ✉2947 Kalakaua Avenue   📞808-922-1928
📞808-924-8980   ✑www.dhbhotel.com, res@dhbhotel.com

This ultra-elegant hotel, secluded from the bustle of Waikiki, is a great place to stay. Located close to the fabled crater, it is an ultra-contemporary establishment. The standard rooms are nondescript but the suites are done in a tasteful, Balinese-themed style, and many come with a kitchen. Located on the ocean, this

13-story facility is one of the most chic resting places around. Continental breakfast is included.

MOANA SURFRIDER RESORT

$$$ 793 ROOMS   ✉ *2365 Kalakaua Avenue*   📞 *808-922-3111, 800-782-9488*
📠 *808-924-4799*   🖥 *www.moana-surfrider.com*

Waikiki was little more than a thatch-hut village when its first deluxe hotel went up in 1901. Today the Moana retains the aura of those early days in its Colonial architecture. Downstairs are restaurants, bars, a lobby and an ancient banyan tree beneath which Robert Louis Stevenson once wrote. A throwback to Colonial times, tea (fee) is served every afternoon at the Banyan Veranda. Be sure to ask for a room in the original section.

HILTON HAWAIIAN VILLAGE

$$$$ 3250 ROOMS   ✉ *2005 Kalia Road*   📞 *808-949-4321*   📠 *808-951-5458*
🖥 *www.hiltonhawaiianvillage.com*

Offering well over 3000 rooms, this deluxe Hilton is the largest resort in the islands and Waikiki's premier family hotel. The grounds provide a Disneyesque atmosphere that keeps children of all ages engaged— fireworks on Friday evening, shopping malls, restaurants and nightly entertainment, not to mention a penguin pool, flamingos, cockatoos and koi ponds. Seaside diversions include paddle boats and surfboards as well as numerous swimming pools to dip in, an acre of sand for sandcastle-making and an ocean of fun. Not to be overlooked, the rooms are attractively furnished and well-cared for and the service is friendly and welcoming.

HALEKULANI

$$$$ 455 ROOMS   ✉ *2199 Kalia Road*   📞 *808-923-2311, 800-367-2343*
📠 *808-926-8004*   🖥 *www.halekulani.com*

Exuding elegance and refinement, the Halekulani, whose name means "house befitting heaven," is where the elite come to get away from it all. If you want to splurge, you can, too. The guest rooms and facilities are luxurious and the personalized service radiates with Hawaiian hospitality. If you don't want to float in the oceanfront swimming pool (which boasts an orchid made of 1.25 million South African glass mosaic tiles that reflect the changing light), you can visit the spa, indulge in an in-room massage or dine in one of their award-winning dining rooms.

ROYAL HAWAIIAN HOTEL

$$$$ 528 ROOMS   ✉ *2259 Kalakaua Avenue*   📞 *808-923-7311, 866-716-8109*
📠 *808-931-7098*   🖥 *www.royal-hawaiian.com*

This grand dame of Hawaiian hotels captures the sense of Old Hawaii. Built in 1927 and affectionately known as the "Pink Palace," the Royal Hawaiian is an elegant, Spanish Moorish–style building complete with colonnaded walkways and manicured grounds. The fabulous Moroccan-style lobby is bedecked with chandeliers. Adjacent to the original building is a 17-story tower that brings the room count to over 500. Worth visiting even if you never check in.

ROYAL KUHIO

385 UNITS ✉2240 Kuhio Avenue ☏808-923-0555 ✎808-923-0720
🖱www.waikikicondos.com, info@waikikicondos.com

A good bet for families, this highrise is just two blocks from Waikiki Beach. One-bedroom units feature fully equipped kitchens and balconies with ocean or mountain views. Studios are $135; one-bedroom units are $145.

RESORTQUEST WAIKIKI BEACH TOWER

104 UNITS ✉2470 Kalakaua Avenue ☏808-926-6400 ✎808-926-7380
🖱www.rqwaikikibeachtower.com, res.awt@resortquesthawaii.com

All units here feature contemporary furniture, washers and dryers, kitchens and beautiful lanais. The kids will enjoy the pool. One-bedroom units begin at $540. Two-bedroom suites for up to six guests start at $640.

WINSTON'S WAIKIKI CONDOS

10 UNITS ✉417 Nohonani Street, Suite 409 ☏808-924-3332, 800-545-1948
🖱www.winstonswaikikicondos.com, patwinston@gmail.com

At Winston's, deluxe one-bedroom condos rent for $99 to $145 (single or double occupancy only). All suites are comfortably furnished with rattan furniture and feature lanais and full and complete kitchens. The units, just one block from the beach, are well-maintained and clean. Washers and dryers are available. Patrick Winston offers special deals for *Hidden Hawaii* readers, so make sure you call ahead and mention this book. One-month minimum stay preferred.

OUTRIGGER WAIKIKI SHORE

29 UNITS ✉2161 Kalia Road ☏808-922-3871, 800-688-7444 ✎808-922-3887
🖱www.outriggerwaikikishore.com, wsr@outrigger.com

There are studios and one- and two-bedroom units here. These condos feature complete kitchens, washer/dryers and great views. Studios are $275 while one-bedroom units start at $355, with a two-night minimum. Two-bedroom units accommodating up to six start at $480.

RESORTQUEST AT THE WAIKIKI BANYAN

267 UNITS ✉201 Ohua Avenue, one block from the beach ☏808-922-0555
✎808-924-7114 🖱www.rqwaikikibanyan.com, res.ban@resortquesthawaii.com

Just one block from the beach, this highrise has one-bedroom units ($205 to $280) for one to five people. These ocean and mountain view units have full kitchens, rattan furniture and lanais, along with many kid-friendly activities.

DINING

This tourist mecca is crowded with restaurants. Since the competition is so stiff, the cafés here are cheaper than anywhere else on the islands. There are numerous American restaurants serving moderately good food at modest prices, so diners looking for standard fare will have no problem. But as you're probably seeking something more exotic, I'll also list some interesting Asian, Hawaiian, health food and other off-beat restaurants.

NICK'S FISHMARKET

$$$$ SEAFOOD ✉*2070 Kalakaua Avenue* ☎*808-955-6333* 📠*808-946-0478*
🖥*www.nicksfishmarket.com, nickwaikiki@aol.com*

If you decide to stop here, plan on eating seafood. You have never seen such a list of fresh fish dishes. Not that much of it will seem familiar, but there is mahimahi, *opakapaka* and *ahi*. Or if you prefer to dine on something you recognize, how about shrimp scampi, abalone, lobster or scallops? The service is attentive.

EZOGIKU

$ JAPANESE ✉*2420 Koa Avenue and 2146 Kalakaua Avenue*
☎*808-922-2473, 808-926-8616* 📠*808-926-2207* 🖥*www.ezogiku.com*

For a just-before-midnight snack—they close at 11:00—or to satisfy cravings for a hot bowl of noodle soup, you're never too far from an Ezogiku. Rub shoulders with Japanese tourists at the counter in one of these hole-in-the-wall eateries serving ramen in a variety of styles, including curry, pork and wonton. There are two locations to choose from in Waikiki.

WAIKIKI SHOPPING PLAZA

$–$$ INTERNATIONAL ✉*2250 Kalakaua Avenue* ☎*808-923-1191*

To find an affordable meal on Kalakaua Avenue, the oceanfront strip, try the bottom floor of this plaza. Here about a dozen ethnic and American restaurants offer takeout food as well as full-course sit-down dinners.

OCEAN TERRACE RESTAURANT

$$$$ AMERICAN ✉*Sheraton Waikiki, 2255 Kalakaua Avenue* ☎*808-922-4422 ext. 71777* 📠*808-931-8530*

The food is pretty standard fare here but the view deserves five stars. Set poolside next to the beach in one of the state's largest hotels, this open-air dining room provides a welcome means to dine on the water. Popular for breakfast, lunch and dinner, the evening menu centers around rotating theme buffets, such as prime rib and lobster night.

THE BEACHSIDE CAFÉ

$$$$ AMERICAN ✉*Moana Surfrider Resort, 2365 Kalakaua Avenue* ☎*808-921-4600* 📠*808-924-4759*

For oceanfront dining, The Beachside is true to its name. With indoor and patio dining and a big buffet bar, it's a standard-fare American restaurant lacking in imagination but filled with beautiful views. Open for breakfast, lunch and dinner, the café serves steak, hamburgers and egg dishes, as well as offering a prime rib and crab leg dinner buffet. Ask for a table outside.

CIAO MEIN

$$$ ITALIAN/CHINESE ✉Hyatt Regency Waikiki, third floor, 2424 Kalakaua Avenue
📞808-923-1234 📠808-237-6152 🖳www.ciaomein.com, myamasaki@hyatt.com

Italian *and* Chinese? Sounds like an odd pairing, but the hybrid menu here is nonetheless delicious on both sides. On the Chinese side try spicy *kung pao* chicken, Szechuan eggplant or the savory flavors of Mongolian sizzle. If you're craving Italian, start with the carpaccio followed by pasta in a light tomato basil sauce. Everything is served family style, which means shared dishes that make this a great place to go with kids or in a group. Ciao Mein's decor is Euro-chic. Dinner only.

CHEESEBURGER IN PARADISE

$–$$ AMERICAN ✉2500 Kalakaua Avenue 📞808-923-3731 📠808-923-1070
🖳www.cheeseburgerland.com, chzyburger@aol.com

Fans whir overhead and a bar sits in the back; sheet music covers and old Matson oceanliner menus stand framed along the walls. Hard to believe someone would create this ambience for their restaurant, then name the place Cheeseburger in Paradise. But burgers it is, plus a selection of breakfast dishes for the morning.

HAU TREE LANAI

$$$$ INTERNATIONAL ✉New Otani Kaimana Beach Hotel, 2863 Kalakaua Avenue
📞808-921-7066 🖳www.kaimana.com, hautreelanai@kaimana.com

Apart from the bustle of Waikiki but still right on the beach is this island-style dining room. Here beneath the interwoven branches of twin hau trees you can enjoy patio dining with a view that extends across Waikiki to the distant mountains. I favor the place for its breakfast (the French toast is delicious), but they also have a lunch and dinner menu that ranges from steamed vegetables to curried chicken to fresh island fish. In the evening the place is illuminated by torches, and soft breezes wisp off the water, adding to the enchantment.

DIAMOND HEAD GRILL

$$$–$$$$ HAWAII REGIONAL ✉W Honolulu Hotel, 2885 Kalakaua Avenue
📞808-922-3734 📠808-791-5164 🖳www.w-dhg.com, info@w-dhg.com

Innovative, high-quality cuisine and excellent service make this restaurant one of Hawaii's best. The pan-seared *ahi* is one of those oh-so-good dishes that makes you want to order it each time you visit. The refined and artful presentation is complemented by the eatery's clean and contemporary decor with deco highlights. There's entertainment Wednesday through Saturday nights. No lunch.

SEASIDE BAR & GRILL

$–$$ AMERICAN ✉2256 Kuhio Avenue 📞808-922-8227 📠808-922-8227

Favored by both tourists and locals for its low prices, the Seaside has a budget-priced early-bird special of steak or mahimahi nightly until 7 p.m. Choose any two items—lobster tail, crab legs, mahimahi, fried

74

shrimp or New York steak—and they'll throw in a house salad as well. The fish is frozen and the place is actually two blocks from the "seaside," but for low-rent dining it's worth considering.

FATTY'S CHINESE KITCHEN

$ CHINESE   ⊠Kuhio Mall, 2345 Kuhio Avenue   ☎808-922-9600

An L-shaped counter with swivel chairs is the most decor you can expect here. The prices on plate lunches and dinners are a throwback, too. With dozens of choices, including many "noodle in soup" dishes, Fatty aims to suit every palate.

KEO'S IN WAIKIKI

$$–$$$ THAI   ⊠2028 Kuhio Avenue   ☎808-951-9355
✐www.keosthaicuisine.com, keos@keosthaicuisine.com

One of the ethnic restaurants most popular with local folks is Keo's. Fulfilling to all the senses, this intimate place is decorated with fresh flowers and tropical plants. The cuisine includes such Southeast Asian dishes as the "evil jungle prince," a sliced beef, shrimp or chicken entrée with coconut milk, fresh basil and red chili, or for breakfast, the Hawaiian Special—eggs with bacon, green onions and soy sauce. You can choose from dozens of fish, shellfish, fowl and meat dishes. The menu offers a lot of variety, and is highly recommended.

CHA CHA CHA RESTAURANT

$–$$ CARIBBEAN-MEXICAN   ⊠342 Seaside Avenue   ☎808-923-7797
☎808-926-7007

The blue skies and green palms of the Caribbean never seem far away in Hawaii, and they feel even closer here. With its tropical color scheme and festive decor, this "Caribe/Mex" eatery serves up Mexican dishes such as burritos, tacos and quesadillas prepared Caribbean-style with unusual spices and sauces.

PERRY'S SMORGY

$–$$ AMERICAN   ⊠2380 Kuhio Avenue   ☎808-926-0184   ☎808-922-1907

A Waikiki standby, Perry's has an inexpensive, prix-fixe buffet at dinner, lunch and breakfast. With an extensive salad bar, plus a host of meat and fish platters, this all-you-can-eat emporium is hard to beat.

ARANCINO

$$ ITALIAN   ⊠255 Beach Walk   ☎808-923-5557   ☎808-922-0105
✐www.arancino.net, info@arancino.net

Authentic Italian specialties at affordable prices draw nightly crowds here. The place has the feel of a New York–style bistro, with excellent, home-style standards like eggplant parmigiana and risotto prepared tableside that are worth the potential 20-minute wait.

hidden

BALI BY THE SEA

$$$$ PACIFIC RIM *Hilton Hawaiian Village, 2005 Kalia Road*
808-949-4321 *808-947-7926*

Dishes like macadamia nut–crusted *opakapaka* and marinated rack of lamb make this place a special favorite. Plush seating, nautical lamps, fresh flowers and soft ocean breezes add to the charm of this elegant restaurant. Dress code. Dinner only. Closed Sunday.

SHORE BIRD BEACH BROILER

$$–$$$ AMERICAN/JAPANESE *Reef Hotel, 2169 Kalia Road* *808-922-2887*
808-926-5372

This beachfront dining room is a great place to enjoy a reasonably priced dinner and an ocean view. This is a cook-your-own-food facility that offers hand-carved steaks, fresh fish, teriyaki chicken and barbecued ribs for dinner. The all-you-can-eat breakfast buffet, with American standards and some Japanese dishes as well, is a good deal. One of the best bargains on Waikiki Beach, the Shore Bird is inevitably crowded, so try to dine early.

LA MER

$$$$ FRENCH *Halekulani Hotel, 2199 Kalia Road* *808-923-2311* *808-926-8004* *www.halekulani.com*

It's not surprising that Waikiki's most fashionable hotel, the Halekulani, contains one of the district's finest restaurants. Situated on an open-air balcony overlooking the ocean, La Mer has a reputation for elegant dining in intimate surroundings. French-inspired dishes include crispy-skin *onaga* fillet, confit tomato with truffle juice and fried basil, and rack of lamb with a dijon mustard crust, provençal-style vegetables and creamy potatoes. Add the filigree woodwork and sumptuous surroundings and La Mer is one of the island's most attractive waterfront dining rooms. Formal attire required. Reservations recommended. Dinner only.

hidden

ORCHIDS

$$$$ HAWAII REGIONAL/INTERNATIONAL *Halekulani Hotel, 2199 Kalia Road* *808-923-2311* *808-926-8004* *www.halekulani.com*

Downstairs from La Mer is this classy yet casual restaurant, serving a mix of Hawaiian and world cuisine like steamed *onaga* with sesame oil and shiitake mushrooms, roasted pepper-spiced duck breast and roasted lamb chops. Orchids is open for breakfast, lunch, dinner and Sunday brunch.

SHOPPING

This tourist mecca is a great place to look but not to buy. Browsing the busy shops is like studying a catalog of Hawaiian handicrafts. It's all

here. You'll find everything but bargains. With a few noteworthy exceptions, the prices include the unofficial tourist surcharges that merchants worldwide levy against visitors. Windowshop Waikiki, but plan on spending your shopping dollars elsewhere.

DUKE'S LANE ✉*Kalakaua Avenue to Kuhio Avenue* One Waikiki shopping area I do recommend is Duke's Lane. This alleyway may be the best place in all Hawaii to buy jade jewelry. Either side of the lane is flanked by mobile stands selling rings, necklaces, earrings, stick pins, bracelets and more. It's a prime place to barter for tiger's eyes, opals and mother-of-pearl pieces.

WAIKIKI SHOPPING PLAZA ✉*2250 Kalakaua Avenue* The main shopping scene is in the malls and this one has five floors of stores and restaurants. Here are jewelers, sundries and boutiques, plus specialty shops like **Borders Express** (808-922-4154), with an excellent line of magazines as well as paperbacks and bestsellers.

ROYAL HAWAIIAN SHOPPING CENTER ✉*2233 Kalakaua Avenue* ☎*808-922-0588* A four-story complex that runs for two blocks along Kalakaua Avenue, from Lewers Street to the Outrigger Waikiki, this is a key shopping destination. On the *makai* side (facing the ocean), it fronts the grounds of the Royal Hawaiian and the Sheraton Waikiki. It is Waikiki's largest mall and features Euro-American designer boutiques, upscale shops, numerous restaurants and fast-food kiosks, as well as an indoor shooting gallery and showroom. A weekly schedule of Hawaiiana and other cultural performances provides an entertaining respite from the pressures of shopping.

LITTLE HAWAIIAN CRAFTS SHOP

✉*Royal Hawaiian Shopping Center* ☎*808-926-2662* Here you'll find an interesting selection of traditional and contemporary Hawaiian crafts including carved koa wood bowls, Niihau shell leis, Hawaiian quilts, ceramics and glassware.

THE UKULELE HOUSE

✉*Royal Hawaiian Shopping Center* ☎*808-923-8587* If you're in the market for a ukulele, stop by this gem, which carries everything from children's souvenir ukes for $10 to musically playable instruments ranging from $80 all the way to $2000-plus for vintage models. This world-famous supplier of vintage and unique ukuleles is also home of the world's largest ukulele. If you would like to try playing a ukulele on your visit to Hawaii, you can take free 30-minute lessons here.

KING'S VILLAGE ✉*131 Kaiulani Avenue at Kalakaua Avenue* This mock Victorian town that suggests how Britain might have looked had the 19th-century English invented polyethylene. The motif may be trying to appear antiquated, but the prices are unfortunately quite contemporary.

WAIKIKI TRADE CENTER ✉2255 Kuhio Avenue With an air of Milanese splendor about it, this glass-and-steel complex is a maze of mirrors. In addition to the stained-glass windows and twinkling lights, there are several worthwhile shops in this strikingly attractive mall.

INTERNATIONAL MARKETPLACE ✉2330 Kalakaua Avenue ☎808-971-2080 A Waikiki institution since 1957, the marketplace is known for its quaint ethnic groupings of Chinese, Japanese, Hawaiian, Indian, Filipino and South Seas crafts and food. It has an ethnic food pavilion, outdoor carts and kiosks, free-standing restaurants, an entertainment amphitheater and, of course, shops. Lots of shops: jewelry, crafts, apparel, gifts and more.

RAINBOW BAZAAR ✉Hilton Hawaiian Village, 2005 Kalia Road Designed in Oriental style, with curving tile roofs and brilliantly painted roof beams, you can stroll along this Asian arcade, past lofty banyan trees and flowering gardens, to stores filled with rare art and Far Eastern antiquities. Worth window shopping.

LOCAL MOTION ✉1958 Kalakaua Avenue ☎808-979-7873 ⌨www.localmotion hawaii.com This island-based company has opened an architecturally distinguished flagship shop for its line of logowear and sporting gear, including surfboards, body boards and backpacks.

ISLAND TREASURES ANTIQUE MALL ✉2301 Kuhio Avenue ☎808-922-8223 You'll find Waikiki's best selection of Hawaiiana in this multi-level complex that's home to a number of individual vendors. Fun for browsing and a purchase if you find something priced right. The shops open in the afternoon and stay open late, which makes it a good tie-in with an evening stroll. Call for hours. Closed Monday.

BAILEY'S ANTIQUES AND ALOHA SHIRTS ✉517 Kapahulu Avenue ☎808-734-7628 ⌨www.alohashirts.com, baileysantiques@webtv.net Looking for a vintage silk shirt? Those famous Hawaiian styles, like the one Montgomery Clift sported in *From Here to Eternity*, are among the alluring items at Bailey's. This place carries over 12,000 Hawaiian shirts, and is the world's largest vintage shirt store. If an original silky is beyond your means, they also have reproductions as well as collectibles like Zippo lighters.

PEGGY'S PICKS ✉732 Kapahulu Avenue ☎808-737-3297 Peggy's sells everything from Hawaiiana to an eclectic array of collectibles at affordable prices. Closed Sunday.

NIGHTLIFE

Hawaii has a strong musical tradition, kept alive by excellent groups performing their own compositions as well as old Polynesian songs. I'm not talking about the "Blue Hawaii"–"Tiny Bubbles"–"Beyond the Reef" medleys that draw tourists in droves, but *real* Hawaiian music. Oahu is the ideal island to seek out Hawaiian sounds. Many of these musicians—Keola Beamer, Kealii Reichel, Henry Kapono, Olomana and the Brothers Cazimero to name a few—may be playing at a local club. Consult the daily newspapers, or tune in to KCCN at 100 on the radio dial. This all-Hawaiian station is the home of island soul.

NICK'S FISHMARKET ✉*2070 Kalakaua Avenue* ☎*808-955-6333* ✆*808-946-0478, nickwaikiki@aol.com* Over at Nick's there's live entertainment nightly except Monday and Tuesday. Expect to hear light rock, jazz, soul or blues while munching on half-price *pupus*.

PARADISE LOUNGE ✉*Hilton Hawaiian Village, 2005 Kalia Road* ☎*808-949-4321* ✆*808-951-5458* On Friday and Saturday nights, a contemporary Hawaiian group stars here. Other forms of live entertainment are offered the rest of the week. Choose between table or lounge seating in this carpeted club, which is decorated with Hawaiian landscapes painted by local artists.

DUKE'S CANOE CLUB

✉*Outrigger Waikiki, 2335 Kalakaua Avenue* ☎*808-922-2268* ✆*808-923-4204* This club offers a beachfront setting, a distant view of Diamond Head, and plenty of atmosphere. Duke refers to Duke Kahanamoku, the Olympic swimming champion and surfer who helped restore surfing to a position of cultural prominence. The decor documents his career with archival photography and memorabilia. It draws overflowing crowds, particularly on Sunday afternoons when Henry Kapono performs.

MAI TAI BAR

✉*Royal Hawaiian Hotel, 2259 Kalakaua Avenue* ☎*808-923-7311* There's Hawaiian music nightly at this tropical haven. Grab an umbrella-topped table on the terrace for primo ocean views.

ESPRIT NIGHTCLUB ✉*Sheraton Waikiki Hotel, 2255 Kalakaua Avenue* ☎*808-922-4422* ✆*808-923-8785* A congenial spot situated right on Waikiki Beach, this cozy club features bands that play music from different eras Wednesday through Sunday and offers spectacular ocean views every night of the week. Cover for non-hotel guests.

SHORE BIRD BEACH BROILER ✉*Outrigger Reef, 2169 Kalia Road* ☎*808-922-2887* A group performs mellow Hawaiian music nightly at this late-night *pupus* spot.

SCRUPLES ✉*2310 Kuhio Avenue* ☎*808-923-9530* ✆*808-926-8804* Tired of the old nine-to-five grind? For a change of pace try this swanky club, where the schedule is eight to four. 8 p.m. to 4 a.m., that is. Promising "dance and romance," this popular nightspot features dancing to Top-40 tunes. Dress code. Cover and two-drink minimum.

THE CELLAR ✉*205 Lewers Street* ☎*808-923-9952* The order of the night here is dancing, with hits spun by a deejay Tuesday through Saturday. It's a top spot for a hot night. Pool tables are available for those not into dancing. Closed Sunday. Cover.

COCONUT WILLY'S BAR & GRILL ✉*2330 Kalakaua Avenue* ☎*808-923-9454* ✆*808-923-0581* Live bands start in the afternoon and continue on into the night here. The 35-and-over crowd turns out to dance to '50s and '60s classics as well as Hawaiian and country tunes.

79

TIKI'S

✉2570 Kalakaua Avenue ☎808-923-8454 ⌨www.tikisgrill.com Bustling until closing time, the bar at this hip spot is frequented by locals and visitors drawn to its casual, relaxed atmosphere, exotic drinks menu and live Hawaiian music.

DIAMOND HEAD GRILL ✉W Honolulu Hotel, 2885 Kalakaua Avenue ☎808-922-3734 ☒808-791-5164 ⌨www.w-dhg.com If you like sophisticated jazz to accompany dinner or drinks Wednesday and Thursday, this is the place to go. The vocalists and musicians are first rate, and the decibel level is suitable for either concentrating on the music, conversation or food, which is some of the best in the Islands. Friday and Saturday nights offer deejay dancing.

MOOSE MCGILLYCUDDY'S ✉310 Lewers Street ☎808-923-0751 ⌨www. moosewaikiki.com, honomoose@aol.com With room for 300 of your closest friends, Moose McGillycuddy's is a prime place to dance to live bands Monday through Saturday. Deejays also spin Top-40 music. Known for its weird pictures, this establishment is easily spotted. Just look for the only building on Lewers Street sporting a stuffed moose head. Occasional cover.

GERMAINE'S LUAU ☎808-949-6626, 800-367-5655 ⌨www.germainesluau. com For an authentic *tourist* experience accompanied by a genuine aloha spirit, join the busloads of Waikiki visitors who are caravanned to Barbers Point for the ultimate in Hawaiian kitsch. At Germaine's you'll get to witness the unearthing ceremony of a pig from its underground *imu* (oven), dine on Hawaiian-style food and watch Polynesian dancers (or join them on stage), all at a beachfront site as the sun sets on the Pacific.

Gay Scene
The gay scene is centered around several clubs on Waikiki's Kuhio Avenue and in Eaton Square, near the corner of Eaton and Hobron streets, not far away.

IN BETWEEN ✉2155 Lauula Street ☎808-926-7060 ⌨www.inbetweenonline. com On a short street near Kuhio and Lewers, this is a great place to bend an elbow with island regulars.

ANGLES WAIKIKI ✉2256 Kuhio Avenue ☎808-926-9766 ⌨www.angles waikiki.com, angles.waikiki@juno.com Clubgoers hang in and out here, where a bar in the center of the room provides a place to socialize, as does the lanai outside. There are pool tables and videos, as well as a dancefloor. Every Wednesday, crowds compete for cash prizes in the Best Chest/Best Buns contest.

FUSION WAIKIKI ✉Paradise Building, 2260 Kuhio Avenue ☎808-924-2422 A spicy gay club open until 4 a.m., this hot spot takes up the second and third floors of the Paradise Building and features dancing to house and underground deejay music. There are male strip shows and female impersonation performances on Friday and Saturday. Cover.

HULA'S BAR AND LEI STAND ✉️*Waikiki Grand Hotel, 134 Kapahulu Avenue* 📞*808-923-0669* Near Diamond Head, Hula's, with an ocean view and a disco complete with strobe-lit dancefloor and videos, rocks nightly until 2 a.m.

VENUS NIGHTCLUB ✉️*1349 Kapiolani Boulevard* 📞*808-951-8671* 🖥️*www.venusnightclub.com* Dance any night of the week 'til 4 a.m. to deejay-spun house, disco and hip-hop mixes at Venus. They also feature a male revue. Dress code. Cover.

BEACHES & PARKS

WAIKIKI BEACH

Famous all over the world, the strand in Waikiki is actually several beaches in one. Kahanamoku Beach, Fort DeRussy Beach, Royal-Moana Beach, Kuhio Beach Park and Queen's Surf form an unbroken string that runs from the Ala Wai Canal to Diamond Head Crater. Together they comprise Waikiki Beach. Along that string of beaches are some of *the* surf spots that have made Waikiki famous including "Canoes" and "Queens." Ask one of the local beach boys where to go for a spot that fits your level of expertise. Bottom fishing will net you *akule*, snapper, *moana*, weke, *ulua*, *menpachi* and bonefish. Snorkeling is so-so. Since going to the beach in this busy enclave also means exploring Waikiki itself, I have placed the beach descriptions in the sightseeing section on the preceding pages.

DOWNTOWN HONOLULU

For a historical and cultural tour of Hawaii's state capital, simply head toward Downtown Honolulu. A financial center for the entire Pacific Rim, Honolulu's importance to both North America and Asia is manifest in the highrise cityscape. The historical significance of this port city is evident from the 19th-century buildings that lead to the financial district in the heart of the city.

SIGHTS

MISSION HOUSES MUSEUM ✉️*553 South King Street* 📞*808-531-0481* 📱*808-545-2280* 🖥️*www.missionhouses.org, info@missionhouses.org* A fitting place to begin your tour of downtown is among the oldest homes in the islands. The buildings here seem to be borrowed from a New England landscape, and in a sense they were. The Frame House, a trim white wooden structure, was cut on the East Coast and shipped around the Horn to Hawaii. That was back in 1821, when this Yankee-style building was used to house missionary families.

Like the nearby Chamberlain House and Depository and other structures here, the Frame House represents one of the missionaries' earli-

Downtown
Honolulu

SAM CHOY'S
BREAKFAST
LUNCH & CRAB
BIG ALOHA BREWERY

PEOPLE'S CAFE

WASHINGTON PLACE

CHAI'S ISLAND BISTRO

Ala Moana Blvd

4 OAHU DOWNTOWN HONOLULU SIGHTS

PEOPLE'S CAFE

PAGE 90

Bargain-priced Polynesian favorites like poi, *lomi* salmon and *kalua* pig

WASHINGTON PLACE

PAGE 84

Politically significant home (now a museum) of Queen Liliuokalani before and after removal from power

SAM CHOY'S BREAKFAST LUNCH & CRAB AND BIG ALOHA BREWERY

PAGE 92

Where local boy Sam Choy helped Hawaii Regional cuisine establish an international reputation

CHAI'S ISLAND BISTRO

PAGE 93

Intimate setting for great Hawaiian music—watch for shows by Jerry Santos, the Brothers Cazimero or Makaha Sons

---

est centers in Hawaii. It was in 1820 that Congregationalists arrived in the islands; they immediately set out to build and proselytize. In 1831, they constructed the Chamberlain House and Depository from coral and used it as the mission store. The neighborhood's Printing Office, built of the same durable material ten years later, was used by the first press ever to print in the Hawaiian language. The Mission Houses complex tells much about the missionaries, who converted Hawaiian into a written language, then proceeded to rewrite the entire history of the islands. The museum is run by the Hawaiian Mission Children's Society. Guided tours daily. Closed Sunday and Monday. Admission.

KAWAIAHAO CHURCH

✉ *957 Punchbowl Street* Opposite the Mission Houses Museum, at South King and Punchbowl streets, is this renowned church. The imposing edifice required 14,000 coral blocks for its construction. Completed in 1842, it has been called the Westminster Abbey of Hawaii because coronations and funerals for Hawaiian kings and queens were once conducted here. Services are still performed in Hawaiian and English every Sunday at 10:30 a.m.; attending them is not only a way to view the church interior, but also provides a unique cultural perspective on contemporary Hawaiian life. Also note that the tomb of King Lunalilo rises in

Downtown Honolulu

POINTS OF INTEREST

- Ⓐ Aloha Tower
- Ⓑ Contemporary Museum
- Ⓒ Foster Botanical Garden
- Ⓓ Hawaii Children's Discovery Center
- Ⓔ Hawaii Maritime Center & Falls of Clyde
- Ⓕ Hawaii State Art Museum
- Ⓖ Honolulu Academy of Arts
- Ⓗ Honolulu Memorial Park
- Ⓘ Honolulu Myohoji Temple
- Ⓙ Iolani Palace
- Ⓚ Kamehameha Statue
- Ⓛ Kawaiahao Church
- Ⓜ Mission Houses Museum
- Ⓝ Royal Mausoleum
- Ⓞ State Capitol Building
- Ⓟ Soto Mission of Hawaii
- Ⓠ Tenrikyo Mission
- Ⓡ Washington Place

front of the church, and behind the church lies the cemetery where early missionaries and converted Hawaiians were buried.

MISSION MEMORIAL BUILDING ⊠*Across South King Street* This brick structure with stately white pillars was constructed in 1916 to honor the same early church leaders held in esteem at Kawaiaho Church. The nearby Renaissance-style building with the tile roof is **Honolulu Hale**, the City Hall. You might want to venture into the central courtyard, an open-air plaza surrounded by stone columns.

IOLANI PALACE

⊠*South King and Richards streets* ☎*808-522-0832* ☏*808-532-1051* ⌨*www.iolanipalace.org, info@iolanipalace.org* If you walk along South King Street in a westerly direction toward the center of Honolulu, this stunning palace will appear on your right. The palace (*iolani* means "bird of heaven" in Hawaiian) is the only state residence of royalty on American soil. The king who commissioned the Iolani Palace in 1882, David Kalakaua, was a world traveler with a taste for the good life. Known as the Merry Monarch, he planned for his coronation the greatest party Hawaii had ever seen. He liked to spend money with abandon and managed to amass in his lifetime a remarkable collection of material goods, not the least of which was his palace. This stunning Victorian-style mansion served as a royal residence until Queen Liliuokalani was overthrown in 1893. Later the ill-starred monarch was imprisoned here; eventually, after Hawaii became a territory of the United States, the palace was used as the capitol building until 1969. Guided tours lead you past the koa staircases, the magnificent chandeliers and the Corinthian columns that lend a touch of European grandeur to this splendid building.

The land around the Palace was significant to the Hawaiian people even before the royalty set up house. A Hawaiian temple stood here until it was probably destroyed in 1819. King Kamehameha III relocated his court from Lahaina to this location in 1845. After his residence was torn down, the current palace incarnation was constructed.

Located on the palace grounds is **Iolani Barracks**, where the Royal Household Guards were stationed, and the **Coronation Pavilion**, upon which the King was crowned. You can tour the palace grounds for free, but there's an admission charge for the building. Reservations are strongly advised; children under five are allowed only in the video theater and basement galleries. Tours are given Tuesday through Saturday. Closed Sunday and Monday.

KAMEHAMEHA STATUE ☎*808-539-4999* ☏*808-539-4996* ⌨*www.judiciary historycenter.org, jhchawaii@yahoo.com* Directly across the street from Iolani Palace rises a statue honoring Hawaii's first king. A huge gilt-and-bronze figure cast in Italy, it is covered with flower leis on special occa-

84

sions. The spear-carrying warrior wears a feather cape and helmet. Behind him stands **Aliiolani Hale**, better known as the Judiciary Building, home to Hawaii's Supreme Court. Back in the days of the monarchy, it served as the House of Parliament. Self-guided tours of the Judiciary History Center are available Monday through Friday, and docent-led tours are available by appointment.

STATE CAPITOL BUILDING ⊠*Bounded by South Beretania, Richards and Punchbowl streets* ☏*808-586-0178* 📠*808-586-0019* Unlike the surrounding structures, this is an ultramodern building, completed in 1969. Encircled by flared pillars that resemble palm trees, the capitol represents a variety of themes. Near one entrance there's a statue of Father Damien, who tended to those with leprosy on Molokai Island; presiding over the other entrance is Queen Liliuokalani, Hawaii's last reigning monarch. The House and Senate chambers are designed in a cone shape to resemble volcanoes, and the open-air courtyard is a commentary on the state's balmy weather. Tours of the capitol building and the legislature are given Monday, Wednesday and Friday.

HAWAII STATE ART MUSEUM ⊠*One Capitol District Building; 250 Hotel Street, second floor* ☏*808-586-0304, 808-586-0908* 🖥*www.hawaii.gov/sfca* Since 1967 the State of Hawaii has set aside a percentage of revenues to fund the State Foundation on Culture and the Arts. The result is an art collection that has grown to more than 5000 pieces ranging from fabrics to paintings, glasswork to bronze sculpture. Art from the collection is exhibited in 285 buildings throughout the State, some of which is highlighted in an excellent historic walking tour booklet of downtown Honolulu. It's available free from the State Foundation for Culture and the Arts. To provide a museum setting for a portion of the collection, the State purchased the historic Richard Street YMCA, a noteworthy 1920s architectural monument across the street from Iolani Palace, and created the Hawaii State Art Museum (HiSAM), with three galleries on the second floor offering a total of 12,000 square feet of exhibit space. Closed Sunday and Monday.

WASHINGTON PLACE

⊠*320 South Beretania Street* ☏*808-586-0248* Home to Hawaii's governors for 80 years, this building steeped in history is now a public museum. Captain John Dominis began construction in 1846, but never got to live here because he died at sea before the house was completed four years later. His famous daughter-in-law, however, made the house a palace. Queen Liliuokalani was living in Washington Place when she was overthrown, marking the end of the Hawaiian monarchy. When she was released from prison, she returned to Washington Place despite several other more comfortable living options. It has been speculated that her residence here was an act of politics and bravery: the home was cramped—at least by royal standards—but located near the new government's center of power. She did not, it would appear, wish to be forgotten. Washington Place has continued to serve its government over the years, providing living quarters for 12 governors and their families. Tours are available Monday through Friday; 48-hour advance reservations are required.

4 OAHU DOWNTOWN HONOLULU SIGHTS

ST. ANDREWS CATHEDRAL ✉Beretania and Alakea streets ☎808-524-2822 🖥808-537-4177 Thought to be the only example of French-Gothic architecture in Hawaii, this cathedral was erected in 1862 of stone shipped from England. Its eight bells have the names of eight Hawaiian monarchs and the dates of their reigns engraved on them, and can perform 40,320 different melodic changes. One of the three Sunday masses is conducted partially in Hawaiian.

HONOLULU ACADEMY OF ARTS ✉900 South Beretania Street ☎808-532-8700 🖥808-532-8787 🖱www.honoluluacademy.org, academypr@honoluluacademy.org Another important cultural point and a jewel in Honolulu's art community is its arts academy. Founder Anna Rice Cooke originally donated over 4000 works in 1927. Today the internationally recognized museum boasts over 34,000 pieces and is worth spending an afternoon perusing. Emphasizing Eastern and Western artworks, the museum may exhibit such items as author James Michener's collection of *ukiyo-e* prints from Japan or the Samuel H. Kress Foundation collection of Italian Renaissance paintings. In addition, traditional arts of Africa, the Pacific and the Americas are also displayed. Several elegantly landscaped courtyards add to the beauty. Closed Monday. Admission.

HAWAII CHILDREN'S DISCOVERY CENTER ✉111 Ohe Street ☎808-524-5437 🖥808-524-5400 🖱www.discoverycenterhawaii.org, info@discoverycenterhawaii.org Let the kids burn off some steam at this 38,000-square-foot discovery center. Four major galleries sponsor interactive exhibits that are hands-on and educational (for example, "Fantastic You" will teach kids everything they need to know about the human body), but don't worry, they'll never catch on. You can picnic (or nap) at the park across the street. Be forewarned: the Center does not accommodate strollers (although it is wheelchair accessible), so bring a carrier. Closed Monday. Admission.

Waterfront

For a tour of Honolulu's waterfront, head down Richards Street from the State Capitol Building toward Pier 7. Next to the Aloha Tower Marketplace, a festive market bazaar with shops, food and music, the imposing and historic *Falls of Clyde* lies berthed.

HAWAII MARITIME CENTER ✉Pier 7, Honolulu Harbor ☎808-523-6151 🖥808-536-1519 🖱www.bishopmuseum.org/exhibits/hmc/hmc.html This fascinating center (adjacent to the *Falls of Clyde*) traces the archipelago's maritime history from the earliest Polynesian voyagers though the whaling ships on up to modern times. Kids and adults alike will enjoy displays and exhibits, some of them interactive, on volcanoes, surfing, sharks and shipwrecks. Another attraction is a whaling exhibit, replete with the skeletal remains of a humpback whale. (The center includes the *Falls of Clyde* in their admission price.) Admission.

A completely restored 1878 sailing ship, the ***Falls of Clyde*** is reputedly the only fully rigged four-masted ship in the world. In the old days it was used to carry sugar and oil across the Pacific. Honolulu was then a harbor filled with tall-masted ships, so crowded at the dock that they bumped one another's gunwales. Part of this proud fleet, the *Falls of Clyde* was built in Scotland and sailed halfway round the world. For a single admission charge (Note: *Falls of Clyde* will be closed until mid-2008) you can tour this marvelous piece of floating history (it's a National Historic Landmark) and, when in port, view the **Hokulea**, a double-hulled canoe that has sailed several times to Tahiti. A 60-foot replica of an ancient Polynesian craft, it follows the traditional designs of the boats used by the early Tahitians. Since 1975, this fragile craft has sailed between Hawaii and French Polynesia by Hawaiian navigators, re-creating more than 100,000 miles of historic sea voyages. Using no modern instruments, navigating by stars and wave patterns, they traced the course of their ancestors.

ALOHA TOWER ⊠*Pier 9* From the Hawaii Maritime Center, follow the roadway along the water until you see the spire along the water's edge. In the early 20th century, when many visitors arrived in luxurious ocean liners, this slender structure was Hawaii's answer to the Statue of Liberty. It greeted guests when they arrived and bade them farewell upon departure. Now dwarfed by the skyscrapers of downtown Honolulu, proud Aloha Tower still commands an unusual view of the harbor and ocean. Any day between 9 a.m. and sunset you can ride an elevator to the tenth-floor observation deck for a crow's-nest view.

KEWALO BASIN HARBOR ⊠*Ala Moana Boulevard and Ward Avenue* ☎*808-594-1849* It's fun to wander the wharves along the waterfront, catching glimpses of the shops and pleasure boats that still tie up around Honolulu's historic port. You can take in the city's fishing fleet, as well as several tour boats, at this harbor, which is also known as Fisherman's Wharf, located midway between Waikiki and Downtown Honolulu.

HONOLULU FISH MARKET

⊠*Near the Honolulu Harbor (Pier 38)* To see where all that delicious seafood you've been eating comes from, stop by the this fish market. Here auctioneers sell the day's catch. For the real experience, get there at 5:30 in the morning. Those not quite as industrious should note it's all over by noon.

FORT STREET MALL From the Honolulu Fish Market it's not far to this seven-block stretch of Downtown Honolulu that is an attractive pedestrian thoroughfare with a few restaurants. The mall is also a good place to spend a little time shopping. Located miles from the Waikiki tourist beat, the stores here cater to local people, so you'll be able to discover objects unobtainable in kitschier quarters.

MERCHANT STREET Fort Street Mall leads you to the center of the Honolulu's old downtown section. The 19th- and early-20th-century buildings in this neighborhood re-create the days before Hawaii became the 50th state, when the islands were almost totally controlled by "The Big Five," an interlocking group of powerful corporations. Today the brick-rococo district remains much the same on the outside. But the interiors of the buildings have changed markedly. They now house boutiques and gourmet restaurants downstairs and multinational corporations on the upper floors.

Chinatown

Heading away from the waterfront all the way to the end of Merchant Street, take a right on Nuuanu Avenue, then a left on Hotel Street. As you walk along this thoroughfare, which seems to change its identity every block or two, you will pass from Honolulu's conservative financial district into one of its most intriguing ethnic neighborhoods, Chinatown.

The Chinese first arrived in Hawaii in 1852, imported as plantation workers. They quickly moved to urban areas after completing their plantation contracts, became merchants and proved very successful. Many settled right here in this weather-beaten district, which has long been a center of controversy and an integral part of Honolulu's history. When bubonic plague hit the Chinese community in 1900, the Caucasian-led government tried to contain the pestilence by burning down afflicted homes. The bumbling white fathers managed to raze most of Chinatown, destroying businesses as well as houses.

Chinatown has undergone a dramatic transformation over the past years in an effort to eliminate some of the seedier elements and red-light businesses. While it still has plenty of character, thanks to its quaint, time-worn stores and abundance of distinctive eateries, a thriving arts community has been established, breathing new life into the neighborhood.

Some of Chinatown's woodframe buildings still suggest the old days and traditions. Wander down side streets like Maunakea Street and you will encounter import stores, Chinese groceries and noodle factories. You might also pop into one of the medicinal herb shops, which feature unique potions and healing powders. There are chop suey joints, acupuncturists and outdoor markets galore, all lending a priceless flavor of the Orient.

MAUNAKEA MARKETPLACE ✉*Hotel and Maunakea streets* ☎*808-524-3409* The ultimate emblem of Chinatown's revitalization is this often-crowded marketplace. This Amerasian shopping mall, with a statue of Confucius and one of Kuan Yin overlooking a brick courtyard, houses a Chinese teahouse and a Chinese art store. The most interesting feature is the produce market, a series of traditional hanging-ducks-and-live-fish stalls housed inside an air-conditioned building.

CHINATOWN WALKING TOURS

✉*76 North King Street* ☎*808-533-3181* 📠*808-533-3184* The best way to visit this neighborhood is on one of the walking tours sponsored by the Chinese Chamber of Commerce. Chinatown today is an eclectic community, containing not only Chinese, but Filipinos, Hawaiians and more recent arrivals from Vietnam and Laos. To fully understand Hawaii's melting-pot population, it's important to visit this vibrant district. The walking tour is given on Monday mornings, and will take you past temples and other noteworthy spots around the neighborhood. Fee.

IZUMO TAISHAKYO MISSION Going north along Hotel Street across Nuuanu Stream, turn right on College Walk and follow it a short distance upstream. You'll pass this Japanese Shinto shrine. Take a minute to stop in to see the bell and gate.

FOSTER
BOTANICAL GARDEN

✉50 North Vineyard Boulevard ✆808-522-7065, 808-522-7066 (reservations) ⌨www.co.honolulu.hi.us/parks/hbg Proceed farther and you will arrive at this 14-acre plot planted with orchids, palms, coffee trees, poisonous plants and numerous other exotic specimens. There are about 4000 species in all, dotted around a garden that was first planted over 150 years ago. You can meditate under a bo tree or wander through a "prehistoric glen," a riot of ancient ferns and unusual palms. Or you can stroll through and marvel at the universe of color crowded into this urban garden. Visitors are advised to bring insect repellent. Admission.

KUAN YIN TEMPLE

✉50 North Vineyard Boulevard When you're done enjoying Foster Botanical Garden, stop by the adjacent temple, where the smell of incense fills the air and Buddhist tranquility pervades. For a brief moment you'll feel like you're in ancient China rather than Honolulu.

CULTURAL PLAZA On the way back to Chinatown, walk along the other side of Nuuanu Stream and stop at this Asian-style shopping mall bounded by Kukui, Maunakea and Beretania streets, and by the stream. You'll find porcelain, Chinese jewelry, housewares, gifts, medicinal herbs, Chinese cake shops and several restaurants. Don't miss the open-air market selling fresh vegetables, tropical fruits, fish, chicken feet, pigs' heads and other exotic items. The market entrance is in the back of the plaza.

HAWAII THEATRE ✉1130 Bethel Street ✆808-791-1306, 808-528-0506 (tickets) ⌨808-528-1675 ⌨www.hawaiitheatre.com On the outskirts of Chinatown is this revitalized theater. After years of painstaking restoration, it is a study in neoclassical architecture. With gilded decor, Corinthian columns and striking mosaics, it has been elevated again to the grand status it enjoyed when the theater first opened in 1922. In 1929, it was the first movie theater in the islands to show movies with sound. Tours are available at this nationally registered historic place. Shows, concerts, festivals, ethnic programs and films are presented here. Closed Monday. Admission.

RESORTQUEST AT THE EXECUTIVE CENTRE HOTEL
$$$$ 125 ROOMS ✉1088 Bishop Street ☎808-539-3000 ℻808-523-1088
🖥www.rqexecutivecentre.com, res.exc@resortquesthawaii.com
This highrise in the financial district, with its location and perks aimed at business folks (computer ports, in-room wi-fi, daily newspaper) make it an ideal spot for a business trip. Other amenities include laundry facilities and complimentary breakfast.

NUUANU YMCA
$ 70 ROOMS ✉1441 Pali Highway ☎808-536-3556 ℻808-521-1181
🖥www.ymcahonolulu.org, tragossnig@ymcahonolulu.org
The Y has inexpensive one-person accommodations for men. Complete athletic facilities are available to make it more enticing.

DINING

Waterfront
As you get away from Waikiki you'll be dining with a more local crowd and tasting foods more representative of island cuisine, so I would certainly advise checking out some of Honolulu's eating places.

FISHERMAN'S WHARF
$$–$$$ SEAFOOD ✉1009 Ala Moana Boulevard ☎808-538-3808 ℻808-521-5210
Right next door to Honolulu's fishing fleet you'll find a tourist dining establishment that's been serving up platters for years. It has an authentic seafront feel because it is where the fishing boats actually come in. There are seafood dishes as well as pasta and steaks. No lunch on weekends.

JOHN DOMINIS
$$$–$$$$ SEAFOOD ✉43 Ahui Street ☎808-523-0955 ℻808-526-3758
🖥www.johndominis.com
Fresh *onaga*, mahimahi, *opakapaka* and *ahi* highlight the vast seafood menu here. A sprawling establishment midway between Waikiki and Downtown Honolulu, it features huge pools filled with live fish. The wood-paneled dining room overlooks the water and the chefs know as much about preparing seafood as the original Polynesians. For land-lubbers, steak and veal are also on the menu. Dinner only except for Sunday brunch.

NICO'S PIER 38
$$ PLATE LUNCHES ✉1133 North Nimitz Highway ☎808-540-1377
℻808-540-1376 🖥www.nicospier38.com
Enjoy a meal of island favorites prepared with the skill and subtleties of chef Nicolas "Nico" Chaize's French culinary training. Plate lunches are elevated to another level with *hoisin* barbecue chicken and homemade hamburger steak with mushroom-onion gravy. Or try the grilled *ahi* baguette sandwich with arugula, tomato and wasabi aioli. In the morning, you can order

sweet bread French toast or a hearty fried rice with ham, Portuguese sausage, bacon and *kamaboko* (fishcake). Breakfast and lunch only. Closed Sunday.

Downtown

PEOPLE'S CAFÉ

$ HAWAIIAN ✉*1310 Pali Highway* ☏*808-536-5789* ✒*808-536-5789*

Near the city's financial center there's a modest restaurant that I particularly like. With a primarily Polynesian menu, this is a good spot to order poi, *lomi* salmon, *kalua* pig and other island favorites. *Ono, ono!* Closed Sunday.

LA MARIANA SAILING CLUB

$$–$$$ AMERICAN/SEAFOOD ✉*50 Sand Island Access Road*
☏*808-848-2800* ✒*808-841-2173*

There is nothing else in Honolulu quite like this. Located on the shores of the Keehi Lagoon and reached through the industrial port area off Sand Island Access Road, La Mariana plays host to an assortment of old salts who dance the hula, sing, party and provide more local color than you'll find just about anywhere else in town. What's more, the food, with a focus on fresh fish, seafood, prime rib and steaks, is good and the service friendly.

WISTERIA RESTAURANT

$$ JAPANESE ✉*1206 South King Street* ☏*808-591-9276* ✒*808-596-0976*

Pleasing local Japanese Hawaiians for years, this is where they come to celebrate birthdays, anniversaries and other milestones. The setting is padded booths—coffeeshop style. The food is Japanese home-style cooking, just like *obachan* (grandma) used to make. The sukiyaki and teriyaki are particularly tasty. No lunch Saturday and Sunday.

Chinatown

MYLAN RESTAURANT

$–$$ VIETNAMESE ✉*1160 Maunakea Street* ☏*808-528-3663*

Right in the heart of Chinatown, it may be small, but this café represents a triple threat to the competition—attractive decor, good prices and excellent food. The menu covers the spectrum of Vietnamese dishes, with a smattering of Italian and vegetarian fare, and the interior, lined with tropical paintings, is easy on the eyes.

CHAR HUNG SUT

$ CHINESE ✉*64 North Pauahi Street* ☏*808-538-3335*

This hole-in-the-wall take-out joint is short on ambience, but locals line up for the shredded pork buns (*manapua*), pork hash, half-moon dumplings, sweet rice cakes and other tasty treats, buying dozens at a time. Get there early or you may be disappointed—favorites can, and do, run out before day's end. Closed Tuesday.

MAUNAKEA MARKETPLACE
✉ *Hotel and Maunakea streets*

There's a little bit of every other ethnic cuisine at the food stalls at this marketplace. Here you'll find vendors dispensing steaming plates of Thai, Chinese, Japanese, Hawaiian, Filipino, Korean, Vietnamese and Italian food. Italian? Small tables are provided.

TAI PAN DIM SUM
$–$$ CHINESE   ✉ *Cultural Plaza, 100 North Beretania Street #167*   ☎ *808-599-8899*

Drawing an overflow crowd of local, Tai Pan is well-loved for its bite-sized delicacies such as *char siu* buns (baked and steamed), shrimp dumplings, bean curd rolls and pork ribs in black bean sauce. The fluorescent-lit room, tightly packed with tables, may lack pizzazz, but the authentic food is flavorful and reasonably priced.

LEGEND BUDDHIST VEGETARIAN RESTAURANT
$ CHINESE   ✉ *100 North Beretania Street*   ☎ *808-532-8218*

For anyone who thinks a meal without meat isn't a meal, a visit here might make a health-food nut out of you. Yes, it's vegan (i.e., no animal products)—but the dim sum is darn good. Run by the same people as Legend Seafood Restaurant, this eatery is located in the same building. No dinner. Closed Wednesday.

TO CHAU
$ VIETNAMESE   ✉ *1007 River Street*   ☎ *808-533-4549*

Here you'll find excellent *pho*, the popular Vietnamese soup, and other simple dishes from that region at very low prices. But be prepared to wait a bit as it usually draws a crowd.

MABUHAY CAFÉ
$–$$ FILIPINO   ✉ *1049 River Street*   ☎ *808-545-1956*

For Filipino food, this café comes recommended by several readers. It's a plainly adorned place on the edge of Chinatown that serves a largely local clientele. The menu is extensive, covering all types of Filipino dishes.

INDIGO
$$–$$$ ASIAN   ✉ *1121 Nuuanu Avenue*   ☎ *808-521-2900*   📠 *808-537-4164*
🖥 *www.indigo-hawaii.com*

One of Chinatown's treats, this Eurasian dining room has bright art on white walls, white tablecloths and dark furniture. You can expect more than a dozen dim sum dishes. The soups and salads include tomato-garlic crab soup and goat cheese wontons. Among the entrées, they offer miso-marinated seared salmon and Mongolian lamb chops with mint-tangerine sauce. What an adventure! No lunch Saturday. Closed Sunday and Monday.

SAM CHOY'S BREAKFAST, LUNCH & CRAB AND BIG ALOHA BREWERY

$$–$$$ HAWAII REGIONAL   ✉580 North Nimitz Highway   ✆808-545-7979
✆808-545-7997   ⌨www.samchoy.com

A giant red neon sign announces that you've arrived at this noisy, bustling restaurant with marine decor accentuated by a dry-docked fishing boat. Chef Sam Choy, a local boy who has helped Hawaii Regional cuisine establish an international reputation, serves crab (Dungeness, Maryland Blue, Florida Gold, Alaskan king) fresh from the open kitchen. There's also lobster, shrimp, fish and, for those unclear on the concept, chicken and beef dishes.

LITTLE VILLAGE

$ CHINESE   ✉1113 Smith Street   ✆808-545-3008

If you're looking for tasty pot stickers, stop at this delightful spot, which specializes in Chinese dumplings stuffed with a wide range of vegetarian and meat fillings. The pan-fried beef and walnut shrimp, garlic spinach and special fried rice are winners, too.

SHOPPING

Downtown

ALOHA ANTIQUE & COLLECTIBLES ✉378 North School Street ✆808-585-8082 If you love those claustrophobic antique stores that have keepsakes stacked to the rafters and spilling into the aisles, then the 900 block of Maunakea Street is calling. This place has everything imaginable in the priceless-to-worthless range.

Waterfront

ALOHA TOWER MARKETPLACE ✉Pier 8 ✆808-528-5700 ⌨www.alohatower.com A California-style affair complete with white stucco walls and curved tile roof, this marketplace is located on the waterfront overlooking Honolulu Harbor. It's tucked between the Hawaii Maritime Museum and Aloha Tower, and is set near one of the busiest parts of the harbor. With its flagstone walkways and open-air courtyards, it's worth stopping by even if buying something is the last thing on your mind. Among the over 70 shops are about 25 devoted to apparel, a handful of galleries and perhaps three dozen specialty shops. Bring back a piece of Hawaii's musical tradition from **Hawaiian Ukulele** (808-536-3228).

Chinatown

CULTURAL PLAZA ✉Corner of Beretania and Maunakea streets ✆808-521-4934 If you're seeking Oriental items, then Chinatown is the place. Spotted throughout this neighborhood are small shops selling statuettes, pottery and other curios. It's also worthwhile wandering through the Cultural Plaza. This mall is filled with Asian jewelers, bookstores and knickknack shops.

OPEN MARKET

✉*Along North King Street between River and Kekaulike streets* Don't miss this great place to shop for fresh foods. There are numerous stands selling fish, produce, poultry, meat, baked goods and island fruits, all at low-overhead prices.

PEGGE HOPPER GALLERY ✉*1164 Nuuanu Avenue* ☎*808-524-1160* 🖰*www.peggehopper.com* At the edge of Chinatown along Nuuanu Avenue are several galleries and shops worthy of a visit. The Pegge Hopper Gallery displays acrylic paintings and the female portraits for which she is renowned. Open Tuesday through Friday or by appointment.

NIGHTLIFE

HONOLULU THEATER FOR YOUTH ✉*Queen Emma's Square* ☎*808-839-9885* 📠*808-839-7018* 🖰*www.htyweb.org, htymail@htyweb.org* A variety of youth- and family-oriented productions are performed by this young theater team at the Tenney Theatre at St. Andrew's Cathedral. The company also tours the neighbor islands. Reservations are recommended.

CHAMBER MUSIC HAWAII ☎*808-489-5038 (tickets)* For something more refined and classical, consider an evening of fine vocal performance from this chamber group, which presents a series of concerts annually at several different locations around the city, including the Honolulu Academy of Arts. They also perform on the windward side of the island.

HONOLULU SYMPHONY ☎*808-524-0815, 808-792-2000 (box office)* The symphony's season runs from September to May, and provides a delightful schedule of programs. They perform at the Neal Blaisdell Center at Ward and King streets.

HAWAII OPERA THEATRE ✉*987 Waimanu Street* ☎*808-596-7372, 808-596-7858 (box office)* 🖰*www.hawaiiopera.org* Here you can see works like Saint-Saens' *Samson and Delilah*, Puccini's *Madame Butterfly* and *Die Fledermaus* by Strauss. This regional company features stars from the international opera scene.

CHAI'S ISLAND BISTRO

✉*Aloha Tower Marketplace, 1 Aloha Tower Drive* ☎*808-585-0011* 🖰*www. chaisislandbistro.com, chai@chaisislandbistro.com* In a fairly intimate setting, where you can get up close and personal, especially if you come early and have dinner, this bistro often hosts Hawaiian entertainers. Call and check who will be there—you're apt to find Jerry Santos, the Brothers Cazimero or Makaha Sons.

THIRTYNINEHOTEL ✉*39 North Hotel Street* ✆*808-599-2552* ⌕*www.thirty ninehotel.com* For a bit of swanky New York culture, join the young fashionistas at this pinnacle of hipness in Honolulu's Chinatown. Dance in the gallery, which is perpetually filled with quality, contemporary art, or sip a cocktail and soak in the well-populated, trés chic atmosphere.

LA MARIANA SAILING CLUB

✉*50 Sand Island Access Road* ✆*808-848-2800* ⌕*808-841-2173* There's nothing quite like a Friday or Saturday evening at La Mariana. A festive group of locals takes over the floor to entertain you with their song and dance. If you're lucky, it will be someone of note who dropped by to talk story or strum his or her uke. There's live piano music nightly.

INDIGO ✉*1121 Nuuanu Avenue* ✆*808-521-2900* An attractive Asian restaurant with a patio, this spot has hip-hop dancing, acoustic jazz and contemporary music Tuesday through Saturday. On several nights the sound is live; other nights it's deejay driven. Closed Sunday and Monday. Occasional cover.

ARTS AT MARK'S GARAGE ✉*1159 Nuuanu Avenue* ✆*808-521-2903* ⌕*www.artsatmarks.com* Stop here for art exhibits, jazz and dance performances, poetry slams and comedy improvisations.

HAWAII THEATRE ✉*1130 Bethel Street* ✆*808-791-1306, 808-528-0506 (tickets)* ⌕*www.hawaiitheatre.com* Shows here run the gamut from the best in Broadway performances to dance troupes, classical music and much more. The **Hawaii International Film Festival** (www.hiff.org) is held here late in the year (among other venues).

REGAL DOLE CANNERY 18 THEATRES ✉*735-B Iwilei Road* ✆*808-528-3653* If you're in the mood for a movie fix, head to this theater complex, a short drive from Chinatown. Hawaii's largest cineplex with 18 screens, it also features Hawaii's best cinematic selection, including foreign films you'll find nowhere else on the island.

BEACHES & PARKS

KAKAAKO WATERFRONT PARK

✉*End of Cooke Street off Ala Moana Boulevard*

🏃 Located near downtown Honolulu and popular with local picnickers, this rock-fringed park has a promenade with an uninterrupted view spanning from Diamond Head to the harbor. There are picnic tables, pavilions, showers, restrooms and large grassy plots. A surfing break offshore is popular, but there's no swimming.

SAND ISLAND STATE RECREATION AREA

✉ *From Waikiki, take Ala Moana Boulevard and Nimitz Highway several miles west to Sand Island Access Road* ✆ *808-587-0300*

🏄 ⛴ This 140-acre park wraps around the south and east shores of Sand Island, with sections fronting both Honolulu Harbor and the open sea. Despite the name, there's only a small sandy beach here, and jet traffic from nearby Honolulu International might disturb your snoozing. But there is a great view of Honolulu. While the swimming and snorkeling are poor here, there are good surf breaks in summer and fishing is usually rewarding. *Papio* and *moano* are the prime catches. Facilities include restrooms and a picnic area.

▲ State permit required for tent camping in the grassy area facing the ocean.

GREATER HONOLULU

Framed by the Waianae Range in the west and the Koolau Range to the east, Honolulu is a nonstop drama presented within a natural amphitheater. Honolulu Harbor sets the stage to the south; at the center lie Waikiki and Downtown Honolulu. Wrapped around these tourist and business centers is a rainbow-shaped congeries of sights and places that, for lack of a better name, constitutes "Greater Honolulu."

Greater Honolulu is where most of the people of Honolulu live. It extends from navy-gray Pearl Harbor to the turquoise waters of the prestigious Kahala district and holds in its ambit some of the city's prettiest territory.

The points of interest are dotted all across the city and require a bit of planning to see. You'll need to ride buses or taxis or rent a car, but it is well worth the extra effort. You'll be away from the crowds of tourists and get a chance to meet the locals and get a singular perspective on island life and culture.

Many of the points of interest below are frequented more by local residents than tourists. Others contain an interesting mix of local folk and out-of-towners. In any case, be sure to take the time to explore some of these outlying spots.

SIGHTS

Kalihi–Nuuanu Avenue Area

The first district in Greater Honolulu is actually within walking distance of Downtown Honolulu, but it's a relatively long walk, so transportation is generally advised. Nuuanu Avenue begins downtown and travels uphill in a northeasterly direction past several noteworthy points.

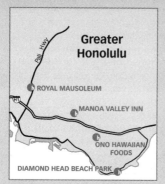

ROYAL MAUSOLEUM
PAGE 96

Revered and beautifully adorned final resting place for Hawaii's 19th-century royal families

MANOA VALLEY INN
PAGE 104

Magnificent 1915 cream-colored Victorian mansion set in the lush Manoa Valley

ONO HAWAIIAN FOODS
PAGE 107

Packed hole-in-da-wall eatery with locals feasting on *laulau*, *kalua* pig, *pipikaula*, *poi* and *haupia*

DIAMOND HEAD BEACH PARK
PAGE 110

Surfing and snorkeling off a twisted ribbon of white sand—near to—but far enough from Waikiki to lose the crowd

SOTO MISSION OF HAWAII ✉1708 Nuuanu Avenue ☎808-537-9409
Home of a meditative Zen sect, Soto Mission is one of the first spots you'll see along Nuuana Avenue. Modeled after a temple in India where the Buddha gave his first sermon, this building is marked by dramatic towers, and beautiful Japanese bonsai plants decorate the landscape.

HONOLULU MYOHOJI TEMPLE ✉2003 Nuuanu Avenue ☎808-524-7790
Here and at the nearby Soto Mission the city seems like a distant memory. This building, placidly situated along a small stream, is capped by a peace tower.

HONOLULU MEMORIAL PARK ✉22 Craigside Place Uphill from Honolulu Myohoji Temple and Soto Mission lies this memorial park. There is an ancestral monument here, bordered on three sides by a pond of flashing carp and a striking three-tiered pagoda. This entire area is a center of simple yet beautiful Asian places of worship.

TENRIKYO MISSION ✉2236 Nuuanu Avenue This is a woodframe temple that was moved here all the way from Japan. One intriguing fact about this fragile structure is that large sections were built without nails.

ROYAL MAUSOLEUM _____

✉2261 Nuuanu Avenue The Hawaiian people have an important center here–the Royal Mausoleum, which is situated across the street from the Tenrikyo Mission. This was the final resting place for two of Hawaii's royal families, the Kamehameha and Kalakaua clans. Together they ruled 19th-century Hawaii. Today the area is a state monument landscaped with palms, ginger, plumeria and other beautiful tropical plants and flowers. Closed weekends.

Punchbowl and Tantalus

It is a few miles from Downtown Honolulu to Punchbowl, the circular center of an extinct volcano. You'll find it northeast of town, at the end of Ward Avenue and just off Prospect Drive, which circles the crater. A youngster in geologic terms, the volcano is a mere 150,000 years old. From the lip of the crater, there is a marvelous vista sweeping down to Diamond Head, across Honolulu and all the way out to the Waianae Range.

NATIONAL MEMORIAL CEMETERY 📞 *808-532-3720* The most important feature in Punchbowl is the National Memorial Cemetery, located in the extinct volcano known as *Puowaina*, Hawaiian for "hill of sacrifice." Over 42,000 war dead have been interred, including victims of both World Wars, as well as the Korean, Spanish-American, Vietnam and Iraq wars. There is also an impressive monument to the "Courts of the Missing," which lists the names of soldiers missing in action. Ironically, of all the people buried here, the most famous was not a soldier but a journalist—Ernie Pyle, whose World War II stories about the average GI were eagerly followed by an entire nation. Near his grave you will also find the burial site of Hawaii's first astronaut, Ellison Onizuka, who died in the *Challenger* space shuttle disaster. Guided walking tours (fee) are offered by the American Legion.

TANTALUS ————————————

You can explore the heights by following Tantalus Drive as it winds up the side of this 2013-foot mountain. Together with Round Top Drive, Tantalus Drive forms a loop that circles through the residential areas hidden within this rainforest. There are spectacular views all along the route, as well as hiking trails that lead from the road into verdant hilltop regions. Here you'll encounter guava, banana and eucalyptus trees as well as wildflowers such as ginger, and an occasional wild pig.

PUU UALAKAA PARK One of the best views in all of the Punchbowl–Tantalus area is found at this lovely retreat located along the drive. The vista here extends from Diamond Head west to Pearl Harbor, encompassing in its course a giant swath of Honolulu and the Pacific. If you were a fan of *Blue Hawaii*, you might recall the view from here. It's where Elvis decides he wants to become a tour guide.

CONTEMPORARY MUSEUM ✉ *2411 Makiki Heights Drive* 📞 *808-526-1322* 📠 *808-536-5973* 🖥 *www.tcmhi.org, info@tcmhi.org* En route to Puu Ualakaa Park, stop by this museum. In addition to changing exhibitions of contemporary art, it features the works of several well-known artists in its sculpture garden and galleries, including David Hockney,

Greater Honolulu

POINTS OF INTEREST

- Ⓐ Battleship Missouri Memorial
- Ⓑ Bishop Museum
- Ⓒ Contemporary Museum
- Ⓓ Japanese Cultural Center of Hawaii
- Ⓔ Lyon Arboretum
- Ⓕ National Memorial Cemetery (Punchbowl)
- Ⓖ Nuuanu Pali Lookout
- Ⓗ Queen Emma's Summer Palace
- Ⓘ Royal Mausoleum
- Ⓙ Soto Mission of Hawaii
- Ⓚ State Capitol Building
- Ⓛ University of Hawaii
- Ⓜ USS Arizona Memorial
- Ⓝ USS Bowfin Submarine Museum

Robert Arneson, Charles Arnoldi and Tom Wesselman. Boasting five galleries, an inspired gift shop and a gourmet café, the museum is nevertheless upstaged by its magnificently landscaped grounds. Closed Monday. Admission.

Cross-Island Express

Along the outskirts of Honolulu, there are several more points of interest. The best way to tour them is while traveling along the two highways that cut across the Koolaus, connecting Honolulu directly with the island's Windward Coast: the Likelike Highway (Route 63) and the Pali Highway (Route 61). The Likelike Highway can be reached from Route H-1, the superhighway that serves Honolulu. Before heading up into the mountains to tour other sites, you will encounter the Bishop Museum near the intersection of Routes 63 and H-1.

BISHOP MUSEUM ✉ *1525 Bernice Street* ☏ *808-847-3511* 📠 *808-841-8968* 🖰 *www.bishopmuseum.org, membership@bishopmuseum.org* Founded in 1889 by Charles Reed Bishop in honor of his late wife, Princess Bernice Pauahi Bishop, the last descendant of the royal Kamehameha family, the Bishop Museum now includes a plethora of artifacts, documents and photographs about Hawaii as well as other Pacific island cultures. Built on the original site of the Kamehameha Schools for Boys, a school established to educate Hawaiian children, the museum was created to augment their education and instill a greater pride in their Hawaiian heritage. The one remaining building from the school, which was relocated in the '60s, is Bishop Hall. The museum is a must-see for anyone interested in Hawaiiana.

Here you'll also find an outrigger canoe, thrones, primitive artworks and fascinating natural-history exhibits. There are drums made with shark skin, and helmets decorated with dog teeth and pearl shells. The 19th-century whaling trade is represented with menacing harpoons and yellowing photographs of the oil-laden ships. Of all the exhibits, the most spectacular are cloaks worn by Hawaiian kings and fashioned from tens of thousands of tiny feathers. (The Hawaiian Hall is under renovation until Spring 2008). There are displays capturing the Japanese, Chinese and Filipino heritage in Hawaii and a hall devoted to other cultures of the Pacific. The museum also houses a planetarium, various children's activities, and a gift shop. The Bishop is truly one of the finest museums of its kind in the world. Admission.

QUEEN EMMA'S SUMMER PALACE

✉ *2913 Pali Highway* ☏ *808-595-6291* 📠 *808-595-4395* 🖰 *www.daughtersof hawaii.org, doh1903@hawaii.rr.com* The other, more scenic road across the mountains is the Pali Highway, Route 61. As it ascends, it passes Queen Emma's Summer Palace. Constructed in 1848, the palace was originally used as a mountain home by King Kamehameha IV and his wife, Queen Emma. Today the gracious white-pillared house is a museum. Here you can view the Queen's personal artifacts, as well as various other period pieces.

The Palace's gardens are especially beautiful; you can almost see the Queen entertaining her guests by the lily pond. The gift shop has a nice selection of local crafts and books. Admission.

NUUANU PALI DRIVE _____ hidden

When visiting Queen Emma's Summer Palace, you can also walk the tree-shaded grounds of this scenic road and follow until it rejoins the highway. This residential boulevard, with its natural canopy and park-like atmosphere, is one of Honolulu's many idyllic hideaways.

NUUANU PALI LOOKOUT Along Pali Highway there is a turnoff to a lookout—a point that must not be missed, and is without doubt Oahu's finest view. Gaze down the sheer, rugged face of the Koolau cliffs as they drop 3000 feet to a softly rolling coastal shelf. Your view will extend from Makapuu Point to the distant reaches of Kaneohe Bay, and from the lip of the cliff far out to sea. It was from these heights, according to legend, that a vanquished army was forced to plunge when Kamehameha I captured Oahu in 1795.

Pearl Harbor

Many people consider a trip here a pilgrimage. It was here on a sleepy Sunday morning, December 7, 1941, that the Japanese launched a sneak attack on the United States naval fleet anchored in the port, immediately plunging the nation into World War II. As Japanese planes bombed the harbor, over 2400 Americans lost their lives. Eighteen ships sank that day in the country's greatest military disaster. Pearl Harbor, several miles northwest of Downtown Honolulu, can be reached by car or bus.

USS ARIZONA MEMORIAL ℡808-422-2771 ℡808-483-8608 ⌨www.nps.gov/usar The battleship USS *Arizona* was hit so savagely by aerial bombs and torpedoes that it plunged to the bottom, entombing over 1100 sailors within its hulk; today they remain in that watery grave. A special USS Arizona Memorial was built to honor them; it's constructed directly above the ship, right in the middle of Pearl Harbor. The memorial includes a shrine with the name of each sailor who died aboard the ship carved in marble. Gazing at this too, too long list of names, and peering over the side at the shadowy hull of the ship, it's hard not to be overcome by the tragic history of the place. Daily from 8 a.m. to 3 p.m., there's a 75-minute program that includes free boat tours out to this fascinating memorial. Remember, no bathing suits, bare feet or bags are permitted.

USS BOWFIN SUBMARINE MUSEUM ✉Pearl Harbor ℡808-423-1341 ℡808-422-5201 ⌨www.bowfin.org Anchored nearby the *Arizona* visitors center, this World War II–era submarine is a window into life beneath the waves. It provides an excellent opportunity to tour the claustrophobic quarters in which 80 men spent months at a time. The accompanying museum, filled with submarine-related artifacts, will help provide an even fuller perspective. Admission.

BATTLESHIP MISSOURI MEMORIAL ✉ *Pearl Harbor* ✆ *808-423-2263,*
888-877-6477 ✍ *www.ussmissouri.org, bigmo@ussmissouri.org* For another perspective on World War II, visit this battleship memorial. Launched in
1944, the *Missouri*, or Mighty Mo as it is usually called, was the last U.S.
battleship ever built. It was aboard this 887-foot vessel on September 2,
1945, that General Douglas MacArthur accepted the surrender of the
Japanese forces, thus ending World War II. The decommissioned battleship is now docked in Pearl Harbor, off Ford Island, within sight of the
USS *Arizona* Memorial. Tours depart from the ticket office of the *Bowfin*
submarine. Guided tours are available (reservations recommended), or
you can tour the Mighty Mo on your own, getting a first-hand glimpse of
its massive armaments, the surrender deck and the commanding
bridge. Plan to spend an hour on the self-guided tour. Admission.

Ala Moana Area

Bordering the *ewa* direction of Waikiki, just Diamond Head–side of
Downtown Honolulu, is Ala Moana (which means "pathway to the
sea"). Its claim to fame is a very large family-oriented park that extends
from the Ala Wai Yacht Harbor along the ocean to Kewalo Basin.

ALA MOANA BEACH PARK Honolulu residents flock here on the
weekends to hold family reunions or company picnics, or to play volleyball, softball or tennis with their friends. The sandy beach that lines
the park is a safe place for swimmers, especially near **Magic Island** (Ala
Moana Regional Park), the peninsula on the east side of the park. Long-
distance swimmers practice swimming the length of the park, while
joggers run alongside the shore to get into shape. Watching the sun set
from this spot is the sport of choice for many locals and tourists alike.

ALA MOANA CENTER ✍ *www.alamoana.com* Across the street from
Ala Moana Beach Park, this shopping center is the shop-'til-you-drop
capital of the islands (and almost anywhere else in the U.S.). In addition to
over 200 shops, Ala Moana Center is the main transfer point for most island buses, so if you ride TheBus, you'll likely end up here at some point.

Moiliili–Kapahulu–Kaimuki Area

Just *mauka* (toward the mountains) of Ala Moana are several working-
class communities—Moiliili, Kapahulu and Kaimuki. They skirt the University of Hawaii on one side and Waikiki on the other. What's best about
these neighborhoods is the handful of restaurants that are far enough
away from the madding crowd of Waikiki to make eating out a pleasure.
Restaurants in every budget category can be found in these enclaves, and
best of all, you'll more than likely be dining with a local crowd.

**JAPANESE CULTURAL CENTER
OF HAWAII**

✉ *2454 South Beretania Street* ✆ *808-945-7633* ✆ *808-944-1123* ✍ *www.*
jcch.com, info@jcch.com In Moiliili, this cultural center sponsors a
permanent exhibit focusing on the history of Japanese culture in
Hawaii. In addition to the gallery, there's a gift shop, traditional

martial arts dojo and teahouse. The Resource Center contains an extensive collection of books, pamphlets, periodicals and oral histories. It also hosts cultural events and festivals marking traditional Japanese holidays; call ahead for details. Closed Sunday and Monday. Admission.

Manoa Valley Area

Residents of a different sort are found in the city's beautiful Manoa Valley, a couple of miles northeast of Waikiki. Among the elegant homes decorating the region are some owned by the New England families that settled in Hawaii in the 19th century.

UNIVERSITY OF HAWAII ⊠*2444 Dole Street* ☎*808-956-8111* ☐*www.hawaii.edu* The state university has its main campus in Manoa; almost 21,000 students and 1300 faculty members attend classes and teach on these beautifully landscaped grounds.

UNIVERSITY OF HAWAII ART GALLERY ⊠*Art Building, University of Hawaii at Manoa* ☎*808-956-6888* ☐*www.hawaii.edu/artgallery, gallery@hawaii.edu* Don't miss the opportunity to visit the university's art gallery. Employing modular and movable walls, it constantly reinvents itself to the configurations of visiting exhibits. Exhibits here have included intricately patterned Japanese fishermen's coats, ethnic clothing from southwest China, and contemporary Korean art. You never know what the gallery will offer up. Closed Saturday and from mid-May to mid-August.

EAST-WEST CENTER

⊠*John Burns Hall, 1601 East-West Road* ☎*808-944-7111* ☐*www.eastwestcenter.org, ewcinfo@eastwestcenter.org* A non-profit research facility, this center is also part of the university. Designed by noted architect I. M. Pei, the center strives to promote the mutual understanding and cooperation among Pacific Rim cultures. The center also contains a number of priceless Asian artworks, a Japanese garden, waterfall and teahouse, well worth viewing.

WAIOLI TEA ROOM ⊠*2950 Manoa Road* ☎*808-988-5800* From campus you can head deeper into Manoa Valley along Oahu Avenue and Manoa Road. You'll pass this cozy dining room tucked into a garden setting where you can enjoy breakfast, lunch or high tea, a bakery and a gift shop. Here also is the Little Grass Shack that was once occupied by novelist Robert Louis Stevenson (or so the story goes), and a small chapel replete with stained-glass windows.

LYON ARBORETUM

⊠*3860 Manoa Road* ☎*808-988-0456* ☐*www.hawaii.edu/lyonarboretum* Farther down Manoa Road is a magnificent 194-acre garden with over 8000 plant species. Also here are research greenhouses, hiking trails and perhaps the world's largest collection of palm trees. Closed weekends.

Diamond Head Beach Park, a twisting ribbon of white sand, nestles directly below the famous crater. Whenever the wind and waves are good, you'll see windsurfers and surfers galore sweeping in toward the shoreline. The coral reef here makes for good skindiving, too. It's a pretty beach, backdropped by the Kuilei cliffs and watched over by the **Diamond Head Lighthouse**.

From Diamond Head, continue east along Diamond Head Road and Kahala Avenue. These will lead through the **Kahala District**, home to the island's elite. Bordered by the ocean and the exclusive Waialae Country Club is a golden string of spectacular oceanfront homes with carefully manicured lawns.

SHANGRI LA _____ h**idden**

For details and tour options contact the Honolulu Academy of Arts ✆ *808-532-3853* ✉ *www.honoluluacademy.org* Tobacco heiress Doris Duke, a socialite celebrity of the mid-20th century, built a fantasy home on a five-acre site on the lava rock headland called Black Point, just to the east of Diamond Head. Duke, who died in 1993, created a museum of the house, which she'd romantically named Shangri La, after the legendary Himalayan valley where peace and good health prevailed. Intrigued by Islamic art, Duke designed the home with Islamic architectural features, furnishings and artworks. The museum is open to a limited number of visitors daily, with departures from the Honolulu Academy of Arts. Advance bookings are recommended for the informative and entertaining docent-led tour.

LODGING

Ala Moana Area
YMCA CENTRAL BRANCH
$ 114 ROOMS   ✉ *401 Atkinson Drive* ✆ *808-941-3344* 📠 *808-941-8821*
✐ *www.ymcahonolulu.org*
An inexpensive place for both men and women across from Ala Moana Park is this YMCA. It's handily situated across the street from Ala Moana Center and a block from the beach. And you're welcome to use the gym, pool, saunas and television room. There's a Vietnamese restaurant on-site. You can also expect the usual Y ambience—long sterile hallways leading to an endless series of identical, cramped, uncarpeted rooms. You will pay several dollars more for a private bathroom, but low prices help make up for the lack of amenities.

PAGODA HOTEL
$$$–$$$$ 359 ROOMS   ✉ *1525 Rycroft Street* ✆ *808-941-6611, 800-367-6060*
📠 *808-955-5067* ✐ *www.pagodahotel.com, pagres@hthcorp.com*
Sufficiently removed from the crowds but still only a ten-minute drive from the beach is this bright, tropical-style hotel. Spacious studio and

one-bedroom units put the accent on rattan furniture. The carpeted rooms feature views of the hotel garden or distant mountains. Units in the adjoining Pagoda Terrace offer kitchens. Ask for a room in the new wing, which is substantially nicer than the old one.

Manoa Valley Area
FERNHURST YWCA
$ 40 ROOMS   ✉ *1566 Wilder Avenue*   📞 *808-941-2231*   📠 *808-945-9478*
🖥 *www.ywcaoahu.org*

In Manoa Valley, the Fernhurst YWCA is an appealing three-story lowrise that provides a residence for women and children (boys up to five years old). Rooms are single or double occupancy with shared baths. Among the facilities are microwaves, laundry, dining room and lounge. Rates include breakfast and dinner.

HOSTELLING INTERNATIONAL—HONOLULU
$ 43 BEDS   ✉ *2323-A Sea View Avenue*   📞 *808-946-0591*   📠 *808-946-5904*
🖥 *www.hiayh.org, hihostel@lava.net*

This dormitory-style crash pad has separate living quarters for men and women, although there is one studio available. Shared kitchen facilities, television lounge, garden patio and laundry are available. Visitors can book island tours through the hostel.

MANOA VALLEY INN
$$ 8 ROOMS   ✉ *2001 Vancouver Drive*   📞 *808-947-6019*   📠 *808-946-6168*
🖥 *www.manoavalleyinn.com, manoavalleyinn@aloha.net*

Hawaii's foremost bed-and-breakfast inn rests in a magnificent old mansion near the University of Hawaii campus. Set in the lush Manoa Valley, this B&B is a 1915 cream-colored Victorian featuring seven guest rooms and an adjacent cottage. Decorated with patterned wallpaper and old-style artworks, the rooms are furnished in plump antique armchairs. Guests enjoy a spacious veranda and lawn. For luxury and privacy, this is a historic jewel.

DINING

Kalihi-Nuuanu Avenue Area

HELENA'S HAWAIIAN FOODS
$ HAWAIIAN   ✉ *1240 North School Street*   📞 *808-845-8044*

Quietly hidden away in a tiny storefront in the Kalihi district, Helena's has been dishing up *kalua* pig, *lomi* salmon and *pipikaula* for more than 50 years. The food is served in tiny dishes, so you can sample a selection. The luau chicken cooked with taro leaves and coconut milk is a knockout. The place only has 13 tables, which means there's often a wait. But it's worth it. Closed Saturday through Monday.

MEG'S DRIVE-IN

$ PLATE LUNCHES ✉ *743 Waiakamilo Road* ☎ *808-845-3943*

Also in Kalihi, Meg's is a small eatery serving breakfast, local-style plate lunches and daily specials. You can take your meal to go or dine on the adjoining lanai. No dinner Saturday. Closed Sunday.

Ala Moana Area

MAKAI MARKET

$ INTERNATIONAL ✉ *Ala Moana Center, 1450 Ala Moana Boulevard*

Right next to Waikiki, in Ala Moana Center, there are numerous ethnic takeout restaurants that share a large dining pavilion. Best of all is **Patti's Chinese Kitchen** (808-946-5002, fax 808-943-4355), a crowded and noisy gathering place. At Patti's you can choose from over 20 entrées plus a side order of fried rice or *chow fun*. The courses include dim sum, orange chicken, beef and broccoli, tofu, beef tomato, sweet-and-sour ribs, barbecued pork and shrimp with vegetables. There's also the **Poi Bowl** (808-949-8444), a takeout stand serving traditional Hawaiian dishes. **Sobeye Noodle Shop** (808-946-7214) features bowls of Japanese soba and udon noodles. Or you can ride the escalator to the upper level of Ala Moana Center. Here **Shirokiya** (808-973-9111), a massive Asian department store, features an informal Japanese à la carte–style buffet. Closed Sunday.

DAIEI FOOD COURT

$ ✉ *801 Kaheka Street* ☎ *808-973-4800*

A few blocks from Ala Moana Center is Daiei, a grocery and department store filled with an amazing variety of Asian and Hawaiian foods and goods. The food court here is an incredibly popular spot with local shoppers.

WARD CENTRE

✉ *1200 Ala Moana Boulevard*

Situated midway between Waikiki and Downtown Honolulu is Ward Centre, a focus for gourmet dining. A warren of wood-paneled restaurants, it features several outstanding eateries.

COMPADRES

$$–$$$ MEXICAN ✉ *Ward Centre, 1200 Ala Moana Boulevard* ☎ *808-591-8307*
☎ *808-593-2901* 🖰 *www.compadresrestaurant.com*

This attractive Mexican restaurant, with oak bar and patio dining, prepares dishes from south of the border as well as salads, steaks and seafood. It specializes in tropical ambience, good food and fishbowl-size margaritas.

RYAN'S GRILL

$$ PAN-ASIAN ✉ *Ward Centre, 1200 Ala Moana Boulevard* ☎ *808-591-9132* ☎ *808-591-0034*

Ryan's is one of Honolulu's hottest after-work hangouts for singles who want to become un-single, and the place is packed from 5 p.m. until after 1 a.m. Comfortable leather chairs and marble-topped tables create a cozy, modern atmosphere. Grilled and steamed fish and fowl, pizzas, salads and fettuccine are among the many culinary options for those who go to eat instead of drink.

PAGODA FLOATING RESTAURANT

$$$ INTERNATIONAL ✉1525 Rycroft Street ☎808-948-8356 📠808-946-4635
🖰www.pagodahotel.com

For prime rib, crab legs, shrimp and vegetable tempura, try this "floating" restaurant. A restaurant-in-the-round, it sits above a pond populated with gaily colored tropical koi. Several cascades and a fountain feed the pond. The surrounding grounds have been carefully landscaped. This full-service restaurant offers breakfast and dinner buffets with changing featured entrées such as oxtail stew, *misoyaki*, butterfish and *kalua* pork.

Moiliili–Kapahula–Kaimuki Area

ALAN WONG'S RESTAURANT

$$$$ HAWAII REGIONAL ✉1857 South King Street ☎808-949-2526
📠808-951-9520 🖰www.alanwongs.com

To go where the local gentry dine, head to Alan Wong's for locally caught fish, home-grown produce and a wealth of poultry and meat dishes like macadamia nut and coconut–crusted lamb chops. One of the *in* places to dine on Hawaiian Regional cuisine, so reservations are suggested. Dinner only.

CHEF MAVRO'S

$$$$ FRENCH ✉1969 South King Street ☎808-944-4714 🖰www.chefmavro.com, chef@chefmavro.com

A star in the Honolulu culinary scene is this top-of-the-line restaurant. Chef George Mavrothalassitis, formerly of the Four Seasons Resort in Wailea, presides over his own corner in Honolulu. The unassuming building on South King Street does not hint at what awaits inside—an elegant yet understated dining room adorned with local artwork. The French-inspired cuisine arrives at the table in an equally sublime presentation. The dishes are five-star and the service impeccable. One claim to fame of Chef Mavro is the perfect pairing of the wine with every item on the menu. A place for that special night. Dinner only. Closed Monday.

SAM CHOY'S DIAMOND
HEAD RESTAURANT

$$$–$$$$ HAWAII REGIONAL ✉449 Kapahulu Avenue, Suite 201
☎808-732-8645 📠808-732-8683 🖰www.samchoy.com

Quantity and quality don't usually come together, particularly where gourmet restaurants are concerned. But at Sam Choy's you can count on platter-size portions of macadamia-crusted chicken breast, grilled Asian-style lamb chops or oven-roasted duck. Considered one of the top Hawaiian cuisine restaurants on the island, it sits with unassuming grace on the second floor of a strip mall. Eat heartily (and well)! Dinner and Sunday brunch.

IRIFUNE
$$ JAPANESE ✉ 563 Kapahulu Avenue ☎ 808-737-1141

This warm and friendly Japanese eatery is frequented by a local crowd. In fact, around dinnertime, you will likely find yourself in line. The decor gives off a fun, casual air: fishing nets, Kabuki masks and other assorted wallhangings. On the menu are tasty curry, sushi, teriyaki and tempura dishes, plus several other Asian delectables. Closed Sunday and Monday.

ONO HAWAIIAN FOODS

hidden

$$ HAWAIIAN ✉ 726 Kapahulu Avenue ☎ 808-737-2275

A must for all true Hawaii lovers, this hole-in-da-wall eatery is located on a busy street. But if you're lucky enough to get one of the few tables, you can feast on *laulau*, *kalua* pig, *pipikaula*, poi and *haupia*. The walls are papered with signed photographs of local notables and the place is packed with locals, notable and otherwise. Closed Sunday.

RAINBOW DRIVE-IN
$ PLATE LUNCHES ✉ 3308 Kanaina Avenue ☎ 808-737-0177

For local-style plate lunches, cruise in to Rainbow's. Popular with *kamaaina* and tourists alike, the menu includes hamburger steak, beef stew, breaded mahimahi, chili and fried chicken served with two scoops of rice and various salads.

AZTECA MEXICAN RESTAURANT
$$ MEXICAN ✉ 3617 Waialae Avenue ☎ 808-735-2492

Waialae Avenue, a neighborhood strip a mile or so outside Waikiki, has developed into a gourmet ghetto. Azteca's is a vinyl-booth-and-plastic-panel eatery that serves a delicious array of Mexican food.

3660 ON THE RISE

hidden

$$$–$$$$ HAWAII REGIONAL ✉ 3660 Waialae Avenue ☎ 808-737-1177
☎ 808-735-6105 ✎ www.3660.com, 3660@cleanwire.net

This award-winning restaurant is a local favorite, blending island ingredients with a definite touch of European cuisine. Try their signature *ahi katsu*: deep-fried *ahi* wrapped in *nori* with a wasabi-ginger sauce. Finish off the meal with Harlequin crème brûlée, which is difficult to describe without salivating but basically involves vanilla-bean custard and chocolate mousse glazed with caramel. Dinner only. Closed Monday.

HALE VIETNAM
$$ VIETNAMESE ✉ 1140 12th Avenue ☎ 808-735-7581 ✎ www.halevietnam.com

For spicy and delicious Asian dishes, it is hard to find a more appealing place than this one. A family restaurant that draws a local crowd, it has traditional Vietnamese soup and a host of excellent entrées.

SHOPPING

Pearl Harbor Area

KAM SUPER SWAP MEET

✉*98-850 Moanalua Road* ☎*808-483-5535* Expect a variety of second-hand items here. It's a great place to barter for bargains, meet local folks and find items you'll never see in stores. It's open on Wednesday, Saturday and Sunday.

Kalihi–Nuuanu Avenue Area

LANAKILA

✉*1809 Bachelot Street* ☎*808-531-0555* 📠*808-533-7264* 🖱*www.lanakila hawaii.org* Scattered around town are several shops that I recommend you check out. Lanakila is a non-profit that includes a gift shop with crafts made by the disabled, and the craftsmanship is superb. There are shell necklaces, woven handbags, monkeypod bowls, Hawaiian pillows and homemade dolls. You'll probably see these items in other stores around the islands, with much higher price tags than here at the "factory." Closed weekends.

SHOP PACIFICA ✉*1525 Bernice Street, near the intersection of Routes 63 and H-1* ☎*808-848-4158* 📠*808-847-8249* Out at the Bishop Museum be sure to stop by this shop, which offers a fine selection of Hawaiiana. There are books on island history and geography, an assortment of instruments that include nose flutes and gourds, plus cards, souvenirs and wooden bowls.

Ala Moana Area

ALA MOANA CENTER ✉*1450 Ala Moana Boulevard* ☎*808-955-9517* 📠*808-949-0985* 🖱*www.alamoanacenter.com* On the outskirts of Waikiki is the state's largest shopping center. This multitiered complex has practically everything. Ala Moana features three department stores: **Sears** (808-947-0252), **Macy's** (808-941-2345) and a Japanese emporium called **Shirokiya** (808-973-9111). You'll also find an assortment of stores selling liquor, tennis and golf supplies, stationery, leather goods, cameras, shoes, tobacco, etc. You name it, they have it. The designer shops, appropriately, are located on the upper levels.

WARD CENTRE ✉*1200 Ala Moana Boulevard* This is one of Honolulu's sleeker shopping malls located on Ala Moana Boulevard. Streamlined and stylized, it's an enclave filled with designer shops, spiffy restaurants, boutiques and children's shops. Adorned with blond-wood facades, brick walkways and brass-rail restaurants, the shopping complex provides a touch of Beverly Hills. Anchoring Ward Centre at the far end is **Borders Books & Music** (808-591-8995), a superstore that is chockablock with everything for your reading and listening pleasure.

They have two floors of paperbacks, hardback, audiotapes and CDs. Just down the walkway, you'll find **Hawaiian Moon** (808-596-2294), a locally owned family business that specializes in island-style clothing that is more hip and contemporary than the aloha wear sold at places like Hilo Hatties. Many of the garments are made from original prints that reflect Hawaii's culture and landscape. In the same complex, **Town & Country Surf Shop** (808-592-5299), offers an excellent selection of surf wear and beach apparel, as well as surf, skate and body boards, and all the accessories and gear needed to enjoy those sports. **Black Pearl Gallery** (808-597-1477), features lustrous Tahitian black pearls that highlight its jewelry collection.

WARD WAREHOUSE ✉ 1020 Ala Moana Boulevard Ala Moana Center may be the biggest, but the smaller Ward Warehouse, between Waikiki and Downtown Honolulu, is a shopping center worth visiting. It features stores such as **Native Books/Na Mea Hawaii** (808-596-8885), which stocks locally crafted items and an extensive collection of books on the islands. **Nohea Gallery** (808-596-0074) displays quilts, jewelry, pottery, glassware, lamps and wooden bureaus—all made in Hawaii by local artists.

Kahala Area

KAHALA MALL ✉ 4211 Waialae Avenue ☎ 808-732-7736 One of Honolulu's more upscale shopping centers is Kahala Mall, where you'll find designer shops galore. This attractive complex also hosts almost 100 moderately priced stores.

NIGHTLIFE

Outside Honolulu there are usually a couple of spots to hear Hawaiian music. Pick up a copy of *Spotlight's Oahu Gold, The Honolulu Weekly* or *This Week Oahu* magazine to see what's going on.

Ala Moana Area

RUMOURS ✉ 410 Atkinson Drive ☎ 808-955-4811 ✎ www.alamoanahotel.com Theme nights are the spice of life here. Salsa is featured on Thursday and "Big Chill" night on Friday highlights '60s music. Located in the Ala Moana Hotel, this club is decorated with artwork and neon fixtures. Open Friday and Saturday nights. Cover.

WARD ENTERTAINMENT CENTER ✉ 1044 Auahi Street This bustling destination is a draw for both tourists and *kamaaina*. On the ground floor, Dave & Buster's restaurant/entertainment center has an extensive video arcade, billiards and shuffleboard. Escalators to the second level lead to a 16-screen movie theater. Or just grab a cup of coffee at Starbucks and enjoy a little people-watching.

KINCAID'S ✉ 1050 Ala Moana Boulevard ☎ 808-591-2005 A harbor view and Hawaiian contemporary music played on Thursday, Friday and Saturday by acoustic guitarists and bands make this a good choice for a relaxing evening. The lounge is part of a popular Honolulu restaurant in Ward Warehouse.

Manoa Valley Area

ANNA BANNANA'S ✉2440 South Beretania Street ✆ 808-946-5190 ✆ 808-946-6959 Over by the University of Hawaii's Manoa campus, Anna Bannana's has been a popular hangout for years. This wildly decorated spot has all types of live entertainment nightly, from open-mic Monday and turntable Tuesday to live bands on the weekend. Occasional cover.

MANOA VALLEY THEATRE ✉2833 East Manoa Road ✆ 808-988-6131 ✆ 808-988-3179 ✍ www.manoavalleytheatre.com A half dozen Broadway and off-Broadway productions with local actors are staged here. Recent offerings include *I Love You, You're Perfect, Now Change* and *Rocky Horror Picture Show.*

BEACHES & PARKS

Pearl Harbor Area

KEAIWA HEIAU STATE RECREATION AREA

✉ To get there from Honolulu, take Route 90 west to Aiea, then follow Aiea Heights Drive to the park.

🏃 Amazing as it sounds, this is a wooded retreat within easy driving distance of Honolulu. Situated in the Koolau foothills overlooking Pearl Harbor, it contains the remains of a *heiau*, a temple once used by Hawaiian healers. There's a forest extending to the far reaches of the mountains and a loop hiking trail. Facilities include picnic area, showers and restrooms.

🏕 Tents only. State permit required.

Ala Moana Area
ALA MOANA REGIONAL PARK

✉ On Ala Moana Boulevard at the west end of Waikiki, across from Ala Moana Center

🏊🎣🏄🚣 This 119-acre park is a favorite with Hawaii residents. On weekends every type of outdoor enthusiast imaginable turns out to swim, snorkel, fish (common catches are *papio*, bonefish, goatfish and *moano*), jog, sail model boats and so on. It's also a good place to surf; there are three separate breaks here: "Concessions," "Tennis Courts" and "Baby Haleiwa" all have summer waves. There's a curving length of beach, a grassy park area, a helluva lot of local color and facilities that include a picnic area, restrooms, showers, concession stands, tennis courts, a recreation building, a bowling green and lifeguards. Fun fact: in the opening credits of *Gilligan's Island*, the ship set sail out of the harbor near here.

Kahala Area

DIAMOND HEAD BEACH PARK

✉ Just beyond Waikiki along Diamond Head Road at the foot of Diamond Head; watch for parked cars.

🏊🎣🏄🏄🚣 Heaven to windsurfers, this twisting ribbon of white sand sits directly below the crater. It's close enough to

Waikiki for convenient access but far enough to shake most of the crowds. The Kuilei cliffs, covered with scrub growth, loom behind the beach. Snorkeling is good—a coral reef extends offshore through this area. There's also a year-round surf break called "Lighthouse." And for the anglers, your chances are good to reel in *ulua*, *papio* or *mamao*. A shower is the sole facility.

KUILEI CLIFFS BEACH PARK AND KAALAWAI BEACH
✉ *Located east of Diamond Head Beach Park*

Extending east from Diamond Head Beach Park, these sandy corridors are also flanked by sharp sea cliffs. Together they extend from Diamond Head Lighthouse to Black Point. The aquatic attractions are the same as at Diamond Head Beach Park and both beaches can be reached from it (or from cliff trails leading down from Diamond Head Road). A protecting reef makes for good swimming at Kaalawai Beach (which can also be reached via a public accessway off Kulumanu Place).

WAIALAE BEACH PARK
✉ *4900 block of Kahala Avenue in Kahala*

Smack in the middle of Honolulu's prestigious Kahala district, where a million dollars buys a modest house, sits this tidy beach. Its white sand neatly groomed, its spacious lawn shaded by palms, Waialae is a true find. It has good swimming and fishing. There are bathhouse facilities, beachside picnic tables and a footbridge arching across the stream that divides the property. To the west of the park lies Kahala Beach, a long, thin swath of sand that extends all the way to Black Point. Snorkeling is best near the Kahala Hotel & Resort.

SOUTHEAST OAHU

Out past Honolulu, beyond the glitter of Waikiki and the gilded neighborhoods of Kahala, the pace slows down, the vistas open up and Oahu begins to look more like a tropical island. The road—Route 72, the Kalanianaole Highway—leads out of Honolulu and hugs the rugged coastline as it climbs up and down and back and forth along the edge of a series of volcanic ridges. The jagged, jade-colored peaks of the Koolau Mountains on one side and the sparkling blue sea on the other provide some of the most striking scenery the state has to offer.

SIGHTS

KOKO HEAD Kalanianaole Highway streams through Hawaii Kai and other residential areas, then ascends the slopes of an extinct volcano, 642-foot Koko Head. Here Madame Pele is reputed to have dug a hole for the last time in search of fiery volcanic matter.

KOKO CRATER The second hump on the horizon is this crater, which rises to over 1200 feet. This fire-pit, according to Hawaiian legend, is the vagina of Pele's sister. It seems that Pele, goddess of volcanoes, was being pursued by a handsome demigod. Her sister, trying to distract the hot suitor from Pele, spread her legs across the landscape.

HANAUMA BAY ✉ *Located on Kalanianaole Highway about 12 miles east of Waikiki* ☎ *808-396-4229* From the top of Koko Head, a well-marked road and sidewalk lead down to one of the prettiest beaches in all Hawaii. The word *hanauma* means "the curved bay," and you will clearly see that Hanauma Bay was once a circular volcano, one wall of which was breached by the sea. This breathtaking place is a marine preserve filled with multicolored coral and teeming with underwater life. Little wonder that Hollywood chose this spot as the prime location for Elvis Presley's movie, *Blue Hawaii*. Elvis' grass shack was right here, and the strand was also a setting in the classic film *From Here to Eternity*.

The swimming and snorkeling are unmatched anywhere and the mazework of coral formations along the bottom adds to the snorkeling adventure. Or you can stroll along the rock ledges that fringe the bay and explore **Toilet Bowl**, a tidepool that "flushes" as the waves wash through it. The best time to come is early morning before other swimmers stir up the waters. Hanauma Bay is an extremely popular picnic spot among local folks, so it is also advisable to visit on a weekday rather than face bucking the crowds on Saturday and Sunday. Because of its popularity, the preserve cuts off entrance to the park when the parking lot is full (another good reason to arrive early). Closed Tuesday. Admission.

From Hanauma Bay the highway corkscrews along the coast. Among the remarkable scenes you'll enjoy en route are views of Lanai and Molokai, two of Oahu's sister islands. On a clear, clear day you can also see Maui, an island that requires no introduction.

HALONA BLOWHOLE At an overlook you will encounter this lava tube through which geysers of seawater blast. During high tide and when the sea is turbulent, these gushers reach dramatic heights. *Halona* means "peering place," and that is exactly what everyone seems to do here. You can't miss the spot, since the roadside parking lot is inevitably crowded with tourists. Between December and April this vista is also a prime whale-watching spot.

SANDY BEACH Just beyond Halona Blowhole spreads this stretch of sand, one of Hawaii's most renowned bodysurfing spots. It's a long, wide beach piled with fluffy sand and complete with picnic areas and showers. Inexperienced bodysurfers are better off enjoying the excellent sunbathing here, since the dramatic shorebreak that makes the beach so popular among bodysurfers is dangerous for beginners.

KOKO CRATER BOTANICAL GARDENS _____

✉ *Kealahou Street, off of Kalanianaole Highway* ☎ *808-522-7060* ⌫ *www.honolulu.gov/parks/hbg* Across from Sandy Beach, a sign points you to a side road that leads up to this 60-acre collection of cacti, plumeria and other water-thrifty plants. A brochure at the start of the two-mile loop trail guides you through the drought-resistant landscape.

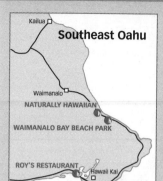

NATURALLY HAWAIIAN

PAGE 116

Hawaii-inspired fine art and homemade gifts including puka-shell necklaces, *koa* wood pieces, prints and paintings

WAIMANALO BAY BEACH PARK

PAGE 118

Sunny beach and shady grove of ironwood trees (known to locals as "Sherwood Forest")—an excellent spot for picnicking, sunbathing and swimming

ROY'S RESTAURANT

PAGE 115

Ultracontemporary. Innovative. Gourmet. Hawaii's Pacific Rim cuisine made to perfection with fresh local ingredients

MAKAPUU POINT Route 72 rounds Oahu's southeastern corner and sets a course along the eastern shoreline. It also climbs to this scenic point from which you can take your first view of the Windward Coast. You will be standing on Makapuu Point. Above you rise sharp lava cliffs, while below are rolling sand dunes and open ocean. The slope-faced islet just offshore is Rabbit Island. The distant headland is Makapuu Peninsula, toward which you are bound.

SEA LIFE PARK HAWAII ✉*Makapuu Point* ☎*808-259-2501* ☎*808-259-7373* ✑*www.sealifeparkhawaii.com* From Makapuu Point's perfect perch you can also spy this marineworld attraction comparable to those in California and Florida. Among the many features at this park is the "Hawaiian Reef Tank," a 300,000-gallon oceanarium inhabited by about 4000 sea creatures. To see it you wind through a spiral viewing area that descends three fathoms along the tank's glass perimeter. At times a scuba diver will be hand-feeding the fish. Swimming about this underwater world are sharks, stingrays, turtles and a variety of lesser-known species. As well as several interactive programs, the park also features a turtle lagoon, penguin habitat and the only known *wholphin* (half whale, half dolphin) living in captivity. Admission.

MAKAPUU BEACH PARK Across the road from Sea Life Park spreads this other fabled but daunting bodysurfing spot set in a particularly pretty location. Nearby black lava cliffs are topped by a white lighthouse and Rabbit Island is anchored just offshore. **Rabbit Island**, located off Makapuu Point, resembles a bunny's head, but was actually

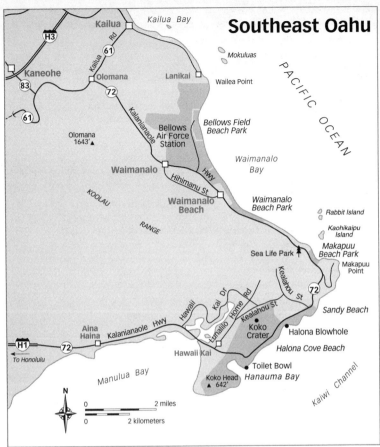

Southeast Oahu

named for a former rabbit-raising farm there. Makapuu Beach itself is a short, wide rectangle of white sand. It's an ideal place to picnic, but when the surf is up, beware of the waves.

KOOLAU RANGE The road from Makapuu Beach continues along the shoreline between soft sand beaches and rugged mountain peaks. During the next 30 miles your attention will be drawn back continually to those rocky crags. They are part of the Koolau Range, a wall of precipitous mountains that vault up from Oahu's placid interior. Their spires, minarets and fluted towers are softened here and there by lush, green valleys, but never enough to detract from the sheer beauty and magnitude of the heights. Light and shade play games along their moss-covered surfaces, while rainbows hang suspended between the peaks. If wind and weather permit, you will see hang gliders dusting the cliffs as they sail from the mountains down to the distant beach.

WAIMANALO The road from Makapuu Beach continues through this old ranching area that today has been turned to fruit and flower cultivation.

OLOMANA PEAK Outside town you will see this peak favored by rock climbers. It is a double-barreled peak that seems to belong in the Swiss Alps.

LODGING

TRADEWINDS BEACH HOUSE

$$–$$$ 6 ROOMS   ✉Waimanalo   ☎808-259-7792, 866-625-6946   📠808-259-0203
🖥www.beachhousehawaii.com, info@beachhousehawaii.com

If you want to follow the footsteps of James Michener and hang out at Waimanalo Beach, you might consider tucking yourself in at this beach house, where you can rent just a room or the whole house. Here you'll find six bedrooms (most with a queen-sized bed and ceiling fan) and a full bath, plus barbecue facilities, a billiard room, and use of a kitchen.

BEACH HOUSE HAWAII

✉Beach lots throughout Waimanalo   ☎808-259-7792, 866-625-6946   📠808-259-0203
🖥www.beachhousehawaii.com, info@beachhousehawaii.com

This is a lodging service that offers rental homes ranging from studios to six-bedroom units, each with private bath, kitchenette, lanai, queen-sized beds, fresh flowers and ceiling fans. Boogieboards, snorkeling gear, beach chairs, a hot tub and a barbecue round out the amenities. Fresh papaya grow on the trees, and for a lazy afternoon in the sun, sink into the hammock with a good book. For those who can't get away from it all, there's even internet access.

DINING

Spotted along Oahu's southeastern shore are a couple of moderately priced restaurants (and an expensive but worthy one) that may prove handy if you're beachcombing or camping. All are located on or near Route 72 (Kalanianaole Highway).

ASSAGGIO HAWAII KAI

$$$ ITALIAN   ✉Koko Marina Shopping Center, 7192 Kalanianaole Highway, Hawaii Kai
☎808-396-0756   📠808-396-0757

This is an excellent neighborhood-style Italian restaurant with an extensive menu. You'll find dishes like butter-steamed Manila clams, linguine chicken and osso buco, as well as a fresh catch-of-the-day and seafood. There are four other locations in Mililani, Ala Moana, Manoa and Kailua, though I like this one for its yacht-club ambience and marina-side seating. No lunch on Sunday.

ROY'S RESTAURANT

$$$–$$$$ HAWAII REGIONAL   ✉6600 Kalanianaole Highway, Hawaii Kai
☎808-396-7697   📠808-396-8706   🖥www.roysrestaurant.com,
honolulu@roysrestaurant.com

Tucked away in unassuming fashion in a business park is one of my favorite dining spots. You'll have to travel all the way to Hawaii Kai, several miles east of Waikiki, to find Roy's. It is, to say the least, ultracontemporary, from the magazine clips framed on the walls to the cylindrical fish tank near the door. One of the most innovative of Hawaii's Pacific Rim cuisine dining rooms, it specializes in fresh local ingredients. Wildly popular, so reserve in advance. Dinner only.

DAVE'S ICE CREAM

$ DESSERT   ✉ *41-1537 Kalanianaole Highway, Waimanalo* ✆ *808-259-0356*

Dave's scoops up gourmet ice cream in flavors like azuki bean, cotton candy and *poha*, made from gooseberries grown on the Big Island. It also serves guava and passion fruit sherbet, among many other selections.

KENEKE'S

$ PLATE LUNCHES   ✉ *41-857 Kalanianaole Highway, Waimanalo* ✆ *808-259-9811*

For breakfast, plate lunches and sandwiches at greasy-spoon prices, drop in here. No gourmet's delight, this tiny eatery is well placed for people enjoying Waimanalo's beaches. No dinner.

SHOPPING

NATURALLY HAWAIIAN

✉ *41-1025 Kalanianaole Highway, Waimanalo* ✆ *808-259-5354* 🖷 *808-259-5350* 🖱 *www.naturallyhawaiian.com* There aren't many places on Oahu more Hawaiian than Waimanalo, so this place fits the landscape nicely. Featuring fine art and homemade gifts, the shop sells puka-shell necklaces, *koa* wood pieces, prints and paintings, and Hawaiian commemorative stamps.

BEACHES & PARKS

HANAUMA BAY NATURE PRESERVE

✉ *Take Kalanianaole Highway (Route 72) to Koko Head, then turn onto the side road near the top of the promontory. This leads to a parking lot; leave your vehicle and walk the several hundred yards down a somewhat steep path to the beach.* ✆ *808-396-4229*

One of Oahu's prettiest and most popular beaches, this bay is located about nine miles east of Waikiki. A curving swath of white sand, it extends for almost a half-mile. The bottom of the bay is a maze of coral reef, and the entire area has been designated a marine preserve; fishing is strictly prohibited. As a result, the skindiving is unmatched and the fish are tame enough to eat from your hand. (Just beware of "Witch's Brew," a turbulent area on the bay's right side, and the "Molokai Express," a wicked current sweeping across the mouth of the bay.) You can also hike along rock ledges fringing the bay and explore some mind-boggling tidepools. Crowded though it is, this is one strand that should not be bypassed (though park officials are now regulating access to prevent overuse). Get here early—April through September the beach closes at 7 p.m., 6 p.m. the rest of the year (it opens at 6 a.m.), and the parking lot fills up quickly. In addition, you are required to watch a short film on the bay's ecosystem and proper snorkeling etiquette. Facilities include a picnic area, restrooms, showers, a snack bar, snorkeling equipment rentals, a gift shop and lifeguards. Closed Tuesday. Parking fee, $1; nonresident day-use fee, $5 per person.

HALONA COVE BEACH

✉ *Stop at the Halona Blowhole parking lot on Kalanianaole Highway (Route 72), about ten miles east of Waikiki. Follow the path from the right side of the lot down to the beach.*

This is the closest you'll find to a hidden beach near Honolulu. It's a patch of white sand wedged between Halona Point and the Halona Blowhole lookout. Located directly below Kalanianaole Highway (Route 72), this is not exactly a wilderness area. But you can still escape the crowds massed on the nearby beaches. Swimming and snorkeling are good when the sea is gentle but extremely dangerous if it's rough. Prime catches are *ulua*, *papio* and *mamao*. There are no facilities.

SANDY BEACH

✉ *Head out on Kalanianaole Highway (Route 72) about 12 miles east of Waikiki.*

A long, wide beach, this is a favorite among Oahu's youth. The shorebreak makes it one of the finest, and most dangerous, bodysurfing beaches in the islands. Surfing is good and very popular but beware of rip currents. Lifeguards are on duty. It's a pleasant place to sunbathe, but if you go swimming, plan to negotiate a pounding shoreline. Anglers try for *ulua*, *papio* and *mamao*. There are picnic areas, restrooms and showers. Should you want to avoid the crowds, head over to Wawamalu Beach Park next door to the east.

MAKAPUU POINT STATE WAYSIDE

✉ *Off Kalanianaole Highway between Sandy Beach and Makapuu Lookout*

This state park encompasses Makapuu Beach, lookout and the lighthouse that overlooks the east Oahu coast. The mile-long asphalted trail leading to the lighthouse has become a popular family excursion; you can take the trail's uphill segments at a leisurely pace. The heat can be draining by midday, so a morning or afternoon hike is recommended, particularly on weekends when crowds abound. Panoramic views are the reward, with brisk tradewinds likely. The two islands offshore nearby are bird sanctuaries. The large one is known as Rabbit Island. The Hawaiians call it Manana Island, which means to stretch out or protrude.

MAKAPUU BEACH PARK

✉ *On Kalanianaole Highway (Route 72) about 13 miles east of Waikiki*

Set in a very pretty spot with lava cliffs in the background and Rabbit Island just offshore is this short, wide rectangle of white sand. It is Hawaii's most famous bodysurfing beach. With no protecting reef and a precipitous shoreline, Makapuu is inundated by awesome swells that send wave riders crashing onto shore. Necks and backs are broken with frightening regularity here, so if the waves are large and you're inexperienced—play the spectator. If you take the plunge, prepare for a battering! Snorkeling is usually poor and surfing is not permitted here. Common catches are *ulua*, *papio* and *mamao*. The only facilities are restrooms and a lifeguard.

WAIMANALO BEACH PARK AND WAIMANALO BAY BEACH PARK

✉ *Waimanalo Beach Park is at 41-741 Kalanianaole Highway (Route 72) about 15 miles east of Waikiki. Waimanalo Bay Beach Park is on Aloiloi Street a mile farther north.*

🏊 🏄 🚻 This spacious 38-acre park is located at the southeast end of Waimanalo's three-and-a-half-mile-long beach. It's studded with ironwood trees and equipped with numerous recreation facilities including a playground, a basketball court and a baseball field. Waimanalo Beach Park and Waimanalo Bay Beach Park, a mile farther north, are both excellent spots for picnicking, swimming, snorkeling, bodysurfing and sunbathing. The latter is farther removed from the highway in a grove of ironwood trees known to local residents as "Sherwood Forest." Waimanalo is a good place to fish for *papio*, bonefish, milkfish and goatfish. There are picnic areas, restrooms and showers at both.

⚠ A county permit required at both of the parks for tent and trailer camping.

BELLOWS FIELD BEACH PARK

✉ *Turn off Kalanianaole Highway (Route 72) toward Bellows Air Force Station. The park is located near Waimanalo, about 17 miles east of Waikiki.*

🏊 🏄 🚣 🚻 One of Oahu's prettiest parks, Bellows is a broad white-sand beach bordered by ironwood trees and a marvelous view of the Koolau mountains. It's a great place for swimming and snorkeling and it's also a good surf spot for beginners; fishing usually rewards with *papio*, bonefish and goatfish. Sounds great, huh? The catch is that Bellows Park is situated on a military base and is open to visitors only from Friday noon until 8 a.m. Monday. Facilities include a picnic area, showers and a restroom.

⚠ County permit required.

WINDWARD COAST

Named for the trade winds that blow with soothing predictability from the northeast, this sand-rimmed shoreline lies on the far side of the pali from Honolulu. Between these fluted emerald cliffs and the turquoise ocean are the bedroom communities of Lanikai, Kailua and Kaneohe and the agricultural regions of the Waiahole and Waikane valleys. As suburbs give way to small farms, this florid region provides a relaxing transition between the busy boulevards of Honolulu and the wild surf of the North Shore.

119

4 OAHU WINDWARD COAST SIGHTS

Kailua, which was previously a quiet suburb, has become a windsurfing mecca, attracting beginning and intermediate sailors from around the world to its shores. A protective reef, a lack of breakers and on-shore trade winds create near perfect conditions for the sport, and the residents of Kailua haven't overlooked the opportunities. Scores of families operate bed and breakfasts in residential neighborhoods, and windsurfers have become a part of the community. It's the kind of low-key place where even the likes of Robin Williams, who reportedly vacations there, can find an escape.

SIGHTS

ULUPO HEIAU

From the southeastern corner of the island, the Kalanianaole Highway flows into Kailua, where it intersects with Route 61, or Kailua Road. If you go right for a quarter of a mile along this road you will encounter Ulupo Heiau (it's behind the YMCA). According to Hawaiian legend, this temple (which stands 30 feet high and measures 150 feet in length) was built by *Menehune*, who passed the building stones across a six-mile-long bucket brigade in a one-night construction project. The *Menehunes*, in case you haven't been introduced, were tiny Hobbit-like creatures who inhabited Hawaii even before the Polynesians arrived. They were reputed to be superhumanly strong and would work all night to build dams, temples and other structures. Several mysterious humanmade objects in the islands that archaeologists have trouble placing chronologically are claimed by mythmakers to be *Menehune* creations.

LANIKAI BEACH A slight detour down Route 61 toward the Pacific will bring you to one of Oahu's premier neighborhoods—Lanikai—and one of its most beautiful beaches—Lanikai Beach. Actually, Lanikai has one of the world's best beaches. The sand is powder-fine; palm trees sway in the wind, providing enough shade to make for ideal sunbathing; and the water, protected by an offshore reef, is the color of Indian turquoise.

MOKULUAS Offshore are two small islands, **Moku Iki** and **Moku Nui**, bird sanctuaries known as the Mokuluas. Moku Iki is off-limits, but you can kayak (or swim) out to dry, barren Moku Nui from Lanikai Beach; you'll find a fine-sand beach, where hundreds of birds will probably be your only company. The strand where you disembark from your kayak has a unique feature—the waves come from both sides of the island and create an enormous clashing sound. Around the back of the island is a little cove where people often swim, though the currents can be dangerous and the surf quite high, so be cautious.

HOOMALUHIA BOTANICAL GARDEN

✉ *45-680 Luluku Road, Kaneohe* ✆ *808-233-7323* 🖷 *808-233-7326* Heading back to the main highway from Lanikai, you will find that Route 72 immediately merges into Route 61, which then continues for two miles to Route 83, the Kamehameha Highway. Above this thoroughfare, spreading across more than 400 acres at the foot of the *pali* is this botanical garden, a relaxing nature conservancy. With sheer cliffs rising on one side and a panoramic ocean view opening in the distance, it is a special place indeed. There is a 32-acre lake (no swimming) as well as a visitors center and hiking trails. Camping is available on weekends (permit required—get one at the garden office, open daily). The fruits, flowers and trees include hundreds of species native to Hawaii as well as tropical regions around the world.

HAIKU GARDENS

✉ *46-336 Haiku Road, Kaneohe* ✆ *808-247-6671* 🖷 *808-247-5886* 🖱 *www. haikugardens.com* The Kahekili Highway carries you to these graceful gardens, located just outside Kailua. Formerly a private estate, the gardens rest in a lovely spot with a lofty rockface backdrop. Within this preserve are acres of exotic plant life, including an enchanting lily pond as well as numerous species of flowers. Hawaii specializes in beautiful gardens; the frequent rains and lush terrain make for luxuriant growing conditions. This happens to be one of the prettiest gardens of all.

VALLEY OF THE TEMPLES ✉ *47-200 Kahekili Highway, Kaneohe* ✆ *808-239-8811* Along the Kahekili Highway you'll encounter this verdant chasm folded between the mountains and the sea. Part of the valley has been consecrated as a cemetery honoring the Japanese. Highlighting the region is the **Byodo-In Temple**. Rimmed by 2000-foot cliffs, this Buddhist shrine is a replica of a 900-year-old temple in Kyoto, Japan. It was constructed in 1968 in memory of the first Japanese immigrants to settle in Hawaii. The simple architecture is enhanced by a bronze bell weighing seven tons that visitors are permitted to ring. A statue of Buddha dominates the site. Walk along the placid reflecting pool with its swans, ducks and multihued carp and you will be drawn a million miles away from the bustle of Honolulu. Admission.

CORAL QUEEN ✆ *808-292-8470* 🖷 *808-236-0722* At Heeia Kea Boat Harbor on Kamehameha Highway, you can take an hour-long glass-bottom boat ride aboard the *Coral Queen*. Closed Sunday. To get there simply follow North Kalaheo Avenue through Kailua, then pick up Kaneohe Bay Drive, and turn right on Route 836, which curves for miles before linking with Route 83.

KANEOHE BAY ✉ *Located along Kamehameha Highway (Route 836), a few hundred yards before it merges with Route 83* Renowned for its coral formations

MALAEKAHANA STATE RECREATION AREA AND GOAT ISLAND

PAGES 125, 131

Tropical wonderland of palms, a curving, white-sand beach and small offshore island with a shallow, well-protected swimming and snorkeling area

ULUPO HEIAU

PAGE 119

Mysterious temple built by the *Menehune*, Hawaii's mythical Hobbit-like creatures who carried giant stones using their superhuman strength

ISLAND TREASURES ART GALLERY

PAGE 128

Exceptional collections of arts and crafts from artists living in Hawaii

HAWAII'S HIDDEN HIDEAWAY B&B

PAGE 125

With that name? Had to—lovely—with outdoor spa, ocean view and location, location, location

and schools of tropical fish that are as brilliantly colored as the coral, this expansive body of water possesses the only barrier reef in Hawaii. Along its shores are ancient Hawaiian fishponds, rock-bound enclosures constructed by the early Polynesians to raise fresh seafood. Though they once lined the shores of Oahu, today only a quarter (about 100) remain in usable condition. Several rest along this Windward Coast. One of the largest is located near Heeia State Park. It's an impressive engineering feat that measures 500 feet in length and once contained an 88-acre fish farm. The stone walls in places are 12 feet thick.

KUALOA RANCH ⊠*Kaneohe* ✆*800-231-7321* ◿*www.kualoa.com* Ancient Hawaiians would have fared well on the television series *Survivor*; they had fishtrapping down pat. Using enclosed brackish water off the coast, fish were bred and maintained in fishponds through ingenious use of makaha, sluice gates that controlled the in- and outflow of water. Designed to allow young fish in and keep the ready-to-eat fish from escaping, the gates also helped control the growth of algae, the lowest but

Windward Coast

POINTS OF INTEREST
- Ⓐ Byodo-In Temple
- Ⓑ Crouching Lion
- Ⓒ Haiku Gardens
- Ⓓ Hoomaluhia Botanical Garden
- Ⓔ Mormon Temple
- Ⓕ Old Sugar Mill
- Ⓖ Polynesian Cultural Center
- Ⓗ Senator Fong's Plantation and Gardens
- Ⓘ Ulupo Heiau

N

MAKAI
MAUKA

0   2 miles
0   2 kilometers

James Campbell National Wildlife Refuge
Kahuku Sugar Mill
Kahuku
Malaekahana State Recreation Area
Goat Island
Laie
Hukilau Beach
Ⓔ
Ⓖ Laie Point
Pounders Beach
83
Kokololio Beach Park
Hauula Beach Park
Hauula
Sacred Falls
Punaluu
Sacred Falls State Park
Punaluu Beach Park
Kahana Bay
Swanzy Beach Park
Kahana Ⓑ
Kaaawa
Ahupuaa O Kahana State Park (Kahana Valley State Park)
Ⓕ
83
Kualoa Regional Park
Waikane
Mokolii Island (Chinaman's Hat)
Waiahole

PACIFIC

OCEAN

Kahaluu
Ⓗ Heeia State Park
Kaneohe Bay
Kaneohe Marine Corps Air Station
Ⓐ
Ⓒ Coconut Island
Kaneohe
Kailua
Mokulua Islands
H3
H3
83
Kailua Beach Park
Ⓓ
Lanikai
Ⓘ
H1
Aiea
Pearl Harbor
Kahekili Hwy
Kamehameha Hwy
Likelike Hwy
63
Pali Hwy
Olomana
Bellows Air Force Station
Pali Lookout
Nuuanu Pali 1186'
H201
61
Waimanalo
78
H1
Honolulu
Waimanalo Beach
72
Honolulu International Airport
RANGE
KOOLAU
Mamala Bay
Waimanalo Bay

most vital rung on the pond food ladder. This ancient technique is still practiced in Oahu's Kaneohe Bay, where the Kualoa Ranch maintains an operational pond and sells its produce.

HEEIA STATE PARK

☎*808-247-3156* Continuing along Route 836 you'll come to this state park, a small greensward located on Kealohi Point, anchored by a lighthouse. Kealohi Point was a significant spot for ancient Hawaiians: it was thought to be a jumping-off point of the soul into the spirit world. This park is a perfect spot for a picnic with lovely views of the bay and the ancient fishpond. Offshore you'll see Coconut Island, made famous in the opening of TV's *Gilligan's Island*. Adjacent to the park is **Heeia Kai Boat Harbor**.

SENATOR FONG'S PLANTATION AND GARDENS ✉*47-285 Pulama Road, Kaneohe* ☎*808-239-6775* ✆*808-239-6469* ⌨*www.fonggarden.com, info@fonggarden.com* High above Kaneohe, gazing down upon the bay, is Senator Fong's. Here you can take an hour-and-a-half long leisure walk throughout 725 acres of gardens and orchards. This luxurious preserve was donated by one of Hawaii's most famous U.S. senators, so be prepared to venture from Eisenhower Valley to Kennedy Valley (sugar cane) to the Johnson Plateau (fruit orchards) to Nixon Valley (gardens) to the Ford Plateau (pine trees). Guides will take you on a one-mile walking tour (that can expand to two miles if you're up for it). Admission.

WAIAHOLE VALLEY AND WAIKANE VALLEY Route 83 soon becomes known as the Kamehameha Highway as it courses past lazy fishing boats then enters these valleys, some of the last places on the island where Hawaiian farmers grow crops in the traditional way. Fruit stands line the highway. The roads off the highway lead to small Hawaiian enclaves, where you'll see taro patches and papaya trees in the backyards.

CHINAMAN'S HAT That cone-shaped island offshore is Chinaman's Hat. It was named for its resemblance to a coolie cap, though the Hawaiians had another name for it long before the Chinese arrived in the islands. They called it Mokolii Island, or "little dragon," and claimed it represented the tail of a beast that resided under the water. Watch for frigate birds and delicate white-tailed tropical birds flying overhead.

OLD SUGAR MILL Just down the road from Kualoa Ranch is Oahu's first sugar mill, which lies in ruin along the side of the road. Built during the 1860s, it fell into disuse soon after completion and has since served only as a local curiosity.

KAAAWA BAY Along Kamehameha Highway you'll pass the community of Kaaawa and **Swanzy Beach Park** (see "Beaches & Parks" section below). A few miles later be on the lookout for the Hawaii Visitors Bureau marker noting **Crouching Lion** (there's also a restaurant by the same name just below the mountain). To the ancient Hawaiians, who had never experienced the king of the jungle, the stone face was, in fact,

that of Kauhi, a demigod from the island of Tahiti who was turned into stone during a struggle between Pele and her sister Hiiaka.

KAHANA BAY

Once the sight of a burgeoning Hawaiian fishing village, this coral-studded bay is now a tranquil spot for a picnic or swim in the sea. Be sure to look out for **Huilua Fishpond**, the oldest of Oahu's many fishponds (it's currently being reconstructed).

KAHANA VALLEY STATE PARK

☎️*808-587-0300* Across the highway from the Huilua fishpond is this state park (it's official name is Ahupuaa o Kahana State Park, but few call it by that moniker). If you like to hike there's a trail up the valley through lush foliage that weaves past old farmsteads. Check out the visitors and orientation centers here. Please be respectful of those who live here.

PUNALUU

After Kahana Valley Park, the highway, still crowding the coastline, traverses the roadside community of Punaluu, legendary home of the demigod Kamapuaa, one of Pele's lovers. There's a long, narrow strand of sand and ocean at **Punaluu Beach Park**, which offers pleasant swimming opportunities because of an offshore reef. (However, use caution when the weather is stormy.)

HAUULA

The roadway continues up to the small town of Hauula with its old **Hauula Door of Faith Church**, a small chapel of clapboard design surrounded by palms. Not far from it is another aging woodframe sanctuary, **Hauula Congregational Christian Church**, built of wood and coral back in 1862.

LAIE

Once thought to have been an ancient place of refuge for Hawaiians, this town is now a stronghold for Mormons. The Hawaii campus of **Brigham Young University** is located here, as well as the **Mormon Temple**. The courtyards and grounds of the temple are open to the public, but only Mormons are permitted to enter the temple sanctuary.

POLYNESIAN CULTURAL CENTER

✉️*55-370 Kamehameha Highway, Laie* ☎️*808-293-3333,   800-367-7060* 📠*888-722-7339* 🌐*www.polynesia.com* The Mormons own this cultural center, Oahu's most popular tourist attraction. Set right on Kamehameha Highway in Laie, it represents one of the foremost theme parks in the entire Pacific, a 42-acre attempt to re-create ancient Polynesia. As you wander about the grounds you'll encounter ersatz villages portraying life in the Marquesas, Tahiti, Fiji, Tonga, New Zealand and old Hawaii. Step over to the Tahitian hamlet and you will experience the rocking *tamure* dance. Or wander onto the islands of Samoa, where the local inhabitants demonstrate how to climb coconut trees. In Tonga a native will be beating tapa cloth from mulberry bark, while the Fijians are pounding rhythms with poles of bamboo. These mock villages are linked by waterways and can be visited in canoes. The boats will carry you past craftsmen preparing poi by mashing taro roots, and others husking coconuts.

The most popular shows are the "Pageant of the Long Canoes," in which the boats head up a lagoon amid a flurry of singing and dancing, and "Horizons." The latter is an evening show similar to Waikiki's Polynesian revues, though generally considered more elaborate. Most of the entertainers and other employees at this Hawaiian-style Disneyland are Mormon students attending the local university. Closed Sunday. Admission.

LAIE POINT ⊠*Head toward the ocean on Anemoku Street, off Kamehameha Highway, then turn right on Naupaka Street* Be sure to take in this point, the town's natural wonder. The headland provides extraordinary ocean views sweeping for miles along the shoreline. Since the breezes and surf are wilder here than elsewhere on the Windward Coast, you'll often encounter waves lashing at the two offshore islets with amazing force. The island with the hole in it is Kukihoolua or, as the locals call it, Puka Rock.

MALAEKAHANA STATE RECREATION AREA

Along the oceanside, a few miles outside of Laie, hidden behind the vines hugging the road is Malaekahana (see "Beaches & Parks" for added description). This gem of a park offers a long strand of white sand lined with ironwood trees. Offshore is Goat Island, or **Mokuauia**, a bird sanctuary you can actually wade over to when the tide is right (be sure to wear reef slippers or some such foot covering and be careful of the currents).

LODGING

PAT'S KAILUA BEACH PROPERTIES

$$ 32 ROOMS ⊠204 South Kalaheo Avenue, Kailua ☎808-262-4128, 808-261-1653
☏808-261-0893 ⌂www.patskailua.com, info@patskailua.com

Out in the suburban town of Kailua, where trim houses front a beautiful white-sand beach, you'll discover Pat's. Overlooking Kailua Beach Park and about 100 yards from the beach sits a cluster of woodframe cottages. Each is equipped with a full kitchen, cable television and a telephone. Some of the furniture is nicked, but these units (from studios to five-bedroom homes) are clean and cozy. They sit in a yard shaded with monkeypod, coconut and breadfruit trees and provide an excellent value.

HAWAII'S HIDDEN HIDEAWAY B&B

$$–$$$ 3 ROOMS ⊠1369 Mokolea Drive, Kailua ☎808-262-6560, 877-443-3299 ☏808-262-6561 ⌂www.ahawaiibnb.com, hhhideaway@yahoo.com

I recommend Hawaii's Hidden Hideaway B&B for more than just its name. It really is a lovely bed and breakfast, with lots of privacy. There are a suite and two studios available; the suite has an outdoor spa with an ocean view. All three have private entrances, parking and decks, and kitchenettes stocked with breakfast goodies. You're quite close to the beaches of Lanikai and Kailua, and a 30-minute or so drive to Waikiki. Three-night minimum stay—not that that will be difficult.

SCHRADER'S WINDWARD COUNTRY INN

$$–$$$ 50 ROOMS ✉47-039 Lihikai Drive, Kaneohe ☎808-239-5711, 800-735-5071 📠808-239-6658 🖋www.schradersinn.com, schrader@lava.net

You can't get much closer to the water than Schrader's. It's an unusual resting place consisting of several woodframe buildings right on the edge of Kaneohe Bay. There are picnic tables, barbecue grills and a pool on the two-acre property, as well as a tour boat that can take you snorkeling, kayaking or sightseeing on the bay. The guest rooms are cottage style with kitchenettes; many have lanais and bay views. Prices include continental breakfast.

ALI'I BLUFFS BED & BREAKFAST

$ 2 ROOMS ✉46-251 Ikiiki Street, Kaneohe ☎808-235-1124, 800-235-1151 📠808-236-4877 🖋www.hawaiiscene.com/aliibluffs, donm@lava.net

This contemporary Hawaiian B&B offers two rooms with private baths: The Victorian room features antiques and vintage paintings; the Circus room has large circus posters, many of them originals, from around the world. Furnished in antiques and Persian rugs, this charming home offers a full breakfast served poolside every morning.

LAIE INN

$–$$ 49 ROOMS ✉55-109 Laniloa Street, Laie ☎808-293-9282, 800-526-4562 📠808-293-8115 🖋www.laieinn.com, laieinn@hawaii.rr.com

A low-slung motel with two floors of rooms surrounding a swimming pool, the Laie Inn is a standard Coke-machine-in-the-courtyard facility located next to the Polynesian Cultural Center.

DINING

BUZZ'S ORIGINAL STEAK HOUSE

$$–$$$ STEAK ✉413 Kawailoa Road, Kailua ☎808-261-4661

Kailua has a collection of eating establishments spread throughout the town. Among them is Buzz's, right across the street from the beach. The place is popular not only with windsurfers, but with Honolulu residents who drive out on the weekends to enjoy the surf and a meal at this upscale beach shack, which has been in business since 1962. Burgers, steaks and seafood are the specialties here, and all entrées include a trip to the salad bar at dinnertime.

TIMES COFFEE SHOP

$ AMERICAN/LOCAL-STYLE ✉153 Hamakua Drive, Kailua ☎808-262-0300

Slide into a booth at this coffee shop, where breakfast brings local favorites (Portuguese sausage omelettes, spam and eggs) and American classics (pancakes, waffles). Fried rice, hamburger steaks, grilled mahimahi and sandwiches make an appearance on the lunch menu. No dinner.

SAENG'S THAI CUISINE

$–$$ THAI   ✉*315 Kailua Road, Kailua*   ✆*808-263-9727*

Saeng's is a freshly decorated ethnic restaurant with a hardwood bar and potted plants all around. Located in a strip mall, it nevertheless conveys a sense of elegance. The menu focuses on vegetarian, seafood and curry dishes. No lunch on weekends.

CINNAMON'S RESTAURANT

$$ CONTINENTAL   ✉*Kailua Square Shopping Center, 315 Uluniu Street, Kailua*
✆*808-261-8724* ✆*808-262-9910* ✎*www.cinnamonsrestaurant.com,*
cinnamonrest@aol.com

Known for years as a prime breakfast and lunch place, Cinnamon's draws a local crowd, which sits beneath the dining room gazebo or out on the patio. The menu is best described as Continental cuisine with local flavors. Try the chicken cashew sandwich or the carrot pancakes—all made from scratch! No lunch Sunday, no dinner.

BACI BISTRO

$$–$$$ ITALIAN   ✉*30 Aulike Street, Kailua*   ✆*808-262-7555* ✆*808-261-2857*
✎*www.restauranteur.com*

Kailua residents will tell you the pastas here are all homemade and beautifully prepared. You have the option of sitting in the small dining room with greenhouse windows or in the romantic covered lanai. There are veal and fish entrées, risotto dishes and an array of antipasti. No lunch on Saturday and Sunday.

KOA PANCAKE HOUSE

$$ AMERICAN   ✉*46-126 Kahuhipa Street, Kaneohe*   ✆*808-235-5772*

This tastefully appointed restaurant features a breakfast bill of fare that includes pancakes and crêpes suzette and a lunch menu with salads, sandwiches, teriyaki chicken and seafood. No dinner.

HALEIWA JOE'S SEAFOOD GRILL

$$–$$$ STEAK/SEAFOOD   ✉*46-336 Haiku Road, Kaneohe*   ✆*808-247-6671*
✆*808-247-5886* ✎*www.haleiwajoes.com*

What sets Haleiwa Joe's apart is its idyllic setting. A terraced dining area overlooks sharp cliffs and peaceful flower beds, making this a choice stop for dinner. The menu consists of steak, seafood and prime rib with a Pan-Asian influence. Dinner only.

SUMO RAMEN AND CURRY HOUSE

$ LOCAL-STYLE   ✉*Kaneohe Shopping Center, 45-934 Kamehameha Highway, Kaneohe*   ✆*808-234-6868*

Serving up tasty local food, ranging from Spam curry to seafood ramen bowls and beef stew, this place is a sure bet. Prices range from $3.50 to $6.50, making it one of the cheapest eateries in the area.

CROUCHING LION INN
$$$–$$$$ AMERICAN   ✉51-666 Kamehameha Highway, Kaaawa   ☎808-237-8511
🖳808-237-7061

The setting is the draw at this vintage 1927 wood-shingle house at the foot of verdant mountains. The food isn't remarkable, but they do have the most extensive menu in the area. Try the specialties: honey garlic shrimp, macadamia chicken and flame-broiled scallops. The beautiful ocean view makes it a worthy stop, even without food. One drawback: It's popular with tour buses, so try to arrive at an off-hour.

SHOPPING

Shopping in the Windward Coast is not a major activity. Kailua and Kaneohe both have large shopping centers but the stores are not noteworthy. There are, however, a few places to stop by and browse.

ISLAND TREASURES
ART GALLERY

✉629 Kailua Road, Suite 103, Kailua   ☎808-261-8131   Peruse an exceptional collection of pottery, wooden boxes, jewelry, paintings, handcrafted wooden furniture, shell candles and etched glass with island designs, all created by artists living in Hawaii.

CROUCHING LION GALLERY   ✉Crouching Lion Inn, 51-666 Kamehameha Highway, Kaaawa   ☎808-237-8545   This gallery sells original paintings and prints by local and international artists, as well as sculpture and handcrafted gift items.

LANCE FAIRLY GALLERY   ✉53-839 Kamehameha Highway, Punaluu   ☎808-293-9009   ⌨www.lancefairly.com   Expect original paintings by local artists, limited-edition prints and enameled tropical fish at this Punaluu shop.

NIGHTLIFE

BOARD RIDERS BAR AND GRILL   ✉201 Hamakua Drive #A, Kailua   ☎808-261-4600   Nights on the Windward Coast are quiet and peaceful, and most people like it that way, aside from the large number of military personnel who frequent the night spots. For those who prefer a bit of action, head to Kailua, where there's always something going on at Board Riders. This sports bar has a pool table and dart boards; on many nights there are dance tunes ranging from reggae to rock. Occasional cover on Friday and Saturday.

BEACHES & PARKS

KAILUA BEACH
✉Off Kalaheo Avenue

Stretching for two miles with white sand all the way and tiny islands offshore, this is one of the prettiest beaches around. It's in the suburban town of Kailua, so you'll trade seclusion for excellent beach facilities. The center of activity is **Kailua Beach Park**, at the end of Kailua Road near the south end of the beach. This 30-acre facility has a grassy expanse shaded by ironwood and coconut trees and perfect for picnicking. There are restrooms and a pavilion. **Kalama Beach County Park** (250 North Kalaheo Avenue), a small park with restrooms in the middle of Kailua Beach, is less crowded. Swimming, surfing and body-surfing are good all along the strand and windsurfing is excellent, but exercise caution.

LANIKAI BEACH

The strand parallels Mokulua Drive. Lanikai can be reached by driving south along the beachfront roads in Kailua.

Everyone's dream house is on the beach at Lanikai. This sandy stretch, varying from 20 to 100 feet in width, extends for over a mile. The entire beach in this residential community is lined with those houses everybody wants. The water is the color of cobalt and the protecting reef offshore makes the entire beach safe for swimming. Lanikai has also become a windsurfing favorite. No facilities; the nearest facilities are at Kailua Beach.

HEEIA STATE PARK

Route 836 (Kamehameha Highway) just outside of Kaneohe

This small pocket park located off of Kamehameha Highway at Kealohi Point is an ideal spot to picnic when traveling around the island. The views of Kaneohe Bay and the ancient Hawaiian fishpond are noteworthy. Numerous indigenous plants thrive here and there are educational programs offered by Friends of Heeia State Park. In addition, there's a pavilion, picnic tables and restrooms.

KUALOA REGIONAL PARK

49-479 Kamehameha Highway (Route 83) about ten miles north of Kaneohe

You could search the entire Pacific for a setting as lovely as this one. Just 500 yards offshore lies the islet of Mokolii, better known as Chinaman's Hat. Behind the beach the *pali* creates a startling background of fluted cliffs and tropical forest. The beach is a long and narrow strip of sand paralleled by a wide swath of grass parkland. Little wonder this is one of the Windward Coast's most popular picnic areas. It is usually a favorite for swimming, snorkeling and fishing, but high bacteria levels during rainy seasons sometimes result in beach closures. Facilities include picnic areas, restrooms and showers.

Tent camping permitted. County permit required.

SWANZY BEACH PARK, PUNALUU BEACH PARK AND HAUULA BEACH PARK

These parks are all located along Kamehameha Highway (Route 83). Swanzy lies about 12 miles north of Kaneohe, Punaluu is about four miles north of Swanzy, and Hauula is about three miles beyond that.

These three county facilities lie along Kamehameha Highway (Route 83) within seven miles of each other. Swimming is generally good at each. Along this coast the most abundant fish is *papio*, followed by bonefish, milkfish and goatfish. Camping is allowed at all except Punaluu, but none compare aesthetically with other beaches to the north and south. Swanzy (open weekends only) is located on the highway but lacks a sandy beach. However, it has the best diving. Its surf break, "Crouching Lion," is for experts only; Punaluu, though possessing a pretty palm-fringed beach, is cramped; and Hauula, a spacious park with a beach and a winter surf break for beginners, is visited periodically by tour buses. So put these beach parks near the bottom of your list, and bring them up only if the other beaches are too crowded. All three beaches have picnic areas and restrooms.

▲ Tent and trailer camping allowed at Hauula Beach Park, as well as at Swanzy Beach Park on weekends. A county permit is required. 808-523-4525.

AHUPUAA O KAHANA STATE PARK

✉ 52-222 Kamehameha Highway (Route 83) about 14 miles north of Kaneohe
☎ 808-587-0300   📠 808-587-0311   🖥 www.hawaii.gov/dlnr/dsp

🚶 🛶 ⚓ This 5228-acre paradise, set on a white-sand beach, offers something for every adventurer. You can pick fruit in a lush forest, picnic in a coconut grove and sightsee an ancient fishpond. You can also fish for *papio*, bonefish, milkfish and goatfish. Swimming is generally good. Surfing is a possibility but is mediocre at best. Facilities include an orientation center, picnic areas and restrooms.

▲ There's tent camping on the beach; $5 per night. No camping on Thursday. State permit required.

KOKOLOLIO BEACH PARK

✉ 55-017 Kamehameha Highway (Route 83) in Laie about 20 miles north of Kaneohe

🛶 ⚓ ⚓ Here's one of the prettiest beaches on the Windward Coast. With trees and a lawn that extends toward the white-sand beach, it's a highly recommended spot for day-tripping. It's also a good beach for swimming and bodysurfing and in winter there are breaks up to six feet, with right and left slide. Common catches include *papio*, bonefish, goatfish and milkfish. There are picnic areas and restrooms.

▲ Camping allowed with county permit.

POUNDERS BEACH

✉ Kamehameha Highway north of Kakela Beach

🛶 ⚓ Named for the crushing shorebreak that makes it a popular bodysurfing beach, this quarter-mile-long strand features a corridor of white sand and a sandy bottom. Swimming is good near the old landing at the western end of the beach. Be careful of currents when swimming anywhere along the beach. Anglers try for *ono*, *moi* and *papio*. There are showers, but no other facilities here.

HUKILAU BEACH

✉ Kamehameha Highway (Route 83) in Laie about 22 miles north of Kaneohe

🛶 🎣 ⚓ ⚓ This privately owned facility fronts a beautiful white-sand beach that winds for more than a mile. Part of the beach is lined with homes, but much of it is undeveloped. Several small islands lie off-shore, and the park contains a lovely stand of ironwood trees. All in all this enchanting beach is one of the finest on this side of the island. Swimming is good; bodysurfing is also recommended. Snorkeling is usually fair and there are small surfable waves with left and right slides. The principal catch is *papio*; milkfish, bonefish and goatfish are also caught. There are no facilities here.

MALAEKAHANA STATE RECREATION AREA AND GOAT ISLAND

✉Kamehameha Highway (Route 83) in Laie about 23 miles north of Kaneohe
📞808-293-1736 📠808-293-2066 🖥www.malaekahana.net

⚊ ⚊ ⚊ ⚊ ⚊ This is a rare combination. The Malaekahana facility is one of the island's prettiest parks. It's a tropical won-derland filled with palm, *hala* and ironwood trees, and graced with a curving, white-sand beach. Goat Island or Mokuauia, lies just offshore. When the tide is right you can wade out to it. Other times, grab a boogie board or surf board and paddle out with a picnic lunch. It's a small, low-lying island covered with scrub growth and scattered ironwood trees. On the windward side is a coral beach; to leeward lies a crescent-shaped white-sand beach. It's a good place to swim because it is shallow and well-protected. There are also good places for snorkeling and, in win-ter, you can paddle out to a break with a left slide. Feel like fish-ing? You may well reel in *papio*, the most abundant fish along here; goatfish, milkfish and bonefish are also caught. Goat Island is now a state bird refuge, so you might see wedge-tailed shear-waters nesting. Whatever activity you choose, make sure you don't disturb the birds. Goat Island will return the favor—there'll be nothing here to disturb you either. Facilities include showers, bathrooms and barbecue pits.

▲ There are two sections to the park. The Laie section includes Goat Island and is administered by the state. The Kahuku section (Puuhonua o Malaekahana, or Place of Refuge) is operated by the Friends of Malaekahana, the first native Hawaiian group to operate a park in the islands.

Laie Section: Tent camping allowed. State permit required.

Kahuku Section: There are rustic cabins available here. These beachfront units include 45 campsites and 7 beach cabins—6 beach houses with two or three bedrooms, private baths and kitchens ($130 per night)—and a four-room cabin with a game room and a commercial kitchen ($250 per night). There are five yurts that sleep two to six people ($50 to $100 per night). Tent sites are $5.20 per person, per night. Cabins are equipped with beds, kitchen facilities and bathrooms. Bring your own bedding and cooking gear and be prepared for very rustic accommodations.

NORTH SHORE

Wide, wide beaches heaped with white, white sand roll for miles along the North Shore, which curves from Kahuku Point in the east to Kaena Point in the west. Although they can compete with the most beautiful beaches anywhere, it's not the sand or their size that is the main attraction here. Rather it is the winter waves, and these waves have made Oahu's North Shore legendary and very busy during surf season. Surfers come from around the world to try their skill at one of the world's most renowned spots for the sport.

If you have ever owned a surfboard, or even a Beach Boys album, you know Waimea Bay and Sunset Beach. The names are synonymous with surfing. They number among the most challenging and dangerous surf spots anywhere. During the winter, 15- to 20-foot waves are as common as bleached hair and beach buggies. The infamous "Banzai Pipeline," where surfers risk limb and longevity as thunderous waves pass over a shallow reef, is here as well.

The surf is not the only thing that's superb. The setting is stunning. Oahu's two mountain ranges form the backdrop, while 4025-foot Mt. Kaala, the island's highest peak, towers above all. Small ranches and farms checkerboard the tableland between the mountains and the sea. The old-time farmers, the surfers and the counterculture types who live in the area all come to Haleiwa for shopping, dining and socializing. Haleiwa, a restored plantation town with old clapboard buildings and wooden sidewalks, preserves the spirit of a rural way of life that is rapidly disappearing.

The plantations that established Oahu's economic base have all closed. In fact, the last sugar mill on the island, located in the North Shore town of Waialua, shut down in 1996, marking the end of a major chapter in Oahu's history. Although the Waialua Sugar Company now no longer processes cane, this low-key village west of Haleiwa still has the feel of a sugar town. The mill, which stands at its center, and the old Bank of Hawaii building, serve as reminders of a past that just yesterday was the present.

As the hub of sugar production has shifted to other areas of the world, the farmers of Oahu have filled the vacuum. Coffee experienced a bum crop when it was first planted here in the early 1800s. Locals gave it a more successful try in 1825, however, and it's now experiencing a production boom. The soil and climate of this island lend themselves to excellent crops of the beans, which thrive in moist soil rich in the organic matter of volcanic rock and leaf mold. The land near Waialua, the sleepy little sugar plantation town, is ideal for coffee production: the absorbent soil is loose enough to drain excess water, and the temperature and elevation further the perfect conditions. The sorghum and wiliwili trees of the North Shore currently protect the crop; ultimately, the recently planted Norfolk pines will become the primary guardian against wind damage to the coffee trees.

KAHUKU The main road along the North Shore begins with the small town of Kahuku, where many residents call home. For a taste of the rural Hawaii of old, take a detour into this little village. Kahuku is also the home of the Kahuku Sugar Mill, a turn-of-the-20th-century plant. In an effort to refurbish the old mill, the entire complex was turned into a shopping mall. The shops never quite made it and now the mall hosts local services (including a health clinic).

JAMES CAMPBELL NATIONAL WILDLIFE REFUGE

✉ 66-590 Kamehameha Highway, Haleiwa ☎ 808-637-6330 ext. 40 Facilitating the recovery of four endangered bird species—the black-necked Hawaiian stilt, Hawaiian moorhen, Hawaiian coot and Hawaiian duck—this wildlife refuge consists of two units: the Punamaoo Pond is a spring-fed marsh; the Kii Unit is made up of former sugar cane waste–settling basins. Free guided tours of the 164-acre wetlands are offered Thursday and Saturday, from late October to late February. Reservations required.

KAIHALULU BEACH If you continue along Kamehameha Highway from the wildlife refuge, you will skirt Kaihalulu Beach, which continues out to **Kahuku Point**, the northernmost point on Oahu. The current here is strong and the rocky bottom makes swimming difficult, but it is a wonderful spot to spend the afternoon beachcombing. The road then makes a bend past **Kuilima Cove**, the windswept white-sand strand fronting the Turtle Bay Resort.

ROADSIDE VENDORS

Roadside vendors at locations along the way sell sweet corn, watermelon, papaya, mango and tropical flowers from local farms and gardens, fresh-caught fish and shrimp from the area's aquaculture ponds. You'll get a warm welcome and a chance to "talk story" with the locals as well as the opportunity to enjoy some of Hawaii's natural treasures.

SUNSET BEACH ✉ Kamehameha Highway Stretching for two miles and averaging 200 feet in width, this is one of Hawaii's largest strands. While Sunset Beach is actually only a single surfing spot, the name has become synonymous with a two-mile-long corridor that includes Banzai Beach and the adjacent Pipeline. When the surf is up you can watch world-class athletes shoot the curl. When it's not, Sunset becomes a great place to swim.

EHUKAI BEACH PARK ✉ Off Kamehameha Highway about seven miles northeast of Haleiwa This is best place to surf on Oahu. Just 100 yards to the west (Ke Nui Road) sits the **Banzai Pipeline**, where a shallow coral shelf

HIDDEN LISTINGS

GIOVANNI'S ALOHA SHRIMP TRUCK
PAGE 139

Traditional two-scoops-of-rice lunch plates topped with lemon and butter or hot and spicy shrimp that locals claim are the best on Oahu

KE IKI BEACH BUNGALOWS
PAGE 138

Eleven wood-framed bungalows spread across an acre-and-a-half of palm-shaded beachfront

PUPUKEA BEACH PARK
PAGE 142

Amazing snorkeling and tidepooling along several sections of rocky shoreline, including highly regarded "Shark's Cove"

PUU O MAHUKA HEIAU
PAGE 134

Once used for human sacrifices, the island's oldest stone temple atop a plateau that offers spectacular views

creates tubular waves so powerful and perfect they resemble pipes. First surfed in 1957, it lays claim to cracked skulls, lacerated legs and some of the sport's greatest feats.

PUU O MAHUKA HEIAU

✉*From Kamehameha Highway, turn left near the Sunset Beach Fire Station onto Pupukea Road, then follow the Hawaii Visitors & Convention Bureau signs.* On a plateau between Sunset Beach and Waimea Bay you'll find Oahu's oldest temple. A split-level structure built of stone, it once was used for human sacrifices. Today there is nothing more menacing than a spectacular view and perhaps a gentle breeze from the ocean.

ST. PETER & PAUL A beautiful religious site built on a former rock-crushing plant, this quaint church, with its steeple constructed from the remaining rocks of the plant, seems to stand watch over Waimea Bay.

WAIMEA VALLEY AUDUBON CENTER ✉*Kamehameha Highway, five miles northeast of Haleiwa* ☎*808-638-9199* 📠*808-638-9197* 🖥*www.waimea.audubon.org, waimea@audubon.org* Here you can wander through a tropical preserve and cultural park stretching across 1800 acres. Once a Hawaiian village, it is crisscrossed with hiking trails and archaeological ruins. Weather permitting, you can picnic and swim at Waimea Falls, or browse the arboretum featuring tropical and subtropical trees from around the world, beautiful botanical gardens including one local Hawaiian species. Then there are the birds that populate the complex; since this nature park serves as a bird sanctuary, it attracts a varied assortment. Activities for visitors include self-guided tours everyday except Monday and Friday. Admission.

WAIMEA BAY Across the road from the Audubon Center looms Waimea Bay, another fabled place that sports the largest surfable waves in the world. When surf's up in winter, the monster waves that roll in are so big they make the ground tremble when they break. Salt spray reaches as far as the highway. Thirty-foot waves are not uncommon. Fifty-foot giants have been recorded; though unsurfable, these are not tidal waves, just swells rising along the incredible North Shore. In December, the Hawaiian Triple Crown—basically the Super Bowl of surfing—takes place. In summer, Waimea is a pretty blue bay with a white-sand beach. The water is placid and the area perfect for picnicking and sunbathing. So when you visit Waimea, remember: Swim in summer, sunbathe in winter.

HALEIWA The Kamehameha Highway crosses Anahula River and a double rainbow–shaped bridge en route to this old plantation town with a new facelift. Fortunately, the designers who performed the surgery on this village had an eye for antiquity. They planned it so the modern shopping centers and other facilities blend comfortably into the rural landscape. The community that has grown up around the new town reflects a rare combination of past and future. The old Japanese, Filipinos and Hawaiians have been joined by blond-mopped surfers and laidback counterculturalists. As a result, this clapboard town with wooden sidewalks has established itself as the "in" spot on the North Shore. Its stylish nonchalance has also proved popular among canny travelers. Despite gentrification, Haleiwa holds on to its relaxed ambience. The surf scene still adds a definite style to Haleiwa.

NORTH SHORE SURF AND CULTURAL MUSEUM ⊠*North Shore Marketplace, 66-250 Kamehameha Highway, Haleiwa* ✆*808-637-8888* ⌕*www.captain rick.com/surf_museum.htm* Surf's up at this museum, which displays related artifacts, boards and old photographs of the local community. A mini-theater shows videos of the sport. The museum also temporarily houses items from an 1824 shipwreck, providing a safe haven for the items while the wreck is being excavated. (There's jewelry for sale that was found by underwater metal detection.) The museum's other claim to fame is its possession of the last two boards used by famed surfer Mark Foo before he was killed in a surfing accident in 1994. Closed Tuesday.

LILIUOKALANI PROTESTANT CHURCH hidden

The little church in Haleiwa is named for the queen who used to summer on the shores of the nearby Anahulu River, Queen Liliuokalani. This Protestant church dates back to the early

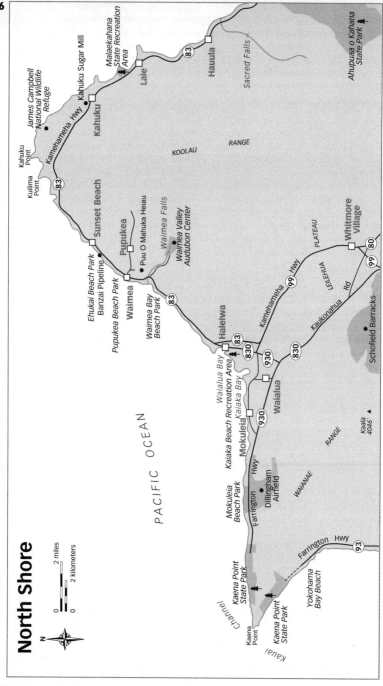

North Shore

N

0   2 miles
0   2 kilometers

PACIFIC OCEAN

James Campbell National Wildlife Refuge

Kahuku Sugar Mill

Malaekahana State Recreation Area

Laie

83

Hauula

Sacred Falls

Ahupuaa o Kahana State Park

Kamehameha Hwy

Kahuku

Kahuku Point

Kuilima Point

83

KOOLAU   RANGE

Sunset Beach

Pupukea

Puu O Mahuka Heiau

Waimea Falls

Waimea Valley Audubon Center

Whitmore Village

80

Ehukai Beach Park

Banzai Pipeline

Pupukea Beach Park

Waimea

Waimea Bay Beach Park

PLATEAU

LEILEHUA

Kamehameha Hwy

99

99

Rd

80

Haleiwa

83

83

830

930

Waialua Bay

Kaiaka Beach Recreation Area

Kaiaka Bay

Mokuleia

Waialua

930

830

Kaukonahua

Schofield Barracks

830

Kaala 4046'

Mokuleia Beach Park

Dillingham Airfield

Farrington Hwy

930

WAIANAE   RANGE

Kaena Point State Park

Farrington Hwy

93

Kaena Point State Park

Yokohama Bay Beach

Kaena Point

Kauai   Channel

1800s, though the current building was constructed in the mid-1900s. If you have a chance to enter the church, take a look at the clock that was donated by the queen—it shows the phases of the moon as well as the hour, day, month and year.

WAIALUA A scenic detour takes you to this former sugar plantation town, via Haleiwa Road. There's not much to see here except the old Waialua Sugar Mill, which has been converted into office space. The mill closed its sugar operation in the mid-'90s and the cane fields around this area are being replanted with Waialua coffee. Plantation houses line the streets and it's an interesting area to look around.

THE ORIGINAL GLIDER RIDE ✆808-637-0207 ✐www.honolulusoaring.com, info@gliderridehawaii.com For a faster route toward Kaena Point, pick up Farrington Highway (Route 930). This country road parallels miles of unpopulated beachfront, past wind-battered Mokuleia Beach and arrives at Dillingham Airfield, where you can take a ride along the Waianae Mountains. With over 30 years of experience, Mr. Bill knows the ins and outs of the countryside. He'll also provide you with a video of your ride. Calling about weather conditions and making reservations are highly recommended.

KAENA POINT

hidden

Beyond Dillingham Air Field, the road continues for several miles between a wild ocean and scrub brush–covered mountains before turning into a very rugged dirt track. Along this unpaved portion of roadway you can hike out about ten miles to Kaena Point on Oahu's northwest corner. This is the legendary point of departure for Hawaiian souls.

LODGING

TURTLE BAY RESORT
$$$$ 443 ROOMS   ✉57-091 Kamehameha Highway, Kahuku ✆808-293-8811, 800-203-3650 📠808-293-9147 ✐www.turtlebayresort.com
For a resort experience in a rustic setting, consider this rural retreat, which sprawls across 880 acres on a dramatic peninsula. With a broad beach at the doorstep and mountains out back, the resort is an overwhelming spot. Add to that riding paths, two golf courses, tennis courts, three swimming pools, a spa and a fitness center. Every guest room features an ocean view.

BACKPACKER'S VACATION INN
$ 21 UNITS   ✉59-788 Kamehameha Highway, Haleiwa ✆808-638-7838 📠808-638-7515 ✐www.backpackers-hawaii.com, bpackers@maui.net
Surfers, scuba divers and budget-minded travelers will love Backpacker's along Oahu's vaunted North Shore. The central building provides hostel-style rooms and features a TV lounge and kitchen. There's also a back house with private rooms that share a kitchen and bath. Like a hostel, it's budget-priced. Across the street, and directly on the beach,

there's a house with private apartments that include their own kitchen and bathroom and are moderately priced. In addition, there are nine restored plantation cabins with kitchens and baths set on a landscaped acre. The inn has guest laundry facilities and barbecue areas, which provide excellent opportunities for meeting other travelers.

KE IKI BEACH BUNGALOWS

$$–$$$ 11 UNITS ✉ 59-579 Ke Iki Road, Haleiwa ☏ 808-638-8229, 866-638-8229 📠 808-638-8823 🖉 www.keikibeach.com, info@keikibeach.com

Offering houses right on the beach, these bungalows are located between the Banzai Pipeline and Waimea Bay. You'll find moderate- and deluxe-priced duplexes and an ultra-deluxe-priced cottage, all on an acre-and-a-half of palm-shaded property. They are basic woodframe buildings with bamboo and rattan furnishings; all units have full kitchens. The complex includes barbecue facilities, hammocks and a wide beach. Accommodations are great for families.

KAWELA BAY BEACH HOUSE

$$$$ 1 UNIT ✉ Kawela Bay Book through Pacific Islands Reservations ☏ 808-262-8133 📠 808-262-5030, pir@aloha.com

Although it's a bit far-flung, located some 30 minutes north of Haleiwa, this beach house is a great choice for those seeking a quiet, oceanfront retreat on the North Shore that doesn't cost an arm and a leg. A cottage on a larger estate, the two-bedroom, one-bath house has a full kitchen and a fold-out couch in the living room. The decor is light and breezy, but it's cozy—while it can sleep four adults and two kids, it's best-suited to a small family or close friends. It sits right on a secluded white-sand beach that has good snorkeling and plenty of privacy.

CONDOS

THE ESTATES AT TURTLE BAY

114 UNITS ✉ 56-565 Kamehameha Highway, Kahuku ☏ 808-293-0600, 888-200-4202 📠 808-293-0471 🖉 www.turtlebay-rentals.com, etbinfo@hawaii.rr.com

Located on the grounds of the Turtle Bay Resort but independently operated, The Estates offers studio, as well as one-, two- and three-bedroom resort condominiums, each with stove, refrigerator, dishwasher, microwave, washer/dryer and cable television. There are five swimming pools and four tennis courts on the property, and guests can arrange golf and horseback riding through the resort. Rates begin at $115 for a studio and up to $300 for a three-bedroom unit.

TURTLE BAY CONDOS

50 UNITS ✉ 56-565 Kamehameha Highway, Kahuku ☏ 808-293-2800 📠 808-293-2169 🖉 www.turtlebaycondos.com

This clean, minimalist-style accommodation has one-, two- and three-bedroom units with kitchen facilities, washer/dryer and private lanais that overlook either a nine-hole golf course or a garden area. In high season, studios are $110; one-bedrooms units with a loft sleeping up to four guests are $165; two-bedroom units with a loft are $215; and three-bedroom units start at $240.

DINING

KAHUKU GRILL

$$–$$$ PLATE LUNCHES   ✉56-565 Kamehameha Highway, Kahuku   ☏808-293-2110

Appropriately enough, you'll find the Kahuku Grill not far from the old Kahuku Sugar Mill. The menu includes Hawaiian plate lunches as well as shrimp, seafood and steak dishes. Open for breakfast, lunch and dinner daily, it's plain and informal.

GIOVANNI'S ALOHA SHRIMP TRUCK

$$ PLATE LUNCHES   ✉Beside The Mill, Kamehameha Highway, Kahuku
☏808-293-1839

Giovanni's serves gourmet plate lunches that the locals claim are the best on Oahu. There's a choice of scampi, lemon and butter shrimp or hot and spicy shrimp, and, like all plate lunches, they come with two scoops of rice. Eleven picnic tables sit under an awning for this rain-or-shine outdoor eating spot.

TURTLE BAY RESORT

$$–$$$ PACIFIC RIM/AMERICAN   ✉57-091 Kamehameha Highway, Kahuku
☏808-293-8811   ☏808-293-9147   ⌨www.turtlebayresort.com

This resort features three dining options. **21 Degrees North** has sweeping ocean views and features contemporary island cuisine. Expect such delights as rosemary-crusted rack of lamb, Muscovy duck and seared *ahi* with wasabi mashed potatoes. At the **Palm Terrace**, overlooking the hotel's lovely grounds, you'll encounter moderate-priced dining in an attractive environment. The restaurant, serving three buffet meals, offers everything from sautéed swordfish to calzone. At the **Hang Ten**, munch on a hamburger or fish tacos while lounging in the sun.

JAMESON'S BY THE SEA

$$–$$$ SEAFOOD   ✉62-540 Kamehameha Highway, Haleiwa   ☏808-637-6272
☏808-637-3225

For relaxed sunset dining overlooking the ocean, try Jameson's. The inviting dining area features tropical touches like potted plants and rattan furnishing. For lunch there are sandwiches, chowders and fresh fish dishes; at dinner they specialize in seafood. Brunch on the weekend.

HALEIWA JOE'S SEAFOOD GRILL

$$–$$$ SEAFOOD   ✉66-011 Kamehameha Highway, Haleiwa   ☏808-637-8005
☏808-637-8861

The seafood here is not the best I've ever had, but the salads are large and refreshing, the coconut shrimp pretty good, and the atmosphere a little more chichi than most casual beachside places. Plus, the patio has a beautiful ocean view.

How to Beat the Heat with a Sweet Treat

Since the early days of Hawaiian royalty, people have complained about Honolulu's shirt-sticking weather. Come summer, temperatures rise and the trade winds stop blowing. Visitors seeking a golden tan discover they're baking without browning. And residents begin to think that their city, renowned as a cultural melting pot, is actually a pressure cooker.

With the ocean all around, relief is never far away. But a lot of folks, when not heading for the beaches, have found another way to cool off: shave ice. Known as ice frappes among the Japanese originators and snow cones back on the mainland, these frozen treats are Hawaii's answer to the Good Humor man.

They're made with ice that's been shaved from a block into thin slivers, packed into a cone-shaped cup and covered with sweet syrup. Health-minded people eat the ice plain or with a low-calorie or sugar-free syrup, but some folks ask for a scoop of ice cream or sweet red beans (*azuki* beans) underneath the shavings. Most people just order it with their favorite syrup flavors—grape, root beer, cola, cherry, orange, lemon-lime, vanilla, fruit punch, banana, strawberry or whatever.

Whichever you choose, you'll find it only costs about a buck at the many stands sprinkled around town. Watch for stands up on the North Shore, too.

MATSUMOTO'S ✉*66-087 Kamehameha Highway, Haleiwa* ✆*808-637-4827*
No doubt you'll see a long line outside this shop, Oahu's most famous shaved ice store.

As a matter of fact, any place where the sun blazes overhead you're liable to find someone trying to beat the heat by slurping up a "snow cone" before it melts into mush.

ROSIE'S CANTINA

$–$$ MEXICAN   ✉*Haleiwa Shopping Plaza, 66-165 Kamehameha Highway, Haleiwa* ✆*808-637-3538* ✆*808-637-5086*

Mexican restaurants in Hawaii had fish tacos long before places on the mainland caught on. True to the islands, Rosie's offers them, rounding out a menu filled with the culinary features found in every south-of-the-border eatery. The breakfast menu features American standbys like pancakes and omelettes, while the dinner menu ranges from tacos and enchiladas to steaks and seafood.

KUA AINA SANDWICH _____

$ AMERICAN/LOCAL-STYLE   ✉*66-160 Kamehameha Highway, Haleiwa* ✆*808-637-6067* ✆*808-637-4858*

Join the surfers who pour into the joint, where they order hamburgers, french fries and mahimahi sandwiches at the counter, then kick back at one of the roadside tables. Great for light meals, this place is a scene and a half.

CHOLOS HOMESTYLE MEXICAN RESTAURANT

$ MEXICAN ✉ North Shore Marketplace, 66-250 Kamehameha Highway, Haleiwa
📞 808-637-3059

Steaming fish tacos smothered in spicy salsa. Salty chips that leave oil on your napkin. Cold beer topped with lime. Mmmm. But I digress. Cholos is ideal after-beach fare. You can dine inside or out, and the gorgeous crafts on display are for sale.

COFFEE GALLERY

$ COFFEEHOUSE ✉ North Shore Marketplace, 66-250 Kamehameha Highway, Haleiwa 📞 808-637-5355 🖥 www.roastmaster.com, coffeegalleryhawaii@yahoo.com

Years ago Haleiwa was home to Da Cuppa Kope, a great café and gathering place. Today it's been supplanted by an even better coffeehouse, the Coffee Gallery, which roasts its coffee on-site. In addition to the best cappuccino on the island, this homespun restaurant, decorated with coffee sacks, serves homemade pastries, bagels, soups and a variety of sandwiches. They also have internet and free wi-fi access.

PARADISE FOUND CAFÉ

$ VEGETARIAN ✉ Inside Celestial Natural Foods, 66-443 Kamehameha Highway, Haleiwa 📞 808-637-4540

Casual is an understatement here, where barefoot beachgoers order up fresh-fruit smoothies, soups, salads and vegetarian delights such as tempeh burritos and tofu lemongrass curry. Vegan substitutions are easily accommodated at this friendly eatery.

CAFÉ HALEIWA

$ AMERICAN ✉ 66-460 Kamehameha Highway, Haleiwa 📞 808-637-5516

At this café surfers swear by the omelettes, pancakes and "the Barrel"— a blend of eggs, potatoes, green salsa and cheese wrapped in a tortilla. Sandwiches and burgers round out the menu. Located in a century-old building featuring local artwork, surfboards and surfing memorabilia, this local favorite also serves an excellent quesadilla. No dinner.

SHOPPING

THE ONLY SHOW IN TOWN ✉ 56-931 Kamehameha Highway, Kahuku 📞 808-293-1295 📠 808-293-8585 Calling itself The Only Show In Town is a slight (very slight) exaggeration, but claiming to be "Kahuku's largest antique and vintage collectible shop" is definitely warranted. Some store specialties include Japanese glass fishing floats, ivory, Coca-Cola memorabilia and unusual beads from around the world. Fittingly, this wonderful antique store is located in the old Tanaka Plantation Store, an early-20th-century woodframe building.

Trendy shoppers head for the little town of Haleiwa. Since Haleiwa is a center for surfers, it's a good place to buy sportswear and aquatic equipment as well as varied artworks and crafts.

STRONG CURRENT ✉ 66-208 Kamehameha Highway, Haleiwa 📞 808-637-3410 🖥 www.strongcurrenthawaii.com Stocking everything imaginable that's related to surfing, this place even has a small "surfing museum," consisting of memorabilia from the sport's early days. Then there are the books, videos, posters, boards and other appurtenances, all relating to a single theme.

IWA GALLERY ⊠*66-119 Kamehameha Highway, Haleiwa* ☏*808-637-4865* Here you'll find a unique collection of artwork by a number of local island artists, including handcrafted candles.

OOGENESIS BOUTIQUE ⊠*66-249 Kamehameha Highway, Haleiwa* ☏*808-637-4422* This shop has a creative selection of women's fashions.

NORTH SHORE MARKETPLACE ⊠*66-250 Kamehameha Highway, Haleiwa* You can watch glass artists fashion whales, sharks, reef fish and other aquatic creatures at **Oceans in Glass** (808-637-5026), pick up a new bikini or swimsuit at **North Shore Swimwear** (808-637-6859) or buy a surfboard and any of the associated gear at **Boardriders Club** (808-637-5026).

NIGHTLIFE

BAY CLUB _____
⊠*Turtle Bay Resort, 57-091 Kamehameha Highway, Kahuku* ☏*808-293-8811* Entertainment is a rare commodity on the North Shore, but you will find contemporary Hawaiian music here, and a Polynesian revue on Friday.

BREAKERS RESTAURANT AND BAR ⊠*66-250 Kamehameha Highway, Haleiwa* ☏*808-637-9898* Haleiwa's most popular bar is Breakers. There's live music on weekend nights, when it's usually packed.

BEACHES & PARKS

SUNSET BEACH
⊠*Kamehameha Highway*

As far as surfing goes, this is the place! I think the best way to do Sunset is by starting from **Ehukai Beach Park** (off Kamehameha Highway about seven miles northeast of Haleiwa). From here you can go left to the "Banzai Pipeline," where crushing waves build along a shallow coral reef to create tube-like formations. To the right lies "Sunset," with equally spectacular surfing waves. Throughout the area the swimming is fair in summer; however, in winter it is extremely dangerous. From September to April, high waves and strong currents prevail. Be careful! Game fish caught around Sunset include *papio*, *menpachi* and *ulua*. Facilities at Ehukai Beach Park include picnic areas, restrooms and showers. Snorkeling here is poor.

PUPUKEA BEACH PARK _____
⊠*Kamehameha Highway at Pupukea Road*

Some of the island's best snorkeling is at this marine reserve on Kamehameha Highway six miles northeast of

Haleiwa. This 80-acre park, fringed by rocky shoreline, divides into several sections. Foremost is "Shark's Cove," located on the north side of the fire station, which contains spectacular tidepools. Underwater caves draw divers (experienced only—there have been a number of drownings in these deep and maze-like caverns).

WAIMEA BAY BEACH PARK
✉Kamehameha Highway (Route 83) about five miles northeast of Haleiwa

If Sunset is *one* of the most famous surfing spots in the world, Waimea is *the* most famous. The biggest surfable waves in the world (40 feet in winter!) roll into this pretty blue bay. There's a wide white-sand beach and a pleasant park with a tree-studded lawn. It's a marvelous place for picnicking and sunbathing. During the winter crowds often line the beach watching top-notch surfers challenge the curl; in summer the sea is flat and safe for swimming; you can also bodysurf in the shorebreak and snorkel when the bay is calm. *Papio, menpachi* and *ulua* are common catches. Facilities include a picnic area, restrooms, showers and a lifeguard.

HALEIWA BEACH PARK
✉Kamehameha Highway (Route 83), Haleiwa

This is an excellent refuge from the North Shore's pounding surf. Set in Waialua Bay, the beach is safe for swimming almost all year. You can snorkel, although it's only fair. Surfing in not possible here but "Haleiwa" breaks are located across Waialua Bay at Alii Beach Park. Facilities include a picnic area, restrooms, showers, a ball field, a basketball court and a playground. The primary catches at Haleiwa are *papio, menpachi* and *ulua*.

HALEIWA ALII BEACH PARK
✉Kamehameha Highway (Route 83), Haleiwa ☎808-637-5051
✆808-637-5052

Across from Haleiwa Beach Park, this is where you go to surf. Swells can top 20 feet here, which is why it's the site of several surfing and bodyboarding tournaments—you can watch the pros do things that seem to defy gravity. If you've come on one of the few days that surfing is not ideal, or if you're a beginner, bring your boogieboard and join the kids on the more manageable waves. If you're visiting in winter, you may be in luck: lifeguards sometimes give free surfing lessons in the morning (it's a good idea to reserve a spot ahead of time; head for the lifeguard tower to sign up). Facilities include a picnic area, restrooms and year-round lifeguards.

KAIAKA RECREATION AREA
✉Haleiwa Road just outside Haleiwa

The setting at this peninsular park is beautiful. There's a secluded area with a tree-shaded lawn and a short strip of sandy beach. A rocky shoreline borders most of the park, so it's more for picnics than water sports. You *can* swim and snorkel but there's a rocky bottom. Fishing is good for *papio*, *menpachi* and *ulua*. The facilities here include a picnic area, showers and restrooms.

▲ Permitted; a county permit is required.

MOKULEIA BEACH PARK AND MOKULEIA BEACH

✉ *On Farrington Highway (Route 930) about seven miles west of Haleiwa. To the west of the park, this beach stretches for miles along a secluded coast. You can hike down the beach or reach its hidden realms by driving farther west along Farrington Highway (Route 930), then turning off onto any of the numerous dirt side roads.*

The 12-acre park contains a sandy beach and large unshaded lawn. An exposed coral reef detracts from the swimming, but on either side of the park lie beaches with sandy ocean bottoms. If you do swim, exercise caution, especially in the winter months; there's no lifeguard. There's good snorkeling and in winter the surf breaks up to ten feet near Dillingham Airfield. Anglers try for *papio*, *menpachi* and *ulua*. Watch for skydivers, who often use the shoreline for their beach landings. Whatever your activity of choice, you'll have to contend with the noise of small planes from nearby Dillingham Airfield. The park is also an excellent starting point for exploring the unpopulated sections of Mokuleia Beach. Facilities include picnic areas, restrooms and showers.

▲ Tent and trailer camping are allowed with a county permit. Unofficial camping along the undeveloped beachfront is common.

MOKULEIA ARMY BEACH
✉ *Route 930 near the Dillingham Airfield*

This is the widest stretch of sand along the Mokuleia shoreline, and probably the most untamed. Once maintained by the Army for the exclusive use of their personnel, it's now open to the public but has no facilities. The high surf in winter poses no challenge to natives, but surfing really isn't recommended; there have been fatalities here. The treacherous waters mean that you'll pretty much have the spot to yourself. Most visitors are locals with a strong sense of loyalty to this largely untouristed spot.

CENTRAL OAHU

From Haleiwa south to Wahiawa you can take Route 803, Kaukoahuna Road, a pretty thoroughfare with excellent views of the Waianaes, or follow Route 99, the Kamehameha Highway, which passes through verdant pineapple fields.

SIGHTS

DOLE PINEAPPLE PLANTATION ✉ *64-1550 Kamehameha Highway, Wahiawa* ☎ *808-621-8408, 800-697-9100* 📠 *808-621-1926* ⌨ *www.dole-plantation.com, sales@*

dole-plantation.com The plantation, often crowded with tourists, sells (who would have guessed?) pineapple products. They offer a self-guided tour, a train ride through the plantation and the World's Largest Maze, a 1.7-mile labyrinth made from more than 11,000 Hawaiian plants that covers two acres. Admission for maze and train ride.

THE PINEAPPLE VARIETY GARDEN *Kamehameha Highway and Kamananui Road, Wahiawa* A plot of land on the highway has been planted with a variety of pineapples, once a major agricultural staple of the island. Nowadays, most pineapples are grown elsewhere so this really is a garden museum.

KUKANILOHO

⌂*Follow the dirt road across from Whitmore Avenue just north of Wahiawa.* The east fork of Route 99 becomes Route 80, which passes near a cluster of sacred stones marking the place where Hawaiian royalty gave birth accompanied by chants, drums and offerings. Studded with eucalyptus trees, this spot has held an important place in Hawaiian mythology and religion for centuries.

HIDDEN LISTINGS

WAHIAWA BOTANICAL GARDENS
PAGE 146
Beautiful colors and fragrances—worth the stop

MAKUA CAVE
PAGE 151
Lava cavern large enough for exploring and snorkeling near Yokohama Bay's turquoise waters

DA POKEMAN FISH MARKET
PAGE 147
Great spot for the raw fish delicacy known as *poke*—cooked fresh-fish specials also winners

HAWAIIAN ELECTRIC BEACH PARK
PAGE 153
White-sand beach featuring "Tracks"—an exciting and challenging surf spot for serious wave riders

KOLEKOLE PASS For a scenic and historic detour from Route 80, follow Route 80 until it links with Route 99. Take Route 99 west, pull up to the sentry station at Schofield Barracks and ask directions to the pass. On that "day of infamy," December 7, 1941, Japanese bombers buzzed through this notch in the Waianae Range. You'll be directed through Schofield up into the Waianaes. When you reach Kolekole Pass, there's another sentry gate. Ask the guard to let you continue a short distance farther to the observation point. From here the Waianaes fall away precipitously to a plain that rolls gently to the sea. There's an astonishing view of Oahu's west coast. If you are denied permission to pass the sentry point, then take the footpath that begins just before the gate, leading up the hill. From near the cross at the top, you will have a partial view of both the Waianaes' western face and the central plateau region.

SCHOFIELD BARRACKS Originally established in 1909 to defend the northern approach to Pearl Harbor, today the barracks are a thriving, self-contained Army community, and one of the largest Army posts outside the continental U.S. Not to mention the fact that this was the location for *From Here to Eternity*, starring Burt Lancaster, Deborah Kerr and Frank Sinatra.

TROPIC LIGHTNING MUSEUM ✉Building 361, Waianae Avenue ✆808-655-0438 🖷808-655-8301, linda.hee@schofield.army.mil The interesting history of the barracks and the 25th Infantry is explained through exhibits and photos at this army building. Tours are available by reservation. Closed Sunday and Monday.

WAHIAWA BOTANICAL GARDENS

✉1396 California Avenue, Wahiawa phone/fax 808-621-7321 🖳www.co.honolulu.hi.us/parks/hbg Spreading across 27 acres, you'll find a handsome retreat studded with tropical vegetation. Plants include orchids, ferns, cacti and bromeliads, as well as Heliconias, palms and gingers that thrive in a cool, moist climate. There are also plants from Africa and Australia, Asian camphor trees and gum trees from New Guinea. A walk through the gardens is a feast for the senses, with fragrant flowers and spices filling the air and colors as vivid as any you've seen before. The garden specializes in introduced and native rainforest plants. Guided tours are available by appointment.

Route H-2 provides the fastest means back to Honolulu; the most interesting course is along Route 750, Kunia Road, which skirts the Waianaes, passing sugar cane fields and stands of pine.

PLANTATION VILLAGE

✉94-695 Waipahu Street, Waipahu ✆808-677-0110 🖷808-676-6727 Along the way back to Honolulu you can take in this partially re-created and partially restored village that spreads across three acres of Waipahu Cultural Park in Waipahu. Comprised of over two dozen buildings, it includes a Japanese Shinto shrine, a company store and a Chinese Society building. Hawaii's many ethnic groups are represented in the houses, which span several architectural periods of the 19th and 20th centuries. Together they provide visitors with a window into traditional life on a plantation. Closed Sunday. Admission.

HAWAII OKINAWA CENTER

✉94-587 Ukee Street, Waipahu ☎808-676-5400 A small center in the town of Waipahu showcases the life and times of Okinawan immigrants to the islands. A gallery features historical items from the sugar era, including a grinder used to make tofu and a kitchen crock distiller for moonshine. You'll also find traditional crafts and a photo display. Closed Sunday.

From Waipahu, Honolulu is about 15 miles east along Route H-1, or you can take Route 750 south to Ewa.

DINING

DA POKEMAN FISH MARKET

$ SEAFOOD ✉36 North Kamehameha Highway, Wahiawa ☎808-622-4629
If you're hankering for fresh fish, including the raw fish delicacy known as *poke*, stop here. The food is simple, cheap, local-style and good, with an emphasis on bentos and plate lunches built around such entrées as teriyaki chicken and beef, pork cutlet and fried chicken. The daily fresh-fish specials are always a winner.

SEOUL INN

$ KOREAN ✉410 California Avenue, Wahiawa ☎808-621-9090
You can order a range of excellent Korean entrées here, including *kalbi* beef, fish *jun* and a number of hot and cold one-dish meals that combine fish, chicken, meat or tofu and abundant fresh vegetables. The meat *jun* is recommended, and the kim chee is hot and spicy; bring your own beer to cut the heat. The casual, dark dining room borders on gloomy, but you can always order take out if you don't warm to the ambience.

SUNNYSIDE

$ AMERICAN ✉1017 Kilani Avenue, Wahiawa ☎808-621-7188
This eatery in Wahiawa is the choice for hearty homestyle meals and delicious baked goods made on the premises. The menu features waffles, pancakes and omelettes, as well as chicken cutlets, hamburgers, teriyaki mahimahi and liver and onions at $5 or less. The fruit and cream pies are legendary and whole pies must be reserved; the chocolate pudding pie should not be missed. Closed Sunday.

OAHU CENTRAL OAHU DINING

ELENA'S HOME OF FINEST
FILIPINO FOODS

$ FILIPINO ✉4-866 Moloalo Street, Waipahu ☎808-676-8005
In Waipahu, Elena's is certainly worth a stop if you're craving a
meal that's authentic, tasty and low-priced. You can start at 6 a.m.
with their trademark omelette filled with pungent pork *adobo*, or
try an early dinner of *pancit* noodles, *sari sari*, roast pig or other
dishes that have the usual Filipino emphasis on fresh vegetables,
pork and distinctive flavor. The homey, simple decor is as down to
earth as the food. Breakfast, lunch and dinner are served.

NANCY'S KITCHEN
$ LOCAL-STYLE ✉Gentry Waipio Shopping Center, 94-1040 Waipio Uka Street,
Waipahu ☎808-676-3438 Check out this delightful spot for delicious local-style breakfasts and authentic Hawaiian fare. A homey eatery, this
is a good choice for a comfortable, low-priced meal away from the
tourist track.

SHOPPING

MILILANI FARMER'S MARKET ✉Mililani High School, 95-1200 Meheula
Parkway, Mililani If you are in the area, check out this farmer's market,
open from 8 a.m. to noon on Sundays.

NIGHTLIFE

NANCY'S KITCHEN ✉Gentry Waipio Shopping Center, 94-1040 Waipio Uka
Street, Waipahu ☎808-676-3438 By day, this low-price local eatery is known
for filling breakfasts and authentic Hawaiian fare. At night it does double duty as a casual sports bar with a family-style ambience.

LEEWARD COAST

Out along the west coast of Oahu, less than 30 miles from the sands of
Waikiki, Hawaiian culture is making a last stand. Here on the tableland
that separates the Waianae Range from the ocean, the old ways still prevail. Unlike the cool rainforests of the Windward Coast or the rain-
spattered area around Honolulu, this is a region of stark beauty, resembling the American Southwest, with rocky crags and cactus-studded
hills. Farther north, the spartan scenery gives way to wide vistas of massive mountains sloping gracefully to the sea.

Hawaiian and Samoan farmers tend small fields and raise chickens.
Side roads off the main highway pass dusty houses and sunblasted
churches before turning into dirt tracks that keep Hawaiian and
Samoan farmers tend small fields and raise chickens. Side roads off the
mainhighway pass dusty houses and sunblasted churches before turning into dirt tracks that keep climbing past truck farms and old home-

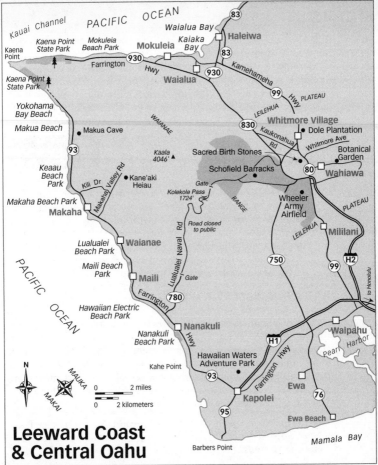

Leeward Coast & Central Oahu

steads. For entertainment, there are birthday luaus, cockfights and slack-key guitar playing.

The Leeward Coast has become the keeper of the old ways, and residents jealously guard the customs and traditions that they see slipping away in the rest of the state. Although there have been reports of outsiders being hassled by local residents, the reality, in fact, is usually the reverse. Here, far from the madding crowds of tourists and tourist businesses, the true spirit of aloha is alive and well. But who knows for how long?

"Second City," a major development built near the town of Ewa, has added thousands of houses to the Central Oahu area, which has led to a dramatic increase in commuter traffic. And in the southwest corner of the island the ultra-modern JW Marriott Ihilani Resort & Spa in the Ko Olina area is only the beginning of the inevitable encroachment along this side of the island.

EWA From Honolulu you can visit the Leeward Coast region by traveling west on Route H-1 or Route 90. If you want to tour what once was a prime sugar-growing area, take Route 90 past Pearl Harbor, then turn left on Fort Weaver Road (Route 760). This country lane leads to the plantation town of Ewa. With its old sugar mill and trim houses, Ewa is an enchanting throwback to the days when sugar was king. This town is a slow, simple place, perfect for wandering and exploring.

HAWAIIAN RAILWAY

✉91-1001 Renton Road, Ewa ☎808-681-5461 ☎808-681-4860 ☐www.hawaiianrailway.com, info@hawaiianrailway.com The transportation of late-19th- to early-20th-century Oahu centered around the railroad. You can experience the past firsthand on a ride aboard this historical train, once owned by the defunct Oahu Railway and Land Company. The ride covers six miles (of the existing ten) and is fully narrated. There are historical locomotives on display, and you can picnic on the grounds. Open Sunday only. Admission.

HAWAIIAN WATERS ADVENTURE PARK
✉400 Farrington Highway, Kapolei ☎808-674-9283 ☐www.hawaiianwaters.com, questions@hawaiianwaters.com Near Oahu's southwest corner, Routes H-1 and 90 converge to become the Farrington Highway (Route 93). From here, follow the signs to Hawaiian Waters, perfect for those who are afraid of getting a little sand in their pants but love to ride waves or splash in the water. There are inner-tube slides, a 60-foot water slide, artificial waves and much more, spread over 25 acres. For less wet fun, mini-golf is also available. Closed Tuesday and Wednesday. A hefty admission.

The first beach you come to along the Leeward Coast is Barbers Point. It's not worth a detour. However, continue along Route 93 and you'll come upon Oahu's latest development.

KO OLINA RESORT

✉92-1480 Aliinui Drive You might want to stop here and take a look at the scenery: Seven lagoons surrounded by silky sand dot this multifaceted complex, that includes a hotel, golf course and marina. It's a beautiful and little visited spot. It does get windy, so hold on to your hat.

HAWAIIAN ELECTRIC BEACH PARK Farrington Highway continues along the coast to Kahe Point. The ugly power plant you see is a good landmark to find Hawaiian Electric Beach Park and a top surfing spot by the name of "Tracks." Keep going along Route 93 and you'll pass the towns of Nanikuli, Maili and Waianae.

WAIANAE If you turn up Mailiilii Street in Waianae, you will pass placid Hawaiian homesteads and farmlands. This side road also provides sweeping views of the Waianae Range. On the northern side of town is Waianae Harbor, a small port hosting small fishing vessels as well as spiffy yachts.

MAKAHA Along Farrington Highway is Makaha Beach, one of Hawaii's most famous surfing spots, and the site of an annual international surfing championship. It's also a great place for shell hunting. The **Makaha Valley**, extending from the ocean up into the Waianae Mountains, is home to the **Kaneaki Heiau**, (off Manunaolu Street; phone/fax 808-695-8174), a 15th-century temple dedicated to the god Lono. Closed Monday and when raining or windy.

MAKUA CAVE

The highway continues along the coastline past several mostly deserted beaches and parks. Across from Kaena Point State Park you'll come upon Makua Cave, a lava cavern large enough for exploring and snorkeling. Beyond that, where the paved road turns to dirt, lies Yokohama Bay, with its curving sand beach and inviting turquoise waters.

KAENA POINT

The road past Yokohama is partially passable by auto, but it's very rough. If you want to explore this scenic point from this side of the island, you'll have to hike. It's about two miles to the northwest corner of Oahu, past tidepools teeming with marine life. On a clear day you can see Kauai from this point. (Don't leave valuables in your car in this area.)

LODGING

JW MARRIOTT IHILANI RESORT & SPA
$$$$ 387 ROOMS   ✉92-1001 Olani Street, Kapolei   ☎808-679-0079, 800-626-4446
📠808-679-0295   🖱www.ihilani.com

To get away from everything, you'll want to dig deep into your pockets for a short stay here. Backed by the Waianaes and facing a curved expanse of ocean, this hideaway is part of the 640-acre Ko Olina Resort. There's a golf course, six tennis courts, four restaurants and a spa. More important, you'll find a string of four lagoons, each with a crescent beach and a cluster of islets that protects the mouth of the lagoon.

CONDOS

MAKAHA SHORES
88 UNITS   ✉84-265 Farrington Highway, Makaha   ☎ 808-696-7121   📠808-696-7121
🖱www.makahashores.com, inquiries@makahashores.com

This resort condo complex overlooks pretty Makaha Beach Park, one of Hawaii's top surfing beaches. There are studios and one- and two-bedroom units, each individually decorated by their owners. The minimum stay is one week. Rates start at $525.

MAKAHA VALLEY TOWERS

586 UNITS   ✉ *End of Kili Drive, Makaha* ✆ *808-695-9568*

A highrise set along the slopes of Makaha Valley, units here range from studios to two-bedrooms, with nightly, weekly and monthly stays available. Rates vary and accommodations are handled by local realtors. One week studios $600, suite (monthly) $2600.

DINING

JW MARRIOTT IHILANI RESORT & SPA

$$–$$$$ INTERNATIONAL   ✉ *92-1001 Olani Street, Kapolei* ✆ *808-679-0079*
✆ *808-679-0800*

By way of resort restaurants, JW Marriott has several deluxe- and ultra-deluxe-priced dining rooms. Foremost is **Azul** (dinner only; brunch on Sunday), where the pork chops come with orange sauce, the lobster is served in *pistou* and the ideas are Mediterranean. **Ushiotei** (dinner only; closed Tuesday and Wednesday) is the ultimate in Japanese cuisine. And **Naupaka**, a poolside terrace serving cross-cultural dishes for breakfast, lunch and dinner, is the Ihilani's answer to informality and easy elegance. Reservations are recommended.

CATHAY INN CHOP SUEY

$–$$ CHINESE   ✉ *86-088 Farrington Highway, Waianae* ✆ *808-696-9477*

A welcome restaurant on this sparsely populated strip of Waianae shoreline, this is a good choice for Chinese food.

HANNARA RESTAURANT

$ KOREAN/HAWAIIAN   ✉ *86-078 Farrington Highway, Waianae*
✆ *808-696-6137*

Offering Korean and Hawaiian cuisines, this simple, often-crowded eatery is consistently good. Breakfast and lunch daily.

L & L DRIVE-INN

$ PLATE LUNCHES   ✉ *85-080 Waianae Valley Road, Waianae*
✆ *808-696-7989* ✆ *808-696-8803*

When I'm in Waianae, I have to stop at L & L, which serves breakfast, lunch and dinner. The breakfast combo includes eggs, Portuguese sausage, Spam and rice. Among the hearty plate lunches offered the rest of the day are breaded pork chop with hamburger steak and shrimp curry with chicken *katsu*.

NIGHTLIFE

JW MARRIOTT IHILANI RESORT & SPA   ✉ *92-1001 Olani Street, Kapolei* ✆ *808-679-0079* **Naupaka Terrace** features nightly live entertainment. The Ihilani is also home to the **Hokulea**, a cozy lounge perfect for a quiet rendezvous. Hours vary with season.

NANAKULI BEACH PARK

✉ 89-269 Farrington Highway (Route 93) about five miles south of Waianae

☎ 808-668-1137

This park is so large that a housing tract divides it into two parts. The main section features a white-sand beach, *kiawe*-studded camping area and a recreation complex. It's simply a park with everything, unfortunately including weekend crowds. Needless to say, the swimming is good; lifeguard on duty. There are winter breaks with right and left slides. Fishing is sparse, but there's still *papio*, *ulua*, *moano* and *menpachi*. Facilities include restrooms, showers, a ball field, a basketball court and a volleyball court.

▲ Tent and trailer camping are allowed, but a county permit is required.

HAWAIIAN ELECTRIC BEACH PARK

✉ Located on Farrington Highway (Route 93) about seven miles south of Waianae

Once privately owned, this park across the highway from a monstrous power plant is now run by the county. There's a rolling lawn with palm and *kiawe* trees, plus a white-sand beach and coral reef. You can swim, snorkel, surf year-round and fish for *papio*, *ulua*, *moano* and *menpachi*. If you're a proficient surfer, you'll probably head for "Tracks," a top surfing break. The drawbacks are the lack of facilities (there are restrooms and a picnic area) and the park's proximity to the electric company.

MAILI BEACH PARK

✉ 87-021 Farrington Highway (Route 93) in Maili a few miles south of Waianae

A long winding stretch of white sand is the high point of this otherwise unimpressive facility. The swimming is good in the summer; reef snorkeling is only fair. Be aware of the reef's steep dropoff. There are winter surf breaks with a right slide. The principal game fish caught here are *papio*, *ulua*, *menpachi* and *moano*. The park contains shade trees and a spotty lawn. There are picnic tables, restrooms and showers.

▲ Permitted weekends only with a county permit. Tent camping, with a county permit, is allowed in the summer at nearby Lualualei Beach Park.

MAKAHA BEACH PARK

✉ 84-369 Farrington Highway (Route 93) in Makaha, two miles north of Waianae

Some of the finest surfing in the world takes place right offshore here. This is the site of international competitions, drawing championship surfers from all across the Pacific. For more relaxed sports, there's a white-sand beach to sunbathe on and some good places to skindive. Swimming and snorkeling are both good when the sea is calm; otherwise, exercise extreme caution. Check with a lifeguard about water conditions. Anglers try for *papio*, *ulua*, *moano* and *menpachi*. The precipitous Waianae Mountains loom behind the park. There are picnic tables, restrooms and showers.

KEAAU BEACH PARK

✉ 83-431 Farrington Highway (Route 93) about five miles north of Waianae

Except for the absence of a sandy beach, this is the prettiest park on the west coast. It's a long, narrow grassy plot spotted with trees and backdropped by the Waianaes. Sunsets are spectacular here, and on a clear day you can see all the way to Kauai. There's a sandy beach just west of the park. Unfortunately, a coral reef rises right to the water's edge, making entry into the water difficult. But once you're in there's great snorkeling, swimming and bodysurfing. In summer there are good surf breaks with a left slide. People fish for *papio*, *ulua*, *moano* and *menpachi*. There are picnic areas, restrooms and showers.

▲ Tent and trailer allowed. County permit required.

KAENA POINT STATE PARK (YOKOHAMA BAY)

✉ At the end of the paved section of Farrington Highway (Route 93), about nine miles north of the town of Waianae

This curving stretch of white sand is the last beach along Oahu's northwest coast. With the Waianae Range in the background and coral reefs offshore, it's a particularly lovely spot. Though officially a state park, the area is largely undeveloped. You can walk from Yokohama Bay past miles of tidepools to Oahu's northwest corner at Kaena Point, a great place to spot porpoises, is the legendary home of Nanue the Shark Man. Yokohama Bay is a prime region for beach lovers and explorers both. When the sea is calm the swimming is good and the snorkeling is excellent but exercise extreme caution if the surf is up. There are summer breaks up to 15 feet over a shallow reef (left slide). Fish caught in this area include *papio*, *ulua*, *moano* and *menpachi*. No facilities.

OUTDOOR ADVENTURES

CAMPING

Along with its traffic and crowds, Oahu has numerous parks. Unfortunately, these disparate elements overlap, and you may sometimes find you've escaped from Honolulu's urban jungle and landed in a swamp of weekend beachgoers. So it's best to plan outdoor adventures far in advance and to schedule them for weekdays when possible.

Currently, camping is allowed at 15 beach parks operated by the City and County of Honolulu. Seven of these parks are on the island's windward side and five on the leeward side. Another two are on the North Shore. Bellows Field Beach Park at Waimanalo on the Windward Coast, only allows camping at its 50 campsites on the weekends. Swanzy Beach Park at Kaaawa, Maili and Kualoa are also weekend-only campgrounds (Kualoa is closed in summer). The others permit tent camping every night except Wednesday and Thursday. There are no trailer hookups.

COUNTY PARKS ✉*Honolulu Municipal Building, 650 South King Street, ground floor, Honolulu, HI 96813* ✆*808-523-4527* Permits are also available at any of the "satellite city halls" around the island. Camping at county parks requires a permit. The free permits can be obtained from the Department of Parks and Recreation.

STATE PARKS ✉*1151 Punchbowl Street, Room 310, Honolulu, HI 96813* ✆*808-587-0300* You can also write in advance for permits State parks allow camping for up to five days, depending on the park. It's first-come, first-served on the first day, but after that visitors may reserve spaces. The Division of State Parks issues the free permits Monday through Friday.

There are four state parks on Oahu with camping facilities. Malaekahana State Recreation Area on the Windward Coast between Laie and Kahuku offers both tent camping and housekeeping cabins. Also on the Windward Coast, Oahu's largest state park **Kahana Valley State Park**, located between Kaaawa and Punaluu, has campsites. Tent camping is available at **Sand Island State Recreation Area** on Sand Island in Honolulu, as well as at **Keaiwa Heiau State Recreation Area** in the hills above Honolulu.

Remember when planning your trip, rainfall is heaviest on the Windward Coast, a little lighter on the North Shore and lightest of all on the Leeward Coast.

OMAR THE TENT MAN ✉*94-158 Leoole Street, Waipahu* ✆*808-677-8785* In central Oahu, Omar sells camping gear. Closed Sunday.

HOOMALUHIA BOTANICAL GARDEN

✉*45-680 Luluku Road, Kaneohe* ✆*808-233-7323*
This garden allows camping on the grounds Friday through Sunday. There is no fee, but a permit is required and no hookups are available. Gates lock at 4 p.m.—no in-and-out privileges afterward.

FISHING

From deep-sea fishing to trolling for freshwater bass, Oahu offers challenges to suit any angler. You can try game fishing out in the

Pacific, head down to the beach for surf-casting or try one of the island's popular lakes.

Most of the island's fishing fleet dock at Kewalo Basin (Fisherman's Wharf) on Ala Moana Drive between Waikiki and downtown Honolulu.

HAWAII FISHING ADVENTURES AND CHARTERS ✉*575 Cooke Street A315* ✆*808-396-2607, 877-388-1376* ✍*www.sportfishhawaii.com* This outfitter books deep-sea fishing trips that go out for blue marlin, yellowfin tuna and mahimahi. Charters leave from Kewalo Basin, and reservations are required (all equipment provided).

SPORT FISHING ✆*808-396-4401* ✍*www.waikikifishing.com* A great company to consider is this one, which runs the *Pacific Blue* and *Ilima* out of Kewalo Basin. Equipment provided.

MAGGIE JOE SPORTFISHING ✆*808-591-8888, 877-806-3474* ✍*www.fish-hawaii.com* Offering quarter-, half- or full-day trips, Maggie Joe's interisland company has four boats.

SNORKELING & SCUBA DIVING

One of the great myths about Oahu is that you need to go far off the beaten track to discover its secret treasures. The fact is that within half an hour of Waikiki are excellent snorkeling and diving opportunities. Only an hour away are excellent reefs easily reached by dive boats. From popular Hanauma Bay, just a short ride from the heart of Honolulu, to Kaena Point on the Leeward Coast, there are snorkeling and diving opportunities for beginners and certified pros alike. Or you can snorkel at Makua Beach, located between Makaha and Yokohama Bay on the Leeward Coast, and swim with the dolphins. Because conditions vary, I strongly recommend seeking instruction and advice from local diving experts before setting out.

Waikiki
WAIKIKI DIVING CENTER ✉*424 Nahua Street, Honolulu* ✆*808-922-2121* ✍*www.waikikidiving.com* This dive center takes divers to different sites around Oahu, depending on the time of year and the weather. The company offers two- to three-day PADI and NAUI courses and sells, rents and repairs diving equipment. It will also take nondivers out on an inexpensive introductory scuba charter so they can see what the sport is all about.

Downtown Honolulu
SEE IN SEA ✉*670 Auahi Street* ✆*808-528-2311, 866-528-2311* ✍*www.seein sea.com* Excursions with this company visit the *Mahi* shipwreck, Fantasy Reef, Turtles Canyon, Airplanes and Makaha Caverns, to name a few. Rentals and instruction are also available.

Southeast Oahu
ALOHA DIVE SHOP ✉*Hawaii Kai Shopping Center, 377 Keahole Street, Hawaii Kai* ✆*808-395-5922* ✍*www.hawaiiaweb.com/html/aloha_dive_shop.htm* This shop runs day trips for certified divers and lesson packages for students at Maunalua Bay in the southeast corner of the island.

CAPTAIN BRUCE ✉*Waianae Boat Harbor* ☎*808-373-3590, 800-535-2487* ✇*www.captainbruce.com* Featuring trips all around the island, including the *Mahi* shipwreck and Makaha Caverns, this dive company is a great option. Waikiki pick-up is available.

Windward Coast
AARON'S DIVE SHOP ✉*307 Hahani Street, Kailua* ☎*808-262-2333, 888-847-2822* ✇*www.hawaii-scuba.com* Choose between beach and boat dives, as well as special night trips at Aaron's.

North Shore
HALEIWA SURF CENTER ✉*Haleiwa Alii Beach Park, Haleiwa* ☎*808-637-5051* Depending on the season, the surf center teaches such sports as snorkeling, surfing, swimming, lifesaving and sailing. This county agency is also an excellent source of information on the island's water sports and facilities.

SURF N' SEA ✉*62-595 Kamehameha Highway, Haleiwa* ☎*808-637-9887* ✇*www.surfnsea.com* Specializing in small groups, this company offers half-day beach and boat dives on the North Shore and Leeward Coast including the *Mahi* shipwreck.

SNUBA

Somewhere between snorkeling and scuba diving is Snuba, created for those who would like to take snorkeling a step further but may not be quite ready for scuba diving. It's a shallow-water dive system that allows underwater breathing. Basically this is how it works. Swimmers wear a breathing device (the same one used in scuba diving) that is connected to a built-in scuba tank that floats on a raft. They also wear a weight belt, mask and fins. The air comes through a 20-foot tube connected to the raft, which follows the swimmer. Groups of six participants are taken out with a guide. They can dive up to 20 feet.

BREEZE HAWAII ✉*3014 Kaimuki Avenue* ☎*808-735-1857* ✇*www.breezehawaii.com* This group offers Snuba tours at Hanauma Bay. Common sightings include an array of fish, eels, dolphins and turtles.

SURFING, WINDSURFING & KITESURFING

Surfing, a sport pioneered centuries ago by Hawaiian royalty, is synonymous with Oahu. Stars bring their boards from all over the world to join international competitions that take advantage of ideal surf and wind conditions. From the 30-foot winter rollers on the North Shore to beginner lessons off Waikiki, this is beach boy and girl territory. Windsurfing is equally popular in areas like Kailua Bay and along the North Shore. Kitesurfing follows principles similar to paragliding, windsurfing and even snowboarding.

If you plan to surf Oahu (or any of the other Hawaiian islands), check out www.globalsurfers.com. This online surf community maintained by surfers offers valuable information on surf spots on Oahu—from beginner breaks like Canoes, Point Panics and Secret, to intermediate breaks like "Monster Mush," "Pyramid Rock" and "Hauula Bowls," to expert-only breaks like "Off-the-Wall," "Pinballs" and "Pipeline." Not only do they inform you about the break, the type of wave, and the length of the ride, they give you the rap on what to wear (board shorts or wet suits), the crowd level, the best board to use, and the ever-important "localism" of the locale. Remember when surfing in Hawaii, give the locals proper respect.

Waikiki

PRIME TIME SPORTS ⊠*Kalia Road* ☎*808-949-8952* For everything "on the water, in the water and under the water" check out Prime Time Sports near Fort DeRussy Beach. They offer beach accessories, equipment sales and rentals, lessons and plenty of friendly advice. Private and group surfing lessons have a "stand and surf" guarantee.

THE ALOHA BEACH SERVICE ☎*808-922-3111* The Aloha Beach Service, in front of the Sheraton Moana Surfrider Hotel, offers lessons and rents long boards.

Greater Honolulu

LOCAL MOTION ⊠*1958 Kalakaua Avenue* ☎*808-979-7873* Near downtown, go to Local Motion for surfboard rentals. Check out their selection of beachwear, boards and equipment for sale.

DOWNING HAWAII ⊠*3021 Waialae Avenue* ☎*808-737-9696* In the Diamond Head area, this shop rents boards. Closed Sunday.

Windward Coast

KAILUA SAILBOARD AND KAYAK COMPANY ⊠*130 Kailua Road, Kailua* ☎*808-262-2555* ⏀*www.kailuasailboards.com, info@kailuasailboards.com* This adventure company will teach you the tricks of the trade or help you brush up on your technique. You can also rent sailboards, boogieboards, long boards, kayaks, snorkeling and kitesurfing equipment here.

NAISH HAWAII ⊠*155-A Hamakua Drive, Kailua* ☎*808-261-6067* ⏀*www.naish .com* In the same area as Kailua Sailboards, Naish offers lessons and rentals. This company manufactures its own boards and also operates a shop filled with the latest in sailboarding and kitesurfing apparel and accessories, as well as long boards.

North Shore

HALEIWA SURF CENTER ⊠*Haleiwa Alii Beach Park, Haleiwa* ☎*808-637-5051* A resource for both the participatory and spectator aspects of surfing and windsurfing is found here. Surf lessons normally run September to April.

SURF N' SEA HALEIWA ⊠*62-595 Kamehameha Highway, Haleiwa* ☎*808-637-9887* ⏀*www.surfnsea.com* Surfing lessons and rentals are also available at this facility. Lessons last two to three hours; price includes all gear.

One of the best ways to enjoy Oahu is aboard a sailboat. From brief cruises off Honolulu to a day-long charter along the North Shore, this is the perfect antidote to the tourist crowds. It's also surprisingly affordable.

HAWAII YACHTS ✆800-908-5250 ✐www.hawaiiyachts.com If you're eager to charter your own yacht, contact this company, which charters all sizes of vessels ranging from fishing boats to luxury yachts.

HONOLULU SAILING COMPANY ✉47-335 Lulani Street, Honolulu ✆808-239-3900, 800-829-0114 ✐www.honsail.com Ever dream of sailing off into the sunset, wind blowing in your hair? Snorkeling trips, swimming in the ocean off Diamond Head, a sunset cruise or a whale-watching venture can all be arranged here. You can even get married at sea by your licensed and uniformed captain. This personable outfit will sail to meet your needs.

ABOVE HEAVEN'S GATE ✉41-1010 Laumilo Street, Waimanalo Bay ✆808-259-5900, 800-800-2933 ✐www.hawaiiweddings.com/sailing Operating charter group cruises to the Diamond Head reef area, this group offers rides aboard a teakwood pirate ship. You can also take a guided Hobie-cat tour off the Windward Coast to undiscovered islands most tourists miss, such as the original location of *Gilligan's Island* or the site where *Jurassic Park* was filmed (by appointment only). Along the way you'll enjoy Waimanalo, Kaneohe, Lanikai and Kailua Bay. You can also learn how to sail this swift 16-foot craft.

KAYAKING

A sport well suited for Oahu, kayaking is an ideal way to explore the island's protected bays, islands and inland rivers. It seems that kayakers are popping up everywhere, particularly around the southeast coast of the island and up the Waimea River.

GO BANANAS ✉799 Kapahulu Avenue ✆808-737-9514 ✐www.gobananas kayaks.com To rent or purchase kayaks and equipment, or to sign up for lessons and tours, consider this shop just outside Waikiki.

KAILUA SAILBOARD AND KAYAK COMPANY ✉130 Kailua Road, Kailua ✆808-262-2555 On the Windward Coast, stop here for kayak rentals and lessons.

WAKEBOARDING & WATERSKIING

Snowboarders with the summertime blues gave rise to wakeboarding. If the thrill of waterskiing is a little *too* thrilling, wakeboarding may be the sport to try. A relatively easy-to-control board is pulled slowly (well, 20–35 m.p.h) behind a boat, while the rider skims the wake. The equipment is much easier to maneuver than waterskis, and when your skills are up to par, you can venture into the fancy stuff: jumps, backrolls, zip-zags.

Waterskiing is more physically demanding than wakeboarding, using every muscle in your body, requiring a higher speed and employing narrower, less agile skis.

HAWAII WATER SPORTS CENTER ✉*Koko Marina Shopping Center, 7192 Kalanianaole Highway, Hawaii Kai* ☎*808-395-3773* ✐*www.hawaiiansportscenter.com* Near Koko Head, this center offers instruction every day. Lessons are 20 minutes long. Reservations required.

SKYDIVING & HANG GLIDING

Both skydiving and hang gliding offer bird's-eye views of Oahu for those with daring.

BIRDSEYE VIEW OF OAHU ✉*328 Ilihau Street, Kailua* ☎*808-381-4296* Birdseye View of Oahu offers daily ultralight airplane and tandem hang-gliding instruction at Kaneohe Marine Base. Call the company, and they'll also give you information on hang gliding in the area.

SKYDIVE HAWAII ✉*68-760 Farrington Highway* ☎*808-637-9700* ✐*www.sky divehawaii.com* You can learn to skydive and participate in a tandem dive with this company at Dillingham Airfield on the North Shore.

PACIFIC INTERNATIONAL SKYDIVING CLUB ✉*68-760 Farrington Highway* ☎*808-637-7472* Another skydiving option at Dillingham Field is this operation.

JOGGING

Jogging is very big on Oahu. There are several popular spots, and though they are never quite deserted, the crowds rarely become unmanageable. Ala Moana Regional Park is a good area for a run; the paved road fronts the beach, and the cool ocean breezes are welcome. Kapiolani Park is another jogger's mecca. Ala Wai Canal is a less-recommended road; it's along a main drag and can get chaotic. Oahu also hosts endless races and marathons. For information on participation, pick up a free copy of *Hawaii Race Magazine*, available at most newsstands.

RIDING STABLES

It's not the Wild West, but Oahu is *paniolo* country. To explore its beaches, valleys and pasturelands, contact the following listings.

KUALOA RANCH HAWAII ✉*49-560 Kamehameha Highway, Kaaawa* ☎*808-237-8515* ✐*www.kualoa.com, activityinfo@kualoa.com* Located on the Windward Coast across from Chinaman's Hat, Kualoa Ranch leads one- and two-hour rides that provide startling views of the ocean and surrounding mountains. Guided rides for kids ages three through seven are available. They also offer many other activities including movie site tours, a jungle expedition and an ocean voyaging tour.

TURTLE BAY RESORT ☎808-293-8811 This resort on the North Shore has riding programs for the general public. They offer 45-minute guided tours. These, and a one-and-one-half-hour evening ride, all take place on the grounds of the hotel, with trails along the beach and through a lovely wooded area.

HAPPY TRAILS RANCH ✉59-231 Pupukea Road, Pupukea ☎808-638-7433 ⌨www.happytrailshawaii.com On the North Shore, this ranch conducts one-and-a-half and two-hour trail rides through a rainforest valley and pastureland. The ranch has peacocks, chickens, a wild boar and six species of ducks. Children will love this place, and they can ride if they are six years or older.

GOLF

Even before Tiger Woods, golf has been a very popular sport among visitors in Hawaii, and no other island has more golf courses than Oahu. With more than 30 to choose from, there's one to suit every level of play. And the scenery is spectacular.

Greater Honolulu
ALA WAI GOLF COURSE ✉404 Kapahulu Avenue ☎808-733-7387 For a round of golf in Honolulu, try Hawaii's first municipal course. The *Guinness Book of World Records* named it the busiest course in the world.

Southeast Oahu
HAWAII KAI GOLF COURSE ✉8902 Kalanianaole Highway ☎808-395-2358 ✆808-395-7726 ⌨www.hawaiikaigolf.com This is a popular spot with both tourists and *kamaaina* and features two 18-hole courses—one executive and one championship.

Windward Coast
WAIMANALO OLOMANA GOLF LINKS ✉41-1801 Kalanianaole Highway, Waimanalo ☎808-259-7926 ⌨www.olomanagolflinks.com A lush setting is offered at this 18-hole course.

BAY VIEW GOLF PARK ✉45-285 Kaneohe Bay Drive, Kaneohe ☎808-247-0451 Stop here for an inexpensive round of golf.

PALI GOLF COURSE ✉45-050 Kamehameha Highway, Kaneohe ☎808-266-7612 Located below the Nuuanu Pali Lookout, this course affords sweeping views of the rugged Koolaus and the windward coastline.

KAHUKU GOLF COURSE ✉56-501 Kamehameha Highway, Kahuku ☎808-293-5842 If you want to play a casual game, try this nine-hole course.

North Shore
THE TURTLE BAY GOLF ✉Kahuku ☎808-293-8574 The links at this resort was created around an existing 100-acre wetland preserve, which serves as home to several endangered Hawaiian birds. One of the two 18-hole courses was designed by Arnold Palmer.

Leeward Coast and Central Oahu

HAWAII COUNTRY CLUB ✉94-1211 Kunia Road, Wahiawa ☎808-622-1744 Set amid fields of sugarcane and pineapple along the Leilehua Plateau in the center of Oahu, this 18-hole, par-72 course is a bit rundown, but offers some challenging holes.

THE MILILANI GOLF CLUB ✉95-176 Kuahelani Avenue, Mililani ☎808-623-2254 Though not particularly demanding, this course provides lovely views of the Koolau and Waianae ranges.

TED MAKALENA GOLF COURSE ✉93-059 Waipio Point Access Road, Waipahu ☎808-675-6052 The flat Ted Makalena Golf Course is not well-maintained, but is still popular with local duffers.

KO OLINA GOLF CLUB ✉92-1220 Aliinui Drive, Kapolei ☎808-676-5309 ✐www.koolinagolf.com Golfers must drive their carts under a waterfall to get to the twelfth hole of this championship course. They will also enjoy the series of lakes, brooks and waterfalls that meanders through the 18-hole course.

MAKAHA GOLF CLUB ✉84-626 Makaha Valley Road, Makaha ☎808-695-9544 Especially beautiful is this course in the Makaha Valley, where sheer volcanic cliffs tower 1500 feet above lush greens, and golfers share the course with birds and peacocks.

TENNIS

Many Oahu resorts offer complete tennis facilities. But don't despair if your hotel lacks nets. There are dozens of public tennis courts in 47 locations around the island. Following is a partial listing.

COUNTY DEPARTMENT OF PARKS AND RECREATION ☎808-692-5561 ✐www.honolulu.gov/parks/programs/tennis Call the County Department of Parks and Recreation for more information on public courts.

Waikiki

KAPIOLANI PARK ✉2740 Kalakaua Avenue Four lighted courts.

DIAMOND HEAD TENNIS CENTER ✉3908 Paki Avenue Ten courts.

Greater Honolulu

ALA MOANA TENNIS CENTER ✉Ala Moana Regional Park, Ala Moana Boulevard Ten lighted courts.

KEEHI LAGOONS ✉Off the Nimitz Highway Twelve courts (four lighted).

MANOA VALLEY DISTRICT PARK ✉2721 Kaaipu Street Four lighted courts.

Windward Coast

KAILUA DISTRICT PARK ✉21 South Kainalu Drive, Kailua Eight lighted courts.

KANEOHE DISTRICT PARK ✉45-660 Keaahala Road, Kaneohe ☎808-266-7652 or 808-955-6676 x29 Six lighted courts.

North Shore
SUNSET BEACH NEIGHBORHOOD PARK ✉59-360 *Kamehameha Highway, Haleiwa* Two lighted courts.

Leeward Coast
WAIANAE DISTRICT PARK ✉85-601 *Farrington Highway, Waianae* Eight courts (two lighted).

BIKING

Oahu is blessed with excellent roads, well-paved and usually flat, and cursed with heavy traffic. About three-quarters of Hawaii's population lives here, and it sometimes seems like every person owns a car.

Honolulu can be a cyclist's nightmare, but outside the city the traffic is somewhat lighter. And Oahu drivers, accustomed to tourists driving mopeds, are relatively conscious of bicyclists. It's certainly possible to bike through Central Oahu. Kamehameha Highway is an option, although it is dotted with steep grades and sections that aren't too bike-friendly. Riders may cruise the Kalanianaole Highway, past Kapiolani Park and around Diamond Head to Hanauma Bay, pedal along the Waianae Coast or zip across the interior from Waialua to Pearl City. Other coastal rides cover the area between Haleiwa and Kahuku and the stretch between Waimanalo Beach and Kaaawa.

If you'd really like to get away from it all, try mountain biking. One of Oahu's most popular mountain bike trails is **Mauna Wili** on the windward side. It starts from the Pali lookout and goes all the way to Waimanalo. Just past Waimea Bay is the **Ke Ala Pupukea** bike path, which goes through Sunset Beach Park and Waimea Bay Beach Park. It also conveniently passes a supermarket.

Keep in mind that the Windward Coast and the North Shore are the wet sides, and the south and west coasts are the driest of all. And remember, rip-offs are a frequent fact of life on Oahu. Leaving your bike unlocked is asking for a long walk back.

THE DEPARTMENT OF TRANSPORTATION ✎*www.state.hi.us/dot/highways/bike/oahu* The Department of Transportation offers a free "Bike Oahu" map that lists detailed routes, road grades and where along the way you can find water and food. The entire brochure is available on their website.

HAWAII BICYCLING LEAGUE ✉*3442 Waialae Avenue #1, Honolulu* ☎*808-735-5756* ✺*808-735-5756* ✎*bicycle@hbl.com* If you'd like a little two-wheeled company, check out the Hawaii Bicycling League, which regularly sponsors weekend bike rides and free annual events.

Bike Rentals
COCONUT CRUISERS ✉*305 Royal Hawaiian Avenue, Waikiki* ☎*808-924-0556* This company rents beach cruisers and mountain bikes.

BLUE SKY RENTALS ✉*1920 Ala Moana Boulevard, Honolulu* ☎*808-947-0101* Blue Sky has mountain, road and children's bikes.

Bike Repairs

EKI CYCLERY ✉1603 Dillingham Boulevard, Honolulu ✆808-847-200 ⌾www.eki cyclery.com In addition to doing repair work, this shop sells accessories and mountain bikes although, watch out, their employers can be a bit unhelpful. With mountain, road and triathlon bikes for sale.

THE BIKE SHOP ✉1149 South King Street, Honolulu ✆808-596-0588 ⌾www. bikeshophawaii.com You can get repair work done here.

ISLAND TRIATHLON & BIKE ✉569 Kapahulu Avenue, Honolulu ✆808-732-7227 This shop does repairs and sells bikes.

HIKING

There are numerous hiking trails within easy driving distance of Honolulu. I have listed these as well as trails in the Windward Coast and North Shore areas. Unfortunately, many Oahu treks require special permission from the state, the armed services or private owners. But you should find that the hikes suggested here, none of which require official sanction, will provide you with ample adventure.

SIERRA CLUB ✉P.O. Box 2577, Honolulu ✆808-538-6616 ⌾www.hi.sierra club.org To hike with a group or to obtain further information on hiking Oahu, contact the local Sierra Club.

HAWAIIAN TRAIL AND MOUNTAIN CLUB ✉P.O. Box 2238, Honolulu, HI 96804 ⌾www.aditl.com/htmc, htmc@aditl.com For regular weekend hikes, contact these folks. E-mail ahead; some hikes are for members only.

THE HAWAII NATURE CENTER ✉2131 Makiki Heights Drive ✆808-955-0100, 888-955-0104 ⌾www.hawaiinaturecenter.org Contact this center for guided hikes one or two times a month. Call ahead to make a reservation. You can also get free maps and general trail information.

All distances listed for hiking trails are one way unless otherwise noted.

Greater Honolulu

If you're staying in Waikiki, the most easily accessible hike is the short jaunt up **Diamond Head** crater. There's a sweeping view of Honolulu from atop this famous landmark. The trail begins inside the crater, so take Diamond Head Road around to the inland side of Diamond Head, then follow the tunnel leading into the crater.

In the Koolau Mountains above Diamond Head there is a trail that climbs almost 2000 feet and affords excellent panoramas of the Windward Coast. To get to the **Lanipo Trail** (3 miles), take Waialae Avenue off of Route H-1. Then turn up Wilhelmina Rise and follow until it reaches Maunalani Circle and the trailhead.

For spectacular vistas overlooking the lush Palolo and Manoa valleys, you can hike **Waahila Ridge Trail** (2 miles). To get there, take St. Louis Heights Drive (near the University of Hawaii campus) and then follow connecting roads up to Waahila Ridge State Recreation Area.

The following trails can be combined for longer hikes. **Manoa Falls Trail** (0.8 mile) goes through Manoa Valley. This is a pleasant jaunt that follows Waihi Stream through a densely vegetated area to a charming waterfall. **Manoa Cliff Trail** (3.4 miles) a pleasant family hike, follows a precipice along the west side of Manoa Valley. And **Puu Ohia Trail** (.75 mile), which crosses Manoa Cliff Trail, provides splendid views of the Manoa and Nuuanu valleys. Both trails begin from Tantalus Drive in the hills above Honolulu. **Makiki Loop Trail** (2.5 miles roundtrip) begins near Tantalus Drive. Composed of three interlinking trails, this loop passes stands of eucalyptus and bamboo trees and offers some postcard views of Honolulu. Another loop trail, **Judd Memorial** (.75 mile), crosses Nuuanu Stream and traverses bamboo, eucalyptus and Norfolk pine groves en route to the Jackass Ginger Pool. To get there, take the Pali Highway (Route 61) several miles north from Honolulu. Turn onto Nuuanu Pali Drive and follow it about a mile to Reservoir Number Two spillway.

You can access a two-mile-long portion of the **Old Pali Road** directly to the right of the Pali Lookout. The narrow paved roadway provides easy hikes that are perfect for family excursions and reward with sweeping panoramas of the Windward Coast. For those with a more strenuous hike in mind, the **Koolaupoko Trail** (9 miles) departs from the Pali Lookout parking lot for magnificent rainforest, valley and ocean views. In places the trail is quite steep and occasionally demanding.

In the mountains above Pearl Harbor, at Keaiwa Heiau State Recreation Area, you will find the **Aiea Loop Trail** (4.8 miles). Set in a heavily forested area, this hike passes the wreckage of a World War II cargo plane. It provides an excellent chance to see some of the native Hawaiian trees—*lehua*, *ohia* and *koa*—used by local woodworkers. (For directions to Keaiwa Heiau State Recreation Area, see the "Greater Honolulu Beaches & Parks" section in this book.)

Another hike is along **Waimano Trail** (7 miles), which climbs 1600 feet to an astonishing vista point above Oahu's Windward Coast. There are swimming holes en route to the vista point. To get there, take Kamehameha Highway (Route 90) west to Waimano Home Road (Route 730). Turn right and go two and a half miles to a point along the road where you'll see a building on the right and an irrigation ditch on the left. The trail follows the ditch.

Southeast Oahu

There are several excellent hikes along this shore. The first few are within ten miles of Waikiki, near Hanauma Bay. From the beach at Hanauma you can hike two miles along the coast and cliffs to the Halona Blowhole. This trek passes the Toilet Bowl, a unique tidepool with a hole in the bottom that causes it to fill and then flush with the wave action. Waves sometimes wash the rocks along this path, so be prepared to get wet (and be careful!).

At the intersection where the short road leading down toward Hanauma Bay branches from Kalanianaole Highway (Route 72), there are two other trails. **Koko Head Trail** (1 mile), a hike to the top of a volcanic cone, starts on the ocean side of the highway. This trek features some startling views of Hanauma Bay, Diamond Head and the Koolau Range. Another hike, along **Koko Crater Trail** (1 mile), leads from the highway up to a 1208-foot peak. The views from this crow's nest are equally spectacular.

Windward Coast

There are several other particularly pretty hikes much farther north, near the village of Hauula. In Hauula, if you turn off of Kamehameha Highway and head inland for about a quarter-mile up Hauula Homestead Road, you'll come to Maakua Road. Walk up Maakua Road, which leads into the woods. About 300 yards after entering the woods, the road forks. Maakua Gulch Trail branches to the left. If you continue straight ahead you'll be on Hauula Trail, but if you veer left onto Maakua Gulch Trail, you'll encounter yet another trail branching off to the left in about 150 yards. This is Papali Trail (also known as Maakua Trail).

Maakua Gulch Trail (3 miles), en route to a small waterfall, traverses a rugged canyon with extremely steep walls. Part of the trail lies along the stream bed, so be ready to get wet. **Hauula Trail** (2.5 miles) ascends along two ridges and provides fine vistas of the Koolau Range and the Windward Coast. **Papali Trail** (2.5 miles) drops into Papali Gulch, then climbs high along a ridge from which you can view the surrounding countryside.

North Shore and Leeward Coast

You can approach the trail to Kaena Point either from the North Shore or the Leeward Coast. It's a dry, rock-strewn path that leads to Oahu's westernmost tip. There are tidepools and swimming spots en route, plus spectacular views of a rugged, uninhabited coastline; it's a great place to spot porpoises, and is the legendary home of Nanue the Shark Man. If you're lucky you may sight nesting albatross or rare Hawaiian Monk seals. Keep your distance as both are protected species and a portion of the point is a wildlife preserve. In ancient times, this was sacred land; it was believed the souls of the dead departed from Kaena to the afterworld, called *Po*, the realm of the spirits. To get to the trailhead, just drive to the end of the paved portion of Route 930 on the North Shore or Route 93 on the Leeward Coast. Then follow the trail out to Kaena Point. It's about two miles via the Leeward Coast, and a half-mile via the North Shore.

TRANSPORTATION

AIR

HONOLULU INTERNATIONAL AIRPORT ⌧*Rodgers Boulevard, Honolulu* ✆*808-861-1260* ✑*www.honoluluairport.com* There's one airport on Oahu and it's a behemoth. The airlines that fly in here are Air Canada, Air New Zealand, Air Pacific, Aloha Airlines, All Nippon Airways, American, American Tran Air, China Airlines, Continental, Continental Air Micronesia, Delta, Hawaiian Airlines, Japan Airlines, JTB Aloha Service, Korean Airlines, Northwest, Quantas Airlines, Rich International, and

United Airlines. Honolulu International Airport is a Pacific crossroads, an essential link between North America and Asia. Honolulu International includes all the comforts of a major airport. You can check your bags; fuel up at a restaurant, coffee shop or cocktail lounge; shop at several stores; or shower.

Ground Transport

To cover the eight or so miles into Waikiki, it's possible to hire a cab for $25 to $30.

ROBERT'S HAWAII ☎808-539-9400, 800-831-5541 🖋www.robertshawaii.com
For $9 (roundtrip $15), Robert's will take you to your Waikiki hotel or condominium.

THEBUS ☎808-848-5555 🖋www.thebus.org City buses #19 and #20 travel through Downtown Honolulu and Waikiki. This is the cheapest transportation, but you're only allowed to carry on baggage that fits on your lap. So, unless you're traveling very light, you'll have to use another conveyance.

BOAT

HAWAII SUPERFERRY ✉One Waterfront Plaza, 500 Ala Moana Boulevard, Suite 300, Honolulu ☎808-531-7400 🖷808-531-7410 🖋www.hawaiisuperferry.com
Providing three-hour rides between Oahu and Maui six days a week, this inter-island ferry is still new to the waters, first setting sail in 2007. More than a mode of transportation, it includes food, entertainment and shopping. Ongoing environmental protection surveys are being held, so it is a good idea to check travel policies prior to boarding or making reservations.

CAR RENTALS

Of all the islands, Oahu offers the most car-rental agencies. At the Honolulu airport, **Avis Rent A Car** (808-834-5536, 800-331-3712), Budget Car and Truck Rental (808-836-1700, 800-527-0700), **Dollar Rent A Car** (866-434-2226), **Hertz** (808-529-6800, 800-654-3011) and **National Car Rental** (808-831-3800, 800-227-7368) all have booths. Their convenient location helps to save time while minimizing the problem of picking up your car.

There are many other Honolulu-based companies offering very low rates but providing limited pick-up service at the airport. I've never found the inconvenience worth the savings. There you are—newly arrived from the mainland, uncertain about your environment, anxious to check in at the hotel—and you're immediately confronted with the Catch-22 of getting to your car. Do you rent a vehicle in which to pick up your rental car? Take a bus? Hitchhike? What do you do with your bags meanwhile?

Though not at the airport, **Alamo Rent A Car** (808-833-4585, 800-462-5266) provides airport pick-up service. **VIP Rental** is a cheaper outfit (234 Beachwalk; 808-922-4605).

If you prefer to go in high style, book a limousine from **Cloud Nine** (808-524-7999, 800-524-7999).

JEEP RENTALS

Adventure Rentals (808-944-3131) provide jeeps and **Dollar Rent A Car** (808-944-1544) has Dodge Durangos for rent. **VIP Car Rental** (808-922-4605) rents Suzuki Samurais and Geo Trackers.

MOPED RENTALS

ADVENTURE ON 2 WHEELS ✉1946 *Ala Moana Boulevard, Honolulu* ☎*808-944-3131* This Waikiki store rents mopeds and bicycles, among other things.

BLUE SKY RENTALS ✉1920 *Ala Moana Boulevard, Honolulu* ☎*808-947-0101* This facility located on the ground floor of the Inn On The Park Hotel rents mopeds.

PUBLIC TRANSIT

Oahu has an excellent bus system that runs regularly to points all over the island and provides convenient service throughout Honolulu. Many of the beaches, hotels, restaurants and points of interest mentioned in this chapter are just a bus ride away. It's even possible to pop your money in the fare box and ride around the entire island.

THEBUS ☎*808-848-5555* ⌨*www.thebus.org* Rumbling along city streets and country roads TheBus operates from 5 a.m. to 10 p.m. (though some lines run past midnight), covering 90 percent of the 60-square-mile island. The fleet of 525 buses travel a combined total of 60,000 miles every day, carrying 260,000 passengers—between 30,000 and 35,000 of them are visitors. There are also express buses traveling major highways at commuter times. Most buses are handicapped accessible and many have bike racks.

If you stay in Waikiki you'll inevitably be sardined into a #19 or #20 bus for the ride through Honolulu's tourist mecca. Many bus drivers are Hawaiian; I saw some hysterical scenes on this line when tourists waited anxiously for their stop to be called, only to realize they couldn't understand the driver's pidgin. Hysterical, that is, *after* those early days when *I* was the visitor with the furrowed brow.

But you're surely more interested in meeting local people than tourists, and you can easily do it on any of the buses outside Waikiki. They're less crowded and a lot more fun for peoplewatching.

For information on bus routes call TheBus. And remember, the only carry-on luggage permitted is baggage small enough to fit on your lap.

169

AERIAL TOURS

The quickest way to see all Oahu has to offer is by taking to the air. In minutes you can experience the island's hidden waterfalls, secluded beaches and volcanic landmarks. Tranquil gliders and hovering whirly-birds all fly low and slow to make sure you see what you missed on the trip over from the mainland. You can also take extended flights that include the outer islands.

MAKANI KAI HELICOPTERS ✉*110 Kapalulu Place, Honolulu* ✆*808-834-5813, 877-255-8532* 🖷*808-837-7867* ✐*www.makanikai.com* This company offers helicopter tours of Waikiki and Honolulu, Hanauma Bay, the Koolau Mountains, Chinaman's Hat, Sacred Falls, Kahana Rainforest and the North Shore. They also take trips to the "Jurassic Park Valley," an area where parts of the movie were filmed. Reservations required.

THE ORIGINAL GLIDER RIDES ✉*Dillingham Airfield, Mokuleia* ✆*808-637-0207* ✐*www.honolulusoaring.com, info@gliderridehawaii.com* To enjoy a one- or two-passenger glider trip, head out here and talk to Mr. Bill. On your 20-minute trip you're likely to see fields of sugar cane, marine mammals, surfers working the North Shore and neighboring Kauai. You'll also enjoy peace and quiet while working your way down from 3000 feet. A videotape of the ride and your reactions makes a memorable souvenir.

WALKING TOURS

OAHU NATURE TOURS ✉*P.O. Box 8059, Honolulu, HI 96815* ✆*808-924-2473* ✐*www.oahunaturetours.com* Offering several different daily eco-tours, Oahu Nature provides an overview of native Hawaiian birds and plants. One focuses on Oahu's volcanic history at Diamond Head Crater. Another tour takes you into the Hawaiian rainforest at 2000-feet elevation in the Koolau Mountains. Equipment, transportation and water are provided. Reservations required. Fee.

CHINATOWN TOURS Chinatown's rich history and culture can be experienced in several inexpensive walking tours that make this exotic place come alive. Explore the markets to find the special ingredients that make up Thai, Vietnamese and Chinese cooking on monthly walks hosted by **Lyon Arboretum** (808-988-0456). The **Chinese Chamber of Commerce** (808-533-3181) offers culinary tours on Monday. For historical background in this fascinating area try the **Hawaii Heritage Center** (116 Smith Street, Honolulu; 808-521-2749).

BIG ISLAND

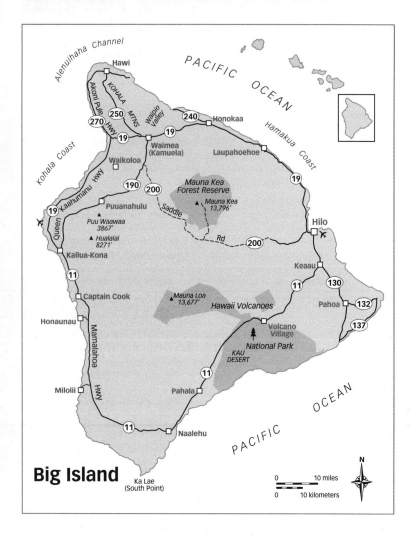

The Big Island, they call it, and even that is an understatement. Hawaii, all 4030 square miles, is almost twice as large as all the other Hawaiian islands combined. Its twin volcanic peaks, Mauna Kea and Mauna Loa, dwarf most mountains. Mauna Loa, the world's largest active volcano, which last erupted in 1984, looms 13,677 feet above sea level. Mauna Kea, rising 13,796 feet, is the largest island-based mountain in the world. It is actually 32,000 feet from the ocean floor, making it, by one system of reckoning, the tallest mountain on earth, grander even

Nevada chain could fit within this single peak.

Kilauea, a third volcano whose seething firepit has been erupting with startling frequency, is one of the world's most active volcanoes. Since its most recent series of eruptions began in 1983, Kilauea has swallowed almost 200 houses. In 1990 it completely destroyed the town of Kalapana, burying a once lively village beneath tons of black lava; then in 1992 it destroyed the ancient Hawaiian village of Kamoamoa and the *heiau* at Wahaula. There is little doubt that the Big Island is a place of geologic superlatives.

But size alone does not convey the Big Island's greatness. Its industry, too, is expansive. Despite the lava wasteland that covers large parts of its surface, and the volcanic gases that create a layer of "vog" during volcanic eruptions, the Big Island is the state's greatest producer of coffee, papayas, vegetables, anthuriums, macadamia nuts and cattle. Its orchid industry, based in rain-drenched Hilo, is the world's largest. Over 22,000 varieties grow in the nurseries here.

Across the island in sun-soaked Kona, one of the nation's two coffee industries operates. Just off this spectacular western coast lie some of the finest deep-sea fishing grounds in the world. Between Hilo and Kona, and surrounding Waimea, sits the Parker Ranch. Sprawling across 225,000 acres, it is one of the world's largest independently owned cattle ranches.

Yet many of these measurements are taken against island standards. Compared to the mainland, the Big Island is a tiny speck in the sea. Across its broadest reach it measures a scant 93 miles long and 76 miles wide, smaller than Connecticut. The road around the island totals only 300 miles, and can be driven in a day, though I'd recommend taking at least five. The island's 158,423 population comprises just 8 percent of the state's citizens. Its lone city, Hilo, has a population nearing 50,000.

But large or small, numbers cannot fully describe the Big Island, for there is a magic about the place that transcends statistics. Hawaii, also nicknamed the Orchid Island and Volcano Island, is the home of Pele, the goddess of volcanoes. Perhaps her fiery spirit is what infuses the Big Island with an unquantifiable quality. Or maybe the island's comparative youth is what makes the elements seem nearer, more alluring and strangely threatening here. It's still growing in size because of lava flows from Kilauea and Mauna Loa. In fact, recent activity has added more than a square mile to the island. The Big Island is geologically the youngest spot on earth, one million years old. Whatever it might be, the Big Island has always been where I feel closest to the Polynesian spirit. Of all the Hawaiian islands, this one I love the most.

It was here, possibly as early as A.D. 400 or as late as the 9th century, that Polynesian explorers may have first landed when they discovered the island chain. Until the advent of the white man, it was generally the most important island, supporting a large population and occupying a vital place in Hawaii's rich mythology. Little wonder then that Kamehameha the Great, the chief who would become Hawaii's first king, was born here in 1753. He established the archipelago's first capital in Kailua and ruled there until his death in 1819.

Within a year of the great leader's passing, two events occurred in Kailua that jolted the entire chain far more than any earthquake. First the king's heir, Liholiho, uprooted the centuries-old taboo system upon which the native Hawaiian religion rested. Then, in the spring of 1820, the first American missionaries dropped anchor off the coast of Kailua-Kona. It was also near here that Captain James Cook, history's greatest discoverer, was slain in 1779 by the same people who had earlier welcomed him as a god. Across the island another deity, Pele, was defied in 1824 when the high chieftess Kapiolani, a Christian, ate *kapu* (forbidden) fruit on the rim of an active lava lake at Kilauea, and suffered no ill consequence.

As stirring as the Big Island's story might be, much of its drama still awaits the visitor. For the land—the volcanoes, beaches and valleys—is as vital and intriguing today as in the days of demigods and kings. This is a place for the adventurer to spend a lifetime.

On the east coast, buffeted by trade winds, lies Hilo, a lush tropical town that soaks up 130 to 200 inches of rain annually. Here anthuriums and orchids are cultivated in a number of spectacular nurseries. Just to the south—smoking, heaving and erupting—sits Hawaii Volcanoes National Park.

The Puna District that straddles the coast between the volcanoes and Hilo has been the site of dramatic eruptions over the past several decades. This region is also home to the island's controversial geothermal power plant.

In the north, from the Hamakua Coast to the Kohala Peninsula, heavy erosion has cut through the volcano to form spectacular canyons such as the Waipio Valley. All along the Hamakua plateau, once thriving sugar plantations, fed by waters from Mauna Kea, now lay fallow from the mountains to the surf.

In startling contrast to these verdant mountains is the desert-like Kau district at the southern tip of the island (and, for that matter, the southernmost point in the United States). Along the west coast stretches the Kona district, a vacationer's paradise. Suntan weather, sandy beaches and coral reefs teeming with tropical fish make this an ideal area to just kick back and enjoy. The island's central tourist area is located here in Kailua-Kona, where Hawaiian royalty settled in the 19th century.

And for something unique to the Big Island, there's Waimea with its rolling grasslands, range animals and *paniolos*, or Hawaiian-style cowboys. In fact, one of the biggest Hereford cattle herds is located here in the center of the island.

It's an island I don't think you should miss, an island that offers a string of luxury resorts as well as time-worn tropical retreats hidden along its other shores. To geologists the Big Island is a natural laboratory in which the mysteries of volcanic activity are a fact of everyday life; to many Hawaiians it is the most sacred of all the islands. To everyone who visits it, Hawaii is a place of startling contrasts and unspeakable beauty, an alluring and exotic tropical island.

KAILUA-KONA AREA

At the center of the tourist scene on the Kona Coast is the contemporary town of Kailua or Kailua-Kona—a reference to the district in which it's located. Here, extending for eight miles along Alii Drive from the King Kamehameha Hotel to Keauhou Bay, is a string of hotels, restaurants, condominiums and shopping malls. Like a little Waikiki, Kailua-Kona is the commercial focus for this side of the island. In recent years, Kailua-Kona and the surrounding region have grown rapidly, and as is true in many parts of the state, infrastructure has not kept pace. Traffic frequently moves very slowly in this part of the island, so take it easy and allow extra time to reach the airport.

SIGHTS

KAILUA WHARF ⊠*Alii Drive* Despite the tinsel and tourist trappings, this old fishing village and former haunt of Hawaiian royalty still retains some of its charm. If you tour the wharf around 4 p.m., the fishing boats may be hauling freshly caught marlin onto the docks. Some of the finest marlin grounds in the world lie off this shoreline and the region is renowned for other deep-sea fish. The wharf itself is a departure point not only for fishing charters but for snorkeling tours and glass-bottom boat cruises as well. It's also a favorite place for viewing Kona's fabled sunsets.

AHUENA HEIAU ⊠*75-5660 Palani Road* ☎*808-327-0123* On the grounds of King Kamehameha's Kona Beach Hotel rests Ahuena Heiau, a culturally significant site that has been reconstructed. Ahuena was once part of Kamakahonu ("the eye of the turtle"), Kamehameha's royal compound. It was here that the exalted Kamehameha retired after uniting Hawaii's islands as a single kingdom. Menacing *kii* (sacred wooden figures) stand guard here, while offerings wrapped in *ti* leaves are still left by the faithful. Unfortunately, a hotel luau facility was built next to the site. Tours of the hotel grounds are available by appointment.

KONA HISTORICAL SOCIETY
⊠*81 Mamalahoa Highway* ☎*808-323-3222* ✐*www.konahistorical.org* For a taste of historic Kailua-Kona, including an informative visit to Hulihee Palace stop here. The 75-minute tour starts with the reign of King Umi in the 15th century and leads to the present day with plenty of stops in between. This tour is recipient of the Historic Hawaii Foundation's Preservation Award and is offered weekday at 9 a.m. and 11 a.m. Twenty-four-hour advance reservations are required. Fee.

HULIHEE PALACE
⊠*75-5718 Alii Drive* ☎*808-329-1877* ☎*808-329-1321* ✐*www.huliheepalace. org* Built in 1838, this small but elegant estate sits on Alii Drive in the middle of town. Today it's a two-story museum housing royal Hawaiian relics. It was built by the brother-in-law of Kamehameha I and later used by King Kalakaua as a summer palace during the 1880s. Of particular interest are the redwood pillars in the Entry Hall, a souvenir of King Kalakaua's trip to California. Also featured is the desk that King David Kalakaua used while in residence. In the Kuhio Room, a stunning *koa* dining table that be-

longed to the Kalakaua family dominates. And of interest in the Kuakini Room is a reproduction of a Hawaiian sled, a *papa holua*. A pair of kahili, Royal Standards, in the Victorian-furnished second-floor Sitting Room adds an eclectic touch, while a cradle and large round container, an *umeke*, made from the trunk of a coconut tree and used as a hat box are attention-getters in Princess Ruth's bedroom. The Kawanakoa Room is dominated by a large *koa* wardrobe commissioned by King Kalakaua. Closed Monday. Admission.

MOKUAIKAUA CHURCH ✉75-5713 *Alii Drive* ☎808-329-1589 Directly across the street from Hulihee Palace is the oldest church in the islands. The first missionaries anchored offshore in 1820 after sailing over 18,000 miles around Cape Horn from Boston. By 1836, with most of the Hawaiians converted to Protestant Christianity, the missionaries dedicated this imposing lava-and-coral structure.

ATLANTIS ADVENTURES ✉Bouganvillea Plaza #303, 75-5656 Kuakini Highway, Kailua ☎808-329-6626, 800-548-6262 🖷808-329-1153 ✎www.atlantisadventures.com Contrasting with the venerable sites in Kona is this 80-ton made-for-tourists submarine. Diving to depths of 120 feet, the 48-passenger sub explores tropical reefs. During the hour-long voyage, passengers view the underwater world through large viewing ports. Admission.

DISAPPEARING SANDS BEACH Almost everything in Kailua sits astride Alii Drive, the waterfront street that extends south from town to Keauhou Bay. Several miles from Kailua, Alii passes Disappearing Sands Beach (or Magic Sands Beach). The lovely white sand here is often washed away by heavy winter surf and then redeposited when the big waves subside as the seasons change.

ST. PETER'S CATHOLIC CHURCH ✉Alii Drive Along the rocky shore of Kahaluu Bay is St. Peter's Catholic Church. This stark blue-and-white clapboard chapel, also known as the "Little Blue Church" precariously perched on a lava foundation, is one of the world's smallest churches and was established in 1889.

HISTORICAL SITES
Located just across Kahaluu Bay are several interesting historical sites: two *heiau* and the **King's Pool**. You can continue on to Keauhou Bay, where a monument marks the **Birthplace of Kamehameha III**.

ASTRONAUT ELLISON S. ONIZUKA SPACE CENTER ✉Kona International Airport, eight miles north of Kailua ☎808-329-3441 🖷808-326-9751 At Kona's airport you can pay your respects to the crew of the space shuttle *Challenger* at an interactive learning center. It's a fitting tribute to Onizuka, who lived in Hawaii, and the other astronauts who died in the 1986 tragedy. Videos and interactive displays trace the astronauts' lives and the development of the space program. Admission.

Kailua-Kona Area

Kaupulehu

KONA VILLAGE RESORT

BIG ISLAND GRILL
HULIHEE PALACE
Kailua-Kona

DISAPPEARING SANDS BEACH

KONA VILLAGE RESORT

PAGE 177

Polynesian style thatched-roof guest cottages offering serenity and solitude in an ancient fishing village

BIG ISLAND GRILL

PAGE 182

Hearty local cuisine a block off the tourist drag, and half a world away

HULIHEE PALACE

PAGE 173

Once King Kalakaua's summer palace, now an elegant two-story museum housing royal Hawaiian relics

DISAPPEARING SANDS BEACH

PAGE 187

A small white strand studded with lava rocks, home to Kona's best surf spot—"Banyans"

ORIGINAL HAWAIIAN CHOCOLATE FACTORY ⊠ *78-6772 Makenawai Street* ✆ *808-322-2626* ✑ *www.originalhawaiianchocolatefactory.com* The Big Island is the only place in the United States where cacao beans, the basic ingredient of chocolate, are grown, and the Original Hawaiian Chocolate Factory is the only operation on the island that grows, harvests, processes and packages all-Hawaiian chocolate. The husband-and-wife operation above Kaeuhou may be the world's smallest chocolate maker. You'll see their product in stores all over the island; if you want to discover where it comes from, call Bob Cooper and arrange a two-hour tour on which you'll see how the cacao trees grow and bear fruit, how the pods are shucked and the beans are fermented and sun-dried, and how they are transformed into chocolate. The Coopers conduct factory tours about five times a week by reservation only.

LODGING

FOUR SEASONS RESORT HUALALAI
AT HISTORIC KAUPULEHU

$$$$ 243 ROOMS ⊠ *72-100 Kaupulehu Drive, Kaupulehu-Kona* ✆ *808-325-8000*
✆ *808-325-8053* ✑ *www.fourseasons.com/hualalai,*
hualalai.reservations@fourseasons.com
Shibui best describes this understated yet elegant bungalow-style guest facility. The resort offers a bit of heaven here on earth. Of

Kailua-Kona Area

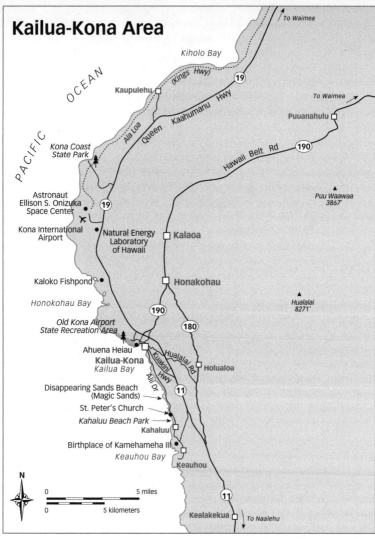

PACIFIC OCEAN

Kiholo Bay

(Kings Hwy)

To Waimea

19

Kaupulehu

Aia Loa

Queen Kaahumanu Hwy

To Waimea

Puuanahulu

Hawaii Belt Rd

190

Kona Coast
State Park

▲ Puu Waawaa
3867'

Astronaut
Ellison S. Onizuka
Space Center   **19**

Kona International
Airport

● Natural Energy
Laboratory
of Hawaii

Kalaoa

Kaloko Fishpond

Honakohau

Honokohau Bay

▲ Hualalai
8271'

Old Kona Airport
State Recreation Area

190

180

Ahuena Heiau

Hualalai Rd

Kailua-Kona
Kailua Bay

Kuakini Hwy

Alii Dr

Disappearing Sands Beach
(Magic Sands)

St. Peter's Church

Kahaluu Beach Park

Holualoa

11

Kahaluu

Birthplace of Kamehameha III

Keauhou Bay

Keauhou

N

| 0 | 5 miles |
| 0 | 5 kilometers |

11

Kealakekua   To Naalehu

course, heaven is pricey. But outdoor enthusiasts will be content with the four oceanfront pools—including a seawater pool made for snorkelers—the Sports Club and Spa with its lap pool, eight tennis courts and rock-climbing wall and the PGA championship golf course designed by Jack Nicklaus. Kids will like the game room and parents will appreciate the "Kids for all Seasons Program." (Children under 18 can share their parents' room at no extra charge.) There are three restaurants for dining. What will make it a "Hidden Hawaii" experience is a visit to the Hawaiian cultural center that extends the *Kaupulehu* traditions of Hawaii to the visitor. They offer such diverse classes as ukulele, the Hawaiian language, *lauhala* weaving and Hawaiian navigation. There are also 31 suites (each with a private lanai and ocean view) on the premises.

KONA VILLAGE RESORT

$$$$ 125 UNITS   ✉P.O. Box 1299, Kaupulehu-Kona, HI 96745
☎808-325-5555, 800-367-5290 📠808-325-5124 ⌨www.konavillage.com, kvr@aloha.net

Of course, when money is no object, this is the place to stay. A very plush, private colony located 14 miles north of Kailua, it's a regal retreat set along a white-sand cove in an ancient Hawaiian fishing village. The individual guest cottages are thatched-roof structures, variously designed to represent the traditional houses of Hawaiian, Tahitian, Fijian, Samoan and other Polynesian groups. There are no TVs, telephones, radios, clocks or air conditioners in the rooms, but you will find serenity, solitude and a well-heeled version of hidden Hawaii, not to mention a fitness center, tennis courts, sailboats and outrigger canoes. Prices are in the stratosphere and are based on the American plan.

HONU KAI BED AND BREAKFAST

$$ 3 UNITS   ✉75-1027 Henry Street, Kailua-Kona, HI 96740 ☎808-329-8676, 800-528-2456 ⌨www.honukaibnbinfo@honukaibnb.com, info@honukai.com

For a more intimate feel, this B&B offers three in-house suites and an adjoining bungalow in a plantation-style home with coastal views. A garden jacuzzi is surrounded by lush vegetation. Each suite has a lanai and is decorated with Hawaiian motifs. A *koi* pond provides Honu Kai with a distinctive feel.

PATEY'S PLACE IN PARADISE

$ 8 UNITS   ✉75-184 Ala Ona Ona Street ☎808-326-7018 📠808-326-7640
⌨www.alternative-hawaii.com/affordable

This conveniently priced hostel in the center of Kailua is small and clean, and boasts a bay view from the huge wraparound deck. There are dormitory-style accommodations for eight people as well as four private rooms that sleep eight and have ocean views. Kitchen facilities, internet access and television rooms are provided.

KONA SEASIDE HOTEL

$$$ 220 ROOMS   ✉75-5646 Palani Road ☎808-329-2455, 800-560-5558
📠808-329-6157 ⌨www.sand-seaside.com

Located across the street from the ocean, this multi-faceted facility features the Tower Wing; the Garden Wing, where the rooms come with mini-kitchenettes; and the Pool Wing, where the rooms are smaller and less fashionable but are conveniently placed around one of the hotel's two swimming pools. While the more expensive rooms add lanais and wall-to-wall carpeting, all the accommodations are tastefully done. A restaurant is adjacent.

Kailua

190

0   0.5 mile

0   0.5 kilometer

N

19 Queen Kaahumanu Hwy

Palani Rd

Luhia St

Kaiwi St

Alapa St

Kopiko St

Pawai Pl

Kuakini Rd

11

Ololi

Ala Onaona

Kalani

Alaka

Alanoe

Lamaokaola

Alahou

Kalawa

Hawaii Belt Rd

A

F

E D Sarona

Kakina

Hualalai

C

182

Hualalai Rd

Kailua Bay

Alii Dr

Kanakai St

Wailua Rd

Kuakini Hwy

Hualalai Rd

11

POINTS OF INTEREST
Ⓐ *Ahuena Heiau*
Ⓑ *Atlantis Adventures*
Ⓒ *Hale Halawai*
Ⓓ *Hawaii Visitors Bureau*
Ⓔ *Hulihee Palace*
Ⓕ *Mokuaikaua Church*
Ⓖ *Old Kona Airport State
    Recreation Area*

Lunapule St

B

Alii Dr

KING KAMEHAMEHA
KONA BEACH HOTEL

hidden

$$$–$$$$ 460 ROOMS   ✉75-5660 Palani Road   ☎808-329-2911,
800-367-2111 📠808-329-4602 ⌨www.konabeachhotel.com,
kbhreservations@hthcorp.com

Anchoring one end of Kailua Bay is the town's most historic
hotel. The "King Kam" is deserving of note. The lobby alone is
worth the price of admission: It's a wood-paneled affair along
which you can trace the history of ancient Hawaii. For its guests,
it has a pool, tennis courts and jacuzzi, plus a host of other
amenities ranging from an activities desk to room service. The
guest rooms themselves are quite spacious, fashionably deco-
rated and well equipped. You'll find plush carpeting, color televi-
sions, air conditioning, refrigerators, coffee makers and lanais
with views of the ocean or mountains.

KONA BAY HOTEL

$$ 143 ROOMS   ✉75-5739 Alii Drive ☎808-329-1393, 800-367-5102 📠808-935-7903
⌨www.unclebilly.com, reservations@unclebilly.com

Part of the Kona Bay Hotel is a section of the old Kona Inn, the rest of which fell to Kailua developers who have perversely transformed it into yet another shopping mall. What remains is a four-story semicircular structure with a pool, bar, restaurant and lounge in the center. The rooms are large, tastefully furnished and quiet. Some have lava walls that provide a pleasant backdrop plus excellent soundproofing. The staff is friendly, and the atmosphere is very appealing. I once spent a relaxing month here and recommend the place.

KONA ISLANDER INN

$–$$ 140 UNITS ✉75-5776 Kuakini Highway ✆808-329-3333, 800-244-4752 📠808-326-4137 🖰www.konahawaii.com, konahawaii@hotmail.com

Set between Alii Drive and Route 11 on Kailua's outskirts, this hotel has a large lobby, an oval pool, a hot tub and a barbecue flanked by MacArthur palms. Several three-story buildings spread across a lush swath of land, all of the studios have small lanais, cable television, microwaves, refrigerators and air conditioning; two have ocean views.

KONA TIKI HOTEL

$–$$ 15 ROOMS ✉75-5968 Alii Drive ✆808-329-1425 📠808-327-9402 🖰www.konatiki.com, reservations@konatiki.com

Here is a quaint hotel neatly situated on the ocean with rooms that are bright and clean. Despite the contrasting decorative themes and the noise from Alii Drive, I recommend this establishment for its ocean-view lanais, oceanfront pool, barbecue, garden and complimentary continental breakfast. Most of the rooms have kitchenettes. Reservations are recommended.

KONA WHITE SANDS APARTMENT HOTEL

$$ 10 UNITS ✉77-6467 Alii Drive ✆808-329-3333, 800-244-4752 📠808-326-4137 🖰www.konahawaii.com, konahawaii@hotmail.com

Located just across the street from Disappearing Sands Beach (the nicest beach along Alii Drive), this is a ten-unit hotel of two-bedroom, two bathroom apartments. Each comes with a kitchenette and ceiling fans. The cinderblock and plasterboard walls are pretty plain, but who needs fancy interior decoration with that knockout ocean view? Rooms are cross-ventilated, and the cooling breeze will probably bring along noise from cars and sun revelers. That's the extra price for living this close to the Kona Coast. Many people are willing to pay it, so you'll have to reserve a room far in advance.

SHERATON KEAUHOU RESORT AND SPA

$$$$ 1021 ROOMS ✉78-128 Ehukai Street, Keauhou ✆808-930-4900, 866-500-8313 🖰www.sheratonkeauhou.com

The Old Kona Surf, after being closed for a number of years, was reborn as the Sheraton Keauhou Resort and Spa. *Keauhou* means "new beginning," and the millions of dollars in renovations poured in did, indeed, create a new beginning. The rooms and suites are luxurious and the ocean views along the 22-acre beachfront are invigorating, but the stark design and setting evoke little in the way of the romantic spirit of the islands. But then again, travelers with kids might want to forgo the romance for the island's largest waterslide—the Manta Ray Super Slide & Pool, positioned at the heart of the resort.

CONDOS

KONA ISLANDER INN RESORT

140 ROOMS ✉ 75-5776 Kuakini Highway ☏ 808-329-3333, 800-244-4752
📠 808-326-4137 🖳 www.konahawaii.com, konahawaii@hotmail.com

Budget accommodations in Kailua-Kona? Well, almost. Centrally located in town, this resort was one of the first condominium complexes built in the area back in the 1960s, and these days it's probably the most affordable. The air-conditioned rooms are studio apartments, each with a single large living/sleeping room, a kitchenette and a lanai. The complex consists of three buildings, each three stories tall, linked by pathways that lead among palm trees and gardens. There's a swimming pool and a hot tub, and a white-sand beach directly across the highway. Daily rates run from $79.95 to $99.95.

SEA VILLAGE

20 UNITS ✉ 75-6002 Alii Drive ☏ 808-329-6438, 800-367-5168
🖳 www.sunquest-hawaii.com, squest@sunquest-hawaii.com

About one mile south of Kailua is the Sea Village, which offers 11 one-bedroom oceanview units ranging from $115 to $160; 9 two-bedroom units with two baths are $135 to $165 for one to four people. There's a swimming pool and tennis courts. Oceanfront, but no beach.

KONA RIVIERA VILLA

12 UNITS ✉ 75-6124 Alii Drive ☏ 808-329-1996, 800-800-6202 📠 808-326-2178
🖳 www.konahawaiirentals.com, knutson@aloha.net

This is a relatively small condo on a lava-rock beach outside Kailua. It's attractively landscaped, has a pool and rents one-bedroom units from $105 to $135 ($85 to $120 from April 15 to December 14). Three-day minimum.

KONA BALI KAI

10 UNITS ✉ 76-6246 Alii Drive ☏ 808-329-9381 📠 808-326-6056
🖳 www.sunquest-hawaii.com, squal@sunquest-hawaii.com

Located on Banyans Beach in Kona, you'll find one of Kailua-Kona's only oceanfront accommodations. The units are roomy and nicely appointed, and include studios and one- or two-bedroom suites, all with fully equipped kitchens and ceiling fans. Other amenities include laundry facilities, a convenience store, a snorkeling shop, barbecue areas and limited maid service. There's a courtyard swimming pool and jacuzzi. Rates start at $195 for a mountain studio.

KONA MAGIC SANDS

13 UNITS ✉ 77-6452 Alii Drive ☏ 808-329-3333, 800-244-4752 📠 808-326-4137
🖳 www.konahawaii.com, konahawaii@hotmail.com

Located on the ocean, next to Disappearing Sands Beach, this complex has studio apartments renting for $105 without air conditioning, $135 with, year-round, single or double.

ASTON KONA BY THE SEA

86 UNITS ✉ 75-6106 Alii Drive ☏ 808-327-2300, 800-321-2558 📠 808-327-2333
🖳 www.rqkonabythesea.com

This is a large, trimly landscaped complex on a lava-rock beach. The suites are one and two bedrooms; all have two baths and a lanai; there's a pool and jacuzzi. Rates start at $80.

DINING

5 BIG ISLAND KAILUA-KONA AREA DINING

O'S BISTRO

$$–$$$ ASIAN   ✉75-1027 Henry Street #102   ☎808-327-6565
📠808-331-2572

Don't let the strip mall setting dissuade you from easing on over to O's. Focus on the fine local art and stellar menu instead. The cuisine varies from Japanese to Thai to Vietnamese to Italian with a single common denominator—everything is prepared with noodles. It's also a showcase for one of Hawaii's finest chefs—Amy Ferguson Ota. If you try the udon Peking duck and *kai choy*, you may be back every day you're on the island. Open for breakfast, lunch and dinner.

KONA COAST SHOPPING CENTER

$ CHINESE/PLATE LUNCHES   ✉74-5586 Palani Road

You'll find several inexpensive short-order joints in this shopping center. **Don's Chinese Kitchen** (808-329-3770) serves tasty, nutritious, inexpensive meals at its cafeteria-style emporium. **Kamuela Deli** (808-334-0017) is a plate-lunch place next door. You can dine on homemade burgers and lunch plates of teriyaki beef or chicken as well as an array of full meals. Of special interest are the Hawaiian-style roast pork and barbecue.

HARBOR HOUSE

$–$$ SEAFOOD   ✉74-425 Kealakehe Parkway   ☎808-326-4166

For the freshest fish, you can't beat Harbor House, a small, open-air eatery right next to the fishing fleet at Honokahau Harbor. Whether you choose the grilled fish entrée, sandwich or fish and chips, you can be assured it's the catch of the day. The bar is a popular happy hour hangout, but don't dawdle if you're hungry, as the place closes at 7 p.m.

OCEAN SEAFOOD CHINESE RESTAURANT

$$ CHINESE   ✉King Kamehameha Mall, 75-5626 Kuakini Highway   ☎808-329-3055

In the King Kamehameha Mall, between the King Kamehameha Hotel and the Kona Industrial Area, you'll come upon this Asian delight. The extensive menu has classics including Peking duck, chow mein, chow fun and hot and sour soup. Suffice it to say that it's all there.

BUNS IN THE SUN

$ DELI   ✉Lanihau Center, 75-5595 Palani Road   ☎808-326-2774

A local breakfast favorite, Buns serves bagels, donuts and pastries accompanied by full-flavored Kona coffee. The little blue-and-white bakery-deli also offers a full line of fresh-made bread, cakes and other baked goods. There's a soup, salad and sandwich lunch menu, and they'll pack you a box lunch for your beach picnic or driving excursion.

SIBU CAFÉ

$$ INDONESIAN   ✉*Banyan Court Mall, 75-5695 Alii Drive*   ☎*808-329-1112*

Indonesian and Southeast Asian dishes are prepared daily for lunch and dinner. Among the tangy favorites at this outdoor café are beef *saté*, tofu and vegetable stir-fry and Balinese chicken (which is marinated, cooked over an open flame, then served with peanut sauce).

BASIL'S RESTAURANT

$–$$ ITALIAN   ✉*75-5707 Alii Drive*   ☎*808-326-7836*

This a hole-in-the-wall bistro punched into a storefront along Alii Drive has reasonably priced Italian food. The menu is pretty standard as is the red-checkered oilcloth interior, but portions are large and tasty.

TRES HOMBRES BEACH GRILL

$–$$ MEXICAN   ✉*Alii Drive and Walua Road*   ☎*808-329-2173*   ☎*808-331-2850*

A great option for Mexican food in this neck of the woods is Tres Hombres. You'll get a good, filling Mexican meal in a comfortable restaurant.

CASSANDRA'S GREEK TAVERN

$$–$$$ GREEK   ✉*75-5719 Alii Drive*   ☎*808-334-1066*

If you care for Mediterranean, Cassandra's has tables out on the patio as well as in a cozy little dining room. Souvlaki, kebabs, moussaka and dolmas dominate the menu, but they also prepare steak and seafood dishes.

AKI'S CAFÉ

$–$$ JAPANESE-AMERICAN   ✉*75-5699 Alii Drive*   ☎*808-329-0090*   ☎*808-334-0318*

You not only can dine inexpensively at Aki's, you can dine under an umbrella overlooking the water. They may not live up to their motto of "fine Japanese and American food," but the cuisine is passable. They offer hamburgers, fish and chips and spaghetti on the American side of the menu, with sushi, stir-fry and curry dishes on the other. For dinner, there's steak, chicken teriyaki and fish *misoyaki*.

PANCHO & LEFTY'S CANTINA & RESTAURANTE

$–$$ MEXICAN   ✉*75-5719 Alii Drive*   ☎*808-326-2171*

If you're seeking a tropical drink and a tropical sunset over the water, then Pancho & Lefty's is the place. Similar food as Tres Hombres, different ambience, higher prices. They also serve Mexican, American and Hawaiian breakfasts.

BIG ISLAND GRILL

$–$$ LOCAL-STYLE   ✉*75-5702 Kuakini Highway, Kona*   ☎*808-326-1153*

Just a block off the main Kona tourist drag, and half a world away, lies a casual family restaurant that's always hopping. Portions are hefty, and the emphasis is on local cuisine, such as the *loco moco*—a burger patty and egg atop rice, smothered in gravy—plate lunches, sandwiches and hamburgers.

KYOTOYA SUSHI SHOP
$ SUSHI ✉North Kona Shopping Center, Kuakini Highway and Kalani Road
📞808-987-8490

At the North Kona Shopping Center you'll find a take-out window with a patio and tables serving, you guessed it, sushi. Closed Sunday.

KONA INN RESTAURANT
$$$–$$$$ AMERICAN ✉75-5744 Alii Drive 📞808-329-4455 📠808-327-9358

The commemorative sign at the Kona Inn tells the tale of the old inn—how it was built back in the steamship era when Kona was gaining fame as a marlin fishing ground. The bad news is that the original hotel was converted into a shopping mall—of which this contemporary namesake is a part. The good news is that the restaurant is quite attractive—an open-air, oceanfront affair with two separate dining facilities. The Kona Inn serves grilled appetizers and sandwiches in its café/grill. The dining room has a separate menu with several fresh fish dishes daily as well as Hawaiian-style chicken.

LULU'S
$$ DELI ✉75-5819 Alii Drive 📞808-331-2633 📠808-329-6766

Set on a second-story terrace overlooking the ocean, Lulu's is one of Kailua's pleasingly windswept addresses. You can lean against the tile bar or sink into a booth, then order from a straightforward sandwiches-salads-and-hamburgers menu.

JAMESON'S BY THE SEA
$$$–$$$$ SEAFOOD ✉77-6452 Alii Drive near Disappearing Sands Beach
📞808-329-3195 📠808-329-0780

This is a lovely waterfront restaurant with an emphasis on fresh local seafood dishes. Tucked unpretentiously into the corner of a large condominium, Jameson's conveys a modest sense of elegance: bentwood furniture, potted palms, a seascape from the lanai or through plate-glass windows and good service. Choose from an enticing menu of fresh local catches, steaks, chicken dishes and other gourmet delights. Lunch and dinner weekdays, dinner only on weekends.

SHOPPING

You might remember that song about how "L.A. is a great big freeway." Well, the Hawaiian version could easily be "Kailua is a great big shopping mall." I have never seen so many shopping arcades squeezed into so small a space. Here are goldsmiths, boutiques, jewelers galore, travel agencies, sandal-makers, knickknack shops, sundries, T-shirt shops and much, much more, all crowded onto Alii Drive.

KONA INN SHOPPING VILLAGE ✉Alii Drive 📞808-329-6573 This shopping center, which parallels the waterfront, features dozens of shops. Because of its convenient location and variety of stores, it is the center of the visitor shopping scene.

COCONUT GROVE MARKETPLACE ✉75-5801 Alii Drive Toward the south end of town, this complex features a selection of restaurants and shops, including the **Collector Fine Art Gallery** (808-331-1100). This gallery features the works of local and international artists, with a great selection of paintings, ceramics, art glass, woodworks, as well as less pricey art objects.

HULIHEE PALACE GIFT SHOP

✉75-5718 Alii Drive ☎808-329-1877 This small store located behind the palace, specializes in Hawaiian handicrafts and literature.

WATERFRONT ROW ✉75-5770 Alii Drive This is one of the more tastefully designed malls, a raw-wood-and-plank-floor shopping complex with perhaps a dozen stores and restaurants.

TROPICAL HEAT WAVE ✉75-5744 Alii Drive ☎808-329-4348 For a selection of affordable arts and crafts, some locally made, some imported, step into this cool store.

KONA MARKETPLACE ✉75-5669 C Alii Drive Within this buzzing complex is the **Kim Taylor Reece Gallery** (808-331-2433), which specializes in artistic photographs of classic hula dancers.

FARMERS MARKETS

✉Alii and Hualalai drives Kona's outdoors "farmers' markets" go well beyond fresh produce, macadamia nuts, coffee and flowers to include hand-crafted art, resortwear, and Hawaiian-themed souvenirs. **Kailua Village Farmers Market** (808-329-6573), where local growers gather under plastic tarps to sell their wares, is a good place to pick up home-grown fruits and vegetables. Open Wednesday through Sunday, 9 a.m. to 5 p.m. North of town, **Alii Gardens Marketplace** (75-6129 Alii Drive; 808-334-1381) offers a huge range of goods. Open Wednesday, Friday, Saturday and Sunday, 9 a.m. to 5 p.m.

NIGHTLIFE

What action there is in Kailua is near the shorefront on Alii Drive. Several of the waterfront nightspots in Kailua shine spotlights in the water so you can watch manta rays gliding along the shore.

HUGGO'S ✉Alii Drive and Kakakai ☎808-329-1493 With its stunning ocean views, this place is usually packed to the gills. Various live bands perform every evening.

LULU'S RESTAURANT & BAR ✉75-5819 Alii Drive ☎808-331-2633 The younger set will gravitate toward the rather raucous Lulu's for its dancefloor and deejays on the weekends, amateur sumo wrestling competition on Wednesday nights and free salsa and line-dancing lessons on Tuesday and Sunday, respectively.

Stargazing

For a different kind of nightlife, turn to the skies for some stargazing. The vast open spaces and crystal-clear air make Hawaii a prime nocturnal viewing spot. A couple of outfitters offer a unique excursion: they'll pick you up and take you to the mountain while providing an informative narrative on the astronomy, geology and geography of Hawaii. After you've experienced a Hawaiian sunset they'll take you mid-mountain, where the highlight of the evening begins: stargazing through portable telescopes with narration provided by knowledgeable experts. The evening concludes with hot chocolate and the peace of the night skies. Contact **Mauna Kea Summit Adventures** (P.O. Box 9027, Kailua-Kona, HI 96745; 808-322-2366, 888-322-2366; www.maunakea.com, e-mail reservations@maunakea.com) or **Hawaii Forest & Trail** (74-5035B Kaahumanu Highway, Kailua-Kona; 808-331-8505, 800-464-1993; www.hawaii-forest.com) to book your excursion.

WINDJAMMER LOUNGE ⊠*Royal Kona Resort, 75-5852 Alii Drive* ✆*808-329-3111* ⌨*www.royalkona.com* For an evening of slow rhythms and dancing cheek to cheek, drop by this lounge, which has live music and entertainment on weekends.

KONA BREWING COMPANY
⊠*75-5629 Kuakini Highway* ✆*808-334-2739* To sample Hawaii's own designer beers, check out this brew pub, serving an exotic array of local flavors in addition to specializing in pizzas and salads.

BIG ISLAND COMEDY CLUB ✆*808-329-4368* For an evening of laughs, call to find out where this ever-moving event is being staged. It's usually at a popular nightspot in Kailua or elsewhere along the coast.

THE OTHER SIDE ⊠*74-5484 Kaiwi Street* ✆*808-329-7226* Catering to both a gay and straight clientele, pool tables, dart boards and recorded sounds are the names of the game here.

BEACHES & PARKS

HALE HALAWAI
⊠*Near the intersection of Alii Drive and Hualalai Road in Kailua*
Here you'll find a small oceanfront park fringed with coconut trees. There's an activities pavilion but no beach. Its central location in Kailua does make the park a perfect place to watch the sunset, though.

OLD KONA AIRPORT STATE RECREATION AREA
⊠*About one-half mile northwest of the King Kamehameha Kona Beach Hotel on Kuakini Highway in Kailua*
⚓ 🏄 ⛱ This white-sand beach parallels Kailua's former landing strip, extending for a half-mile along a lava-crusted

shore. Very popular with Kailuans, it's a conveniently located spot for catching some rays (sun, that is). The water is shallow, with a rocky bottom. There are a few sand channels for entering the water; and there is a sandy inlet good for kids just north of the lighthouse. This area offers excellent diving. Principal catches are threadfin, big-eyed scad, bonefish, *papio* and especially mullet. Facilities include a picnic area, restrooms and showers. The park gate is closed every evening at 8 p.m.

KAMAKAHONU

✉ *West end of Alii Drive, adjacent to the pier*

This snippet of sand hugs the south-most corner of Kailua Bay adjacent to the pier. It's a popular spot with local kids and guests at the adjacent King Kamehameha's Kona Beach Resort. Kayakers and distance swimmers also take advantage of the calm beachside to access the waters of Kailua Bay. The restored Ahuena Heiau provides a great backdrop for a swim. Both the beach and temple were part of Kamehameha's royal compound, called *Kamakahonu*, "the eye of the turtle." Snorkeling offers great view of tropical fish.

HONOKOHAU BEACH

✉ *To get there take Kaahumanu Highway a couple miles north from Kailua. Turn onto the road to Honokohau Small Boat Harbor. From the north side of the harbor, walk about 600 yards farther north to the beach.*

This was once Kailua's nude beach, but prohibitions are now in effect. Folks come for miles to soak up the sun on this long narrow strand; it's bordered by a lagoon, backdropped by distant mountains, protected by a shallow reef and highly recommended for the adventurous. Since the water is well-protected, it's good for swimming, although a bit shallow. There are recommended spots for skindiving south of the small-boat harbor but stay away from the harbor itself since sharks are ubiquitous. Surfers enjoy Honokohau's waves. Rather than fish here, try Kaloko Pond about one-half mile north. There are no facilities here.

MAHAIULA BEACH—KEKAHA KAI STATE PARK

✉ *The beach is located 2.6 miles north of Keahole Airport. Drive down an unpaved ocean road about 1.5 miles to the parking lot. Take the turnoff marked State Park, about five miles north of the Kona international airport.*

A not-very-good road, partly paved, mostly bumpy, leads to beautiful Mahaiula Beach with its white sands and clear blue waters. At the head of a well-protected and deep bay, the swimming is great, as are the snorkeling and diving. In ancient times this coast was (and is) one of the richest in marine resources. There are restrooms, but you must bring your own water. The posted 7 p.m. gate closing should be taken seriously.

MAKALAWENA BEACH

North of Mahaiula Beach. It can be reached along the coastal foot trail from Mahaiula Beach (about 30 minutes each way). This is on private land, so for off-trail activities you need permission from the owner.

🏃 🏖 🐟 🚣 Makalawena, the next beach to the north of Mahaiula, is another beautiful stretch of North Kona coast. Sand dunes are the backdrop for this shoreline made up of intricate caves. If you're a shell collector or birder (Opaeula Pond here is a waterbird sanctuary), this is the place to go. Now and then the modern world intrudes, since the beaches are not far from the jets departing Kona International.

DISAPPEARING SANDS BEACH

Alii Drive, four miles south of Kailua

🏖 🤿 🚣 A small strand studded with volcanic rocks, this spot is also called Magic Sands. It seems that the white sand periodically washes away, exposing a lava shoreline. When still carpeted with sand, this is a very crowded place—a favorite area for swimming and bodysurfing. Kona's best surfing spot is just north of here at "Banyans," with breaks year-round over a shallow reef. For anglers, the major catches include mullet, threadfin, big-eyed scad, bonefish and *papio*. Restrooms and showers are the only facilities.

KAHALUU BEACH PARK

Alii Drive, five miles south of Kailua

🏖 🐟 🤿 🚣 Set along the south shore of Kahaluu Bay, this county park is fringed with palm trees. The salt-and-pepper beach is small and often crowded. Swimming is excellent here since the cove is partially protected by outlying rocks. Tropical fish abound, making this a recommended place for snorkeling, especially beginners. Surfing is good near the reef during periods of high surf. Anglers fish for mullet, threadfin, big-eyed scad, bonefish and *papio*. The bay is also a good spot for throw-netting and surround-netting. Facilities include picnic areas, pavilions, showers and restrooms.

KOHALA COAST

Stretching from the northern boundary of Kona to the northwestern tip of the Big Island are the districts of South and North Kohala. One element that comes as a visual shock to many first-time visitors to the Big Island's west coast is the endless stretch of black lava that blankets this dry terrain. Standing in the windshadow of both Mauna Loa and Mauna Kea, this region projects the bald unreality of a moonscape. But the ragged shoreline has been trimmed with stands of palm trees and sections along the roadways are splashed with bougainvillea.

During the last several decades South Kohala, which includes some of the island's prettiest beaches, saw the building of one upscale resort after another. Farther north, where Kohala Mountain forms a 5000-foot-high spine, the territory remains much as it has for decades. As the Kaahumanu Highway (Route 19) gives way to the northerly Akoni Pule Highway (Route 270), the landscape eventually changes from dry and barren to tropical and luxurious.

Geologically, the Kohala Coast was the section of the island that first rose from the sea. Later, as the volcanoes that formed Kohala Mountain became extinct, the region evolved into a center of historical importance. Kamehameha I was born and raised along this wind-blasted coastline and it was here that he initially consolidated his power base. The region is filled with ancient *heiau* as well as more recent cemeteries that date to the era when sugar dominated the local economy.

Exploring this region from Kailua-Kona you will find that Kaahumanu Highway cuts across a broad swath of lava-crusted country. This area is becoming increasingly developed with both high-end resort properties and is also slated for an extensive new community of homes, shops, schools and parks for native Hawaiians, through the state Department of Hawaiian Homelands. There are views of Maui to the north, Mauna Kea to the east and Hualalai to the south.

The site of the Puukohola *heiau* and the main harbor for this stretch of coast, Kawaihae, also offers several shops and restaurants and makes a good stop en route to North Kohala or Waimea.

SIGHTS

South Kohala

Waikoloa's Anaehoomalu Bay provides a dividing line between the districts of North Kona and South Kohala, which runs from Anaehoomalu to a border with North Kohala 20 miles beyond Kawaiahae. Old lava flows, mostly from Hualalai, dominate the landscape, with grasses the primary groundcover.

WAIKOLOA For evidence of Kohala's historic significance you need look no farther than Waikoloa, located between Honokaa and Waimea. While the area is now heavily developed with tourist resorts, it is also the site of the **Waikoloa Petroglyph Field**. Here you can wander amidst a forbidding lava field etched with ancient symbols. The contrast, with a modern golf course on one side and primitive rock carvings on the other, is ironic to say the least. The path to the petroglyphs is .3-mile in length and begins at the Kings' Shops Mall in Waikoloa. This rough lava course is part of the King's Trail, a mid-19th-century trail built for horseback riders making the 32-mile trip from Kailua to Puako.

HILTON WAIKALOA VILLAGE ⊠425 Waikoloa Beach Drive, Waikoloa ☎808-886-1234 ☏808-886-2900 ✐info@hiltonwaikaloavillage.com Not exactly a hidden destination, this is worth a look-see if you are staying on the Kohala Coast. The Hilton Waikoloa, the closest thing to a theme park you'll find on the island, offers a four-acre swimming and snorkeling la-

Kohala Coast

SUSHI ROCK
BAMBOO RESTAURANT
LAPAKAHI STATE HISTORICAL PARK
Hawi
Kawaihae
Puako
"69" BEACH

SUSHI ROCK

PAGE 196

Hawi's dining gem with super fresh fish in colorful, original sushi rolls—dine indoors or al fresco

BAMBOO RESTAURANT

PAGE 196

Wonderfully restored 1920s general store turned gallery, restaurant and live Hawaiian music venue

LAPAKAHI STATE HISTORICAL PARK

PAGE 191

Preserved ancient Hawaiian village with fishing shrines, canoe sheds, housing sites and burial plots

"69" BEACH

PAGE 199

Fallen *kiawe* trees providing tiny hideaways on a white-sand shoreline in a rocky cove perfect for snorkeling

goon, an interactive dolphin guest program, waterfalls, lush gardens and numerous dining spots. You can ride a tram or hop onto a mahogany canal boat (you'll feel like you're on the jungle ride at Disneyland, but without the hippos coming up for air) to tour the facility. Better yet, stroll around and gaze at the stunning artworks that adorn the lobbies and gardens of this massive facility. (Reservations are required for the dolphin encounters.)

ANAEHOOMALU BEACH ✉*A half-mile off Kaahumanu Highway, about 25 miles north of Kailua near the 76-mile marker* The Outrigger Waikoloa fronts one of Hawaii's most beautiful beaches, Anaehoomalu. This area, with its sheltered cove and natural ponds, was once a gathering place for Hawaiian royalty. Sea turtles and other marine life call this bay home. (See "Beaches & Parks" below.)

PUAKO PETROGLYPH FIELD _____

✉*A short spur off Mauna Lani resort's main road* Going north on the Kaahumanu Highway you'll pass a desolate desert of black lava before coming to the community of Puako. It's an easy walk on the Malama Petroglyph Trail to the extensive petroglyph field. There are hundreds of examples of this Hawaiian art form at

Kohala Coast

Alenuihaha Channel

PACIFIC OCEAN

Birthplace of Kamehameha I

Mookini Heiau

Halaula

Hawi

Kapaau

270

Keokea Beach Park

Kapaa Beach Park

Kamehameha Rock

Mahukona Beach Park

Lapakahi State Historical Park

Pololu Valley Lookout

Akoni Pule HWY

Kohala Mountain Rd

KOHALA MTNS

N

0 ____ 5 miles
0 ____ 5 kilometers

270

250

WAIPIO VALLEY

Kawaihae

Spencer Beach Park
Kawaihae Bay

Waiaka

To Honokaa

19

19

Puukohola National Historic Site

Waimea (Kamuela)

Hapuna Bay
Waialea Bay

Puako

Hapuna Beach State Park

190

19

Kohala Coast

Waikoloa Petroglyph Field

Waikoloa

Trail

Anaehoomalu Beach

Hilton Waikoloa Village

HWY

Kiholo Bay

Kaupulehu

Kiholo

Mamalahoa

Trail

Kaahumanu

19

Queen

King's

190

Puuanahulu

200

▲ Puu Waawaa 3867'

To Kailua-Kona

Puako, with warriors and outriggers, surfers and sailing ships some of the numerous themes. (It is not permitted to do stencil work on either the old petroglyphs or the contemporary examples that line the trail.)

PUUKOHOLA NATIONAL HISTORIC SITE

North of Mauna Kea Beach Hotel lies the harbor of **Kawaihae**, one of the island's busiest ports and the locale of two major *heiau*, **Mailekini** and **Puukohola**, which have been dedicated as the Puukohola National Historic Site. Kamehameha built the impressive triple-tiered Puukohola in 1791 after a prophet related that doing so would ensure his victory over his rivals. At the temple dedication, the ambitious chief aided the prophecy by treacherously slaying his principal enemy. Measuring 224 feet by 100 feet, it was built of lava rocks and boulders that were fitted together using no mortar.

PUA MAU PLACE BOTANIC & SCULPTURE GARDEN ✉10 Ala Kahua Drive, Kawaiahae ☎808-882-0888 ⌨www.puamau.org, irinaprinap@turquoise.net Only one-third of this garden's 45 acres has been planted, but the results are already colorfully spectacular, highlighted by towering hedges of bougainvillaea, and giant plumeria interspersed with giant bronze insect sculptures with a sci-fi appeal. Take the book describing Pua Mau's plants for a self-guided walking tour. Admission.

North Kohala
North Kohala includes much of the mountainous peninsula that provides the Big island with its northernmost lands. The landscape rises from a coastal plain to the lushly forested slopes of the Kohala Mountains.

LAPAKAHI STATE HISTORICAL PARK

✉12 miles north of Kawaihae ☎808-882-6207 ☎808-882-6208 Along Akoni Pule Highway (Route 270) is a preserved village that provides a unique glimpse into ancient Hawaiian ways. This is definitely worth a leisurely look-see. Dating back 600 years, this one-of-a-kind site includes fishing shrines, canoe sheds, house sites and burial plots.

MOOKINI HEIAU

✉Reached by taking a left at the Upolu airfield, then following the dirt road for a mile and a half. Make sure you visit this *heiau*, one of the oldest (possibly as old as A.D. 800) and most historically significant archaeological sites from old Hawaii, linked by legend to the arrival of the priest Paao from Tahiti. A holy place, it measures 250 feet by 130 feet. The **Birthplace of Kamehameha I**, marked with a plaque, lies one-third mile (and two gates) farther west along the same road. The boulders here are reputed to be the original birthstones. The isolated setting is seldom visited, which adds to the spiritual sense of discovery the site offers.

HAWI AND KAPAAU The old plantation town of Hawi, with its trim houses and freshly painted storefronts, harkens back to an earlier era. Back in the 1980s, when the sugar cane industry was in decline, the town looked rather forlorn. But by the beginning of this century it had been completely restored by artists and entrepreneurs. Like neighboring Kapaau, it shows its new face in the form of small galleries and local shops. Both are charming enclaves adorned with small churches and relics from the days when sugar was king.

KAMEHAMEHA STATUE

Pride of Kapaau is the original Kamehameha Statue, a nine-ton creation cast in bronze. The more famous Honolulu monument is actually a replica of this gilt figure. Crafted in Florence around 1879 by an American sculptor, the original disappeared at sea on its way to Hawaii but was later recovered and installed here.

The **courthouse** behind the Kamehameha statue is equally historic, providing a glimpse of small-town life enhanced by informational signs. Senior citizens often man a desk and "talk story" with those with questions or aloha to share.

BOND ESTATE

✉*Off Route 270, Kapaau* A marked side road off Route 270 just east of Kapaau leads through a macadamia orchard to the Bond Estate. One of Hawaii's best preserved missionary estates, it dates back to 1841, when it was built by Reverend Elias Bond and his wife, Ellen. Their Maine background is reflected in the New England–style architecture of the stone house, church, school and plantation buildings. Bond designed the property as a self-sufficient farm to sustain his family, his parishioners and the school where Ellen educated teachers for the 32 one-room schoolhouses the Bonds would eventually establish around the Kohala district. The family eventually converted the farm into a sprawling sugar cane plantation, which became the largest employer in the area and flourished for 100 years. A 1973 earthquake damaged the buildings, and two years later the sugar operation shut down for good. The buildings are on the National Register of Historic Places.

POLOLU VALLEY LOOKOUT

Along this lush, rainy side of the peninsula are taro patches and pandanus forests. Past the **Kamehameha Rock** (a large boulder that the mighty conqueror reputedly carried from the sea), Route 270 ends at Pololu Valley Lookout. The view here overlooking Pololu Valley extends along the monumental cliffs that guard Hawaii's north coast. A half-mile trail leads down to a lovely beach, but watch out for the treacherous riptides.

KOHALA MOUNTAIN

You can climb the back of this mountain along Route 250 (Kohala Mountain Road) from Hawi. This completes a loop tour of North Kohala. Rising to 3564 feet, the road rolls through cactus-studded range country and offers startling views down steep volcanic slopes to the sea. En route are cattle ranches, stands of

Norfolk pine and eucalyptus, and curving countryside covered with sweet grasses and wildflowers.

LODGING

South Kohala

For years the Kohala district was a placid region strewn with lava and dotted by several pearly beaches. A single resort stood along its virgin coastline. Today, a series of upscale resorts can be found.

WAIKOLOA BEACH MARRIOTT RESORT

$$$$ 545 ROOMS   ✉69-275 Waikoloa Beach Drive, Waikoloa   ☎808-886-6789, 800-922-5533   ✆808-886-3601   ⌨www.waikoloabeach.com

This sprawling resort stands along the golden strand of Anaehoomalu Beach, one of Hawaii's most beautiful beaches. The resort boasts an airy lobby decorated with teak furnishings. Guest rooms with rattan furnishings and neutral tones are quite roomy and comfortable, and you can wander the 15 acres of lovely gardens and discover ancient petroglyph fields and a royal fishpond.

MAUNA LANI BAY HOTEL AND BUNGALOWS

$$$$ 343 ROOMS   ✉68-1400 Mauna Lani Drive, Kohala Coast   ☎808-885-6622, 800-367-2323   ✆808-885-1484   ⌨www.maunalani.com, reservations@maunalani.com

This 3200-acre resort rests on a white-sand beach. Designed in the shape of an arrowhead, this luxurious facility offers two golf courses, six tennis courts, a spa and fitness center and five restaurants, several of which are award winners. With brilliant green gardens set against black lava, the landscape combines curving lawns and palm-ringed fishponds. Each guest room is spaciously laid out and designed in a pastel motif.

THE FAIRMONT ORCHID, HAWAII

$$$$ 539 ROOMS   ✉1 North Kaniku Drive, Kohala Coast   ☎808-885-2000, 800-845-9905   ✆808-885-5778   ⌨www.fairmont.com/orchid, orc.orchidwholesale@fairmont.com

With grounds that are spacious, beautifully landscaped and maintained, the Orchid sits on a lovely crescent of white sand that is ideal for swimming. Rooms are spacious, with earth-toned walls. There are a large oceanside swimming pool, 11 tennis courts, four restaurants, fitness center, with the resort's two 18-hole golf courses adjacent.

HAPUNA BEACH PRINCE HOTEL AT MAUNA KEA RESORT

$$$$ 350 ROOMS   ✉62-100 Kaunaoa Drive, Kohala Coast   ☎808-880-1111, 800-882-6060   ✆808-880-3142   ⌨www.hapunabeachhotel.com, reservations@princehawaii.com

The sprawling Hapuna Beach Prince is nestled into the bluffs above a wide expanse of sandy beach. The posh resort features beautifully landscaped grounds and offers two golf courses, tennis courts, a spa and children's programs. The guest rooms are decorated in shades of peach and beige, and most have large lanais and ocean views.

KOHALA VILLAGE INN

$–$$ 19 ROOMS   ✉55-514 Hawi Road, Hawi ☎808-889-0404

✐www.kohalavillageinn.com, info@kohalavillageinn.com

In the small rustic town of Hawi near Hawaii's northwestern tip, this inn and an adjacent restaurant are the hottest spots around. But there's still privacy and quiet aplenty out back in the sleeping quarters. Rooms in this establishment feature tin roofs, private baths, ceiling fans, internet access and handsome hardwood floors, and face a small courtyard. The place is tidy. There are also rooms in an adjacent building.

CONDOS

One way to avoid the high cost of the five-star Kohala Coast resorts is to rent a condominium in one of the many complexes.

VISTA WAIKOLOA

125 UNITS   ✉Waikoloa Beach Resort, 69-1010 Keana Place, Waikoloa

☎800-822-4252 ℻808-883-9818 ✐www.southkohala.com, info@southkohala.com

The Vista is a three-story condominium complex along Waikoloa Beach that offers air-conditioned two-bedroom luxury suites with large windows and kitchens complete with dishwashers. The dining areas are on private 380-square-foot lanais. There's a heated outdoor pool as well as whirlpools, an exercise room, and washers and dryers. Three-night minimum stay. Prices range from $182 to $360 a night.

MAUNA LANI POINT VILLAS

116 UNITS   ✉68-1050 Mauna Lani Point Drive, Kohala Coast ☎800-642-6284

℻808-885-5015 ✐www.classicresorts.com, info@classicresorts.com

Spread across 19 oceanfront acres, these luxuriously appointed condos are close to a white-sand beach. They also have access to the resort's beaches, jogging trails and a 27-acre historic preserve. Some of the units can fit up to four people; prices range from $350 to $495 a night for one-bedroom units; two-bedroom units run from $465 to $695 a night. Three-night minimum stay required.

PUAKO BEACH CONDOMINIUMS

38 UNITS   ✉Puako Beach Drive, Puako ☎808-882-7000, 800-332-7081

✐www.vacationbigisland.com, seaside@aloha.net

This is the only condominium complex in the secluded beachfront community of Puako. It's a long four-story structure located next to the Puako Store, across the street from the beach and one mile from the luxuriant white sands of Hapuna Beach State Park. All 38 units are air-conditioned, mostly three-bedroom, two-bath units designed to sleep up to six, with a king-size bed, a queen-size bed and two twins. Most units have views of the ocean in front and Mauna Kea in back. The grounds are nicely landscaped with flower gardens, and there are a round swimming pool and a children's wading pool. The nightly rate is

$195, except during the Christmas holiday when it is $200 a night with a two-week minimum.

195

DINING

South Kohala

Dining out in South Kohala means resort dining, which includes a wide range of upscale hotel restaurants, with additional restaurants, including inexpensive fast food options like pizza and tacos at the Queen's Court at the Kings' Shops at Waikoloa.

GRAND PALACE CHINESE RESTAURANT

$$–$$$ CHINESE ✉ *Kings' Shops at Waikoloa Beach Resort, 69-275 Waikoloa Beach Drive, Waikoloa* ✆ *808-886-6668*

Outside the expensive resorts, you'll find the Grand Palace a welcome change along Hawaii's northwestern shore. The menu offers plenty of choices, with seafood the specialty of the house. With sizzling noodle dishes and traditional favorites such as wonton soup and egg foo young, this place provides delicious meals at an affordable price.

VILLAGE STEAK HOUSE

$$$ STEAK ✉ *Hilton Waikoloa Village, 69-425 Waikoloa Beach Drive, Waikoloa* ✆ *808-883-9644*

Whether you're a duffer or not this dining facility boasts plate-glass views of the Waikoloa Village Golf Course. Selections such as filet mignons, porterhouses, New York strips and T-bone steaks are no surprise, but you can also find fresh fish, shrimp and chicken entrées. Daily specials round out the menu. No dinner Sunday and Monday.

BAY TERRACE

$–$$ CONTINENTAL ✉ *Mauna Lani Bay Hotel, 68-1400 Mauna Lani Drive, Kohala Coast* ✆ *808-885-6622* ✆ *808-885-1478*

The Mauna Lani Bay Hotel hosts some well-known, formal and very expensive restaurants. At the Bay Terrace there's an ever-changing menu. The offerings may include fresh, tropical fruit, smoked turkey benedict or brioche French toast.

CANOE HOUSE

$$$$ PACIFIC RIM ✉ *Mauna Lani Bay Hotel, 68-1400 Mauna Lani Drive, Kohala Coast* ✆ *808-885-6622* ✆ *808-885-1478*

One of the Big Island's most highly regarded dining rooms, specializing in Pacific Rim cuisine and offering spectacular sunsets as an appetizer, the Canoe House delivers fine food and a fine time. The menu, which changes frequently, is a creative mix of island and Asian dishes. Dinner only. Reservations strongly recommended.

BLUE DOLPHIN RESTAURANT

$$$ PACIFIC RIM/MEDITERRANEAN   ✉*61-3616 Kawaihae Road, Kawaihae*
☎*808-882-7771*   📠*808-880-1995*

For a comfortable outdoor dining pavilion where you can enjoy Pacific/
Mediterranean dishes like *nori*-wrapped tempura *ahi* with tropical
fruit salsa or sautéed mahimahi with hot buttered macadamia nuts
stop here. Call for dinner hours. Closed on rainy days.

CAFÉ PESTO

$$–$$$$ ITALIAN   ✉*Kawaihae Shopping Center, Suite 101, Kawaihae*
☎*808-882-1071*   📠*808-882-1459*   ✑*www.cafepesto.com, cafepesto@excite.com*

If you cast anchor in the town of Kawaihae, consider this Italian eatery.
Gourmet pizza is the specialty at this simple café. But you'll also find
pastas prepared with Asian flair, risottos and fresh fish.

TRES HOMBRES BEACH GRILL

$$–$$$ MEXICAN   ✉*Kawaihae Shopping Center, Kawaihae*   ☎*808-882-1031*

The food is Mexican but the theme is surfing here. Incidentally, there is
a great display of surfing memorabilia and some of the bar counters are
even fashioned from surfboards.

KAWAIHAE HARBOR GRILL & SEAFOOD BAR

$$–$$$$ SEAFOOD   ✉*Route 270, Kawaihae*   ☎*808-882-1368*   📠*808-882-7005*

Located across from Kawaihae Harbor, this grill and seafood bar's
menu runs from burgers to catch-of-the-day, pastas to steak. Alfresco
seating is a pleasant option at this casual restaurant known for its fresh
fish. For dessert, try the *lilikoi* (passion fruit) cheesecake.

North Kohala

BAMBOO RESTAURANT

$$–$$$ PACIFIC RIM/LOCAL-STYLE   ✉*Akoni Pule Highway, Hawi*
☎*808-889-5555*   📠*808-889-6192*   ✑*www.thebamboorestaurant.info*

Up near Kohala's northern tip, in the well-preserved historic
town of Hawi, is a wonderful restaurant located in the 1920s-era
general store turned gallery. This eatery is decorated with tropi-
cal plants and art, and the menu offers a mix of Pacific regional
and "local style" cuisine and includes such items as Thai coconut
prawns and grilled fresh island fish in a variety of preparations.
All meats and produce served are locally grown. There's Hawai-
ian music Friday and Saturday nights. Definitely worth a stop.
Reservations suggested. Closed Sunday night and Monday.

SUSHI ROCK

$$ SUSHI   ✉*Akoni Pule Highway, Hawi*   ☎*808-889-5900*
✑*wobounds@aol.com*

This is a little dining gem in Hawi, offering super fresh fish and
chicken dishes, and a variety of colorful, original rolls served at

indoor and outdoor tables. The menu includes all the old favorites, along with some innovations, such as roasted local fish
with macadamia nuts and fruit with avocado. You can even pick
up some Japanese dinnerware in the gift shop inside the restaurant. Locals drive from afar to dine here.

KOHALA COFFEE MILL

$ COFFEEHOUSE/DESSERTS ✉ *Akoni Pule Highway, Hawi* 📞 *808-889-5577,*
877-301-7683 🖳 *808-889-5062*

In the center of Hawi is a café that serves coffee, smoothies, shaved ices,
homemade fudge and pastries, but especially Tropical Dreams Ice
Cream. Created locally, Tropical Dreams whips up exotic flavors like
mango, white chocolate ginger and lychee.

HULA LA'S MEXICAN KITCHEN & SALSA FACTORY

$ MEXICAN ✉ *Kohala Trade Center, Hawi* 📞 *808-889-5668*

At Hula La's Mexican Kitchen & Salsa Factory, nachos, soft tacos and
green chicken enchiladas are only part of the full menu. Food is
freshly prepared and delicious.

KOHALA DINER

$ DINER ✉ *Just off Akoni Pule Highway about one mile east of Hawi*
📞 *808-889-0208* 🖳 *808-884-5051* ✑ *www.kohaladiner.wp.net*

For a taste of funky, traditional Hawaii there's this diner. Set in a
tinroof plantation building with bare walls and plastic tablecloths, it serves breakfast, lunch and dinner at super-low prices.

SHOPPING

South Kohala

RESORT SHOPPING Shopping in Kohala was once a matter of un-
covering family-owned crafts shops in tiny towns. Now that it has become a major resort area, you can browse designer stores in several
top-flight hotels. Simply drive along Akoni Pule Highway between
Kailua and the Kohala Peninsula; you'll encounter, from south to north,
the **Royal Waikoloan**, **Hilton Waikoloa Village**, **Mauna Lani Bay Hotel**
and the **Mauna Kea Beach Hotel**. Each of these resort complexes features an array of boutiques, knickknack shops, jewelers, sundries and
other outlets.

KINGS' SHOPS AT WAIKOLOA ✉ *Waikoloa Beach Drive, Waikoloa* Set on
the road leading in to the Waikoloa resort complex, this mall contains
clothing stores, a sundries shop and several other promising enterprises. One must-stop shop is the **Ukulele House** (808-886-8587)
where a beautiful and diverse collection of Hawaii's signature instruments are found. Choices start at under $25 and price upward into the
hundreds. It's fun browsing even if you have no intention of making
a purchase.

THE GALLERY AT BAMBOO

✉*Akoni Pule Highway, Hawi* ✆*808-889-1441* The tiny town of Hawi, another of the island's clapboard plantation towns, hosts several artist shops. The Gallery at Bamboo has a marvelous collection of island clothes, jewelry and Hawaiian art.

KOHALA BOOK SHOP ✉*54-3885 Akoni Pule Highway, Kapaau* ✆*808-889-6400*

✎*www.kohalabooks.com* Hawaii's largest used bookstore isn't located in Honolulu, but in small town Kapaau. The book shop's selection includes many hard-to-get classics of Hawaiiana as well as a well-stocked contemporary bookshelf. Leave yourself some time to browse. Closed Sunday.

ACKERMAN GALLERIES ✉*Akoni Pule Highway, Kapaau* ✆*808-889-5971*

✎*www.ackermangalleries.com* Along Akoni Pule Highway, in the falsefront town of Kapaau, you'll find these galleries. Divided into two different stores on opposite sides of the street, Ackerman's features fine art in one location (closed Sunday) and crafts items in the other.

NIGHTLIFE

HONU BAR ✉*Mauna Lani Bay Hotel, 68-1400 Mauna Lani Drive, Kawaihae* ✆*808-885-6622* This bar features live music on weekends and is one of several places in this spacious resort to dance, listen to Hawaiian music or imbibe. Some guests, however, may prefer a game of chess, pool or backgammon.

PANIOLO LOUNGE AND POLO BAR ✉*The Fairmont Orchid, 1 North Kaniku Drive, Kohala Coast* ✆*808-885-2000* Board games and billiards are what's on tap in this stylish setting.

CLIPPER LOUNGE ✉*Royal Waikoloan, Kaahumanu Highway, Waikoloa* ✆*808-886-6789* The night scene at this resort centers around this watering hole that offers live bands as a backdrop.

BAMBOO RESTAURANT

✉*Akoni Pule Highway, Hawi* ✆*808-889-5555* Locals and visitors alike head here for Hawaiian music on Friday and Saturday nights. Reservations recommended.

BEACHES & PARKS

ANAEHOOMALU BEACH

✉*A half-mile off Kaahumanu Highway, about 25 miles north of Kailua near the 76-mile marker, fronting the Outrigger Waikoloa*

An enchanting area, this is one of the island's most beautiful beaches. There are palm trees, two ancient fishponds filled with barracuda, and a long crescent of white sand. Turn from the sea and take in the gorgeous mountain scenery. Or explore the nearby petroglyph field and archaeological ruins. This beach is very popular and often crowded since it's fronted by a major resort complex. Swimming is excellent along this partially protected shore; there is no lifeguard on duty. Snorkeling is good for beginners but it lacks the scenic diversity elsewhere. Mullet, threadfin, big-eyed scad, bonefish and *papio* are among the usual catches here. Facilities include picnic tables, restrooms and an outdoor shower; there are restaurants in the adjacent Marriott Waikoloa Beach.

SECRET POND AT MAUNA LANI

✉ *Adjacent to the series of fish ponds at the Mauna Lani Resort, 68-1400 Mauna Lani Drive*

🏃 🏊 Secret Pond's cool fresh waters are reached on the trail that leads past the fishponds to the coast. The pool was created in the 19th century when stream waters were enclosed by a lava rock wall. The crystal blue-green waters are inviting, although the pool is too small for much of a swim.

"69" BEACH OR WAIALEA BAY

✉ *Near the entrance to Hapuna Beach Park, about five miles south of Kawaihae. From Kaahumanu Highway, turn into the park entrance. Then take the paved road that runs southwest from the park (between the beach and the A-frames). Go about six-tenths of a mile on this road and then turn right on a dirt road (the road at the very bottom of the hill). When the road forks, after about one-tenth mile, go left. Follow this road another one-tenth mile around to the beach.*

🏊 🐟 🎣 No, it's not what you might think. This lovely beach is named for a numbered utility pole at the road turn-off rather than for licentious beach parties. The white-sand shoreline extends several hundred yards along a rocky cove. Despite houses nearby, the spot is fairly secluded; fallen *kiawe* trees along the beachfront provide tiny hideaways. It's a good place to swim but exercise caution. When the water is calm it's also a good spot for snorkeling. Surfers paddle out to the breaks near the southwest end of the bay and off the northwest point. There are no facilities here.

HAPUNA BEACH STATE PARK

✉ *On Kaahumanu Highway, three miles south of Kawaihae*

🏊 🐟 ⛱ Here's one of the state's prettiest parks. A well-tended lawn—studded with *hala*, coconut and *kiawe* trees—rolls down to a wide corridor of white sand that extends for one-half mile, with points of lava at either end. Maui's Haleakala crater looms across the water. This is a popular and generally crowded place. Unfortunately, a major resort hotel was built at one end of the beach. Swimming is excellent at the north end of the beach but beware of dangerous currents when the surf is high. Snorkelers enjoy the coral and fish near the rocks and cliffs at the end of the beach. *Papio*, red bigeye, mullet, threadfin and *menpachi* are often caught here. Facilities include picnic areas, restrooms and showers.

⚓ ☎ *808-974-6200* No tent or trailer camping is allowed. However, screened A-frame shelters, located on a rise above the beach, can be rented. These cottages, which cost $20 per night, are equipped with a table, sleeping platforms and electricity; they sleep up to four people. Bring your own bedding and cooking utensils. Toilet and kitchen facilities are shared among all six A-frames.

SPENCER BEACH PARK
✉ *Off Kawaihae Road about one mile south of Kawaihae*

Lacking the uncommon beauty of Anaehoomalu or Hapuna, this spacious park is still lovely. There's a wide swath of white sand, backed by a lawn and edged with *kiawe* and coconut trees. Swimming is excellent here and snorkeling will satisfy beginners and experts alike. Anglers try for *papio*, red bigeye, mullet, threadfin and *menpachi*. There are plenty of facilities: picnic area, restrooms, showers, a large pavilion, volleyball and basketball courts and electricity. This is the only county park with a nighttime security patrol. Also, the gates close you in from 11 p.m. to 6 a.m.

⚓ Both tent and trailer camping are allowed; $3 per night. County permit and reservations are required. This is a very popular place to camp so reserve early—capacity is limited.

MAHUKONA BEACH PARK
✉ *Off Akoni Pule Highway about 13 miles north of Kawaihae*

This now-abandoned harbor village and boat landing lies along a rocky, windswept shore. The lawn is shaded with *kiawe* trees; there's no sandy beach here at all. Nicer areas lie to the south, but if you seek a site far from the frenzied crowd, this is a good retreat. The rocks make for poor access for swimming but snorkeling is good. Frequent catches include threadfin, mullet, *menpachi*, *papio* and red bigeye. Facilities include a picnic area, restrooms, showers and electricity. There's no drinking water.

⚓ Tent and trailers are allowed; $3 per night. County permit required.

KAPAA BEACH PARK
✉ *Off Akoni Pule Highway about 14 miles north of Kawaihae*

Besides a spectacular view of Maui, this rocky, wind-plagued park has little to offer. It does have a miniature cove bounded by *kiawe* trees, but lacks any sand, which is sometimes nice to have on a beach. Swimming is difficult because of the rocks. Kapaa offers good diving but the entrance is rocky and the currents are tricky. Fishing is probably your best bet here since you can stand on the rocks and try for threadfin, mullet, red bigeye, *papio* and *menpachi*. Picnic areas and restrooms are the only facilities. There's no drinking water.

⚓ Tents and trailers are allowed, but the terrain is very rocky for tent camping; $3 per night.

KEOKEA BEACH PARK

✉ *About six miles past Hawi. Take Akoni Pule Highway and turn at the sign. Follow the winding road one mile.*

Seclusion is the password to this beautiful little park with its cliff-rimmed cove and tiered lawn fringed by *hala* and palm trees. Set way out on the Kohala peninsula, this retreat receives very heavy rainfall. You can swim here but only with extreme caution. It's an excellent area for spearfishing but is often plagued by high wind and high surf. Mullet, *papio*, red bigeye, threadfin and *menpachi* are the main catches here. There are picnic areas, drinking water, restrooms and showers.

▲ Tent and trailers are allowed; $3 per night. County permit required.

WAIMEA

Just 15 miles from the tablelands of Honokaa and ten miles from the Kohala Coast, at an elevation of 2670 feet, sits Waimea. Covered with rolling grasslands and bordered by towering mountains, Waimea (also called Kamuela) is cowboy country. Here, *paniolo*, Hawaiian cowboys, ride the range on one of the world's largest independently owned cattle ranches. Founded by John Palmer Parker, an adventurous sailor who jumped ship in 1809, Parker Ranch extends from sea level to over 9000 feet. In a typical year the 150,000-acre ranch is home to between 30,000 and 35,000 head of cattle.

The cool rustic countryside, seemingly incongruous in a tropical retreat like Hawaii, is dotted with carpenter's Gothic houses and adorned with stables, large grassy lawns and picket fences. Like every place that's discovered, and word is out on Waimea, growth has had its impact with lots of in-migration from the mainland and Honolulu and second-home communities for the wealthy in the vicinity. There are a lot more houses, served by several small malls. There are several haute cuisine restaurants worthy of lunch or dinner, and plenty of bed-and-breakfasts to make for a cozy stay.

SIGHTS

PARKER RANCH VISITORS CENTER ✉ *67-1435 Mamalahoa Highway, Kamuela* ☎ *808-885-7655* 📠 *808-885-7561* 🌐 *www.parkerranch.com, info@parkerranch. com* The museum here presents a history of the Parker family that will carry you back 160 years with its displays of Victorian-era furniture and clothing. In addition to the artifacts and family mementos, there is a movie that tells the story of the Parker family from its earliest days to the present. Admission.

HISTORIC PARKER RANCH HOMES ✉*Mamalahoa Highway, one-half mile west of town* ☎*808-885-5433* ℡*808-885-6602* ✐*www.parkerranch.com, visitor@parkerranch.com* Here you can view the Parker family's original 1840s-era ranch house and the adjoining 1862 home (which doubles as a museum filled with extraordinary French Impressionist artwork). While the original home was built of *koa* and contains a collection of antique calabashes, the latter-day estate boasts lofty ceilings, glass chandeliers and walls decorated with the work of Pissaro and Corot, among others. The manicured gardens and homes give visitors a chance to see a bygone Hawaiian era. There's also an art gallery, Puuopelu Gallery, on the property. Closed Sunday. Admission.

IMIOLA CONGREGATIONAL CHURCH ✉*65-1084 Mamalahoa Highway, Waimea* ☎*808-885-4987* For a splendid example of *koa* woodworking, visit this church on the east side of town. Built in 1832, this clapboard church has an interior fashioned entirely from the native timber.

HAKALAU FOREST NATIONAL WILDLIFE REFUGE

✉*Twelve miles from Hakalau* ☎*808-443-2300* Established in 1985, this wildlife refuge is divided into two sections. Both segments were chosen for their diversity of endemic species of flora and fauna. There are the 5000-acre Kona Forest Unit, upcountry of Kealakekua Bay, which is closed to the public, and the 33,000-acre preserve at Maulua, on the upper slopes of Mauna Kea. The upper portion of Maulua is open to activities such as birdwatching and hiking. Hawaiian owls, hoary bats, hawks and colorful forest songbirds like *apapane* and *akiapolaau* all make their home here. There are no facilities, and no maintained trails. Access is limited to weekends. To reach this isolated acreage means taking the Saddle Road, following the turnoff to Hale Pohaku and the observatories atop Mauna Kea. Turn right where unpaved Mana/Keanakolu Road intersects the summit road. From here it's 12 miles to Hakalau. For entry approval call the refuge between 7 a.m. and 4 p.m.; those approved are given the combination to the locked gate.

LODGING

WAIMEA GARDENS BED AND BREAKFAST
$$$ 3 ROOMS   ✉ *P.O. Box 563, Kamuela*   ☎ *808-885-8550*   📠 *808-885-0473*
✐ *contact@waimeagardens.com*
Situated at the foot of the Kohala Mountains, this bed and breakfast offers another lodging option with its three distinctive studios: one with a fireplace, another with a hot tub and private garden, and a third with a private deck and garden. Benches, which dot the water's edge along the stream out back, are perfect for an afternoon of relaxation. Tropical fruit, breads and pastries start each day.

KAMUELA INN
$$ 30 ROOMS   ✉ *Kawaihae Road*   ☎ *808-885-4243, 800-555-8968*   📠 *808-885-8857*
✐ *www.hawaii-inns.com*
Checking in here you'll find modest one- and two-room units, as well as suites. These are clean and bright with private baths. All units are equipped with cable TV and some have refrigerators. Guests are served a continental breakfast.

WAIMEA COUNTRY LODGE
$$ 21 ROOMS   ✉ *65-1210 Lindsey Road*   ☎ *808-885-4100, 800-367-5004*
📠 *808-885-6711*   ✐ *www.castleresorts.com*
Set amid the Kohala Mountains in the cowboy town of Waimea is a "lodge" that's really a multi-unit motel with exposed-beam ceilings and furniture of knotty pine. Guest rooms are large, carpeted and equipped with telephones, shower-tub combinations and color televisions; some have small kitchenettes.

DINING

PANIOLO COUNTRY INN
$$–$$$ STEAK   ✉ *65-1214 Lindsey Road*   ☎ *808-885-4377*
If you're hankering for a steak up here in *paniolo* country, then ride on in to this eatery. There are branding irons on the walls and sirloins on the skillet. The booths are made of knotty pine and dishes have names like "Lone Ranger" and "bucking bronco." You can order barbecued chicken, baby back ribs, a "south of the border" special or the veggie quesadillas.

DANIEL THIEBAUT

$$$$ PACIFIC RIM ⊠*65-1259 Kawaihae Road* ✆*808-887-2200* ✎*808-887-0811* ⌔*www.danielthiebaut.com, reservations@danielthiebaut.com*

Chef Daniel Thiebaut blends his French training with local foods and Asian flavors to create exceptional Pacific Rim cuisine at his namesake restaurant. Artfully presented entrées such as duck breast and Hunan-style rack of lamb fill the menu. Located in a century-old general store, the interior retains much of its old warmth and feel with polished hardwood floors and period furnishings. Dinner and Sunday brunch only.

HAWAIIAN STYLE CAFE

$ LOCAL-STYLE/PLATE LUNCHES ⊠*64-1290 Kawaihae Road* ✆*808-885-4295*

Paniolo and other locals hang out at the counter here. It's a funky little diner where the portions are huge and the prices ridiculously low. Breakfast might be an omelet bigger than your plate or a stack of buttermilk pancakes 12 inches in diameter. For lunch, you can fill up on cholesterol with a big, fat, juicy hamburger and a heaping pile of fries. The place is justly known for its *luau* plate (served only on alternating Fridays), featuring *laulau*,

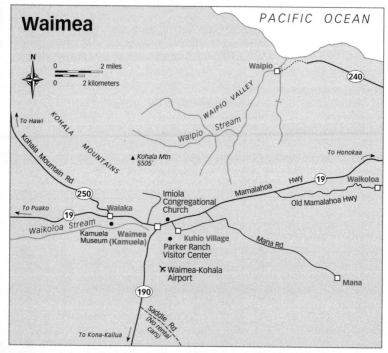

kalua pig, *lomi* salmon, chicken long rice and pickled vegetables. "All-you-can-eat" might be an understatement; it's likely to be all you'll need to eat for your entire stay on the island. Breakfast and lunch only.

MERRIMAN'S

$$$–$$$$ HAWAII REGIONAL   ✉Opelo Plaza, Kawaihae Road
📞808-885-6822 📠808-885-8756 🖥www.merrimanshawaii.com,
office@merrimanshawaii.com

Waimea's first contribution to Hawaii regional cuisine is Merriman's, a very highly regarded restaurant that has received national attention. The interior follows a neo-tropical theme and the menu is tailored to what is fresh and local. Since the locale is not simply Hawaii, but upcountry Hawaii, the cuisine combines the seashore and the cattle ranch. You might find fresh fish with spicy *lilikoi* sauce or steak with *kiawe*-smoked tomato sauce; gourmet vegetarian dishes round out the fare. I highly recommend it. No lunch Saturday and Sunday.

WAIMEA RANCH HOUSE

$$$–$$$$ STEAK   ✉65-1144 Mamalahoa Highway 📞808-885-2088

Dark *koa* panels accented with cowboy gear and photos of *paniolo* create a Western ambience here. The cuisine is heavy on the meat—steaks and lamb—but also cooks up tasty pasta dishes. Thin-crust pizza and tangy caesar salads make for a great lunch. Closed Tuesday.

TAKO TACO TAQUERIA

$ MEXICAN   ✉64-1066 Mamalohoa Highway, Waimea 📞808-887-1717

For a healthy twist on standard Mexican fare, try this nifty taqueria. The chef takes extra care with the authentic sauces and portions are hearty, without being sloppy. A number of vegetarian choices are available. You can eat in the dining room or the garden, and there's live music most nights.

SHOPPING

WAIMEA CENTER ✉65-1158 Mamalahoa Highway, Kamuela In the center of Waimea is the aptly named Waimea Center, the shopping complex in Waimea's cattle country. This modern center features boutiques, knickknack shops and more.

PARKER SQUARE ✉Kawaihae Road The claim here is that they specialize in "distinguished shops." Particularly recommended is the **Gallery of Great Things** (808-885-7706), a store that fulfills the promise of its name. Look for locally made arts and crafts as well as contemporary and tribal art and work representing Polynesia, Indonesia and the Pacific Rim. Also, **Bentley's Home Collection** (808-885-5565) offers everything from clothing to greeting cards.

DAN DELUZ'S WOODS

✉ *64-1013 Mamalahoa Highway* ☎ *808-885-5856* Dan Deluz's Woods has beautifully handcrafted bowls, boxes and carvings, as well as knickknacks such as letter openers and bookmarks. *Koa, milo,* mango, *kamani, hau* and sandalwood and other Hawaiian woods are turned into a variety of stunning pieces. The owner, in the business for decades, is a master of his trade. Worth a stop.

NIGHTLIFE

KAHILU THEATRE ✉ *Parker Ranch Center, 67-1186 Lindsey Road* ☎ *808-885-6017* ⬧ *www.kahilutheatre.org* There's not much to do at night in *paniolo* country except listen to the cows moo. If you're lucky, something will be happening at the 490-seat Kahilu Theatre, which offers dance performances, concerts, plays and current movies.

KONA/KAU DISTRICT

South of Kailua lies the Kona/Kau district, a region often overlooked by Big Island visitors. The land at this end of the island was formed from the lava flows of Hualalai and Mauna Loa. Black- and green-sand beaches hug the rugged coastline, while coffee trees and windswept grasslands cling to the ragged hillsides. Small towns, unspoiled by tourism, sit along the highway, lost in a time warp of tropical reveries. The southernmost point in the United States is here, as are coffee plantations, historic landmarks and other gems to discover.

SIGHTS

KONA COFFEE COUNTRY

Along the lower slopes of Hualalai just above Kailua lies coffee country. This 20-mile-long belt, located between the 1000- and 2000-foot elevation and reaching south to Honaunau, is an unending succession of plantations glistening with the shiny green leaves and red berries of coffee orchards. If you prefer your vegetation decaffeinated, there are mango trees, banana fronds, macadamia nut orchards and sunbursts of wildflowers. To make sure you remember that even amid all the black lava you *are* still in the tropics, old coffee shacks and tinroof general stores dot the countryside.

So rather than heading directly south from Kailua, make sure you take in the full sweep of Kona's coffee country. Just take Palani Road (Route 190) uphill from Kailua, then turn right onto Route 180. This winding road cuts through old Kona in the heart of the growing region—watch

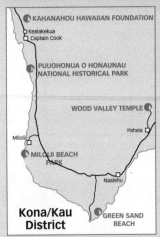

Kona/Kau District

KAHANAHOU HAWAIIAN FOUNDATION

PAGE 218

School for native musical arts sells bamboo nose flutes, dancing sticks and hand-wrought hula drums

PUUHONUA O HONAUNAU NATIONAL HISTORICAL PARK

PAGE 210

Beachfront refuge that is one of the Hawaiian's most sacred spots and the Big Island's finest example of ancient architecture

WOOD VALLEY TEMPLE

PAGE 212

Serene resting place with rooms to rent within 25 beautifully landscaped acres of a Buddhist retreat

MIILOLII BEACH PARK

PAGE 220

Thriving fishing village with vintage South Sea charm, fringed with reefs for wonderful snorkeling

GREEN SAND BEACH

PAGE 211

Uniquely and truly green sand colored by the Olivine eroding from an adjacent cinder cone

for orchards of the small trees. Before the coast road was built, this was the main route. Today it's somewhat off the beaten track, passing through funky old country towns like Holualoa before joining the Mamalahoa Highway (Route 11) in Honalo.

HOLUALOA ✉️*Route 190* In the heart of coffee country, this village retains its small-town feel, even with its trendy collection of galleries along Mamalahoa Highway, a two-lane road that winds through the three-block-long heart of town.

Coastal Area
KONA HISTORICAL SOCIETY MUSEUM AND GIFT SHOP ✉️*Mamalahoa Highway, Kealakekua* 📞*808-323-3222* 📠*808-323-2398* 🖥️*www.konahistorical.org, khs@konahistorical.org* On Mamalahoa Highway, you'll encounter the old Greenwell Store, a lava stone building that dates to 1875, and a perfect

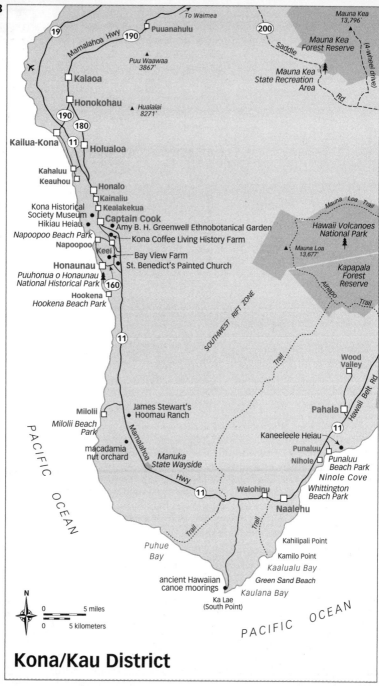

Kona/Kau District

place to combine shopping with museum browsing. The Kona Historical Society Museum and Gift Shop has taken over this former general store (now on the National Register for Historic Places). Today it's filled with artifacts from Kona's early days plus notecards, calendars and other items. Of particular interest are the marvelous collections of photos and antique bottles. Closed Saturday and Sunday.

AMY B. H. GREENWELL ETHNOBOTANICAL GARDEN

⊠*Off Mamalahoa Highway* ☎*808-323-3222* ⊘*www.konahistorical.org* This main route continues south along the western slopes of **Hualalai**. Located on an ancient Hawaiian agricultural site, this garden spreads across 12 acres of upland countryside. The land is divided into four vegetation zones, varying from seaside plants to mountain forests, and is planted with hundreds of Polynesian and native Hawaiian species. On a self-guided tour, you can wander through fields cleared by Hawaiians in pre-contact days and view the plants that were vital to early island civilizations. Guided tours are offered the second Saturday of every month at 10 a.m. or by appointment. Closed Saturday and Sunday.

KONA COFFEE LIVING HISTORY FARM

⊠*At the 110-mile marker on Mamalahoa Highway, Captain Cook* ☎*808-323-2006* 🖷*808-323-957* ⊘*www.konahistorical.org, coffeefarm@konahistorical.org* Across the road from the Greenwell Garden is this living history farm. Known locally as Uchida Farm, this seven-acre working coffee farm depicts the daily life of immigrant farmers from the 1920s to the 1940s, when small family farms dominated the rural Kona landscape and life in the district revolved around the annual coffee cycle. Access to the grounds is by guided tour only, during which you can view the orchards, a Japanese-style farmhouse, gardens and old processing mills. Closed Saturday and Sunday. Fee.

UCC HAWAII COFFEE FACTORY OUTLET ⊠*82-5810 Napoopoo Road, Captain Cook* ☎*808-328-5662* 🖷*808-328-5663* ⊘*www.ucc-hawaii.com, info@ucc hawaii.com* Near the town of Captain Cook, Napoopoo Road leads down to Kealakekua Bay. First it passes this factory outlet. I don't know about you, but I'm a confirmed "caffiend," happily addicted to java for years. So it was mighty interesting to watch how the potent stuff goes from berry to bean to bag, with a few stops between. For a fee, the Roastmaster tour lets you roast your own batch of Kona coffee to take home in personalized bags. If you haven't tried Kona coffee, one of the few brews grown in the United States, this is the time.

KEALAKEKUA BAY Don't miss this marine reserve and outstanding snorkeling spot with technicolor coral reefs and an array of tropical fish species. Spinner dolphins swim close to shore in this area. This exceptional spot is best reached by kayak. Or you can get there on one of the many snorkeling trips offered. Kealakekua Bay is also where you can also check out the reconstructed temple, **Hikiau Heiau**, where Captain James Cook once performed a Christian burial service for one of his crewmen. Captain Cook himself had little time left to live. Shortly after the ceremony, he was killed and possibly eaten by natives who had originally welcomed him as a god. A white obelisk, the **Captain Cook Monument**, rises across the bay where the famous mariner fell in 1779. The cliffs looming behind the Captain Cook marker in Kealakekua Bay are honeycombed with **Hawaiian burial caves**.

PUUHONUA O HONAUNAU NATIONAL HISTORICAL PARK

⊠*Four miles south of Kealakekua Bay on Route 160* ☎*808-328-2288* 📠*808-328-8251* 🖰*www.nps.gov/puho* This ancient cultural site, also known as the Place of Refuge, was one of the many sites established by the *alii* (chiefs) so that *kapu* breakers and refugees had places to flee for sanctuary. Once inside the Great Wall, a lava barricade ten feet high and 17 feet wide, they were safe from pursuers. Free booklets are available for self-guided tours to the royal grounds, *heiau* and menacing wooden images of Native Hawaiian gods that made this beachfront refuge one of Hawaii's most sacred spots. The *heiau*, dating back to the 16th and 17th centuries, are among the finest examples of ancient architecture on the Big Island. Also explore the house models, built to traditional specifications, the royal fishpond and the displays of ancient arts and crafts. Picnic tables and a sandy sunbathing area offer a place to relax—and don't miss the fascinating tidepools along the lava shoreline. (There's also great snorkeling here in the area just offshore from the boat ramp.) If you can, time your visit to Puuhonua o Honaunau for late afternoon and stay long enough to enjoy the sunset. Facing west, the setting sun silhouettes the rebuilt Hale o Keawe in vibrant color. You may be the only one there, which adds to a marvelous sense of the past that comes to life with serenity and power. Admission.

PAINTED CHURCH ⊠*84-5140 Painted Church Road, Honaunau* ☎*808-328-2227* 📠*808-328-8482* St. Benedict's is my favorite church in all the islands. An imaginative Belgian priest, hoping to teach his parishioners through color and imagery, transformed this rickety wooden chapel into a painted church by covering the interior walls with murals. He depicted several religious scenes and painted a vaulted nave behind the altar to give this tiny church the appearance of a great European cathedral. The charming exterior is carpenter's Gothic in style with a dramatic spire.

BAY VIEW FARM ⊠*Painted Church Road, Honaunau* ☎*808-328-9658 800-662-5880* 📠*808-328-8693* 🖰*www.bayviewfarmcoffees.com,   bayview@aloha.net* Here you can tour a mill that produces Kona coffee. The trees here, like many you'll see along the roadside, are pruned to six or eight feet. Each will produce about 20 pounds of berries, which, after being picked by hand, will eventually produce two pounds of beans. Like peas in a pod, there are two beans per berry. A pulping machine squeezes them out of the red berry skin. Next, the beans are dried for up to a week and are turned every hour during daylight. Finally, the outer husks are removed and the beans are graded and bagged for shipping. Small amounts of the premium beans are roasted on the premises (you can watch) and served as free samples (you can also buy more, of course).

SOUTHERN MAUNA LOA There is little except you, alternating bands of greenery and dark lava, and the black macadam of the Mamalahoa Highway as you proceed toward the southern extremities of the Big Island. Here along the lower slopes of Mauna Loa, lifeless lava fingers cut across lush areas teeming with tropical colors. The contrast is overwhelming: Rounding a bend, the road travels from an overgrown land of poinsettias and blossoming trees to a bleak area torn by upheaval, resembling the moon's surface. Once past the lava flows that have ravaged the countryside, you'll discover a terrain that, though dry and windblown, is planted with macadamia nut orchards and fields of cattle-range grasses.

MILOLII Take the Mamalahoa Highway south from Kailua for about 33 miles. Turn off onto a well-marked, winding, one-lane, macadam road leading five miles down to this quaint Hawaiian fishing village. Despite the homes being built, it's quiet and remote, offering a glimpse of life as it once was in Hawaii. Please be respectful of the community living here. (See "Beaches & Parks" section below for more information.)

Continuing south, Mamalahoa Highway passes the late **James Stewart's Hoomau Ranch** (87-mile marker), then a sprawling **macadamia nut orchard**. Eventually, the road arrives at the South Point turnoff.

SOUTH POINT ROAD South Point Road leads through 11 miles of rolling grassland burned dry by the summer sun to the nation's southernmost point. En route you'll pass a cluster of windmills that draw energy from the trades that blow with ferocity through this region. Fishermen have built **platforms** along the sea cliff here to haul their catches up from the boats that troll these prime fishing grounds.

There are also **ancient Hawaiian canoe moorings** in the rocks below South Point Road, and the remains of a *heiau* near the light tower. Some archaeologists believe that South Point was one of the places where Polynesian discoverers first settled.

GREEN SAND BEACH hidden

Another local feature, Green Sand Beach, is a two-mile hike along the waterfront from the Kaulana boat ramp. Olivine eroding from an adjacent cinder cone has created a beach with a decidedly greenish hue. It's a hot hike, so if you go, make sure you take water. A rough shorebreak may make swimming risky.

PUNALUU BEACH PARK From Mamalahoa Highway, continue on to **Naalehu**, the nation's southernmost town, and then on to Punaluu Beach Park. With its palm trees and enchanting lagoon, Punaluu's black-sand beach is simply gorgeous. The tourist complex detracts from the natural beauty, but to escape the madding mobs the explorer need wander only a couple of hundred yards east to the rocky remains of **Kaneeleele Heiau**. Or venture about one-third mile south to **Ninole Cove**. Although there's a condominium complex nearby, this spot is a bit more secluded. Many of the stones along Ninole's pebbly beach are filled with holes containing "baby" stones that are said to multiply.

From Punaluu to Volcanoes National Park, the highway passes through largely uninhabited grassland and abandoned sugar cane areas. **Pahala**, the only town along this stretch, is a plantation colony.

WOOD VALLEY TEMPLE _____

✉ *P.O. Box 250, Pahala, HI 96777* ✆ *808-928-8539* 🖥 *www.nechung.org* For an interesting side trip, go through Pahala to Wood Valley Temple, where a Tibetan Buddhist monk and his followers have taken over an old Japanese temple. Situated on 25 acres, the temple was dedicated in 1980 by the Dalai Lama. A tranquil yet dynamic place, it is painted in floral colors and adorned with a gilded statue of the Buddha. A donation of $5 per person to visit the temple and grounds is requested.

LODGING

Coffee Country
KONA HOTEL
$ 11 ROOMS ✉ *Route 180, Holualoa* ✆ *808-324-1155*

For a funky country place high in the mountains overlooking the Kona Coast, check in here. Catering primarily to workers, this 11-unit hotel remains a real sleeper. It might be difficult to book a room during the week, but on weekends, the lunchpail crowd heads home and you can rent a small place at an unbelievably low rate. Shared bathroom facilities. It's five miles to the beaches and action around Kailua, but if you're after an inexpensive retreat, this is the place.

Coastal Area
H. MANAGO HOTEL
$ 62 ROOMS ✉ *Mamalahoa Highway, Captain Cook* ✆ *808-323-2642*
📠 *808-323-3451* 🖥 *www.managohotel.com, mail@managohotel.com*

Here, you'll have a varied choice of accommodations. Rooms in the creaky old section have communal baths. The battered furniture, torn linoleum floors and annoying street noise make for rather funky living here. Rooms in the "newer" section rise in price as you ascend the stairs. First-floor accommodations are the least expensive and rooms on the ethereal third floor are the most expensive, but all reside in the budget range. The only advantage for the extra cost is a better view. All these rooms are small and sparsely furnished—but you'll find visual relief in the marvelous views of mountain and sea from the tiny lanais. There's also a restaurant and television room in the old section.

KEALAKEKUA BAY BED AND BREAKFAST

$$–$$$ 3 ROOMS   ✉P.O. Box 1412, Kealakekua, HI 96750   ☎808-328-8150, 800-328-8150   📠808-328-8866   ⌨www.keala.com, kbaybb@aloha.net

With manicured grounds leading to a tiled-roof villa, this bed and breakfast combines picture-perfect views of Kealakekua Bay with its assortment of accommodations. Three light and airy suites are available. The Alii includes a jacuzzi tub to relax in, but all rooms have private entrances, private baths and refrigerators. Native Hawaiian prints, wicker furniture and ceiling fans adorn each room, including the lounge and dining room. The Ohana Kai cottage has two bedrooms, two-and-a-half baths, a kitchen, laundry, and a private lanai and garden, sleeping up to six.

KEALAKEKUA INN

$$ 5 ROOMS   ✉81-6652 Mamalahoa Higway, Kealakekua   ☎808-322-6521   ⌨www.vrbo.com/121988, chosley@hawaii.rr.com

For a Victorian English country inn smack in the middle of Big Island coffee country, this inn rents four well-appointed suites in a newly constructed house, along with a separate historic studio with an old-style Japanese *furo* bath. Or rent the whole place. It's at a cool 1500-foot elevation, with sweeping views.

DRAGONFLY RANCH

$$–$$$$ 5 UNITS   ✉Route 160, Honaunau   ☎808-328-2159   ⌨www.dragonflyranch.com, reservations@dragonflyranch.com

One of the more unusual places to stay on the Big Island is this ranch. Spread across two acres, the Dragonfly is billed by owner Barbara Moore as a "healing-arts center." The grounds are luxurious and the atmosphere is decidedly New Age. The "honeymoon suite" has an outdoor bed (screened in), complete with mirrored canopy, a sunken bath and shower. Three of the five units are private and have partial kitchen facilities, or, for a small fee, you can participate in the family-style dinner. Don't expect condo-style living, but do prepare yourself for an experience.

THE HORIZON GUEST HOUSE

$$$$ 4 UNITS   ✉P.O. Box 957, Honaunau, HI 96726   ☎808-328-2540, 888-328-8301   📠808-328-8707   ⌨www.horizonguesthouse.com, contact@horizonguesthouse.com

Upcountry Honaunau has several noteworthy bed and breakfasts that cater to the gay and lesbian community. One such place is the Horizon Guest House that has 40 acres of privacy with spectacular views from rooms and the pool and jacuzzi. There are four suites to choose from, all with private lanais. It's located on Route 11 near the 100-mile marker and the Hookena Beach turnoff.

KALAEKILOHANA

$$$ 4 UNITS ✉94-2152 South Point Road, Naalehu ☎808-939-8052
⌨www.kau-hawaii.com, kk@kau-hawaii.com

The many charms of the Kau District and Hawaiian culture can be explored using a room at peaceful Kalaekilohana—located on the road to Ka Lae, or South Point—as home base. The guest suites within this rambling, gracious inn include private baths and a full morning meal. The hosts are extremely attentive, offering live music, cultural workshops and helpful touring tips for guests. Gay-friendly.

MARGO'S CORNER

$–$$ 2 UNITS ✉P.O. Box 447, Naalehu, HI 96772 ☎808-929-9614
⌨www.margoscorner.com, info@margoscorner.com

If camping is your idea of vacation fun, check out this unique spot. Margo's caters to bicyclists looking for refuge from highrise hotels and staid inns. Hot showers and dinner are provided, and sleeping quarters consist of a number of tent sites situated in a large yard filled with pine trees and organic gardens. For the less adventurous, the "Rainbow Cottage" with a queen-sized bed, a private bath and a view of the garden is available, or try the "Adobe Suite" that sleeps six and includes a sauna. Also here are a health food store and a community library. Ask about the art retreats. No smoking. Reservations are required.

SHIRAKAWA MOTEL

$ 12 ROOMS ✉P.O. Box 467, Naalehu, HI 96772 ☎808-929-7462
📠808-929-7462 ⌨www.shirakawamotel.com, shirak@hialoha.net

The country's southernmost caravansary located on the Mamalahoa Highway in Waiohinu sits on stunningly beautiful grounds. Once when I stopped by, a rainbow lay arched across the landscape and birds were loudly rioting in the nearby hills. Located 1000 feet above sea level, this corrugated-roof hostelry offers rooms with faded furniture. Three rooms have functional kitchenettes. Without cooking facilities, the bill is even less. A spacious two-room suite with a kitchen is also available.

SEA MOUNTAIN AT PUNALUU

$$–$$$$ 76 UNITS ✉Off Mamalahoa Highway, Punaluu ☎808-928-6200,
800-444-6633 📠808-928-8075 ⌨www.viresorts.com, seamtn@hialoha.net

This retreat is a welcome contradiction in terms—a secluded condominium. Situated in the arid Kau District south of Hawaii Volcanoes National Park, it rests between volcanic headlands and a spectacular black-sand beach. A green oasis surrounded by lava rock and tropical vegetation, the complex contains a golf course, pool, tennis courts and jacuzzi. The condos are multi-unit cottages (moderate to deluxe) that are well-decorated and include a bedroom, sitting room, kitchen and lanai; slightly larger units are available (deluxe to ultra-deluxe).

WOOD VALLEY TEMPLE

hidden

$$ 9 ROOMS   ✉ *Four miles outside Pahala*   ☎ *808-928-8539*

✐ *www.nechung.org, nechung@aloha.net*

For a serene resting place, bed down at this Buddhist retreat and guesthouse, which has dormitory-style and private rooms. Set on 25 landscaped acres, it provides a serene resting place. The guest rooms are pretty basic but have been pleasantly decorated and are quite comfortable. Baths are shared and guests have access to the ample kitchen facilities. Call for reservations; two-night minimum.

DINING

Coffee Country

From Kailua south, the Mamalahoa Highway heads up *mauka* into the mountains above the Kona Coast. There are several restaurants in the little towns that dot the first 15 miles. All sit right on the highway.

HOLUAKOA CAFE

$ CONTINENTAL   ✉ *76-5900 Mamalahoa Highway, Holualoa*   ☎ *808-322-2233*

At the north end of Holualoa is this European-style cafe, where the sandwiches and baked goods make a great alfresco breakfast or lunch. The changing menu also includes salads, soups and quiche. Closed Sunday.

TESHIMA RESTAURANT

$$ JAPANESE   ✉ *79-7251 Mamalahoa Highway, Honalo*   ☎ *808-322-9140*

South of Kona, traditional Japanese food can be found here, where the entire family works to keep this long-time eatery going. Specialties include teriyaki and tempura, with a light batter that isn't greasy. It's simple, but clean, and the food is good.

ALOHA ANGEL CAFÉ

$$–$$$ AMERICAN   ✉ *79-7384 Mamalahoa Highway, Kainaliu*   ☎ *808-322-3383*

✐ *www.alohatheatre.com, info@alohatheatre.com*

Back in the days of the sugar plantations, and before television, nearly every one of Hawaii's small towns had their own movie theater. Today most of them are gone or have been transformed into various enterprises. The Aloha Angel Café started its life as the snackbar of the Aloha Theatre in 1932. It offers a full menu as well as freshly baked pastries. There's additional seating on the lanai if you prefer an ocean view. Note one of the theater's old film projectors on display in front. Closed Tuesday and Wednesday after 2:30 p.m.

EVIE'S ORGANIC CAFÉ

$$ AMERICAN/DELI   ✉ *Mango Court on Mamalahoa Highway, Kainaliu*

☎ *808-322-0739*   ✐ *evie@turquoise.net*

Perusing the menu here reveals a "groaning board" of organic delights: steamed veggies with lemon tahini, the local catch, Alaskan salmon, focaccia and pizza. For dessert you'll find homemade chocolate dream cake (wheat-free), *lilikoi* and coconut tapioca, and sugar-free apple crisp à la mode (made with, of course, organic ice cream). Evie's weeknight cabaret, which takes place in the small open-air dining area, makes it a unique venue. Call for reservations—there aren't many tables. No dinner Saturday and Sunday.

Coastal Area
MANAGO HOTEL

$$ AMERICAN ✉*Mamalahoa Highway, Captain Cook* ☏*808-323-2642*
📠*808-323-2451* 🖰*www.managohotel.com, mail@managohotel.com*

This small hotel has a full-sized dining room for its guests, and while the fare and service aren't the best, it is convenient, so long as you arrive during the prescribed meal times (7 to 9 a.m., 11 a.m. to 2 p.m. and 5 to 7:30 p.m.). It's got a dining hall feel to it, with the decidedly average food and limited menu one might expect, although it's locally famous for its thick pork chops.

HONG KONG CHOP SUEY

$ CHINESE ✉*Kealakekua Ranch Center, Mamalahoa Highway, Captain Cook*
☏*808-323-3373*

In Kealakekua Ranch Center, a shopping center in the town of Captain Cook, there is one low-priced eatery. This is it. It's one of those Chinese restaurants that have (literally) over 100 items on the menu. Closed Tuesday.

KEEI CAFÉ

$$–$$$ HAWAIIAN-AMERICAN ✉*Mile marker 112-113, Mamalahoa Highway, Captain Cook* ☏*808-322-9992*

Housed in a plantation-style building, this café serves Hawaiian-American and eclectic fusion cuisine, among the best in the area. From Thai curry, Brazilian seafood chowder, pork chops in peppercorn gravy and catch-of-the-day fish specials to peanut-miso salad, vegetarian black beans and tofu fajitas, everything is made from scratch using local ingredients. Leave room for the heavenly coconut flan. Closed Sunday, no dinner Monday.

COFFEE SHACK

$$ AMERICAN ✉*85-5799 Mamalahoa Highway, Honaunau*
☏*808-328-9555* 🖰*www.coffeeshack.com*

From the outside, the Coffee Shack may look something like a brownish mobile home teetering on the brink of a cliff, but the view from hundreds of feet above the surf is part of what makes this roadside diner south of Captain Cook so special. The breakfast menu features eggs benedict and luau-bread french toast among its offerings. Lunch selections include pizzas and fish sandwiches on homemade bread. Breakfast and lunch only.

MISTER BILL'S
$$–$$$ AMERICAN ✉*Mile marker 78, Mamalahoa Highway* ☏*808-929-7447*
📠*808-929-8129*

For a comfortable meal, try this spot. The menu includes steak, prawns and chicken. In an area lacking in full-service dining facilities, this restaurant and full bar is a welcome oasis. There is a kid's menu.

SHAKA RESTAURANT
$$ AMERICAN/PLATE LUNCHES ✉*Mamalahoa Highway, Naalehu* ☏*808-929-7404*

Down in Naalehu, you'll find the nation's southernmost restaurant. There are full-course breakfasts; at lunch they serve sandwiches, plate lunches, homemade pizzas and salads; the dinner menu has beef, seafood and chicken dishes. There's also a full bar.

PUNALUU BAKE SHOP
$ BAKERY ✉*Mamalahoa Highway, Naalehu* ☏*808-929-7343*
🖂*www.punaluubakeshop.com, ckoi@punaluubakeshop.com*

At latitude 19 degrees, four minutes north of the equator, the Punaluu Bake Shop is the southernmost bakery in the U.S. and it's a pleasant stop when cruising the Mamalahoa Highway. While it's famous for Hawaiian sweet bread (free samples!), the cases are also filled with other delectable treats such as *malasadas* (Portuguese pastries) and *anpans* (Japanese pastries). In addition, it serves island ice cream and Kau coffee. The Punaluu Bake Shop folks provide a comfortable spot to enjoy a snack; you'll find a small botanical garden and visitors center as well. No dinner.

SHOPPING

After escaping the tourist traps in Kailua, you can start seriously shopping in South Kona. Since numerous shops dot the Mamalahoa Highway as it travels south, I'll list the most interesting ones in the order they appear.

Coffee Country

HALE 'O KULA GOLDSMITH GALLERY ✉*Old Holualoa post office, 76-5942 Mamalahoa Highway, Holualoa* ☏*808-324-1688* Check out Sam Rosen's shop for artful designs in gold, platinum and silver. Closed Sunday and Monday.

CINDERELLA'S ANTIQUES ✉*Mamalahoa Highway, Holualoa* ☏*808-322-2474* If you're an antique hound, this is your kind of place. They also feature collectibles.

STUDIO 7 GALLERY ✉*76-5920 Mamalahoa Highway, Holualoa* ☏*808-324-1335* Among the area's most noteworthy art galleries, this beautifully designed multiroom showplace displays pottery, paintings, sculpture and prints. Closed Sunday and Monday.

HOLUALOA GALLERY ✉*76-5921 Mamalahoa Highway, Holualoa* ☎*808-322-8484* Artist Matthew Lovein creates *raku*-style wishing jars from a Holualoa workshop; his elegant pottery artwork is for sale at this gallery. Closed Sunday and Monday.

KONA ARTS CENTER ✉*Mamalahoa Highway, Holualoa* Housed in an old coffee mill, is the arts center, where local artists gather to create their wares.

KIMURA LAUHALA SHOP

✉*Mamalahoa Highway, Holualoa* ☎*808-324-0053* For locally made hats and baskets woven from pandanus and bamboo, and sold at phenomenally low prices, turn off the main road onto Hualalai Road, and check out Kimura's. Closed Sunday.

BLUE GINGER GALLERY ✉*79-7391 Mamalahoa Highway, Kainaliu* ☎*808-322-3898* On display here is an impressive array of crafts items produced by local artisans. There are ceramics, custom glass pieces, woodwork and hand-painted silk scarves.

PARADISE FOUND ✉*Mamalahoa Highway, Kainaliu* ☎*808-322-2111* This is a recommended store, which features contemporary and Hawaiian-style clothes.

Coastal Area

KEALAKEKUA'S GRASS SHACK ✉*Konwena Junction, Kealakekua* ☎*808-323-2877* "There's a place in Hawaii that is very dear to me . . . I want to go back to my little grass shack in Kealakekua, Hawaii." Yes, there really is a little grass shack in Kealakekua and it's been one of my favorite shopping stops. Scaled down from its previous incarnation, Kealakekua's Grass Shack still offers a large selection of Hawaiian products, including bowls, jewelry and mirrors made from *koa, kou, milo,* mango and norfolk pine woods. You can also find handmade woven *lauhala* hats, baskets, carved figurines, etched glass, Niihau shell leis and hula accessories. You probably, however, won't see the *humuhumunukunukapuaa* go swimming by.

KAHANAHOU HAWAIIAN FOUNDATION

✉*Mamalahoa Highway, Kealakekua* ☎*808-322-3901* This apprentice school teaching Hawaiians native arts sells hand-wrought hula drums and other instruments, as well as masks and other crafts. It also serves as an introduction to Hawaiian music as you view bamboo nose flutes, musical bows, dancing sticks and ceremonial drums.

BONG BROTHERS COFFEE COMPANY ✉*84-5227 Mamalahoa Highway, Honaunau* ☎*808-328-9289* 🖂*808-328-8112* 🌐*www.bongbrothers.com* Given their catchy moniker, it was probably inevitable that the Bong Brothers, a long-established Kona coffee growing and roasting operation, would open a retail location. Bong, the Chinese coffee growers' family name, has nothing to do with *pakalolo* paraphernalia, but don't tell that to the folks who have made Bong Brothers (and Bong Sistah) T-shirts a hot Big Island souvenir. You'll find them on sale at Bong Brothers on Route 11 in Honaunau, along with local fruits such as cherimoya, star fruit and sugarloaf pineapples. The shop also serves fresh-squeezed juices and smoothies, as well as homemade soups and, of course, coffee straight from their own roasting room. Closed Saturday.

NIGHTLIFE

EVIE'S ORGANIC CAFÉ ⊠*Mango Court on Mamalahoa Highway, Kainaliu* ☏*808-322-0739* On weeknights, come to Evie's for an evening of cabaret. Be sure to reserve a table if you want to enjoy a meal during the show.

ALOHA PERFORMING ARTS COMPANY ⊠*P.O. Box 794, Kealakekua* ☏*808-322-9924* This company produces an ongoing series of theatrical performances, including popular hits such as *Little Shop of Horrors* and *A Christmas Carol*. They often perform at the Aloha Theatre. Call for information.

BEACHES & PARKS

NAPOOPOO BEACH PARK
⊠*Kealakekua Bay; in the town of Captain Cook, take Napoopoo Road, which leads four miles down to Kealakekua Bay; turn right at the end of the road.*

Small boats occasionally moor off this black-rock beach on Kealakekua Bay. Set amidst cliffs that rim the harbor, it's a charming spot, drawing caravans of tour buses on their way to the nearby Hikiau Heiau. Kealakekua Bay, one mile wide and filled with marine life, is an underwater preserve that attracts snorkelers and glass-bottom boats. In the bay there are good-sized summer breaks. Just north, at "Ins and Outs," the surf breaks year-round. Anglers can try for mullet, *moi*, bonefish, *papio* and big-eyed scad are the common catches. Napoopoo's gray-sand beach was washed away by a storm in 1992, leaving a bouldered beach in its place. The steep incline makes ocean access risky. A picnic area, showers and restrooms are available. There's a soda stand just up from the beach.

KEEI BEACH
⊠*Kealakekua Bay; Take the Mamalahoa Highway to Captain Cook, then follow Napoopoo Road down to Kealakekua Bay. At the bottom of the hill, go left toward the Puuhonua o Honaunau National Historical Park. Take this road a half-mile, then turn right onto a lava-bed road. Now follow this extremely rough road another half-mile to the beach.*

This salt-and-pepper beach extends for a quarter-mile along a lava-studded shoreline. Situated next to the creaky village of Keei, this otherwise mediocre beach offers marvelous views of Kealakekua Bay. It is far enough from the tourist area, however, that you'll probably encounter only local people along this hidden beach. Darn! The very shallow water makes swimming safe, but limited. Try the north end. Plenty of coral makes for good snorkeling. Mullet, threadfin, bonefish, *papio* and big-eyed scad are common catches here. There are no facilities.

HOOKENA BEACH PARK

✉️ *Take the Mamalahoa Highway south from Kailua for about 21 miles to Hookena. Turn onto the paved road at the marker and follow it four miles to the park.*

Popular with adventurous travelers, this is a wide, black-sand beach bordered by sheer rock walls. Coconut trees abound along this lovely strand, and there's a great view of the South Kona coast. This is a recommended beach for swimming. Near the cliffs south of the beach are some good dive spots. Mullet, threadfin, bonefish, *papio* and big-eyed scad are among the most common catches. A picnic area and restrooms are the only facilities. There is no drinking water, but cooking and bathing water is available.

⚠️ Tent camping is allowed; $3 per night. County permit required.

MILOLII BEACH PARK

✉️ *Take the Mamalahoa Highway south from Kailua for about 33 miles. Turn off onto a well-marked, winding, one-lane macadam road leading five miles down to the village.*

Even if you don't feel like a character from Somerset Maugham, you may think you're amid the setting for one of his tropical stories. This still-thriving fishing village is vintage South Seas, from tumbledown shacks to fishing nets drying in the sun. Unfortunately, however, houses have been springing up over the last few years. There are patches of beach near the village, but the most splendid resources are the tidepools, some of the most beautiful I've ever seen. This area is fringed with reefs that create safe but shallow areas for swimming, and wonderful spots for snorkeling. Exercise extreme caution if you go beyond the reefs. This beach is a prime area for mullet, bonefish, *papio*, threadfin and big-eyed scad. Facilities include restrooms, picnic area and a volleyball court. There's no running water.

⚠️ Permitted only in the seaside parking lot. Get there early and you can park a tent beneath the ironwood trees with the sea washing in just below; $3 per night. County permit required.

MANUKA STATE WAYSIDE

✉️ *On Mamalahoa Highway, 19 miles west of Naalehu*

This lovely botanic park, almost 2000 feet above sea level, offers a beautiful ocean view. The rolling terrain is planted with both native and imported trees and carpeted with grass. The only facilities are restrooms and a picnic area.

⚠ No tent and trailers are allowed here, but you can park your sleeping bag in the pavilion. No electricity. A state permit is required.

WHITTINGTON BEACH PARK
✉ *Across from the abandoned sugar mill on Mamalahoa Highway, three miles north of Naalehu*

🏄 ⛴ 🏖 A small patch of lawn dotted with coconut, *hala* and ironwood trees make up this pretty little park. It's set on a lava-rimmed shoreline near the cement skeleton of a former sugar wharf. There are some marvelous tidepools here. Access to the water over the sharp lava rocks is rough on the feet. But once you're in, the snorkeling is very good and there's a surf break in summer with a left slide. Mullet, *menpachi*, red bigeye, *ulua* and *papio* are the most frequent species caught. Facilities consist of picnic area, restrooms and electricity.

⚠ Tent and trailer camping are allowed; county permit required.

PUNALUU BEACH PARK
✉ *About a mile off Mamalahoa Highway, eight miles north of Naalehu*

🏖 ⛴ 🏖 A black-sand beach fringed with palms and bordered by a pleasant lagoon, this area, unfortunately, is regularly assaulted by tour buses. Still, it's a place of awesome beauty, one I would not recommend bypassing. One reason for the hubbub is the appearance of the endangered green sea turtles, which should not be disturbed. For more privacy, you can always check out Ninole Cove, a short walk from Punaluu. This attractive area has a tiny beach, grassy area and lagoon, which is a good swimming spot, perfect for children, during calm conditions. Exercise caution when swimming outside the lagoon. The snorkeling is only mediocre. Surfers attempt the short ride over a shallow reef (right slide). Principal catches are red bigeye, *menpachi*, *ulua* and *papio*. Facilities include a picnic area, restrooms, showers and electricity.

⚠ Tents and trailers are allowed; county permit required.

HAWAII VOLCANOES NATIONAL PARK

Covering 344 square miles and extending from the Puna shoreline to the 4090-foot summit of Kilauea to the summit crater of Makuaweoweo atop 13,677-foot Mauna Loa, this incredible park is deservedly the most popular attraction on the Big Island. Its two live volcanoes, still-young Kilauea (one of the world's most active volcanoes) and towering Mauna Loa make the region as elemental and unpredictable as the next volcanic eruption.

Currently, the 20-year-plus-long eruption of Kilauea, which resulted in the loss of several hundred homes and the coastal town of Kalapana in 1991, continues unabated. As a result, a visit to the coast when lava is flowing into the sea has been an experience enjoyed by millions under the watchful eye of National Park Service rangers.

Unlike Washington's Mt. St. Helens or Mt. Pinatubo in the Philippines, Hawaii's volcanic eruptions are generally less dangerous. Their lava is released in rivers that flow, largely underground, to the sea, where lava erupts in tall fountains. The release of cinder and ash creates cone-shaped craters called cinder cones. Don't make the park a day trip; it's worth as much time as you can spare.

SIGHTS

Contained within this national park are rainforests, black-sand beaches, rare species of flora and fauna, and jungles of ferns. If you approach the park from the southwest, traveling up the Mamalahoa Highway (Route 11), the following points of interest begin within a mile of the park boundary.

1790 FOOTPRINTS At the trailhead for **Kau Desert Trail**, you can follow a short (1.5 miles round trip) path that leads to 1790 Footprints, an area where, according to legend, Halemaumau's hellish eruption overwhelmed a Hawaiian army in 1790. The troops, off to battle Kamehameha for control of the island, left the impressions of their dying steps in molten lava—or so the story goes. According to Park officials, the tracks were left in hot mud by travelers, not warriors. Either way, the tracks can still occasionally be seen in the very fragile hardened ash layers.

TREE MOLDS ⊠ *Turn off Manalahoa Highway on to Mauna Loa Road. Take the first right-hand turn.* Lava flowing through a *koa* forest created these amazing fossils, an eerie sight. The molten rock ignited the trees and then cooled, leaving deep pits in the shape of the incinerated tree trunks. (Bring mosquito repellent.)

KIPUKA PUAULU ⊠ *Backtrack to Mauna Loa Road and take the left fork.* Also known as **Bird Park**, this is a mile-long nature trail leading through a densely forested bird sanctuary. *Kipuka* means an "island" surrounded by lava and this one is filled with more than 30 species of Hawaiian trees, including *koa*, *kolea* and *ohia*. If the weather's clear, you can continue along this narrow, winding road for about ten miles to a **lookout** perched 6662 feet high on the side of Mauna Loa.

KILAUEA VISITOR CENTER ✉*Go back to the Manalahoa Highway to Crater Rim Drive and turn left.* ☏*808-985-6000* 📠*808-985-6004* ⊲*www.nps.gov/havo, havo_interpretation@nps.gov* This visitor center provides a walk-through forest, a film on recent eruptions, a bookstore and an information desk. Parking is available here or along Crater Rim Drive.

VOLCANO ART CENTER___ h*idden*

✉*P.O. Box 129, Volcano, HI 96785* ☏*808-967-7565* 📠*808-967-8512* ⊲*www.volcanoartcenter.org* Across the road from the visitors center, on the rim of Kilauea at **Volcano House**, there's a hotel and restaurant. An earlier Volcano House, built in 1877, currently houses the Volcano Art Center, right next to the visitor complex. Here you'll find notable exhibits and gallery works by local artists whose creations relate to the Hawaiian environment and heritage. They also host classes in the Hawaiian language and Hawaiian arts such as hula and lei making, as well as painting, ceramics, glass and photography.

SULPHUR BANKS You can either walk the ten-minute trail or drive along Crater Rim Drive to get to this odoriferous sightseeing spot. Here, green, red, brown and yellow hues are painted by deposits of crystal that form on the rocks when the gas reaches the surface. Other minerals, including opal, earthy hematite and gypsum, form by the weathering of the rock. These solfataras, or fumaroles, are vents that issue steam, hydrogen sulfide and other gases. Kilauea releases tons of sulphuric gases every day. *Take note:* People with heart conditions, pregnant women and those with breathing problems should avoid this area, as well as Halemaumau Crater, since these gases are unhealthy for them.

STEAM VENTS Just beyond the Sulphur Banks you can take a steam bath by simply approaching the railing of the less smelly vents. The steam is caused by groundwater hitting the heated lava. On cooler days you'll find more steam. Steam vents are located on the edge of Kilauea Caldera. A meadow is formed by alterations to the soil that prevent the growth of trees and shrubs. Be careful around the steam vents; they can actually burn you. You'll find larger vents around the crater if you hike around it.

KILAUEA CALDERA From the Steam Vents pick up Crater Rim Drive, one of the islands' most spectacular scenic routes. This 11-mile loop passes lava flows and steam vents in its circuit around and into Kilauea Caldera. It also takes in everything from a rainforest to a desert and provides views of several craters.

Hawaii Volcanoes National Park

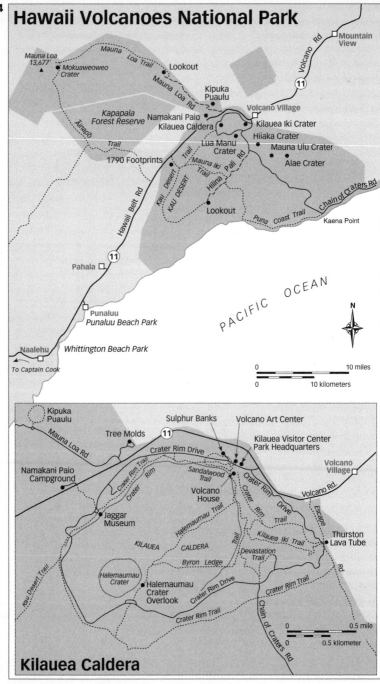

Mauna Loa
13,677'

Mokuaweoweo
Crater

Mauna Loa Trail

Lookout

Mauna Loa Rd

Kipuka
Puaulu

Volcano Rd

Mountain
View

11

Kapapala
Forest Reserve

Namakani Paio

Kilauea Caldera

Volcano Village

Kilauea Iki Crater

Lua Manu
Crater

Hiiaka Crater

Mauna Ulu Crater

'Āinapō Trail

1790 Footprints

Mauna Iki
Trail

Kaʻū Desert Trail

KAŪ DESERT

Hilina Pali Rd

Alae Crater

Lookout

Puna Coast Trail

Chain of Craters Rd

Kaena Point

Hawaii Belt Rd

11

Pahala

PACIFIC OCEAN

N

Punaluu
Punaluu Beach Park

Naalehu

Whittington Beach Park

To Captain Cook

0   10 miles

0   10 kilometers

Kipuka
Puaulu

Tree Molds

Mauna Loa Rd

11

Sulphur Banks

Crater Rim Drive

Volcano Art Center

Kilauea Visitor Center
Park Headquarters

Crater Rim Trail

Crater Rim

Namakani Paio
Campground

Sandalwood
Trail

Volcano House

Crater Rim Drive

Volcano
Village

Volcano Rd.

Escape Rd

Jaggar
Museum

Halemaumau Trail

KILAUEA   CALDERA

Crater Rim Trail

Kilauea Iki Trail

Thurston
Lava Tube

Kaʻū Desert Trail

Byron Ledge

Devastation
Trail

Halemaumau
Crater

Halemaumau
Crater
Overlook

Crater Rim Drive

Crater Rim Trail

Chain of Craters Rd

Crater Rim Trail

0   0.5 mile

0   0.5 kilometer

Kilauea Caldera

If Kilauea is active, plan a visit to the eruption zone at dusk. Keep in mind that viewing the volcanic eruption may require a one- or two-mile-long trek to the eruption zone. Hikers should bring water and wear hiking shoes with a decent tread to navigate the hardened lava rock trail and handle the ground heat generated by cooling lava. Bring a flashlight. You'll need it if you're heading back from a dusk viewing. The best viewing is from 20 minutes before sunset until 20 minutes after. (Sunset ranges between 5:30 p.m. mid-winter and 7:30 p.m. mid-summer.) This is the stuff of lifetime memories.

THURSTON LAVA TUBE Proceeding clockwise around Kilauea Caldera, the road leads near this well-lit cave 450 feet long set amid a lush tree-fern and *ohia* rainforest. The tube itself, created when outer layers of lava cooled while the inner flow drained out, reaches heights inside of ten feet. You can walk through the tunnel and along nearby **Devastation Trail**, a half-mile paved asphalt trail that cuts through a skeletal forest of *ohia* trees regrowing after being devastated in a 1959 eruption.

HALEMAUMAU CRATER This pit, which erupted most recently in 1982, is the traditional home of Pele, the goddess of volcanoes. Even today steam and sulfurous gas blast from this hellhole, filling the air with a pungent odor and adding a sickly yellow-green luster to the cliffs. Halemaumau is actually a crater within a crater, its entire bulk contained in Kilauea's gaping maw.

Around the southern and western edges of Kilauea Caldera, the road passes part of the **Kau Desert**, a landscape so barren that astronauts bound for the moon were brought here to train for their lunar landing.

JAGGAR MUSEUM ☎808-967-8186 At this museum, adjacent to the U.S.G.S. park observatory, you can catch an eagle's-eye glimpse into Halemaumau Crater and take in a series of state-of-the-art displays on volcanology. Then the road continues on to a succession of steam vents from which hot mists rise continually.

CHAIN OF CRATERS ROAD _____

The Mamalahoa Highway zips into Hilo from the Kilauea Crater area. Once you could take a more interesting route by following Chain of Craters Road down to the Puna district. But now a lava flow several miles wide has closed part of the road. The 20-mile-long section that is still open skirts several pit craters, traverses miles of decades-old lava flows, and descends 4000 feet to the coast. Near the sea, a two-mile trail leads to an excellent collection of **petroglyphs at Puuloa**. The Chain of Craters Road then hugs the cliffs of the shoreline until it abruptly ends, buried for ten miles under lava flows as much as 75 feet deep.

VOLCANO VILLAGE This small rural enclave lies one mile Hilo-side of the main entrance to Hawaii Volcanoes National Park. The village itself includes a few shops and restaurants on Old Volcano Road, which parallels Route 19 for about one mile. The rest consists of a grid of country roads fronting homes nestled amidst lush vegetation of endemic fern and *koa* forest interspersed with flowering ginger, camellia and other flowering exotics that prosper in the wet, temperate climate.

VOLCANO GARDEN ARTS ✉️ *19-3834 Old Volcano Road* 📞 *808-985-8979* 🖥️ *www.volcanogardenarts.com, volcanogardenarts@hawaii.rr.com* Volcano Village's population includes both Native Hawaiians and an assortment of mainland escapists, including many artists and other creative types who revel in its rural isolation and spiritual energy. Ira Ono, one of Volcano's long-term residents and a key multimedia artist-in-residence, operates this working gallery, in the vintage 1908 Hopper Estate. The workshop-cum-gallery-cum-sculpture-garden offers special classes in various arts throughout the year. Closed Sunday and Monday.

LODGING

There are quite a number of lovely bed and breakfasts along the Puna/Kau coast in Volcano Village, which plays host to those *akamai* (smart) enough to plan a dusk visit to the eruption site, about 40 to 45 minutes from park headquarters. Since you want to be there at dusk to see the lava at its most awesome, a stay in Volcano is the right choice. The volcano isn't a good day trip. It's more than two hours on dark, twisting, country roads to Kona and Kohala hotels. Besides, the night sky, undimmed by civilization, is a spectacle of brilliant stars and fragrant breezes, which makes an evening walk something memorable.

VOLCANO HAWAII ACCOMMODATIONS 📞 *808-967-8662,* *800-733-3839* 🖥️ *www.lavalodge.com, info@lavalodge.com* This central agency can help book reservations at a variety of area B&Bs.

VOLCANO PLACES 📞 *808-967-7990, 877-967-7990* 🖥️ *www.volcanoplaces.com* This booking agency has information on cottage rentals.

VOLCANO HOUSE
$$–$$$$ 42 ROOMS   ✉️ *Near the entrance to Hawaii Volcanoes National Park on Route 11* 📞 *808-967-7321* 📠 *808-967-8429* 🖥️ *www.volcanohouse.com, reservations@volcanohousehotel.com*
Perched 4000 feet above sea level on the rim of Kilauea Crater and situated in Hawaii Volcanoes National Park, this hotel provides a unique resting place where you can watch the steam rise from Halemaumau Crater or study the rugged contours of slumbering Kilauea. Standard rooms are unfortunately located in a separate building behind the main hotel. For a view of Kilauea, ask for a "crater view," from a superior or deluxe room on the volcano side. The rooms are decorated in an ever tidy and cozy fashion, with wall-to-wall carpeting but no TV or radio. And you certainly won't need an air conditioner at these breathless heights.

KILAUEA LODGE
$$$–$$$$ 15 ROOMS   ✉️ *19-3948 Old Volcano Road, Volcano Village* 📞 *808-967-7366* 📠 *808-967-7367* 🖥️ *www.kilauealodge.com, stay@kilauealodge.com*
The lodge does not rest on the lip of the crater, but that doesn't prevent it from being the finest place in the area to stay. Set on tropically wooded grounds, this hideaway nevertheless conveys a mountain at-

Hawaii Volcanoes National Park Campgrounds

$ 📞*808-985-6017*

The main campground at Hawaii Volcanoes National Park, **Namakani Paio Campground** (off Route 11, 31.5 miles southwest of Hilo) is situated in a large, open grassy area dotted with eucalyptus and *ohia* trees at an elevation of 4000 feet. Although there are a handful of designated campsites, it's mostly a matter of simply picking a clear spot, first-come, first-served, and pitching your tent there. The campground has water and restrooms, and there are fire grills and picnic tables in a central pavilion. Bring your own firewood—none is available on-site. There are no reservations and no check-in. Open year-round; seven-day maximum stay.

Located just above the campground of the same name, **Namakani Paio Cabins** are ten extremely basic cabins operated by the Volcano House hotel. Each sleeps up to four people, with one double bed and twin-size bunk beds, all bare-mattress. Amenities include a picnic table and an outdoor barbecue grill. Cabin occupants use the campground restrooms and drinking water supply. Showers are available at the hotel. Rates are $40 a night for two people, $8 per additional person, plus $20 for optional linen rental and a $12 key deposit. Reservations are required; make them through the reception desk at the Volcano House (808-967-7321).

The national park's **Kulanaokuaiki Campground** (five miles southwest from Chain of Craters Road on Hilina Pali Road) has eight campsites. Located in the middle of the Kau Desert at an elevation of 2700 feet, it offers the remote feel of wilderness camping without the hike. There is a vault toilet but no water; bring plenty. The developed campsites have picnic tables and barbecue grills; bring your own firewood. There are no reservations and no check-in. Open year-round.

mosphere. Some guest rooms have fireplaces; all have private baths. This coziness carries over into an inviting common room furnished with rocking chairs and a tile fireplace. The lodge, built in 1938 as a YMCA camp, rests at the 3700-foot elevation and combines the best features of a Hawaiian plantation house and an alpine ski lodge. It also provides a memorable contrast to the ocean-oriented places that you'll probably be staying in during the rest of your visit. A two-bedroom cottage with a hot tub is also available. Full breakfast is included.

HALE OHIA COTTAGES

$$–$$$ 8 ROOMS   ✉*11-3968 Hale Ohia Road, Volcano Village*
📞*808-967-7986, 800-455-3803* 📠*808-985-8887* 🖥*www.haleohia.com, reservations@haleohia.com*

The wood-shingled buildings at these 1931 cottages are conveniently located just outside park headquarters on beautifully landscaped grounds. Hale Lehua, Ihilani and #44 cottages are freestanding structures with fireplaces and kitchenettes. There are also five suites (two in the main house and three in another cottage), all with private baths and entrances. The spacious two-story, three-bedroom Hale Ohia suite is well-suited to family travelers, with three bedrooms, a large living space, a full kitchen and a covered lanai with room for barbecuing.

KULANA _____ hidden

$ 3 ROOMS   ✉P.O. Box 190, Volcano Village, HI 96785   ✆808-985-9055
🖳www.discoverkulana.com, discoverkulana@yahoo.com

Billing itself as a smoke-, alcohol-, drug- and drama-free zone, Kulana is a women-centric artistic and spiritual retreat near Volcano. Clean, comfortable, shared and private rooms, cabins and camping are available for stays ranging from a day to more than a month. While there, you can pursue artistic projects, attend workshops or just hang out in the *ohia* forest.

DINING

VOLCANO HOUSE RESTAURANT

$$$ AMERICAN   ✉Near entrance to Hawaii Volcanoes National Park
✆808-967-7321   📠808-967-8429   🖳www.volcanohousehotel.com

If you're looking for a vista, this eatery—perched on the rim of Kilauea Crater—affords expansive views. Located at 4000-foot elevation in Hawaii Volcanoes National Park, this spacious dining room looks out on sheer lava walls and angry steam vents, and on a clear day, the imposing bulk of Mauna Loa. If you can tear yourself away from the stunning scenery, there's buffet-style breakfast and lunch, and an ample dinner menu highlighted by fresh fish, prime rib, linguini marinara and a variety of seafood dishes.

KILAUEA LODGE

$$$–$$$$ AMERICAN   ✉Old Volcano Road, Volcano Village   ✆808-967-7366
🖳www.kilauealodge.com, e-mail stay@kilauealodge.com

For those languorous evenings when time is irrelevant and budgets forgotten, there is Kilauea Lodge. You can sit beside a grand fireplace in an atmosphere that mixes tropical artwork with alpine sensibility. The exposed-beam ceiling and elegant hardwood tables comfortably contrast with a menu that features seafood Mauna Kea, duck a l'orange, catch of the day and chicken Milanese. Dinner only.

LAVA ROCK CAFÉ

$$ AMERICAN   ✉Old Volcano Road, Volcano Village   ✆808-967-8526
📠808-967-8090   🖳www.volcanovillage.com

In L.A. there's the Hard Rock Café; in Volcano Village, it's the Lava Rock Café. Breakfast, lunch and dinner feature "magma mini meals," but only at dinner can you get a "volcanic eruption." The lasagna, T-bones and fajitas are, presumably, burning hot. The Lava Rock also serves as an internet café for e-mail junkies. No dinner Sunday or Monday.

THAI THAI RESTAURANT

$$ THAI   ✉19-4084 Old Volcano Road, Volcano Village   ✆808-967-7969

A welcome addition to the Volcano dining scene is this cute, casual eatery that whips up a good selection of curries, with your choice of island fish, chicken, pork or tofu, along with an array of other Thai entrées. The food is fresh and quite tasty, so it tends to get very busy at night.

KIAWE KITCHEN

$$–$$$ AMERICAN   ✉ *Old Volcano Road at Haunani Road, Volcano Village*
📞 *808-967-7711*

When hiking around the park gives you a hearty appetite, this kitchen is ready to serve up big, satisfying portions in a cozy setting. *Kiawe* (mesquite) charcoal adds smoky flavor to crispy pizzas, hot sandwiches and breads, while massive salads, cold sandwiches and pasta round out the menu.

PUNA DISTRICT

That bulging triangle in the southeast corner of the Big Island is the Puna District, a kind of living geology lab where lush rainforest is cut by frequent lava flows from the East Rift Zone of Kilauea. Here at the state's easternmost point, black-sand beaches, formed when hot lava meets the ocean and explodes into crystals, combine with anthurium farms and papaya orchards to create a region both luxurious and unpredictable. There are lava tubes, arches and caves galore, all formed by the lava that flows inexorably down from the rift zones of Kilauea.

While in Puna, visitors should not wander off-road. This was, and likely still is, a prime locale for growing *pakalolo*, as marijuana is known in Hawaii. (*Paka* translates as "weed," *lolo* as "crazy.") Ill-conceived State and Federal drug eradication efforts have made for some bad energy concerning marijuana cultivation. The end result has been counter-productive, driving up prices without stopping the flow, pushing more money into an illegal pipeline.

SIGHTS

KEAAU & PAHOA Route 130 will carry you through the tumble-down plantation town of Keaau and near the artistic little community of Pahoa, and along Route 137, an enchanting country road that hugs the coast.

LAVA FLOWS In 1990, lava flows poured through Kalapana, severing Routes 130 and 137 (which have since been reconnected) and covering many houses. Kalapana, once home to more than 400 people, was largely destroyed. Today, a few isolated houses form oases in a desert of black lava. Just above the town, where the roadway comes to an abrupt halt, you can see how the lava crossed the road. Since the latest series of volcanic eruptions began on the Big Island in 1983, the Puna District has been in constant turmoil. Between 1983 and 2002, some 525 acres of new land mass has been created through Kilauea volcano's ongoing eruptions. The volcano produces 300,000 to 1 million square yards of lava per day, with much of it flowing over existing lava flows.

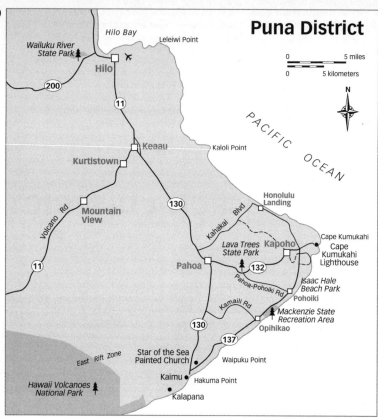

Puna District

0   5 miles
0   5 kilometers

STAR OF THE SEA PAINTED CHURCH

✉ *Between mile markers 19 and 20, Highway 130, Kaimu* The former Star of the Sea Painted Church in Kalapana used to be my favorite church in all the Hawaiian Islands. An imaginative Belgian priest, hoping to add color and imagery to the mass, covered the interior walls of this tiny, spired carpenter's Gothic chapel with murals depicting religious scenes and painted a vaulted nave behind the altar to give the little church the appearance of a European cathedral. In 1990, when a slow-moving lava flow destroyed much of Kalapana, villagers lifted the church off its foundation and trucked it to safety just hours before the lava would have engulfed it. The Catholic Church decommissioned it and sold it to the Kalapana Ohana Association for "$1 and love," and it was moved to a three-acre site leased from the state along the Kalapana-Pahoa Highway. The association was awarded a small government grant to convert it into a Native Hawaiian cultural center, but the *hoolaulea*, or celebration, they organized to raise matching funds was scheduled for September 15, 2001—and cancelled at the last minute because of the tragic events half a world away. Today, it still stands forlorn by the roadside as volunteers from the 40-member Kalapana Ohana Association work to keep it from deteriorating. Open daily.

After exploring the area of recent volcanic action, you can backtrack along the coast via Route 137, which proceeds northeast through jungly undergrowth and past dazzling seascapes to the tiny villages of **Opihikao** and **Pohoiki** or continue on Route 137 past Kapoho where the paved road ends.

RED ROAD

 idden

At the end of Route 137 you'll find a red dirt and cinder road, appropriately named Red Road. At times the coastline is in sight, at times it is hidden by tall ironwoods and lush vegetation. The road undulates, following the contour of the landscape, giving the drive a roller coaster feel. The rural landscape provides an away-from-it-all feeling, which characterizes Puna's rustic appeal.

CAPE KUMUKAHI LIGHTHOUSE

 idden

At the end of the Red Road is the Cape Kumukahi Lighthouse on the state's easternmost point. It too was spared. Today you can see where the wall of lava parted, flowed around the beacon, then closed again as it continued to the sea. In the process, it added about 500 yards of land to the point—an awesome demonstration of how young this Big Island really is. It is rumored that the lighthouse keeper at the lighthouse had given an old woman a meal just before the lava flowed down to the sea. Could it be that Madame Pele spared the lighthouse after enjoying a satisfying dinner?

Now return to Route 132 and head west back toward Pahoa. The road passes more of the **1960 lava flow**, which covered almost 2000 acres and totally leveled the small village of Kapoho.

LAVA TREES STATE PARK ✉Head south on Highway 130 from Pahoa. Turn east on Highway 132. Park entrance is 3 miles down the road on the left. The park, recently cleared of alien plant species in an effort to restore the native Hawaiian ecosystem, is about halfway between Pahoa and the coast at Pohoiki. An eruption, circa 1790, caused the grotesque formations at Lava Tree State Park. Here the molten rock swamped a grove of *ohia* trees, then hardened around the skeletons to create a fossil forest. When fissures in the earth drained the molten lava, these petrified trees were left as a lonely legacy. In strange and exotic fashion, these giant skeletons, mixed with fresh growth, loom above huge cracks in the landscape.

PAHALA PLANTATION COTTAGES

$$–$$$$ 4 UNITS   ✉P.O. Box 940, Pahala, HI 96777   ☎808-928-9811
✐www.pahala-hawaii.com, mahalo@aloha.net

If you're harkening for a taste of old Hawaii, with all the modern amenities, these cottages offer delightful lodgings in a sleepy, pretty little town that got even slower when sugar died. Three comfortable rental cottages and the former plantation manager's house offer one to seven bedrooms in a decidedly rural setting.

BUTTERFLY INN

$ 2 ROOMS   ✉P.O. Box 6010, Kurtistown, HI 96760   ☎808-966-7936, 800-546-2442;
✐www.thebutterflyinn.com, the.butterfly.inn@prodigy.net

After a long day traversing the dense growth of tropical flowers and macadamia and fruit trees, guests are grateful for a soak in a hot tub, a stint in the steam house or a minute with one of the nearby masseuses. All this and more are obtainable at the Butterfly Inn, an all-women lodging, where women bring their own food (and sometimes share in the bounty of the garden), located between Hilo and the village of Volcano. Rooms are cozily decorated, and there's an enclosed deck.

KAILANI OCEANSIDE RETREAT

$$–$$$$ 48 UNITS   ✉RR 2, Box 4500, Pahoa, HI 96778   ☎808-965-7828,
800-800-6886   📠808-965-0527   ✐www.kalani.com, kalani@kalani.com

In the beautiful Puna District, a volcanic region fringed with black-sand beaches, this is a marvelous place to retreat from the world. Situated on Route 137, 15 miles from Pahoa, it sits just above the ocean on 120 acres. In addition to lodging, this New Age resort provides a lifestyle. There are weekly classes in hula, weaving and lei making, plus programs in dance, yoga and massage. The facilities include a watsu pool, two jacuzzis and a sauna, an Olympic-sized swimming pool and volleyball courts. Guests stay in multi-unit lodges, sharing a spacious living room, or in private cottages; treehouse units with ocean views are also available. Sleeping accommodations are basic but appealing, with pine walls; the room decorations are made by local artists. Campsites are available at budget prices. Special events for gays and lesbians are planned during the year. Meals are $43 a day per person.

DINING

LUQUIN'S MEXICAN RESTAURANT

$$ MEXICAN   ✉Old Government Road, Pahoa   ☎808-965-9990

A friendly Mexican eatery serving a variety of dishes from south of the border can be found in the rustic town of Pahoa. You'll find all the familiar favorites on the menu, from *huevos rancheros* to enchiladas, as well as fish tacos smothered in deliciously *picante* red chili salsa. There's a cantina bar, and the old-time Pahoa-style atmosphere is enhanced by a colorful paint job.

NING'S THAI CUISINE

$–$$ THAI   ✉15-2955 Pahoa Road, Pahoa   ☎808-965-7611

Pahoa has slim pickings for good eating, but happily Ning's serves up red, yellow, green and massaman curries that are a cut above, even in these bleak culinary realms. The dining room sits right on the wooden boardwalk that runs through the town, allowing you to soak up the quirky ambience.

BLACK ROCK CAFÉ

$$ AMERICAN   ✉Old Government Road, Pahoa   ☎808-965-1177

For more traditional fare consider this booth-lined shrimp-and-steak eatery. They offer a half-dozen different beef dishes as well as spaghetti, baby back ribs and a catch-of-the-day fish entrée.

PAOLO'S BISTRO

$$ ITALIAN   ✉333 Pahoa Road, Pahoa   ☎808-965-7033

An excellent entry in Pahoa's Italian restaurant scene, Paolo's specializes in Tuscan-style cuisine, highlighting fish dishes and freshly made pasta with pesto or olive oil and garlic. The short menu is supplemented by daily specials. Ingredients are straight from the farm, and the emphasis is on quality rather than quantity. The atmosphere is family-friendly and there's a gazebo in the back for outside dining. Closed Monday.

SHOPPING

PAHOA Out in the volcano region, on the road down to the Puna District, you'll pass through the tiny town of Pahoa. Either side of Route 130, the main drag, is lined with falsefront buildings. Each one seems to contain yet another ingenious craft shop run by a local resident.

BEACHES & PARKS

MACKENZIE STATE RECREATION AREA

hidden

✉Route 137, nine miles northeast of Kaimu

🏖 This beautiful 13-acre park lies in an ironwood grove along a rocky coastline. King's Highway, an ancient Hawaiian trail, bisects the area. There is no swimming, snorkeling or surfing because a sea cliff borders the park. There's good shore fishing from rock ledges but be careful! Occasional high waves break on these ledges. Picnic area and pit toilets are the only facilities. There's no drinking water.

⛺ Tent camping; state permit required.

ISAAC HALE BEACH PARK

✉ *Route 137, about two miles northeast of MacKenzie State Recreation Area*

⚓ 🚶 🏊 🎣 This small park on the Puna coast is pretty but rundown. There's a patch of black sand here and some hot springs nearby. A boat landing ramp makes this a popular park with local folks. Swimming is okay when the sea is calm. There are both summer and winter breaks in the center of the bay. The most common catches here are *papio*, *moi*, mountain bass, *menpachi*, red bigeye, *ulua* and goatfish. A picnic area and restrooms are the only facilities.

⛺ Tent and trailer camping. County permit required. I much prefer nearby MacKenzie State Recreation Area for overnighting.

HILO

There's one thing you'll rarely miss in this tropical city—rain. Hilo gets about 130 inches a year. The Chamber of Commerce will claim it rains mostly at night, but don't be deceived. It's almost as likely to be dark and wet at midday. There is a good side to all this bothersome moisture—it transforms Hilo into an exotic city crowded with tropical foliage, the orchid capital of the United States.

Hilo is the closest you will approach in all Hawaii to a Somerset Maugham–style South Seas port town. With its turn-of-the-20th-century stores, many badly needing a paint job, and old Chinese shops, it's a throwback to an era when tourists were few and Hawaii was a territory.

Sections of town, especially around Waianuenue Avenue, have been extensively refurbished and the entire downtown area is looking fresher than it has in decades. While Hilo still has plenty of old-fashioned charm and an enduring sense of character, it's no longer uncommon to see tourists meandering through the streets, where they find many more shops and restaurants to tempt them.

SIGHTS

IMILOA ASTRONOMY CENTER OF HAWAII ✉ *600 Imiloa Place* 📞 *808-969-9700* 📠 *808-969-9748* 🖥 *www.imiloahawaii.org, info@imiloahawaii.org* The Big Island is known as an international astronomy hub, and it plays up that connection well in this facility. Located in a blocks-long complex of buildings that serve as headquarters for the various Mauna Kea observatories, Imiloa is instantly recognizable by its three, cone-shaped structures, roofed with shiny titanium. Although it's a bit confusing to navigate the center itself, there's a good mix of Hawaiian culture and hands-on scientific exhibits, including a theater screening short 3-D films. But the real treat is the 40-minute planetarium show, which shows how the Polynesians navigated by the stars. This is a great place to spend a rainy day in Hilo, especially with kids. Admission. Closed Monday.

SHIPMAN HOUSE BED & BREAKFAST
PAGE 239

Restored historic inn with rooms lovingly decorated in original furnishings dating back to the monarchy

PUKA PUKA KITCHEN
PAGE 241

Hole-in-the-wall with just three tables serving healthy plate lunches along Hilo's pretty bayfront

LILIUOKALANI GARDENS
PAGE 235

Vibrantly colored Japanese gardens filled with Hawaiian and Asian trees and dotted with pagodas and arched bridges

RICHARDSON OCEAN PARK
PAGE 245

Black-sand beach backdropped by Mauna Kea, with a lava outcropping for wonderfully protected snorkeling

NANI MAU GARDENS ✉*421 Makalika Street* ☎*808-959-3500* ✏*808-959-3501* ✐*garden@nanimau.com* Hilo's rain-soaked environment is a boon for commercial flower growers. This is one place to see how this industry operates, as well as delight in their lovely gardens. With 20 acres and over 2000 plant varieties, including every flowering plant in the islands, Nani Mau (which means "forever beautiful") is one of the largest orchid growers in the islands. It's a botanical wonderland, opened to the public in 1972. For a small fee you can wander the garden, with its numerous tropical trees and plants, waterfalls and museum. Anthurium and orchid lovers will be quite content to spend the afternoon here.

LILIUOKALANI GARDENS

✉*Banyan Drive and Lihiwai Street* Banyan Drive is a green thumb's delight. Sweeping past Hilo's nicest hotels, this waterfront road is shaded with rows of giant banyan trees. Plaques proclaim the dignitaries who planted them, including Franklin D. Roosevelt, Babe Ruth and Amelia Earhart. Next to this verdant arcade are

236

POINTS OF INTEREST

- Ⓐ Boiling Pots
- Ⓑ County Library
- Ⓒ East Hawaii Cultural Center Gallery
- Ⓓ Liliuokalani Gardens Museum
- Ⓔ Lyman House Memorial
- Ⓕ Naha & Pinao Stones
- Ⓖ Nani Mau Gardens
- Ⓗ Pacific Tsunami Museum
- Ⓘ Suisan Fish Market
- Ⓙ Wailoa Visitor Center

Hilo

Downtown Hilo

the Liliuokalani Gardens, 19 acres exploding with color. These Japanese gardens, featuring both Hawaiian and Asian trees, are dotted with pagodas and arched bridges.

COCONUT ISLAND From Banyan Drive, a short footbridge crosses to this palm-studded islet in Hilo Bay. It's an old Hawaiian sanctuary that presents a dramatic view of Hilo Bay and, on a clear day, of Mauna Kea and Mauna Loa as well.

SUISAN COMPANY LIMITED

✉85 Lihiwai Street ☎808-935-9349 ✆808-935-211 ✎www.suisan.com
Be sure to check out this local institution, started in 1907 by a small group of Waiakea fishermen. Anglers bring their fresh catches—*ahi*, mahimahi, reef and bottom fish, whatever's jumping—here for sale. Great photo ops! If you'd like to sample some of the fresh fish, buy some tasty *poke ahi* (raw tuna chunks seasoned with chili peppers, seaweed, green onions and soy sauce), a favorite Hawaiian dish. Better set your alarm. Things get going around 6 a.m.

WAILOA RIVER STATE PARK ✉Piopio Street, off Kamehameha Avenue ☎808-933-0416 Fronting Hilo Bay is this state park, where grassy picnic areas surround beautiful **Waiakea Fishpond**. Across one of the pond's arching bridges, at **Wailoa Visitors Center**, there are cultural and local art exhibits and an information desk. The center also hosts cultural demonstrations.

LYMAN HOUSE ✉276 Haili Street ☎808-935-5021 ✆808-969-7685 ✎www. lymanmuseum.org, info@lymanmuseum.org Located in downtown Hilo, this is a fascinating example of a 19th-century missionary home. Built in 1839, the house is furnished with elegant period pieces that create a sense of this bygone era (the house is open to guided tours only). Also on the property is a Hawaiian history museum focusing on Hawaiian culture and the islands' many ethnic groups, and an excellent collection of rocks and minerals. Among the museum's highlights is a 3-D map of the entire Hawaiian chain, from ocean floor to mountain top. Closed Sunday. Admission.

PACIFIC TSUNAMI MUSEUM ✉130 Kamehameha Avenue ☎808-935-0926 ✆808-935-0842 ✎www.tsunami.org, tsunami@tsunami.org Tsunamis are capable of inconceivable amounts of devastation and destruction, as the world witnessed in Southeast Asia in December 2004. To learn more about this form of natural disaster, visit this little museum that recaptures in photos, videos and interactive displays the tsunamis that periodically wreak havoc on Hilo. Most notorious was the one in 1946, which swept a half-mile inland and killed 94 people on the Big Island. Computers lead visitors through the history and physics of these infamous phenomena and survivors present first-hand accounts in the museum's videotaped oral histories. Closed Sunday.

GUIDED TOUR ✉️*329 Kamehameha Avenue* 📞*808-935-8850* Drop into the Hilo Mainstreet Program Office to pick up a self-guided tour of the town. It leads you to 17 sites of historic and architectural significance in Hilo's tropical enclave.

DOWNTOWN LANDMARKS Grassroots initiatives have brought about a partial revitalization of what remains of the diminishing number of wood-frame buildings that give Hilo a distinctive look. Luckily there have been some notable successes, including the surprisingly elegant **Palace Theater** (c. 1925), a restored landmark that's home to top-notch live theater and musicals. The **old Police Station** (c. 1928) is now an arts complex (the East Hawaii Cultural Center), while the classic **Kress Building** now houses shops and multiscreen movie theaters and a charter school, each a hopeful sign for the future.

EAST HAWAII CULTURAL CENTER GALLERIES ✉️*141 Kalakaua Street* 📞*808-961-5711* 📠*808-935-7536* 💻*www.ehcc.org, arts@ehcc.org* These galleries display the work of local and international artists in a series of exhibits that change monthly. The building itself, an old police station built in 1928 that has achieved historic landmark status, is a work of art. Closed Sunday and the last week of every month.

NAHA & PINAO STONES

✉️*300 Waianuenue Avenue, Hilo* Fronting the library on nearby Waianuenue Avenue are these sacred stones. According to legend, whoever moved the massive Naha Stone would rule all the islands. Kamehameha overturned the boulder while still a youth, then grew to become Hawaii's first king. The smaller Pinao Stone is believed to have guarded a temple or palace entrance.

RAINBOW FALLS Head west on Waianuenue Avenue to the foaming cascade in Wailuku River State Park. Here, particularly in the morning, spray from the falls shimmers in spectral hues. It's another two miles to **Boiling Pots**, where a series of falls pours turbulently into circular lava pools. The rushing water, spilling down from Mauna Kea, bubbles up through the lava and boils over into the next pool.

KAUMANA CAVES Kaumana Drive, branching off Waianuenue Avenue, leads five miles out of town to these caves. A stone stairway leads from the roadside down to two fern-choked lava tubes, formed during Mauna Loa's devastating 1881 eruption. Explore the lower tube, but avoid the other—it's dangerous.

PANAEWA RAINFOREST ZOO & GARDENS ✉️*One mile off the Mamalahoa Highway several miles south of town* 📞*808-959-7224* 📠*808-981-2316* 💻*www.hilozoo.com, cohzoo@interpac.net* Located in a lush region that receives over 125 inches of rain annually, this modest facility houses numerous rainforest animals as well as other species. There are capuchin monkeys, water buffalo and tigers, plus an array of exotic birds that include crowned cranes, parrots, Hawaiian hawks, whistling tree ducks and nenes. Don't miss Namaste, a white Bengal tiger.

The main hotel district in this rain-kissed city sits astride the bay along Banyan Drive. Most hotels offer moderately priced accommodations, while a few are designed to fit the contours of a more slender purse.

SHIPMAN HOUSE BED & BREAKFAST

$$$$ 5 ROOMS ✉*131 Kaiulani Street* ☎*808-934-8002, 800-627-8447*
📠*808-934-8002* 🖥*www.shipmanhouse.com, bighouse@bigisland.com*

The former home of the cattle rancher W. H. Shipman and his wife Mary, this historic inn has been lovingly restored by the Shipmans' great-granddaughter Barbara Ann and her husband Gary. Much of the furnishings are original and date back to the monarchy, including a Steinway piano Queen Liliuokalani sometimes played while a guest here. Jack London and wife Charmian also spent time at this gracious Victorian. Nowadays, there are five spacious accommodations (two in the detached guest cottage) that are individually decorated with period pieces and fresh flowers. A hula *halau* practices on the premise, and guests are invited to join in on Wednesday-night classes.

DOLPHIN BAY HOTEL

$$ 18 UNITS ✉*333 Iliahi Street* ☎*808-935-1466* 📠*808-935-1523*
🖥*www.dolphinbayhotel.com, john@dolphinbayhotel.com*

On a tree-lined residential street just across the Wailuku River sits this comfortable two-story establishment. Studios, one-bedroom apartments (which can accommodate up to four) and a two-bedroom unit (housing as many as six) come with kitchenettes. Rooms upstairs have exposed-beam ceilings; all units have cinderblock walls, but personal touches like fresh flowers and fruit, and a garden with a running spring, make this a good choice.

WILD GINGER INN

$ 17 ROOMS ✉*100 Puueo Street* ☎*808-935-5556, 800-882-1887* 📠*808-969-1225*
🖥*www.wildgingerinnhilo.com*

This vintage-1940s Hawaiian-style inn is surrounded by flowering trees and trimly manicured grounds. Here you'll find 17 inexpensive guest rooms attractively furnished with wood floors and ceiling fans. There's a laundry room, a large garden and a spacious lobby. It also features an open-air lobby that's tastefully tiled and equipped with a very inviting hammock.

HILO BAY HOTEL

$$–$$$ 144 ROOMS ✉*87 Banyan Drive* ☎*808-935-0861, 800-367-5102*
📠*808-935-7903* 🖥*www.unclebilly.com, reservations@unclebilly.com*

The theme here is Polynesian, and proprietor "Uncle Billy" carries it off with flair: wicker furniture, thatch and *tapa* in the lobby, a restaurant/cocktail lounge, a bayside swimming pool and several carp ponds dotted about the tropical gardens. Standard rooms have wall-to-wall carpeting, televisions, telephones and air conditioning. The rooms are plainly furnished, located away from the water and rent for a moderate price. Superior rooms (which overlook the gardens, are larger, more attractive and come with ocean views) can be reserved for slightly more. Oceanfront rooms are also available and rent for deluxe prices.

NANILOA VOLCANOES RESORT

$$–$$$ 307 ROOMS   ✉ *93 Banyan Drive*   ☎ *808-969-3333*   📠 *808-969-6622*
🖥 *www.naniloaresort.com, res@hottours.us*

This is a high-rise affair located right on the water with guest rooms that are comfortably furnished and nicely adorned. Restaurants, bars, a lounge and a spa are among the many amenities here, but the most alluring feature is the landscape—the tree-studded lawn is fringed with tidepools and volcanic rock. Add outdoor swimming pools, a spacious lobby and friendly staff and you have the perfect nesting spot in town. Guests also have access to the Naniloa Country Club's nine-hole golf course across the street.

HILO SEASIDE HOTEL

$$ 133 ROOMS   ✉ *126 Banyan Way*   ☎ *808-935-0821, 800-560-5557*
📠 *808-969-9195*   🖥 *www.hiloseasidehotel.com, info@hiloseasidehotel.com*

Near the far end of tree-lined Banyan Drive lies this charming place, which is actually on a side street fronting Reed's Bay, an arm of Hilo Bay. Owned by the Kimis, a Hawaiian family, it has the same friendly ambience that pervades their other hotels. There's a large lobby decorated with tile, *koa* wood and bamboo. A carp pond complete with footbridges dominates the grounds. The rooms are small and plainly decorated. Most are wallpapered and equipped with telephone, television and a combination shower-tub (perfect for soaking away a rainy day). The lanais overlook lush gardens and the hotel swimming pool. All in all, for friendly ambience and a lovely setting, the Seaside is a prime choice.

ARNOTT'S LODGE

$ 29 ROOMS   ✉ *98 Apapane Road*   ☎ *808-969-7097*   📠 *808-935-6442*
🖥 *www.arnottslodge.com, mahala@arnottslodge.com*

On the outskirts of Hilo in a low-key residential area just one block from the waterfront is a clean, bright attractive hostel. There are two dormitory rooms available as well as 20 semiprivate and 9 private singles and doubles. Hiking and snorkeling trips are frequently arranged. With low prices, and full kitchen and laundry facilities provided, it's one of the area's best bargains.

DINING

Scattered throughout Hilo are numerous cafés, lunch counters and chain restaurants serving low-cost meals. More importantly, this is a great town for ethnic eating on a budget.

PUKA PUKA KITCHEN

$ PLATE LUNCHES   ✉*270 Kamehameha Avenue*   📞*808-933-2121*

This is a hidden gem, named for its hole-in-the-wall locale along Hilo's pretty bayfront. It's tiny, with just three tables, but you can order takeout, and its savory lamb pita wraps and hearty, yet healthful, versions of the local plate lunch are worth a visit. Lunch only.

CAFÉ PESTO

$$–$$$ ITALIAN   ✉*S. Hata Building, 308 Kamehameha Avenue*   📞*808-969-6640*
📠*808-969-4858*   🖱*www.cafepesto.com*

You can dine or take out at this appealing eatery located in the historic S. Hata Building. A downtown Hilo gathering place, they serve traditional wood-fired pizza, calzone and risotto, as well as organic chicken, fresh fish and organic salads.

REUBEN'S MEXICAN FOOD

$$ MEXICAN   ✉*336 Kamehameha Avenue*   📞*808-961-2552*

There are more than three dozen dishes on the menu here, numbered one to thirty-seven, and they cover the entire territory. Whether you're searching for enchiladas, *camarones empanizados*, beef tostadas, carne asada or huevos rancheros, you'll find it here.

PESCATORE

$$–$$$ ITALIAN   ✉*235 Keawe Street*   📞*808-969-9090*

For creative Italian cuisine, this is the place to go. Its yellow exterior, green tablecloths, red chairs, lace curtains and candles in wine bottles create a colorfully romantic atmosphere. The menu offers such entrées as marinated lamb chops, sautéed chicken breast in lemon caper sauce and pasta *puttanesca* with anchovy sauce, but as the name suggests, the specialty is fresh seafood, from a traditional cioppino (fisherman's stew) full of lobster, shrimp, scallops and clams to unique sashimi Italian-style. Breakfast served daily.

OCEAN SUSHI DELI

$$ SUSHI   ✉*239 Keawe Street*   📞*808-961-6625*

This is a good place to pick up a fresh meal of sushi if you can only make a selection from the extensive menu of both traditional favorites and new creations. A few other fish and noodle dishes round out the menu. Although it looks a bit dumpy, the food makes it worth a visit. Closed on Sunday.

ROYAL SIAM

$$$–$$$$ THAI   ✉*70 Mamo Street*   📞*808-961-6100*

Thailand is represented at this Asian eatery with a warm ambience, friendly staff, local crowd and exceptional cuisine. You'll find *pad thai* and traditional Thai curries.

242

NORI'S SAIMIN AND SNACKS

$ JAPANESE   ✉688 Kinoole Street #124   ☎808-935-9133

A hole-in-the-wall local favorite well-hidden behind a bowling alley, Nori's has nonetheless grown so popular over the years that it even has its own line of souvenir T-shirts, hats, beach towels and packaged snacks. The atmosphere is boisterous, and it's open until midnight or so. *Saimin*, noodles similar to ramen, comes prepared in assorted ways—green and flavored with *wasabi*, fried with Spam, or in seaweed soup, to name a few. There are also other choices. Try the *ahi* tuna burger.

MIYO'S

$-$$ JAPANESE   ✉Waiakea Villas Shops, 400 Hualani Street   ☎808-935-2273   📠808-935-2273

Home-style Japanese meals are made fresh at Miyo's. A selection of vegetarian specialties, sashimi, tempura and sesame chicken are served in a simple setting of wooden tables and shoji screens. The dining room overlooks a lagoon that meanders out to Hilo Bay. Closed Sunday.

DON'S GRILL

$-$$ AMERICAN   ✉485 Hinano Street   ☎808-935-9099   📠808-961-0162

This is one of those all-American places where dinner comes with soup or salad, hot vegetables, a fresh roll and your choice of mashed potatoes or fries. In this case it's Hawaiian all-American, so the menu switches from pork chops to teriyaki beef, rotisserie chicken to tofu stir-fry, and barbecued ribs to breaded calamari. Very popular with the local folk. Closed Monday.

NIHON RESTAURANT & CULTURAL CENTER

$$-$$$ JAPANESE   ✉123 Lihiwai Street   ☎808-969-1133

Right next to Suisan fish market, Nihon, a Japanese dining establishment, is a bit light on the culture, but the food is well prepared. Scenic views of Hilo Bay are accented by artwork from local artists. Specialties include noodle dishes, tempura, sukiyaki and sushi. Closed Sunday.

UNCLE BILLY'S FISH AND STEAKHOUSE

$$-$$$ SEAFOOD/STEAK   ✉Hilo Bay Hotel, 87 Banyan Drive   ☎808-935-0861   🖥www.unclebilly.com, resv@unclebilly.com

Located at the Hilo Bay Hotel, this eatery sports Hawaiian decor. In addition to its rattan furnishings, the cozy restaurant hosts Polynesian dinner shows nightly. The menu is filled with surf-and-turf dishes priced reasonably. There's no lunch here, but they do offer breakfast and dinner daily.

KEN'S HOUSE OF PANCAKES

$ AMERICAN   ✉1730 Kamehameha Avenue   ☎808-935-8711   📠808-961-5124   🖥khop@interpac.net

A local institution, voted Best Breakfast by locals eight years in a row, Ken's has to top the list for all-American fare. If you've ever been to a Denny's or Howard Johnson's, you've been in Ken's. Endless rows of naugahyde booths, a long counter next to the kitchen, uniformed waitresses—the classic roadside America motif. The cuisine is on par with the decor and you'll find 200 items on the menu, but it's a great place to join locals for breakfast (yummy banana pancakes) and it's a good late-night option—open 24 hours.

HARRINGTON'S

$$$–$$$$ SEAFOOD/STEAK   ✉135 Kalanianaole Street   📞808-961-4966
📠808-961-4975

Hilo's foremost steak-and-seafood restaurant is found in this waterfront dining room that is particularly popular with locals. Here you can dine in a congenial atmosphere to the strains of Hawaiian music in the background. Harrington's also has a relaxing bar scene and can be counted on for good food with a view. No lunch on weekends.

HILO BAY CAFÉ

hidden

$$–$$$ PACIFIC RIM   ✉Waikea Center, 315 Makaala Street
📞808-935-4939

Although the setting isn't promising—between two cellular phone stores in a big-box shopping mall at the Waikea Center—the fresh, creative food at this café transcends its pedestrian locale. The warm, contemporary décor suits an eclectic menu that is shaped by local, Asian and West Coast influences. A range of meals are offered, from vegan pot pies and crab cake sandwiches to fresh fish specials and ricotta tater tots served with a sweet-spicy marmalade made from jalapeños and Big Island *ohelo* berries. Open for breakfast, lunch and dinner.

SHOPPING

PRINCE KUHIO PLAZA ✉111 East Puainako Street 📞808-959-3555 The most convenient way to shop in Hilo is at this full-facility complex with everything from small crafts shops to swank boutiques to a sprawling department store. The Big Island's largest mall, it's a gathering place for local shoppers and a convenient spot for visitors. But bargains and locally crafted products are probably what you're after. So it's a good idea to window-shop and check out prices, then do your buying at smaller shops.

THE MOST IRRESISTIBLE SHOP IN HILO ✉256 Kamehameha Avenue 📞808-935-9644 This store doesn't quite live up to its bold name but does create a strong attraction with jewelry, clothing, ceramics, books and toys. They also feature works by local artists.

BASICALLY BOOKS ✉160 Kamehameha Avenue 📞808-961-0144 If maps, guidebooks, globes, gifts, Hawaiian music and volumes on Hawaiiana sound more inviting, Basically Books is an excellent choice.

HANA HOU ✉*164 Kamehameha Avenue* &*808-935-4555* ✐*hanahou.hilo@ verizon net* Here is a shop filled with "vintage and contemporary island treasures." Among those keepsakes are old Hawaiian song sheets, Matson menus and aloha shirts. Closed Sunday.

SIG ZANE DESIGNS ✉*122 Kamehameha Avenue* &*808-935-7077* ✐*www. sigzane.com* Specializing in "distinct island wearables, bedding and gifts," this shop has its own designer line of island dresses and aloha shirts. Closed Sunday.

THE BOOK GALLERY ✉*259 Keawe Street* &*808-935-4943* For beach-reading materials, try this well-stocked independent book store.

DAN DELUZ WOODS

✉*Mile marker 12, Route 11* &*808-968-6607* ✇*808-968-6019* A great spot for original woodwork is south of Hilo at Dan DeLuz Woods. The beautiful pieces are fashioned from banyan, sandalwood, *koa* and *milo*, all priced reasonably. The DeLuzes, the craftspeople who own the shop, do all their carving in a separate workshop. If you'd like a description of how the bowls are made, they're happy to provide an informal tour.

HILO FARMERS MARKET

✉*Corner of Mamo and Kamehameha streets* &*808-933-1000* There is a farmers' market in Hilo on Wednesday and Saturday. Tie it in to a visit to the volcano if you're headed that way.

NIGHTLIFE

THE CROWN ROOM ✉*Naniloa Volcano Resort, 93 Banyan Drive* &*808-969-3333* ✐*www.hottours.us* The main entertainment scene centers around the big hotels along Banyan Drive. By far the best place is the Naniloa Volcano Resort. This hotel has a nicely appointed nightclub, which usually books local groups, but every once in a while it imports a mainland band for special events. There's usually a cover charge and two-drink minimum.

WAIOLI LOUNGE ✉*Hilo Hawaiian Hotel, 71 Banyan Drive* &*808-935-9361* The lounge at the Hilo Hawaiian Hotel has live music on weekends. Usually it's a contemporary trio.

HARRINGTON'S ✉*135 Kalanianaole Avenue* &*808-961-4966* This popular waterfront restaurant hosts a Hawaiian guitarist on Friday and Saturday nights.

UNIVERSITY OF HAWAII AT HILO PERFORMING ARTS CENTER ✉*200 East Kaiwili Street* &*808-974-7310* You also can frequently catch a play, Hawaiian cultural event or live concert on campus. Both local and mainland talent are featured.

KALAKAUA PARK

⊠*On the corner of Kinoole Street and Waianuenue Avenue*

This pretty little park, located on a busy city street corner, has a grand old banyan tree and a pleasant picnic area. A bronze statue of King Kalakaua adds dignity to the park grounds.

REED'S BAY BEACH PARK

⊠*At the end of Banyan Drive*

Reed's Bay, a banyan-lined cove, is a marvelous picnic spot. The bay is actually an arm of Hilo Bay, but unlike the larger body of water, it offers excellent swimming in smooth water (though an underwater spring keeps the water cold). There is also an adjacent body of water popular with the locals. They call it "ice pond" due to its cold waters. Facilities include picnic areas, drinking water, showers and restrooms.

ONEKAHAKAHA, KEALOHA AND LELEIWI COUNTY PARKS

⊠*All three parks are located within five miles of Hilo, east along Kalanianaole Avenue.*

None of these three parks have sand beaches, but all possess lava pools or other shallow places for swimming. They also have grassy plots and picnic areas, plus restrooms and showers. If you fish along these shores, chances are good you'll net *papio*, threadfin, mountain bass, mullet, big-eyed scad, mackerel scad, milkfish, bonefish or goatfish. Kealoha Park offers good snorkeling, surfing, spearfishing and throw-netting.

RICHARDSON OCEAN PARK

⊠*Take Kalanianaole Avenue to within a quarter-mile of where the paved road ends; watch for the sign to Richardson Ocean Park. The beach is behind and to the right of the center.* ☎*808-961-8695* ✈*808-961-8696*

This black-sand beach, south of Hilo Bay, is without doubt the finest beach in the area. From there you can see Mauna Kea hulking in the background. Coconut palms and ironwood trees fringe the beach, while a lava outcropping somewhat protects swimmers. The protected areas also make for good snorkeling. This is one of the best spots around Hilo for surfing as well as bodysurfing and bodyboarding. Winter break with right slides. Mornings and evenings are the prime times, but at all times beware of currents, riptides and sharp reefs. Park officials warn beginners to learn the sport at a less treacherous location. Lifeguards are on duty every day. Facilities here include restrooms and outdoor showers.

SADDLE ROAD

Cutting across the island, Saddle Road climbs from Hilo to an elevation of over 6500 feet (bring a sweater!). The eastern section is heavily wooded with *ohia* trees and ferns and is often fog-shrouded. The central portion includes stark fields of lava only intermittently broken by *kipuka*, "islands" of trees surrounded by lava but left alive—micro-ecosystems that are home to rare native plants and birds. The western portion traverses rolling pastures. The Saddle is a stark landscape, a mosaic of decades-old flows from Mauna Loa's and Mauna Kea's grass-covered cinder cones. You cross lava flows from 1855 and 1935 while gaining elevation that will provide you with the finest view of these mountains anywhere on the island. Before setting out, pack warm clothing and check your gas gauge—there are no service stations or stores en route. And consult your car rental agency: Some do not permit driving on Saddle Road. But the drive may become much easier to traverse in the near future—a road improvement project is in progress along Saddle Road, which is likely to continue until early 2009. For up-to-date information, visit www.cflhd.gov.

SIGHTS

ONIZUKA CENTER FOR INTERNATIONAL ASTRONOMY
📞808-961-2180 📠808-969-4892 Near the 28-mile marker of Saddle Road, the road to Mauna Kea leads 13 miles up to the 13,796-foot summit. The first six miles are passable by passenger car and take in a lookout and the center. There's a free star-gazing program from 6 to 10 p.m. Four-wheel-drive vehicles are recommended for the trip to the summit, although most cars can handle it without problems.

MAUNA KEA OBSERVATORY
Beyond this point you will need a four-wheel-drive vehicle. Be sure to call ahead since the visitor station at the center sponsors tours of the summit and star-gazing opportunities. At the summit you'll find the observatory complex, one of the finest observatories in the world, but be prepared for freezing temperatures. You'll also be treated to some of the most otherworldly views imaginable.

MAUNA KEA STATE RECREATION AREA

✉On the Saddle Road about 35 miles west of Hilo About midway along the Saddle Road, situated on the tableland between Mauna Kea and Mauna Loa at 6500-feet elevation, is this excellent base camp for climbing either mountain. With its stunning mountain views, sparse vegetation and chilly weather, this rarefied playground hardly seems like Hawaii. For remoteness and seclusion, you can't choose a better spot.

PANIOLO COUNTRY
Saddle Road continues past a United States military base, then descends through stands of eucalyptus windbreaks into Waimea cattle country. Here you can pick up the Mamalahoa Highway (Route 190) southwest to Kailua, only 87 miles from Hilo. Passing through sparsely populated range country over 2000 feet in elevation, this road has sensational views of the Kona Coast and Maui.

MAUNA KEA STATE RECREATION AREA

✉ *On the Saddle Road about 35 miles west of Hilo*

This 20-acre park, located within the Mauna Kea Forest Reserve, offers spectacular views of both Mauna Kea and Mauna Loa. Dress warmly—at an elevation of 6500 feet, the park can be quite chilly. There are plenty of scenic trails for hiking. A picnic area and restrooms are the only facilities.

▲ No tents or trailers are allowed. The cabins can be rented from the **Division of State Parks** (75 Aupuni Street, Hilo, HI 96721; 808-974-6200). The individual cabins, each accommodating up to six people, have two bedrooms, a kitchenette and an electric heater. Bring water for washing and drinking. Rates are $35 for one to four people and $5 for each additional person. Sometimes (depending on water availability) there are also fourplex cabinettes. These aren't as nice as the individual cabins. They are one-bedroom units crowded with eight bunks; cooking is done in a community dining and recreation area next door.

HAMAKUA COAST

Route 19, the Mamalahoa Highway, leads north from Hilo along the rainy, windswept Hamakua Coast. Planted with papaya, macadamia nuts, taro and ginger root, among other crops and teeming with exotic plant life, this elevated coastline is as lushly overgrown as Hilo.

A softly rolling plateau that edges from the slopes of Mauna Kea to the sea, the region is cut by sharp canyons and deep gulches. Waterfalls cascade down emerald walls and tumbling streams lead to lava-rock beaches. Beautiful is too tame a term for this enchanting countryside. There are stands of eucalyptus, shadowy forests and misty fields of sugar cane. Plantation towns, built between 1900 and 1910, filled with pastel-painted houses adorned with flower gardens, lie along the route.

SIGHTS

SCENIC DRIVE Several miles outside Hilo, follow the signs to the Scenic Drive. This old coast road winds past abandoned cane fields and shantytowns before rejoining the main highway. Alexander palms line the road. Watch for Onomea Bay: There you'll see a V-shaped rock formation where a sea arch collapsed in 1956.

HAWAII TROPICAL BOTANICAL GARDEN

✉ *On the Four Mile Scenic Route, seven miles north of Hilo* ☎ *808-964-5233*
📠 *808-964-1338* 🖱 *www.hawaiigarden.com, htbg@ilhawaii.net* You might
want to stop by this exotic nature preserve with streams, waterfalls, rugged coastline and over 2000 plant species. This jungle
garden, edged by the Pacific and inhabited by shore birds and giant sea turtles, is a place of uncommon beauty. Admission.

AKAKA FALLS STATE PARK On Route 19, you'll soon come to a
turnoff heading inland to this state park. Don't bypass it! A short nature
trail leads past bamboo groves, ferns, ti and orchids to Akaka Falls,
which slide 442 feet down a sheer cliff face, and Kahuna Falls, 400 feet
high. This 66-acre preserve is covered in a canopy of rainforest vegetation. There are birds of paradise, azaleas and giant philodendrons
whose leaves measure as much as two feet.

HAKALAU GULCH

Countless gulches ribbon the landscape between Hilo and
Honokaa. For a unique tour, take the road from Hakalau that
winds down to this gulch. Literally choked with vegetation, this
gorge extends to a small beach. Towering above the gulch is the
highway bridge.

LAUPAHOEHOE POINT A side road several miles north of Hilo
corkscrews down to a hauntingly beautiful peninsula from which 24
students and teachers were swept away by the 1946 tidal wave. Here
gently curving palm trees and spreading lawns contrast with the lash of
the surf.

LAUPAHOEHOE TRAIN MUSEUM ✉ *Between mile markers 25 and 26
on Route 19* ☎ *808-962-6300* 📠 *808-962-6957* 🖱 *www.thetrainmuseum.com* Beginning in 1899 and lasting until 1946—when sugar was king—railways
were the main source of transportation on the Big Island. Nowadays
all that's left of the railroads are relics found in this museum, housed
in a former railroad employee's home. Here you'll find railroad artifacts, photos, memorabilia and a chance to "talk story" with the museum's volunteers, many of whom have spent their lives in the community. Admission.

WORLD BOTANICAL GARDENS

✉ *Near mile marker 16 on Route 19 in Umauma* ☎ *808-963-5427* 📠 *808-963-
5427* 🖱 *www.wbgi.com, info@wbgi.com* It's a jungle out there. But at
these gardens they're trying to make a tropical paradise out of it.
Among the features are a football field–sized children's maze, a
300-acre botanical garden, a pathway through a dense and very
beautiful rainforest, and a vista point overlooking a triple-tiered
waterfall; many more features are under development. Be sure

Hamakua Coast

WAIPIO WAYSIDE

PAGE 250

Preserved 1930s rural bed-and-breakfast inn offering an organic tropical breakfast and plenty of aloha

KAMAAINA WOODS

PAGE 252

Splendid assortment of native wood bowls made on site in an open-view factory

KALOPA STATE RECREATION AREA

PAGE 253

Ideal hiking on untouched wooded expanses ripe for exploring

WORLD BOTANICAL GARDENS

PAGE 248

Tropical paradise complete with rainforest, a giant children's maze, and a vista point overlooking a triple-tiered waterfall

to try the complimentary fruit and juice. Guided tours are available. Bring mosquito repellent. Admission.

PLANTATION TOWNS Along Route 19 the town of **Paauilo** offers a glimpse of vintage Hawaii: decaying storefronts and tinroof cottages. Then it's on to **Honokaa**, a village caught in a lazy-paced time warp and the one-time world center of macadamia nut growing.

WAIPIO VALLEY AND LOOKOUT

Head out Route 240 to the island's largest valley. Most people get to see Waipio from this scenic lookout where Route 240 comes to an abrupt end. From the lookout you can see the mile-long black sand beach that marks Waipio's border with the sea. Tall ironwoods mark the site that was once a *heiau*, with the taro patches that pay homage to the Hawaiian past. The steep road that makes its way to the valley floor requires four-wheel drive. It's narrow (in some places only wide enough for one vehicle), steep (with up to a 38 degree gradient), with sheer dropoffs that have hosted more than one vehicle.

WAIPIO VALLEY TOURS Taro patches and tumbledown cottages still dot the valley. From the lookout point at road's end, a jeep trail drops sharply into Waipio. Explorers can hike down or take an hour-and-a-half tour in a four-wheel-drive van with the **Waipio Valley Shuttle and Tours** (808-775-9518). Another agency with tours is **Waipio**

Valley Wagon Tour (808-775-9518) Its tour is part four-wheel-drive, part mule-drawn, GM shock-equipped wagon. Both tours travel several miles up into the valley for eye-boggling views of 1200-foot **Hiilawe Falls**. Both are closed Sunday.

If you hike into Waipio Valley, be prepared for some heavy-duty puffing and panting on the way up, and take heed of no trespassing signs. Camping requires a permit, with unimproved campsites just behind the beach.

LODGING

WAIPIO WAYSIDE

$$–$$$ 5 ROOMS   ✉P.O. Box 840, Honokaa, HI 9672 ☎808-775-0275, 800-833-8849 ⬚www.waipiowayside.com, info@waipiowayside.com

This is prime bed-and-breakfast country that benefits from a rural setting and hosts with plenty of aloha. The five-room Waipio Wayside, on Route 240 between Honokaa and Waipio, offers a convenient base for exploring the valley. The 1930s home has been nicely updated, preserving the feel of the past. An organic tropical breakfast is served communally.

HOTEL HONOKAA CLUB

$–$$ 20 ROOMS   ✉Route 240, Honokaa ☎808-775-0678, 800-808-0678
📠808-775-0678 ⬚www.hotelhonokaa.com, manager@hotelhonokaa.com

Perched on a hillside above the Hamakua Coast, this place has a

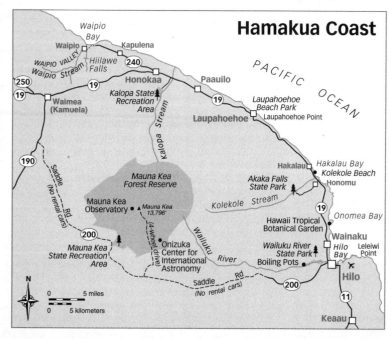

Hamakua Coast

boardinghouse atmosphere. The rooms upstairs are kept thoroughly scrubbed and freshly painted; they're quite adequate. A modest price buys a splendid ocean view, color television plus a tiny private bathroom. Or trade the cable TV away and you can have a small cubicle with community bathroom at even less cost. These rooms are smaller and lack the view, but they're just as clean as the upstairs rooms. Dorm-style hostel accommodations are also available. A continental breakfast is included for hotel stays.

MOUNTAIN MEADOW RANCH

$$ 2 UNITS ✉46-3895 Kapuna Road, Honokaa, HI 96727 ✆808-775-9376
⌕www.mountainmeadowranch.com, info@mountainmeadowranch.com

At this caravansary in Ahualoa (about five minutes upcountry of Honokaa toward Waimea), you're surrounded by pastureland and tall eucalyptus that scent the air. There are a separate one-bedroom cottage or a two-bedroom suite that can be rented as a two-bedroom booking. Breakfast includes home-brewed coffee, local fruits, breads, pastries and cereal. Rooms are spacious, beds comfortable—fluffy and warm for the cool night air. Owner Gay George is a most pleasant hostess.

DINING

JOLENE'S KAU KAU KORNER

$ PLATE LUNCHES ✉45-3625 Mamane Street, Honokaa ✆808-775-9498

Jolene's has plate lunches, burgers and sandwiches during daylight hours. At dinner, they move on to mahimahi, shrimp and vegetable tempura, stir-fry beef and grilled chicken with pineapple. It's a simple café but reasonably priced with good-sized portions and local color. Closed weekends.

TEX DRIVE-IN & RESTAURANT

$$ AMERICAN ✉Route 19, Honokaa ✆808-775-0598

Oversize portions, and the fact that on some nights it's the only restaurant in town, makes Tex's a Honokaa landmark and gathering place. Local specialties and standard fare like hamburgers dominate the fast-food menu.

SHOPPING

OHANA GALLERY

✉Honomu ✆808-963-5467 On the road to Akaka Falls in Honomu, you'll happen upon a gallery with a wide array of work by local artists and craftspeople. Of particular note are photographs of the volcano erupting on the Big Island. The gallery also serves as an informal area information center. Closed Sunday and Monday.

KAMAAINA WOODS

✉️ *Lehua Street, Honokaa* 📞 *808-775-7722* 📠 *808-775-2074* 🖱️ *www.huli hands.com* Be sure to stop by this shop with its splendid assortment of handmade bowls and decorations. With items fashioned from *milo*, mango and *koa*, this shop is practically a museum. And if you are interested in learning more about these woods, you can view the factory through the window. Closed Saturday and Sunday.

WAIPIO VALLEY ARTWORKS

✉️ *48-5416 Kukuihaele Road* 📞 *808-775-0958* Located near the Waipio Valley Lookout, this shop is also cluttered with woodcarvings. Made from several different woods, some of these creations are extremely beautiful. They also feature paintings, ceramics and other locally crafted items.

NIGHTLIFE

HONOKAA PEOPLE'S THEATRE ✉️ *Honokaa* 📞 *808-775-0000* 📠 *808-775-9963* This 1930 structure with an Old West–style facade and a portico over the sidewalk is one of the last motion picture houses in Hawaii with a single big screen. Besides showing first-run films and independent and art films, the renovated theater is used for occasional live dance performances and music concerts.

BEACHES & PARKS

KOLEKOLE BEACH PARK

✉️ *Just off Mamalahoa Highway (Route 19) about 12 miles northwest of Hilo*

Located at the mouth of a wide gulch lush with tropical vegetation, this comfortable park has a large and pleasant grassy area. A stream and waterfall tumble through the park down to the rocky, surf-torn shore. The sandy beach and natural beauty of the place make it very popular among local residents. You can swim in the stream but the ocean here is forbiddingly rough. (Don't swim in the water if you have open cuts; Hawaii's streams teem with bacteria.) Threadfin, *menpachi*, *papio* and *ulua* are the common catches. Facilities consist of a picnic area, restrooms and electricity; there is no drinking water, but spring water is available for cooking and showers.

▲ Tent and trailer; $3 per night. County permit required.

LAUPAHOEHOE BEACH PARK

✉️ *One mile off Route 19 down a well-marked twisting road, about 27 miles northwest of Hilo*

Set on a low-lying peninsula that was inundated by the 1946 tidal wave, this hauntingly beautiful park is still lashed by heavy surf. A precipitous *pali* and lava-strewn shoreline surround the area.

Swimming, snorkeling and surfing are good at times, but usually very dangerous. You can fish for *ulua*, *papio*, *menpachi* and *moi*. Facilities include a picnic area, restrooms, showers and electricity.

▲ Tent and trailer camping; $3 per night. County permit required.

KALOPA STATE RECREATION AREA

✉ *Take Route 19 southeast from Honokaa for about three miles. A well-marked paved road leads from the highway another two miles to the park.*

A wooded retreat set in the mountains above the Hamakua Coast, this 100-acre park has both untouched expanses ripe for exploring and several beautifully landscaped acres. Ranging from 2000 to 2500 feet elevation, it's a great place for hiking or just for escaping. There are picnic areas, restrooms, showers and cabins.

▲ Tent camping is permitted and cabins are also available. Reservations: 808-974-6200.

WAIPIO BEACH

✉ *You can reach the main section of beach by wading the stream, a dangerous task when waters are full. Otherwise it requires a bridge crossing upstream followed by a walk (or drive) to the shore.*

🏃 🏖 Waipio's mile of gray sands are dissected by the waters of Waipio Stream after a journey that begins six miles upstream. With a steep break and often unpredictable currents, swimming requires a careful reading of daily conditions. The setting provides wonderful views of the valley's steep walls. The remains of an ancient *heiau* are situated in an ironwood grove that backs the beach.

OUTDOOR ADVENTURES

CAMPING

There are few activities on the Big Island more pleasurable than camping. Beautiful state and county parks dot the island, while enticing hiking trails lead to remote mountain and coastal areas.

No matter what you plan to do on the island, keep in mind that the Kona side is generally dry, while the Hilo side receives considerable rain. Also remember that the mountains can be quite cold and usually call for extra clothing and gear.

Camping at county parks requires a permit. These cost $5 per person per day ($2 for ages 13 through 17, $1 for children). Although RV camping is allowed in many county parks, no special parking or electrical hookups are provided.

COUNTY DEPARTMENT OF PARKS AND RECREATION
✉101 Pauahi Street, Suite 6, Hilo, HI 96720 ☎808-961-8311 📠808-961-8411
🌐www.hawaii-county.com

NORTH KONA PERMIT OFFICE
✉75-5530 Kuakini Highway ☎808-327-3560 🌐www.hawaii-county.com

STATE DEPARTMENT OF LAND AND NATURAL RESOURCES
✉75 Aupuni Street, Hilo, HI 96720 ☎808-974-6200 📠808-974-6222

HILO SURPLUS STORE (FOR CAMPING GEAR)
✉148 Mamo Street, Hilo ☎808-935-6398 📠808-935-0967 🌐ddeatty@aol.com

FISHING

The waters off the Kona Coast are among the Pacific's finest fishing grounds, particularly for marlin. Many charter boats operate out of Kailua; check the phone book for names or simply walk along the pier and inquire.

KONA CHARTER SKIPPERS ASSOCIATION ✉74-857 Iwalani Place, Kailua-Kona ☎808-329-3600, 800-762-7546 🌐www.konabiggamefishing.com, konafish@hawaii.rr.com One of the larger outfits, they sponsor daily charters for marlin, yellowfin tuna, *ono*, mahimahi and other gamefish. Using boats 31 to 54 feet in length, they take out up to six passengers per boat for half- and full-day trips. Private charters are also available.

SEA WIFE ✉P.O. Box 2645 Kailua-Kona, HI 96745 ☎888-329-1806 🌐seawifeii@hawaii.rr.com With Captain Tim Cox at the helm, this fishing vessel sets out Monday through Saturday from Honokohau Harbor in pursuit of marlin, mahimahi, *ono* and tuna.

PAMELA ✉Honokohau Harbor, Kailua-Kona ☎808-329-3600, 800-762-7546 📠808-334-0941 Head up to the tuna tower to survey the fishing scene aboard this 38-foot Bertram that focuses on marlin, short-nosed spearfish, mahimahi, yellowfin and wahoo.

CHARTER DESK ✉Honokohau Harbor, Kailua-Kona ☎808-329-5735 🌐www.charterdesk.com Located in the Honokohau Marina, this service can arrange half- or full-day excursions and also tailor the trip to guest requests.

SNORKELING & SCUBA DIVING

The Big Island's coastal waters offer some of the most enticing dive sites in Hawaii. Good visibility, lava and coral formations and, of course, an intriguing variety of marine life assure plenty of fun. Whether you choose a beach or boat dive, you'll find the waters relatively uncrowded.

Simply stated, Hawaii's Kona Coast offers some of the world's most spectacular diving. All along this western shoreline lie magnificent submerged caves, lava flows, cliffs and colorful coral reefs.

Protected from prevailing trade winds by Mauna Kea and Mauna Loa, Kona enjoys the gentlest conditions. Usually the weather is sunny, the surf mild and the water clear (visibility is usually in the 100-foot range). Locals claim they get about 345 ideal diving days a year. It's small wonder, then, that adventurers travel from all over the world to explore Kona's underwater world.

What will you see if you join them? The Kona Coast has over 650 species of reef fish including the brightly colored yellow tang, the aptly named raccoon butterflyfish, the trumpetfish, the coronetfish, the cow-eyed porcupine pufferfish, and the black, yellow and white moorish idol. Large marine animals abound as well, including green sea turtles, hawksbill turtles, manta rays, spotted eagle rays, pilot whales, pygmy killer whales and humpback whales.

Kailua–Kona Area

Kamakahonu Beach, the sand patch next to Kailua's King Kamehameha Kona Beach Hotel, is a crowded but convenient snorkel site. There are corals and many species of fish here, but watch out for heavy boat traffic along the wharf. On the south side of the pier, at the small beach where the Ironman Triathlon swim begins, is good snorkeling.

Ski Hawaii

During your island tour you'll inevitably pull up behind some joker with a bumper sticker reading "Think Snow." Around you trade winds may be bending the palm trees, sunbronzed crowds will be heading to the beach, and the thermometer will be approaching 80°. Snow will be the furthest thing from your mind.

But up on the 13,796-foot slopes of Mauna Kea, you're liable to see a bikini-clad skier schussing across a mantle of newly fallen snow! Any time from December until April or May, there may be enough dry snow to create ski runs several miles long and fill bowls a half-mile wide and almost a mile long. The slopes range from beginner to expert: Some have a vertical drop of 4500 feet. This is some of the world's highest skiing available.

Situated above the clouds about 80 percent of the time, this snow lover's oasis is baked by a tropical sun many times more powerful than at the beach. So it's easy to tan and easier yet to burn.

Combined with the thin air and winds up to 100 miles per hour, Hawaii's ski slopes are not for the faint-hearted or fair-skinned. But if you're seeking an incredible adventure and want a view of the Hawaiian islands from a 13,000-foot crow's nest, the heights of Mauna Kea await. There are no lifts and no groomed trails; beneath the snow is hard lava rock and cinder. A four-wheel-drive vehicle is required to get you there. It's the same road used to get to the observatories.

SKI GUIDES HAWAII ✉ *P.O. Box 1954, Kamuela, HI 96743* ☎ *808-885-4188* ✎ *www.skihawaii.com, christopher@langan.net* To hit the slopes, check in with this outfit. They offer all-day downhill skiing and snowboarding tours on Mauna Kea and cross-country skiing on Mauna Loa. The ski season lasts from November through July. This is not an inexpensive trip—but then again, skiing never is. Reservations recommended and deposit required.

256

Old Kona Airport State Recreation Area, just a stone's skip north of town, affords excellent diving on either side. The entry is rocky, but once in, you'll find the waters spectacular. Some glass-bottom boats tour this area.

Honokohau Beach has some good spots south of the small-boat harbor. **Kaloko-Honokohau National Historic Park**, north of Honokohau Harbor, has a trail that leads to an excellent beach and snorkeling site.

Kahaluu Beach Park, with its easy entry to the water and complete beach services including restrooms, lifeguard, picnic tables and showers, is the best spot for beginners. The waters here are too shallow for great scuba diving, which means they're all the better for snorkeling.

Across from Napoopoo Beach Park, at the **Captain Cook Monument,** is an excellent diving spot—so good, in fact, that it draws diving tours and glass-bottom boats and lots of odd looking masked-and-finned mammals.

Keei Beach features a lot of coral and, reportedly, a sea grotto. At **Puuhonua o Honaunau National Historical Park**, also known as the Place of Refuge, there are two natural steps carved into the rocky shoreline that allow for easy entry directly into swarms of reef fish. Because of the abundance of colorful marine life, the accessible location, the easy entry and the variety of depths, this is one of the coast's best spots for snorkelers and scuba divers alike. **Hookena Beach Park** offers good dive spots near the cliffs south of the beach. **Milolii** has excellent diving areas as well as fascinating tidepools.

OCEAN ECO TOURS ⊠Honokohau Harbor, 74-425 Kealakehe Parkway, Suite 15, Kailua-Kona ☎808-324-7873 🖷808-331-1936 🖳www.oceanecotours.com, ecoinfo@oceanecotours.com Specializing in teaching beginners to catch the perfect wave, Ocean Eco Tours offers surfing lessons every day.

HONU SAILING ⊠Honokohua Harbor, Kailua ☎808-896-4668 🖳www.sailkona.com Whole day, half-day and sunset trips with snorkeling are this outfitter's specialty.

KAMANU CHARTERS ⊠P.O. Box 2021, Kailua-Kona, HI 96745 ☎808-329-2021, 800-348-3091 🖷808-329-8424 🖳www.kamanu.com, info@kamanu.com Rather than heading out to Molikini with all the other folks, this charter company takes you to a hidden cove that teems with fish and otherworldly coral formations. You're bound to see a slinky eel, needlenose fish and tons of parrot fish. If you're lucky, spinner dolphins cavort alongside the boat as you make your way back to the marina. A lively crew makes the day even more special.

SANDWICH ISLE DIVERS ⊠Kona Marketplace, Kailua-Kona ☎808-329-9188 888-743-3483 🖳www.sandwichisledivers.com This is a full-service dive shop that offers repairs and instruction, and has a boat for dive trips. Trip destinations include Turtle Pinnacles, Pine Trees, Golden Arches, Kaiwi Point and Kaloko Arches and more locations along the Kona Coast and beyond. They also conduct a night manta ray dive.

SEA PARADISE SCUBA ⊠78-7128 Kaleopapa Street, Keauhou ☎808-322-2500, 800-322-5662 🖳www.seaparadise.com Lava tubes, caverns, caves and other fascinating formations at 40 locations south of Kailua are the highlights with this company.

BIG ISLAND DIVERS ✉*Kaahumanu Plaza, 75-5467 Kaiwi Street, Kailua-Kona* ☏*808-329-6068* ⏴*www.bigislanddivers.com* This outfit offers daytime and night dives along the Kona Coast.

Kohala Coast

Anaehoomalu Beach is good for beginners, but it lacks the scenic diversity of other areas. There's good diving at the end of the road leading to Puako, but it's rocky. **"69" Beach** (or Waialea Bay) features good underwater opportunities when the surf is mild. **Hapuna Beach State Park** has an area that abounds in coral and fish near the rocks and cliffs at the end of the beach. **Spencer Beach Park** is filled with coral and suits beginners and experts alike.

Mahukona Beach Park is an old shipping area littered with underwater refuse that makes for great exploring. **Kapaa Beach Park** offers good diving, but it has a rocky entrance and tricky currents. **Keokea Beach Park**, an excellent spearfishing area, is often plagued by wind and high surf.

KOHALA DIVERS ✉*Kawaihae Shopping Center, Kawaihae* ☏*808-882-7774* ⏴*www.kohaladivers.com* This full-service diving center provides scuba and snorkeling lessons as well as gear rental. There is a two-tank boat dive available, or go out on their 42-foot custom dive boat.

Hilo

Dives on Hilo are done mostly from the shore and include lots of sealife sightings. Some of the best spots are Leleiwi, Pohoiki, Reed's Bay and Richardson's Beach.

NAUTILUS DIVE CENTER ✉*382 Kamehameha Avenue, Hilo* ☏*808-935-6939* ⏴*www.nautilusdivehilo.com* The only dive shop in Hilo, Nautilus has been operating one- and two-tank shore dives off the Hilo Coast as well as all over the island since 1982. You'll see a variety of marine life, including sea turtles, as well as coral formations and caves. Closed Sunday.

SURFING & WINDSURFING

For surfing U.S.A., consider the dynamic Kona Coast as well as Hilo Bay. Winter is peak season for surfing popular spots such as "Lyman's" and "Banyan's." Also popular is "Pohiki" in the Puna area near the Kilauea volcano.

Windsurfing is good year-round. Try Anaehoomalu Beach on the Kona Coast or the South Point area.

OCEAN ECO TOURS ✉*Honokohau Harbor, 74-425 Kealakehe Parkway, Suite 15, Kailua-Kona* ☏*808-324-7873* ☏*808-331-1936* ⏴*www.oceanecotours.com, ecoinfo@oceanecotours.com* Specializing in teaching beginners to catch the perfect wave, Ocean Eco Tours offers surfing lessons every day.

257
5 BIG ISLAND OUTDOOR ADVENTURES SURFING & WINDSURFING

HONOLUA SURF COMPANY ✉75-5744 Alii Drive, Kailua-Kona ☎808-329-1001 At the Kona Inn Shopping Village, Honolua sells surfboards and boogieboards and recommends the best locations.

PACIFIC VIBRATIONS ✉75-5702 Likana Lane, Kailua-Kona ☎808-329-4140 These friendly folks will outfit you for a day of surfing and they're a great resource for info about local outdoor activities.

OCEAN SPORTS HAWAII ✉Outrigger Waikoloa Resort, Waikoloa ☎808-886-6666 ext. 1, 888-724-5234 ⌂www.hawaiioceansports.com Sailboards and lessons can be found here.

SAILING & PARASAILING

One of the authentic pleasures of a Big Island visit is a sail along the Kona or Kohala coast. Choose from a pleasure sail or take an adventure trip that includes a snorkeling excursion.

FAIR WIND BIG ISLAND OCEAN GUIDES ✉78-7130 Kaleiopapa Street, Kailua-Kona ☎808-322-2788, 800-677-9461 ⌂www.fair-wind.com The calm waters off Kona provide ideal conditions for Fair Wind's two catamarans that travel to Kealakekua Bay for snorkeling and sightseeing on daily morning and afternoon tours.

HONU SAILING ✉Honokohua Harbor, Kailua ☎808-896-4668 ⌂www.sailkona.com Whole day, half-day and sunset trips with snorkeling are this outfitter's specialty.

UFO PARASAIL ✉Kailua-Kona ☎808-325-5836, 888-359-4836 ⌂www.ufoparasail.net For those who want to get above it all, give parasailing a try. You are strapped to a parachute that is towed aloft by a motorboat.

KAMANU CHARTERS ✉P.O. Box 2021, Kailua-Kona, HI 96745 ☎808-329-2021, 800-348-3091 ☎808-329-8424 ⌂www.kamanu.com, info@kamanu.com Rather than heading out to Molikini with all the other folks, this charter company takes you to a hidden cove that teems with fish and otherworldly coral formations. You're bound to see a slinky eel, needlenose fish and tons of parrot fish. If you're lucky, spinner dolphins cavort alongside the boat as you make your way back to the marina. A lively crew makes the day even more special.

MAILE GULF STAR ✉Kawaihae Harbor ☎800-726-7245 ⌂www.adventuresailing.com The *Maile Gulf Star* is a 50-foot sailboat available for a variety of trips around the Big Island.

KAYAKING

As serene or challenging an adventure as you want, exploring Big Island waters in a kayak can be one of the best ways to view the coast. Many tour companies pair a trip with other activities, such as snorkeling, which can make for an extra memorable day.

KONA BOY ✉Mamalahoa Highway near mile marker 113 ☎808-322-3600 ⌂www.konaboys.com Guided sea tours on the island's west side are the name of the game here. Rentals of dive, surf, racing or touring kayaks are also available. Kona Boy is a resource for maps, information and advice on sea kayaking.

ALOHA KAYAK CO. ✉*79-7428 Mamalahoa Highway, Honalo* ☎*808-322-2868,* *877-322-1444* ✍*www.alohakayak.com, info@alohakayak.com* The Big Island's only Hawaiian-owned and -operated kayak company is Aloha Kayak Co. These knowledgeable folks will rent you equipment and take you on exciting tours that include cliff-jumping, snorkeling and even swimming through lava tubes.

WHALE WATCHING & BOAT TOURS

Between November and May, when about 600 humpback whales inhabit Hawaiian waters, a popular spectator sport is spotting these behemoths in the channels around the islands. The rest of the year, outfitters seek out the lesser-known whales and other marinelife attractions.

CAPTAIN DAN MCSWEENEY'S WHALE WATCHING ADVENTURES ✉*Honokohau Harbor, Kailua-Kona* ☎*808-322-0028, 888-942-5376* ✆*808-322-2732* Captain Dan McSweeny's operates three-hour cruises. If you don't see whales, the company will give you another trip at no charge.

CAPTAIN ZODIAC ✉*Honokohau Harbor* ☎*808-329-3199* ✍*www.captain zodiac.com* Zip along the Kona coast on one of the four-hour trips made twice daily. You may see whales, dolphins, sea turtles and other marine life as you journey along the coast and visit sea caves and lava tubes. There's a stop at Kealakekua Bay for snorkeling.

GOLF

Some of the best golfing in the country is found on the Big Island. From stunning links on the Kohala Coast to community courses in the Hilo area, this island has everything you need for a golf-oriented vacation. Sunny conditions on the Kona side mean you generally don't need to worry about taking a rain check.

Kailua-Kona Area
HAWAII COUNTRY CLUB ✉*72-3890 Hawaii Belt Road (Route 190), Kalaoa* ☎*808-325-6625* Located on the slopes of Hualalai, about seven miles north of Kailua-Kona, this course offers cool Upcountry play between 2000 and 3000 feet above sea level. Play is hilly with narrow fairways that favor accuracy. The views are rewarding.

KONA COUNTRY CLUB ✉*78-7000 Alii Drive, Kailua-Kona* ☎*808-322-2595* At Kona's, a pair of 18-hole golf courses are ideal for those who want to bunker down. Bring along your camera to capture memorable views of the ocean course. Or head uphill to fully enjoy the challenging Mauka course. If you're looking for over-water holes and hidden hazards, you've come to the right place.

Kohala Coast
The Kohala Coast is where the monied set swings their clubs. So if you're going to play golf at these five-star luxury resorts, bring a fat wallet.

WAIKOLOA VILLAGE GOLF COURSE ✉Waikoloa ☎808-883-9621
This is an 18-hole, par-72 layout that also includes a driving range and practice greens. This windy course, designed by Robert Trent Jones, Jr., has great views of Mauna Kea and Mauna Loa.

WAIKOLOA BEACH RESORT GOLF COURSE ✉Waikoloa ☎808-886-7888 The golf course at this resort was also designed by Robert Trent Jones, Jr. It heads through petroglyph fields.

WAIKOLOA KINGS' GOLF COURSE ✉Waikoloa ☎808-886-7888 Waikoloa Kings' has a popular course adjacent to the beach resort course.

MAUNA LANI GOLF COURSE ✉68-1310 Mauna Lani Drive, Kohala Coast ☎808-885-6655 At this posh resort there are two 18-hole links built across rugged lava beds. If you miss the fairway, don't expect to find your ball out there in the volcanic landscape. There's also a driving range and practice greens.

Kona/Kau District

SEA MOUNTAIN GOLF COURSE ✉Route 11, Punaluu ☎808-928-6222
Sea Mountain is a popular 18-hole course located south of Kilauea volcano. It's beautifully landscaped with coconut and banyan trees.

Hawaii Volcanoes National Park

VOLCANO GOLF AND COUNTRY CLUB ✉99-1621 Pii-Mauna Drive, Volcanoes National Park ☎808-967-7331 This is the only course I know located in the vicinity of an erupting volcano. The high elevation (4000 feet) will give your ball an extra lift on this 18-hole course.

Hilo

NANILOA COUNTRY CLUB ✉120 Banyan Drive, Hilo ☎808-935-3000
This is a nine-hole, par-35 course overlooking Hilo Bay. The narrow course may look easy but don't be deceived: Water hazards and trees along the fairways create plenty of challenges.

HILO MUNICIPAL GOLF COURSE ✉340 Haihai Street, Hilo ☎808-959-7711 One of the best bargains on the islands, this 18-hole course has great views of the water and the mountains. Be sure to reserve tee times on the weekends. You can sharpen your skills on the driving range and practice greens.

Hamakua Coast

HAMAKUA COUNTRY CLUB ✉Mile Marker 751, Route 19, Honokaa ☎808-775-7244 Another inexpensive choice, this country club is located on the north shore about 40 miles from Hilo. The nine-hole course bans power carts. While it lacks the amenities of the resort links, Hamakua has a nice neighborhood feel.

RIDING STABLES

Saddle up and survey the Big Island's lush Kohala Mountains on horseback. Some outfitters even provide *paniolo*-style trips.

HAWAII FOREST & TRAIL ✉ _74-5035B Kaahumanu Highway, Kailua-Kona_ ☏ _808-331-8505, 800-464-1993_ ✎ _www.hawaii-forest.com, info@hawaii-forest.com_ An eco-friendly group, they offer four types of trips, including mule trips through the Kohala Mountains, where sweeping views of the coastline, Pololu Valley and Haleakala are the attraction. The guides are friendly and informative.

PANIOLO ADVENTURES ✉ _Mile 13.2 on Kohala Mountain Road (Route 250), North Kohala_ ☏ _808-889-5354_ ✎ _www.panioloadventures.com_ You can re-enact life as a _paniolo_ on an 11,000-acre cattle ranch in the lovely North Kohala mountains. These folks even outfit you with a duster, hat and boots to make the experience more realistic. Take one of five guided rides offered daily that range in elevation from sea level to 4800 feet, or schedule a private one.

DAHANA RANCH ✉ _P.O. Box 1293, Kamuela, HI 96743_ ☏ _808-885-0057, 888-399-0057_ 📠 _808-885-7853_ ✎ _www.dahanaranch.com_ Dahana Ranch operates a gorgeous spread. Besides offering packages of _paniolo_ entertainment and a chance to "brand, rope and pen," they also have rides for the less dedicated. Their one-and-a-half-hour tour takes in views of the working ranch as well as the surrounding valley and mountains. The two-and-a-half-hour option includes participation in an authentic cattle drive. Reservations required.

KINGS' TRAIL RIDES O' KONA ✉ _Kealakekua_ ☏ _808-323-2388_ ✎ _www.konacowboy.com, sales@konacowboy.com_ If you want a land and sea adventure, this outfitter offers a riding/snorkeling combo. Riders descend the Kaawaloa Trail to Kealakekua Bay. Lunch is included, and children over seven with riding experience can participate.

NAALAPA TRAIL RIDES ✉ _Waipio Valley Artworks, Kukuihaele Village Road, Kukuihaele_ ☏ _808-775-0419_ ✎ _www.naalapastables.com_ In Waipio Valley, this group will take you on a two-hour ride through taro patches and waterfalls and (it goes without saying) past magnificent views, Monday through Saturday. They also offer excursions in the Kohala Mountains seven days a week.

BIKING

The Big Island offers very good roads and many unpopulated stretches that make it ideal for bikers. Much of the island is mountainous with some fairly steep grades in the interior. Saddle Road, the roads to Waimea, and the road from Hilo up to Volcanoes National Park will all make a heavy breather of you, but the coast roads are generally flat or gently rolling. Most roads have shoulders and light traffic. Keep in mind that the northeast side of the island receives heavy rainfall, while the Kona side is almost always sunny. But wet side or dry, the scenery is spectacular throughout.

BACKROADS ✉ _801 Cedar Street, Berkeley, CA 94710_ ☏ _800-462-2848, 510-527-1555_ 📠 _510-527-1444_ ✎ _www.backroads.com_ How about a 300-mile bike ride to get you going? This well-respected adventure outfitter offers you the opportunity to really see the Big Island. If you enjoy biking with others, check out their website. On their Big Island adventure trip you will visit sacred Hawaiian grounds, coffee farms, green-sand beaches, and the southernmost point of the United States as well as spin along lush coastlines and, to test your worth, pedal a 4000-foot climb. (For those who don't need to show their metal, there is a van you can ride in.) In the evening you get to rejuvenate at upscale resorts. It's a six-day, five-night jaunt, with prices in the steep Mauna Kea range. But, what a work out!

Bike Rentals

DAVE'S BIKE AND TRIATHLON SHOP ✉75-5669 Alii Drive, Kailua-Kona ☎808-329-4522 Dave's rents mountain and cross-training bikes—with shuttles to and from Kailua hotels—and does repairs. If you want, you can ship your bike and Dave's will have it assembled before you arrive.

HAWAIIAN PEDALS ✉75-5744 Alii Drive, Kailua-Kona ☎808-329-2294 ⌨www.hawaiianpedals.com Hybrids as well as gear and accessories can be found here. Rental times range from five hours to a couple of weeks.

HP BIKEWORKS ✉74-5583 Luhia Street, Kailua-Kona ☎808-326-2453 ⌨www.hpbikeworks.com Hawaiian Pedal's sister company, HP Bikeworks, rents front- and full-suspension mountain bikes.

There are no bike rentals in Hilo.

Bike Repairs

MID-PACIFIC WHEELS ✉1133-C Manono Street, Hilo ☎808-935-6211 The folks here will do repair work or sell you bike accessories.

HIKING

Of all the islands in the chain, Hawaii has the finest hiking trails. The reason? Quite simply, it's the Big Island's size. Larger than all the other islands combined and boasting the highest peaks, the Big Island offers the greatest diversity to explorers.

Mauna Loa and Mauna Kea, each rising over 13,000 feet, provide rugged mountain climbing. To the north, the Kohala Mountains feature trails through dense tropical terrain and along awesome cliffs. In Volcanoes National Park, hikers can experience the challenge of walking through a lava wasteland and into the belly of an active volcano.

Along much of Hawaii's shoreline lies a network of trails that have been under study by the Department of the Interior. Originally a series of access trails for the Hawaiians, they were paid for by local farmers to tax collectors. In 1823, William Ellis, a missionary, tried to follow them to circumnavigate the island. In more recent times, a group of journalists recreated—to the best of their ability—his route.

The plantations in the northeast destroyed any trails in that corner of the island. The sections that remain contain archaeological sites that should be left unmolested. Some people have proposed National Trail status for the network, but until then you'll need a topographic map, re-

spect for private property and archaeology, and a yen for adventure to
tackle the trails that the Hawaiians once tread.

Hawaii's official hiking trails run through three areas: Volcanoes
National Park, Kau Desert and the Kohala Mountains. These are popular and well-defined trails, many of which are described below. Permits
are required for any overnight backcountry camping within the bound-
aries of Hawaii Volcanoes National Park, which includes the Kau
Desert. Apply the morning of your trip at the Kilauea Visitor Center.
Permits are free, but first-come, first-served. All distances listed for hiking trails are one way unless otherwise noted.

Kohala Coast

Stretching along Kohala peninsula's northeast coast is a series of sheer
cliffs and wide valleys rivaling Kauai's Na Pali Coast in beauty. At either
end of this rainswept *pali* are lush, still valleys that can only be reached
by hiking trails. To camp legally in this area can be a challenge, since
you need a permit or permission wherever you go, and the land could
be State, corporate or owned by one of the dozens of property holders.
If you want to camp, start by asking questions at the State Department
of Land and Natural Resources; 808-974-4221.

Pololu Valley Trail (0.5 mile) descends from the Pololu Valley Lookout
at the end of Akoni Pule Highway to the valley floor 400 feet below.
There you'll find a secluded beach (beware of the riptides) and a series
of trails that lead up through the Kohala Mountains.

Kona/Kau Area

From Volcanoes National Park's southern section several trails lead
into the hot, arid Kau Desert. All are long, dusty trails offering solitude
to the adventurous hiker.

Kau Desert Trail (3.5 miles) branches off Crater Rim Trail and drops
2000 feet en route to the lookout at the end of Hilina Pali Road. The
shelter along the way, at Kipuka Pepeiau, provides a welcome resting
place on this lengthy trek.

Mauna Iki Trail (3.6 miles) leads from Mamalahoa Highway (Route
11) to Hilina Pali Road. The trail passes near Footprints Trail, where a
sudden volcanic eruption in 1790 engulfed a Hawaiian army at war
with Kamehameha.

Hawaii Volcanoes National Park

The most interesting and easily accessible trails lead through the
Kilauea Caldera area. The caldera, three miles long and 4000 feet above
sea level, can be explored either by hiking along one extended trail or
over several shorter connecting trails.

Crater Rim Trail (11.6-mile loop) begins near the park headquarters
and encircles Kilauea Caldera. An excellent introduction to the volcanoes, this lengthy loop trail passes steam vents, the Kau Desert, the
fractured Southwest Rift area and a fascinating fern forest. The views
from along the rim are spectacular.

Sulphur Banks Trail (0.3 mile) begins at park headquarters and parallels Crater Rim Drive past steam vents and sulphur deposits.

Halemaumau Trail (3.5 miles) starts near Volcano House, then descends into Kilauea Caldera. The trail crosses the crater floor and affords astonishing views down into steaming Halemaumau crater, then climbs back up to join Crater Rim Trail. This has got to be one of the park's finest hikes.

Kilauea Iki Trail (5 miles) loops from the Thurston Lava Tube parking lot down into Kilauea Iki crater and returns via Crater Rim Trail. Crossing the crater floor, the trail passes over a lava crust beneath which lies a pool of hot rock. Rainwater percolates through the crust, reaches the hot rock, and emerges as steam. The pool was once hot but has cooled significantly (the eruption was in 1959).

Sandalwood Trail (1.5-mile loop) loops from near the Volcano House past sandalwood and *ohia* trees and then along the side of Kilauea Caldera.

Byron Ledge Trail (4 miles) branches off Halemaumau Trail, crosses the Kilauea caldera floor, and then climbs along Byron Ledge before rejoining Halemaumau. This makes an excellent connecting trail.

Starting within the Kapapala Forest Reserve at 5650 feet, the **Ainapo Trail** (3.5 miles) takes hikers on a moderately challenging trek past mesic *koa* and *ohia* trees. On the way up to the Ainapo Trail Shelter at Halewai, you'll catch sight of mountain goats and sheep. More experienced hikers can climb the rest of the fog-covered trail (7.5 miles) and will be rewarded with views from the rim of the Mokuaweoweo Caldera in Hawaii Volcanoes National Park. The trailhead begins at the cattle-guard between the 40- and 41-mile markers on the Mamalahoa Highway between Volcano and Pahala. This hike requires permits from the Division of Forestry and Wildlife in Hilo (808-974-4221). Reservations for the shelter can be made up to 30 days in advance.

Volcanoes National Park's premier hike is along **Mauna Loa Trail**. This tough 18-mile trek, requiring at least three days, leads to the top of the world's largest shield volcano. Cold-weather equipment and a sturdy constitution are absolute necessities for this challenging adventure. Permits are required for this hike.

Climbers usually hike seven miles the first day from the trailhead at the end of Mauna Loa Strip Road up to Red Hill (Pu'u 'Ula'ula). At this 10,035-foot way station, there is a rudimentary cabin with eight bunks with mattresses, but no provisions. A hearty 11-mile trek the second day leads to the rim of Mauna Loa's summit caldera, and to the Mokuaweoweo cabin (located on the rim). The return trip takes one or two days, depending on how fast you want to come down.

Beware of altitude sickness and hypothermia, and be sure to register for a permit at park headquarters before and after hiking. Purification tablets or filters for the water and white gas for the stoves are essential; there are no stoves provided in the cabin. Don't treat this as a casual jaunt; it's a real trek. Planning will ensure your safety and enjoyment.

(A single-lane paved road climbs from Saddle Road to an area near Mauna Loa summit. This alternative hiking route lacks the adventure but reduces the time needed to ascend Mauna Loa. This road is not open to rental cars.)

Hamakua Coast
Waipio Valley Trail begins from Waipio Valley lookout at the end of Route 24. Waipio is a broad, lush, awesomely beautiful valley ribboned with waterfalls and rich in history. From the trailhead, a jeep trail drops steeply for one mile to the valley floor. Here the trail joins one road leading up into the valley and another heading to the beach. The high road goes toward 1200-foot Hiilawe Falls and to an abandoned Peace Corps training camp.

TRANSPORTATION

AIR

Two airports serve commercial flights to the Big Island—Hilo International Airport (General Lyman Field) and Kona International Airport.

KONA INTERNATIONAL AIRPORT ✆ 808-329-2484 The main landing facility is Kona International Airport. Many mainland visitors fly here rather than to Honolulu to avoid Oahu's crowds. Aloha Airlines, American Airlines, Hawaiian Airlines and United Airlines provide service directly to Kailua-Kona from the mainland. Canada 3000 (seasonally) and Japan Airlines (daily) fly directly from their respective countries.

Passengers flying between the islands use Aloha Airlines or Hawaiian Airlines. They provide frequent jet service from Oahu and the other islands to both Hilo and Kona. Other inter-island carriers include Island Air, Pacific Wings and Paragon Air. ATA has direct flights to and from Hilo from the West Coast of California

This facility has snack bars, cocktail lounges, duty-free shops, a restaurant and souvenir shops, but no lockers or bus service. A ten-mile cab ride into town costs about $30.

HILO INTERNATIONAL AIRPORT Hilo International Airport (General Lyman Field), once the island's main jetport, is now more like a small city airport. The airlines that operate here are Aloha Airlines, ATA, go!, Hawaiian Airlines, Island Air and Pacific Wings.

You'll find a cafeteria-style restaurant, cocktail lounge, gift shop, newsstand and lockers, but no bus service. Covering the two miles into town means renting a car, hailing a cab, hitching or hoofing.

CAR RENTALS

When choosing a rental agency, check whether they permit driving on the Saddle Road across the island and on South Point Road, both good paved roads with few potholes and many points of interest. I think it's quite unfair, even irrational, that some rental companies revoke insurance coverage if you drive these thoroughfares. But my protests will be of little benefit in case of an accident. So check first or be prepared to take your chances! It's wise to remember that you will be driving farther on the Big Island than on other islands, sometimes through quite rural areas; it may sound obvious, but remember to watch your gas gauge.

Several companies have franchises at the Hilo and Kailua-Kona airports. Among these are **Avis** (808-935-1290, 808-327-3000, 800-331-1212), **Budget Rent A Car** (808-329-8511, 800-527-0700), **Dollar Rent A Car** (800-800-4000), **Hertz Rent A Car** (808-935-2896, 808-329-3566, 800-654-3011), **National Rent A Car** (808-935-0891, 808-329-1674, 800-227-7368) and **Thrifty Car Rental** (800-367-5238).

Alamo Rent A Car (808-961-3343, 808-329-8896, 800-327-9633) is located outside the Hilo International Airport and Kona Airport. **Harper Car & Truck Rental** (808-969-1478, 800-852-9993) is located inside the Kona airport but you must take a shuttle to reach its Hilo location.

JEEP RENTALS

Budget Rent A Car (808-329-8511, 800-527-0700) rents four-wheel drives. With offices in Hilo and Kona, **Harper Car & Truck Rental** (808-969-1478, 800-852-9993) offers four-wheel-drive vehicles and allows travel on the Saddle Road and Mauna Kea summit road.

PUBLIC TRANSIT

HELE-ON BUS ✉*County Hawaiian Transit* ✆*808-961-8744* ✆*808-961-8745* ✎*heleonbus@co.hawaii.hi.us* The Hele-On Bus provides cross-island service Monday through Saturday between Hilo and Kailua-Kona. There are also limited intra-city buses serving Hilo. The Hele-On runs Monday through Saturday; fares range from 75¢ for short rides to $6 for the Hilo–Kailua cross-island run.

The Hilo bus terminal is on Kamehameha Avenue at Mamo Street. You'll see few bus stops indicated on the island. The official stops are generally unmarked, and you can hail a bus anywhere along its route. Just wave your hand. When it's time to get off, the driver will stop anywhere you wish.

For information and schedules, contact the County Hawaiian Transit.

AERIAL TOURS

Thanks to the Kilauea eruption, the Big Island offers a wide variety of flightseeing options. In addition to the lava flows, you'll see remote coastlines, the slopes of Mauna Kea and coffee plantations. Bring your camera because the lava flow is one of Hawaii's greatest sightseeing opportunities.

BIG ISLAND AIR ✉*Kona Airport* ☎*808-329-4868* 🖂*808-329-0855* 🖰*www.big islandair.com, info@bigislandair.com* For a spectacular circle island tour featuring Kilauea and the north end valleys and waterfalls, hop on board. Flights last about 1 hour and 45 minutes.

BLUE HAWAIIAN HELICOPTER ✉*Hilo International Airport; Queen Kaahumanu Highway, Waikoloa* ☎*808-961-5600, 800-786-2583* 🖰*www.bluehawaiian.com* Here you have a choice from a range of flights lasting from 30 minutes up to two hours. Passengers view the valleys and waterfalls on the island's northern end, as well as volcanic activity at Kilauea. They fly out of two locations.

SAFARI HELICOPTERS ✉*P.O. Box 1941, Lihue, Kauai, HI 96766; Hilo Commuter Air Terminal, Hilo International Airport, Hilo* ☎*808-969-1259, 800-326-3356* 🖰*www.safarihelicopters.com, info@safarihelicopters.com* Safari's two tours both emphasize viewings of the Kilauea Volcanic system, with its lava tubes to the ocean, cinder cones and much more. One tour adds a visit to the waterfalls near Hilo to the itinerary.

MAUI

Residents of Maui, Hawaii's second-largest island, proudly describe their Valley Isle by explaining that "Maui *no ka oi.*" Maui is the greatest. Few of the island's visitors have disputed the claim. They return each year, lured by the enchantment of a place possessing 33 miles of public beaches, one of the world's largest dormant volcanoes, beautiful people, a breeding ground for rare humpback whales and a climate that varies from subtropic to subarctic.

Named after one of the most important demigods in the Polynesian pantheon, Maui has retained its mythic aura. The island is famous as a chic retreat and jet-set landing ground. To many people, Maui *is* Hawaii.

But to others, who have watched the rapid changes during the past several decades, Maui is no longer the greatest. They point to the 2.4 million tourists (second only to Oahu) who visited during a recent year, to the condominiums and resort hotels now lining the prettiest beaches and to the increasing traffic over once-rural roads. And they have a new slogan. "Maui is *pau.*" Maui is finished. Overtouristed. Overpopulated. Overdeveloped.

Today, among the island's 141,320 population, it seems like every other person is in the real estate business. On a land mass measuring 729 square miles, just half the size of Long Island, their goods are in short supply. During the 1970s and 1980s, land prices shot up faster than practically anywhere else in the country, although the 1990s saw prices decline.

Yet over 75 percent of the island remains unpopulated. Despite pressures from land speculation and a mondo-condo mentality, Maui still offers exotic, untouched expanses for the explorer. Most development is concentrated along the south and west coasts in Kihei, Wailea and Kaanapali. The rest of the island, **269** though more populated than neighboring islands, is an adventurer's oasis. The second-youngest island in the chain, Maui was created between one and two million years ago by two volcanoes. Haleakala, the larger, rises over 10,000 feet, and offers excellent hiking and camping within its summit caldera, the largest such dormant volcanic crater in the world. The earlier of the two firepits created the West Maui Mountains, 5788 feet at their highest elevation. Because of their relative age, and the fact they receive 400 inches of rainfall a year, they are more heavily eroded than the smooth surfaces of Haleakala. Between the two heights lies Central Maui, an isthmus formed when the lava from each volcano flowed together.

The twin cities of Kahului and Wailuku, Maui's commercial and civic centers, respectively, sit in this saddle. Until the 1990s, most of the island was planted in sugar, which became king in Maui after the decline of whaling in the 1860s. Today, a road through what remains of the cane fields leads south to the sunsplashed resorts and beaches of Kihei, Maalaea, Wailea and Makena.

Another road loops around the West Maui Mountains. It passes prime whale-watching areas along the south coast and bisects Lahaina, an old whaling town that is now the island's sightseeing capital. Next to this timeworn harbor is the resort area of Kaanapali, a two-mile stretch of beach backed by hotels, condominiums and a full range of resort facilities. Beyond Kaanapali lies eight miles of coast lined with crescent beaches and lava rock promontories with another collection of hotels, condos and homes at Honokawai, Kahana and Napili. Past Napili the Kapalua Resort adds an upscale alternative, with several hotels and condos and three of Hawaii's best golf courses. Head past Kapalua and the landscape becomes wilder, with a series of deep wilderness valleys and grassy headlands that offer magnificently wild coastal views. You'll want to take a break in rustic Kahakuloa, where taro is still grown and the lifestyle is reminiscent of old Hawaii. From Kahakuloa, the road continues around West Maui, returning you to Wailuku and Kahului.

The road girdling Haleakala's lower slopes passes equally beautiful areas. Along the rainswept northeast coast are sheer rock faces ribboned with waterfalls and gorges choked with tropic vegetation. The lush, somnolent town of Hana gives way along the southeast shore to a dry, unpopulated expanse that is always ripe for exploration.

On the middle slopes of Haleakala, in Maui's Upcountry region, small farms dot the landscape. Here, in addition to guavas, avocados and lychee nuts, grow the sweet Kula onions for which the Valley Isle is famous.

Back in the days of California's gold rush, Maui found its own underground nuggets in potatoes: Countless bushels were grown in this area and shipped to a hungry San Francisco market. Today the crop is used to prepare Maui potato chips.

Because of its strategic location between Oahu and Hawaii, Maui has played a vital role in Hawaiian history. Kahekili, Maui's last king, gained control of all the islands except Hawaii before being overwhelmed by Kamehameha in 1790. Lahaina, long a vacation spot for island rulers, became a political center under Hawaii's first three kings and an important commercial center soon after Captain Cook sighted the island in 1778. It served as a supply depot for ships, then as a port for sandalwood exports. By the 1840s, Lahaina was the world capital of whaling. Now, together with the other equally beautiful sections of the Valley Isle, it is a mecca for vacationers.

270 Maui's magic has cast a spell upon travelers all over the world, making the island a vacation paradise. Like most modern paradises, it is being steadily gilded in plastic and concrete. Yet much of the old charm remains. Some people even claim that the sun shines longer on the Valley Isle than any other place on earth. They point to the legend of the demigod Maui who created his own daylight savings by weaving a rope from his sister's pubic hair and lassoing the sun by its genitals. And many hope he has one last trick to perform, one that will slow the course of development just as he slowed the track of the sun.

LAHAINA

Maui's top tourist destination is a waterfront enclave that stretches for over two miles along a natural harbor, but measures only a couple of blocks deep. Simultaneously chic and funky, Lahaina has gained an international reputation for its art galleries, falsefront stores and waterfront restaurants.

It also happens to be one of Hawaii's most historic towns. A royal seat since the 16th century, Lahaina was long a playground for the *alii*. The royal surfing grounds lay just south of today's town center, and in 1802, Kamehameha I established his headquarters here, taking up residence in the Brick Palace, the first Western-style building in Hawaii.

Although the Hawaiian capital moved to Honolulu in 1850, Lahaina remained a favorite vacation spot for several kings, including Kamehameha III, IV and V, and Queen Liliuokalani. All had second homes in the area and returned often to indulge in those favorite Hawaiian pastimes—rest and relaxation.

It was in Lahaina that the first high school and first printing press west of the Rockies were established in 1831. From Lahaina, Kamehameha III promulgated Hawaii's first constitution in 1840, and established a legislative body that met in town until the capital was eventually moved to Honolulu.

During the 1820s, this quaint port also became a vital watering place for whaling ships. At its peak in the mid-1840s, the whaling trade brought over 400 ships a year into the harbor.

To the raffish sailors who favored it for its superb anchorage, grog shops and uninhibited women, Lahaina was heaven itself. To the stiff-collared missionaries who arrived in 1823, the town was a hellhole—a place of sin, abomination and vile degradation. Some of Lahaina's most colorful history was written when the Congregationalists prevented naked women from swimming out to meet the whalers. Their belligerent brethren anchored in the harbor replied by cannonballing mission homes and rioting along the waterfront.

The town declined with the loss of the whaling trade in the 1860s, and was transformed into a quiet sugar plantation town, serving the Pioneer Sugar Mill that opened during the same decade. Hawaii's first phone line was installed from Lahaina to Haiku in 1877, but not until

Lahaina–Kaanapali Area

KIMO'S
HALE PAI
Lahaina
I'O
OLOWALU BEACHES
Olowalu

HALE PAI

PAGE 277

1837 printing house that published Hawaii's first money and a newspaper written in the Hawaiian language

KIMO'S

PAGE 284

Traditional Hawaiian music at a waterfront gathering place with tropical drinks and the sun setting in the ocean

I'O

PAGE 279

Innovative Pacific Rim cuisine that creatively incorporates local ingredients like sweet papaya from the Hana rainforests

OLOWALU BEACHES

PAGE 285

Offshore by the coral reef: great snorkeling and killer surfing
On the beach: Maui diamonds!

developers began building resorts in nearby Kaanapali a century later did the town fully revive.

During the 1960s, Lahaina was designated a national historic landmark and restoration of many important sites was begun. By the 1970s, the place was a gathering spot not only for the jet set but the ultra hip as well. Clubs like the Blue Max made Lahaina a hot nightspot where famous musicians came to vacation and jam.

Today, Lahaina retains a gentrified charm with shops, galleries, clubs and restaurants lining Front Street, an oceanside "Main Street." It resembles Manhattan when it comes to parking, especially in summer. (Lots on Dickenson Street have reasonable rates. If you're parking at a meter, the price of parking can be astronomical if you get a ticket.) Luckily, most points of interest lie within a half-mile of the old sea wall that protects this narrow thoroughfare from the ocean, so the best way to explore the town is on foot.

SIGHTS

LAHAINA HARBOR Start your tour on Wharf Street, and take a stroll along the docks to this lively harbor. In addition to tour boats, pleasure crafts from around the world put in here or cast anchor in the

Lahaina Roads just offshore. During the heyday of the whaling industry in the 1840s, the Auau Channel between Lahaina and Lanai was a forest of masts.

PIONEER INN ✉*658 Wharf Street* ☎*808-661-3636* 📠*808-667-9366* 🖥*www.pioneerinnmaui.com, info@pioneerinnmaui.com* Across Wharf Street sits this rambling historic hostelry built in 1901. With its second-story veranda and landscaped garden, this aging woodframe hotel is a great place to bend an elbow and breathe in the salt air.

HAUOLA STONE

Just north of the Pioneer Inn a Hawaii Visitors Bureau sign points out the chair-shaped Hauola Stone, a source of healing power for ancient Hawaiians, who sat in the natural formation and let the waves wash over them.

BRICK PALACE

There is nothing left of this two-story structure commissioned in 1798 by Kamehameha I. Located just inshore from the Hauola Stone and built by an English convict, the palace was used by the king in 1802 and 1803 (although some say he preferred to stay in his grass shack next door). Today the original foundation has been outlined with brick paving.

BANYAN TREE ✉*Front and Hotel streets* To the south of the Brick Palace, a banyan tree, the largest in the U.S. and among the oldest in the islands, extends its rooting branches across almost an entire acre. Planted in 1873 to mark the advent of Protestant missionaries in Maui 50 years earlier, this shady canopy is a resting place for tourists and mynah birds alike.

OLD COURTHOUSE ☎*808-667-9175* 📠*808-661-4779* 🖥*www.visitlahaina.com, web.request@visitlahaina.com* The sprawling giant presses up against the Old Courthouse, constructed in 1859 from coral blocks taken from the home built for King Kamehameha III. The historic building is home to the **Lahaina Town Action Committee**, where you can pick up maps and brochures, including one that provides all the details needed for a self-guided walking tour of Lahaina.

LAHAINA ARTS SOCIETY ☎*808-661-0111* 📠*808-661-9149* 🖥*www.lahainaarts.org* A self-proclaimed "training ground" for local artists, the arts society is also a non-profit association located in the courthouse. Art shows are presented under the banyan tree.

LAHAINA HERITAGE MUSEUM ✉*Second floor of the Old Courthouse* ☎*808-661-1959* With varying exhibits, such as a selection of traditional canoes, this museum offers information of interest to both locals and visitors. One display features a three-dimensional map of Maui and includes a brief history of Lahaina.

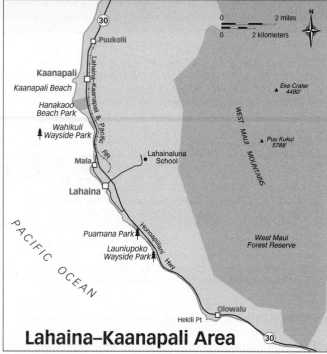

Lahaina–Kaanapali Area

OLD FORT Those stone ruins on either side of the courthouse are the remains of the Old Fort, built during the 1830s to protect Lahaina from the sins and cannonballs of lawless sailors. The original structure was torn down two decades later to build a jail, but during its heyday the fortress guarded the waterfront with numerous cannons.

BALDWIN HOME ☎808-661-3262 ✉808-661-9309 ⬦www.lahainarestoration. org, lrf@hawaii.rr.com Across Front Street from the Old Fort is the Baldwin Home, Lahaina's oldest building. Constructed of coral and stone in the early 1830s, the place sheltered the family of Reverend Dwight Baldwin, a medical missionary. Today the house contains period pieces and family heirlooms, including some of the good doctor's rather fiendish-looking medical implements. Beneath the hand-hewn ceiling beams rests the Baldwin's Steinway piano; the dining room includes the family's china, a fragile cargo that made the voyage around Cape Horn; and in the master bedroom stands a four-poster bed fashioned from native *koa*. Admission.

Next door to the Baldwin Home is the **Master's Reading Room**, an 1834 storehouse and library. It is home to the Lahaina Restoration Foundation and not open to the public.

WO HING MUSEUM ✉858 Front Street ☎808-661-5553 A Chinese gathering place that dates to 1912, the Wo Hing Museum has been lovingly restored. While the temple has been converted into a small museum, the old cookhouse adjacent is used to show films of the islands made by Thomas Edison from 1898 through 1906, during the early days of motion pictures. Admission.

HOLY INNOCENTS' EPISCOPAL CHURCH ✉*561 Front Street* ☎*808-661-4202* ☏*808-661-8667* ✐*www.holyimaui.org, holyinno@hawaii.rr.com* A small structure dating from 1927, this waterfront church has maintained its original beauty. Very simple in design, the sanctuary is filled with exquisite paintings. The Hawaiian madonna on the altar and the tropical themes of the paintings are noteworthy features. Services are Sunday at 7 a.m. and 10 a.m.

WAIOLA CEMETERY

✉*Wainee Street* With its overgrown lawn, dotted with eroded tombstones, this cemetery contains graves dating to 1829. Queen Keopuolani, the wife of Kamehameha I and the mother of Hawaii's next two kings, is buried here. So is her daughter, Princess Nahienaena, and Governor Hoapali, who ruled Hawaii from 1823 to 1840. Surrounded by blossoming plumeria trees, there are also the graves of early missionaries and Hawaiian commoners.

WAIOLA CHURCH ✉*535 Wainee Street* ☎*808-661-4349* ☏*808-661-1734* Maui's first Christian services were performed in 1823 on the grounds of Wainee Church next door to the cemetery. Today's chapel, renamed the Waiola Church, built in 1953, occupies the spot where the Wainee church was constructed in 1832. The earlier structure, Hawaii's first stone church, seated 3000 parishioners and played a vital role in the conversion of the local population to Christianity and Western ways.

LAHAINA HONGWANJI TEMPLE ☎*808-661-0640* A little farther north from the Waiola Church on Wainee Street sits a temple honoring Hawaii's Japanese-American heritage and boasting three distinctive turrets. The building dates from 1927, but the Buddhist Hongwanji sect has been meeting at this site since 1910.

HALE PAAHAO ✉*Corner of Prison and Wainee streets* ☎*808-667-1985* Beyond the temple rise the menacing walls of old Hale Paahao, a prison built by convicts in 1854 and used to house rowdy sailors as well as more hardened types. The coral blocks used to build this local hoosegow were taken from the Old Fort on Front Street.

EPISCOPAL CEMETERY Just north of the jail along Wainee Street sits the Episcopal Cemetery and **Hale Aloha**. Walter Murray Gibson, a controversial figure in 19th-century Hawaiian politics who eventually became an adviser to King David Kalakaua, is buried here. Hale Aloha, completed in 1858 and restored in 1974, served as a church meetinghouse.

MARIA LANAKILA CHURCH ✉*Wainee and Dickenson streets* Near the cemetery is this lovely white-washed building with interior pillars that

Lahaina

to Kaanapali

to Hale Pai &
Lahainaluna
School

to Kihei

Mala

Mala
Wharf

Baby
Beach

Lahaina Harbor

Lahaina

Maluulu o
Lele Park

Kamehameha Iki Park

Auau Channel

Puamana

0   0.25 mile
0   0.25 kilometer

N

Honoapiilani Hwy
Sugar Cane Train
Lahaina-Kaanapali & Pacific RR
Kahoma

Stream

Front St
Kenui St
Ala Moana St
Puunoa Pl
Baker St
Wainee St
Papalaua St
Liuakini St
Panaewa St
Dickenson St
Hotel St
Wharf St
Canal St
Prison St
Hale St
Wainee St
Shaw St
Honoapiilani Hwy
Mill St (private)
Ailo St
Ilikahi St
Kauaula St
Aholo St
Pualei St
Puapihi St
Kauaula St
Lahainaluna Rd
Kuhua St
Aki St
Paeohi St
Aki St
Kelawea St
Kalena St
Liu St
Ikena St
Kuialua St
Hinau St
30
30
Mill St (private)

POINTS OF INTEREST

- **A** Atlantis Submarines
- **B** Baldwin Home/
  Master's Reading Room
- **C** Hale Aloha & Episcopal Cemetery
- **D** Hale Paahao
- **E** Hauola Stone
- **F** Holy Innocents' Episcopal Church
- **G** Lahaina Hongwanji Temple
- **H** Lahaina Jodo Mission
- **I** Lahaina Shingon Mission
- **J** Maria Lanakila Church
- **K** Old Courthouse
- **L** Pioneer Inn
- **M** Pioneer Mill
- **N** Seamen's Cemetery
- **O** Sugar Cane Train Depot
- **P** Waiola Church and Cemetery
- **Q** Wo Hing Museum

was built in 1928 to replace a 19th-century chapel. Adjacent is the **Seamen's Cemetery**, a poorly maintained ground where early sailors were laid to rest.

LAHAINA SHINGON MISSION ✉️*682 Luakini Street between Hale and Dickenson streets* 📞*808-661-0466* 📠*808-661-0466* 🖥️*http://hokoji.com, info@hokoji.com* A simple plantation-era structure with an ornately gilded altar, this mission was built in 1902 by a Japanese monk and his followers. It now represents another gathering place for Maui's Buddhists.

SUGAR CANE TRAIN ✉️*The main station is off Hinau Street in Lahaina.* 📞*808-667-6851, 800-499-2307* 📠*808-661-8389* 🖥️*www.sugarcanetrain.com* The proverbial kids-from-eight-to-eighty set will love this reconstructed 1890s-era steam train. Operating near the West Maui resort area, the Lahaina–Kaanapali & Pacific Railroad engine and passenger cars chug along a six-mile route midway between the mountains and ocean. Various package tours are available with the train rides, including a sunset dinner train ride, complete with live Hawaiian entertainment. Admission.

FRIENDS OF MOKUULA
✉️*505 Front Street #221, Lahaina* 📞*808-661-3659* 🖥️*www.mokuula.com, friends@mokuula.com* Beneath a county park in Lahaina, archaeologists have uncovered one of the islands' most historical sites—Mokuula. It is thought to have once been the political and spiritual center of Maui, with royal residences and a royal mausoleum there, as well as Mokuhinia, a natural wetland and fishpond. Carbon dating shows it to be one of the earliest signs of human existence in the islands. Friends of Mokuula is an organization created to try and restore the site.

ATLANTIS SUBMARINES ✉️*Wharf Cinema Center, 658 Front Street* 📞*808-667-2224* 📠*808-661-1210* 🖥️*www.atlantisadventures.com* Oceanic adventurers might want to take an opportunity to stop in at this unique attraction and reserve an underwater tour. The voyage takes you aboard a 48-passenger submersible down more than 100 feet. En route you may see close-up views of technicolor coral reefs and outlandish lava formations. A trip to the depths requires deep pockets; these 90-minute excursions aren't cheap. The tour departs from the Pioneer Inn Hotel.

LAHAINA JODO MISSION ✉️*12 Ala Moana Street* 📞*808-661-4304* For a journey of a spiritual nature, don't miss this mission, a Buddhist enclave one-half mile north of Lahaina on Ala Moana Street. There's a temple and a three-tiered pagoda here, as well as the largest ceremonial bell in Hawaii. The giant bronze Buddha, with the West Maui Mountains in the background, is a sight to behold. It rests amid stone walkways and flowering oleander bushes in a park-like setting. The temple grounds are open to the public from dawn to dusk.

LAHAINALUNA SCHOOL 📞*808-662-4000* For a splendid view of Lahaina, turn off Route 30 onto Lahainaluna Road, pass the now-closed, century-old **Pioneer Mill**, and head *mauka* (toward the mountains) to Lahainaluna School. Established by missionaries in 1831, it is one of the country's oldest schools west of the Rockies. Today this historic facility serves as a public high school for the Lahaina area.

HALE PAI

📞 808-667-7040 📠 808-667-7040 ✉ lrf@hawaii.rr.com A printing house dating to 1837, this press printed Hawaii's first money and many religious tracts and primers produced in the islands. The first newspaper west of the Rockies was also printed here, written mostly in the Hawaiian language. Hale Pai is open as a museum and research library and houses a working reproduction of the original printing press. Closed Saturday and Sunday.

LODGING

BEST WESTERN PIONEER INN

$$$ 34 ROOMS   ✉ 658 Wharf Street   📞 808-661-3636, 800-457-5457
📠 808-667-5708   🖥 www.pioneerinnmaui.com, info@pioneerinnmaui.com

To fully capture the spirit of Lahaina, there's only one place to stay—the Pioneer Inn. Located smack on Lahaina's waterfront, this wooden hostelry is the center of the area's action. On one side, sloops, ketches and glass-bottom boats are berthed; on the other side lies bustling Front Street with its falsefront shops. The Inn is noisy, vibrant and crowded with tenants and tourists. On the ground floor, you can hunker down over a glass of grog at the saloon, or stroll through the Inn's lushly planted courtyard. Accommodations are located in the section overlooking the courtyard. These are small and plainly decorated, with telephones, wi-fi, overhead fans, air conditioning and lanais. A swimming pool completes the picture.

LAHAINA INN

$$–$$$ 12 ROOMS   ✉ 127 Lahainaluna Road   📞 808-661-0577, 800-669-3444
📠 808-667-9480   🖥 www.lahainainn.com, inntown@lahainainn.com

My Oscar for most original inn goes to this colorfully eclectic boutique hotel. Constructed in the early 20th century, this beauty was fully restored and appointed in Gay Nineties finery. Each room is wall to ceiling with gorgeous antiques—leaded glass lamps, mirrored armoires, original oil paintings, cast-iron beds and brass locks. Attention to detail is a way of life: the place simply exudes the aura of another era. If you don't stay here, stop by and visit.

PLANTATION INN

$$$–$$$$ 19 ROOMS   ✉ 174 Lahainaluna Road   📞 808-667-9225, 800-433-6815
📠 808-667-9293   🖥 www.theplantationinn.com, info@theplantationinn.com

While the building is actually quite modern, the Plantation Inn possesses the look and ambience of an early-20th-century hostelry. Modeled after the plantation architecture of an earlier era, most rooms are individually decorated in period furniture and adorned with either poster, brass or canopy beds, stained-glass windows and tile bathrooms. Combining the atmosphere of the past with the amenities of the present, guest rooms also feature televisions, wi-fi, refrigerators and air conditioning, as well as VCRs on request. There's a pool with a shaded pavilion and jacuzzi on the premises. Full breakfast included.

OUTRIGGER AINA NALU RESORT

$$$$ 135 UNITS ✉️*660 Wainee Street* 📞*808-667-9766, 800-462-6262*
📠*808-661-3733* 🖥*www.outrigger.com, reservations@outrigger.com*

Set on the waterfront near bustling Front Street, this resort is a warren of woodframe buildings spread across lushly landscaped grounds. The ambience is an odd combination of tropical retreat and motel atmosphere. It features 135 trimly decorated units, some of which are small studios (with kitchens) and one- or two-bedroom efficiencies. Amenities include two swimming pools, laundry facilities, a tennis court and a picnic area.

CONDOS

PUAMANA

35 UNITS ✉️*34 Pualima Place* 📞*808-667-2712 (Reservations through Klahani Resorts),*
800-628-6731 📠*808-661-5875* 🖥*www.klahani.com, klahani@hotmail.com*

Perhaps the nicest complex to stay at on this side of the island, this 28-acre retreat is about a mile southeast of Lahaina. A townhouse complex, Puamana's 1920s-era sugar plantation rests along a rock-strewn beach. The oceanfront clubhouse, open to guests, was once the plantation manager's house, and the landscaped grounds are still given over to mango, plumeria and torch ginger trees. Guests stay in low-slung plantation-style buildings that sport shake-shingle roofs and house from two to six units. One-bedroom gardenview units start at $190; two-bedroom units are $275. To round out the amenities there are three pools and a tennis court. There's a three-night minimum that increases to seven nights during the Christmas season.

LAHAINA SHORES HOTEL

199 ROOMS ✉️*475 Front Street* 📞*808-661-4835, 800-642-6284* 📠*808-661-4696*
🖥*www.classicresorts.com, info@classicresorts.com*

Though it's more expensive than many others, Lahaina Shores has the advantage of a beachfront location. This sprawling condominium complex offers studio apartments beginning at $200, while one-bedroom units start at $275. With a swimming pool, jacuzzi and the nearby beach, it's quite convenient.

DINING

SUNRISE CAFÉ

$ AMERICAN/DELI ✉️*Around back at 693A Front Street* 📞*808-661-8558*

One of my favorite light-food stops is a devil-may-care place called the Sunrise Café. Set in a tiny clapboard building with a fresh, airy look, it serves salads, sandwiches and espresso, plus such entrées as smoked kalua pork, grilled chicken breast and mango barbecue chicken. The service is laidback—Maui style. The café serves breakfast and lunch.

PIONEER INN GRILL

$$–$$$ SEAFOOD   ✉️*658 Wharf Street*   📞*808-661-3636*   📠*808-667-5708*

This historic restaurant brings back the Lahaina of old. The main dining room is a cozy anchorage dotted with nautical fixtures and specializing in regional fare. The emphasis is on the "bounty of Hawaii;" in other words, fresh fish, Upcountry produce and local herbs. Select one of the day's fresh fish specials and you can't go wrong. Breakfast begins at 7 a.m.

I'O — hidden

$$$$ PACIFIC RIM   ✉️*505 Front Street, Lahaina*   📞*808-661-8422*
📠*808-661-8399*   🖱️*www.iomaui.com*

I'o is the name and creative food is the game. Brainchild of Chef James McDonald, this beachfront restaurant offers both indoor and patio seating in an area that was a favored spot of ancient Hawaiian royalty. The decor is an undersea world of fantasy set against a backdrop of high-tech fixtures. This is the style that matches the chef's cuisine; for example, he creates a New Age salad utilizing an old Hawaii staple, hand-picked *pohole* fern shoots and sweet papaya from the Hana rainforests, served with a roasted garlic pesto. The local fish preparations are amazing. Dinner only.

CHEESEBURGER IN PARADISE

$$ AMERICAN   ✉️*811 Front Street*   📞*808-661-4855*

I can't say much for the nomenclature, but the prices are worth note here. This is a rare catch indeed—an inexpensive restaurant smack on the Lahaina waterfront that serves three meals a day and features live rock-and-roll music nightly. Granted, you won't find much on the menu other than hamburgers, salads and sandwiches. But if some couples can live on love, why can't the rest of us live on ocean views?

KIMO'S

$$–$$$ SEAFOOD/STEAK   ✉️*845 Front Street*   📞*808-661-4811*   📠*808-667-6077*
🖱️*www.kimosmaui.com, tskimos@aol.com*

The preferred style of dining in Lahaina is steak and seafood at one of the waterfront restaurants along Front Street. And the common denominator is the ever-popular, usually crowded Kimo's, where you can enjoy all the tropical amenities while dining on fresh fish, lobster or prime rib. They have live Hawaiian music Friday through Wednesday evenings.

LONGHI'S

$$$–$$$$ MEDITERRANEAN   ✉️*888 Front Street*   📞*808-667-2288*
🖱️*www.longhis.com, longhi@longhis.com*

Informality is the password at this European-style café that specializes in Mediterranean dishes. The menu changes daily and is never written down; the waiter simply tells you the day's offerings. Usually there'll be several pasta dishes, sautéed vegetables, salads, a shellfish creation, steak, a wine-soaked chicken or veal dish and perhaps eggplant parmigiana. Longhi's prepares all of its own bread and pasta, buys Maui-grown produce and imports many cheeses from New York. The dinners reflect this diligence. Breakfasts and lunches are cooked with the same care. Definitely recommended, especially for vegetarians, who can choose from many of the dishes offered. This is the original location; there's another one in Honolulu and one in Wailea.

BUBBA GUMP SHRIMP CO.

$$–$$$ AMERICAN ✉*889 Front Street* ☎*808-661-3111* 📠*808-667-6650*
🖱*www.bubbagump.com*

You won't have to flag down your server here. At this family-friendly eatery, which pays homage to the movie *Forrest Gump*, you just display the "Run Forrest Run" sign on your table, and the service comes to you. Featuring "shrimp any way you can think of eating it," and other American-style food, it is also filled with *Gump* memorabilia.

THAI CHEF RESTAURANT

$$ THAI ✉*878 Front Street* ☎*808-667-2814* 📠*808-661-0466*

In the Old Lahaina Shopping Center, this cozy dining spot offers an inviting assortment of Southeast Asian dishes. Try the green papaya salad, sautéed chili chicken or seafood with red curry sauce. No lunch on Saturday and Sunday.

ALOHA MIXED PLATE

$ PLATE LUNCHES ✉*1285 Front Street* ☎*808-661-3322*
📠*808-661-3087*

Voted Best Plate Lunch by locals, this neighborhood favorite on the edge of town is a beach shack by day serving *saimin, udon,* burgers and plate lunches. The patio is a great place to soak up the beach scene.

OLD LAHAINA LUAU

$$$$ LOCAL-STYLE ✉*1251 Front Street, behind the Lahaina Cannery Mall*
☎*808-667-1998, 800-248-5828* 📠*808-661-3087*
🖱*www.oldlahainaluau.com, info@oldlahainaluau.com*

Slightly (I said *slightly*) off the tourist track is the Old Lahaina Luau. Dinner here is based on the traditional luau—from the grass hut buildings to the menu of roast pork, *kalua* pig, sweet potato, mahimahi and poi. Reserve early, show up on time and be prepared to make an evening of Hawaiian feasting.

DAVID PAUL'S LAHAINA GRILL

$$$$ PACIFIC RIM ✉*127 Lahainaluna Road* ☎*808-667-5117,*
800-360-2606 📠*808-661-5478* 🖱*www.lahainagrill.com,*
davidpauls@lahainagrill.com

Headlining Pacific Rim cuisine, David Paul's is an intimate dining room with a personalized touch. According to founding chef

David Paul Johnson, the menu represents "a gathering of technique, flavors and skills from around the world, utilizing local ingredients to translate each dish into an exceptional dining experience." Tequila shrimp with firecracker rice, steamed Hawaiian lobster with a foie gras–chanterelle sauce, Kona coffee–roasted rack of lamb or macadamia-smoked pork chop were on the regularly changing menu when I was there. Dinner only.

GERARD'S RESTAURANT

$$$$ FRENCH   ⊠ *174 Lahainaluna Road*   ✆ *808-667-6077, 877-661-8939*
✆ *808-667-5392*   ✐ *www.gerardsmaui.com, gerard@maui.net*

An evening here is a defining experience in Lahaina dining. You'll encounter a French restaurant in a Victorian setting with tropical surroundings. Housed in the Plantation Inn, a bed and breakfast reminiscent of early New Orleans, Gerard's provides a chandelier-and-patterned-wallpaper dining room as well as a veranda complete with overhead fans and whitewashed balustrade. The chef prepares fresh fish, rack of lamb, duck *confit* and puff pastry with shiitake mushrooms. Of course, that is after having started off with *ahi* steak tartar or crab bisque. Dinner only. Highly recommended for a splurge.

ERIK'S SEAFOOD AND SUSHI BAR

$$$–$$$$ SEAFOOD   ⊠ *843 Wainee Street*   ✆ *808-669-4806*   ✆ *808-662-8784*

From the aquariums, captain's chairs and marlin trophies, you could never guess what they serve at this nautical gem. What a surprise to discover a menu filled with crabmeat-stuffed prawns, lobster-stuffed chicken breast, salmon and local fish. Early-bird specials are a hit with the budget-minded.

LOCAL FOOD

$ PLATE LUNCHES   ⊠ *222 Papalaua Street*   ✆ *808-667-2882*

Right off the highway in Anchor Square, facing the West Maui Mountains is this takeout stand that sells plate lunches and juices.

SANSEI RESTAURANT & SUSHI BAR

$$$ PACIFIC RIM/SUSHI   ⊠ *600 Office Road, Lahaina*   ✆ *808-669-6286*
✆ *808-669-0667*   ✐ *www.sanseihawaii.com*

Sansei has developed a cult following among both locals and tourists alike for its Pacific Rim sushi. One version incorporates spicy crab, mango, and various vegetables with sweet Thai chili sauce for dipping instead of the usual soy and wasabi. In another, smoked salmon, Maui onions and cream cheese combine to create the "bagel roll." The tuna sashimi is cut thin and covered with Thai fish sauce and peanuts. It's sushi quite unlike any you've ever tasted. And there's also a selection of entrées, including lobster and blue crab ravioli. Dinner only.

COMPADRES

$$ MEXICAN   ✉ *Lahaina Cannery Mall, 1221 Honoapiilani Highway*   ✆*808-661-7189*   ≈*808-661-7137*

A great place to sip a margarita or enjoy a Mexican meal with an island flair is this light, bright and airy eatery. The tropical ambience is as appealing as the steaming dishes served here. Especially popular are the fajitas and pork carnitas, but the menu also offers burgers, salads and vegetarian dishes. Breakfast, lunch and dinner—they open at 8 a.m.

ATHENS GREEK RESTAURANT

$ GREEK   ✉*Lahaina Cannery Mall, 1221 Honoapiilani Highway*   ✆*808-661-4300*

If you like Greek food, you'll want to stop at this fast-food stand at the Lahaina Cannery Mall where the gyros are generously stuffed with fresh ingredients and the shish kebabs come in chicken, fish and beef varieties (go for the fish). Take your meal to a nearby table and catch the passing scene.

CHEZ PAUL

$$$$ FRENCH   ✉*Honoapiilani Highway, Olowalu, four miles south of Lahaina*   ✆*808-661-3843*   ≈*808-667-5692*   ⌨*www.chezpaul.com, chezpaul@maui.net*

Near the top of the cognoscenti's list of gourmet establishments is this unlikely looking French restaurant in Olowalu. The place is several miles outside Lahaina in a renovated building that also houses Olowalu's funky general store. But for many years this little hideaway has had a reputation far transcending its surroundings. You'll probably drive right past the place at first, but when you do find it, you'll discover a menu featuring such delicacies as homemade duck pâté with mustard seed, grilled rack of lamb with mango chutney, island fish poached in champagne and several other tempting entrées. While the tab is ethereal, the rave reviews this prim dining room receives make it worth every franc. Dinner only.

SHOPPING

Lahaina's a great place to combine shopping with sightseeing. Most shops are right on Front Street in the historic wooden buildings facing the water. For a walking tour of the stores and waterfront, start from the Pioneer Inn at the south end of the strip and walk north on the *makai* or ocean side. Then come back along the *mauka*, or mountain, side of the street.

LAHAINA PRINTSELLERS ✉*505 Front Street* ✆*808-667-7843, 800-669-7843* ≈*808-667-5634* ⌨*www.printsellers.com* This is one of my favorite Maui shops. It has an astounding collection of maps and engravings from Polynesia and other parts of the world.

WHARF CINEMA CENTER ✉*658 Front Street* ✆*808-661-8748* ≈*808-661-5871* The Wharf is a multilevel complex of shops and restaurants. The cinema itself is small, but the movies are first-run if you're in the mood for a film while you're on Maui.

THE GECKO STORE ✉️703 Front Street 📞808-661-1078 This is the only shop I've seen with a sand floor. It stocks inexpensive beachwear as well as T-shirts and toys, many with a gecko theme.

CÉLÉBRITÉS ✉️764 Front Street 📞808-667-0727 ✐www.celebrityfineart.com, celebrities@maui.net A trendy showcase for the artistic work of several musicians and actors, the collection here includes John Lennon, Miles Davis, the Rolling Stones' Ronnie Wood and Paul Stanley. They also have album cover art and pieces signed by the Beatles and the Stones.

LAHAINA GALLERIES ✉️828 Front Street 📞808-667-2152, 800-228-2006 ✐www.lahainagalleries.com This gallery is of special note not only for the contemporary and classic artworks but also because of the imaginative ways in which they're displayed. Even if you're not just dying to write that five-figure check, stop by for a viewing.

SGT. LEISURE ✉️855B Front Street 📞808-667-0661 Stop here to browse an array of imaginative T-shirts.

CONTEMPORARY VILLAGE GALLERY
✉️180 Dickenson Street 📞808-661-5559 This gallery features paintings by contemporary Hawaiian artists. Amid the tourist schlock is some brilliant artwork.

BANYAN TREE GALLERY
✉️648 Wharf Street, Suite 103, first floor of the Old Courthouse 📞808-661-0111 Stop here if you're in the market for local artwork; on display are pieces by a number of Maui artists.

LAHAINA CANNERY MALL ✉️1221 Honoapiilani Highway This massive complex of stores housed in an old canning factory is the area's most ambitious project. **Na Hoku** (808-661-1731) is where you can pick up Hawaiian heirlooms, jewelry, Tahitian and Akoya pearls, or designs by Kabana and Steven Douglas. **Maui Playworks** (808-661-4766; www.mauiplayworks.com) is the place to pick up stunt and sport kites including box and bird designs. Here you'll also find windsocks, kaleidoscopes, games and a wide array of toys. Complete flying instructions, including tips on where to launch your kite, are provided by the helpful staff.

LAHAINA CENTER ✉️900 Front Street On the corner of Front and Papalana streets is this shopping mall, a sprawling complex of theaters, stores and restaurants. Among the shops here is **Hilo Hattie Fashion Center** (808-667-7911), where you and your honey can buy those matching aloha outfits.

Front Street's the strip in Lahaina—a dilapidated row of buildings from which stream some of the freshest sounds around.

ART NIGHT

If it's Friday in Lahaina, you can browse the town's art galleries, which sponsor a special Art Night every week. This is a great opportunity to meet some of the artists who have made Lahaina an international art scene. The artists, who welcome visitors at galleries where their work is displayed, talk story and add a unique personal touch to a night on the town.

PIONEER INN GRILL ✉*658 Wharf Street* ☎*808-661-3636* The seagoing

motif complete with harpoons, figureheads and other historical nautical decor sets the scene here. Tucked into a corner of the Pioneer Inn, and usually packed to the bulkheads with a lively crew, it's a great place to enjoy a tall cold one while listening to live music Tuesday, Wednesday and Thursday.

BLUE LAGOON TROPICAL BAR AND GRILL ✉*Wharf Cinema Center,*

658 Front Street ☎*808-661-8141* You can relax and enjoy a drink at the courtyard here adjacent to the Pioneer Inn Grill. Occasional live music.

MOOSE MCGILLYCUDDY'S ✉*844 Front Street* ☎*808-667-7758* 📠*808-*

667-5168 ✎*mooses@maui.net* Make your way to this hot club offering a large dancefloor for a variety of live music acts. The house is congenial and the drinks imaginatively mixed; for contemporary sounds with dinner, arrive before 9 p.m. Cover on Tuesday.

CHEESEBURGER IN PARADISE ✉*811 Front Street* ☎*808-661-4855*

Lounge in "paradise" and groove to a variety of performers playing fun tunes from 4:30 'til close—around 10 p.m.—every night. There is no dancefloor, however.

KIMO'S

✉*845 Front Street* ☎*808-661-4811* Lahaina's favorite pastime is watching the sun set over the ocean while sipping a tropical concoction at a waterfront watering place. A prime location for this very rewarding activity is Kimo's, which features traditional Hawaiian music Wednesday through Sunday, and Top 40 hits on Friday and Saturday.

MAUI THEATRE

✉*Old Lahaina Center, 878 Front Street* ☎*808-661-9913, 877-688-4800*
📠*808-661-5363* ✎*www.ulalena.com* Both high-tech and culturally beautiful, this ensemble is constantly evolving. The mix is one

part live theater with two parts Broadway musical and one part Cirque du Soleil. What makes its production *'Ulalena* unique is the story—it is a manifestation of the ancient Hawaiian *kumulipo* (creation chant) combined with Hawaii's mythology and history through the ages. The number of performances changes seasonally, so call for the schedule. Admission.

WARREN & ANNABELLE'S ✉ *900 Front Street* ✆ *808-667-6244* 📠 *808-667-6245* 🖥 *www.warrenandannabelles.com, lisa@warrenandannabelles.com* Reserve a table here for a "magical" entertainment experience. "Warren" is Warren Gibson, a master at sleight-of-hand magic. "Annabelle" is the ghost of a woman who lived in Lahaina during the whaling era and lost her sweetheart to the sea. She can still be seen (or rather, heard) at her piano, playing tunes for the return of her lost love. Appointed in turn-of-the-20th-century splendor, Annabelle's Parlor is also a restaurant/lounge. The waitstaff sings while helping guests call out song requests to Annabelle. After the preliminaries, doors open to the theater for an entertaining, interactive magic show. Unlocking the secret passage to enter the parlor is also part of the fun. The show runs Monday through Saturday. Reservations strongly recommended. Admission.

BEACHES & PARKS

PAPALAUA WAYSIDE COUNTY PARK

✉ *About ten miles south of Lahaina on Honoapiilani Highway*

Kiawe trees and scrub vegetation spread right to the shoreline here. There are sandy patches between the trees large enough to spread a towel, but I prefer sunbathing at beaches closer to Lahaina. Bounded on one side by Honoapiilani Highway, this narrow beach extends for a mile to join a nicer, lawn-fringed park; then it stretches on toward Olowalu for several more miles. If you want to be alone, just head down the shore. Swimming is good, snorkeling is okay out past the surf break and surfing is excellent at Thousand Peaks breaks and also very good several miles east in Maalaea Bay. There's an outhouse and picnic area at the county park.

▲ Tent camping. County permit required.

OLOWALU BEACHES

✉ *Go south from Lahaina on Honoapiilani Highway for about six miles.*

To the north and south of Olowalu General Store lie narrow corridors of white sand. This is a great spot to hunt for Maui diamonds. Swimming is very good, and south of the general store, where road and water meet, you'll find a coral reef ready for snorkeling. A growing green sea turtle population can be seen by snorkelers at the 14-mile marker. Surfers will find good breaks with right and left slides about a half-mile north of the general store. *Ulua* are often caught from Olowalu landing. There are no facilities, but there is a market nearby.

LAUNIUPOKO COUNTY PARK
✉*Three miles south of Lahaina on Honoapiilani Highway*

There is a seaside lawn shaded by palm trees and a sandy beach at this family-friendly park. A rock seawall slopes gently for entering swimmers, but offers little to sunbathers. It's located near the West Maui Mountains, with views of Kahoolawe and Lanai. When the tide is high, it's a good place to take children to swim safely and comfortably in the tidal pool on the other side of the seawall. Otherwise, swimming and snorkeling are mediocre. Beginning surfers can try their boards here. There is good surf-casting from the seawall and south for three miles. The park has a picnic area, restrooms and showers.

PUAMANA COUNTY PARK
✉*About two miles south of Lahaina on Honoapiilani Highway*

A narrow beach and grass-covered strip wedged between Honoapiilani Highway and the ocean, this seafront is dotted with ironwood trees. The excellent views make this a choice spot for an enjoyable picnic. Facilities include portable restrooms and showers.

KAMEHAMEHA IKI PARK
✉*On Front Street next to the 505 Front Street Mall*

The one thing going for this park is its convenient location in Lahaina. Otherwise, it's heavily littered, shadowed by a mall and sometimes crowded. If you do stop by, try to forget all that and concentrate on the sandy beach, lawn and truly startling view of Lanai directly across the Auau Channel. Recent attempts to add more of a native Hawaiian feel to the park include a site where visitors can watch the ongoing construction of traditional wooden canoes. Swimming is okay, snorkeling's good past the reef and, for surfing, there are breaks in the summer near the seawall in Lahaina Harbor. This surfing spot is not for beginners! Threadfin and *ulua* are common catches here. Restrooms and tennis courts are across the street at Maluulu o Lele Park near the playing field.

BABY BEACH
✉*Take Front Street north from Lahaina for about a half-mile. Turn left on Puunoa Place and follow it to the beach.*

This curving stretch of white sand is the best beach in Lahaina. It lacks privacy but certainly not beauty. From here you can look back to Lahaina town and the West Maui Mountains or out over the ocean to Kahoolawe, Lanai and Molokai. Or just close your eyes and soak up the sun. Swimming is good and well protected, if shallow. Snorkeling is only fair. In summer there are breaks nearby at Mala Wharf; left slide. Threadfin is often caught.

WAHIKULI COUNTY PARK
✉*Between Lahaina and Kaanapali on Honoapiilani Highway*

Just off the road between Lahaina and Kaanapali, facing Lanai and Molokai is this narrow stretch of beach and lawn. There are facilities aplenty, which might be why this pretty spot is so popular and crowded. Swimming is very good, but snorkeling is only fair. (There's a better spot just north of here near the Lahaina Canoe Club.) The most common catches here are *ulua* and threadfin. Facilities include picnic areas, showers and restrooms; there are tennis courts up the street at the Civic Center.

HANAKAOO BEACH PARK
✉Between Lahaina and Kaanapali on Honoapiilani Highway

Conveniently located beside Kaanapali Beach Resort, this long and narrow park features a white-sand beach and grassy picnic ground, and is referred to by locals as Canoe Beach. Practically every Saturday, this is the place to watch Hawaiian canoe racing. The road is nearby, but the views of Lanai are outstanding. Swimming is good, snorkeling fair, but surfing poor. Common catches include *ulua* and threadfin. There are picnic areas, restrooms and showers.

KAANAPALI– KAPALUA AREA

Even in the case of Maui's notorious land developers, there is method to the madness. The stretch of coastline extending for six miles along Maui's western shore, crowded to the extreme with hotels and condominiums, is anchored by two planned resorts. Like handsome bookends supporting an uneven array of dog-eared paperbacks, both Kaanapali and Kapalua add class to the arrangement.

SIGHTS

Kaanapali
Supporting the south end of the area, this 500-acre enclave extends along three miles of sandy beach and includes six hotels, a half-dozen condominiums, two golf courses and an attractive shopping mall. Back in the 19th century it was a dry and barren segment of the sugar plantation that operated from Lahaina. Raw sugar was hauled by train from the mill out to Black Rock, a dramatic outcropping along Kaanapali Beach, where the produce was loaded onto waiting ships.

BLACK ROCK In 1963, Kaanapali's first resort opened near this black lava divide and development soon spread in both directions. Important to developers, who built the Sheraton Maui Hotel around it, Black Rock (Puu Kekaa) is a volcanic cinder cone from which ancient Hawaiians believed that the dead departed the earth in their journey to the spirit world. According to legend, the great 18th-century Maui chief Kahekili proved his bravery by leaping from the rock to the ocean below. It is near the sacred area around Black Rock that divers harvest precious black coral from an underwater shelf.

WHALERS VILLAGE MUSEUM ✉Whalers Village, 2435 Kaanapali Parkway, Kaanapali ☎808-661-5992 ☎808-661-8584 ✎www.whalersvillage.com Kaanapali's modern-day contribution to Pacific culture is the museum within

Whalers Village. This facility comprises an outdoor pavilion and a museum that details Lahaina's history of whaling. Outdoors, you'll find a 30-foot-long whale skeleton and a whaling longboat on display. The "golden era of whaling" is also portrayed in scrimshaw exhibits, a scale-model whaling ship, harpoons and other artifacts from the days when Lahaina was one of the world's great whaling ports. Self-guided audio tours are available. There's a wonderful shop on site, with a selection of fossilized whale ivory scrimshaw in addition to Victorian-era antiques.

An early chief, Piilani, built a road through the area in the 16th century and gave his name to modern-day Route 30, the Honoapiilani Highway. Translated as "the bays of Piilani," the road passes several inlets located north of Kaanapali that have been developed in haphazard fashion. Honokowai, Kahana and Napili form a continuous wall of condominiums that sprawls north to Kapalua Bay and offers West Maui's best lodging bargains.

Kapalua

The bookend holding the north side in place is Kapalua, a former pineapple plantation that was converted into a luxurious 1500-acre resort. Here two major hotels, three golf courses and several villa-style communities blanket the hillside from the white sands of Kapalua Bay to the deep green foothills of the West Maui Mountains. Like the entire strip along Maui's western flank, Kapalua enjoys otherworldly sunsets and dramatic views of Lanai and Molokai.

29

PUEONE O HONOKAHUA

☎ 808-669-620 The Kapalua area includes one of Maui's most important cultural zones. This 14-acre preserve, near the Ritz-Carlton, Kapalua, was the site of fishing shrines and *heiau* where the ancient Hawaiians worshipped their gods and made astronomical observations. Today you can see a burial ground dating back to A.D. 950 and portions of the King's Highway, a 16th-century stone road around Maui. Also extant are the outlines of terraced taro patches farmed by early inhabitants. Although this land has been claimed in turn by King Kamehameha III, the sugar king H. P. Baldwin, and lastly the Maui Land and Pineapple Company, the state now protects and preserves it as a native Hawaiian sanctuary. The Ritz-Carlton conducts a free tour called "A Sense of Place" at the preserve every Friday from 10 a.m. to noon.

LODGING

In the Kaanapali-Kapalua area the modestly priced hotel is not an endangered species, it's totally extinct! So prepare yourself for steep tariffs.

Kaanapali
HYATT REGENCY MAUI

$$$$ 806 ROOMS ✉ 200 Nohea Kai Drive, Kaanapali ☎ 808-661-1234, 800-233-1234 📠 808-667-4498 🖥 www.maui.hyatt.com, hrmsales@maui.net

Ever since this classic-style resort was built in 1980, with its atrium lobby, Asian artwork and freeform swimming pool, it has set the standard for quality. Unlike more recent hotels, in which the size of guest rooms is sacrificed for the sake of lavish grounds, the Hyatt Regency maintains an ideal balance between public and private areas. If you're seeking beautiful surroundings, friendly service and beachfront location, this 806-room extravaganza is the ticket. They also boast a 16-inch reflecting telescope that probes deep space seven nights a week: reservations required.

KAANAPALI BEACH HOTEL

$$$$ 430 ROOMS ✉ 2525 Kaanapali Parkway, Kaanapali ☎ 808-661-0011, 808-667-5978 📠 808-667-5978 🖥 www.kbhmaui.com, res@kbhmaui.com

This retreat sits right on the beach and sports three restaurants and a large lobby. Guest rooms enjoy private lanais and guests lounge around a grassy courtyard, lush gardens and a whale-shaped swimming pool. In addition, there's a giant checkerboard; Hawaiian arts and crafts demonstrations are presented throughout the week.

SHERATON MAUI RESORT

$$$$ 510 ROOMS ✉ 2605 Kaanapali Parkway, Kaanapali ☎ 808-661-0031, 888-488-3535 📠 808-661-0458 🖥 www.sheraton.com/maui, sheraton.maui@sheraton.com

At Black Rock, the sacred lava promontory where cliff divers plunged into the Pacific, the ancient tradition is reenacted as part of a nightly

8888888888888
8888888888888
6 **MAUI** KAANAPALI-KAPALUA AREA LODGING

torch-lighting ceremony here. The rooms and suites are spread across 23 acres of spacious landscaped grounds. The hotel's distinctive architecture (it is partially built atop the rock) places some rooms near the water's edge. Decorated with rattan furniture and tropical prints, all the rooms are trim and comfortable. You can watch the sunset from several restaurants and lounges, swim in a 140-yard pool or enjoy snorkeling along Black Rock.

ROYAL LAHAINA RESORT

$$$$ 516 ROOMS   ✉2780 Kekaa Drive, Kaanapali   ☎808-661-3611, 800-222-5642 📠808-661-6150 🖱www.2maui.com

Spread across 27 acres and encompassing 10 tennis courts, 3 swimming pools, 2 restaurants, a coffee shop and a white-sand beach that extends for a half-mile is this upscale resort. Rooms in the highrise hotel price in the ultra-deluxe category, while the rates for the nicest accommodations, the multiplex cottages that dot the landscaped grounds, head for the sky. (Note that some readers were neither impressed by the prices nor the accommodations.)

Kapalua

RITZ-CARLTON, KAPALUA

$$$$ 445 ROOMS   ✉1 Ritz-Carlton Drive, Kapalua   ☎808-669-6200, 800-241-3333 📠808-669-2028 🖱www.ritzcarlton.com

Unique among Ritz-Carltons, the Kapalua sits above the ocean on

Kaanapali–Kapalua Area

grounds that overlook not only the formal gardens and manicured lawns associated with this chain, but a sacred resting place for ancient Hawaiian spirits. It was this burial ground that initially put the hotel at odds with Hawaiian culture but then led it to become one of the strongest supporters of the Hawaiian people in the islands. The spacious guest rooms and suites are well-appointed with contemporary furnishings rooted in Hawaiian tradition and include private lanais. The grounds are as beautiful as they are sacred. The usual five-star hotel amenities include a spa and fitness center, two golf courses, four restaurants and 24-hour room service. Kapalua Bay, one of three beaches here, has been designated among the best beaches in America.

CONDOS

Most condominiums in this area are on the beach or just across the road from it. They are ideally situated for swimming or sunbathing; the major drawback, ironically, is that there are so many other condos around.

Kaanapali

KAANAPALI ALII

264 UNITS ✉50 Nohea Kai Drive, Kaanapali ☎808-667-1400, 800-642-6284 📠808-667-1145 🖥www.classicresorts.com, info@classicresorts.com

This place ranks as one of Maui's better buys. Here the immense 1500- to 1900-square-foot suites can easily be shared by two couples or a family. All condo units have large living and dining rooms, full kitchens, sitting areas and two baths. Fully carpeted and furnished with rattan, contemporary artwork and potted palms, these units start at $405 and top out at $930. The contemporary highrise facility rests along the beach and has a pool, fitness center and tennis court.

THE WHALER ON KAANAPALI BEACH

360 UNITS ✉2481 Kaanapali Parkway, Kaanapali ☎808-661-4861, 800-922-7866 📠808-661-8315 🖥www.resortquesthawaii.com, res.wha@resortquesthawaii.com

Adjacent to the shops of Whalers Village, The Whaler offers spacious units with *koa* parquet floors and some rattan furniture. With its twin 12-story towers, this oceanfront condominium boasts marble baths. Prices range from $255 to $750.

RESORTQUEST KAANAPALI SHORES

430 UNITS ✉3445 Lower Honoapiilani Road, Kaanapali ☎808-667-2211, 800-922-7866 📠808-661-0836 🖥www.kaanapalishores-maui.com

Bright and tropical hotel room–style accommodations are available here. Standard hotel rooms start at $225; studios are available from $275, double with a balcony and full kitchen; and one-bedroom units with a garden view and full kitchen start at $300.

MAUI ELDORADO

204 UNITS ✉2661 Kekaa Drive, Kaanapali ☎808-661-0021, 888-339-8585 📠808-667-7039 🖥www.outrigger.com

If you're willing to move away from the beach, you'll save money at this premium resort, an Outrigger-managed property located along the Kaanapali golf course. The condominiums are spacious and well-appointed, and some have ocean views. Studios go for $299; one-bedroom units start at $329; and two-bedrooms are available from $539. Overall, the complex is a bit austere, but it's a bargain in this neighborhood.

Kaanapali to Kapalua

PAPAKEA RESORT

158 UNITS ✉3543 Lower Honoapiilani Road, Honokowai ✆808-669-4848, 800-922-7866 📠808-665-0662 🖥www.resortquesthawaii.com, res.pap@resortquesthawaii.com

The cool, island-style units here provide a pleasant retreat. Ranging from $290 studios to $680 three-bedroom units, all 158 condominiums come with spacious lanais.

MAUI SANDS

76 UNITS ✉3600 Lower Honoapiilani Road, Honokowai ✆808-669-1900, 800-367-5037 🖥www.mauiresortmanagement.com, mrm.reservations@yahoo.com

One-bedroom apartments at this beachfront abode run from $95, while two-bedroom units start at $190 for one to four people. There is a seven-night minimum year-round and a ten-night minimum in December and January.

HALE MAUI

12 UNITS ✉3711 Lower Honoapiilani Road, Honokowai ✆808-669-6312 📠808-669-1302 🖥www.halemauivacationrental.com, halemaui@maui.net

With a private path leading to the water, Hale Maui offers easy access to the ocean. It has spacious one-bedroom apartments for $105, which include kitchens and secluded balconies. The drawback to this budget rate is that there is no pool—but you won't miss it with the beach practically in your backyard.

KALEIALOHA

67 UNITS ✉3785 Lower Honoapiilani Road, Honokowai ✆808-669-8197, 800-222-8688 📠808-669-2502 🖥www.mauicondosoceanfront.com, info@mauicondosoceanfront.com

The one-bedroom apartments at this tranquil oceanfront oasis start at $135 double; $10 each additional person.

POLYNESIAN SHORES

52 UNITS ✉3975 Lower Honoapiilani Road, Honokowai ✆808-669-6065, 800-433-6284 📠808-669-0909 🖥mauicondosrentals.com, info@mauicondosrentals.com

Tucked between tropical gardens, this laid-back townhouse has one-bedroom apartments that start at $145 double; two-bedroom units, $185 for four; three-bedroom apartments, $245 for four. All units have ocean views.

MAHINA SURF

56 UNITS ✉4057 Lower Honoapiilani Road, Kahana ✆808-669-6068, 800-367-6086 📠808-669-4534 🖥www.mahinasurf.com, mahinasf@maui.net

When you're not sunbathing beachside, you can relax indoors here and still watch the waves. One-bedroom units start at $140 double ($125 to $175 from April 15 to December 14); two-bedroom accommodations range from $155 to $205. There are oceanfront views with a lava-rock beach. There's a three-night minimum stay. Closed Sunday.

KAHANA REEF

18 UNITS ✉ *4471 Lower Honoapiilani Road, Kahana* ✆ *808-879-5445, 800-822-4409*
🖷 *808-874-6144* 🖎 *www.resortquestmaui.com, info@resortquestmaui.com*

With studio and one-bedroom apartments for $155 to $170 single or double, this bright, contemporary resort has you covered for a bargain price. All units are oceanfront; they require a four-night minimum stay.

NAPILI POINT RESORT

115 UNITS ✉ *5295 Lower Honoapiilani Road, Napili* ✆ *808-669-9222, 800-669-6252*
🖷 *808-669-7984* 🖎 *www.napili.com*

Located on a lava rock coastline, this resort is a short walk from sandy Napili Bay beach. One-bedroom condos at Napili Point Resort are $229 to $309 for up to four people (reduced rates in low season). Two-bedroom units start at $289. Here sliding doors lead out to oceanview patios.

OUTRIGGER NAPILI SHORES RESORT

152 UNITS ✉ *5315 Lower Honoapiilani Road, Napili* ✆ *808-669-8061, 800-688-7444*
🖷 *808-669-5407* 🖎 *www.outrigger.com, reservations@outrigger.com*

A beautifully landscaped lowrise resort with newly renovated studios and one-bedrooms running from $219 to $335, this Outrigger offers sublime accommodations. The units are individually decorated with tropical themes and the complex is graced by gardens of plumeria and hibiscus. The pool and beach areas are idyllic.

THE NAPILI BAY

34 UNITS ✉ *33 Hui Drive, Napili* ✆ *808-661-3500, 888-661-7200* 🖷 *808-661-2649*
🖎 *www.mauibeachfront.com, beachfrt@maui.net*

Studio apartments at The Napili Bay are $145 double for oceanfront views. In addition to private lanais, there's a common barbeque area.

NAPILI KAI BEACH RESORT

162 UNITS ✉ *5900 Honoapiilani Road, Napili* ✆ *808-669-6271, 800-367-5030*
🖷 *808-669-0086* 🖎 *www.napilikai.com, stay@napilikai.com*

All 162 units—studios, one-, two- and three-bedroom affairs—range in price from $230 to $1150 at this calm island paradise. Most come with kitchens. All are fully carpeted and have private lanais, rattan furniture, picture windows and direct access to an impressive beach.

Kapalua
KAPALUA VILLAS

380 UNITS ✉ *500 Office Road, Kapalua* ✆ *808-669-8088, 800-545-0018*
🖷 *808-669-5234* 🖎 *www.kapaluavillas.com*

Face it: there are few words in the English language more romantic than "villa." And there are few condominiums on Maui more alluring than Kapalua Villas. Situated on a 1650-acre resort and surrounded by two golf courses and an ocean, they offer views that sweep past the mountains and out to the neighbor islands. The units are lowrise structures with sunken tubs, large lanais, and rattan and wicker furniture. Individually owned and decorated, the accommodations provide direct access to swimming, golf and tennis. One-bedroom units range from $269 to $559; two-bedroom units run from $379 to $779.

Kaanapali

SWAN COURT

$$$$ HAWAII REGIONAL ✉*200 Nohea Kai Drive, Kaanapali*
✆*808-661-1234*

Overlooking serene tropical gardens, this open-air establishment defines the ultimate Maui experience. Guests enter this upscale restaurant in the Hyatt Regency Maui via a grand staircase. With a waterfall and gliding swans in the background, you can choose from a variety of daily-changing entrées such as Hunan marinated lamb chops, grilled lobster satay with coconut and lemongrass, island-style bouillabaisse with macadamia sambal and sautéed *ono* with marinated shrimp won tons. For dessert, there's a daily soufflé selection and dessert sampler. Formal dress required. No lunch.

TROPICA

$$$-$$$$ SEAFOOD/INTERNATIONAL ✉*Westin Maui, 2365 Kaanapali Parkway, Kaanapali* ✆*808-667-2525*

For an elegant dining experience at a reasonable price, grab a table here. Feast on fare prepared on rotisseries, grills and in wood ovens, as well as fresh seafood, while watching the sun set over the bordering beach. Dinner only.

NICKY'S PIZZA

$ PIZZA ✉*Whalers Village, 2435 Kaanapali Parkway, Kaanapali* ✆*808-667-0333*

One way to eat at a reasonable price is by stopping at the takeout stands on the lower level of Whalers Village. There are tables inside or out in the courtyard. Nicky's serves an assortment of pies (including by the slice) plus spaghetti and meatballs and salads.

LEILANI'S ON THE BEACH

$-$$$ STEAK ✉*Whalers Village, 2435 Kaanapali Parkway, Kaanapali*
✆*808-661-4495* ✆*808-667-9027* ✎*www.leilanis.com*

The sunsets are otherworldly at Leilani's, a breezy veranda-style dining room. Trimmed in dark woods and lava rock, the upstairs dining room is dominated by an outrigger canoe that hangs suspended from the ceiling. On the menu you'll find rack of lamb, ginger chicken and teriyaki steak. Downstairs, you can relax and take in the scene from the umbrella shade of the Beachside Grill, where cocktails accompany burgers, sandwiches and salads. Frequently there is live rock-and-roll in the afternoon. Touristy but appealing.

HULA GRILL

$$$ SEAFOOD/HAWAII REGIONAL ✉*Whalers Village, 2435 Kaanapali Parkway, Kaanapali* ✆*808-667-6636* ✆*808-661-1148* ✎*www.hulagrill.com*

Peter Merriman, the chef extraordinaire who earned his reputation with a restaurant on the Big Island, transported his brand of Hawaii regional cuisine across the Alenuihaha Channel to open Hula Grill in Kaanapali. Specializing in seafood, this 1930s-era beach house has wok-charred *ahi*, seafood dim sum dishes and an array of entrées that includes Macadamia nut–crusted mahi-mahi, grilled herbed *ono* and pizza baked in the *kiawe* oven. For landlubbers there's Maui-raised steak and goat cheese pizza.

GIOVANI'S TOMATO PIE RISTORANTE

$$ ITALIAN   ✉2291 Kaanapali Parkway   ☎808-661-3160   ✆808-661-5254

Located near the entrance to Kaanapali Beach Resort, this casual eatery offers delicious Italian fare. A patio restaurant overlooking a golf course, it's a pretty place to dine on pizza, pasta and other traditional favorites. The restaurant features a menu that includes veal marsala, chicken parmesan and shrimp scampi. Dinner only.

KAANAPALI MIXED PLATE RESTAURANT

$$ INTERNATIONAL/LOCAL-STYLE   ✉Kaanapali Beach Hotel, 2525 Kaanapali Parkway, Kaanapali   ☎808-661-0011   ✆808-667-5616   🖥www.kbhmaui.com, info@kbhmaui.com

An all-you-can-eat buffet is available here at a price that is surprisingly out of place for this expensive hotel. A complete breakfast is offered; lunch and dinner include a few entrées, a salad bar, soup and dessert buffets. Meat-eaters will revel in the dinner buffet's all-you-can-eat prime rib.

BASIL TOMATOES ITALIAN GRILLE

$$$ ITALIAN   ✉At the entrance to the Royal Lahaina Resort, 2780 Kekaa Drive, Kaanapali   ☎808-662-3210   ✆808-661-5254

Located on the scenic Kaanapali North Course, this cozy eatery features northern Italian versions of veal chop, fresh fish, lasagna and a variety of pastas. Flavorful food and an intimate setting make this a top choice for dinner. Dinner only.

Kaanapali to Kapalua

DOLLIE'S PUB AND CAFÉ

$$ DINER   ✉4310 Lower Honoapiilani Road, Kahana   ☎808-669-0266   ✆808-665-0614

A favorite with locals, Dollie's offers fettuccine alfredo, sandwiches, salads and pizza. Voted Best of Maui by local write-in vote, this is a sports-on-the-TV bar (nine satellite TVs, two 42-inch flat screens) with a small kitchen and adjacent dining room.

ROY'S KAHANA BAR AND GRILL

$$$–$$$$ PAN-ASIAN   ✉Kahana Gateway Shopping Center, 4405 Honoapiilani Highway, Kahana   ☎808-669-6999   🖥www.roysrestaurant.com, kahana@roysrestaurant.com

One of Maui's leading restaurants, Roy's eschews the waterfalls, swans, tinkling pianists and other accoutrements of the island's top dining rooms. Instead, this spacious second-story establishment looks like a gallery with its exposed-beam ceiling, track lighting and paintings. The open kitchen serves up such creations as fresh seared lemongrass *shutome* with Thai basil peanut sauce, *kiawe*-grilled filet mignon with garlic mashed potatoes and Chinese barbecue cabernet, grilled ginger chicken with shoyu glaze and garlic chive rice and blackened *ahi* with soy-mustard butter. Reservations are a must!

FISH & GAME BREWING COMPANY & ROTISSERIE

$$$–$$$$ SEAFOOD/STEAK   ✉*Kahana Gateway Shopping Center, 4405 Lower Honoapiilani Road, Kahana* ✆*808-669-3474* ✐*www.fishandgamerestaurant.com, info@fishandgamerestaurant.com*

A good choice for food, libations and conversation is this big-portions-for-big appetites restaurant. The name is quite a mouthful, but this establishment boasts three dining rooms as well as a microbrewery. The open-hearth rotisserie oven, along with the gleaming copper vats, dominate the first room. The main dining room contains an exhibition kitchen and live lobster tank, while the private dining room showcases a fireplace and leather wingback chairs. Fresh fish and seafood are island-caught; for the carnivorous, there's roasted meats and the tastiest rack of lamb on the island. Sports fans will also enjoy the large-screen TVs in the bar. Breakfast on weekends during football season.

CHINA BOAT

$$ CHINESE   ✉*4474 Lower Honoapiilani Road, Kahana* ✆*808-669-5089* ✆*808-669-6132*

For Mongolian beef, *kung pao* chicken or hot Szechuan bean curd, make a stop at this serene eatery. At this family-style restaurant, you can ease into a lacquered seat and take in the Japanese *ukiyoe* prints that adorn the place. Adding to the ambience are lava walls that showcase beautiful Chinese ceramic pieces. Patio dining is also available. No lunch on Sunday.

MAUI TACOS

$ MEXICAN   ✉*Napili Plaza, 5095 Napilihau Street, Napili* ✆*808-665-0222, 888-628-4822* ✐*www.mauitacos.com, eatmaui@maui.net*

In addition to its namesake, Maui Tacos has chimichangas, tostadas, burritos, quesadillas and enchiladas. Nothing fancy, just a few formica booths and tables with molded plastic chairs. But the salsa's fresh daily, the beans are prepared without lard and the chips are made with cholesterol-free vegetable oil. Egg burritos and huevos rancheros are served for breakfast. Frozen yogurt and fruit smoothies are also available.

SEA HOUSE RESTAURANT AT NAPILI BEACH RESORT

$$$$ SEAFOOD/HAWAII REGIONAL   ✉*5900 Lower Honoapiilani Road, Napili* ✆*808-669-1500* ✆*808-669-5740*

Perched on the white sandy beach along one of the most beautiful bays on Maui, you'll find an eatery noted for fresh island fish (offered four different ways). For landlubbers there's steak, free-range chicken and pasta. The *pupus* menu offers a wonderful selection of island specialties. Open for breakfast, lunch and dinner.

THE PLANTATION HOUSE RESTAURANT

$$$–$$$$ MEDITERRANEAN/HAWAII REGIONAL   ✉*2000 Plantation Club Drive, Kapalua* ☎*808-669-6299* 📠*808-661-0466*
🖥*www.theplantationhouse.com, info@theplantationhouse.com*

Maui aficionados agree that this restaurant is among the island's best. Capturing their accolades is a spacious establishment with panoramic views of the Kapalua region and a decor that mixes mahogany and wicker with orchids and a roaring fire. Not to be upstaged by the surroundings, the chef prepares fresh island fish seven different ways. The most popular is the "plantation Oscar"—the fish is pan sauteed, then served with butter braised asparagus and sauteed crabmeat with a lemon *beurre blanc*. For lighter appetites there are salads, pastas, honey-guava scallops and, for lunch, a wide range of soups and sandwiches. Breakfast is also served.

SHOPPING

WHALERS VILLAGE ✉*2435 Kaanapali Parkway, Kaanapali* ☎*808-661-4567*
This sprawling complex combines a shopping mall with a museum. Numbered among the stores you'll find gift emporia featuring coral and shells, a shirt store with wild island designs, other stores offering fine men's and women's fashions.

And then there are the displays. Within this mazework mall you'll discover blunderbusses, scrimshaw pieces, the skeletal remains of leviathans and whaling boats with iron harpoons splayed from the bow. Practically everything, in fact, that a whaler (or a cruising shopper) could desire.

Several shops in this split-level complex should not be missed. For instance, **Lahaina Printsellers Ltd.** (808-667-7617) purveys "fine antique maps and prints." **Sgt. Leisure** (808-891-9256) sells brightly colored resortwear and T-shirts. At **Blue Ginger Designs** (808-667-5793) original styles in women's and children's clothing are featured.

For serious shoppers, ready to spend money or be damned, there is nothing to compare with the neighboring hotels. Set like gems within this tourist cluster are several world-class hotels, each hosting numerous elegant shops.

HYATT REGENCY MAUI ✉*210 Nohea Kai Drive, Kaanapali* ☎*808-661-1234*
Foremost in hotel shopping is this Hyatt, along whose wood-paneled lobby are stores that might well be deemed mini-museums. There are art galleries, a fabric shop, clothing stores, jewelry stores and more—set in an open-air lobby that is filled with rare statuary and exotic birds.

HAWAIIAN QUILT COLLECTION

✉*210 Nohea Kai Drive, Kaanapali* ☎*808-667-7660* This is another favorite Hyatt Regency shop, where you'll find wallhangings, quilting supplies and an array of quilts. All quilts are Hawaiian related and made by the owner.

LA BAREDA ✉100 Nohea Kai Drive, Kaanapali ✆808-667-5082 An excellent place to find inexpensive Hawaiian souvenirs, stop here for items such as sarongs, straw hats, jewelry and T-shirts. This shop in the Maui Marriott hotel is also knee-deep in key chains, pennants and ceramic pineapples.

PLANTATION COURSE GOLF SHOP ✉2000 Plantation Club Drive, Kapalua ✆808-669-8877 Here you'll find an impressive collection of jackets, shirts, sweaters, sweatshirts and shorts, some with a tropical flair. This is also a good place to look for the work of signature designers.

NIGHTLIFE

HULA GRILL

✉2435 Kaanapali Parkway ✆808-667-6636 ✇808-661-1148 ✍www.hula pie.com Possibly the prettiest place in these parts to enjoy a drink 'neath the tropic moon is the bar here. Located in the Whalers Village mall, this beach house–style gathering place is decorated with original Hawaiian outrigger canoes. It features live Hawaiian music and hula nightly until 10:30 p.m. The place is located right on the water, so you can listen to a slow set, then stroll the beach.

HYATT REGENCY MAUI ✉200 Nohea Kai Drive, Kaanapali ✆808-661-1234, 800-233-1234 ✇808-667-4498 Hawaiian musicians perform nightly within the Hyatt at the **Weeping Banyan**, an open-air lounge. **Spats Trattoria** (cover) offers deejay dance music on Saturday.

'ONO SURF BAR & GRILL

✉Westin Maui, 2365 Kaanapali Parkway, Kaanapali ✆808-667-2525 There's nightly music and Hawaiian entertainment at this tropical bistro within the Westin Maui.

LAGOON BAR ✉Sheraton Maui, 2605 Kaanapali Parkway, Kaanapali ✆808-661-0031 The Sheraton Maui is a prime nightspot both early and later in the evening. Just before sunset you can watch the torch-lighting and cliff-diving ceremony from the Lagoon Bar.

ROYAL OCEAN TERRACE LOUNGE ✉2780 Kekaa Drive, Kaanapali ✆808-661-3611 You can find occasional Hawaiian-style entertainment at this beachfront watering hole on the grounds of the Royal Lahaina Resort. Arrive early and you can watch the sunset between Lanai and Molokai, followed by the ubiquitous torch-lighting ceremony.

THE LEHUA LOUNGE ✉Kapalua Bay Hotel, 1 Bay Drive ✆808-669-5656 In the lobby of the Kapalua Bay Hotel, you can enjoy live music nightly over cocktails and great views of the Pacific.

MASTERS OF HAWAIIAN SLACK-KEY GUITAR CONCERT SERIES

✉ *Napili Kai Beach Resort, Napili* 📞 *888-669-3858* If you're a fan of authentic island music, check out this concert series, held on Wednesday evenings. It's hosted by slack-key king George Kahumoku Jr., and features guest musicians and informal talk story sessions that give it an intimate, backyard-jam-session feel.

BEACHES & PARKS

KAANAPALI RESORT BEACHES
✉ *Take the public right-of-way to the beach from any of the Kaanapali resort hotels.*

The sprawling complex of Kaanapali hotels sits astride a beautiful white-sand beach that extends for three miles. Looking out on Lanai and Molokai, this is a classic palm-fringed strand. The entire area is heavily developed and crowded with tourists glistening in coconut oil. But it is an extraordinarily fine beach where the swimming is very good and the skindiving excellent around Black Rock at the Sheraton Maui. The beach has no facilities, but most of the resorts have public restrooms and there are restaurants nearby.

HONOKOWAI BEACH PARK
✉ *North of Kaanapali in Honokowai on Lower Honoapiilani Road (which is the oceanfront section of Route 30)*

Compared to the beaches fronting Kaanapali's nearby resorts, this is a bit disappointing. The large lawn is pleasant enough and the beach ample, with a reef that projects right to the shoreline. Still, the view of Molokai is awesome. In the shallow reef waters the swimming and snorkeling are good; surfing is nonexistent. Friendly to kids, the park features a playground, while the reef waters are ideal for youngsters to splash in. *Ulua* and threadfin are among the most frequent catches. Picnic tables, restrooms and showers are available.

NAPILI BAY
✉ *Several miles north of Kaanapali, with rights-of-way to the beach from Lower Honoapiilani Road via Napili Place or Hui Drive*

You'll find wall-to-wall condominiums along this small cove. There's a crowded but beautiful white-sand beach studded with palm trees and looking out on Molokai. Swimming and snorkeling are delightful and the surfing here is particularly good for beginners.

KAPALUA BEACH
✉ *There's a right-of-way to the beach from Lower Honoapiilani Road near the Napili Kai Beach Club.*

This is the next cove over from Napili Bay. It's equally beautiful, but, sadly, has also suffered from the hands of developers. The crescent of white sand that lines Kapalua Bay is bounded on either end by rocky points and backdropped by a line of coconut trees and the Kapalua Bay Hotel. Swimming and snorkeling are excellent; beginners will be especially delighted by the multitude of colorful fish so close to the shore.

D. T. FLEMING PARK
✉*At the Ritz-Carlton, Kapalua, about seven miles north of Kaanapali just off Honoapiilani Highway*

🐬 🦀 🏊 🛶 One of Maui's nicest beach parks, D. T. Fleming has a spacious white-sand beach and a rolling lawn shaded with palm and ironwood trees with a nice view of Molokai's rugged East End. Unfortunately, a major resort resides just uphill from the beach. Sometimes windy, the park is plagued by rough and dangerous surf during the winter. Use caution! You'll find good swimming and body-surfing and fair snorkeling during the summer. There are also good breaks nearby at Little Makaha, named after the famous Oahu beach. For anglers the prime catches are *ulua* and *papio*. There are restrooms, a picnic area and showers.

NORTHWEST MAUI

To escape from the crowds and commotion of the Kaanapali–Kapalua area and travel north on the Honoapiilani Highway is to journey from the ridiculous to the sublime. As you curve along the edge of the West Maui Mountains, en route around the side of the island to Kahului and Wailuku, you'll pass several hidden beaches that lie along an exotic and undeveloped shore. This is a region of the Valley Isle not frequented by the tourist crowd.

SIGHTS

HONOKOHAU BAY Near the rocky beach and lush valley at this serene bay, the Honoapiilani Highway (Route 30) becomes the Kahekili Highway (Route 340). This macadam track snakes high above the ocean, hugging the coastline. From the highway rises a series of multi-hued **sandstone cliffs** that seems alien to this volcanic region and creates a picturesque backdrop to the rocky shore.

KAHAKULOA ————————————

As the road continues, the scenery is some of the most magnificent on Maui. Down a dirt side road sits the rustic village of Kahakuloa. Nestled in an overgrown valley beside a deep blue bay, the community is protected by a solitary headland rising directly from the sea. Woodframe houses and churches, which appear ready to fall to the next gusting wind, are spotted throughout this enchanting area. Kahakuloa is cattle country, and you'll find that the villagers live and farm much as their forefathers did

Northwest Maui

HONOLUA BAY

PAGE 302

Some of the finest surf breaks in all Hawaii, with picture-perfect, 15-foot tubes during winter months

MOKULEIA BEACH

PAGE 302

Shallow cover of white sand bounded by cliffs, looks across the waves to Molokai

KAHAKULOA

PAGE 300

A glimpse of Maui's traditional village life in a rustic seaside town nestled within an overgrown valley

back when most of Maui was unclaimed terrain. It was from the shoreline near Kahakuloa that the Polynesian canoe *Hokulea* left on its famous voyage.

The road ascends again outside Kahakuloa. Opening below you, one valley after another falls seaward in a series of spine-backed ridges. Above the road, the mountain range rises toward its 5788-foot summit at Puu Kukui.

WAIHEE There are lush gulches farther along as the road descends into this quiet plantation town. Here rolling countryside, dotted with small farm houses, slopes from the roadside up to the foothills of the West Maui Mountains.

SACRED SPOTS

You're still on the Kahekili Highway, but now once again it really is a highway, a well-traveled road that leads toward Kahului. Located just northwest of town, a side road leads to two sacred spots. The first, **Halekii Heiau**, overlooking Kahului Bay and Iao Stream, dates from the 1700s. Today this temple, once as large as a football field, is little more than a stone heap. **Pihana Kalani Heiau**, a short distance away, was once a sacrificial temple.

Before driving this route, as well as the back road from Hana to Ulupalakua, remember that the car rental agencies will not insure you over these winding tracks. Many cover the roads anyway, and I highly recommend that you explore them both if weather permits.

MOKULEIA BEACH OR SLAUGHTERHOUSE BEACH

✉ *Take Honoapiilani Highway for exactly eight-tenths of a mile past D. T. Fleming Park. Park on the highway and take the steep path down about 100 yards to the beach.*

This lovely patch of white sand is bounded by cliffs and looks out on Molokai. Set at the end of a shallow cove, the beach is partially protected. Swimming, snorkeling and surfing are all good. This is part of a marine sanctuary so fishing is not permitted. There are no facilities here.

HONOLUA BAY

✉ *About one-and-a-third miles north of D. T. Fleming Park on Honoapiilani Highway, the dirt road to the beach is open only to cars with boats in tow. Park with the other cars along the highway and follow the paths to the beach.*

A rocky beach makes this cliff-rimmed bay unappealing for sunbathers, but there are rich coral deposits offshore

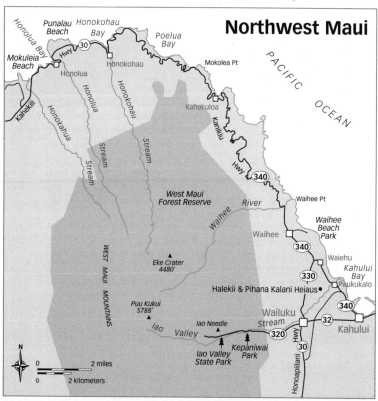

Northwest Maui

Honolua Bay
Punalau Beach
Honokohau Bay
Poelua Bay
Mokuleia Beach
Hwy 30
Honolua
Honokohau
Mokolea Pt
PACIFIC OCEAN
Kahakuloa
Kahekili
Honokohua Stream
Honolua Stream
Honokohau Stream
Kaniau
Hwy 340
West Maui Forest Reserve
Waihee River
Waihee Pt
Waihee
Waihee Beach Park
340
Waiehu
Eke Crater 4480'
330
Kahului Bay
Paukukalo
Halekii & Pihana Kalani Heiaus
WEST MAUI MOUNTAINS
Puu Kukui 5788'
Wailuku
Waikuku Stream
340
Iao Needle
Iao Valley
Kepaniwai Park
320
Hwy 32
Kahului
Iao Valley State Park
30
Honoapiilani Hwy
N
0   2 miles
0   2 kilometers

and beautiful trees growing near the water. In winter you're likely to find crowds along the top of the cliff watching surfers work some of the finest breaks in all Hawaii: perfect tubes up to 15 feet. Swimming is good, but the bottom is rocky. Snorkeling is excellent, particularly on the west side of the bay. No fishing is allowed; this is part of a marine sanctuary. There are no facilities (and usually very few people) here.

HONOKOHAU BAY ⟨hidden⟩

✉ *About six miles north of D. T. Fleming Park on Honoapiilani Highway*

This rocky beach is surrounded by cliffs. To the interior, a lush valley rises steadily into the folds of the West Maui Mountains. When the water is calm, swimming and snorkeling are good. The surf offers rugged, two- to twelve-foot breaks. Keep in mind the changeable nature of this wave action, since it can vary quickly from the gentle to the dangerous. Milkfish, *papio*, leatherback, *moano* and big-eyed scad are the principal species caught in these waters.

CENTRAL MAUI

Central Maui is defined not by what it is but by what lies to the east and west of it. On one side Haleakala lifts into the clouds; on the other hand loom the West Maui mountains, a folded landscape over 5000 feet in elevation. Between them, at the center of the island, sits an isthmus, some areas planted in sugar cane and pineapple. Never rising more than a few hundred feet above sea level, it houses Kahului along its northern edge and serves as the gateway to both the Lahaina–Kaanapali and Kihei–Wailea areas. Three highways cross the isthmus separating West Maui from the slopes of Haleakala. From Kahului, Mokulele Highway (Route 350) tracks south to Kihei through this rich agricultural area. The Kuihelani Highway (Route 380), running diagonally and through open stretches, joins the Honoapiilani Highway (Route 30) in its course from Wailuku along the West Maui Mountains. The low-lying area that supports this network of roadways was formed by lava flows from Haleakala and the West Maui Mountains.

SIGHTS

ALEXANDER & BALDWIN SUGAR MUSEUM ✉ *3957 Hansen Road, Puunene* ☎ *808-871-8058* ⌖ *www.sugarmuseum.com* This museum, an award-winning nonprofit organization, is across from the largest operating sugar plantation in Hawaii. It provides a brief introduction to Hawaii's main crop. Tracing the history of sugar cultivation in the islands, its displays portray everything from early life in the cane fields, the multi-ethnic plantation life, to contemporary methods for producing refined sugar. Closed Sunday except in July and August. Admission.

MAUI TROPICAL PLANTATION ✉1670 Honoapiilani Highway ☎808-244-7643 🖱www.mauitropicalplantation.com A 60-acre enclave complete with orchards and groves displaying dozens of island fruit plants, this plantation boasts avocados, papayas, bananas, pineapples, mangoes, coffee and macadamia nuts growing in lush profusion. There's a coffee-roasting room and a tram that will carry you through this ersatz plantation. Admission for tram.

MAUI OCEAN CENTER, THE HAWAIIAN AQUARIUM ✉192 Maalaea Road, Maalaea ☎808-270-7000 🖂808-270-7070 🖱www.mauioceancenter.com, info@mauioceancenter.com Truly both a learning center and a star attraction is this center and aquarium. It's a journey through the living ocean in both open-air and interior exhibits, each of which are interactive in touch, sight and sound. Showcasing not only Hawaii's unique marine life, from the coral reef to the open ocean, this aquarium also dedicates an exhibit to its host culture, showcasing the language, history and lore of Hawaii. Locally trained marine naturalists are on hand to answer questions and give presentations. In the Shark Dive, certified scuba divers (15 years old and older) can dive in the Open Ocean Exhibit and be surrounded by sharks and rays. Admission.

KAHOOLAWE Down the road from McGregor Point, you'll see three islands anchored offshore. As you look seaward, the portside islet is **Molokini**, the crescent-shaped remains of a volcanic crater. Kahoo-

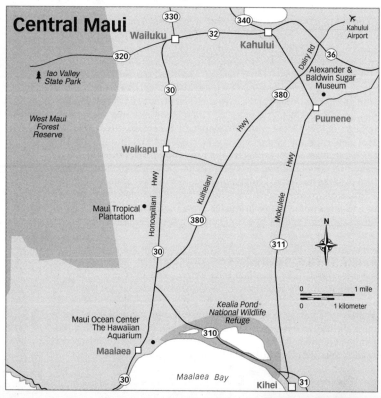

lawe, a barren, desiccated island once used for naval target practice, sits in the center. Located seven miles off Maui's south coast, it is a bald, windblasted place, hot and arid. Hawaiian activists long demanded an end to the bombing of this sacred isle by the U.S. Navy. After years of demonstrations, their demands were finally acknowledged in 1994 when the island was turned over to the state of Hawaii. The humpbacked island to starboard is **Lanai**. As you continue toward Kaanapali, **Molokai** sails into view.

DINING

SEASCAPE MAALAEA RESTAURANT
$$ SEAFOOD ⊠*Maalaea Harbor Village, 192 Maalaea Road, Maalaea;* ✆*808-270-7403*

This restaurant offers seafood, which is what you'd expect from its location on the Maalaea Harbor, right next door to the Maui Ocean Center. It's open for lunch only, and you can dine outdoors on salads, entrees and pastas, all made from fresh, local seafood. There's a children's menu, too.

BEACHES & PARKS

MAALEA BAY
🛶 🏃 Past the small boat harbor here, the highway hugs the southwest coast. There are excellent lookout points along this elevated roadway, especially near the lighthouse at **McGregor Point**. During whale season you might spy a leviathan from this landlocked crow's nest. Just offshore there are prime whale breeding areas.

KIHEI–WAILEA–MAKENA AREA

Stretching from Maalaea Bay to Makena is a near continuous succession of beautiful beaches that make Kihei and Wailea favored resort destinations. Second only to the Lahaina–Kaanapali area in popularity, this seaside enclave rests in the rainshadow of Haleakala, which looms in the background. Maui's southeastern shore receives only ten inches of rain a year, making it the driest, sunniest spot on the island. It also experiences heavy winds, particularly in the afternoon, which sweep across the island's isthmus, which Hawaiians called the "Land of Mirages," or *Kula o ka Mao Mao*.

SIGHTS

Kihei
Since the 1970s, this long, lean stretch of coast has become a developer's playground. Kihei in particular, lacking a master plan, has grown by accretion from a small local community into a haphazard collection of condominiums and mini-malls. It's an unattractive, six-mile strip lined by a golden beach.

Kihei-Wailea-Makena Area

LIHI KAI

PAGE 311

Tranquil tropical oasis with eight wood-paneled beach cottages painted in cool greens and earth tones

DA KITCHEN EXPRESS

PAGE 314

Genuine plate lunches, including ethnic favorites like teriyaki chicken and traditional Hawaiian dishes like *laulau* and *kalua* pork

BLACK SANDS BEACH

PAGE 319

Secluded, long, narrow, salt-and-pepper beach—a great escape from the crowds at nearby Makena State Beach

AHINI-KINAU PRESERVE

PAGE 308

Vast 2000-acre land and ocean preserve with stunningly scenic hiking trails and coral-rich snorkeling sites

KEALIA POND NATIONAL WILDLIFE REFUGE

✉️*On Mokulele Highway near the 6-mile marker* 📞*808-875-1582* Situated strategically along this beachfront are cement **pillboxes**, reminders of World War II's threatened Japanese invasion. Placed along Kihei Road just north of town, they are not far from this refuge, a reserve of over 700 acres frequented by migratory waterfowl like green wing teals, mallards and pintails, as well as Hawaiian stilts and Hawaiian coots. You can take a nature walk here on a wooden boardwalk over the wetlands. Closed weekends.

Wailea

To the south lies this urbane answer to the random growth patterns of its scruffy neighbor. Wailea is a planned resort, all 1450 manicured acres of it. Here scrubland has been transformed into a flowering oasis that is home to top-class hotels and condos, as well as the required retinue of golf courses, tennis courts and overpriced shops. Like Kihei, it is blessed with beautiful beaches.

Home to some of Maui's most luxurious resorts, Wailea is the place to find Picasso originals, 50,000-square-foot spas and villas designed to keep a smile on the face of a high roller. Plantation- and Mediterranean-style architecture, accented by polished limestone tile and granite boulders imported from Mount Fuji, make this swank resort area an international retreat.

Connected by a mile-and-a-half-long ocean walk, and lining five crescent beaches, the resort's luxury properties comprise a self-contained retreat. Covering an area three times the size of Waikiki, Wailea has matured from a series of five crescent beaches separated by lava rock promontories into an elegant mix of hotels, condominiums, golf courses (there are three 18-hole championship links and two clubhouses), tennis court and water sports facilities.

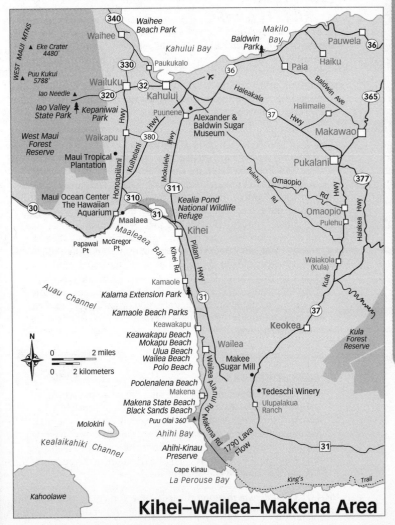

Kihei–Wailea–Makena Area

Adjacent to Wailea, the Makena area is a quiet, less populated area with a single hotel (the Maui Prince) and several small condominiums sharing a full range of resort facilities, including two 18-hole golf courses.

Now a peaceful cove, **Makena Landing**, located on Makena Road, was once a port as busy as Lahaina. During the California gold rush, prevailing winds prompted many San Francisco–bound ships coming up from Cape Horn to resupply here. Fresh fruits and vegetables, badly needed by the would-be miners, were traded in abundance. Later local ranchers delivered their cattle to market by tethering them to longboats and swimming the animals out to steamers waiting just offshore from Makena Landing.

MAKENA STATE BEACH ✉*Along Makena Alanui about four miles beyond Wailea* The setting, dominated by the upcountry slopes of Haleakala and the dry mix of *kiawe* and cactus that provide ground cover, is highlighted by the wide and luxurious sands of the beach here, which I highly recommend visiting. Makena remains one of Maui's finest strands. A hippie hangout in the 1960s and early 1970s, it still retains a freewheeling atmosphere, especially at nearby **Little Beach** (also known as Baby Beach), Maui's most famous nude beach.

AHIHI–KINAU PRESERVE
Past Makena State Beach the road gets rough as it presses south to Ahihi–Kinau Preserve. Encompassing over 2000 acres of land and ocean bottom, this preserve harbors an amazing array of marine life and contains the remains of an early Hawaiian fishing village. Almost 100 larval fish species and about two dozen species of stony coral have been found in this ecologically rich reserve. You can hike on a restored portion of the stone-lined Royal Road that in pre-contact times circled the island. The landscape of lava-scarred lowlands is dominated by the green upcountry pastures of Haleakala's mid-level slopes. This was the route of the annual Makahiki procession, when chiefs and their tax collectors made the rounds of the royal dominions, collecting praise and tribute.

LA PEROUSE BAY
The road continues on, bisecting the **1790 lava flow**, which resulted from Haleakala's last eruption. The flow created Cape Kinau, a thumb-shaped peninsula dividing Ahihi Bay and La Perouse Bay. The bay is named for the ill-starred French navigator, Jean-François de la Pérouse, who anchored here in 1786, the first Westerner to visit Maui. After a brief sojourn in this enchanting spot, he sailed off and was later lost at sea.

MOLOKINI Anywhere along this coastline you can gaze out at this crescent-shaped islet that is a favorite spot among snorkelers. Resting in the Alalakeihi Channel three miles west of Maui, it measures a scant 19 acres in area and rises 165 feet above sea level. The island is actually a tuff cone created by volcanic eruptions deep underwater that solidified into a hard substance called tuff. Black coral divers harvested the surrounding waters until the 1970s. According to Hawaiian legend, Molokini was created when the volcano goddess Pele cut a rival lover—a lizard—in two, turning the tail into Molokini and the head into the cinder cone near Makena Beach. Maui's sands run white, gold, salt and pepper, green—even garnet—depending on what Madame Pele decided to spew years ago.

LODGING

Hotels are rare in Kihei. And in Wailea, a hotel in anything less than an ultra-deluxe price range is a contradiction in terms.

Kihei
NONA LANI COTTAGES
$$–$$$ 8 ROOMS   ✉️*455 South Kihei Road, Kihei*   📞*808-879-2497, 800-733-2688*
📠*808-891-0273* 🖥️*www.nonalanicottages.com, nona@nonalanicottages.com*
With eight wooden cottages, Nona Lani provides a little relief from the mondo-condo Kihei madness. They're situated across busy Kihei Road from a white-sand beach. Each is a one-bedroom unit with lanai, all-electric kitchen and a living room capable of housing one or two extra sleepers. There's wall-to-wall carpeting and a shower-tub combination, plus TV and air conditioners in all bedrooms, but no phone. (Be forewarned: we've had complaints, so you might want to check it out first.) There is a four-night minimum from April 16 to December 15; seven-night minimum from December 16 to April 15. Rooms without kitchens also available; there is a three-night minimum.

ASTON MAUI LU RESORT
$$$–$$$ 120 ROOMS   ✉️*575 South Kihei Road, Kihei*   📞*808-879-5881, 866-774-2924*
📠*808-879-4627* 🖥️*www.maui-lu.com*
Spread across 28 acres, this lavish resort is tropically landscaped with palm trees and flowering plants. Within the grounds, which are across the street from a beach, you'll find a Maui-shaped pool and two tennis courts. The guest rooms are furnished in standard fashion and located in a series of interconnecting buildings with some accommodations on the beach.

MAUI COAST HOTEL
$$$–$$$$ 265 ROOMS   ✉️*2259 South Kihei Road, Kihei*   📞*808-874-6284, 800-895-6284* 📠*808-875-4731* 🖥️*www.mauicoasthotel.com*
Check in to this facility across the street from the beach. It's light, airy, modern and has a pool, outdoor jacuzzis, tennis courts, a pool bar and a cluster of nearby restaurants. There's poolside entertainment nightly.

BEST WESTERN MAUI OCEANFRONT INN
$$$–$$$$ 86 ROOMS   ✉️*2980 South Kihei Road, Kihei*   📞*808-879-7744* 📠*808-874-0145* 🖥️*www.mauioceanfrontinn.com, mtidalgo@mauioceanfrontinn.com*
Down the road from Maui Coast you'll find a series of six buildings designed in mock-Hawaiian style and sandwiched between the highway

and a white-sand beach. There are 86 rooms and two one-bedroom ocean view suites, all attractively decorated and featuring air conditioning, television and refrigerator. There's also a workout facility.

Wailea
FAIRMONT KEA LANI HOTEL

$$$$ 413 ROOMS   ✉4100 Wailea Alanui, Wailea   ☎808-875-4100, 800-659-4100   🖷808-875-1200   ⌨www.fairmont.com, info@kealani.com

This all-suite 22-acre resort is done in southern Mediterranean style. Turning its back on Hawaiian royalty, the Eurocentric lobby would look familiar to Louis XIV. Seven waterfalls, four fountains and a swim-up bar create attractions decadent enough for the Sun King himself. Among the accommodations are 413 suites and 37 villas, each appointed with oak fixtures, floral prints and mirrored doors. The Roman-style baths feature Italian marble (of course) and all the two-story villas come with their own plunge pool.

FOUR SEASONS RESORT MAUI

$$$$ 380 ROOMS   ✉3900 Wailea Alanui, Wailea   ☎808-874-8000, 800-332-3442   🖷808-874-6449   ⌨www.fourseasons.com

This lushly landscaped Four Seasons is the ultimate among ultimate destinations. The only Maui resort we know to feature a trompe l'oeil artwork in the lobby, it's a windswept, Hawaiian palace–style complex set on a luxurious beach. Furnished with wicker and rattan, most of the plantation-style guest rooms offer ocean views. Casablanca fans, tropical plants and marbletop vanities add to the comfort. Louvered doors open onto spacious lanais. Reflecting pools, waterfalls and fountains give the public areas an elegant tropical air. This all comes at a hefty price tag.

Makena
MAUI PRINCE HOTEL

$$$$ 310 ROOMS   ✉5400 Makena Alanui, Makena   ☎808-874-1111, 800-321-6284   🖷808-879-8763   ⌨www.princeresortshawaii.com, reservationshphw@hiprince.com

Its remote location makes the Maui Prince an unusual find. Built around a courtyard adorned with lush tropical gardens and lily ponds, the establishment rewards those willing to drive a few extra minutes to Maui's southernmost retreat. Here you're likely to be lulled to sleep by the sound of the surf. Decorated with heliconia and bougainvillea, the rooms and suites open onto lanais. This V-shaped hotel is next door to two of Maui's top golf courses.

CONDOS

Kihei
LEILANI KAI

8 UNITS   ✉1226 Uluniu Street, Kihei   ☎808-879-2606   🖷808-875-3745   ⌨www.lkresort.com, lkresort@msn.com

A cozy eight-unit apartment hotel, the Leilani is located right on the beach. Studio apartments are $110 double; one-bedroom units are $130 double; two bedrooms will run you $145 for one to four people.

KIHEI KAI

24 UNITS ✉ *61 North Kihei Road, Kihei* ☎ *808-891-0780, 888-778-7717* 📠 *808-891-9403* 🖥 *www.kiheikai.com, kiheikai@maui.net*

Oceanside one-bedroom apartments here are $130 to $145 double ($120 to $165 from mid-April to mid-December). Each has television, phone, full kitchen and lanai. Closed Sunday.

MANA KAI MAUI RESORT

98 UNITS ✉ *2960 South Kihei Road, Kihei* ☎ *808-879-1561, 800-367-5242* 📠 *808-879-7825* 🖥 *www.crhmaui.com, res@crhmaui.com*

A highrise condo, Mana Kai has "hotel units" that consist of the extra bedroom and bath from a two-bedroom apartment ($280 to $300 in peak season), i.e. they lack kitchens. One-bedroom units with kitchens are $245 to $265. The condo has a beachfront location as well as an adjoining restaurant and bar.

LIHI KAI

8 UNITS ✉ *2121 Iliili Road, Kihei* ☎ *808-879-2335* 📠 *808-879-0358* 🖥 *www.lihikai.com*

This tropical oasis has eight beach cottages with full kitchens, six of which rent for $175 single or double, while the two deluxe cottages rent for $200. The décor is tranquil with cool greens and earth tones and cheerful wood paneling. There are also carports and covered lanais at this comfortable property near two beaches. To be sure of getting a cottage, it's best to make reservations far in advance.

KAMAOLE BEACH ROYALE

65 UNITS ✉ *2385 South Kihei Road, Kihei* ☎ *808-879-3131, 800-421-3661* 📠 *808-879-9163* 🖥 *www.mauikbr.com, davi@aloha.com*

Across the street from a beach park, is this seven-story condo with one-bedroom apartments for $120 double; two-bedroom units for $145 to $160 double; three-bedroom units for up to $180. Add $10 for each additional person. No credit cards.

Makena
POLLYMAKENA

2 UNITS ✉ *For reservations contact Maui Tropical Vacations, P.O. Box 641, Haiku, HI 96708* ☎ *866-720-7898* 📠 *708-575-1764* 🖥 *paulas@maui.net.com*

This is a pair of oceanfront villas just a hop, skip and a jump from Makena Beach. Ideal for families or small groups, the larger villa has three bedrooms and a loft; the smaller unit has two bedrooms and sleeps up to five people. Rates range from $550 to $850. Beautifully appointed, they're filled with a fascinating assortment of treasures collected by the charming owner, Parks Hay. A hammock surrounded by tiki torches adorns the front yard and creates a small island of relaxation; a teeming tidepool fronts one of the complexes. PollyMakena is set on "Wedding Cove," so you're bound to witness at least one ceremony during your stay, adding to the romance of this special place.

Gay Lodging
SUNSEEKER RESORT

16 ROOMS   ✉ *551 South Kihei Road, Kihei*   ☎ *808-879-1261, 800-532-6284*
📠 *808-874-3877*   ✇ *www.mauisunseeker.com, info@mauisunseeker.com*

Sunseeker is a small, personalized place where oceanview studios complete with kitchenettes start at $120 double and one-bedrooms from $145 double. Add $45 for each additional person.

JACK & TOM'S CONDOS OR COTTAGE

✉ *Maui Suncoast Realty, 2837 Panepoo, Kihei, HI 96753*   ☎ *808-874-1048, 800-800-8608*
📠 *808-879-6932*   ✇ *www.mauisuncoast.com, mauijack@aol.com*

For gay-friendly accommodations, you can either stay at Jack & Tom's Condos or Cottage or they can direct you to any of the other facilities they manage. All condos have air conditioning; all have cable TV, ceiling fans and kitchen and laundry facilities. Prices range roughly from $80 to $200

ANDREA'S MAUI CONDOS

✉ *P.O. Box 10799, Truckee, CA 96162*   ☎ *800-289-1522*   ✇ *www.mauicondos.com,*
andrea@mauicondos.com

Another booking agency with both a straight and gay clientele, Andrea's has one-, two- and three-bedroom oceanfront condos (priced from $125 to $875) surrounded by lush gardens. Amenities include tennis courts, a pool, a jacuzzi, a sauna and a putting green.

DINING

Kihei
STELLA BLUES CAFÉ & DELICATESSEN

$$–$$$ DINER   ✉ *Azeka Place II, 1279 South Kihei Road, Kihei*   ☎ *808-874-3779*
📠 *808-879-3037*   ✇ *www.stellablues.com*

At Stella Blues, you can dine indoors or outside beneath a sidewalk umbrella. The bill of fare includes vegetarian dishes, pastas and sandwiches. Breakfast, lunch and dinner.

ROYAL THAI CUISINE

$ THAI   ✉ *Azeka Place Shopping Center, 1280 South Kihei Road, Kihei*
☎ *808-874-0813*

If you'd like something from Southeast Asia, stop here. The chairs are wood and the menu includes *dozens* of selections such as crab legs, chili shrimp, cashew chicken or seafood combinations. No lunch on Sunday.

VIETNAMESE CUISINE

$$ VIETNAMESE   ✉ *Azeka Place I, 1280 South Kihei Road, Kihei*   ☎ *808-875-2088*
Although its name isn't very original, the food is. Choose from wraps

filled with chicken, pork, shrimp or beef, vegetarian entrées and such authentic dishes as the claypot specials, which feature meat or fish simmered in tasty broths.

THAILAND CUISINE

$$ THAI ✉1819 South Kihei Road, Kihei ☎808-875-0839 📠808-874-8961

What makes this place stand out among the island's Thai restaurants is the ambience. Lush green plants, hand-woven textiles and hand-embroidered silks are everywhere. The dishes are an enticing combination of traditional Thai favorites made with island produce. The chef uses an imaginative blend of spices, herbs, roots and leaves to enhance the natural flavors of the key ingredients, like chicken, beef or shrimp. The Vegetarian Lovers selections are actually vegan. No lunch on Sunday; dinner is served nightly.

SANSEI SEAFOOD RESTAURANT AND SUSHI BAR

$$–$$$ JAPANESE-PACIFIC RIM ✉Kihei Town Center, 1881 South Kihei Road, Kihei ☎808-879-0004

It's easy to run up a tab at a sushi bar, unless you happen to be dining at this spot where discounts are the order of the day. You'll receive 25 percent off your food if you dine between 5:30 and 6 p.m. Tuesday through Saturday and 50 percent off when eating from 5 to 6 p.m. Sunday and Monday or 10 p.m. to 1 a.m. on Thursday, Friday and Saturday nights. At those prices, it's easy to load up on traditional sushi—with a few nods to local ingredients, such as mangoes and Kula greens—or try one of the entrées, which are a blend of Japanese and Pacific Rim cuisine.

ALEXANDER'S FISH, CHICKEN & CHIPS

$–$$ SEAFOOD ✉1913 South Kihei Road, Kihei ☎808-874-0788 📠808-875-0535

A perennial favorite that keeps folks coming back because the food is so *ono* is Alexander's, which faces Kihei Road in Kalama Village. It's a casual, open-air café that serves savory, lightly battered island fish. Choose from *ahi*, *ono* or mahimahi, with cole slaw and french fries or rice. Chicken and ribs are also on the menu. Take-out is a plus for condo vacationers.

BADA BING RESTAURANT & RAT PACK LOUNGE

$$ ITALIAN ✉1945 South Kihei Road, Kihei ☎808-875-0188 📠808-875-4508

Bada-boom, bada-bing, it's a beautiful thing! (Or so Brooklynites say.) Any way you say it, Bada Bing is a great find. Tucked into the colorful ramshackle buildings of Kihei's Kalama Village, this establishment's interior is spacious, with an outdoor lanai under huge shade trees. House specialties like chicken marsala or piccata are good choices, as is the shrimp scampi. Antipasti offerings include spinach, artichoke and roasted garlic dip with croutons. After dinner, swing into the Rat Pack Lounge Wednesday through Saturday nights.

SURFSIDE SPIRITS AND DELI

$ DELI ✉1993 South Kihei Road, Kihei ☎808-879-1385

This place has a take-out delicatessen serving sandwiches, salads and slaw, as well as plate lunches.

THE SPORTS PAGE GRILL & BAR

$ AMERICAN ✉2411 South Kihei Road, Kihei ☎808-879-0602 ☏808-874-9078

The hot dogs here—like the Boston Red Sox version topped with baked beans and cheese—pay tribute to baseball teams. The sandwiches immortalize famous sports stars. There's the Bonnie Blair ham, Yogi Berra corned beef and cheese and Fred Couples Par 3 club.

DA KITCHEN EXPRESS

$ LOCAL-STYLE/PLATE LUNCHES ✉2439 South Kihei Road, Kihei ☎808-875-7782

For genuine local-style tastes in a clean, inviting diner, stop here in the Rainbow Mall. They offer a variety of dishes that represent the different ethnicities that make up the population of Hawaii. Plate lunches, which are composed of a hot entrée, two scoops of white rice and macaroni, potato or green salad, are the way to go. Teriyaki beef and chicken *katsu* are favorites, as are the traditionally Hawaiian dishes *laulau* and *kalua* pork. Breakfast, lunch and dinner.

GREEK BISTRO

$$–$$$ MEDITERRANEAN ✉Kai Nani Village, 2511 South Kihei Road, Kihei ☎808-879-9330

Did you say Greek? No problem. Located near the Rainbow Mall is this bistro with a full selection of Mediterranean dishes such as moussaka, souvlaki, lamb kebabs and dolmas. Dinner only.

FIVE PALMS BEACH GRILL

$$$$ HAWAII REGIONAL ✉Mana Kai Maui Resort, 2960 South Kihei Road, Kihei ☎808-879-2607 ☏808-874-4803 ✐www.fivepalmsrestaurant.com, fivepalmsres@cs.com

The Five Palms Beach Grill's open-air views of the coast combined with a Hawaii Regional–style menu draw a lively crowd that toasts and dines its way through sunset. The casual atmosphere belies the sophisticated cuisine, which includes dishes such as wok-fried *opakapaka* with curry sauce and jasmine rice and *Pulehu* rack of lamb. Five Palms is also open for breakfast and lunch.

Wailea

TOMMY BAHAMA'S TROPICAL CAFÉ

$$$$ AMERICAN/CARIBBEAN ✉3750 Wailea Alanui, Wailea ☎808-875-9983 ☏808-875-1398 ✐www.tommybahama.com

A visit to Tommy Bahama's is like a walk into a 1940s movie set on a South Seas island. You'll find soft green wainscoting, bold tropical fabrics and fresh tropical flowers beneath gently rotating ceiling fans. An open-air lanai invites relaxation, especially with a cocktail from the

Bungalow Bar. The menu is more of a tribute to the restaurant's Florida roots. There are Caribbean-style names for the dishes, such as Mama Bahama's Jerk Chicken Sandwich and Salmon St. Croix. But the quality of the cuisine is excellent, and the desserts are to die for.

CHEESEBURGER ISLAND STYLE

$$ AMERICAN   ✉3750 Wailea Alanui, Wailea   ✆808-874-8990   ✆808-875-6640
🖱www.cheeseburgerland.com

A fun and casual restaurant at The Shops at Wailea is this spot for cheeseburgers. It's a sister restaurant to Lahaina's Cheeseburgers in Paradise. Along with a familiar decor of tropical prints, bamboo and co-conut wood, this Cheeseburger also sports a Hawaiian memorabilia and logo shop. The owners think they provide the best cheeseburger on the island and I have to agree—it's juicy and delectable, and comes with sautéed onions on a sesame-seed bun. The "Beef-Less in Wailea" veggie burgers are worth a try, too.

CAFÉ KULA

$–$$ AMERICAN   ✉ 3850 Wailea Alanui, Wailea   ✆808-875-1234   ✆808-874-2478

This café at the Grand Wailea Resort has a terrace dining area that offers light, healthy breakfast, lunch and dinner choices. Start the day with a breakfast burrito, quiche, smoothie or pastries. For lunch try the margherita pizza or caesar salad served with chicken or *ahi*.

Makena
HAKONE

$$$–$$$$ JAPANESE   ✉Maui Prince Hotel, 5400 Makena Alanui, Makena
✆808-874-1111   ✆808-879-8763

This is the kind of restaurant you'd expect to find at any self-respecting Japanese-owned resort. The shoji screens, Japanese fans and a sushi bar are authentic; the ocean views are entirely Hawaiian. Start with tempura or miso soup. Entrées include sashimi, sukiyaki and New York steak. Better yet, go on Saturday night when they have the Japanese buffet and try a little bit of everything. Outstanding. Reservations are required. Dinner only. Closed Sunday and Monday.

PRINCE COURT

$$$–$$$$ HAWAII REGIONAL   ✉5400 Makena Alanui, Makena
✆808-874-1111, 808-875-5888

A tranquil oceanfront setting makes the Prince Court the place to enjoy Hawaiian regional cuisine. At this signature restaurant in the Maui Prince Hotel, you can choose from a seasonally chang-ing menu that may begin with *panko*-crusted crab cakes, oysters on the half shell or warm lobster and grapefruit salad. The bill of fare continues with such dishes as tempura-crusted *ahi* with gin-ger butter or seafood mixed grill (tiger shrimp, catch of the day, lobster and scallops). Tropical foliage adds to the elegance. Dinner only except for Sunday brunch.

SHOPPING

Shopping in Kihei is centered in the malls and doesn't hold a lot of promise. You'll find swimwear shops and an assortment of other clothing outlets, but nothing with style and panache. Foremost among the malls is **Azeka Place Shopping Center**, which stretches along the 1200 South block of Kihei Road.

Kihei

MAUI CLOTHING COMPANY'S OUTLET STORE ✉*Kihei Gateway Plaza, 362 Huku Lii Place #106, Kihei* ☎*808-879-0374* You're likely to find a bargain or two at this outlet store if resortwear and Maui logowear are your thing. There's plenty to choose from.

KALAMA VILLAGE SHOPPING CENTER ✉*1941 South Kihei Road, Kihei* An open-air market with about 20 vendors, this is a funky counterpoint to Kihei's other shopping spots. Here you'll find T-shirts, shells, jewelry and souvenirs sold at cut-rate prices by local people. If you're a Kona coffee fan, check out the **Bad Ass Coffee Company** (808-877-5477). There are flavorful blends, pure mild Kona and hearty roasts.

If you don't find what you're searching for at any of these addresses, there are countless other strip malls along Kihei Road.

Wailea

THE SHOPS AT WAILEA ✉*3750 Wailea Alanui, Wailea* ☎*808-891-6770* In the already posh Wailea resort, is this center of elegance. With the look of a Mediterranean seaside village, complete with water fountains, the center is home to several shop-'til-you-drop possibilities. The Shops are comprised of two wings at two levels, and the storefronts lining the East Wing parallel the likes of Rodeo Drive and 5th Avenue. Notable jewelry stores include the Maui-based **Bernard Passman Gallery**. Speaking of art, Wailea boasts galleries galore—**Lahaina Galleries**, **Dolphin Galleries**, **Ki'i Gallery**, **Wyland Galleries**, **Elan Vital Galleries** and **Celebrités**. Complimentary shuttles run from Wailea hotels to The Shops every 30 minutes.

HANA KA LIMA
✉*3700 Wailea Alanui, Wailea* ☎*808-879-1922*
A wonderful place to buy high-quality handicrafts is this market held in the lobby of the Wailea Marriott every Friday from 9 a.m. to 2 p.m. Artists and craftspeople from around the island sell a variety of crafts including stone carvings, paintings, bead jewelry, and scrimshaw. Some artists even demonstrate their skills.

NAPUA GALLERY ✉*3860 Wailea Alanui, Suite 210, Wailea* ☎*808-874-0510* ☎*808-874-2522* 🖳*www.napuagallery.com, napuagallery@earthlink.net* The Grand Wailea Resort Hotel & Spa is home to a $30 million art collection. At the

NaPua Gallery, you can see original Warhol paintings and original Picasso lithographs. Available for purchase are paintings, mixed-media works and sculpture by leading contemporary artists of Hawaii.

MANDALAY IMPORTS ⌂3900 Wailea Alanui, Wailea ☎808-874-5111 Here you'll find Thai silk, designer dresses, lacquer chests and Chinese opera coats. This shop in the Four Seasons Resort at Wailea also sells innovative necklaces and ceramic vases, and carries fashions by Joseph Ribkoff and fabrics by Anne Namba, a famous Honolulu designer.

NIGHTLIFE

KIHEI KALAMA VILLAGE ⌂1913 South Kihei Road, Kihei Bar hoppers and pub crawlers will love this village, a souvenir bazaar by day and busy bar scene by night. Seven bars, each with a different personality, are clustered here, including the raucous **Life's a Beach** (808-891-8010), the stately **Tastings Wine Bar & Grill** (808-879-8711) and the Polynesian-style **South Shore Tiki Lounge** (808-874-6444).

RAT PACK LOUNGE ⌂1945 South Kihei Road, Kihei ☎808-875-0188 Get your laugh on at this lounge with their Friday-night comedy shows.

SUNSET TERRACE LOUNGE ⌂3550 Wailea Alanui, Wailea ☎808-879-4900 This lounge, located at the Renaissance Wailea Beach, is a pleasant spot to see live Hawaiian entertainment when day turns to night.

KUMU BAR AND GRILL

⌂3700 Wailea Alanui, Wailea ☎808-879-1922 Live Hawaiian entertainment is a nightly feature at this Wailea Marriott bar. Come for dinner or have a drink poolside as you enjoy an appealing island show.

FERRAROS ⌂3900 Wailea Alanui, Wailea ☎808-874-8000 This venue at the Four Seasons Resort Maui at Wailea features live Italian music perfectly timed for enjoying a sunset drink.

MOLOKINI LOUNGE

⌂Maui Prince Hotel, 5400 Makena Alanui, Makena ☎808-874-1111 Sip a tropical cocktail and enjoy a live hula show at this resort lounge.

BEACHES & PARKS

KIHEI BEACH
This narrow, palm-fringed beach that runs from Maalaea Bay to Kihei can be seen from several points along Kihei Road and is accessible from the highway. The entire stretch is dotted with small parks and picnic areas and doesn't actually go by a specific name. There are buildings and numerous condominiums along this strip, but few large crowds on the beach. Beach joggers take note: You can run for miles along this unbroken strand, but watch for heavy winds

in the afternoon. Shallow weed-ridden waters make for poor swimming and only fair snorkeling (you'll find better at Kamaole beaches). For those anglers in the crowd, bonefish, *papio*, mullet, goatfish, *ulua*, *moano* and mountain bass are all caught here. There are picnic tables and restrooms at Kihei Memorial Park, which is midway along the beach.

KALAMA EXTENSION PARK
✉ *On South Kihei Road, across from Kihei Town Center*

This is a long, broad park (36 acres) that has an ample lawn but very little beach. Rather than lapping along the sand, waves wash up against a stone seawall. Backdropped by Haleakala, Kalama has stunning views of West Maui, Lanai and Kahoolawe. The in-line skating rink features a view so compelling you could easily lose concentration and run into a fellow skater. This park is an excellent place for a picnic but, before you pack your lunch, remember that it, like all Kihei's beaches, is swept by afternoon winds. For surfers there are summer breaks over a coral reef; left and right slides. Snorkeling and fishing are fair; swimming is poor. There are picnic areas, restrooms, a shower and tennis courts.

KAMAOLE BEACH PARKS (I, II AND III)
✉ *On South Kihei Road near Kihei Town Center*

Strung like beads along the Kihei shore are these three beautiful beaches. Their white sands are fringed with grass and studded with trees. With Haleakala in the background, they all offer magnificent views of the West Maui Mountains, Lanai and Kahoolawe—and all are windswept in the afternoon. Each has picnic areas, restrooms, lifeguard and showers. Swimming is very good on all three beaches. The best snorkeling is near the rocks ringing Kamaole III. Goatfish is the main catch for anglers.

KEAWAKAPU BEACH
✉ *On South Kihei Road between Kihei and Wailea*

Ho hum, yet another beautiful white-sand beach... Like other nearby parks, Keawakapu has marvelous views of the West Maui Mountains and Lanai, but is plagued by afternoon winds. The half-mile-long beach is bordered on both ends by lava points. The swimming is good, but Keawakapu is not as well protected as the Kamaole beaches. Snorkelers explore the area around the rocks. The fishing is excellent. There are no facilities except showers.

MOKAPU AND ULUA
✉ *On Makena Alanui in Wailea between the Grand Wailea Resort and the Four Seasons Resort at Wailea*

These are two crescent-shaped beaches fringed with palms and looking out toward Lanai and Kahoolawe. Much of their natural beauty has been spoiled by the nearby hotels and condominiums. The beaches have landscaped miniparks and are popular with bodysurfers. Swimming and snorkeling are both good; restrooms and a shower are available.

WAILEA BEACH
✉ *In Wailea on Makena Alanui, adjacent to the Renaissance Wailea Beach Resort*

Another lovely white-sand strip, once fringed with *kiawe* trees, is now dominated by two very large, very upscale resorts, part of the ultramodern Wailea development here. Swimming is good (the beach is also popular with bodysurfers) and so is snorkeling. Restrooms and showers are available.

POLO BEACH

✉ *Off Makena Alanui on Kaukahi Road in Wailea, adjacent to the Kea Lani Hotel*

Though not quite as attractive as Wailea Beach, Polo still has a lot to offer. There's a bountiful stretch of white sand and great views of Kahoolawe and Molokini. The beach, popular with bodysurfers, has a landscaped minipark with picnic tables, restrooms and showers. Swimming is good here and the snorkeling is excellent.

POOLENALENA (OR PAIPU) BEACH PARK

✉ *On Makena Alanui about one-and-one-fifth mile before (north of) the Maui Prince Hotel*

Once known by locals as Chang's Beach, this is a lovely white-sand strand that has been transformed into an attractive facility frequented by people from throughout the area. The beach has restrooms; unfortunately it also has as its neighbor the Maui Prince Hotel. Swimming is good, snorkeling fair and fishing very good—many species are caught here.

BLACK SANDS BEACH OR ONEULI BEACH

✉ *On Makena Alanui, four-fifths mile past the Maui Prince Hotel. Turn right on the dirt road at the north end of Red Hill, then bear right and go one-third mile to the beach.*

This is a long, narrow, salt-and-pepper beach located just north of Red Hill, a shoreline cinder cone. Fringed with *kiawe* trees, this stretch of beach is less attractive but more secluded than nearby Makena and much rockier. Facilities are nonexistent. Swimming and snorkeling are both fair, but the fishing is very good, many species being caught here.

There is unofficial camping but it's illegal and not recommended.

MAKENA STATE BEACH

✉ *From Wailea Shopping Village, go about four-and-one-half miles south on Makena Alanui. Turn right into the parking lot.*

Much more than a beach, Makena is an institution. Over the years, it's been a countercultural gathering place. There are even stories about rock stars jamming here during Makena's heyday in the early 1970s. Once a hideaway for hippies, today the beach is increasingly popular with mainstream tourists. So far, in my mind, this long, wide corridor of white sand curving south from Red Hill is still the most beautiful beach on Maui. On the strand in front of the Maui Prince, morning snorkeling excursions on the southern side bring you close up and personal with sea turtles and exotic coral. Watch the swells. They can get dicey. There are toilets.

LITTLE BEACH (PUU OLAI BEACH OR "BABY BEACH")

✉ *Follow Makena Alanui for about four-and-one-half miles south from Wailea Shopping Village. Watch for Red Hill, the large cinder cone on your right. Just past Red Hill, turn right into the parking lot for Makena Beach. From here a path leads over Red Hill to Little Beach.*

🏊 🏄 🤿 ⛺ This pretty stretch of white sand next to Makena Beach, just across Red Hill, is a nude beach. It's also popular with the island's gay crowd. But if you go nude here or at Makena, watch out for police; they regularly bust nudists. Swimming is good (bodysurfing is especially good here) and you can snorkel near the rocks at the north end of the beach. The fishing is fair, though access is difficult. Beware of strong currents. There are no facilities.

⛺ Camping, though unofficial, is very popular here, but beware of thieves.

KAHULUI–WAILUKU AREA

The island, the commercial, civic and population center in the adjoining towns of Kahului and Wailuku. With no clear dividing place, these two municipalities seem at first glance to be "twin towns." They drift into one another as you climb uphill from Kahului Harbor toward the mountains. Kahului is significantly younger than its neighbor, however, and focuses its daily life around commerce. Back in 1890, when it was Maui's largest town, Kahului was deliberately destroyed by fire to kill rats that were spreading an epidemic of bubonic plague. Maui's main airport is here, together with a skein of shopping malls and a few hotels that line a blue-collar waterfront. Wailuku presents a more rolling terrain and is the seat of government for Maui County.

SIGHTS

Kahului

With its bustling harbor and busy shopping complexes, this town offers little to the sightseer. The piers along the waterfront, lined with container-cargo ships and weekly cruise ships, are the embarkation point for Maui's sugar and pineapple crops. Established as a sugar town more than a century ago, Kahului has a commercial feel about it.

KANAHA POND WILDLIFE SANCTUARY

Coming from the airport along Kaahumanu Avenue (Route 32), you can stop and wander through this wildlife sanctuary. Once a royal fishpond, this is now an important bird refuge, especially for the rare Hawaiian stilt and Hawaiian coot. There are two one-mile loop roads through the reserve (closed during breeding sea-

HIDDEN LISTINGS

IAO VALLEY STATE MONUMENT

PAGE 324

Moss-mantled cliffs surrounding a sacred royal burial ground, once off-limits to all but the *alii*

HAWAII NATURE CENTER

PAGE 322

Interactive museum where environmental educators lead daily hikes into stunning Iao Valley

KEPANIWAI COUNTY PARK AND HERITAGE GARDENS

PAGES 322, 329

Romantic picnic spot and Japanese gardens with arched bridges, pagodas and coconut grove

SAM SATO'S

PAGE 326

Genuine local eats, featuring *manju* (a bean cake pastry), dry *mein* (a noodle-dish) and classic *saimin*

son, April through August); a permit from the State Division of Forestry is required to hike the trails. The observation area is open year-round.

Wailuku

The highway leads uphill to this historic town, Maui's administrative center. Older and more interesting than Kahului, Wailuku sits astride the foothills of the West Maui Mountains at the entrance to Iao Valley. A mix of woodframe plantation houses and suburban homes, it even boasts a multi-story civic building.

HAPPY VALLEY For a short tour of the aging woodfront quarter, take a right on Market Street and follow it several blocks to Happy Valley. This former red-light district still retains the charm, if not the action, of a bygone era. Here you'll discover narrow streets and tinroof houses framed by the sharply rising, deeply creased face of the West Maui Mountains.

KAAHUMANU CONGREGATIONAL CHURCH ✉*103 South High Street, Wailuku* ☎*808-244-5189* Just across the road from the county government buildings rests this picturesque church. Queen Kaahumanu attended services here in 1832 when the church was a grass shack, and requested that the first permanent church be named after her. Now Maui's oldest church, this grand stone-and-plaster structure was constructed in 1876, and has been kept in excellent condition for its many visitors. With a lofty white spire, it is the area's most dramatic man-made landmark.

BAILEY HOUSE MUSEUM ✉*2375-A Main Street* ✆*808-244-3326* 🖫*www. mauimuseum.org, baileyh@aloha.net* Near Main Street, you'll find this museum, run by the Maui Historical Society. Lodged in the dwelling of a former missionary, the displays include 19th-century Hawaiian artifacts, remnants from the early sugar cane industry and period pieces from the missionary years. This stone-and-plaster house (started in 1833) has walls 20 inches thick and beams fashioned from hand-hewn sandalwood. Together with an adjoining seminary building, it harkens back to Wailuku's days as an early center of Western culture. Closed Sunday. Admission.

PAPER AIRPLANE MUSEUM ✉*Maui Mall, 70 East Kaahumanu Avenue, Kahului* ✆*808-877-8916* An unusual place, this museum features the world's largest collection of paper airplanes. On display are some 2500 models, ranging from the size of a postage stamp to crafts with wing spans of six feet, along with exhibits that depict Hawaii's aviation history. The gift shop has some fun items, too. Closed Sunday.

KEPANIWAI COUNTY PARK AND HERITAGE GARDENS

Up the road from the Paper Airplane Museum, there's an outdoor cultural showcase to discover. Backdropped by Iao Valley's adze-like peaks, this adult playground features lovely Japanese and Chinese monuments as well as a taro patch. There are arched bridges, a pool and an Oriental garden. The houses of Hawaii's many cultural groups are represented by a Hawaiian grass hut, New England saltbox (complete with white picket fence), Filipino bamboo house and a Portuguese villa. On this site in 1790 Kamehameha's forces overwhelmed the army of a Maui chief in a battle so terrible that the corpses blocking Iao Stream gave Kepaniwai ("damming of the waters") and Wailuku ("bloody river") their names.

HAWAII NATURE CENTER

✉*875 Iao Valley Road* ✆*808-244-6500* 📠*808-244-6525* 🖫*www.hawaii naturecenter.org* After exploring Kepaniwai County Park and Heritage Gardens, continue up to the Nature Center, situated on the edge of Iao Valley, off the gateway to Iao Valley State Monument. It features an interactive nature museum designed for adults as well as children. The Nature Center also hosts hikes every day into the Iao Valley, complete with environmental educators. Admission.

JOHN F. KENNEDY PROFILE Uphill from the Nature Center you'll see Hawaii's answer to Mt. Rushmore, chiseled by nature. Ironically,

Kahului-Wailuku Area

323

6 MAUI KAHULUI-WAILUKU AREA SIGHTS

PACIFIC OCEAN

Kahului Airport

Kanaha Pond Wildlife Sanctuary

Kanaha Ponds

36

Pulehu Rd

Hansen Rd

370

Haleakala Hwy

Hana Hwy

Amala Pl

Keolani Pl

36A

Alamana St

Papa Rd

Dairy Rd

Hulilki St

Hoohana St

36

32A Hobron Ave

Puunene Ave

350

West Papa Ave

311

Alexander & Baldwin Sugar Museum

Puunene

Kuihelani Hwy

380

Maluhia St

Wharf St

32

Lono Ave

Ave

Lono Ave

Kamehameha Ave

KAHULUI-WAILUKU AREA SIGHTS

Kahului Bay

Kahului Harbor

Hoaloha Park

340 Rd

Kahului

Wakea Ave

Kea St

Arno St

Maalo St

Onehee St

South Papa Ave

0   0.5 mile
0   0.5 kilometer

N

Kahului Beach Rd

Kanaloa Ave

Kaahumanu Ave

Kaahumanu Congregational Church

Mahalani St

Waiale Reservoirs

Waiehu Beach Rd

340

Lower Main St

Iao Stream

Wailuku

Mill St

Pualani Rd

Halekii & Pihana Kalani Heiaus

to Waihee

330

Kahekili Hwy

Market St

Vineyard St

Main St

Wells St

Iao

HAPPY VALLEY

320

Tropical Gardens of Maui

to Iao Valley

Bailey House Museum

Keanu St

Kaohu St

Koa Dr

Waiale Rd

Honoapiilani Hwy

Hopoi Village

Hopoi Reservoir

this geologic formation, which bears an uncanny resemblance to the former president, was never noticed until after his assassination.

IAO VALLEY STATE MONUMENT

Surrounded by those same moss-mantled cliffs, Iao Valley provides an excellent view of **Iao Needle**, a single spire that rises to a point 1200 feet above the valley (and 2250 feet above sea level). With the possible exception of Haleakala Crater, this awesome peak is Maui's most famous landmark. A basalt core that has withstood the ravages of erosion, the "Needle" and mist-filled valley have long been a place of pilgrimage for Hawaiians. In ancient times the area was set aside by the ruling chiefs as a sacred site, off limits to commoners. Kakae, the ruler of Maui in the late 1400s, declared the valley the sacred burial place of Hawaiian royalty. It is said that the bones of many of the chiefs were concealed in caves to prevent their enemies from stealing them. In fact, it was *kapu* (prohibited) for anyone other than the *alii* to venture up the valley, except during the Makahiki festival, when Iao Needle was used as an altar. Nowadays, you can join the spirits of the *alii* and enter the valley. Be sure to explore the paths from the parking lot that lead across Iao Stream and up to a vista point. Appreciate your visit here: In ancient times the sacred area around the Iao Valley, which translates to "Valley of Dawning Inspiration" or "Supreme Light," was off limits to commoners. When you take a walk through the area you will understand why it is so precious for Hawaiians.

LODGING

The hotel strip in the harbor town of Kahului lies along the beach on Kahului Bay.

Kahului
MAUI SEASIDE HOTEL
$$ 187 ROOMS   ✉ *100 West Kaahumanu Avenue, Kahului* ✆ *808-877-3311, 800-560-5552* 🖷 *808-877-4618* 🖱 *www.mauiseasidehotel.com, info@mauiseasidehotel.com*
This family-owned hotel consists of two separate complexes sitting beside each other along Kaahumanu Avenue (Route 32). There is a pool, restaurant and lounge. Rooms in the older poolside wing are a bit less expensive: clean, but lacking in decorative flair, the surroundings are quite adequate. Just a few well-spent dollars more places you in a larger, more attractive room in a newer complex, which has more upscale appointments. Both facilities feature phones, TVs, refrigerators and air conditioning. Some include kitchenettes. Ask about discounts.

MAUI BEACH HOTEL
$$–$$$ 147 ROOMS   ✉ *170 Kaahumanu Avenue, Kahului* ✆ *808-877-0051, 888-649-3222* 🖷 *808-242-0865*
With its air-conditioned guest rooms done in tropical decor, this is

about as inexpensive as things get on Maui. While conveniently located in Kahului, it is not your made-in-paradise setting, with "oceanfront" meaning the waters of Kahului Harbor. The grounds are appealingly studded with palms, and there is a pleasant pool area with a small adjacent beach, plus two restaurants and a sundries and snack shop. The attitude is island-style friendly.

Wailuku
ALOHA NORTH SHORE HOSTEL

$ 10 UNITS   ⊠ *2080 West Vineyard Street, Wailuku*   ℡ *808-986-8095, 866-946-7835*
℡ *808-242-0865*   ✑ *www.northshorehostel.com, info@northshorehostel.com*

Another clean, trim hostel-cum-hotel with shared rooms and private singles or doubles is found here. There are laundry and kitchen facilities, as well as free high-speed wireless internet access; baths are shared. Your seventh night is free, and there is complimentary airport shuttle service.

BANANA BUNGALOW

$ 38 ROOMS   ⊠ *310 North Market Street, Wailuku*   ℡ *808-244-5090, 800-846-7835*
℡ *808-244-3678*   ✑ *www.mauihostel.com, info@mauihostel.com*

A kind of resort for low-budget travelers, this hotel/hostel caters to windsurfers, surfers and adventurers. It offers a jacuzzi, garden and fruit trees, internet access, cable TV and movies. The folks here conduct their own free tours and have a free airport drop-off. There are laundry facilities and a community kitchen and, of course, hammocks.

THE OLD WAILUKU INN AT ULUPONO

$$$ 10 ROOMS   ⊠ *2199 Kahookele Street, Wailuku*   ℡ *808-244-5987, 800-305-4899*
℡ *808-242-9600*   ✑ *www.mauiinn.com, mauibandb@aol.com*

Built by a wealthy island banker as a wedding gift for his daughter-in-law, this "queen" of historic homes reflects the Hawaii of past generations. The theme of Ulupono and its landscaped grounds are a tribute to Hawaii's poet laureate of the 1920s and '30s, Don Blanding. There are seven individually decorated bedrooms dedicated to an island flower or plant, each with a matching Hawaiian quilt and its own bath. Common areas are the breakfast room, living room, and library, which holds all of Don Blanding's books. The Vagabond's House offers three more lavish rooms. The plantation era at its gentle best.

DINING

Kahului
MAUI MALL

$ CHINESE/DESSERT   ⊠ *70 East Kaahumanu Avenue*   ℡ *808-871-1307*
✑ *www.mauimall.com*

The best place in Kahului for a quick, inexpensive meal is at one of several shopping arcades along Kaahumanu Avenue (Route 32). For common fare, head over to the Maui Mall. Here you can drop in at **Siu's Chinese Kitchen** (808-871-0828), where they serve three meals a day. To round off the calorie count, you can try a cup of *guri guri* sherbet at **Tasaka Guri Guri Shop** (808-871-4513).

MARCO'S GRILL & DELI

$$–$$$ ITALIAN   ✉*444 Hana Highway, Kahului* ☎*808-877-4446* 📠*808-873-0011*

The white booths and black-tile tables are an appealing touch at Marco's. So is the attention to detail at this family-operated Italian restaurant. They blend their own coffee and grind their own meat for sausages and meatballs. The result is a menu that ranges from chocolate cinnamon French toast at breakfast to submarine sandwiches and vodka rigatoni later in the day. In addition to pasta entrées, they serve seafood dishes.

RAINBOW DINING ROOM

$$$ JAPANESE/AMERICAN   ✉*170 Kaahumanu Avenue, Kahului* ☎*808-877-0051* 📠*808-871-5797*

Overlooking the pool, this spacious open-air restaurant in the Maui Beach Hotel serves a Japanese buffet; breakfast features American cuisine. The former includes shrimp tempura, scallops, mixed vegetables, yakitori chicken, teriyaki steak, many different types of Japanese salad and a host of other dishes. No lunch.

KAU KAU CORNER FOOD COURT

$ INTERNATIONAL   ✉*270 Dairy Road, Kahului* ☎*808-877-2400*

Stop here for a variety of foods at reasonable prices. You'll find a sushi restaurant, a shop that sells noodles, excellent Vietnamese food and sandwiches at **Ba Le** (808-661-5566) and the best of the bunch, **Maui Ocean Grill** (808-893-0263), which serves fish and chips, hearty salads, plate lunches, grilled fish and yummy fried ice cream.

DOWN TO EARTH DELI & CAFÉ

$ VEGETARIAN   ✉*305 Dairy Road, Kahului* ☎*808-877-2661* 📠*808-877-7548*

Want something on the healthy side? This place serves veggie burgers, vegetarian subs and other heart-smart fare in the corner of a full-service natural foods supermarket.

BANGKOK CUISINE

$–$$ THAI   ✉*395 Dairy Road, Kahului* ☎*808-893-0026*

The promise here is "authentic Thai food," though their menu offers decidedly non-traditional food: Cornish game hen in a sauce of garlic and black pepper, eggplant beef, and evil prince shrimp, but their dining room does sport a more authentic vibe. Dinner on Sunday only.

Wailuku

SAM SATO'S

$ LOCAL-STYLE   ✉*1750 Wili Pa Loop, Wailuku* ☎*808-244-7124*

Up the road apiece in Wailuku there are numerous ethnic restaurants guaranteed to please both the palate and the purse. Sam's features local noodle dishes. Open for breakfast and lunch, it specializes in *manju* (a bean cake pastry), dry *mein* (a noodle dish) and the ubiquitous *saimin*. Closed Sunday.

SAENG'S THAI CUISINE

$–$$ THAI   ✉*2119 Vineyard Street, Wailuku* ☎*808-244-1567*

In a tropical garden setting, Saeng's sits in a beautifully designed building embellished with fine woodwork and adorned with Asian accoutrements. The menu, which lists three pages of dishes from Thailand, is like an encyclopedia of fine dining. Meals, which are served in the dining room or out on a windswept veranda, begin with *sateh* and spring rolls, venture on to dishes like the "evil prince" and "tofu delight," and end over tea and tapioca pudding. No lunch Saturday and Sunday.

A SAIGON CAFÉ

$–$$ VIETNAMESE ⌗*1792 Main Street, Wailuku* ☏*808-243-9560* 🖷*808-243-9566*
Though this café doesn't advertise itself with even a sign on the outside, business still flourishes. You'll find a small space inside, but a big menu that includes vegetarian, clay pot, seafood and even steak entrées.

TASTY CRUST

$–$$ AMERICAN ⌗*1770 Mill Street, Wailuku* ☏*808-244-0845* 🖷*808-242-7170*
This friendly eatery is famous for its breakfasts, especially pancakes, which it serves in the morning as well as at lunch and dinnertime. If you'd rather not have breakfast in the evening, try the hamburger steak plate. No dinner on Monday.

TOKYO TEI

$ JAPANESE ⌗*1063-E Lower Main Street, Suite C-101, Wailuku* ☏*808-242-9630*
Wailuku's low-rent district lies along Lower Main Street, where ethnic restaurants cater almost exclusively to locals. These are informal, family-owned, formica-and-naugahyde-chair cafés that serve good food at down-to-earth prices. You'll find Japanese food at Tokyo Tei. Closed Monday.

SHOPPING

Kahului

For everyday shopping needs, you should find the Kahului malls very convenient. Two sprawling centers are strung along Kaahumanu Avenue (Route 32).

MAUI POTATO CHIP FACTORY

⌗*295 Lalo Street, off Route 380, Kahului* ☏*808-877-3652* Always a favorite with locals, Maui potato chips have by now become a worldwide phenomenon. One of the most popular brands is "Kitch'n Cook'd," which is made at this family-owned and operated potato chip factory. This place has been around since the 1950s, annually increasing in popularity, and it now brings in orders from around the globe. These chips are hard to find in mainland stores, but you can stock up on them here where they're freshly made. No tours. Closed Sunday.

KAAHUMANU CENTER

⌗*275 Kaahumanu Avenue* This is Maui's most contemporary shopping mall, with **Macy's** (808-877-3361), **Sears** (808-877-2221), a photo studio, **Border's Express** (808-871-6112), boutiques, shoe stores, candy stores, a sundries shop and a jeweler.

MAUI SWAP MEET

⌗*South Puunene Street, next to the Kahului Post Office, Kahului* ☏*808-877-3100* Bargain hunters can find heaps of deals at this swap meet, held every Saturday morning from 7 a.m. to noon. It costs just 50 cents to peruse the booths packed with T-shirts, homemade food, aloha wear, music and all sorts of unusual goodies.

FUN FACTORY ✉70 East Kaahumanu Avenue, Kahului ☎808-872-4320 ✍www.mauimall.com If you have children in tow, take a break and head here. There are enough video games and other electronic attractions to keep them busy for hours.

SUMMERHOUSE BOUTIQUE ✉395 Dairy Road, Kahului ☎808-871-1320 This place might be called a chic dress shop. But they also sell jewelry and natural fiber garments.

Wailuku

Up in Wailuku, a tumbledown town with a friendly face, you'll find the little shops and solicitous merchants that we have come to associate with small-town America. Along North Market Street are several imaginative shops operated by low-key entrepreneurs.

GOTTING LTD. ✉34 North Market Street, Wailuku ☎ 808-244-7779 ✍www.gottingltd.com High-end oriental antiques, including a prized collection of Buddhas and estate pieces, are showcased here. Closed Sunday.

BROWN & KOBAYASHI ✉38 North Market Street, Wailuku ☎808-242-0804 This antique store specializes in rare pieces from the Orient.

BIRD OF PARADISE ✉56 North Market Street, Wailuku ☎808-242-7699 Check out this shop for collectible Hawaiiana including old records, sheet music, bric-a-brac and plantation-style furnishings. Closed Sunday.

MAUI HISTORICAL SOCIETY BAILEY HOUSE MUSEUM ✉2375-A Main Street, Wailuku ☎808-244-3326 Some of the island's most reasonably priced souvenirs are found at the historical society, located in the Bailey House Museum. Here you'll find an outstanding collection of local history books and art prints. *Koa* bookmarks and Maui-made soaps are also popular.

NIGHTLIFE

MEGAPLEX ✉Maui Mall, 70 East Kaahumanu Avenue, Kahului ☎808-249-2222 If you're in the mood for a movie, check out the offerings at this 12-screen complex.

ALE HOUSE ✉355 East Kamehameha Avenue, Kahului ☎808-877-9001 The crowd is mostly local at this tavern, which has live music most nights of the week. Call ahead to find out the current schedule.

BEACHES & PARKS

HOALOHA PARK
✉On Kaahumanu Avenue (Route 32), Kahului

🚶 🏖 ⚓ Located next to the Kahului hotels, this is one of Kahului's two beaches, but unfortunately the nearby harbor facilities detract from the natural beauty of its white sands. What with heavy boat traffic on one side and several hotels on the other, the park is not recommended. There are much better beaches in other areas of the island. Swimming and snorkeling are poor; surfers will find good breaks (two to six feet, with a left slide) off the jetty mouth near the north shore of

Kahului Harbor. It is, however, a good spot to beachcomb, particularly for Maui diamonds. Goatfish, *papio* and triggerfish can be hooked from the pier; *ulua* and *papio* are often caught along the shore.

KEPANIWAI COUNTY PARK AND HERITAGE GARDENS

⊠*In Wailuku on the road to Iao Valley*

🚶 This beautiful park is carefully landscaped and surrounded by sheer cliffs. You'll discover paths over arched bridges and through Japanese gardens, plus pagodas, a thatch-roofed hut, a taro patch and banana, papaya and coconut trees. An ideal and romantic spot for picnicking, it has picnic pavilions and restrooms.

WAIHEE BEACH PARK

⊠*Outside Wailuku on the rural road that circles the West Maui Mountains. To get there from Route 340 in Waiehu, turn right on Halewaiu Road and then take the beach access road from Waiehu Golf Course.*

🏊 🎣 🛶 This park is used almost exclusively by local residents. Bordered by a golf course and shaded with ironwood trees and *naupaka* bushes, it has a sandy beach and one of Maui's longest and widest reefs. There's a grassy area perfect for picnicking, established picnic areas and restrooms with showers. Beachcombing, *limu* gathering and fishing are all good. Swimming and snorkeling are okay, though the reef is rather shallow.

HANA HIGHWAY

The Hana Highway (Route 360), a smooth, narrow road running between Kahului and Hana, is one of the most beautiful drives in all Hawaii. Following the path of an ancient Hawaiian trail, it may in fact be one of the prettiest drives in the world. The road courses through a rainforest, a luxurious jungle crowded with ferns and African tulip trees, and leads to black-sand beaches and rain-drenched hamlets. The vegetation is so thick it seems to be spilling out from the mountainside in a cascade of greenery. You'll be traveling the windward side of Haleakala, hugging its lower slopes en route to a small Hawaiian town that receives 70 inches of rain a year.

There are over 600 twists and turns and 54 one-lane bridges along this adequately maintained paved road. It'll take at least three hours to drive the 51 miles to Hana. To make the entire circuit around the south coast, plan to sleep in Hana or to leave very early and drive much of the day. If you can, take your time—there's a lot to see.

SIGHTS

Paia

About seven miles east of Kahului, you'll pass the quaint, weather-beaten town of Paia. This old sugar plantation town, now a burgeoning artist colony and windsurfing mecca, has been painted in nursery col-

Kahului · JACQUES NORTHSHORE · Pauwela · Kailua

Hana Highway

ALOHA COTTAGES
HANA COAST GALLERY · Hana
RED SAND BEACH

JACQUES NORTHSHORE

Reasonably priced, exceptionally flavored Pacific Rim cuisine with a hint of the chef's French and Italian origins

ALOHA COTTAGES

Simple cottages perched among banana trees on a hillside overlooking picturesque Hana Bay

HANA COAST GALLERY

Native Hawaiian art, including beautiful serigraphs, model *koa* racing canoes and ceremonial objects

RED SAND BEACH

Lofty cliffs, a precarious hiking trail and one of the most secluded and exotic beaches in all the islands

ors. Along either of Paia's two main streets, plantation-era buildings have been freshly refurbished.

MANTOKUJI BUDDHIST TEMPLE On the eastern side of town this Buddhist temple celebrates the setting sun every day by sounding its huge gong.

HOOKIPA BEACH PARK One of the world's premier windsurfing spots can be found about three miles east of town. Brilliantly colored sails race along the horizon as windsurfers perform amazing acrobatic stunts, cartwheeling across the waves. The latest craze is kite surfing. You can watch riders "kite the surfzone," jump, jibe or ride upwind.

Within the next ten miles the roadway is transformed, as your slow, winding adventure begins. You'll drive past sugar cane fields, across verdant gorges, through valleys dotted with tumbledown cottages and along fern-cloaked hillsides.

TWIN FALLS Route 36 becomes Route 360, beginning a new series of mileage markers that are helpful in locating sites along the way. Near the two-mile marker, a short trail leads to this idyllic swimming hole (the path begins from the west side of the Hoolawa Stream bridge on the right side of the road).

HUELO A tiny "rooster town" (so named because nothing ever seems to be stirring except the roosters), Huelo is known for the **Kaulanapueo Church**. A coral chapel built in 1853, this New England–style sanctuary strikes a dramatic pose with the sea as a backdrop.

WAIKAMOI RIDGE Farther along the highway from Huelo you'll see picnic areas and a nature trail. Here you can visit a bamboo forest, learn about native vegetation and explore the countryside. Remember to bring mosquito repellent, especially if you're planning a rainforest hike.

PUOHOKAMOA FALLS ✉ *11-mile marker* Another picnic area is nestled beside a waterfall and large pool. If you packed a lunch, this is a perfect place to enjoy it. Trails above and below the main pool lead to other waterfalls.

KAUMAHINA STATE WAYSIDE ✉ *12-mile marker* A few zigzags beyond Puohokamoa Falls, you'll find a tree-studded park that overlooks Honomanu Gulch and Keanae Peninsula. From here the road descends the gulch, where a side road leads left to **Honomanu Bay** (14-mile marker) and its black-sand beach.

KEANAE ARBORETUM
✉ *16-mile marker* Above Keanae Peninsula, you'll pass this verdant arboretum. You can stroll freely through paved trails in these splendid tropical gardens, which feature many native Hawaiian plants including several dozen varieties of taro. Another section of the gardens is devoted to exotic tropical plants and there is a mile-long trail that leads into a natural rainforest.

KEANAE PENINSULA ✉ *17-mile marker* Just past the arboretum, turn left onto the road to the Keanae Peninsula. This rocky, windswept point offers stunning views of Haleakala. You'll pass rustic houses, a patchwork of garden plots and a coral-and-stone church built around 1860. A picture of serenity and rural perfection, Keanae is inhabited by native Hawaiians who still grow taro and pound poi. Their home is a lush rainforest—a quiltwork of taro plots, banana trees, palms—that runs to the rim of a ragged coastline.

WAILUA ✉ *18-mile marker* A side road descends to this Hawaiian agricultural and fishing village. Here is another luxurious checkerboard where taro gardens alternate with banana patches and the landscape is adorned with clapboard houses. The town is known for St. Gabriel's Church, a simple structure made completely of sand and coral, dating from 1870.

PUAAKAA STATE WAYSIDE ✉ *22-mile marker* Back on the main road, there's yet another picnic area and waterfall. The cascade tum-

Hana Highway

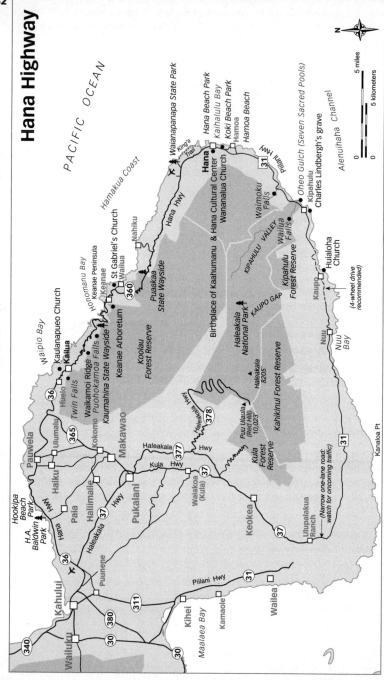

PACIFIC OCEAN

N

5 miles

5 kilometers

Waianapanapa State Park
Hana Beach Park
Kaihalulu Bay
Koki Beach Park
Hamoa
Hamoa Beach

King's Trail

Hana

Birthplace of Kaahumanu & Hana Cultural Center
Wananalua Church

Hana Hwy

Piilani Hwy

31

Oheo Gulch (Seven Sacred Pools)
Charles Lindbergh's grave
Kipahulu

Alenuihaha Channel

Hamakua Coast

Waimoku Falls
Wailua Falls

KIPAHULU VALLEY

Kipahulu
Forest Reserve

St Gabriel's Church
Wailua

Nahiku

Hana Hwy

Huialoha Church

Puaakaa State Wayside

Honomanu Bay
Keanae Peninsula
Keanae

360

Keanae Arboretum

Koolau Forest Reserve

Haleakala National Park

KAUPO GAP

Kaupo

Nuu

(4-wheel drive recommended)

Nuu Bay

Waipio Bay

Kaulanapueo Church
Kailua

Haleakala 8205

Kahikinui Forest Reserve

Twin Falls
Waikamoi Ridge   Puohokamoa Falls
Kaumahina State Wayside

36

Huelo

Kokomo

365

Ulumalu

Puu Ulaula (Red Hill) 10,023

Haleakala Hwy

378

Makawao

Pauwela

Kula Forest Reserve

Hookipa Beach Park

Haleakala   377   Hwy

Paia

Haiku

Kula   Hwy

Hwy

37

Waiakoa (Kula)

(Narrow one-lane road: watch for oncoming traffic)

Kanaloa Pt

H.A. Baldwin Park

36

Hana   Hwy

Hana

Haliimaile

Hwy

37

Pukalani

Hwy

Haleakala

Keokea

31

Utupalakua Ranch

37

Puunene

Kahului

340

Wailuku

380

311

Piilani   Hwy

31

Wailea

30

Kihei

Kamaole

30

Maalaea Bay

bles into a natural pool in a setting framed by eucalyptus and banana trees. Puaakaa means, by the way, "plenty of pigs."

NAHIKU

✉*25-mile marker* Past the wayside, another side road bumps three miles through this tiny picturesque town to a bluff overlooking the sea. The view spreads across three bays all the way back to Wailua. Directly below, the ocean pounds against rock outcroppings, spraying salt mist across a stunning vista. Set in one of the wettest spots along the entire coast, Nahiku village is inundated by rainforest and graced by yet another 19th-century church. America's first domestic rubber plantation opened in Nahiku in 1905. You can still see a few remaining rubber plants in the area.

KAHANU GARDEN

📞*808-248-8912* 📠*808-248-7210* 🖰*www.ntbg.org*
For a cultural treat, turn off Route 360 at Ulaino Road following the signs to this part of the National Tropical Botanical Gardens. The focus here is on native Hawaiian plants and culture. A highlight of the 90-minute tour is a look at the massive **Piilanihale heiau**, which overlooks a moody stretch of coast. The enormous platform (almost 160,000 square feet), built of moss- and algae-covered lava rocks, is the largest of the ancient *heiau* sites remaining in Hawaii. The power of the past can be felt here, especially with the soulful expertise that tour guides impart on a visit. The sense of authenticity makes this a true encounter with Polynesian Hawaii. You can visit the garden on a self-guided tour. Closed Saturday and Sunday. Admission.

WAIANAPANAPA STATE PARK Several miles before you reach Hana, be sure to stop here where you will find a black-sand beach and two lava tubes, **Waianapanapa** and **Waiomao caves**. Hawaiian mythology tells of a Hawaiian princess who hid from her cruel husband here, only to be discovered by him and slain. Now every spring the waters hereabouts are said to run red with her blood. Offshore are several sea arches, and nearby is a blowhole that spouts periodically.

HELANI FARM AND GARDENS ✉*Hana Highway* 📞*808-248-8274, 800-385-5241* 📠*808-248-8274* 🖰*bj4flowers@aol.com* Just before the town of Hana, on the right, is this sprawling oasis of tropical plant life. Only a section of the gardens is currently open to the public, but it's worth a stop as there's a wealth of flowering plants, trees and vines. You'll also find fruit trees, baobab trees, papyrus, ginger plants and even a carp pond. Visits by appointment only.

BLUE POOL As you approach the town of Hana, take the Ulaino Road turnoff going left and follow it to the end. You'll cross a streambed that empties into this pristine freshwater pool, named for the cobalt color of its icy water. There's limited parking just before the streambed in the grassy meadow (perfect for a quiet picnic); the pool is on the left.

HANA LAVA TUBE ✉ *P.O. Box 40, Hana, HI 96713* ☎ *808-248-7308* 🖥 *www.maui cave.com, info@mauicave.com* On your way to or from the pool along the same road, watch for the Hana Lava sign and make a point to visit the island's largest underground lava tube system, created from a flow 1000 years ago. Self-guided tours, lasting approximately 40 minutes, are available; no guided tours are offered. Visitors can also walk through the Red Ti botanical maze. Closed Sunday. Admission.

Hana

To reach this secluded hamlet, you can take the old Hawaiian shoreline trail (see the "Hiking" section at the end of this chapter) or continue on along the highway. This Eden-like town, carpeted with pandanus, taro and banana trees, sits above an inviting bay. Known as "heavenly Hana," it's a ranch town inhabited primarily by folks of Hawaiian ancestry. Because of its remote location it has changed little over the years. The rain that continually buffets Hana makes it a prime agricultural area and adds to the luxuriant, unsettling beauty of the place.

Because of its strategic location directly across from the Big Island, Hana was an early battleground in the wars between the chiefs of Maui and the Big Island, who conquered, lost and regained the region in a succession of bloody struggles. During the 19th century it became a sugar plantation, employing different ethnic groups who were brought in to work the fields. Then, in 1946, Paul Fagan, a San Francisco industrialist, bought 14,000 acres and created the Hana Ranch, turning the area into grazing land for Hereford cattle and opening the exclusive Hotel Hana-Maui. That year, Hana hosted the only mainland American baseball team ever to conduct spring training in Hawaii, when Fagan brought the Pacific Coast League's San Francisco Seals to the islands. Arriving with the players was a squadron of sportswriters who sent back glowing dispatches on "Heavenly Hana," helping to promote the destination and the Hotel Hana-Maui.

HANA BAY
Here you can stroll the beach, explore the wharf and take a short path along the water to a plaque that marks the **Birthplace of Kaahumanu**, King Kamehameha I's favorite wife and a key player in the 1819 overthrow of the ancestral Hawaiian religious system. To reach this sacred spot, pick up the trail leading from the boat landing on the right side of the bay. It leads along the base of **Kauiki Hill**, a cinder cone covered with ironwood trees that was the scene of fierce battles between Kahekili, the renowned Maui chief, and the Big Island chief Kalaniopuu.

MOUNT LYONS Near the Hotel Hana-Maui (where you can request a key to open the gate), you can drive or hike up a short road to this camel-humped hill with the cross on top. From this aerie, a memorial to Paul Fagan, there's a fine view of Hana Bay and the surrounding coastline.

HANA CULTURAL CENTER

✉4974 Uakea Street 📞808-248-6622 📠808-248-7898 ✉hccm@aloha.net

An enticing little museum, the center displays such artifacts from Hana's past as primitive stone tools, rare shells and Hawaiian games. There are antique photographs and elaborately stitched quilts.

COURTHOUSE Built in 1871, this is a modest but appealing structure containing five small benches and the original desk for the judge. Be sure to wander through the **Kauhale Complex**, a replica of a Hawaiian village complete with thatched huts to explore.

WANANALUA CHURCH ✉Hauoli Street and Hana Highway A lovely chapel built from coral blocks during the mid-19th century, this church has been beautifully refurbished. Today, services are conducted in English and Hawaiian. Located atop an ancient *heiau*, stately and imposing in appearance, it is a perfect expression of the days when Christianity was crushing the old Hawaiian beliefs.

From Hana to Ulupalakua

The backroad from Hana around the southeast side of Maui is one of the island's great adventures. It leads along the side of Haleakala past dense rainforest and tumbling waterfalls to an arid expanse covered by lava flows, and then opens onto Maui's vaunted Upcountry region. Since a five-mile stretch is unpaved and other sections are punctuated with potholes, car rental companies generally do not permit driving on parts of this route; so check with them in advance or be prepared to take your chances. Also check on road conditions: The road is sometimes closed during periods of heavy rain.

WAILUA FALLS ✉45-mile marker Past Hana, the road, now designated the Piilani Highway and renumbered as Route 31 (with mileage markers that descend in sequence), worsens as it winds toward an overgrown ravine where this fall and another waterfall pour down sharp cliff faces.

OHEO GULCH ✉42-mile marker Also known as the Seven Sacred Pools, in the Kipahulu District of the Haleakala National Park is a series of waterfalls that tumble into two dozen pools before reaching the sea. "In fact," says Mark Tanaka-Sanders, chief ranger for Haleakala National Park, "there are 24 pools in the area." Who's responsible for the miscount? "Blame it on the tourist industry," he says. "It's also important to know that the Hawaiian people do not consider these pools sacred." They refer to them as the pools at Oheo. The pools are rock-bound, some are bordered by cliffs, and several provide excellent swimming holes. This is an eerie and beautiful place from which you can see up and down the rugged coastline. Used centuries ago by early Hawaiians, they still offer a cool, refreshing experience.

CHARLES LINDBERGH'S GRAVE

✉41-mile marker. To find the grave, continue 1.2 miles past Oheo Gulch. Watch for the church through the trees on the left. Turn left onto an unpaved road and drive several hundred yards, paralleling a stone fence. Turn left into the churchyard. This prominent grave rests on a promontory overlooking the ocean. The great aviator spent his last days here and lies buried beside **Palapala Hoomau Church** in a grave he designed for himself. The church was built in 1857 of limestone coral, and about one hundred years later was restored by Samuel Pryor, the man who introduced Lindbergh to the area. Pryor had a picture of Jesus dressed in Hawaiian robes painted on a window of the church (and reportedly buried his pet monkeys nearby). The whitewashed chapel and surrounding shade trees create a place of serenity and remarkable beauty.

KIPAHULU Not far from Lindbergh's grave the paved road gives way to dirt at this rustic town. It's five miles to the nearest pavement, so your car should have good shock absorbers; sometimes the weather makes it impassable. The road rises along seaside cliffs, some of which are so steep they jut out to overhang the road. This is wild, uninhabited country, ripe for exploration.

HUIALOHA CHURCH Built in 1859, this church rests below the road on a wind-wracked peninsula. Once when I visited this aging worship hall, horses were grazing in the churchyard. Nearby you'll encounter the tinroof town of **Kaupo**, with its funky general store. You'll feel like you've entered a time warp . . . and maybe you won't want to return to the present. Located directly above the town is **Kaupo Gap**, through which billowing clouds pour into Haleakala Crater.

NUU BAY'S The road bumps inland, then returns seaward to this bay's rocky beach. From here the rustic route climbs into a desolate area scarred by lava and inhabited with scrub vegetation. The sea views are magnificent as the road bisects the **1790 lava flow**. This was the last volcanic eruption on Maui; it left its mark in a torn and terrible landscape that slopes for miles to the sea.

ULUPALAKUA RANCH It's several miles farther until you reach Ulupalakua Ranch, a lush counterpoint to the lava wasteland behind. With its grassy acres and curving rangeland, the ranch provides a perfect introduction to Maui's Upcountry region.

LODGING

Paia

THE INN AT MAMA'S FISH HOUSE

$$$$ 4 ROOMS   ✉799 Poho Place, Paia   ☎808-579-9764, 800-860-4852   ✉808-579-8594   ✍www.mamasfishhouse.com, inn@mamasfishhouse.com
Owners of north shore Maui's Mama's Fish House have installed

picturesque beachfront cottages next to their restaurant, and named them accordingly. Located just east of Paia at Kuau Cove, the inn consists of four two-bedroom units, all facing the ocean, plus two one-bedroom garden-view units. True to form, the owners have named each cottage after a Hawaiian fish. Their beachfront property is known for its lush, tropical gardens and swaying coconut palm grove. Each unit is furnished in bold, Hawaiian print decor, including fresh tropical flowers as well as a complete kitchen and private lanai.

Hana

HOTEL HANA-MAUI

$$$$ 70 ROOMS ✉P.O. Box 9, Hana, HI 96713 ☎808-248-8211, 800-321-4262
☏808-248-7202 ⌨www.hotelhanamaui.com

One of Hawaii's finest resting places is this luxurious retreat on a hillside above Hana Bay. From ocean views to tropical landscapes to rolling lawns, this friendly inn is a unique, world-class resort. Spread across the 70-acre grounds are cottage-style accommodations, all elegantly designed to capture the tranquility of Hana. The hotel's award-winning wellness complex sponsors a variety of hiking excursions and nature walks, as well as yoga, tai chi and aqua exercise classes. The adjacent pool, landscaped with lava walls and palm trees, enjoys a spectacular setting. The staff has been here for generations, lending a sense of home to an enchanting locale. Rates for this getaway of getaways are stratospheric, but I highly recommend it.

CAMP KEANAE

$ 8 UNITS ✉Hana Highway, Keanae ☎808-248-8355 ☏808-244-6713
⌨www.mauiymca.org, ymcacampkeanae@aol.com

A very convenient accommodation located on the Hana Highway in Keanae is the Maui YMCA's Camp Keanae. For just $15 a night, both men and women are welcome to roll out their sleeping bags on bunks in the dormitory or one of five cabins. The camp overlooks the sea, and comes with hot showers, laundry facilities, full-size gym, kitchen and outdoor cooking area. A pair of two-bedroom oceanview cottages sleep up to four people ($125 per night); both have full kitchens. Guests must provide their own bedding for the dorms. Reservations required.

ALOHA COTTAGES

$$ 5 ROOMS ✉83 Keawa Place, Hana ☎808-248-8420

Perched on a hillside above Hana Bay, the Aloha has three two-bedroom cottages, one three-bedroom cottage and one studio that are situated among banana trees; most feature hardwood floors and redwood walls. The decor is simple, the kitchens are all-electric and many of the furnishings are rattan. Representing one of Hana's best bargains, the cottages have been recommended many times over the years by readers and friends. There are only five units at this small complex, so advance reservations are a good idea.

HANA KAI MAUI RESORT

$$$–$$$$ 18 UNITS ✉1533 Ukea Road, Hana ☎808-248-8426, 800-346-2772
📠808-248-7482 🖅www.hanakaimaui.com

You can also consider heading down toward the water to the Hana Kai Maui. Located smack on a rocky beach, this pair of two-story buildings sits amid lush surroundings. The ornamental pool is a freshwater affair fed by toe-dipping spring water. The location and exotic grounds rate a big plus. Both studio apartments and one-bedroom condominiums are available.

HANA ACCOMMODATIONS

$$–$$$ 4 UNITS ✉Locations throughout Hana ☎808-248-7868, 800-228-4262
📠808-248-8240 🖅www.hana-maui.com

This agency offers cottages and studios. Scattered throughout the Hana area are homes with either mountain or ocean views; each unit is fully equipped with (or has access to) a kitchen. Many of the accommodations are decorated with tapa-cloth designs and Hawaiian paintings. Most are cooled with ceiling fans and all have outdoor grills perfect for a private feast. Some facilities are within walking distance of the beach and ancient Hawaiian fishponds. Gay-friendly.

HANA MAUI TRAVEL

$$–$$$ 11 UNITS ✉P.O. Box 536, Hana, HI 96713 ☎808-248-7742, 800-548-0478
📠808-248-7319 🖅www.hanamauitravel.com, info@hanamauitravel.com

Another travel agency offers a similar selection of accommodations—including studios and homes—in several price ranges. Here you can settle into a place on Hana Bay or on an idyllic hillside. Some guest units sit atop lava-rock bluffs overlooking the ocean, others are found in secluded five-acre settings. Most accommodations come with lanais, outdoor barbecues and full kitchens.

Don't forget the cabins at **Waianapanapa State Park** (for information, refer to the "Beaches & Parks" section later in this chapter).

Gay Lodging
THE HUELO POINT LOOKOUT

$$$$ 4 UNITS ✉P.O. Box 790117, Paia, HI 96779 ☎808-573-0914, 800-871-8645
📠808-573-0227 🖅www.mauivacationcottages.com, dreamers@maui.net

Set on two acres and bounded by pastureland that stretches to the ocean on three sides is this beautiful lookout. There's lodging in three cottages—the Rainbow, Star Honeymoon and Haleakala, each with king-sized beds and heated towel rails. Also available is a lookout house, a two-story home complete with a full kitchen, dining room, and space for up to eight people. You can also enjoy your own private hot tub, one of two outdoor showers or the shared pool.

NAPULANI O'HANA

$–$$$ 1 UNIT ✉P.O. Box 118, Hana, HI 96713 ☎808-248-8935

Offering spacious accommodations within a few miles of Hana, and a mile and a half from the ocean is Napulani. It's a ranch-style house set on four acres, with decks overlooking the flower-filled gardens; some of the bathroom floors are decorated with handprinted fish. Enjoy the bananas and papaya served in season.

Paia

Paia, once an artsy little town that has since been discovered, is located just a few miles out on the Hana Highway. There are several worthwhile restaurants to choose from. If you don't select any of them, however, be forewarned—there are no pit stops between here and Hana.

PAIA FISH MARKET

$–$$ INTERNATIONAL ✉Corner of Baldwin Avenue and Hana Highway, Paia
📞808-579-8030

If you're craving a tasty fish sandwich, this is the place to go. When you're not in the mood for seafood, this eatery also offers hamburgers, pasta and Mexican dishes such as fajitas. It's is a casual place with plenty of flowers, and prints of water sports on the walls.

CAFÉ MAMBO

$–$$ DINER/DELI ✉30 Baldwin Avenue, Paia 📞808-579-8021

For box lunches, drop in here. Open for breakfast and lunch, this light and airy café serves a variety of items including spinach-nut burgers and mahimahi sandwiches. The menu also offers patrons basic breakfast selections, deli sandwiches, vegetarian options and plain old burgers.

THE FRESH MINT RESTAURANT

$ VEGETARIAN ✉115 Baldwin Avenue, Paia 📞808-579-9144

This is the prime address hereabouts for vegan and vegetarian food. Place your order at the counter—there are salads, sandwiches and hot entrées that include Thai specialties. Dinner only.

JACQUES NORTHSHORE

$$ PACIFIC RIM ✉ 120 Hana Highway, Paia 📞808-579-8844
📠808-579-8014 ✉northshorebistro@aol.com

The look is decidedly young and attractive at Jacques Northshore. The Pacific Rim menu of chef Jacques Pauvert hints of French and Italian origins. The fresh fish means a variety of things, depending on the catches of the day. Rich-sauced pastas like smoked chicken breast are hard to resist. The full sushi bar features an excellent selection. Reasonable prices make Jacques a find for value as well as taste. If you're headed back to the coast after a Haleakala sunset, stop here for dinner. You won't regret it. Dinner only.

CHARLEY'S

$–$$ INTERNATIONAL ✉142 Hana Highway, Paia 📞808-579-9453 📠808-579-8789

Since 1971, Charley's has been a favorite spot to drop in for breakfast (and lunch and dinner). Macadamia-nut pancakes, French toast, Cajun *ono* benedict—you name it, they've got it. At lunch you can try the Woofer burger (Charley's is named after a Great Dane); if you prefer the meatless menu, there are veggie burgers, salads or sandwiches. Dinner entrées include "catch of the day," New York steaks, pasta, pizza and calzones. It's a comfortable atmosphere to dine in and practically open all the time.

MAMA'S FISH HOUSE

$$$$ SEAFOOD ✉799 Poho Place, off Hana Highway ☎808-579-8488, 800-860-4852 ✎www.mamasfishhouse.com, info@mamasfishhouse.com

This oceanfront nook is simply decorated: shell leis, an old Hawaiian photo here, a painting there, plus potted plants. During lunch, the varied menu includes Hawaiian seafood sandwiches and salads as well as fresh fish specialties. Other than a few steak and poultry dishes, the dinner menu is entirely seafood. Evening entrées include seafood provençal and fresh Hawaiian lobster. There are always at least four varieties of fresh fish provided by fishermen who bring their catch directly to Mama's, where it is prepared ten different ways. Reservations are highly recommended.

Hana

If you plan to stay in Hana for any length of time, pack up some groceries along with your raingear. You'll find only three restaurants along the entire eastern stretch of the island. Luckily, they cover the gamut from budget to ultra-deluxe.

TUTU'S AT HANA BAY

$ PLATE LUNCHES ✉Hana Bay ☎808-248-8224

Within whistling distance of the water, Tutu's whips up French toast and *loco moco* (rice, hamburger and an egg smothered with brown gravy) for breakfast and plate lunches, sandwiches and burgers for lunch.

HANA RANCH RESTAURANT

$$$-$$$$ AMERICAN ✉Hana Highway ☎808-248-8255

This small establishment, decorated with blond wood, provides marvelous ocean views. A flagstone lanai is perfect for outdoor dining. Open for lunch (either buffet-style or à la carte) and dinner on Wednesday, Friday and Saturday. Wednesday is pizza and pasta night; Friday and Saturday offer steak, fresh fish and baby-back ribs. Reservations are highly recommended.

KAWIKI

$$$$ HAWAII REGIONAL ✉Hana Highway ☎808-270-5285, 800-321-4262 📠808-248-7202 ✎www.hotelhanamaui.com

Hana's premier restaurant is the main dining room in the Hotel Hana-Maui. This extraordinary resort, perched on a hillside overlooking the ocean, provides three gourmet meals a day to its guests and the public alike. The menu blends contemporary cuisine with a regional Hawaiian influence, while ingredients are from Hana-grown produce and the seafood comes from local fishermen: baby greens with local tropical fruits, macadamia nuts and vanilla vinaigrette, for instance, or seared, rare, *ahi* tuna with pumpkin pureé and young pumpkin shoot tempura.

SHOPPING

Paia, just seven miles outside Kahului, is my favorite place to shop on Maui. Many fine artisans live in the Upcountry area and come down to sell their wares at the small shops lining the Hana Highway. The town itself is a work of art, with old wooden buildings that provide a welcome respite from the crowded shores of Kaanapali and Kihei. I'll mention just the shops I like most. Browse through town to see for yourself. If you discover places I missed, please let me know.

Paia

MAUI CRAFTS GUILD

✉ *43 Hana Highway, Paia* ☎ *808-579-9697* On display at this cooperative gallery is a large range of handmade items all by local artists. Here you'll find anything from pressed hibiscus flowers to sculptures. There are also fabrics, ceramics, jewelry, baskets, woodwork and other Maui-made items.

PAIA TRADING COMPANY ✉ *106 Hana Highway, Paia* ☎ *808-579-9472* This shop has a few interesting antiques and a lot of junk. Among the more noteworthy items: turquoise and silver jewelry, wooden washboards, apothecary jars and antique glassware. Closed Sunday.

MAUI GIRL AND CO. ✉ *12 Baldwin Avenue, Paia* ☎ *808-579-9266* Around the corner from Paia Trading Company on Baldwin Avenue lies another shop worth browsing. It features a fine selection of women's beachwear.

Hana

HANA COAST GALLERY

✉ *Hana Highway, Hana* ☎ *808-248-8636* One of my stops in Hana is this gallery, located in the Hotel Hana-Maui. It features native Hawaiian art and artifacts and fine paintings by Hawaiian artists. Also here are beautiful serigraphs, model *koa* racing canoes, ceremonial objects, feathered art, fiber collages and painted tapa cloth.

NOE NOE ✉ *Hana Highway, Hana* ☎ *808-270-5294* Also on the grounds of the Hotel Hana-Maui is this tropical shop with casual and evening wear for men and women.

HASEGAWA GENERAL STORE ✉ *5165 Hana Highway, Hana* ☎ *808-248-8231* Stop here for everything you could possibly want or need. This store stocks everything from groceries, clothing, sandals and hardware to placemats, movie rentals, film and cards. The original Hasegawa's burned down years ago, but the name is still famous.

6 MAUI HANA HIGHWAY SHOPPING

CHARLEY'S ✉142 Hana Highway, Paia ☎808-579-9453 If you're looking for something to do in the evening, this place offers live music most every night. Check to see if they have something scheduled. You might even run into Willie Nelson, who favors dining at this local restaurant when he's in town. Cover on most nights.

PANIOLO BAR

✉Hana Highway, Hana ☎808-248-8211 In the early evening, you can enjoy a duo singing Hawaiian music at this bar in the Hotel Hana-Maui. As relaxed as Hana itself, this low-key establishment is always inviting.

BEACHES & PARKS

H. A. BALDWIN PARK

✉About seven miles east of Kahului on the Hana Highway

🏖️ 🏑 ⛱️ This spacious county park is bordered by a playing field on one side and a crescent-shaped beach on the other. Palm and ironwood trees dot the half-mile-long beach where you can go shell collecting and gaze out to West Maui. The swimming is good, as is the bodysurfing, but beware of currents; the snorkeling cannot be recommended. For surfing there are winter breaks, with a right slide. Fishing for threadfin, mountain bass, goatfish and *ulua* is good. Facilities include a picnic area with large pavilion, showers and restrooms.

HOOKIPA BEACH PARK

✉Just off the Hana Highway about three miles east of Paia near Mama's Fish House

🏖️ 🏑 🏄 For serious surfers, kitesurfers and windsurfers this is the best spot on Maui. It's *not* the place for a novice to try out the sports. The beach itself is little more than a narrow rectangle of sand paralleled by a rocky shelf. Offshore, top-ranked windsurfers or kitesurfers may be performing airborne stunts. On any given day you're likely to see a hundred sails with boards attached skimming the whitecaps. The swimming is good only when the surf is low. There are picnic areas, restrooms and showers.

HONOMANU BAY

✉Off the Hana Highway, about 30 miles east of Kahului. Turn off onto the dirt road located east of Kaumahina State Wayside; follow it to the beach.

🏑 A tranquil black-sand-and-rock beach surrounded by pandanus-covered hills and bisected by a stream, this is a beautiful and secluded area. There are no facilities, and the water is often too rough for swimming, but it's a favorite with surfers.

WAIANAPANAPA STATE PARK

✉ *Just off the Hana Highway about four miles north of the town of Hana*

Set in a heavenly seaside locale, this park is one of Hawaii's prettiest public facilities and is a very popular park. The entire area is lush with tropical foliage and especially palmy pandanus trees. There's a black-sand beach, sea arches, a blowhole and two legendary caves. But pack your parkas; wind and rain are frequent. Swimming and snorkeling are good—when the water is calm—as is the fishing. Facilities here include a picnic area, restrooms and showers.

▲ ✉ *54 South High Street, Suite 101, Wailuku, HI 96793* ☎ *808-984-8109*

There are sites for up to 60 people on a grass-covered bluff overlooking the sea. There are also plain but attractive accommodations renting for $45 for up to four people. Two additional people are allowed at $5 each. Each cabin contains a small bedroom with two bunk beds, plus a living room that can double as an extra bedroom. All cabins are equipped with bedding and complete kitchen facilities, and some have ocean views. A state permit is required. The cabins are rented through the Division of State Parks.

HANA BEACH PARK

✉ *Off the Hana Highway at Hana Bay*

Tucked in a well-protected corner of Hana Bay, this park has a large pavilion and a curving stretch of sandy beach. It's a great place to meet local folks. Swimming is fine; snorkeling is good near the lighthouse; and beginning surfers will find both summer and winter breaks on the north side of the bay (left slide). Some days are very calm, however. Bonefish, *ulua* and *papio* are routinely taken here and *moilii* run in the months of June and July. As well as the concrete picnic area, there are restrooms and showers and there's a snack bar across the street.

RED SAND BEACH

✉ *This is one place where getting to the beach becomes an adventure. It is located on the far side of Kauiki Hill in Hana. Follow Uakea Road to its southern terminus. There is a grassy plot on the left between Hana School and the parking lot for the Hotel Hana-Maui's sea ranch cottages. Here you will find a trail leading into the undergrowth. It traverses an overgrown Japanese cemetery and curves around Kauiki Hill, then descends precipitously to the beach. Be careful!*

Known to the Hawaiians as Kaihalulu ("roaring sea") Beach, this is one of the most exotic and truly secluded beaches in all the islands. Protected by lofty cliffs, it can be reached by hiking a precarious trail. A volcanic cinder beach, the sand is reddish in hue and coarse underfoot. Most dramatic of all is the lava barrier that crosses the mouth of this natural amphitheater, protecting the beach and creating an inshore pool. Popular with nudists and adventures, it's technically illegal to visit. Swimming, snorkeling and fishing are all good. There are no facilities.

HAMOA BEACH

✉ *Follow the Hana Highway south from Hana for a little over a mile. Turn left on Haneoo Road and follow it for a mile to Hamoa.*

Located at the head of Mokae Cove, this stretch of salt-and-pepper sand with rock outcroppings at each end is a pretty place. Unfortunately, the Hotel Hana-Maui uses the beach as a semiprivate preserve. There are restrooms and a dining pavilion that are available only to guests, so a sense of segregation pervades the beach.

KOKI BEACH PARK

✉ *Half a mile back up the Haenoo Road toward the highway*

A sandy plot paralleled by a grassy park, this beach is more welcoming than Hamoa. Backdropped by lofty red cinder cliffs, Koki can be very windy and the ocean is plagued by currents. With a small island and sea arch offshore, it is also very pretty. Swimmers should exercise caution.

OHEO GULCH

✉ *In Haleakala National Park's Kipahulu section (about ten miles south of Hana)*

The stream that tumbles down Haleakala through this gulch forms several large pools (popularly known as the Seven Sacred Pools) and numerous small ones. The main pools descend from above the Hana Highway to the sea. This is a truly enchanting area swept by frequent wind and rain, and shadowed by Haleakala. It overlooks Maui's rugged eastern shore. You can swim in the chilly waters and camp nearby. There are picnic facilities and outhouses; bring your own drinking water. Watch your step and be careful here; frequent accidents have been reported.

▲ Primitive, meadow-style camping is available on a bluff above the sea. No permit is required and there are no restrictions on the number of occupants, but there is a three-day limit. However, to enter Haleakala National Park a $10 per vehicle fee is required. The permit is good for up to seven days.

UPCOUNTRY

Maui's Upcountry is a belt that encircles Haleakala along its middle slopes and ranges from lush in the north to dry in the south. Situated between coastline and crater rim, it's home to a sparse but growing population, and is ideal for camping, hiking or just wandering. Here the flat agricultural fields that blanket central Maui give way to curving hills of ranch land filled with grazing horses. You may also spot axis deer, Hawaiian owls and pheasants.

HALIIMAILE GENERAL STORE

PAGE 350

Former plantation store turned chic dining spot with a creative contemporary spin on preparing fresh local fish and Big Island beef

ENCHANTING FLORAL GARDEN

PAGE 345

Sprawling eight-acre floral fantasy where blossoms drip from vines and trees in great swaths of vibrant color

POLIPOLI SPRING STATE RECREATION AREA

PAGE 351

Ethereal hiking trails through dense forest and up to the summit of a 6200-foot volcano

Farmers plant tomatoes, cabbages, carrots, giant strawberries and the region's famous sweet Kula onions. Proteas, those delicate flowers native to Australia and South Africa, grow in colorful profusion. Hibiscus, jacarandas, silver oak and other wildflowers sweep along the hillsides like a rainstorm. And on the region's two ranches—35,000-acre Haleakala Ranch and 20,000-acre Ulupalakua Ranch—Angus, Hereford and Brangus (Braham-Angus hybrids) cattle complete a picture far removed from Hawaii's tropical beaches.

SIGHTS

Home to *paniolo*, Hawaii's version of the Western cowboy, the Upcountry region lies along the highways that lead to the crest of Haleakala. Route 37, Haleakala Highway, becomes the Kula Highway as it ascends to the Kula uplands.

KULA'S SURFING GOAT DAIRY ✉ *3651 Omaopai Road* ☎ *808-878-2780*
An interesting stop early on Route 37 is this goat dairy, one of two in Hawaii. It offers tours, which include cheese-tastings.

ENCHANTING FLORAL GARDEN

✉ *Route 37, 10-mile marker, Kula* ☎ *808-878-2531* 📠 *808-878-1805* 🖰 *www.flowersofmaui.com, info@flowersofmaui.com* It's impossible to tell from the road the beauty within this "enchanting" garden. The eight-acre floral fantasy, however, is in spectacular bloom much of the year, thanks to dedicated owners Kazuo and Kazuko Takeda, who have spent nearly a decade planting and nurturing an amazing array of flowers. Blossoms drip from vines and trees in great swaths of vibrant color with the Maui lowlands for a backdrop. Admission.

CHURCH OF THE HOLY GHOST ✉*12-mile marker* Just outside the village of Waiakoa and still in use, this church is a unique octagonal chapel, built along this stretch of road in 1897 for Portuguese immigrants working on Maui's ranches and farms.

MAKEE SUGAR MILL Route 37 angles southwest through Ulupalakua Ranch to the ruins of this once flourishing enterprise built in 1878.

TEDESCHI VINEYARDS ☎*808-878-1266* 🖷*808-876-0127* ✎*www.mauiwine. com, info@mauiwine.com* A currently flourishing business, Tedeschi sits just across the road from the Makee sugar mill. Here at Hawaii's oldest winery you can stop for a taster's tour, sampling a pineapple wine called Maui Blanc, and a sweet dessert wine from pineapple and passionfruit called Maui Splash. The tasting room is located in a building that once served as a retreat for King Kalakaua. This building also houses a gift shop and a history room that includes information about the area—the original families, how the area developed, and the first *paniolo*. A picnic in the lush surroundings that include century-old trees is a bonus.

GRANDMA'S COFFEE HOUSE ✉*9232 Kula Highway* ☎*808-878-2140* Just past Keokea Park on Kula Highway (Route 37), you'll see Grandma's, a local gathering place. Four generations of the Franco family, owners of the coffee shop, have been growing coffee on the slopes of Haleakala and picking the beans by hand. These beans are roasted at the shop in a century-old roaster. Boasting panoramic views, this place can also brag about its homemade breakfasts, fresh-baked goodies, and hot lunch specials; the coffee, of course, is very good, too.

SUN YAT SEN PARK Continuing along Route 37, on the right you'll see a sign for this park. What will really draw your attention, though, are the statues that seem to pop up out of the dry grass. They have a distinctly Asian flair because they are monuments to the Chinese immigrants who first settled Upcountry Maui. China's leader from the early 20th century, Sun Yat Sen actually visited Maui and stayed at the Pioneer Hotel in Lahaina, which may be one more reason why the park was named after him.

KULA BOTANICAL GARDENS

✉*638 Kekaulike Avenue, Kula* You can also turn up Route 377 to this excellent place for picnicking. The landscaped slopes contain an aviary, a pond, a gift shop and a "Taboo Garden" with poisonous plants and over 60 varieties of protea, the flowering shrub that grows so beautifully in this region. Look for the big black iron gate. Admission.

Upcountry

Upcountry

PACIFIC OCEAN

Hamakua Coast

Pauwela

Lower Paia

Twin Falls

36

360

Hana Hwy

Hana Hwy

Haiku

Ulumalu

365

36

Paia

to Hana

Spreckelsville

to Kahului & Wailuku

37

Haleakala

Haliimaile

Kokomo

Koolau Forest Reserve

Hwy

Makawao

University of Hawaii Agricultural Station

37

Makawao Ave

Olinda

Pukalani

377

390

394

Rd

Omaopio

Rd

Olinda

Pulehu Rd

Kula Hwy

Haleakala Hwy

Omaopio

Enchanting Floral Garden

Pulehu

Pulehu Rd

37

Sunrise Protea Farm

Church of the Holy Ghost

Haleakala Hwy

Haleakala Hwy

378

Walakoa

Kula

377

Kula Botanical Gardens

Keokea

Kula Forest Reserve

Puu Ulaula (Red Hill) 10,023'

Haleakala National Park

Keokea Park

Boundary Trail

Skyline Trail

Haleakala 8205'

Sun Yat Sen Park

37

Plum Tr.

Polipoli Spring State Recreation Area

Kahikinui National Park

Makee Sugar Mill

Ulupalakua Ranch

Tedeschi Vineyards

(Narrow one-lane road: watch for oncoming traffic)

31

N

0 2 miles

0 2 kilometers

MAUI UPCOUNTRY SIGHTS

6

SUNRISE PROTEA FARM ✉*378 Haleakala Crater Road* 📞*808-876-0200* 📠*808-876-0107* 🖱*www.sunriseprotea.com* One of the several farms nearby is this family-owned homestead, devoted primarily to proteas. They offer fresh or dried bouquets of these South African native flowers.

POLIPOLI SPRING STATE RECREATION AREA If you make a right from Route 377 onto the road marked for Polipoli before you get to Kula Botanical Gardens, you'll eventually reach this state park. This recreation area is the starting point for uncrowded, easy hikes on Haleakala's upper slopes. Head to Polipoli in the morning and you'll likely catch sight of hang gliders taking off on flights to the lowlands below. Note: The final half of the road to Polipoli is extremely rough; a four-wheel-drive vehicle is recommended. (For more information on trails, see "Hiking" at the end of the chapter.)

MAKAWAO Another intriguing place is Maui's latest "art" destination. It's not Lahaina's Front Street—surprise, surprise—but rather the tiny town of Makawao, where battered buildings and falsefront stores replete with hitching posts create an Old West atmosphere. This is the capital of Maui's cowboy country, similar to Waimea on the Big Island, with a rodeo every Fourth of July. Over the years, Makawao has been transformed from an Old West cow town to a thriving arts center.

LOOP TOURS —————————————
From Makawao the possibilities for exploring the Upcountry area are many. There are two loop tours I particularly recommend. The first climbs from town along Olinda Road (Route 390) past **Pookela Church**, a coral sanctuary built in 1843.

Olinda Road continues through a frequently rain-drenched region to Tree Growth Research Area, jointly sponsored by state and federal forestry services. You can circle back down toward Makawao on Piiholo Road past the **University of Hawaii Agricultural Station**, where you will see more of the area's richly planted acreage.

The second loop leads down Route 365 to the Hana Highway. Turn left on the highway for several miles to Haiku Road, then head left along this country lane, which leads into overgrown areas, across one-lane bridges, past banana patches and through this tinroof town, **Haiku**.

LODGING

KULA LODGE
$$$ 5 UNITS ✉*Haleakala Highway, Kula* 📞*808-878-1535, 800-233-1535* 📠*808-878-2518* 🖱*www.kulalodge.com, info@kulalodge.com*
A mountain lodge on the road to the summit of Haleakala offers a cold-air retreat that is well-situated for anyone who wants to catch the sum-

mit sunrise. For years, Kula Lodge has rented five chalets, some with fireplaces, sleeping lofts and sweeping ocean and mountain views. The individual chalets are carpeted wall-to-wall and trimmed with stained-wood paneling. The central lodge features a cheery restaurant, bar and stone fireplace. An appealing mountain hideaway.

DINING

NICK'S PLACE

$ INTERNATIONAL   ✉Pukalani Terrace Center, Haleakala Highway, Pukalani   ☎808-572-8258

In the town of Pukalani, there are several good dining spots at the Terrace Center. Among them is this cafeteria serving Japanese-Chinese-American fare. Choose from such à la carte items as *chow fun*, tempura, Portuguese sausage, stew or corned-beef hash; together they make a hearty meal. At breakfast, try the eggs with Portuguese sausage.

GRANDMA'S COFFEE HOUSE

$$ COFFEE HOUSE/DELI   ✉9232 Kula Highway   ☎808-878-2140   ☎808-878-2792
✎www.grandmascoffee.com

Stop in here for hot, fresh-ground coffee. For four generations the Franco family, owners of the shop, has been growing coffee, picking beans by hand and roasting them in a century-old roaster. They also offer delicious, home-cooked breakfasts such as scrambled eggs or waffles as well as hot lunch items. No dinner.

MAKAWAO STEAK HOUSE

$$$ STEAK/SEAFOOD   ✉3612 Baldwin Avenue, Makawao   ☎808-572-8711
☎808-572-7103

For something a step more upscale, consider going farther Upcountry to Makawao's. Redwood plank walls hold original paintings by some of the best-known local artists. The popular menu serves a mix of surf-and-turf dishes; unfortunately there is only the salad bar to satisfy vegetarians. But then what righteous vegetarian would go to a steakhouse? Dinner only.

CASANOVA ITALIAN RESTAURANT & DELI

$$$–$$$$ ITALIAN   ✉1188 Makawao Avenue, Makawao   ☎808-572-0220
☎808-572-4978

Go Mediterranean at Casanova's, a stylish bistro that serves Italian-style seafood, pasta dishes and pizza. For something faster, cheaper and more casual, you can try the adjacent deli.

POLLI'S RESTAURANT

$$ MEXICAN   ✉1202 Makawao Avenue, Makawao   ☎808-572-7808
☎808-572-0080

Across the street from Casanova's is this sombreros-on-the-wall-and-oilcloth-on-the-tables eatery offering a full selection of Mexican dishes for lunch and dinner. A local gathering place popular with residents throughout Maui's Upcountry, Polli's has become an institution over the years. It will inevitably be crowded with folks dining on tacos, burritos and tamales, as well as burgers, sandwiches and ribs.

HALIIMAILE GENERAL STORE

$$$–$$$$ HAWAII REGIONAL   ✉*900 Haliimaile Road, Haliimaile*
📞*808-572-2666* 📠*808-572-7128* 🖱*www.bevgannonrestaurants.com,*
dole900@aol.com

Upcountry's contribution to Hawaii regional cuisine is this general store. A former plantation store that has been converted into a chic gathering place, it puts a creative spin on contemporary cuisine and serves roast duckling, fresh island fish and beef from the Big Island. No lunch on Saturday and Sunday.

KULA LODGE RESTAURANT

$$$ AMERICAN   ✉*Haleakala Highway, Kula* 📞*808-878-1535, 800-233-1535*
🖱*www.kulalodge.com, info@kulalodge.com*

On the lower slope of Haleakala, Kula Lodge Restaurant enjoys a panoramic view of the island. Through picture windows you can gaze out on a landscape that rolls for miles to the sea. The exposed-beam ceiling and stone fireplace lend a homey feel, as do the homemade pastries. Specialties include rack of lamb, pasta dishes and vegetarian entrées.

SHOPPING

Baldwin Avenue in the Western-style town of Makawao has developed over the years into a prime arts-and-crafts center. Housed in the false-front stores that line the street you'll find galleries galore and a few boutiques besides.

THE COURTYARD ✉*3620 Baldwin Avenue, Makawao* An attractive wood-frame mall, this complex contains **Hot Island Glass** (808-572-4527), with a museum-quality collection of handblown glass pieces made in the store. Also here is **Viewpoints Gallery** (808-572-5979), which puts many of the higher-priced Lahaina galleries to shame.

GECKO TRADING COMPANY ✉*3621 Baldwin Avenue, Makawao* 📞*808-572-0249* Gecko is a small boutique that features contemporary fashions at reasonable prices, as well as other gift items.

GOODIE'S ✉*3633 Baldwin Avenue, Makawao* 📞*808-572-0288* Check out this place for gift items: crystal mobiles, locally made jewelry, picture frames. There are also women's fashions, men's shirts and handmade Hawaiian baskets.

HUI NOEAU VISUAL
ARTS CENTER

✉*2841 Baldwin Avenue, Makawao* 📞*808-572-6560* 🖱*www.huinoeau.com,*
info@huinoeau.com What put Makawao on the arts-destination map was this visual arts center. Located on the outskirts of

Makawao, the 1917 Mediterranean-style Baldwin mansion offers rotating educational exhibits, and regular workshops on painting, printmaking, ceramics, sculpture and much, much more. For the artistically impaired but pocketbook inclined, works by Maui artists are available for purchase.

CURTIS WILSON COST GALLERY ✉*Route 377 (Haleakala Highway), Kula* ☎*808-878-6544, 800-810-2678* In the Kula Lodge complex, this gallery sells prints, limited editions and originals by Curtis Wilson Cost. The emphasis is on local landscapes and ocean scenery.

PROTEAS OF HAWAII ✉*417 Mauna Place, Kula* ☎*808-878-2533* Specializing in gift boxes, proteas and tropical floral arrangements, this shop also sells orchids and anthuriums. Closed weekends.

NIGHTLIFE

CASANOVA ITALIAN RESTAURANT ✉*1188 Makawao Avenue, Makawao* ☎*808-572-0220* Upcountry is pretty quiet in the evenings, however, there are live bands here on Saturday nights and deejay music on Wednesday and Friday. One of Upcountry's only nightspots, they feature a range of live acts—from local Mauian to internationally known. Cover.

BEACHES & PARKS

POLIPOLI SPRING STATE RECREATION AREA

idden

✉*From Kahului, take Haleakala Highway (Route 37) through Pukalani and past Waiakoa to Route 377. Turn left on 377 and follow it a short distance to the road marked for Polipoli. About half of this ten-mile road to the park is paved. The second half of the track is extremely rough and often muddy. It is advisable to take a four-wheel-drive vehicle.*

🏃 Located at 6200-foot elevation on the slopes of Haleakala, this densely forested area is an ideal mountain retreat. Monterey and sugi pine, eucalyptus and Monterey cypress grow in stately profusion; not far from the campground there's a grove of redwoods. From Polipoli's ethereal heights you can look out over Central and West Maui, as well as the islands of Lanai, Molokai and Kahoolawe. Miles of trails, some leading up to the volcano summit, crisscross the park. Polipoli has a picnic area, restrooms and running water.

▲ ☎*808-984-8109* There is meadow-style camping (a state permit is required) that holds up to 20 people; the cabin houses up to ten people and rents at $45 per night for the first four guests, and an extra $5 for each additional guest. The cabin (three bedrooms) is sparsely furnished and lacks electricity. It does have a wood heating stove and a gas cooking stove. It can be rented from the Division of State Parks. It's recommended to bring in drinking water.

✉️ *West of Hawi and Kapaau at the 27-mile marker*

This is a pleasant picnic spot on a rocky beach at Route 37 in Keokea. There's a rolling lawn with picnic tables, barbecue grills and restrooms.

HALEAKALA NATIONAL PARK

It seems only fitting that the approach to the summit of Haleakala is along one of the world's fastest-climbing roads. From Kahului to the summit rim—a distance of about 40 miles along Routes 37, 377 and 378—the macadam road rises from sea level to 10,000 feet, and the silence is broken only by the sound of ears popping from the ascent.

At the volcano summit, 10,023 feet in elevation, you look out over an awesome expanse—seven miles long, over two miles wide, 21 miles around. This dormant volcano, which last erupted around 1790, is the central feature of a 30,183-acre national park that extends all the way through the Kipahulu Valley to the sea. The crater floor, 3000 feet below the rim, is a multihued wasteland filled with cinder cones, lava flows and mini-craters. It's a legendary place, with a mythic tradition that's as vital as its geologic history. It was from Haleakala ("House of the Sun") that the demigod Maui lassoed the sun and slowed its track across the sky to give his mother more daylight to dry her tapa cloth.

Technically, by the way, this area is an "erosional depression," not a crater. The converging headwaters of eroding valleys met at the top of the mountain and scooped out the seven-mile by two-mile bowl. Later eruptions studded the floor with cinder cones and lava flows. "Erosional depression" is cumbersome compared to "crater," so if you are like me and still say crater, you can at least claim to know the difference.

In the afternoon the volcano's colors are most vivid, but during the morning the crater is more likely to be free of clouds. One of Maui's favorite rituals is a predawn trip to the top of Haleakala to watch the sun rise. Unfortunately, the weather can be foggy and cold. Besides that, getting up early is probably the last thing you want to do on vacation. If so, consider the alternative: Sleep late, take your time getting to the top and arrive in time for sunset. But, then again, you'll miss a dazzling, almost religious experience. In any case, call 808-877-5111 to check on the weather before making the trip up!

Remember that it takes an hour and a half to two hours to reach the summit from Kahului, longer from the Kaanapali–Kapalua area. Be sure to bring warm clothes since the temperature drop from sea level to 10,000 feet can be 30° or more, which means the temperature may be below freezing. You might even encounter snow. The air is very thin, so pace yourself.

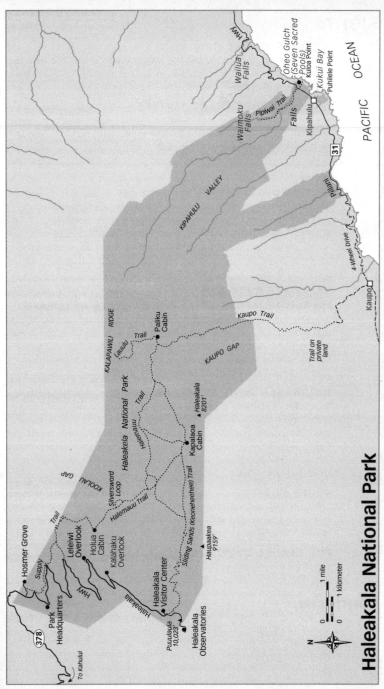

Haleakala National Park

SIGHTS

HOSMER'S GROVE On the way up to the summit (6800 feet) you'll pass this grove, a picnic area and campground (permit not required) surrounded by eucalyptus, spruce, juniper and cedar, as well as some native trees, like *ohia* and *mamanae*.

NATIONAL PARK HEADQUARTERS ☏808-572-4400 ✎www.nps.gov/hale Located at the 7030-foot elevation, these headquarters contain an information desk and maps, and make a good starting point. You may be lucky enough to see the Hawaiian state bird, the nene, which frequents the area around headquarters. Be sure to keep your distance during nesting season.

LELEIWI OVERLOOK The first crater view comes at this overlook, an 8800-foot perch from where, on a clear day, you'll be able to see all the way from Hana across the island to Kihei. Here at sunrise and sunset, under correct meteorological conditions, you can see your shadow projected on the clouds and haloed by a rainbow. To experience this "Specter of the Brocken," stand atop the volcano rim looking toward the cloud-filled crater with the setting sun at your back.

KALAHAKU OVERLOOK Up the hill, a side road leads to this 9324-foot aerie that offers a unique view of several cinder cones within the volcano. Just below the parking lot are numerous **silverswords**. Related to sunflowers, these spike-leaved plants grow only on Maui and the Big Island. They remain low bristling plants for five to fifty years or more before blooming into a flowering stalk. Each plant blossoms once, sometime between May and November, and then dies.

HALEAKALA VISITORS CENTER The best view of the wilderness area is farther up the road at 9745-feet elevation, where you'll find an information desk, as well as a series of exhibits about the volcano. From this vantage point you can gaze out toward Koolau Gap to the north and Kaupo Gap to the south. Several peaks located along the volcano loom out of the clouds; cinder cones, including 600-foot Puu o Maui, rise up from the crater floor.

WHITE HILL From the visitors center a short trail heads up here. Composed of andesite lava and named for its characteristic light color, this mound is dotted with stone windbreaks once used as sleeping places by Hawaiians who periodically visited the summit of Haleakala.

PUU ULAULA OVERLOOK It's a short drive to this summit. From the plate-glass lookout you can view the Big Island, Molokai, Lanai, West Maui and the wilderness area itself. On an extremely clear day this 360° panorama may even include a view of Oahu, 130 miles away.

HALEAKALA OBSERVATORY Perched high above atmospheric haze and the lights of civilization, Haleakala is also an excellent spot for stargazing. The white dome-like structure you see is the observatory, an important center for satellite tracking and television communications. (This area is closed to the public.)

While the views along the volcano rim are awesome, the best way to see Haleakala is from the inside looking out. With 36 miles of hiking trails, two campsites and three cabins, the wilderness provides a tremendous opportunity for explorers. Within the belly of this monstrous volcano, you'll see such geologic features as cinder cones and spatter vents. The Hawaiians marked their passing with stone altars, shelters and adze quarries. You may also spy the rare nene, as well as chukar partridges and pheasants.

VOLCANO FLOOR

The volcano floor is a unique environment, one of constant change and unpredictable weather. Rainfall varies from 12 inches annually in the southwestern corner to 200 inches at Paliku. Temperatures, usually hovering between 55° and 75° during daylight, may fall below freezing at night. Campers should come prepared with warm clothing and sleeping gear, a tent, poncho, lantern and stove (no open fires are permitted). Don't forget the sunblock, as the elevation on the bottom averages 6700 feet and the ultraviolet radiation is intense.

HIKING TRAILS Within the wilderness area you can explore three main trails. **Sliding Sands Trail**, a steep cinder and ash path, begins near the Haleakala Visitors Center. It descends from the rim along the south wall to Kapalaoa cabin, then on to Paliku cabin. In the course of this ten-mile trek, the trail drops over 3000 feet. From Paliku, the **Kaupo Trail** leaves the crater through Kaupo Gap and descends to the tiny town of Kaupo, eight miles away on Maui's southeast coast. **Halemauu Trail** (8 miles) begins from the road three-and-a-half miles beyond National Park Headquarters and descends 1400 feet to the crater floor. It passes Holua cabin and eventually joins Sliding Sands Trail at the Kapalaoa cabin.

LODGING

HALEAKALA NATIONAL PARK CAMPING

✉For more information, write Haleakala National Park, attention: cabins, P.O. Box 369, Makawao, HI 96768 ☏808-572-4400 ✐www.nps.gov/hale

There are campgrounds at Holua and Paliku that require a permit from National Park Headquarters. Permits are given out on a first-come, first-served basis, so plan accordingly. Camping is limited to two days at one site and three days total at both. The campgrounds have pit toilets and nonpotable running water. A 12-person cabin is available at each campsite and at Kapalaoa. Equipped with wood and gas stoves, pit toilets, cooking utensils, bunks and limited nonpotable water, these primitive facilities are extremely popular. So popular, in fact, that guests are chosen by a monthly lottery two months in advance.

OUTDOOR ADVENTURES

The opportunities for adventuring on the Valley Isle are numerous and the conditions for several activities are outstanding. Whale watching, for example, is top-notch on Maui as humpbacks return each year to the waters off Lahaina to give birth. For cyclists, there are thrilling rides down the slopes of Haleakala and challenging courses on Hana's curving coast. Maui is also home to several of the world's premier windsurfing spots including Hookipa Beach on the island's north shore. In addition, Maui has more miles of swimmable beach than any of the other islands in the chain.

CAMPING

Though extremely popular with adventurers, Maui has very few official campsites. The laws restricting camping here are more strictly enforced than on other islands. The emphasis on this boom island favors condominiums and resort hotels rather than outdoor living, but you can still escape the concrete congestion at several parks and unofficial campsites (including one of the most spectacular tenting areas in all Hawaii—Haleakala Wilderness Area).

COUNTY PARKS ⊠ *700 Halia Nakoa Street, Unit 2, Wailuku, HI 96793* ✆ *808-270-7389* Camping at county parks requires a permit. These are issued for a maximum of three consecutive nights at each campsite, and cost $3 per person per night, those under 18 cost 50¢. Permits can be obtained in person at **War Memorial Gym** adjacent to Baldwin High School, Route 32, Wailuku, or by writing the **Department of Parks and Recreation Permit Department**, County Parks Permit Office at the same address.

STATE PARKS ⊠ *54 South High Street, Room 101, Wailuku, HI 96793* ✆ *808-984-8109* State park permits are free and allow camping for five days. They can be obtained in person at the Division of State Parks in the State Building on South High Street, or by writing the Division of State Parks at the same address. You can also rent cabins at Waianapanapa and Polipoli state parks through this office.

If you plan on camping in the Haleakala Wilderness Area, you must obtain a permit on the day you are camping from Haleakala National Park headquarters, located on the way to the valley. These permits are allocated on a first-come, first-served basis.

Remember, rainfall is heavy along the northeast shore around Hana, but infrequent on the south coast. Also, Haleakala gets quite cold; you'll need heavy clothing, rain gear and sleeping gear.

It is best to bring along your own camping gear, but in a pinch check **Airgas Gaspro** (365 Hanakai Street, Kahului; 808-877-0056). **Sears** (275 Kaahumanu Avenue, Kahului; 808-877-2206) at Kahului's Kaahumanu Center also carries camping gear.

More and more adventure tours are becoming eco-tours. Combining the usual tourist activities with a dose of conservation, eco-tours are an edifying way to soak up the beauty and culture of Hawaii while "leaving only footprints."

PATHS IN PARADISE ✉ *P.O. Box 667, Makawao, HI96768* ☎ *808-264-4827* 🖱 *www.mauibirdhikes.com* The flora and fauna of Maui, as well as traces of the ancient Polynesians, are the focus of this group. The company's owner/operator is an environmentalist who will lead you on half- and full-day hikes to explore Hawaii's endangered nature.

OCEAN PROJECT ✉ *Lahaina* ☎ *808-661-6706* 🖱 *oceanproject@prodigy.net* An excellent educational opportunity awaits you at this marine research center studying the coral reefs of Maui. These folks have extensive knowledge and build their events around your interests. At the beach, they'll give you a "class" in the subject of your choice (for example, identification of fish and coral species or the behavior of giant green sea turtles), and then take you snorkeling for an up-close look at what you just learned. The sessions are about two to three hours long and will change the way you view those pretty-colored fish.

SNORKELING & SCUBA DIVING

Maui offers a wide variety of snorkeling and diving opportunities ranging from Black Rock off Kaanapali to Honolua Bay, not to mention Olowalu, Ahihi–Kinau Natural Area Reserve and Ulua Beach. While most of the dive operators are located near the island's south coast resorts, there are also good diving and snorkeling opportunities on the north shore at Paia's Baldwin Beach Park, as well as Hana's Waianapanapa State Park. From Maui it's also easy to reach neighboring destinations such as the Molokini Crater Marine Preserve and reefs off Lanai.

Molokini, a crescent-shaped crater off Maui's southern coast, offers one of the island's great snorkeling adventures. Every day dozens of boatloads of people pull up to dive the remarkably clear waters. Visibility at Molokini typically ranges between 80 and 150 feet, conditions so clear you can spot fish before even entering the water. During winter months, you're also likely to see the humpback whales cavorting nearby.

Lahaina
LAHAINA EXTENDED HORIZONS ✉ *Mala Wharf, Lahaina* ☎ *808-667-0611, 888-348-3628* 🖱 *www.scubadivemaui.com* This company offers half-day excursions to Lanai's west coast. Dive through caverns and lava tubes in search of dolphins, turtles and whales.

OCEAN RIDERS ADVENTURE RAFTING ✉ *Mala Wharf, Lahaina* ☎ *808-661-3586* 🖱 *www.mauioceanriders.com* Specializing in snorkeling trips, Ocean Riders sets out from Maui to Lanai or Molokai on full-day snorkel trips accompanied by schools of tropical fish and topped with a continental breakfast and lunch.

LAHAINA DIVERS INC. ✉143 Dickenson Street, Lahaina ☎808-667-7496, 800-998-3483 ✐www.lahainadivers.com A well-liked dive operator, their retail store provides equipment and accessories. Scuba classes and trips are available year-round depending on the weather. Equipment repair and service are also available.

Kihei–Wailea–Makena Area

MAUI CLASSIC CHARTERS ✉1279 South Kihei Road, Suite 110, Kihei ☎808-879-8188, 800-736-5740 ✐www.mauicharters.com Come here for half-day dives into the coral gardens of the Molokini crater along with catamaran snorkeling excursions.

MAUI DIVE SHOP ✉1455 South Kihei Road, Kihei ☎808-879-3388, 800-542-3483 ✐www.mauidiveshop.com A recommended tour operator that also rents snorkel and scuba equipment, they have ten locations in Maui.

MIKE SEVERNS DIVING ✉Kihei Boat Ramp, Kihei ☎808-879-6596 ✐www.mikesevernsdiving.com, severns@mauigateway.com Well-known by underwater photographers, Mike Severns runs trips for certified divers to Molokini and Makena. Dives focus on the southwest rift of Haleakala, a fascinating place to study marine life. Led by informative guides, these trips are an excellent way to see Maui's hidden marine life.

SCUBA SHACK ✉2349 South Kihei Road, Kihei ☎808-879-3483, 877-213-4488 ✐www.scubashack.com, wetanku@maui.net This full-service operator features scuba and snorkeling trips to Molokini Crater. Visibility of 150 feet makes this marine reserve a favorite place to splash down.

MAUI SUN DIVER ✉Kihei ☎808-879-3337, 877-879-3337 ✐www.mauisundivers.com Maui Sun provides all gear and offers everything from beginner trips to certification classes to night dives. A true part of "Hidden Hawaii," you won't find them on land. They dive mainly in the Kihei-Wailea-Mahena area, but will take you wherever the weather is best.

ED ROBINSON'S DIVING ADVENTURES ✉Kihei ☎808-879-3584, 800-635-1273 ✐www.maui-scuba.com Experienced divers should sign on with Ed Robinson's. A prominent oceanic photographer, Robinson leads half-day scuba excursions aboard the *Seadiver II* and *Sea Spirit* to the Lanai Cathedrals, Molokini and other favored dive sites.

KAI KANANI SAILING CHARTERS ✉5400 Makena Alanui, Maui Prince Hotel ☎808-879-7218 ✐www.kaikanani.com This company operates the 65-foot *Kai Kanani*, which departs from Makena Beach, and goes closer to the largely submerged volcano than other touring vessels. Prices include all equipment, food and drink.

SURFING, WINDSURFING & KITESURFING

If you must go down to the sea again, why not do it on a board? For surfing, *Maalaea*, Honolua Bay and Hookipa are consistent world-class venues. La Perouse is an expert's heaven. For beginners try Launipoka County Park or the Kaanapali Coast.

Pro windsurfers and kitesurfers will want to head to Hookipa. Pros at other things should confine their windsurfing and kitesurfing to Kanaha, Kihei and Spreckelsville.

Lahaina

GOOFY FOOT SURF SCHOOL ✉505 French Street, Suite 123, Lahaina 📞808-244-9283 🌐www.goofyfootsurfschool.com Check out this surf school, which gives beginner- to advanced-level lessons and leads surf safaris.

MAUI OCEAN ACTIVITIES ✉In front of the Hyatt Regency Maui, 200 Nohea Kai Drive, Lahaina 📞808-667-2001 📠808-667-4346 🌐www.mauiwatersports.com, beaches@maui.net This operator offers surfing and windsurfing lessons on the adjacent beach. Ninety-minute windsurfing lessons come with a guarantee of success. Four-person surfing classes are also offered, weather permitting. Rentals are available.

Kahului–Wailuku Area

MAUI WINDSURF COMPANY ✉22 Hana Highway, Kahului 📞808-877-4816, 800-872-0999 📠808-877-4606 🌐www.mauiwindsurfcompany.com, info@mauiwindsurfcompany.com Maui Windsurf can help work windsurfing into your visit, either with a car rack and sails or with lessons. Instruction is held in the calmer waters at Kanaha, near the airport. Hookipa's more powerful winds are recommended only for experts.

SECOND WIND SAIL SURF & KITE ✉111 Hana Highway, Kahului 📞808-877-7467 🌐www.secondwindmaui.com At this place, you can get everything you need for a day (or longer) of surfing, windsurfing or kitesurfing. They offer equipment rental and sales and extensive instruction.

LIGHTNING BOLT ✉55 East Kaahumanu Avenue, Kahului 📞808-877-3484 🌐www.lightningboltmaui.com You can buy surfing gear at this spot, the oldest surf shop on Maui.

Hana Area

KAI NALU SURF TOURS ✉536 Kahua Place, Paia 📞808-579-9937 📠808-579-9937 🌐www.mauisurfing.com, nalu@maui.net Kai Nalu will take you on two- or four-day excursions to lesser-known Maui surfing spots.

FISHING

The deep blue sea around Maui can be nirvana for sportfishing enthusiasts. For deep-sea fishing you'll have to charter a boat, and freshwater angling requires a license, which can be obtained at sportfishing stores.

There is also good fishing from the shore in many places. For information on the best spots, ask at local fishing stores, or try the following beaches: Hoaloha Park, Launiupoko County Park, Honokowai Beach Park, D. T. Fleming Park, Honokohau Beach, Keawakapu Beach, Poolenalena Beach Park, Black Sands Beach, Little Beach and Waianapanapa State Park.

For information on seasons, licenses and official regulations, check with the Aquatic Resources Division of the State Department of Land &

Natural Resources. Choose between party boats, diesel cruisers and yachts custom-designed for trolling. All outfits provide equipment and bait. Just bring your own food and drinks and you're in business. Occasionally, your skipper may head for the productive game fishing waters between Maui and the Big Island. It's a treacherous channel, however, so you're more likely to fish the leeward side of the island or off neighboring Lanai.

Lahaina

WEST MAUI SPORTS & FISHING SUPPLY ✉*1287 Front Street* ✆*808-661-6252, 888-498-7726* ✐*wmauispt@maui.net* Contact this company for trips in search of marlin, mahimahi, wahoo and tuna. If a deep-sea excursion is not for you, rent a pole for shore fishing.

LUCKEY STRIKE CHARTERS ✉*Lahaina Harbor* ✆*808-661-4606* ✐*www.luckeystrike.com* Luckey Strike fishes for marlin, mahimahi, wahoo and tuna with light and medium tackle. Light-tackle bottom fishing and customized live-bait fishing trips are also available.

HINATEA ✉*27 Lahaina Harbor* ✆*808-667-7548* This is a sportfishing boat that offers trips into coastal waters. On half- and full-day trips you'll fish for marlin, mahimahi and *ono*.

Kihei–Wailea–Makena Area

CAROL ANN CHARTERS ✉*Maalaea Harbor* ✆*808-877-2181* In the Kihei area, contact Carol Ann's for four-, six- and eight-hour fishing trips great for catching marlin, tuna, mahimahi and *ono*. She runs a 33-foot Bertrum.

RASCAL CHARTERS ✉*Maalaea Harbor* ✆*808-874-8633* ✐*www.rascalcharters.com, info@rascalcharters.com* Rascal fishes for *ahi*, *ono*, mahimahi and marlin. They also run six- and eight-hour trips aboard a 41-foot Hatteras.

SAILING & WHALE WATCHING

From mid-December until the middle of May, it is prime whale-watching season on Maui. Humpback whales, measuring about 40 feet and weighing over 40 tons, migrate as many as 4000 miles from their summer home in Alaska. On the journey south, they consume tons of krill and tiny fish, then fast while in Hawaii. It is in the waters off Maui that they give birth to their young, babies that can weigh as much as three tons and gain up to 100 pounds a day.

These cetaceans are a protected species and power crafts are required by law to keep their distance. But these restrictions are not so severe as to unduly interfere with the many sailing vessels that offer whale-watching opportunities off the Maui coast. You can also enjoy dive trips or pure performance rides on these beautiful vessels.

A prime area for whale watching lies along Honoapiilani Highway between Maalaea Bay and Lahaina, particularly at McGregor Point. So while you're visiting Maui, always keep an eye peeled seaward for vaporous spume and a rolling hump. The place you're standing might suddenly become an ideal crow's-nest.

Between 2000 and 3000 of the world's 10,000 humpbacks make the annual migration to Maui's southwestern coast each year. Today they are an endangered species, protected by federal law from whalers. Several local organizations study these leviathans and serve as excellent information sources.

PACIFIC WHALE FOUNDATION ✉*300 Maalaea Road, Suite 211, Wailuku* ✆*808-249-8811, 800-942-5311* ✐*www.pacificwhale.org* You can count on this foundation to issue daily reports over local radio stations during whale season. This same organization conducts "eco-adventure cruises," the profits from which help fund their whale protection projects. They have snorkeling tours to Molokini and whale-watching cruises, both led by marine naturalists. Most interesting is their dolphin adventure, where you snorkel Lanai's untouched coral reefs and see spinner and bottlenose dolphins in one of the island's many hidden coves.

Lahaina

TRILOGY EXCURSIONS ✉*Lahaina Harbor* ✆*808-661-4743, 888-225-6284* ✆*808-667-7766* ✐*www.sailtrilogy.com* Trilogy specializes in half- and full-day sailing adventures. They also offer whale-watching trips aboard a 41-foot sloop, as well as snorkeling excursions, scuba trips, instruction and joysailing. Special trips include Molokini crater and Lanai. Trilogy receives high praise from repeat clients who climb aboard the 50-foot catamaran for excursions to Lanai. Once on the nearby island, they can swim and snorkel Hulopoe Bay Marine Reserve, enjoy a Hawaiian barbecue and tour Lanai City. Trips depart from Lahaina and Maalaea harbors and Kaanapali Resort beach.

SCOTCH MIST SAILING CHARTERS ✉*Lahaina Harbor* ✆*808-661-0386* ✐*www.scotchmistsailingcharters.com, info@scotchmistsailingcharters.com* This charter company offers half-day snorkeling trips. Whale watching, sailing and champagne-and-chocolate sunset sails are also available.

AMERICA II ✉*Lahaina Harbor* ✆*808-667-2133, 888-667-2133* ✐*www.sailingon maui.com* Imagine the thrill of big-time yacht racing when you sail aboard this 65-foot America's Cup contender. There are morning whale-watching excursions from December 15 through April and tradewind and sunset sails year-round. The trips last two hours and include soft drinks and snacks.

CINDERELLA ✉*Maalaea Harbor* ✆*808-244-0009* For an intimate experience, try the six-passenger *Cinderella*, a 50-foot luxury sailboat.

LAHAINA CRUISE COMPANY ✉*658 Front Street, Lahaina* ✆*808-661-8397, 877-500-6284* ✐*www.mauiprincess.com* This company offers whale-spotting cruises from mid-December to May. They also have fine-dining sunset dinner cruises, Molokini crater snorkel tours, and four package tours to Molokai, from a van tour to a car rental package.

Kaanapali–Kapalua Area

KAPALUA KAI ✉*Kaanapali* ✆*808-667-5980* ✆*808-667-5980* ✐*www.sailing maui.com* This is a popular catamaran offering picnic-and-snorkeling and sunset sails. It sails Maui's most scenic waters and features whale-watching excursions in winter months. Scuba trips also available.

PARASAILING & HANG GLIDING

Lahaina and Kaanapali Beach are perfect places to become airborne. Wonderful views of Maui's west side and neighboring Molokai add to the fun. The typical parasailing trip includes 30 to 45 minutes shuttling out and back to the launch point and eight to ten minutes in the air.

WEST MAUI PARASAIL ✉Lahaina Harbor, Lahaina ☎808-669-6555 ⌨www.westmauiparasail.com If you go through this outfitter, you'll rise as high as 900 feet on a single or tandem ride. Closed mid-December to mid-May.

UFO PARASAIL ✉Whalers Village, Kaanapali ☎808-661-7836 UFO lets you ascend up to 800 feet and also fly with a companion.

HANG GLIDING MAUI ✉Hana Airport, Kahului ☎808-572-6557 ⌨www.hangglidingmaui.com For hang gliding from some of the most beautiful spots on the island, try this Maui operator. They also operate motorized hang gliding in Hana. Reservations required.

KAYAKING

Cruising Maui's coastline by kayak offers close-up views of sealife as well as neighboring islands and perhaps the largest seasonal population of humpback whales.

Kihei–Wailea–Makena Area

KELII'S KAYAK TOURS ✉P.O. Box 959, #420, Kihei, HI 96753 ☎808-874-7652, 888-874-7652 ⌨www.keliiskayak.com, info@keliiskayak.com An easy-going kayaking excursion along the Makena Bay area can be had with Kelii's. Rising early in the morning, you get a quick lesson on ocean kayaking, and then venture off the shoreline in search of Maui's sea life. Those lazy-looking sea turtles bobbing alongside you don't have to work as hard as you do. The trip concludes with a dip in the sea for an up-close-and-personal snorkeling adventure. Kelii's also offers north shore tour excursions in the Honolua Bay/Honokohau area and west shore departures in Lahaina.

SOUTH PACIFIC KAYAKS ✉95 Halekuai Street, Kihei ☎808-875-4848, 800-776-2326 ⌨www.southpacifickayaks.com Kayak rentals and tours can also be arranged through South Pacific. Their naturalist-guided trips include snorkeling, and you're likely to see whales, sea turtles and dolphins, depending on the season.

Kahului–Wailuku Area

MAUI SEA KAYAKING ✉Puunene ☎808-572-6299 ⌨www.maui.net In Central Maui, this company offers day trips to Maui and Lanai and full-moon trips to Molokini. Or they'll lead you on an overnight "romance" retreat, for which a guide will arrange a seaside campsite that is off the beaten track and inaccessible by car. In the morning, the guide will return to prepare your breakfast and lead the way back to civilization. They also lead kayak and wave-ski surfers to beaches good for surfing. Maximum four people.

Rafting trips are the adventurous way to enjoy the Maui coast. Easily combined with dive and whale-watching trips, these sturdy craft are a great way to reach hidden coves and beaches.

Lahaina

OCEAN RIDERS ADVENTURE RAFTING ✉️*Mala Wharf, Lahaina* 📞*808-661-3586* 🖱️*www.mauioceanriders.com* Ocean Riders will take you out to Lanai and, weather permitting, Molokai, for a glorious day of snorkeling, as well as whale watching during whale season. All trips are aboard rigid-hull inflatable boats.

CAPTAIN STEVE'S RAFTING EXCURSIONS ✉️*Mala Wharf, Lahaina* 📞*808-667-5565* 🖱️*www.captainsteves.com* A great company offering tours is Captain Steve's, which heads out regularly in search of tropical fish, dolphins and exotic birdlife. One trip not to miss circumnavigates Lanai.

HAWAII OCEAN RAFTING'S ✉️*P.O. Box 381, Lahaina, HI 96767* 📞*808-667-2191* 🖱️*www.hawaiioceanrafting.com* Full- and half-day trips are offered aboard Hawaii Ocean's vessel, a motorized raft that takes you to a variety of different snorkeling spots while spinner dolphins leap picturesquely in your wake.

Kihei–Wailea–Makena Area

BLUE WATER RAFTING ✉️*Kihei Boat Ramp, Kihei* 📞*808-879-7238* 🖱️*www.bluewaterrafting.com* Come here for both rafting and snorkeling trips to the very popular Molokini and the Kanaio coast.

RIDING STABLES

Maui's volcanic landscape, beaches and sculptured valleys are choice sites for equestrian excursions. A variety of rides are available across the island—from the shoreline of Hana to the slopes of Haleakala, you can count on seeing wildlife, lava fields and those famous Maui sunsets.

Kihei–Wailea–Makena Area

MAKENA STABLES ✉️*8299 South Makena Road, Makena* 📞*808-879-0244* 🖱️*www.makenastables.com, info@makenastables.com* This group leads trail rides across the scenic 20,000-acre Ulupalakua Ranch on the south slope of Haleakala. Mountain trails cross a 200-year-old lava flow. Choose among a two-and-a-half-hour morning ride or a three-hour sunset ride. Possibilities include overlooking La Perouse Bay or going through Kalua Olapa, which is an old, inactive volcanic vent, and sunset rides. Private rides are available by arrangement.

Hana Highway

LAHAINA STABLES ✉️*P.O. Box 37, Lahaina, HI 96767* 📞*808-667-2222* 📠*808-661-5750* Offering morning, noon and evening rides, this company presents history, views of the islands and sunsets along Laniopoko Valley. Lunch provided for midday rides. Eight riders maximum.

Upcountry and Haleakala

THOMPSON RANCH AND RIDING STABLES ✉️*Polipoli Road, Kula*
📞*808-878-1910* Ride through pastureland on short day and sunset trips
that offer views of the other islands. Excursions are suitable for children.

PONY EXPRESS ✉️*Crater Road, Kula* 📞*808-667-2200* 📠*808-878-2821* 🖥️*www.*
ponyexpresstours.com For tours of Haleakala National Park, these tour
guides offer rides down the trail into the crater. On the seven-and-a-
half-mile roundtrip (which takes three and a half to four hours) you'll
learn about the unique plant and animal life found in the crater, as well
as Hawaiian myths and stories. Remember: the altitude is 10,000 feet so
dress in layers (you need long pants and closed-toe shoes) because it
gets hotter as you go down the trail. (No pregnant women allowed and
you must be over 10 and under 65 to ride.)

CHARLIE'S TRAIL RIDES AND PACK TRIPS 📞*808-248-8209*
Charlie's provides overnight horseback trips from Kaupo through
Haleakala. There is a six-person maximum on overnight trips. Two-
and four-hour trips outside the park are also available. Meals can be included in the travel package for groups of four to six.

GOLF

With more than a dozen public and private courses, Maui is golf
heaven. Choices on the Valley Isle range from country club links to inexpensive community courses. Also, several resorts offer a choice of
championship courses ideal for golfers looking for a change of pace.
These are open to the public for a hefty fee. Consider reserving tee-
times before your visit, especially during the high season. Some courses
allow you to book up to a month in advance.

Lahaina

KAANAPALI GOLF COURSES ✉️*2290 Kaanapali Parkway, Lahaina* 📞*808-*
661-3691 🖥️*www.kaanapali-golf.com, emailus@kaanapali-golf.com* These courses
are among the island's finest. The championship par-71 North Course,
designed by golf course architect Robert Trent Jones, Sr., has a slight incline. The easier South Course is intersected by Maui's popular sugar
cane train.

Kaanapali–Kapalua Area

KAPALUA RESORT ✉️*2000 Village Road, Kapalua* 📞*877-527-2582* With
three courses, this resort is one of the best places to golf on Maui. For a
real challenge, try the par-73 Plantation Course built in the heart of
pineapple country. The oceanfront Bay Course and the mountainside
Village Course, which ascends into the foothills, were created by Arnold
Palmer himself.

Kihei–Wailea–Makena Area

WAILEA GOLF CLUB ✉️*100 Wailea Golf Club Drive* 📞*808-879-2966* 🖥️*www.*
waileagolf.com Located in the heart of the Wailea Resort complex, this
club offers three courses, all with ocean views. The 18-hole old "blue
course" is the least challenging and heads uphill along the slopes of

Haleakala. The "emerald course" is lined with lush tropical flowers, trees and shrubs. The "gold course" is the longest and most challenging, with 93 bunkers. There are two clubhouses on the premises.

MAKENA GOLF CLUB ✉5415 Makena Alanui, Makena 📞808-879-3344 📠808-879-2834 🖥www.makenagolf.com Located next to the Maui Prince Hotel are these two 18-hole courses. Designed by Robert Trent Jones, Jr., the "North" and "South" courses are intended to blend into the natural Hawaiian landscape while offering high-challenge golf. Rolling terrain and beautiful views of the neighbor islands make these links a treat.

Kahului–Wailuku Area
WAIEHU MUNICIPAL GOLF COURSE ✉340 Kahekili Highway, Waiehu 📞808-243-7400 This is the island's only publicly owned course. With a front nine on the shoreline and a challenging back nine along the mountains, this course offers plenty of variety. Other amenities include a driving range and practice green.

KALIHI GOLF COURSE ✉2500 Honoapiilani Highway, Waikapu 📞808-242-4653 This somewhat hilly, par-72 course was designed by Nelson and Wright. Three holes have lakes or ponds. There's a restaurant and pro shop on the premises, as well as a practice range, a chipping green and two putting greens.

Hana Highway
MAUI COUNTRY CLUB ✉48 Nonohe Place, Paia 📞808-877-7893 This is a relatively easy nine-hole course open to the public on Mondays.

Upcountry and Haleakala

PUKALANI COUNTRY CLUB
✉360 Pukalani Street 📞808-572-1314 Boasting the highest elevation of all Maui's courses, this 18-hole public course on the slopes of Haleakala is a sleeper with great views. Bring a jacket or sweater because these links can get cool.

TENNIS

If you're an avid tennis fan, or just in the mood to whack a few balls, you're in luck. Public tennis courts are easily found throughout the island. Almost all are lighted and convenient to major resort destinations.

Lahaina
PARKS AND RECREATION DEPARTMENT 📞808-661-4685 Call here for more information on public tennis courts.

LAHAINA CIVIC CENTER ✉1840 Honoapiilani Highway Five lighted courts.

MALU-ULU-OLELE PARK ✉Front and Shaw streets 📞661-4685 Four lighted courts.

Kaanapali–Kapalua Area

HYATT REGENCY MAUI ✉ *200 Nohea Kai Drive, Kaanapali* ✆ *808-661-1234*
Six courts. Fee for non-guests.

KAPALUA TENNIS GARDEN ✉ *100 Kapalua Drive, Kapalua* ✆ *808-669-5677* Ten courts. Fee.

Kihei–Wailea–Makena Area

KALAMA PARK ✉ *1910 South Kihei Road* ✆ *808-879-4364* Four lighted courts.

WAIPUILANI PARK ✉ *Waipuilani Road* ✆ *808-879-4364* Six courts.

MAKENA RESORT TENNIS CLUB ✉ *Makena Resort, 5400 Makena Alanui, Makena* ✆ *808-879-8777* Six courts. Fee.

WAILEA TENNIS CLUB ✉ *131 Wailea Iki Place, Wailea* ✆ *808-879-1958* Eleven courts. Fee.

Kahului–Wailuku Area

KAHULUI COMMUNITY CENTER ✉ *Onehee and Uhu streets* Four courts.

WAR MEMORIAL COMPLEX ✉ *1580 Kaahumanu Avenue* Four courts.

PUBLIC COURTS ✉ *Wells and Market streets* ✆ *808-270-7389* Seven courts.

Hana Highway

HANA BALL PARK ✉ *Hauoli and Uakea streets* Two courts.

Upcountry and Haleakala

EDDIE TAM MEMORIAL CENTER ✉ *931 Makawao Avenue, Makawao* Two lighted courts.

MAYER HANNIBAL TAVARES COMMUNITY CENTER ✉ *91 Pukalani Street* ✆ *808-572-8122* One court.

BIKING

If you've ever wanted to zip down a mountainside or go off-road in volcanic highlands, you've come to the right place. While Maui is best known for its downhill cycling trips, there are also many other challenging adventures. For example, you can enjoy the remote route from Hana to Ulupalakua or head from Kapalua to Wailuku via Kahakuloa.

As of late 2007, bike tours are not permitted in Haleakala National Park due to safety concerns. Many tours now begin outside the park or from different locations. Independent biking is still allowed in the park.

MAUI MOUNTAIN CRUISERS ✉ *381C Baldwin Avenue, Paia* ✆ *808-871-6014, 800-232-6284* 🖰 *www.mauimountaincruisers.com* For a friendly cruise on single-gear beach cruisers, contact this shop. They serve breakfast or lunch on sunrise or mid-day rides, stopping for lunch at the Sunrise Market and Protea Farm.

ALOHA BICYCLE TOURS ✉ *Kula* ✆ *808-249-0911, 800-749-1564* 🖰 *www.mauibike.com* This is a family-run operation that bills itself as a ride-at-

your-own-pace tour company with a support van. Sounds like an especially good idea along these gorgeous routes. Minimum age is 14.

MAUI DOWNHILL ✉ *199 Dairy Road, Kahului* ☎ *808-871-2155, 800-535-2453*
📠 *808-871-6875* 🖥 *www.mauidownhill.com* Here you'll enjoy sunrise daytrips
and mid-morning runs. The longer trips include a no host meal;
helmets, windbreakers, suits and insulated gloves are provided for
all rides.

HIKING

Many people complain that Maui is overdeveloped. The wall-to-wall
condominiums lining the Kaanapali and Kihei beachfront can be pretty
depressing to the outdoors lover. But happily there is a way to escape.
Hike right out of it.

The Valley Isle has many fine trails that lead through Hana's rainforest,
Haleakala's magnificent valley, up to West Maui's peaks and across the
south shore's arid lava flows. Any of them will carry you far from the
madding crowd. It's quite simple on Maui to trade the tourist enclaves
for virgin mountains, untrammeled beaches and eerie volcanic terrain.

Most trails you'll be hiking are composed of volcanic rock. This is a very
crumbly substance, so be extremely cautious when climbing rock
faces. In fact, you should avoid steep climbs if possible. Stay on the
trails: Maui's dense undergrowth makes it very easy to get lost. If you
get lost at night, stay where you are. Because of the low latitude, night
descends rapidly here; there's practically no twilight. Once darkness
falls, it can be very dangerous to move around. You should also be careful to purify all drinking water. And be extremely cautious near streambeds as flash-flooding sometimes occurs, particularly on the windward
coast. This is particularly true during the winter months, when heavy
storms from the northeast lash the island.

For those ready to take a dip in Iao Stream, be aware that you might be
in the water with *leptospirosis*. This bacterium penetrates the body
through broken skin or such orifices as the nose, mouth and ears. Flu-
like symptoms are the results . . . unless you have a severe case, which
can lead to kidney, liver or heart damage. Consult the Hawaii State
Department of Health at 808-244-4288 for further information.

It's advisable to wear long pants when hiking in order to protect your
legs from rock outcroppings, insects and spiny plants. Also, if you're going to explore Haleakala volcano, be sure to bring rain and cold-
weather gear; temperatures are often significantly lower than at sea
level and this peak occasionally receives snow.

One note: A number of trails pass preserved cultural or historical sites.
Please do not disturb these in any way.

For more information, contact the Division of Forestry and Wildlife, Na
Ala Hele Trails and Access Program (54 South High Street, Room 101,
Wailuku, HI 96793; 808-984-8100, 808-873-3509, fax 808-984-8111;
www.hawaiitrails.org).

Before arriving in Maui, you might want to obtain hiking maps; they are available on Oahu from **Hawaii Geographic Maps & Books**. They also sell informational guides and books useful for hiking (P.O. Box 1698, Honolulu, HI 96806; 808-538-3952, 800-538-395).

If you're uncomfortable about exploring solo, you might consider an organized tour. The **National Park Service** provides information to hikers interested in exploring Haleakala National Park. What follows is a basic guide to most of Maui's major trails (Haleakala National Park, P.O. Box 369, Makawao, HI 96768; 808-572-4400, fax 808-572-1304; www.nps.gov/hale).

HIKE MAUI ✉P.O. Box 330969, Kahului, HI 96733 ✆808-879-5270 📠808-893-2575 💻www.hikemaui.com This company has been offering hiking tours longer than anyone else on the island. They emphasize natural history, and their affection for their subject matter shows. One of the hikes wanders through Kipahula Valley, on the track of waterfalls and streams. You can swim through clear pools past ferns and hanging vines, then lunch at the top of a 200-foot waterfall. They also have volcano and coastline hikes.

All distances listed for hiking trails are one way unless otherwise noted.

Kihei–Wailea–Makena Area

King's Highway Coastal Trail (5.5 miles) follows an ancient Hawaiian route over the 1790 lava flow and is considered a desert region. The trail begins near La Perouse Bay at the end of the rugged road that connects La Perouse Bay with Makena Beach and Wailea. It heads inland through groves of *kiawe* trees, then skirts the coast and finally leads to Kanaloa Point. From this point the trail continues across private land. Because segments of the trail pass through the Ahihi–Kinau Natural Area Reserve, which has stricter regulations, call Na Ala Hele Trails and Access Program for more information (808-873-3508).

Kahului–Wailuku Area

The main hiking trails in this region lie in Iao Valley, Wailuku and along Kakekili Highway (Route 340).

Iao Stream Trail (1 mile) leads from the Iao Valley State Monument parking lot for half a mile along the stream. The second half of the trek involves wading through the stream or hopping across the shoreline rocks. But your efforts will be rewarded with some excellent swimming holes en route. You might want to plan your time so you can relax and swim. Watch for falling rocks and flash floods!

KANAHA POND WILDLIFE SANCTUARY ✆808-984-8100 Not far from Kahului Airport on Route 360, birders will be delighted to find a trail meandering through this wildlife sanctuary (2 miles). This jaunt follows two loop roads, each one mile long, and passes the natural habitat of the rare Hawaiian stilt, the Hawaiian duck (a species re-introduced to Maui in 1991) and the Hawaiian coot. The trails in the Kanaha Pond area are closed during bird-breeding season (April–August). The pond-kiosk area, which has a short observation "peninsula," is open year-round, but to hike on the trail, you'll need a permit from the State Division of Forestry.

Northwest of Kahului, along the Kahekili Highway, are two trails well worth exploring, the Waihee Ridge Trail and Kahakuloa Valley Trail.

Waihee Ridge Trail (2.5 miles) begins just below Maluhia Boy Scout Camp outside the town of Waihee. The trail passes through a guava thicket and scrub forest and climbs 1500 feet en route to a peak overlooking West and Central Maui. The trail summit is equipped with a picnic table rest stop.

Hana Highway

Hana-Waianapanapa Coastal Trail (3 miles), part of the ancient King's Highway, skirts the coastline between Waianapanapa State Park and Hana Bay. Exercise extreme caution near the rocky shoreline and cliffs. The trail passes a *heiau*, sea arch, blowhole and numerous caves while winding through lush stands of *hala* trees.

Waimoku Falls Trail (2 miles) leads from the visitors center parking lot at Oheo Gulch up to Waimoku Falls. On the way, it goes by several pools and traverses a bamboo forest. (Mosquito repellent advised.) Contact Haleakala National Park Headquarters for information on this trail.

Upcountry

The main trails in Maui's beautiful Upcountry lie on Haleakala's southern slopes. They branch out from Polipoli Spring State Recreation Area through the Kula.

Redwood Trail (1.7 miles) descends from Polipoli's 6200-foot elevation through impressive stands of redwoods to the ranger's cabin at 5300 feet. There is a dilapidated public shelter in the old CCC camp at trail's end. A four-wheel drive is required to reach the trailhead.

Plum Trail (1.7 miles) begins at the CCC camp and climbs gently south to Haleakala Ridge Trail. The route passes plum trees as well as stands of ash, redwood and sugi pine. There are shelters at both ends of the trail.

Tie Trail (0.5 mile) descends 500 feet through cedar, ash and sugi pine groves to link Redwood and Plum Trails. There is a shelter at the Redwood junction.

Polipoli Trail (0.6 mile) cuts through cypress, cedars and pines en route from Polipoli Campground to Haleakala Ridge Trail.

Boundary Trail (4 miles) begins at the cattle guard marking the Kula Forest Reserve boundary along the road to Polipoli. It crosses numerous gulches planted in cedar, eucalyptus and pine. The trail terminates at the ranger's cabin.

Waiohuli Trail (1.4 miles) descends 800 feet from Polipoli Road to join Boundary Trail. Along the way it passes young pine and grasslands, then drops down through groves of cedar, redwood and ash. There is a shelter at the Boundary Trail junction.

Skyline Road (6.5 miles) begins at 9750 feet, near the top of Haleakala's southwest rift, and descends more than 3000 feet to the top of Haleakala Ridge Trail. The trail passes a rugged, treeless area resembling the moon's surface. Then it drops below timberline at 8600 feet and eventually into dense scrub. The unobstructed views of Maui and the neighboring islands are awesome. Bring your own water.

Haleakala Ridge Trail (1.6 miles) starts from Skyline Trail's terminus at 6550 feet and descends along Haleakala's southwest rift to 5600 feet. There are spectacular views in all directions and a shelter at trail's end.

TRANSPORTATION

AIR

Three airports serve Maui—Kahului Airport, Kapalua–West Maui Airport and Hana Airport. The latter two are exclusively interisland.

KAHULUI AIRPORT The Kahului Airport is the main landing facility and should be your destination if you're staying in the Central Maui region or on the southeast coast in the Kihei–Wailea–Makena area. Aloha Airlines, American Airlines, Continental Airlines, Delta Air Lines, Hawaiian Airlines, Northwest Airlines, United Airlines and a couple of charter companies offer nonstop service from the mainland.

KAPALUA–WEST MAUI AIRPORT This airport serves the Lahaina–Kaanapali area. **Island Air** (808-669-0255) flies into the facility.

HANA AIRPORT Hana's airport is really only a short landing strip and a one-room terminal that sits near the ocean in Maui's lush northeastern corner. **Island Air** (808-669-0255) lands in this isolated community. And don't expect very much ground transportation waiting for you. There is no bus service, though there is a car rental agency.

BOAT

LAHAINA CRUISE COMPANY ☎808-667-6165 One of the few day-trip services in Hawaii is provided by this company. Their 118-foot *Maui Princess* and 100-foot *Molokai Princess* provide trips Monday through Saturday between Maui and Molokai. The price is not cheap.

HAWAII SUPERFERRY ✉One Waterfront Plaza, 500 Ala Moana Boulevard, Suite 300, Honolulu ☎808-531-7400 ☎808-531-7410 ☐www.hawaiisuperferry.com This inter-island ferry provides three-hour rides between Oahu and Maui six days a week. More than a mode of transportation, the ferry includes food, entertainment and shopping. Ongoing environmental protection surveys are an integral part of this new seafaring operation, which first set sail in December 2007. Still a burgeoning endeavor, it is a good idea to check travel policies prior to boarding or making reservations.

EXPEDITIONS ✉*658 Front Street #127, Lahaina* ☎*808-661-3756* This group operates out of Maui and links Lahaina with Manele Bay on Lanai. There are five boats per day in each direction. The 45-minute trip provides a unique way to travel between the islands.

CAR RENTALS

If, like most visitors to Maui, you arrive at the airport in Kahului, you certainly won't want for car rental agencies. There are quite a few with booths right at the airport. A number of others are located around town. Most agencies require a credit card and renters to be 25 years old.

In Kahului, the airport car-rental agencies are as follows: **Avis Rent A Car** (808-871-7575, 800-331-1212), **Budget Rent A Car** (808-871-8811, 800-527-0700), **Dollar Rent A Car** (808-877-2732, 800-800-4000), **Hertz Rent A Car** (808-877-5167, 800-654-3131) and **National Car Rental** (808-871-8851, 800-227-7368).

The rental agencies outside the airport include companies that rent older model cars at very competitive rates. One of these is **Word of Mouth Rent A Used Car** (808-877-2436, 800-533-5929; www.maui rentacar.com), which strongly recommends reservations.

If you find yourself in the Lahaina–Kaanapali area wanting to rent a car, try **Avis Rent A Car** (808-661-4588, 800-331-1212), **Budget Rent A Car** (808-661-8721, 800-527-0700), **Dollar Rent A Car** (808-667-2651, 800-800-4000), **Hertz Rent A Car** (808-661-7735, 800-654-3131) or **National Car Rental** (808-667-9737, 800-227-7368). All of these agencies have courtesy phones at the Kapalua–West Maui Airport.

Kihei is served by **Avis Rent A Car** (808-874-4077, 800-331-1212). For a cheaper alternative, try **Kihei Rent A Car** (808-879-7257, 800-251-5288).

Dollar Rent A Car (808-248-8237, 800-800-4000) is the sole company in Hana.

JEEP RENTALS

There are several companies on the island of Maui that rent four-wheel-drive vehicles. If you want to venture on the unpaved roads forbidden by front-wheel drives, check to see if it's okay to take the jeep. Some outfits offering jeeps are **Adventures Rent A Jeep** (190 Papa Place, Kahului; 808-877-6626, 800-701-5337) and **Budget Rent A Car** (808-871-8811, 808-661- 8721, 800-527-0700).

PUBLIC TRANSIT

There is almost no public transportation on Maui and the little that is provided lies concentrated in one small sector of the island.

MAUI PUBLIC TRANSIT The Maui Public Transit travels between Wailea, Lahaina, Kaanapali and Kapalua with stops at major resorts (Robert's Hawaii; 808-871-4838—ask for public transit).

AKINA BUS SERVICE &808-879-2828 Akina Bus Service operates private buses in the Lahaina–Kaanapli area.

SPEEDI SHUTTLE &877-242-5777 ⊲www.speedishuttle.com This company offers transportation from Kahului Airport to resorts on the west to the southside of the island. (It's recommended that you call at least a day in advance, though last-minute pickups are sometimes available.)

AERIAL TOURS

Much of Maui's best scenery is reached via serpentine roads or steep mountain drives. While the views are stunning, the best way to get a bird's-eye view is from the air. Helicopters, fixed-wing aircraft and gliders all make it easy to see the volcanic uplands, waterfall splashed cliffs and dreamy back-country beaches.

ALEXAIR ✉Kahului Heliport &808-871-0792, 888-418-8458 A Maui-based helicopter-tour company, they offer a wide range of tours, from 20 to 60 minutes long, as well as private charters.

PARAGON AIR ✉Kahului Airport &808-244-3356, 800-428-1231 ⊜808-573-8218 ⊲www.paragon-air.com, wings@maui.net If you prefer to see Maui and a bit more, come here. Travel aboard a nine-passenger Piper Navajo Chieftain or a six-passenger Partenavia over Maui to the Big Island or Molokai. On Molokai, passengers land and journey by foot or mule to visit Kalaupapa, the leper colony made famous by the work of Father Damien.

SUNSHINE HELICOPTERS ✉Kahului Heliport &808-871-0722, 800-469-3000 ⊜808-871-0682 ⊲www.sunshinehelicopters.com Sunshine offers tours that include whale watching when in season, waterfalls, island circumnavigation and private charters.

BLUE HAWAIIAN HELICOPTERS ✉Kahului Heliport &808-871-8844, 800-745-2583 ⊲www.bluehawaiian.com This company has accumulated its share of accolades. The company has also been used in the making of several blockbuster films such as *Jurassic Park* and *Pearl Harbor*. They offer a standard roster of tours using their ultra-quiet ECO-Stars.

LANAI

Lanai

Kalohi Channel

Polihua
Beach

Shipwreck Beach

Auau Channel

Keanapapa
Pt

Garden of
the Gods

Kanepuu Hwy

MAUNALEI VALLEY

430

Keomuku

PACIFIC OCEAN

Honopu Bay

Koele

Lanai City

Lanaihale
3370'

Makaiwa
Pt

Kaumalapau Hwy

440

Kaumalapau

PALAWI BASIN

Manele Rd

Mt
Waiakeakua
3065'

440

Naha

N

Shark Island

Palaoa Pt

Manele Bay

Kealaikahiki Channel

0   5 miles

0   5 kilometers

Eight miles from Maui, across the historic whaling anchorage at Lahaina Roads, lies the pear-shaped island of Lanai. In profile the island, formed by an extinct volcano, resembles the humpback whales that frequent its waters. It rises in a curved ridge from the south, then gradually tapers to the north. The east side is cut by deep gulches, while the west is bounded by spectacular sea cliffs rising 1500 to 2000 feet. Lanaihale, the island's tallest peak, stands 3370 feet above sea level.

First discovered by Captain Cook's men in 1779, Lanai was long avoided by mariners, who feared its reef-shrouded shores and saw little future in the dry, barren landscape. You can still see testaments to their fear in the rotting hulks that lie off Shipwreck Beach.

Ancient Hawaiians believed Lanai was inhabited only by evil spirits until Kaululaau, son of the great Maui chief Kakaalaneo, killed the spirits. Kaululaau, a Hawaiian-style juvenile delinquent who chopped down fruit trees with the gay abandon of young George Washington, had been exiled to Lanai by his father for his destructive behavior. After the wild youth redeemed himself by making the island safe from malevolent spirits, Lanai was settled by Hawaiians and controlled by powerful Maui chiefs.

Most archaeologists doubt that the native population, which lived from taro cultivation and fishing along the eastern shore, ever exceeded 2500. Even periods of peak population were punctuated by long intervals when the island was all but deserted. Lying in Maui's wind shadow, Lanai has a rainfall that ranges from 40 inches along its northeast face to a meager 12 inches annually in the barren southwest corner.

Like Molokai, its neighbor to the north, Lanai for centuries was a satellite of Maui. (Even today it is part of Maui County.) Then in 1778 it was overwhelmed by the forces of Kalaniopuu, the king of the Big Island. Later in the century, an even more powerful monarch, Kamehameha the Great, set up a summer residence along the south coast in Kaunolu.

During the 19th century, Lanai was a ranchers' island with large sections of flat range land given over to grazing. Missionaries became active saving souls and securing property in 1835 and by the 1860s one of their number had gained control of Lanai's better acreage. This was Walter Murray Gibson, a Mormon maverick whose life story reads like a sleazy novel. Despite being excommunicated by the Mormon church, Gibson went on to become a formidable figure in Hawaiian politics.

Gibson was not the only man with a dream for Lanai. George Munro, a New Zealand naturalist, came to the island in 1911 as manager of a plantation complex that originally tried to grow sugar on the island and then turned to cattle raising. While his herds grazed the island's tablelands, Munro worked in the rugged highlands. He extended the native forest, planting countless trees to capture moisture and protect eroded hillsides. He restored areas ravaged by feral goats and imported the stately Norfolk pines that still lend a mountain ambience to Lanai City. And, most important, Munro introduced an ecological awareness that, with any luck, will continue to pervade this enchanting island.

The land that Gibson and Munro oversaw changed hands several times until James Dole bought it in 1922 for a mere $1.1 million. Dole, descended from missionaries, was possessed of a more earthly vision than his forebears. Pineapples. He converted the island to pineapple cultivation, built Lanai City, and changed the face of Lanai forever.

Filipinos, now about 50 percent of the island's population, were imported to work the fields. They bent to their labors all over Lanai, wearing goggles and gloves to protect against the sharp spines that bristled from the low-lying plants. Pineapples are cultivated through plastic sheets to conserve precious water and harvesting is done by hand. Up until the early 1990s, you could see hundreds of acres covered in plastic. Downtown Lanai would roll up the streets at 9 p.m., but the lights would burn bright in the pineapple fields as crews worked through the night loading the hefty fruits onto conveyor belts.

That was yesterday, back when Lanai retained something of an ambiguous reputation. Most tourists, hearing that Lanai was nothing but pineapples and possessed only 20 miles of paved roads and a single ten-room hotel, left the place to the antelopes and wild goats.

Now, however, the sleeping midget has awakened. You still rent your car in an old gas station with scuffed floors and deer trophies on the wall. And there are still only 30 miles of paved roads on the island. But nothing else here is the same.

Stores have been renovated, old plantation homes have received fresh coats of paint, and two small clusters of homes have been constructed on the outskirts of town. Castle & Cooke, the conglomerate that owns the island (specifically 98 percent of the island's property), poured millions into the place, building two resorts and transforming little Lanai into luxurious Lanai. The Four Seasons Resort Lanai at Manele Bay, a 250-room oceanfront extravaganza, opened in 1991 just one year after the christening of the Four Seasons Resort Lanai, The Lodge at Koele, a rustic but refined 102-room resort situated along Lanai's forested mountain slopes.

Now the days of pineapple cultivation are over. The output has dropped from a peak of about 16,000 acres to a mere 200 acres, sufficient to supply island needs and give visitors a glimpse at what life was like "back when." Fields are being converted to alfalfa and oats; cattle raising has been reintroduced; and the island's Filipino and Japanese population have quit the plantation and are now working to serve the visitors who make their way to Lanai to enjoy the posh resort hotels and a plethora of outdoor activities like golf, tennis, biking and horseback riding.

In the midst of all the change, this lovely little isle has retained its charm. Even now only a fraction of Lanai's 140 square miles is developed. The rest of the island is laced with a network of jeep and hiking trails guaranteed to keep the heartiest adventurer happy. Covered in scrub vegetation along much of its surface, Lanai still supports several rare endemic bird species, including the *pueo*, *uau* and *iiwi*. In fact, while touring Lanai you're bound to meet more of the island's wildlife than its human citizenry. Asian Axis deer roam everywhere while the mouflon, which look like big horn sheep, tend to be found in the lower elevations of the island. Also keep an eye out for wild turkeys and ring-neck pheasants.

Here is an entire island that fits the description "Hidden Hawaii." Almost all of Lanai's 3200 citizens live in rustic Lanai City at the island's center, and most tourists are concentrated at The Lodge at Koele one mile away or along Hulope Beach at the Four Seasons Resort Lanai at Manele Bay. Just beyond these clusters lie mountains, rainforests, ranchlands and remote beaches—untouched realms ripe for exploration.

LANAI CITY

Situated at 1645 feet, Lanai City is a trim community of corrugated-roof houses and small garden plots. Tourist brochures present the place as a quaint New England village. Most of the houses were constructed around the 1920s in traditional company-town fashion. They are square boxes topped with tin roofs and tend to look alike. Norfolk pines break the monotony, and many homes are freshly painted in a rainbow assortment of hues.

SIGHTS

Lanai City is still a company town, but today the company is harvesting tourists instead of planting pineapples. Several housing develop-

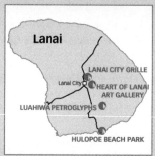

ments and condominium complexes have been built on the outskirts to house hotel employees. With everything centered around the town square, Lanai City embraces almost the entire population of the island. Situated at the center of the island at an elevation midway between the beach and the mountain peaks, it is cool and breezy with a temperate climate.

LANAI CULTURAL AND HERITAGE CENTER ⬦*Old Dole Building, Suite 126, Lanai Avenue* ☎*808-565-7177* ⬦*www.lanaichc.org* This cultural center gives visitors a first-hand look at the 1000-year history of Lanai. Historic photos of this island's immigrants—Filipino, Japanese, Portuguese, Puerto Rican and Korean—are highlighted as well as Hawaiian and plantation era materials. Closed weekends.

DOLE PARK ⬦*Located in the center of Lanai City* The focal point of this "city" is its pine-filled park, a perfect spot to enjoy a book or romp with the kids. Because of its location, you'll be able to watch all the locals going about their daily business.

FOUR SEASONS RESORT LANAI, THE LODGE AT KOELE ⬦*One Keomoku Highway* ☎*808-565-4000* ⬦*808-565-4561* ⬦*www.fourseasons.com/koele* The main "sight" in town is this posh mountain resort. It sits amidst a pine forest in a spectacular hillside setting. Pathways lead through manicured fruit and Japanese gardens, sprawling banyan trees and along a koi-filled reflecting pool.

HOTEL LANAI

$$–$$$ 11 ROOMS ✉828 Lanai Avenue ☎808-565-7211, 877-665-2624
📠808-565-6450 ✎www.hotellanai.com, hotellanai@wave.hicv.net

Brightly painted, this modest mountain retreat was once the only inn on the entire island. Set 1600 feet above sea level and surrounded by Norfolk pines, it offers clean, medium-sized rooms equipped with private baths. The lodge was built in the '20s, as was most of Lanai City, but has been given a lovely face lift. It features a restaurant and lounge, and is a local gathering place at dinnertime. A lot of folks hang out in the lobby here, making for a warm, friendly atmosphere, and the staff is congenial. Choose between small- and medium-sized standard accommodations and rooms with lanais. There's a cottage in the back and a U-shaped structure with only ten rooms, so reservations can be troublesome. It's advisable to arrange transportation with the hotel at the time of making reservations.

FOUR SEASONS RESORT LANAI, THE LODGE AT KOELE

$$$$ 102 ROOMS ✉One Keomoku Highway ☎808-565-7300, 800-321-4666
📠808-565-4561 ✎www.fourseasonsresort.com/koele

This fashionable lodge is a study in style and decorum. The most noteworthy feature is the lobby, a vaulted-ceiling affair faced on either end with a stone fireplace that rises to the roofline. Etched-glass skylights extend the length of the room, illuminating the "great hall." The plantation-style guest rooms are done with four-poster beds, hand-stenciled walls, statuettes and decorative plates. To make sure you remember that even here amid the Cook pines you are still in Hawaii, an overhead fan beats the air in languid motions.

Backdropped by mountains and surrounded by miles of grasslands, the emphasis at The Lodge is on staying put. There are porches lined with wicker chairs, a croquet court, a swimming pool and two jacuzzis that look out on field and forest, and a congenial staff to take care of every request. Five-night minimum at Christmastime.

DREAMS COME TRUE ON LANAI

$$ 4 ROOMS ✉547 12th Street, Lanai City ☎808-565-6961, 800-566-6961
📠808-565-7056 ✎www.dreamscometruelanai.com, hunters@aloha.net

You can discover for yourself whether Dreams Come True on Lanai. That's what Michael and Susan Hunter, two local jewelry makers, claim can happen when you stay in the house they transformed in 1990 into a bed and breakfast. Set in Lanai City and surrounded by fruit trees and flowering gardens, the house (which comfortably accommodates up to ten) is decorated with hand-carved screens and furniture that the owners transported from Sri Lanka and Bali. There's a large living room for guests as well as a selection of double rooms; some have canopied four-poster beds, and all have private baths with Italian marble and whirlpool tub.

378

BAMBOO GARDEN RETREAT

$$–$$$ 7 ROOMS ✉P.O. Box 630523, Lanai City, HI 96763 ☎808-565-9307
808-565-6593 bambooretreat@yahoo.com

Located on the outskirts of Lanai City, these accommodations are an ideal vacation haven for families or group gatherings. With seven bedrooms, a sun room and six baths, this plantation home sleeps from two to twenty people. Amenities abound, including a full kitchen, washer and dryer and (too) many televisions. The garden, with its bamboo and palm trees, creates an island of solitude on an island of solitude. Swedish and Shiatsu massage is also available. Guests are welcome to use the kitchen or laundry. There's also a non-refundable reservation fee. Discounts for weekly rates.

DINING

LANAI CITY GRILLE

$$$$ HAWAII REGIONAL ✉828 Lanai Avenue ☎808-565-7211

Lanai Hotel's dining room has undergone a major transformation. Its new incarnation, Lanai City Grille, offers fresh food from the island's bounty. Right-out-of-the-water seafood, organic meats and the signature rotisserie chicken are all inspired by award-winning chef Bev Gannon. An impressive wine list adds to the experience. Best of all, the aloha spirit has not changed.

CANOES LANAI

$ AMERICAN ✉419 7th Street ☎808-565-6537

Around since the 1920's, this luncheonette is where locals drop in for breakfast and lunch. They swear it has the best hamburgers in town. No dinner. Closed Wednesday.

PELE'S OTHER GARDEN

$$ DELI/ITALIAN ✉8th and Houston streets ☎808-565-9628, 888-764-3354
808-565-7613 pogdelibistro@wave.hicv.net

A New York–style deli by day, an Italian restaurant at night, Pele's is a popular local establishment. During the day you can get overstuffed, made-to-order sandwiches, pasta, salads, pizzas, soup and much more. Come nightfall, tablecloths transform the deli into an Italian bistro; you'll find a variety of appetizers, salads and pizzas as well as pasta dishes. The desserts and coffee are tempting. Closed weekends.

BLUE GINGER CAFÉ

$–$$ AMERICAN ✉409 7th Street at Ilima Avenue ☎808-565-6363 808-565-6306
gabilay@aloha.com

This café rests in an old plantation house and serves three solid meals a day. Traditional paintings and simple drawings of tropical fish adorn the place and the red paint on the cement floor has worn away almost completely. But the white walls shine and the dinners are served piping hot. Try the fried salmon or mahi sandwiches.

Lanai City

to Kanepuu Hwy &
Shipwreck Beach

Lodge at Koele

430

Cavendish
Golf Course

to Garden
of the Gods

Lanai Ave.

3rd St
4th St

Houston St
Gay Ln
5th St

Jacaranda St
Nani

6th St
Lanai

7th St

Dole Park
8th St

Caldwell Ave

Fraser

Koali St

Kiele

9th St

Awalua

Ilima St

430

Gay Ln

Pakali St

13th St

6th St

Puulani Pl

9th St

Hotel Lanai

10th St

Queens Ave

11th St

12th St

Queens
Ave

N

0   0.25 mile
0   0.25 kilometer

Kaumalapau   Hwy

440

Manele

440

Rd

to Airport

to Manele Bay

FOUR SEASONS RESORT LANAI, THE LODGE AT KOELE

On Lanai, isolation is the engine of ingenuity. Confronted with all that land and so few people, the Lodge at Koele transformed sections of the island into an organic garden, hog farm and cattle ranch. After adding a master chef, they had the ingredients for two gourmet restaurants that would be the pride not only of tiny Lanai but any island. Meals in The Terrace and The Formal Dining Room (jackets are required) are as enticing as the hotel's sumptuous surroundings.

THE TERRACE

$$$–$$$$ AMERICAN   ✉Four Seasons Resort Lanai, The Lodge at Koele   ✆808-565-4000   📠808-565-4561   ✐www.fourseasons.com/koele

Here the day begins with Belgian waffles or bacon and eggs (fresh from the farm). By evening the chef progresses to shrimp cocktails with jicama slaw and oven-roasted veal chop with creamy herbed polenta, as well as vegetarian specialties.

THE FORMAL DINING ROOM

$$$$ AMERICAN ✉*Four Seasons Resort Lanai, The Lodge at Koele* ☎*808-565-4000* 📠*808-565-4561* 🖥*www.fourseasons.com/koele*

The menu changes here every four months or so, but imagine lobster with morel mushroom ragout, and Big Island sweet corn soup with shrimp beignet. It overlooks the back of the lodge grounds, with views of the fishpond, fountain and orchid house. Dinner only.

CAFE 565

$ AMERICAN/FILIPINO ✉*408 Eighth Street* ☎*808-565-5687*

An eclectic menu that includes submarine sandwiches, pizza, calzone, pancit noodles and lumpia spring rolls is offered up at this eatery that's open weekdays for lunch (from 10 a.m.) and dinner.

SHOPPING

DIS 'N DAT ✉*418 8th Street* ☎*808-565-9170* Don't go home without visiting this shop brimming with lots of dis 'n dat—from exotic wood carvings and boxes to cool jewelry (especially earrings and necklaces). Located in a landmarked building, it's in the hub of laidback Lanai City.

LANAI ART CENTER

✉*339 7th Street* ☎*808-565-7503* 📠*808-565-9654* 🖥*www.lanaiart.org, lap@ wave.hicv.net* Both a cultural gathering place and gallery, this art center offers such artworks as *koa*-framed originals, greeting cards, ukuleles, stunning photographs, handcrafted jewelry and ceramics. Traveling artists can stock up on their supplies here as well. Check with the center for ongoing classes and workshops.

HEART OF LANAI ART GALLERY

✉*758 Queens Street (behind Hotel Lanai)* ☎*808-565-7815* 🖥*www.lanaion line.com/merchants/heart_of_lanai.htm, den@aloha.net* Granted, it doesn't have much competition, but this shop would be remarkable regardless of where it was located. Many of the paintings and sculptures are done by local artists and depict the plantation culture that was once Lanai's lifeblood but is now fast becoming its legacy. Open for tea and cookies from 2:30 p.m. to 4:30 p.m., Tuesday through Saturday; call ahead if you want to come at some other time. Closed Sunday.

THE LOCAL GENTRY ✉*363-B 7th Street* ☎*808-565-9130* 🖥*locgent@aloha.net* In the heart of Dole Park is this small clothing boutique. If you forgot your swimsuit or sandals, or if you're short on shorts, they have them. They feature clothing from San Francisco City Lights, Putumayo, Tiki, Big Blue, Allen Allen and others.

GIFTS WITH ALOHA ✉*363 7th Street* ☎*808-565-6589* 📠*808-565-9129* 🖥*www .giftswithaloha.com, shop@giftswithaloha.com* This boutique, run by the genial

Duprees, features Lanai and Hawaiian artists. Watercolor originals, pottery and wood pieces along with tempting jams, jellies and sauces, hats and casual resort wear round out the offerings at this Lanai-style (i.e., laidback) store. Closed Sunday.

MIKE CARROLL GALLERY

✉ *443 7th Street* ☎ *808-565-7122* ✐ *www.mikecarrollgallery.com, kathy@mike carrollgallery.com* Landscapes and wildlife of Lanai are celebrated in the oil paintings of local artist Michael Carroll, as well as other local artists. Stop by to see what new works are on the easel.

COFFEE WORKS LANAI ✉ *Corner of Ilima and 6th streets* ☎ *808-565-6962* ✐ *www.coffeeworkshawaii.com* Stop in here for gourmet coffee beans and teas to take home. If you're tired of all of this shopping, stop in for an espresso, a shake or an ice cream.

FOUR SEASONS GIFT SHOP ✉ *Four Seasons Resort Lanai, The Lodge at Koele* ☎ *808-565-7300* Cards, clothing and snacks are for sale at this hotel shop.

HOTEL LANAI GIFT SHOP ✉ *828 Lanai Avenue* ☎ *808-565-7211* Stop at this gift shop for simple souvenirs and gift items.

NIGHTLIFE

Visitors find this a great spot to get the sleep they missed in Lahaina or Honolulu. If rest isn't a problem, Lanai may be a good place to catch up on your reading or letter writing. One thing is certain—once the sun goes down, there'll be little to distract you. But on an average evening, even these night owl's nests will be closed by midnight (*pupus* are served until 11 p.m.).

LANAI CITY GRILLE ✉ *Hotel Lanai, 828 Lanai Avenue* ☎ *808-565-7211* You can have a drink while listening to local gossip at Hotel Lanai's restaurant, or join the locals on Fridays for a *pau hana* (finished work) musical gathering. Closed Monday.

FOUR SEASONS RESORT LANAI, THE LODGE AT KOELE

✉ *One Keomoku Highway* ☎ *808-565-7300* Mix with the gentry here where the lounge possesses a kind of gentlemen's library atmosphere with an etched-glass-and-hardwood interior. In addition to its plush lounge, the Lodge at Koele features hula dancers on weekends at lunchtime or other live entertainment in the lobby (the "great hall") at night.

NORTHEAST LANAI

From Lanai City, Route 430 (Keomuku Road) winds north through hot, arid country. The scrub growth and red soil in this barren area resemble a bleak Southwestern landscape, but the sweeping views of Maui and Molokai could be found only in Hawaii.

By the way, those stone piles—called *ahu*—along the road were placed by passing hikers honoring a local tradition (with no basis in Hawaiian culture) in which columns of three or so stones are built to help ensure good luck. The layering of rocks along a road is also known as macadam, a construction technique from the 1800s.

SIGHTS

SHIPWRECK BEACH Near the end of Keomuku Road you can turn left onto a dirt road. This dirt road leads past colonies of intermittently inhabited squatters' shacks, many built from the hulks of vessels grounded on this nearby beach. The coral reef paralleling the beach has been a nemesis to sailors since whaling days. The remains of more than 200 shipwrecked vessels dot the coastline of this small island and the rusting remains of a barge and a 1950s-era oil tanker still bear witness to the navigational hazards along this coast. Needless to say, this is one of the best areas in Hawaii for beachcombing. Look in particular for the Japanese glass fishing floats that are carried here on currents all the way from Asia.

PETROGLYPHS

At the end of the dirt road near Shipwreck Beach, a path marked with white paint leads to clusters of ancient petroglyphs depicting simple island scenes.

Those interested in extensively exploring the coast can hike all the way from Shipwreck eight miles west to Polihua Beach along jeep trails and shoreline. Back on the main road (continuing straight ahead as if you had never made that left turn that led to Shipwreck Beach) you will discover that the macadam gives way to a dirt road that leads along the northeast shore for 12 teeth-clicking miles. It was along this now-deserted coast that the ancient Hawaiian population lived. Numbering perhaps 2000 in pre-Western times, they fished the coast and cultivated taro.

KAHEA HEIAU

The ghost town of **Keomuku**, marked by a ramshackle church that's been partly refurbished, lies six miles down Keomuku Road. It's another mile and a half to this holy place that many claim is the reason Keomuku was deserted. It seems that stones from this temple were used to build the nearby Maunalei Sugar Company plantation despite warnings against disturbing the sacred rocks. So when the plantation failed in 1901 after its sweet water mysteriously turned brackish, the Hawaiians had a heavenly explanation. It was shortly after this incident that most of the rest of Lanai's populace moved up to Lanai City, leaving only spirits along the coast.

Several miles farther, past numerous salt-and-pepper-colored beaches, the road ends at the old Hawaiian village of Naha. Today nothing remains of this once prosperous colony.

MUNRO TRAIL ⊠*Off Route 430 (Keomuku Road)* Northwest of Naha is this seven-mile, jeep-required trail named for New Zealand naturalist George Munro. It begins in Koele about a mile north of Lanai City and climbs through rainforest and stands of conifers en route to **Lanaihale**, the highest point on Lanai. From this 3370-foot perch you can see every major Hawaiian island except Kauai.

On the way to Lanaihale, about two miles up the trail, you'll pass **Hookio Gulch**. The ridge beyond is carved with a defense work of protective notches made by warriors who tried futilely to defend Lanai against invaders from Hawaii in 1778.

A footpath leads to an overlook above 2000-foot deep **Hauola Gulch**, Lanai's deepest canyon. Here you may see axis deer clinging to the sharp rockfaces, seeming to defy gravity as they pick their way along the heights.

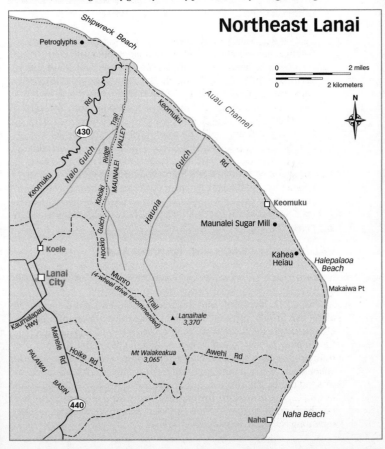

This knife-edge ridge, little more than 100 feet wide in places, is studded with ironwood and eucalyptus trees, as well as the stately Norfolk pines that New Zealand naturalist George Munro personally planted along the heights. From this aerie the slopes fall away to reveal the twin humps of Maui. The Big Island rests far below you, anchored in open ocean. The sea itself is a flat, shimmering expanse.

From Lanaihale you can either turn around or continue and descend through open fields to Hoike Road, which connects with Route 440. Be sure to check road conditions and try to go early in the morning before clouds gather along the ridgetop. While it's rough going at times, the trail affords such magnificent views from its windswept heights that it simply must not be ignored by the adventurous sightseer.

BEACHES & PARKS

SHIPWRECK BEACH

✉ *Ten miles north of Lanai City. Head north on Route 430 (Keomuku Road) and turn left at the end of the paved road.*

This strand is actually a string of small sandy patches that stretches for eight miles along the north coast, all the way to Polihua Beach. The glass fishing balls, driftwood and occasional nautilus shells on the beach make this a beachcomber's paradise. The remains of misguided ships that gave the beach its name also add to the allure. It's often windy. You can swim here but the water is shallow and you must beware of sharp coral—a protecting reef is 200 yards offshore. Windsurfers consider Shipwreck one of the prime spots in the islands. Snorkeling is not advised because of sharks. There's good diving for lobsters, but again, be cautious! You'll find good fishing for *ulua, papio* and octopus in the area between the squatters' houses and the petroglyphs. There are no established facilities at the beach. (See the "Northeast—Shipwreck Beach & Naha" section above for more details.)

HALEPALAOA BEACH AND NAHA BEACH

✉ *Take Route 430 north from Lanai City and continue on after it turns southward and becomes a dirt road. The dirt road extends for about 12 miles, ending at Naha; Halepalaoa Beach is about seven miles out along the dirt road.*

A string of salt-and-pepper-colored-sand beaches lies along the 12-mile dirt road to Naha. While most are unattractive and crowded with shoals, they do offer great views of Molokai, Maui and Kahoolawe. The Naha road winds in and out along the seafront, with numerous access roads leading to the shore. The prettiest strand is Halepalaoa Beach, a mile-long white-sand corridor partially bordered by sand dunes. These are swimming beaches; most are well-protected by shoals, but the waters are shallow. Snorkeling is a possibility here but beware of currents. You can also fish here. Several beaches, including Naha, have small picnic areas.

SOUTHEAST LANAI

Heading south from Lanai City on Route 440 (Manele Road), you'll be traveling through the Palawai Basin, the caldera of the extinct volcano that formed the island. This was also the heart of Lanai's once extensive pineapple plantation.

LUAHIWA PETROGLYPHS

To locate the petroglyphs, head south from Lanai City on Route 440. Turn left at the first dirt road. Follow the lower road as it curves along the bottom of the hillside. After passing below a watertank and pipeline, the road forks and you follow the left fork. The road goes into a horseshoe curve; when you come out of the curve there will be black boulders on the hillside above you to the left. Spread across a few acres, they contain the petroglyphs. The explorer can detour off the main highway to these ancient drawings. Finding them requires obtaining explicit directions, then driving through a field, and finally climbing a short distance up a steep bluff. But the Luahiwa petroglyphs—portraying human figures, deer, paddles and turtles—are among the finest rock carvings in Hawaii and are definitely worth the search. As you approach each cluster of boulders, you'll see pictographic stories begin to unfold. One in particular depicts a large outrigger canoe, sails unfurled, being loaded Noah-style with livestock. Preparing, perhaps, for the ancient migration north to the Hawaiian islands?

MARINE LIFE CONSERVATION CENTER Manele Road leads through agricultural fields and winds down to the twin bays at **Manele Small Boat Harbor** and **Hulopoe Bay**, which together comprise a marine life conservation area.

PUU PEHE

Just offshore from the cinder cone that separates the two harbors is a sea stack known not only for its beauty but for its legends as well. Puu Pehe was a lovely Maui girl kidnapped by a Lanai warrior who kept her hidden in a sea cave. One day when he went off in search of water, a huge sea wave swept the girl to her death. Stricken with grief and remorse, the young warrior buried her on top of the rock island and then jumped to his death from its heights.

The small-boat harbor at Manele, rimmed by lava cliffs along the far shore, contains ruins of ancient Hawaiian houses. You'll also see an old wooden chute protruding from the rocks, a loading platform used years ago to lead cattle onto ships. Today this rock-rimmed anchorage is a mooring place for fishing boats and yachts.

RUINS _____ hidden

Hulopoe offers the island's finest beach, a crescent of white sand with gentle waves, crystalline waters and a fine park facility. You'll find the stone ruins of an ancient Hawaiian home and canoe house at the north end of the beach. Just above the beach, on the grounds in front of the plush Four Seasons Resort Lanai at Manele Bay, stands the remains of an *ahu* or traditional Hawaiian shrine.

LODGING

FOUR SEASONS RESORT LANAI AT MANELE BAY

$$$$ 236 ROOMS   ✉ 1 Manele Bay Drive 📞808-565-7700, 800-321-4666 📠 808-565-3868
🖥 www.fourseasons.com/manelebay, reservations.man@fourseasons.com

While The Lodge at Koele is situated at 1600-feet elevation in Lanai City, eight miles from the ocean, this resort—Lanai's other fashionable resting spot—is a traditional beachfront retreat. Set on a bluff overlooking the best beach on the island, it is an extravaganza designed along both Asian and Mediterranean lines and surrounded by artistically planted gardens. Elegance here is in no way subdued: It speaks from the stone floors and white columns, the dark-paneled library and the recessed ceilings. The two-tiered lobby combines art deco windows with stylized Asian murals; the lower level is a terrace with glass doors that open onto ocean views.

Guest accommodations look out on either the beach or the grounds, which are sculpted into five different theme gardens—Japanese, Bromeliad, Hawaiian, Chinese and Kamaaina. Each room is spacious, done in soft gold hues and decorated with Asian armoires and color sketches of Hawaiian flora. The four-poster beds are accented with quilts and upholstered throw pillows. Add a pool, three tennis courts, a spa and a workout room and you will realize that once-sleepy little Lanai has joined the 21st century.

DINING

Outside Lanai City the dining choices—a grand total of three—are concentrated at the Four Seasons.

OCEAN GRILLE

$$ AMERICAN   ✉ Four Seasons Resort Lanai at Manele Bay 📞 808-565-2000
📠 808-565-2483 🖥 www.fourseasons.com/manelebay

Here, ladies and gentlemen, lunch is served on a bougainvillea-covered terrace. Set poolside just above the beach, this patio dining facility features island salads, including a seasonal fruit offering. There is also a standard assortment of sandwiches.

HULOPOE COURT RESTAURANT

$$$ HAWAII REGIONAL ✉ *Four Seasons Resort Lanai at Manele Bay*

📞 *808-565-2000* 📠 *808-565-2483* 🖱 *www.fourseasonsresort.com/manelebay*

This spacious resort offers more formal dining in its high-ceiling dining room equipped with glass doors that open onto a veranda overlooking the ocean. Island murals adorn the walls and pineapple-motif chandeliers dominate the room. The decor blends Asian and Polynesian styles while the menu features Hawaii Regional cuisine. Breakfast and dinner only.

IHILANI DINING ROOM

$$$$ MEDITERRANEAN ✉ *Four Seasons Resort Lanai at Manele Bay* 📞 *808-565-2000*

📠 *808-565-2483* 🖱 *www.fourseasonsresort.com/manelebay*

Sweeping views of Hulopoe Bay star at the Ihilani. The menu features Mediterranean cuisine and specializes in lamb, bouillabaisse and fresh fish dishes. The service is formal, and the wine list and cheese cart are extensive. Dinner only. Closed Sunday and Monday.

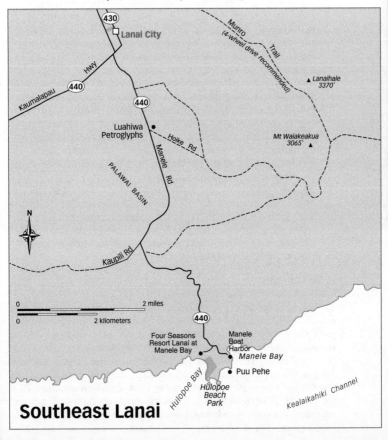

Southeast Lanai

NIGHTLIFE

HALE AHE AHE LOUNGE ⊠*Four Seasons Resort Lanai at Manele Bay* ☎*808-565-2000* 🖷*808-565-2483* ⬚*www.fourseasons.com/manelebay* Down along Hulopoe Beach at the Four Seasons, is this lounge, which combines several different settings, each equally inviting. The lounge itself has dark textured walls, a hardwood bar and a clubby ambience. Out on the terrace you can settle into a comfortable armchair or lean against the rail and enjoy the ocean view. The adjacent **Holokai Room** is a game room complete with a pool table, a wide-screen TV and an air of relaxed elegance. The Hale Ahe Ahe lounge is open for hors d'oeuvres only.

BEACHES & PARKS

HULOPOE BEACH PARK

⊠*Take Route 440 (Manele Road) south from Lanai City for seven miles*

🏊 🏄 ⚓ 🛶 Lanai's finest beach also possesses the island's only fully developed park. Set in a half-moon inlet and fringed with *kiawe* trees, this white-sand beach is an excellent spot for all sorts of recreation. Spinner dolphins are often seen here. Part of a marine life conservation area, Hulopoe has a lava terrace with outstanding tidepools along its eastern point. There is also a wading area for children at this end of the park. If you continue a short distance along this eastern shoreline you'll encounter **Puu Pehe Cove**, a small beach with abundant marine life that is excellent for swimming and snorkeling. Little wonder that Hulopoe is the island's favorite picnic spot. It's also recommended for surfing and fishing. Prime catches are threadfin, *ulua* and bonefish. This is the most accessible surf-casting beach on the island. There are restrooms and showers.

▲ ⊠*P.O. Box 630310, Lanai City, HI 96763* ☎*808-565-2970, 808-565-8206* ⬚*www.islandoflanai.com* This is it—the only campground on the island! There are sites at the far end of the beach. Expect to pay a $5 registration fee plus a charge of $5 per camper per day. Permits are issued by Castle & Cooke Resorts or from the Hulopoe park ranger. Three-night maximum stay.

MANELE BAY

⊠*On Route 440 south of Lanai City*

🏊 🏄 🛶 Primarily a small-boat harbor, this cliff-fringed inlet is populated by sailboats from across the Pacific. Carouse with the crews, walk along the jetty or scramble up the rocks for a knockout view of Haleakala on Maui. It's a very good place for swimming since the harbor is well protected, but you need to be wary of boat traffic. Because Manele Bay is part of a marine preserve the snorkeling is notable and the fishing is limited. Only pole fishing is allowed—no nets. There's a park for picnicking, and just around the corner at Hulopoe Beach are facilities for camping, swimming and other sports.

SOUTHWEST LANAI

SIGHTS

KAUMALAPAU HARBOR A southwesterly course along Route 440 (Kaumalapau Highway) will carry you steadily downhill for about six miles to this busy little harbor, which was built by pineapple interests and used primarily to ship the fruit on barges to Honolulu. During the heyday of Lanai's pineapple industry, more than a million pineapples a day were loaded onto waiting ships. On either side of Kaumalapau, you can see the *pali*, which rises straight up as high as 1000 feet, protecting Lanai's southwestern flank. These lofty sea cliffs are an ideal vantage point for watching the sunset.

KAUNOLU VILLAGE

The most interesting point along Route 440 involves a detour near the airport and a journey down a *very* rugged jeep trail to this village. A summer retreat of Kamehameha the Great and now a national historic landmark, this ancient fishing commu-

Southwest Lanai

nity still contains the ruins of more than 80 houses as well as stone shelters, petroglyphs and graves. Pick your way through it carefully, lest you step on a ghost. Kamehameha's house, once perched on the eastern ridge, looked across to **Halulu Heiau** on the west side of Kaunolu Bay. Commanding a dominant view of the entire region, these rocky remains are bounded on three sides by cliffs that vault 1000 feet from the ocean.

KAHEKILI'S LEAP Warriors proved their courage here by plunging more than 60 feet into the water below. If they cleared a 15-foot outcropping and survived the free fall into 12 feet of water, they were deemed noble soldiers worthy of their great king.

SHARK ISLAND Just offshore from Kahekili's Leap lies this rock formation that bears an uncanny resemblance to a shark fin. Could it be that warriors skilled enough to survive Kahekili's Leap had then to confront the malevolent spirit of a shark?

NORTHWEST LANAI

SIGHTS

KANEPUU PRESERVE ✉ *Take Kanepuu Highway about 20 minutes northwest from Lanai City.* One of Hawaii's (and the Earth's) most fragile ecosystems is found on the west side of Lanai. Home to 48 species of native plants, and covering 590 acres, this preserve has dry land forests similar to those that once covered much of the lowlands of the islands. Plants that grow in this area are found nowhere else on Earth, including the *aiea* and *lama* trees. A prime birdwatching area, it's a special place to walk

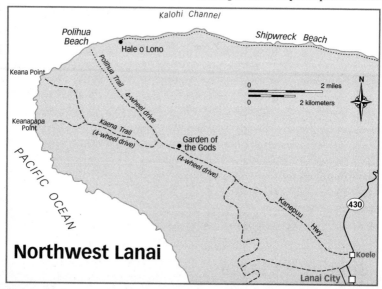

Northwest Lanai

through. There is a self-guided tour using maps at the forest entry, or you can contact the Nature Conservancy of Hawaii (808-537-4508), which protects this special spot, for tours.

LANAI OUTDOOR ADVENTURES CAMPING

GARDEN OF THE GODS

From Lanai City, a graded pineapple road passes through an eerie stand of iron-wood trees, then disintegrates into an un-graded dirt track that leads about seven miles to this garden. This heavily eroded area resembles the Dakota Badlands and features multihued boulders that change color dramatically during sun-rise and sunset. A fantasyland of stone, the Garden of the Gods is planted with ancient lava flows tortured by the elements into as many suggestive shapes as the imagination can conjure. The colors here vibrate with psychedelic intensity and the rocks loom up around you as though they were the gods themselves—hard, cold, dark beings possessed of untold power and otherworldly beauty. This is a spot not to be missed.

BEACHES & PARKS

POLIHUA BEACH

✉ *About 11 miles from Lanai City through rugged grasslands and the Garden of the Gods*

A wide white-sand beach situated along Lanai's northwest shore, this isolated strand, with stunning views of Molokai and Oahu, rivals Kauai's trackless beaches. Swimming is allowed here but exercise extreme caution—strong winds and currents prevail throughout this region. The water here is some-times muddy but when it's clear, and when the Fish and Game Division declares it "in season," you can dive for lobsters. Once a prime nesting beach for green sea turtles, Polihua Beach is an ex-cellent spot to watch whales as they pass close by the shoreline. According to local anglers, this is the best spot on the island for fishing. Common catches include *papio*, *ulua*, bonefish, threadfin and red snapper. There are no facilities here. In order to reach Polihua you'll need to drive over a rugged jeep trail. For specific di-rections and road conditions, check with the jeep rental garages.

OUTDOOR ADVENTURES

CAMPING

LANAI COMPANY ✉ *P.O. Box 630310, Lanai City, HI 96763* 📞 *808-565-2970* With so much virgin territory, Lanai should be ideal for camping. But here, as on the other islands, landowners restrict outdoors lovers. The villain is the outfit that manages the island. It permits island residents to camp where they like, but herds visitors into one area on the south coast. This campsite is located at Hulopoe Beach Park. Reservations are recommended; $5 for camping permit plus $5 per camper per night.

> # The Road to Adventure
>
> The really interesting places on Lanai lie outside town, and most require driving or hiking over jeep trails. It's advisable to get specific directions wherever you go, since the maze of dirt roads can confuse even the most intrepid pathfinder. Where possible, I've included directions; otherwise, check with the jeep rental shop in Lanai City or at the hotels.
>
> To be extra safe, ask about road conditions, too. The slightest rain can turn a dusty jeep road into a slick surface, and a downpour can transmogrify it into an impassable quagmire. I once dumped a jeep into a three-foot ditch when the trail to Polihua Beach collapsed. It had been raining steadily for three days and the soft shoulder couldn't support the weight of a vehicle. I was 11 miles from Lanai City with the wheels hopelessly embedded and an hour left until dark.
>
> The way back led past pretty menacing country, heavily eroded and difficult to track through. Rain clouds brought the night on in a rush. I gathered up my poncho and canteen, convinced myself that the worst to come would be a cold and wet night outdoors, and began trekking back to civilization. Fortunately, after five miserable hours I made it. But the entire incident could have been avoided if I had first checked road conditions and had allowed at least several hours of daylight for my return.
>
> This shouldn't discourage you, though. With the proper precautions, exploring Lanai can be a unique experience, challenging but safe.

FISHING

SPINNING DOLPHIN CHARTERS OF LANAI ✆808-565-7676 📠808-565-7572 🖊www.sportfishinglanai.com If you have a hankering to catch marlin, mahi or *ono*, contact this private sportfishing charter out of Lanai. Ahi and aku (tuna) are found year-round in the waters around Lanai. You can go out for half-day, three-quarter-day or full-day runs. They also offer whale-watching and snorkel tours.

KAYAKING

LANAI ECOADVENTURE CENTRE ✉328 8th Street, Lanai City ✆808-565-7373 🖊www.adventurelanai.com This facility features sea kayaking/snorkel combo trips. Explore the reef and the shipwreck on the island's east side or the volcanic history to the west.

SNORKELING & SCUBA DIVING

The waters off Lanai are teeming with reef fish and coral formations, enough to make any scuba diver content. One area of Lanai—**Cathedrals**—is considered the best dive site in Hawaii. Expect to float among Hawaiian green turtles, butterfly fish, black sturgeons and eels. Another favored spot is **Kaunalu**, with its calm waters and technicolor reef fish.

A number of outfitters that operate out of Maui provide everything you'll need (including refreshments) to test the waters off Lanai. Trip departure times can vary by season.

TRILOGY EXCURSIONS ✉️*Lahaina Harbor, Maui* 📞*808-661-4743, 888-225-6284* 📱*808-667-7766* 🌐*www.sailtrilogy.com* A PADI dive center, this company conducts snorkel/sail trips with an on-board naturalist from Lahaina Harbor to Hulopoe Beach Park on Lanai. Guests enjoy a light breakfast, a barbecue chicken lunch and an hour-long guided van tour through Lanai's old plantation town. Other options include beach dives at Hulopoe Bay, all-day adventure dives and sunrise dives at Cathedrals.

SCOTCH MIST SAILING CHARTERS ✉️*Lahaina Harbor, slip 2, Maui* 📞*808-661-0386* 📱*808-669-6634* 🌐*www.scotchmistsailingcharters.com* Scotch Mist offers half-day snorkeling trips from Maui to various locations, at the captain's discretion.

GOLF

THE EXPERIENCE AT KOELE ✉️*Four Seasons Resort Lanai,The Lodge at Koele, 1 Keomoku Highway, Lanai City* 📞*808-565-7300* Golfers won't be disappointed when they tee off in Lanai. The premier course on the island is this one designed by Greg Norman and Ted Robinson. Set against the backdrop of forested hills and steep gorges, it lies in the verdant central highlands. Green 17 is completely surrounded by a lake. Reserve tee times up to 90 days in advance.

CAVENDISH GOLF COURSE ✉️*Keomoku Road near the Four Seasons Resort Lanai, Lanai City* This nine-hole course—where the locals play—is open to the public as well.

CHALLENGE AT MANELE ✉️*Manele Bay Hotel* 📞*808-565-7700* Try this 18-hole golf course at the Manele Bay Hotel. Designed by Jack Nicklaus, it lies on natural lava outcroppings and follows towering cliffs. The signature hole, number 12, demands a 200-yard tee shot across the ocean. Hotel guests can reserve tee times up to 90 days in advance (30 days for non-guests).

TENNIS

LANAI GYMNASIUM ✉️*Frasier Avenue, Lanai City* 📞*808-565-6979* 📱*808-565-9144* 🌐*margie.sabin@mauicounty.gov* Two lighted courts.

FOUR SEASONS RESORT LANAI AT MANELE BAY ✉️*Near Hulopoe Beach* 📞*808-565-7700* Three courts. Fee. Guests only.

ARCHERY & SPORTING CLAYS

LANAI PINE ARCHERY ✉️*One mile north of The Lodge at Koele on Keamoku Highway* 📞*808-559-4600* 📱*808-565-4508* Ready to test your skills at a medieval sport? Lanai Pine has a range for archers of all skills and ages.

Instructors provide safety tips and pointers. If bows and arrows are too tame for you, try your luck at shooting clay targets at **Lanai Pine Sporting Clays**, run by the same people. Games include skeet, wobble traps and compact sporting. Clays are launched to simulate running patterns of various animals and birds. The staff offers instruction.

RIDING STABLES

THE FOUR SEASONS RESORT LANAI, THE LODGE AT KOELE
✉ *1 Keomoku Road, Lanai City* ☎ *808-565-7300* You can arrange horseback riding and equestrian tours here. Choose between five rides that take you on various trails around the lodge. The Koele Ride is an hour-long leisurely walking ride that follows a wooded trail and gives riders stunning views of Maui, Molokai and Lanai City.

BIKING

There are a few nice rides from Lanai City, but all are steep in places and pass over pockmarked sections of road. One goes south eight miles to Manele Bay and the beach at Hulopoe, another diverts west to busy little Kaumalapau Harbor, and the last heads north 14 miles to Shipwreck Beach. The island is a mountain biker's paradise.

LANAI CITY SERVICE INC. ☎ *808-565-7227* This is a good place to obtain information about Lanai road, including **Munro Trail**, which is perfect for those in good shape and into mountain biking.

LANAI ECOADVENTURE CENTRE ✉ *328 8th Street, Lanai* ☎ *808-565-7373* ✎ *www.adventurelanai.com* Road and mountain bike tours and rentals are available through this center.

FOUR SEASONS RESORT LANAI, THE LODGE AT KOELE
LANAI CITY ☎ *808-565-7300* Both road and mountain bikes are available through the Lodge.

HIKING

Hikers on Lanai are granted much greater freedom than campers. Jeep trails and access roads are open to the public; the only restriction is that hikers cannot camp along trails. Since most of the trails lead either to beaches or points of interest, you'll find them described in the regional sightseeing and "Beaches & Parks" sections above. All distances for hiking trails are one way unless otherwise noted.

In addition to these listings, there are two other trails to consider. The **Ancient Graveyard Trail** (.5 mile) winds to a picturesque graveyard that has been used since ancient times.

The **Koloiki Ridge Trail** (5 miles) leads through forest lands and the Cathedral of Pines (a group of pines resembling a gothic church) to a ridge that runs between Naio Gulch and Maunalei Valley. This moderately difficult hike provides views of Molokai and Maui.

LANAI ECOADVENTURE CENTRE ✉ *328 8th Street, Lanai City* 📞 *808-565-7373* 🖱 *www.adventurelanai.com* Guided hikes, including overnight camping trips, are offered by this company.

TRANSPORTATION

AIR

LANAI AIRPORT There are no direct flights from the mainland to Lanai. Inter-island airlines currently servicing this destination include Hawaiian Airlines, Aloha Airlines, Marjet and Mokulele Airlines. Island Air flies propeller-driven planes and features competitive rates.

Planes to Lanai land at this airport amid an endless maze of grassland and tilled fields four miles from downtown Lanai City. This tiny landing strip has a small gift shop and a courtesy telephone for car rentals (you'll be picked up in a shuttle). There are no lockers or public transportation. A few rooms house airline offices.

If you're staying at any of the island hotels, they will provide transportation into town, as will any of the island's car rental agencies if you're renting a vehicle from them.

BOAT

EXPEDITIONS ✉ *658 Front Street, Suite 127, Lahaina, HI 96761* 📞 *808-661-3756, 800-695-2624* 🖱 *www.go-lanai.com* This ferry service operates out of Maui and links Lahaina with Manele Bay on Lanai. There are five boats per day in each direction. The 45-minute crossing provides a unique way to arrive on the island and if you're lucky, a chance to spy spinner dolphins and flying fish.

CAR & JEEP RENTALS

LANAI CITY SERVICE INC. ✉ *1036 Lanai Avenue* 📞 *808-565-7227* This service, which is affiliated with Dollar Rent A Car, rents automatic compact cars with free mileage as well as new and reliable jeeps. But renting a car on Lanai is like carrying water wings to the desert: There's simply nowhere to go. Rental cars are restricted to pavement, while most of Lanai's roads are jeep trails: four-wheel drive is the only way to fly.

LANAI ECOADVENTURE CENTRE ✉ *328 8th Street, Lanai City* 📞 *808-565-7373* The first time I visited the island of Lanai, I rented a vintage 1942 jeep. The vehicle had bad brakes, no emergency brake, malfunctioning windshield wipers and no seat belts. It was, however, equipped with an efficient shock absorber—me. Today, you can rent jeeps here. (Be aware that the rental car collision insurance provided by most credit cards does not cover jeeps.)

BOAT TOURS

TRILOGY EXCURSIONS ☎*808-661-4743, 888-225-6284* ✐*www.sailtrilogy.com, cnielsen@sailtrilogy.com* There are boat tours of Lanai offered by this Maui-based outfit. They'll take you on a full-day excursion, leaving from Lahaina Harbor. Breakfast and lunch are provided, as well as snorkeling equipment and instruction. You'll also go on a one-hour van tour of the island.

GUIDED TOURS

RABACA'S LIMOUSINE SERVICE ☎*808-565-6670* If you'd rather not do the driving, Rabaca's offers tours around the island in limousines or Suburbans ($73.50 an hour) or, if you prefer, 4 x 4s ($50 an hour). There's a two-hour minimum. They also offer 24-hour service.

MOLOKAI

Between the bustling islands of Oahu and Maui lies an isle that in shape resembles Manhattan, but which in spirit and rhythm is far more than an ocean away from the smog-shrouded shores of the Big Apple. Molokai, Hawaii's fifth-largest island, is 38 miles long and 10 miles wide. It's the only island in the chain, aside from privately owned Niihau, where Hawaiians make up a majority of the population. Along with Lanai, Molokai is really hidden Hawaii. The slender isle was created by three volcanoes that mark its present geographic regions: one at West End where the arid Mauna Loa tableland rises to 1381 feet, another at East End where a rugged mountain range along the north coast is topped by 4970-foot Mount Kamakou, and the third, a geologic afterthought, which created the low, flat Kalaupapa Peninsula.

Considering that the island measures a modest 260 square miles, its geographic diversity is amazing. Arriving at Hoolehua Airport near the island's center, travelers feel as though they have touched down somewhere in the American Midwest. Red dust, dry heat and curving prairie surround the small landing strip and extend to the west end of Molokai. This natural pastureland gives way in the south-central region to low-lying, relatively swampy ground and brown-sand beaches with murky water.

The prettiest strands lie along the western shore, where Papohaku Beach forms one of the largest white-sand beaches in the state, and at the east end around Halawa Valley, a region of heavy rainfall and lush tropic vegetation. To the north is the vaunted *pali*, which rises in a vertical wall 3000 feet from the surf, creating the tallest sea cliffs in the world. Here, too, is an awesome succession of sharp, narrow valleys cloaked in velvet green.

Kaunakakai, a sleepy port town on the south shore, is the islands hub. From here a road runs to the eastern and western coasts. Kalaupapa and the northern *pali* are accessible overland only by mule and hiking trails.

Even in a region of islands, Molokai has always been something of a backwater. To the early Hawaiians it appeared desiccated and inhospitable. The rich Halawa Valley was settled in the 7th century and the island developed a haunting reputation for sorcery and mystical occurrences. In ancient times it was also called *pule-oo*, or "powerful prayer," and was revered for the potency of its priests. They were purported to have such power they could pray someone to death. According to legend, Molokai was the child of the god Wakea and his mistress Hina, whose cave still lies along the southeastern edge of the island.

When Captain James Cook "discovered" the island in November 1778, he found it bleak and inhospitable. Not until 1786 did a Western navigator, Captain George Dixon, bother to land. When Kamehameha the Great took it in 1795, he was actually en route to the much grander prize of Oahu. His war canoes are said to have loomed along four miles of shoreline when he attacked the island at Pakuhiwa Battleground and slaughtered the island's outnumbered defenders.

The next wave of invaders arrived in 1832 when Protestant missionaries introduced the Polynesians to the marvels of Christianity. Around 1850 a German immigrant named Rudolph Meyer arrived in Molokai, married a Hawaiian chieftess, and began a reign as manager of the Molokai Ranch that lasted for almost a half-century.

Leprosy struck the Hawaiian Islands during the 19th century, and wind-plagued Kalaupapa Peninsula became the living hell to which the disease's victims were exiled. Beginning in 1866, people with the disease were torn from their families and literally cast to their fates along this stark shore. Here Father Damien de Veuster, a Belgian priest, the Martyr of Molokai, came to live, work and eventually die among the afflicted. Pope John Paul II beatified Father Damien in recognition of his service to leprosy victims banished to Kalaupapa.

For years Molokai was labeled "The Lonely Isle" or "The Forgotten Isle." By 1910 a population that once totaled 10,000 had decreased to one-tenth the size. Then in 1921, Polynesians began settling homesteads under the Hawaiian Homes Act, which granted a 40-acre homestead to anyone with over 50 percent Hawaiian ancestry. Molokai eventually became "The Friendly Isle," with the largest proportion of native Hawaiians anywhere in the world (except for the island of Niihau, which is closed to outsiders). With them they brought a legacy from old Hawaii, the spirit of aloha, which still lives on this marvelous island. Young Hawaiians, sometimes hostile on the more crowded islands, are often outgoing and generous here.

During the 1920s, while Hawaiians were being granted the hardscrabble land that had not already been bought up on the island, Libby (which later sold out to Dole) and Del Monte began producing pineapples across the richer stretches of the island. The company towns of Maunaloa and Kualapuu sprang up and Molokai's rolling prairies became covered with fields of spike-topped fruits. Over the years competition from Asia became increasingly intense, forcing Dole to shut its operation in 1975 and Del Monte to pull out in 1982.

As elsewhere in Hawaii, the economic powers realized that if they couldn't grow crops they had better cultivate tourists. During the 1970s thousands of acres along the island's western end were allocated for resort and residential development and the sprawling Kaluakoi Resort was built. In 1996, vandals opposed to which had earlier closed access to several beaches and evicted a number of former plantation workers from their homes.

Today the island's population numbers under 8000. There isn't a single traffic light here, and the weak economy has saved Molokai from the ravages of development that plagued the rest of Hawaii during the 1980s. Change is coming, but like everything on Molokai, it is arriving slowly. Time still remains to see Hawaii as it once was and to experience the trackless beaches, vaulting seacliffs, sweeping ranchlands and forested mountains that led ancient Hawaiians to believe in the mystical powers of Molokai.

KAUNAKAKAI TO EAST END

You don't need a scorecard, or even a map for that matter, to keep track of the sightseeing possibilities on Molokai. Across its brief expanse, the Friendly Isle offers several rewards to the curious, none of which are difficult to find.

First, of course, is the falsefront town of Kaunakakai, a commercial hub that more resembles a way station on the road to Dodge City. From here, a simple two-lane road, Route 450 (Kamehameha V Highway), threads its way along the southern shore in search of the Halawa Valley at the far east end of the island.

SIGHTS

KAUNAKAKAI It is only too appropriate that this place gained its greatest fame from someone who never existed. Known for a song written about "The Cock-eyed Mayor of Kaunakakai," the town has in fact had only one mayor—whether he was cock-eyed, no one will say. This somnolent village, with its falsefront buildings and tiny civic center, is administered from Maui. Poor but proud, it possesses a population of fewer than 3000, and has a main drag (Ala Malama Street) that extends a grand total of three blocks but still represents the hub of Molokai.

KAUNAKAKAI WHARF ⊠*Just off of Route 460 on Kaunakakai Place* Nearby, extending seaward almost a half-mile and offering a mooring place for a few fishing boats, charter outfits, and private sailboats is the local wharf. It's a good place to gaze out on the island of Lanai, and an ideal vantage from which to take in the green slopes that rise toward the ridgeline of Molokai. Kids love to swim off the Kaunakaki Wharf, where a roped-off area keeps them safe from the boats. It's also a great place to meet local children.

RUINS Close to the pier landing rest the rocky remains of **Kamehameha V's Summer Home**, where Hawaii's king luxuriated during the late 19th century.

HALAWA BEACH PARK

PAGE 409

A heavenly beach with coconut palms, ironwood trees and waterfalls near some of Molokai's best surfing

KAMAKANA FINE ARTS GALLERY

PAGE 408

Master-crafted Niihau shell leis, *pahu* drums, and *lauhala* hats from over 124 local artists

KANEMITSU'S BAKERY

PAGE 406

Locally popular spot for baked goods and egg dishes served with Portuguese sausage or that other island favorite: Spam

ILIILIOPAE HEIAU

PAGE 402

Ancient center of sorcery and human sacrifice with a massive stone temple measuring 100 yards by 40 yards

---

WASTEWATER RECLAMATION FACILITY _____

✉ *Off Maunaloa Highway on the ocean side just before Kaunakakai* ✆ *808-553-5341* 🖷 *808-553-4251* For birdwatching, you'll want to check out this facility, where the nutrient-rich (read bug-infested) water is a year-round hit with endangered species such as the Hawaiian coot and stilt. In the winter, keep an eye out for the occasional shoveler, green-winged teal, wandering tattler and other migratory waterfowl. Visitors are advised to check in with plant personnel upon arrival. Closed Saturday and Sunday.

From Kaunakakai to Halawa Valley, a narrow macadam road leads past almost 30 miles of seascapes and historic sites. Route 450 runs straight along the south shore for about 20 miles, presenting views across the Kalohi and Pailolo channels to Lanai and Maui. Then the road snakes upward and curves inland before descending again into Halawa Valley.

FISHPONDS

Due to the calm, shallow waters along the southeastern shoreline, this area once supported one of the greatest concentrations of fishponds in Hawaii. Numbering as many as five dozen during the pre-Western period, these ancient aquaculture structures were built of lava and coral by commoners to raise fish for Hawaiian royalty. Small fish were trapped within these stone pens, fattened and eventually harvested. You will see the rebuilt remains of several as you drive along the coast, including **Kalokoeli Fishpond**, two miles east of Kaunakakai, **Keawanui Fishpond**, about 12 miles east of town, and **Ualapue Fishpond**, a mile farther east.

PAKUHIWA BATTLEGROUND

About five miles from town lies **Kawela**, once an ancient city of refuge, now known as the place where two battles were fought at Pakuhiwa Battleground. In his drive to become Hawaii's first monarch, Kamehameha the Great launched a canoe flotilla that reportedly extended four miles along this shore.

NENE O MOLOKAI ✉*P.O. Box 580, Kaunakakai* ☎*808-553-5992* 🖷*808-553-9029* 🖱*www.aloha.net/~nene, nene@aloha.net* For a face-to-feather encounter with the endangered *nene*, Hawaii's state bird, a close relative of the Canadian goose, swing by this nonprofit facility. Birds are raised on this beachfront location, which is open for educational visits (by appointment only).

KAMALO WHARF ✉*Just past the ten-mile marker on Route 450 (indicating that you are ten miles east of Kaunakakai)* A dirt road leads to this wharf, an old pineapple and cattle shipping point. Once a major commercial center (by Molokai standards!), it is now a gathering place for occasional fishermen and boats.

ST. JOSEPH CATHOLIC CHURCH A half-mile from Kamalo Wharf is St. Joseph's, a tiny chapel built by Father Damien in 1876. A statue of the bespectacled priest, clad in a cape and leaning on a cane, graces the property. A small cemetery completes this placid tableau.

SMITH AND BRONTE LANDING A sign on Route 450 (past the 11-mile marker) designates this landing, an inhospitable spot where two aviators crash-landed after completing the first civilian transpacific flight in 1927. The 25-hour flight from California, scheduled to land in

Kaunakakai

Honolulu, ended abruptly when the plane ran out of gas. (An opening in the trees past the 12-mile marker reveals the aforementioned Keawanui Fishpond, one of Molokai's largest.)

OUR LADY OF SEVEN SORROWS CATHOLIC CHURCH ⊠*14 miles east of Kaunakakai* Set back from the road on Route 450 in a clearing framed by mountains is this quaint church. Originally built by Father Damien in 1874 and reconstructed almost a century later, it's a pretty chapel surrounded by coconut trees and flanked by a small cemetery.

ILIILIOPAE HEIAU

⊠*15 miles east of Kaunakakai* ✆*For permission and directions, call Pauline at 808-558-8148* One of the largest in the islands, this temple rests hidden in the underbrush on private land just inland from the highway. Measuring about 100 yards in length and 40 yards in width, it was once a center of sorcery and human sacrifice that today consists of a stone platform and adjoining terraces. This is also the trailhead for the Wailau Valley Trail. According to legend, the heiau's stones were all transported from this distant valley and assembled in a single night. Kamani trees were often planted around *heiau*. Considered sacred in many Polynesian cultures, their seeds, gum and bark have been used for medicinal purposes.

MAPULEHU MANGO GROVE Near Iliiliopae Heiau is this mango grove, a stand of over 2000 fruit trees that were planted in 1926 and now represent one of the largest such groves in the world.

SUGAR MILL The ruins of the island's first sugar mill stand near Route 450's 20-mile marker. All that remains of this early factory, which burned down a century ago, is a solitary stack.

MOKU HOONIKI ISLAND

Just beyond Route 450's 20-mile marker is **Kumimi Beach**, which presents your first view of this popular diving destination, as well as otherworldly vistas of Maui.

Beyond Kumimi Beach the road begins a sinuous course along a string of pearl-white beaches, then climbs above a rocky coastline.

PUU O HOKU RANCH
As you curve upward into Molokai's tropical heights, the roadside flora becomes increasingly colorful and dense. First you encounter the open pastures and rolling ranchland of this 14,000-acre working organic ranch.

HALAWA VALLEY
As the road winds high above this valley it offers several vista points from which to view the V-shaped canyon below bounded by green walls. (*Halawa* means curve.) I love to wander the windswept beach, or hike deep into the valley, which has been inhabited by Hawaiians for 1300 years. Ancient *heiau* and the remains of a once-rich agricultural industry are some of the highlights of this lush rainforest where tropical greenery gives way to white surf and then aquamarine ocean. A river bisects this luxuriant region. At the far end, surrounded by sheer walls, two waterfalls—**Hipuapua** and **Moaula**—spill down the mountainside. Obviously East End has withheld its most spectacular scenery until the last.

Archaeologists believe that Molokai's first settlement was established in this valley, possibly as early as the 7th century. The ancient Hawaiians terraced the surrounding slopes, planting taro and living off the largesse of the sea. In 1946 (and again in 1957) a tidal wave swept through the valley, leveling buildings and leaving salt deposits that destroyed the agricultural industry. Today you can drive down into the valley, where you'll find a park, a lovely curve of sandy beach, freshwater Halawa Stream, an old church and several other structures.

GUIDED HIKES
A hiking trail leads to 250-foot Moaula Falls and 500-foot Hipuapua Falls, but please note, however, that this trail has been closed by the landowner and is not open to the public. To embark on a guided tour of the area contact **Molokai Outdoors** (808-553-4477) or **Visitors Association** (800-274-9303).

LODGING

HOTEL MOLOKAI
$$–$$$ 35 ROOMS   ✉*Kamehameha V Highway*   ✆*808-553-5347, 800-535-0085*
📠*808-553-5047* 🖥*www.hotelmolokai.com, hotelmolokai@aloha.net*

Two miles east of Kaunakakai is this lowrise hotel with faux-Polynesian architectural details. The accommodations are small but comfortable, and have rattan furnishings, tropical prints; some units also have kitchenettes, refrigerators and ceiling fans. There is an oceanside pool and a pleasant lounge area with an adjacent restaurant and cocktail lounge. The hotel fronts a narrow beach, and shallows offshore are not suitable for ocean swimming, but they're great for fishing, kayaking and wind-

Kaunakakai to East End

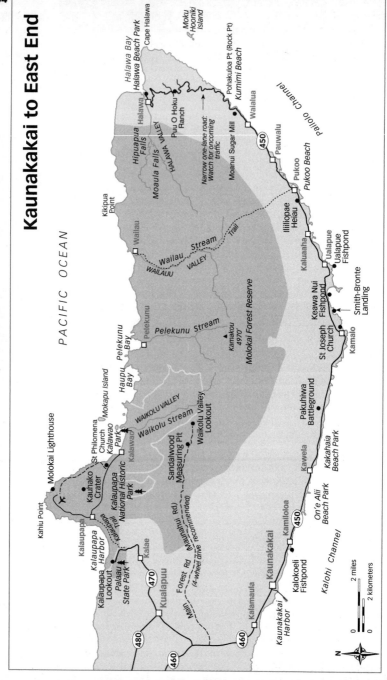

PACIFIC OCEAN

Kahiu Point

Molokai Lighthouse

Kalaupapa Lookout

Palaau State Park

Kualapuu

470

480

460

460

Main Forest Rd (4-wheel drive recommended)

Maunahui Rd

Kaunakakai

Kamiloloa

450

Kalokoeli Fishpond

Kaunakakai Harbor

Kalamaula

Kalohi Channel

0   2 miles
0   2 kilometers

N

Kahulako Crater

St Philomena Church

Kalawao Park

Kalaupapa National Historic Park

Kalawao

Kalaupapa Harbor

Kalae

Kalaupapa Trail

Mokapu Island

Haupu Bay

Pelekunu Bay

Pelekunu

WAIKOLU VALLEY

Waikolu Stream

Waikolu Valley Lookout

Sandalwood Measuring Pit

Kamakou 4970

Molokai Forest Reserve

Pelekunu Stream

Kikipua Point

Wailau

WAILAUU VALLEY

Wailau Stream

Trail

On'e Alii Beach Park

Kawela

Pakuhiwa Battleground

Kahahaia Beach Park

St Joseph Church

Kamalo

Smith-Bronte Landing

Keawa Nui Fishpond

Kaluaaha

Ualapue

Ualapue Fishpond

Iliiliopae Heiau

Pukoo

Pukoo Beach

Pauwalu

450

Moanui Sugar Mill

Narrow one-lane road: Watch for oncoming traffic

HALAWA VALLEY

Moaula Falls

Hipuapua Falls

Puu O Hoku Ranch

Halawa

Halawa Bay

Halawa Beach Park

Cape Halawa

Moku Hooniki Island

Pohakuloa Pt (Rock Pt)

Kumimi Beach

Walalua

Pailolo Channel

surfing. The grounds are nicely landscaped with plenty of tall palms that provide a tropical feel.

KAMALO PLANTATION BED & BREAKFAST

$$ 1 ROOM ✉HCO1, Box 300, Kaunakakai, HI 96748 ☎808-558-8236
📠808-558-8236 🖳www.molokai.com/kamalo, kamaloplantation@aloha.net

If privacy is what you're after, you'll love this bed & breakfast. Set on five acres of orchards and tropical gardens, the secluded cottage lies in the middle of lush grounds. Screen windows let in the tropical smell of the flowering trees, and a private lanai is perfect for the breakfast of homemade bread and fresh fruit from the orchard. The cottage also has a full kitchen.

MOANUI BEACH HOUSE

$$$ 2 ROOMS ✉Kamehameha V Highway at the 20-mile marker ☎808-558-8236
📠808-558-8236 🖳www.molokai.com/kamalo, kamaloplantation@aloha.net

Ten miles east of Kamalo Plantation on a sandy beach ideal for whale watching is this beach house. Decorated Polynesian style, with vaulted ceilings, the house has two bedrooms with king-size beds, one and a half bathrooms, a living and dining area and a large kitchen. All the home amenities, including TV and VCR, as well as beach gear and grill, are included. Complimentary breakfast breads and fruit are provided with coffee and tea. There's a three-night minimum.

A'AHI PLACE BED AND BREAKFAST

$ 3 ROOMS ✉215 Aahi Street, Kaunakakai ☎808-553-8033
🖳www.molokai.com/aahi

In a tropical garden east of Kaunakakai is A'ahi Place. Here you'll find a cedar cottage with kitchen and bath, two full-sized beds, as well as two backpacker's rooms, and lanais surrounded by fragrant tropical flowers and swaying palms. Best of all—there are no phones to interrupt your thoughts.

PUU O HOKU RANCH

$$$$ 11 ROOMS ✉PO Box 1889, Kaunakakai, HI 96748 ☎808-558-8109
📠808-558-8100 🖳hoku@aloha.net

Located on the remote northeastern side of the island, this rustic cottage offers plenty of privacy. It sits on open conservation land and afford views of Maui in the distance. A living room/dining room, fireplace and lovely furnishings make this a perfect place to retreat from the hustle and bustle of city life. If you're there between December and April, you might even spy a migrating humpback whale. Three-night minimum stay.

KA HALE MALA

$$ 1 UNIT ✉P.O. Box 1582, Kaunakakai, HI 96748 ☎808-553-9009
🖳www.molokai-bnb.com, cpgroup@aloha.net

On the south shore near the five-mile marker, Ka Hale Mala (The Garden House) is a quick walk to the beach. Gourmet breakfasts are included in the moderate host rate, or you can stay there on your own for a lower price. The spacious four-room apartment (that sleeps up to four) is surrounded by a tempting tropical garden—tangelos, pomme-los, figs, *kau* oranges, papayas, limes, breadfruit and more—that you're allowed to pick from. Yum.

CONDOS

Molokai offers a variety of home and condo rentals, too many to mention in a guidebook. From one-bedroom facilities to spacious homes, you can probably find something to meet your budgetary needs. One place to look is www.visitmaui.com—check the Molokai listings. Property-management and realty companies are also available in Kaunakakai and Maunaloa. A few include **Friendly Isle Realty** (800-600-4158) and **Swenson Real Estate** (800-558-3648).

MARC MOLOKAI SHORES SUITES

102 UNITS   ✆ *808-553-5954, 800-535-0085*   📠 *808-553-3241*

🖥 *www.marcresorts.com, aloha@marcresorts.com*

Marc Molokai offers oceanfront accommodations with full kitchen, lanai and color television. A series of low-slung buildings that forms a U-shaped configuration around a landscaped lawn extending to the beach sits among palm trees, a swimming pool, shuffleboard and barbecue areas. Rates start at $170.

DINING

A gourmet food-lover will starve on Molokai, but someone looking for a square meal at fair prices should depart well-fed. The budget restaurants are clustered along Ala Malama Street in Kaunakakai.

KANEMITSU'S BAKERY

$ LOCAL-STYLE/BAKERY   ✉ *Ala Malama Street, Kaunakakai*

✆ *808-553-5855*

This bakery serves tasty meals at appetizing prices. A local institution, it's a simple café with molded seats, formica tables and an interesting folk-art mural presenting a map of Molokai. The lunch special varies but the price is low whether you are dining on beef, chopped steak or hamburger steak. Kanemitsu's is a favorite with the breakfast crowd, which is drawn in by the bakery as well as by the menu of omelettes, hot cakes and egg dishes served with Portuguese sausage or that island favorite, Spam. No dinner. Closed Tuesday.

OUTPOST NATURAL FOODS

$ DELI   ✉ *70 Makaena Place, Kaunakakai*   ✆ *808-553-3377*   📠 *808-553-5857*

Outpost has a takeout counter at the back of its tiny health food store. Here you can fuel up with delicious sandwiches, salads and smoothies that are both nutritious and inexpensive. There are also burritos and daily specials. No dinner. Takeout counter closed Saturday and Sunday.

OVIEDO'S LUNCH COUNTER

$ FILIPINO   ✉145 Puali Place, Kaunakakai   ✆808-553-5014

If you're into Filipino fare, try Oviedo's. This mom-and-pop restaurant serves up spicy steaming dishes at low prices. You'll find plank-board walls surrounding a few plastic chairs and yellow formica tables. The steam-tray cuisine includes chicken papaya, pig's feet, turkey tail *adobo* and mango beans. Open for lunch and early dinner.

MOLOKAI DRIVE INN

$ AMERICAN/LOCAL-STYLE   ✉15 Kamoi Street, Kaunakakai
✆808-553-5655   ✆808-553-3693

You're hungry? You want take-out? Why not try this drive inn. At breakfast you'll find the usual (eggs and hotcakes) or the unusual (shrimp omelettes, fried rice, banana pancakes or eggs and Spam). For lunch or dinner try the ox tail or the Chinese plate— or stick to burgers if you must.

MOLOKAI PIZZA CAFÉ

$–$$ PIZZA   ✉Kaunakakai Place, Kaunakakai   ✆808-553-3288   ✆808-553-5400
✉molopizza@cs.com

This is an excellent neighborhood pizzeria located just outside of town. Clean and modern, this local hangout is a great place for a tasty lunch or a quick-and-easy dinner. In addition to pizza, they serve deli sandwiches on homemade bread. Kids love the rides and arcade games.

HULA SHORES

$$ HAWAII REGIONAL   ✉Hotel Molokai, Kamehameha V Highway
✆808-553-5347

Open daily, this oceanfront dining room in Hotel Molokai offers island-fresh vegetables, fish from the ocean, and, for landlubbers in your party, the "turf" of surf and turf: steaks. All this comes with home-grown Hawaiian ukulele and slack-key guitar players serenading you in the evening.

SHOPPING

You needn't worry about falling into the shop-'til-you-drop syndrome on Molokai. Long before you have even begun to think about being tired you will have visited every store on the island. Shopping is still an adventure here, since the few stores operating are all owned by local people and provide a window into life on Molokai.

MOLOKAI ISLAND CREATIONS ✉63 Ala Malama Street, Kaunakakai ✆808-553-5926 Ala Malama Street, Kaunakakai's main street, offers a modest row of shops. This one specializes in clothing, jewelry, glassware and gift items mostly made by Molokai artists.

MOLOKAI FISH & DIVE ✉*61 Ala Malama Street, Kaunakakai* ☎*808-553-5926* "Home of the original Molokai T-shirt designs," this shop features its signature clothing and souvenirs as well as beach items and sporting equipment.

IMPORTS GIFT SHOP ✉*82 Ala Malama Street, Kaunakakai* ☎*808-553-5734* Stop here for casual wear, cultured pearls and Hawaiian heirloom jewelry.

MOLOKAI SURF ✉*130 Kamehameha Highway, Suite 103, Kaunakakai* ☎*808-553-5093* Surfers can get both their surfwear and information where to wear it here. Closed Sunday.

KAMAKANA FINE ARTS GALLERY

✉*2 Kamoi Street, Suite 310, Kaunakakai* ☎*808-553-8520* ⌨*www.molokaifinearts.com, kgallery@aloha.net* Be sure to stop at this gallery across the street from Molokai Drive Inn in Kaunakakai. Finely turned bowls, blown glass, *Niihau* shell leis, *pahu* drums, *lauhala* hats, oil paintings and wood sculptures are just some of the objects you'll find. Over 124 of Molokai's artists are featured here. Closed Sunday.

NIGHTLIFE

HULA SHORES ✉*Hotel Molokai, Kamehameha V Highway* ☎*808-553-5347* There's not much nightlife around these parts, except at this bar. Here you can sip fabulous mixed drinks and listen to the strums of Hawaiian music and think about all the things you don't need to do on your visit to Molokai.

BEACHES & PARKS

O'NE ALII PARK
✉*2.5 miles east of Kaunakakai on Route 450* ☎*808-553-3204* ☎*808-553-3206*

This spacious park has a large grass-covered field and coconut trees plus a narrow beach with an excellent view of Lanai. A reef far offshore makes this area very shallow and affords ample protection. It's excellent for children. Snorkeling, though, is only mediocre. As for surfing, all the action is far out on the reef and it's rarely any good. Surfcasting isn't bad here but it's even better farther to the east. The most common catches are *manini*, red and white goatfish, parrotfish, *papio*, *ulua*, milkfish and mullet. Facilities here include a picnic area, restrooms, showers and electricity at the pavilion.

▲ Mainly tent camping; no hookups, $3 per person per night. Very popular and therefore sometimes crowded and noisy. County permit required.

KAKAHAIA BEACH PARK
✉*Six miles east of Kaunakakai on Route 450*

This long, narrow park wedged tightly between the road and the ocean is the site of the Kakahaia National Wildlife Refuge. Since the water is both shallow and murky, swimming and snorkeling are not recommended. Picnicking, surfing and fishing are much the same as at O'ne Alii Park. Day use only.

PUKOO BEACH

✉*The old Neighborhood Store 'n' Snack Bar, located on Route 450 near 16-mile marker, is your landmark. Just past here, traveling east, turn into the second driveway on the right. This access road leads a short distance to the beach.*

🛶 This crescent-shaped strand is mirrored by another curving beach just to the west. Maui lies directly across the channel and there are also marvelous views of Lanai. With a shallow, rocky bottom, this beach provides only mediocre swimming. However, it's very popular with anglers. There are no facilities.

KUMIMI BEACH, POHAKULOA POINT AND OTHER EAST END BEACHES

✉*Along Route 450 between the 18- and 22-mile markers*

🪸 🐟 🏄 🛶 Beginning near the 18-mile marker on Route 450, and extending for about four miles, lies this string of small sandy beaches. These are among the island's loveliest, featuring white sands and spectacular views of the islands of Maui and Lanai. The swimming is very good, but beware of heavy currents and high surf. Plentiful coral makes for great snorkeling and good lobster diving. There are numerous surfing breaks throughout this area. Pohakuloa Point (or Rock Point), located eight-tenths of a mile past the 20-mile marker, is one of Molokai's top surfing spots. Barracuda are sometimes caught in the deeper regions. Also bonefish, mountain bass, threadfin, *manini*, red and white goatfish, *ulua*, *papio*, parrotfish, milkfish and mullet.

HALAWA BEACH PARK

✉*30 miles east of Kaunakakai on Route 450*

🪸 🐟 🏄 🛶 Set in lush Halawa Valley, one of Molokai's most splendid areas, the park is tucked neatly between mountains and sea on a grassy plot dotted with coconut palms and ironwood trees. Cliffs, waterfalls, two pocket beaches—altogether a heavenly spot, though sometimes rainy and almost always windy. This is an okay place to swim because it is partially protected by the bay, but exercise caution anyway. Snorkeling is good, though the water is sometimes murky. It's one of the very best spots on the island for surfing. Fishing is also notable; the reefs studding this area make it a prime locale for many of the species caught along East End Beaches. The park is a bit weatherbeaten and overgrown and although there are a picnic area and restrooms, the running water must be boiled or treated chemically.

🏕 📞*808-558-8109* Not permitted in the park, but people camp on the other side of Halawa Stream on property owned by Puu o

Hoku Ranch. You will have to park and carry your gear to where you want to camp.

KAUNAKAKAI TO WEST END

Generally, if you are not pointed east on Molokai, you are headed westerly. The thoroughfare that carries you across the prairie-like plains of west Molokai is Route 460, also called the Maunaloa Highway, another two-lane track. Along the way you can venture off in search of the plantation town of Kualapuu and the vista point overlooking Kalaupapa, but eventually you will arrive at road's end out in the woodframe town of Maunaloa. From this red-dust municipality it's a short jaunt to Papohaku Beach, Molokai's western shore. If nothing else, Molokai's West End is rich in myth and history. As Hawaiian storytellers recount, the region around Maunaloa, the volcano that formed this side of the island, was once a cultural focus of the Polynesians. It was here that the hula originated; from the slopes of Maunaloa the goddess Laka spread knowledge of the sensuous dance to all the other islands.

IMPORTANT NOTE: At press time, Molokai Ranch, which owns 60 thousand acres of property on the island, closed its operations. As a result, their businesses and many access roads will be closed indefinitely. Contact the Molokai Visitors Bureau (800-800-6367, 808-553-3876) for updated information.

SIGHTS

KAPUAIWA COCONUT GROVE ✉*Route 460 one-and-a-half miles west of Kaunakakai* Just a mile west of the cock-eyed town of Kaunakakai on Route 460 is this coconut grove, planted in the 1860s by Kamehameha V. This magnificent stand of coconut palms, once 1000 in number, consists of particularly tall trees. The grove creates the sensation of being in a tropical dream sequence, with hundreds of palm trees flashing green and yellow fronds and extending to the lip of the ocean. Some appear to stand in columns, but others have bent so far to the wind they have fallen out of formation. Pay a visit toward sunset, when the palms are memorably silhouetted by tropic skies for a wonderful end-of-day setting. You may not enter the grove. Heed the warnings or you may get conked by a falling nut. These trees are not the trimmed-back kind made safe for the unwary. Adjacent to the grove is the **Kalanianaole Community Hall**, a unique early-20th-century cultural landmark that still serves the community but is considering plans for renovation.

CHURCH ROW Strung like rosary beads opposite Coconut Grove are seven tiny churches. Dubbed "Church Row" it includes Protestant, Mormon, Jehovah's Witness and several other denominations. Like sentinels protecting the island from the devil, they too are gathered in

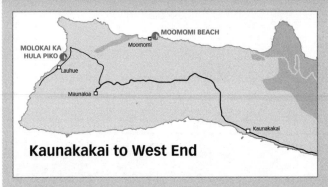

Kaunakakai to West End

MOLOKAI KA HULA PIKO

PAGE 416

A mile-long hike to a sunrise ceremony and beachfront festival honoring Molokai's hula tradition

MOOMOMI BEACH

PAGE 418

Locally loved remote beach with fabulous reef snorkeling—and endangered green sea turtles

rows. The most intriguing are the oldest, tiny woodframe structures with modest steeples. These one-room chapels lack worldly frills like stained glass and are furnished with creaky wooden pews that seat a few dozen parishioners. Stop by and inquire about services; visitors are always welcome.

MOLOKAI PLUMERIAS ✉*About two miles west of Kaunakakai* ☎*808-553-3391* ✐*www.molokaiplumerias.com* This family-run company will take you on a tour of their ten-acre plumeria farm. Plumeria, with the scent of heaven, are the primary flowers used in lei making. Your guide will teach you about the flower, allow you to pick your own and provide you with the necessary tools to create a lei. There are no regularly scheduled tours, so make reservations in advance. Closed weekends.

MAIN FOREST ROAD ✉*Take Route 460 west from Kaunakakai. There is a white bridge a little more than three-and-a-half miles from town, just before the four-mile marker. Take a right on the dirt road just before the bridge.* For a splendid tour of Molokai's mountainous interior, take a drive or hike on this road (Maunahui Road). It is bumpy and requires four-wheel-drive vehicles along its ten-mile length.

MOLOKAI FOREST RESERVE ✉*About 3.5 miles northwest of Kaunakakai on Route 460. Turn east on Molokai Forest Road.* Deer, quail, pheasant, doves and chukkar partridge populate the route here. Numerous secondary roads

Kaunakakai to West End

PACIFIC OCEAN

Kaloi Channel

Kaiwi Channel

Laau Point

POINTS OF INTEREST

- A Kalaupapa Lookout
- B Kapaiwa Coconut Grove
- C Kauhako Crater
- D Kolo Wharf
- E Molokai High School
- F Molokai Lighthouse
- G Molokai Museum and Cultural Center
- H Molokai Plumerias
- I Molokai Ranch
- J Moomomi Dunes
- K Phallic Rock
- L Purdy's Natural Macadamia Nut Farm
- M R.W. Meyer Sugar Mill
- N Sandalwood Measuring Pit
- O St. Philomena Church
- P Waikolu Valley Lookout

Kalawao Park

WAIKOLU VALLEY

Kalaupapa National Historic Park

(Maunahui Rd.)

Kalawao

Kahiu Point

Kalaupapa Harbor

Kalaupapa Trail (pedestrian)

Kalae

Palaau State Park

Kualapuu

470

Forest Rd. (4-wheel drive recommended)

Kaunakakai

450

Main Rd.

460

Kalamaula

480

Lihi Pali

Puu Kapele Ave

Hoolehua

Farrington Ave

Moomomi Ave

Kiowea Park

Molokai Airport

Maunaloa Rd

(Private Road)

Kawaaloa Beach

Moomomi

Keonelele Beach

Mokio Point

DESERT STRIP

(Private Road)

Kaluakoi Rd

(Private Road)

460

Kolo

Maunaloa

(Private Road)

Halena

Laauhue

Papohaku Beach Park

Kawakiu Beach

Ilio Point

(Private Road)

Haleolono

Hale O Lono Beach

Kaluakoi Rd

N

0 2 miles

0 2 kilometers

and trails lead to the very edge of this mammoth forest reserve, through which the main road passes. These side roads offer excellent possibilities for adventurous hikers. Four-wheel drives only.

LUA MOKU ILIAHI

✉*About 15 miles from the ocean along Maunahui Road* Adjacent to Maunahui Road, the main road passes this area known to the English-speaking world as the **Sandalwood Measuring Pit**. This depression, dug into the earth to match the hull size of an old sailing vessel, was used by 19th-century Hawaiians to gauge the amount of sandalwood needed to fill a ship. Four-wheel drives only.

WAIKOLU VALLEY LOOKOUT

A mile east from Lua Moku Iliahi is **Waikolu Picnic Grove**, a heavily wooded retreat ideal for lunching or camping. Here you'll find picnic facilities and an outhouse. (State permit required to camp.) Across the road is this lookout, which perches above Waikolu Valley, which descends precipitously 3000 feet to the sea.

KAMAKOU PRESERVE

☎*808-553-5236 ext. 207* 📠*808-553-9870* 🖥*www.nature.org, hike_molokai@tnc.org* Stop here to explore this 2774-acre sanctuary managed by the Nature Conservancy. Home to more than 200 plants that live only in Hawaii, and accessible only by four-wheel drive, the preserve is a lush rainforest and an important watershed for Molokai. There are several forest birds, including the *apapane* and *amakihi*. The forest is open to the public year-round and once a month there is a guided hike into the preserve. Call ahead for information on visiting the preserve or to check the condition of the Main Forest Road (which may be closed in wet weather).

KUALAPUU

A side trip along Route 470 leads past this tinroof town. Filled with modest plantation houses, it harkens back to an earlier era when Molokai cultivated pineapples rather than tourists. Today its claim to fame is a 1.4-million-gallon reservoir that is reportedly the largest rubber-lined water tank in the world.

MOLOKAI MUSEUM AND CULTURAL CENTER

✉*Route 470, Kalae* ☎*808-567-6436* **Kalae** is home to the R. W. Meyer Sugar Mill, which is the highlight of this museum and cultural center. There is an 1878 steam-generated operation that has been restored in sparkling fashion. The mule-driven cane crusher, copper clarifiers and dependable old steam engine are ready and waiting for Molokai to return to its old ways. There are also well-presented displays and heirlooms of the German immigrant family that owned the mill, as well as native Molokai artifacts. Closed Sunday. Admission.

KALAUPAPA LOOKOUT

✉*Route 470 ends at this lookout.* Here cliffs as green as Ireland fall away in dizzying fashion to reveal a softly sloping tableland 1600 feet below, the Kalaupapa Peninsula. Fringed by white-sand beaches, this geologic afterthought extends more than two miles out from the foot of the *pali*. A lighthouse and landing strip occupy the point of the peninsula. Nearer the cliffs, a cluster of houses comprises the famous leper colony; while neighboring Kauhako Crater, a nicely rounded circle far below you, represents a vestige of the volcano that created this appendage. Ringed by rock and water, protected by the tallest sea cliffs in the world, Kalaupapa Peninsula is a magnificent sight indeed.

PHALLIC ROCK ——————— **h**idden

A short hike from Kalaupapa Lookout, this unusual rock protrudes obscenely from the ground amid an ironwood stand as thick as pubic hair. This geologic formation, so realistic it almost seems sculpted, was said to represent the Hawaiian fertility god, who was turned to stone when his wife caught him admiring a beautiful young girl. Legend says that a woman offering gifts and spending the night here will return home pregnant.

KALAUPAPA COLONY At this secluded spot several patients with what was once labeled leprosy and is now called Hansen's Disease, a chronic infectious bacterial disease that causes sores and ulcers and destroys tissue, live in solitude. Doctors have been able to control the affliction since 1945 with sulfone drugs, and all those living here are free to leave. But many are aging, and have lived on this windswept peninsula most of their lives. This is their home and this is where they choose to live.

To visit Kalaupapa, you can fly, hike or ride muleback; there are no roads leading to this remote destination. Once there you must take a guided tour; no independent exploring is permitted. And no children under 16 are allowed. Bus tours are organized by **Molokai Mule Ride** (808-567-6088, 800-567-7550; www.muleride.com). For flight information, check **Molokai Air Shuttle** (808-567-6847) from Honolulu. **Paragon Air** (808-244-3356, 800-428-1231; www.paragon-air.com) flies from Maui and Honolulu.

As far as I'm concerned, the mule ride is the only way to go. The Molokai Mule Ride conducts tours daily, weather permitting, except Sunday when the park is closed. You saddle up near the Kalaupapa Lookout and descend a 1700-foot precipice, among the tallest sea cliffs in the world. Kalaupapa unfolds below you as you switchback through lush vegetation on a three-mile-long trail. The ride? Exhilarating, frightening, but safe. And the views are awesome.

PURDY'S NATURAL MACADAMIA NUT FARM ✉*Lihipali Avenue, Hoolehua* ✆*808-567-6601* Route 480 will take you into the town of **Hoolehua**, where you'll find Purdy's Nut Farm. Located right behind the island's only high school, this small grove of 70-year-old macadamia nut trees is open to the public for free tours and tastings. The owner will explain the growing cycles of the trees and demonstrate harvesting. Visitors can taste the raw product and also sample the nut after it's been naturally roasted, a process that cuts down greatly on the fat and calories found in nuts sold in stores. Closed Sunday and Monday.

WEST END Route 460 continues over dry rolling plains toward Molokai's West End. This arid plateau, windswept and covered by deep red, iron-rich soil, was once planted in pineapple. Today Molokai Ranch, which still owns much of the region, has turned to hay cultivation to feed cattle. Before it was planted with pineapple, Molokai's West End was once a rich adze quarry. The rock, vital to a Stone Age society, was fashioned into tools that were in turn used to create weapons, canoes, bowls and other necessities.

MAUNALOA Like the pineapple industry itself, Route 460 ends here. With the departure of Dole's operations in 1975, this company town assumed the dusty, falsefront visage of the Wild West after the mines petered out and the saloons shut down. That's all begun to change in the past few years as the Molokai Ranch, which owns just about all of Maunaloa, has started a revitalization program that has seen the more ramshackle plantation houses replaced by contemporary homes, some of the town's more historic buildings upgraded, and several new buildings added, including a lovely 22-room lodge and Molokai's first movie

Molokai Pilgrimage

The ultimate Molokai experience is the pilgrimage to the Kalaupapa leper colony isolated on a 12-square-mile lava tongue that protrudes from the north shore.

The story of the remaining residents goes back to 1866 when the Hawaiian government began exiling people with leprosy to this lonely spot on Molokai's rain-plagued north coast. In those days Kalaupapa was a fishing village, and lepers were segregated in the old settlement at Kalawao on the windy eastern side of the peninsula. The place was treeless and barren—a wasteland haunted by slow death. Victims were shipped along the coast and pushed overboard. Abandoned with insufficient provisions and no shelter, they struggled against both the elements and the disease.

To this lawless realm came Joseph Damien de Veuster—Father Damien. The Belgian Catholic priest, arriving in 1873, brought a spirit and energy that gave the colony new life. He built a church, attended to the afflicted and died of leprosy 16 years later. In 1995, Pope John Paul II made Father Damien "The Blessed Father Damien." Perhaps it is the spirit of this "Martyr of Molokai" that even today marks the indescribable quality of Kalaupapa. There is something unique and inspiring about the place, something you will have to discover yourself.

On the tour you will learn that Kalaupapa has been designated a national historical park. Among the points of interest within this refuge are numerous windblasted structures, a volcanic crater and several monuments. You'll visit St. Philomena Church, built by Father Damien in the 1870s, and Kalawao Park, an exotically beautiful spot on the lush eastern side of the peninsula. Father Damien's grave is also located here.

After touring this peninsula you will know that this is a very spiritual place.

theater. The old post office and general store provide links to Maunaloa's days as a pineapple town, and the overall feeling remains rustically charming, albeit with an increasingly gentrified air.

PAPOHAKU BEACH PARK Any tour of West End should of course finish at the west end. This sparkling three-mile long swath of white sand would be a fitting finale to any tour. Reached by taking Kaluakoi Road from Route 460 and driving through the rolling hills of Kaluakoi Villas, Papohaku is one of the largest beaches in the state. During World War II troops practiced shore landings along this coast. But today you will have the beach and surrounding sand dunes almost entirely to yourself.

MOLOKAI KA HULA PIKO

If you're in town in mid- to late May, you'll want to experience this event, which honors the tradition that claims the hula was first danced on Molokai. A mile-long hike to a sunrise ceremony on a hillside leads to where the dances were said to have originated. Cameras are not allowed and decorum is the rule at this spiritual rite. Later in the day beachfront festivities at Papohaku Beach Park include hula and general high spirits. It can be hard to find a room or car during the event, so plan accordingly. Call the Molokai Visitors Association (800-800-6367) for information and updates.

LODGING

MOLOKAI LODGE

$$$$ 22 ROOMS ✉P.O. Box 259, Maunaloa, HI 96770 ✆808-660-2824, 888-627-8082 📠808-552-2773 🖳www.molokairanch.com, info@molokairanch.com

The two-story lodge in Maunaloa, designed and decorated with the town's plantation past in mind—offers rooms that exude a sense of intimacy and charm, with rattan furnishings and '30s-style Hawaiian prints. Rooms are spacious and individually decorated with cheerful upcountry decor. All offer long, unobstructed views of West Molokai's rolling hills, with the ocean in the distance. The eight-acre property includes a day spa, swimming pool, game room and lounge. There's also a wide range of activities offered to guests: mountain biking, horseback riding, kayaking and cultural hikes. Or you can participate in a cattle roundup at the Paniolo Roundup; and the Cattle Drive, where you'll join *paniolo* as they move cattle from one pasture to another. The staff couldn't be more friendly or helpful.

THE BEACH VILLAGE

$$$$ 40 UNITS ✉P.O. Box 259, Maunaloa, HI 96770 ☎808-660-2824, 888-627-8082 ✆808-552-2773 ◢www.molokairanch.com, info@molokairanch.com

If there is such a thing as luxury camping, a stay here would be it. Affiliated with Molokai Lodge, their idea of "roughing it" includes spacious aluminum-frame "tentalows," canvas-sided bungalows that come with queen-sized beds, overhead fans, solar-heated bathrooms and private wooden decks for lounging about. Three hearty meals are served buffet-style in the dining pavilion.

CONDOS

KALUAKOI VILLAS

23 UNITS ✉1131 Kaluakoi Road, Maunaloa ☎808-552-2721, 800-367-5004 ✆808-552-2201 ◢www.castleresorts.com

Far from the madding crowd on the west end of Molokai, you will find these villas. The cottage-like accommodations are set near a luxurious three-mile-long beach. This is Molokai's premier resting spot, offering both seclusion and comfort. Here you'll find the essence of plush living: a wasp-waisted pool and a view of Oahu across the channel. Studios (starting at $145 a night) and one-bedroom units (starting at $185 a night) have kitchenettes. The spacious cottage villas are $250 a night and come with a full kitchen.

PANIOLO HALE RESORT

15 UNITS ✉Lio Place ☎800-367-2984 ◢www.molokai-vacation-rental.com, rent@island-realestate.com

Located just off the shore of Kepuhi Beach, this resort has units starting at $115 per night. They feature oak floors and beamed ceilings and walls of glass doors that open onto screened lanais. Access to a pool and barbecue area round out the traditional amenities (dishwasher, washer and dryer). Three night minimum.

DINING

KUALAPUU COOKHOUSE

$ LOCAL-STYLE ✉Farrington Street, Kualapuu ☎808-567-9655

This is a family-owned and -operated restaurant serving breakfast, lunch and dinner daily. Here you'll find local and mainland dishes to fit a budget-sized pocketbook. You'll understand why they call this the Friendly Isle when you step inside. Closed Sunday.

SHOPPING

MAUNALOA HIGHWAY SHOPS ☎808-552-2364 ✆808-552-2988 Over on Molokai's West End in the red-dust town of Maunaloa you'll stumble upon two great shops that share the same unmarked building and the same telephone. **Big Wind Kite Factory** has an astonishing assortment of high flyers. There are diamond kites, dancer kites, windsocks and rainbow-tail kites. You can even pick up flags and banners here. At **The Plantation Gallery** there are aloha shirts, batik sarongs, tribal art, shell necklaces and other original pieces by over 30 Molokai craftspeople. They also have the largest collection of books about Hawaii and Hawaiian culture on the island and an extensive selection of Hawaiian music CDs.

WEST SUNDRIES STORE ✆ *808-552-2320* In Kaluakoi Villas, this shop carries (what else?) sundries.

BEACHES & PARKS

PALAAU STATE PARK

✉ *Take Route 460 six miles west from Kaunakakai, then follow Route 470 (Kalae Highway) about six more miles to the end of the road.* ✆ *808-567-6923*

🚶 Set in a densely forested area, this 233-acre park is ideal for a mountain sojourn. Several short trails lead to petroglyphs, a startling phallic rock, and the awesome Kalaupapa Lookout. The trail down to Kalaupapa Peninsula is also nearby, but requires a permit. There are picnic area, restrooms and a pavilion.

⛺ State permit required. Tent camping only.

MOOMOMI BEACH

✉ *Take Route 460 west from Kaunakakai to Hoolehua. Go right on Route 481 (Puupeelua Avenue), then left on Farrington Avenue. Farrington starts as a paved road, then turns to dirt. After 2.2 miles of dirt track, the road forks. Take the right fork and follow it a half-mile to the beach. A four-wheel-drive vehicle may be required. Be warned: the road may be impassible.*

A small, remote beach studded with rocks and frequented only by local people—what more could you ask? While Moomomi is a small pocket beach, many people use the name to refer to a three-mile length of coastline that extends west from the pocket beach and includes two other strands, **Kawaaloa Beach** and **Keonelele Beach**. Moomomi offers good swimming, but use caution because the bottom is rocky and the beach is only partially protected. The snorkeling is very good along reefs and rocks. As for surfing, there are fair breaks at the mouth of the inlet. There's good surf-casting from the rocky headland to the west. Keonelele Beach forms the coastal border of the Moomomi Dunes, a unique series of massive sand dunes that extend as far as four miles inland, covering Molokai's northwestern corner; this is also known as the Desert Strip. The preserve protects five endangered plant species and is a habitat for the endangered Hawaiian green sea turtle. The only facilities are a pavilion and restrooms.

HALENA AND OTHER SOUTH COAST BEACHES

✉ *Route 460 to Maunaloa* ✆ *For current information about road access contact Molokai Ranch at 808-552-2791*

🚣 🛶 🎣 ⛺ 🏊 Don't tell anyone, but there's a dirt road running several miles along a string of trackless beaches on the south shore. The first one, Halena, is a very funky ghost camp with a few primitive facilities. To the west lies **Hale O Lono Beach**, with its pleasant bay and lagoon. To the east is **Kolo Wharf** (an abandoned pier collapsing into the sea), plus numerous fishponds, coconut groves and small sand beaches. This is an excellent area to explore, camp, hike, fish (bass, threadfin, *enenue*, red goatfish) and commune with hidden Hawaii. The swimming is also good if you don't mind muddy water. It's wise to boil or chemically treat the water if you intend to drink it. *Note*: Only Hale O Lono Beach has a public-access road; the other two are located on Molokai Ranch. As you first enter town (before the road curves into the main section), you'll see houses on the left and a dirt road extending perpendicularly to the right.

Now, to get to Halena, take a right at the fork, then a quick left (there are signs posted), then drive a few hundred yards to the end. The shore is nearby; simply walk west along the beach several hundred yards.

To get to Hale O Lono Beach, walk about a mile west along the beach from Halena.

To get to Kolo Wharf and the other beaches, go straight where the road forks. Kolo is two miles east over an equally rugged road. Sand beaches, coconut groves and fishponds extend for another six miles past Kolo. Then the road turns inland, improving considerably, and continues for seven miles more until it meets the main road two miles west of Kaunakakai.

KAWAKIU BEACH

✉ *Take Route 460 west from Kaunakakai. At the Kaluakoi Villas, head to the road near the back 9. Drive north until you hit the beach. It's a tricky route, so you may want to check in with the hotel staff for further details; they warn against making the trip without a four-wheel drive.*

🚶 🚣 🏊 This idyllic spot is my favorite Molokai campground. Here a small inlet, tucked away in Molokai's northwest corner, is edged by a beautiful beach with a sandy bottom. Nearby is a shady grove of *kiawe* trees, fringed by the rocky coastline. On a clear night you can see the lights of Oahu across Kaiwi Channel. This is a very good place to swim because the inlet offers some protection, but exercise caution. Snorkeling is good in summer near the rocks when the surf is low. People fish here for mountain bass, threadfin, *enenue* and red goatfish. There are no facilities.

▲ That shady grove is a perfect site to pitch a tent.

PAPOHAKU BEACH PARK

✉ *Take Route 460 for about 14 miles from Kaunakakai. Turn right onto the road to the Kaluakoi Villas. Continue past the villas (don't turn onto the villas road) and down the hill. Follow this macadam track, Kaluakoi Road, as it parallels the beach. Side roads from Kaluakoi Road and Pohakuloa Road(an adjoining thoroughfare) lead to Papohaku and other beaches.*

⚓ 🏊 🚿 This splendid beach extends for three miles along Molokai's west coast; it's an excellent place to explore, collect puka shells, or just lie back and enjoy the view of Oahu. Backed by *kiawe* trees and low sand dunes, Papohaku is the largest beach on the island, averaging 100 yards in width. Swimming is excellent, but use caution; sit out on the beach and observe the wave action before jumping in. There's not much rock or coral here so the snorkeling is only mediocre. You'll find good breaks for surfing when the wind isn't blowing from the shore. Use caution, especially in the winter months. The beach is also popular with bodysurfers. The fishing is good, usually for mountain bass, threadfin, *enenue* and red goatfish. There are picnic areas, restrooms and showers.

▲ Tent only. County permit required.

OUTDOOR ADVENTURES

CAMPING

With so little development and such an expanse of untouched land, Molokai would seem a haven for campers. Unfortunately, large segments of the island are owned by Molokai Ranch and other private interests; with the exception of a few beaches on Molokai Ranch property, these tracts are closed off behind locked gates.

PAPOHAKU BEACH AND O'NE ALII PARK 📞 *808-553-3204* 🖨 *808-553-3206* There are a few parks for camping. A county permit is required for both of these. Permits are $3 per person a day (50 cents for children) and are obtained at the County Parks and Recreation office in Kaunakakai. Hours are 8 a.m. to 4 p.m., Monday through Friday, so get your permit in advance.

Camping at Palaau State Park is $5 per person per night and requires a permit from the Department of Land and Natural Resources (808-984-8109) on Maui, or from the park ranger (808-567-6923).

MOLOKAI LODGE AND BEACH VILLAGE ✉ *P.O. Box 259, Maunaloa, HI 96770* 📞 *808-552-2741* 🖨 *808-552-2773* 🖥 *www.molokairanch.com* For information on camping at Molokai Ranch, contact this company, Monday through Friday 8 a.m. to 4:30 p.m.

🖥www.molokaifishanddive.com Molokai Fish & Dive sells camping gear.

RIDING STABLES

MOLOKAI FISH & DIVE ✉P.O. Box 576, Kaunakakai, HI 96748 ☎808-553-5926, 866-282-3483 🖥fishanddive@mobettah.net For the *paniolo* (cowboy) set, there are a couple of different opportunities on Molokai to check out. Molokai Fish & Dive (don't let the name mislead you, you won't be riding a seahorse!) offers a horseback ride along the Kaupoa Beach Trail, with visits to a number of historical sites along the way. For the rodeo set, there's the Paniolo Roundup, an opportunity where you can compete with one another in the Molokai Ranch Rodeo Arena. Here you'll round up and sort cattle and do team penning. The high point of the round-up experience arrives when guests put what they have learned into action during the penning race. Of course, you'll be taught how to do all this by real Hawaiian *paniolo*. Yee haw!

SNORKELING & SCUBA DIVING

Not the most ideal island for underwater adventures, despite having the largest reef system in the United States and the highest bog in the world, Molokai does have a few technicolor gems to offer. The best diving spots are centered off the offshore island of Mokuhooniki. But that area is for pros only, and is only decent when the weather cooperates, which doesn't happen often. On Molokai itself, stop at the **20-mile marker** on the east side of the island heading out to Halawa Valley. Keep an eye open for Dragon Tail, a lava outcropping that zigzags into the Pailolo Channel. There's a large offshore reef here where you're likely to see long skinny trumpet fish, sturgeon and maybe a few green sea turtles.

If you're not traveling with gear, the following outfitter rents equipment.

MOLOKAI FISH & DIVE ✉61 Ala Malama Street, Kaunakakai ☎808-553-5926 🖥www.molokaifishanddive.com Check out this outfitter for mask, fin and snorkel rentals.

KAYAKING

LANI'S KAYAK ✉P.O. Box 826, Kaunakakai, HI 96748 ☎808-558-8563 For a scenic paddling adventure, Lani's has full-day North Shore trips that take in breathtaking sea cliffs and lush greenery. Its two-and-a-half-hour Southeast tour features turtles and waterfalls.

MOLOKAI FISH & DIVE ✉61 Ala Malama Street, Kaunakakai ☎808-553-5926 🖥www.molokaifishanddive.com Guided and unguided ocean kayak tours, including an exploration of the old Kolo wharf are offered here. Your guides will share their knowledge of the ancient Hawaiian fish ponds. Reservations strongly recommended.

HOTEL MOLOKAI'S OUTDOOR ACTIVITIES ✉*Kamehameha V Highway, Kaunakakai* ✆*808-553-4477* ✑*www.hotelmolokai.com* One- and two-person kayak rentals are available at Hotel Molokai. They also have car carriers for rent.

FISHING

Depending on the weather, deep-sea fishing charters will take you to various spots that are within ten to twenty miles of Molokai. Here you're likely to catch mahimahi, tuna, marlin and *ono*.

ALYCE C COMMERCIAL AND SPORT FISHING ✉*Kaunakakai* ✆*808-558-8377* ✑*www.alycecsportfishing.com* Alyce C offers half-, three-quarter- and full-day excursions—all equipment included. Bring your own food and drink. They also operate whale-watching tours from late December to early April.

MOLOKAI ACTION ADVENTURES ✉*Kaunakakai* ✆*808-558-8184* This action adventures company provides all the equipment for half- or full-day charters.

BIKING

Traffic is light and slow-moving, making Molokai an ideal place for two-wheeling adventurers. The roads are generally good, with some potholes out East End near Halawa Valley. The terrain is mostly flat or gently rolling, with a few steep ascents. Winds are strong and sometimes make for tough going.

MOLOKAI FISH & DIVE ✉*61 Ala Malama Street, Kaunakakai* ✆*866-282-3483* ✑*www.molokaifishanddive.com* For those in good shape and who like to climb, contact this shop for their advanced mountain-bike tour on rugged terrain at Molokai Ranch. Afternoon tours are for beginners and feature a single-track or ranch-road descent to Hale O Lono. All in all, the ranch features 100 miles of trails.

HIKING

Molokai features some splendid country and numerous areas that seem prime for hiking, but few trails have been built or maintained and most private land is off-limits to visitors. Some excellent hiking possibilities, but no official trails, are offered along the beaches described above. Palaau State Park also has several short jaunts to points of interest.

The only lengthy treks lead to the island's rugged north coast. Four valleys—Halawa, Wailau, Pelekunu and Waikolu—cut through the sheer cliffs guarding this windswept shore.

PELEKUNU TRAIL The Pelekunu Trail begins several hundred yards beyond the Waikolu Valley Lookout. It is unmaintained and extremely difficult. Traversing Nature Conservancy property, the trail leads to a lookout point and then drops into the valley. This is for skilled hikers only.

WAILAU TRAIL ✉P.O. Box 125, Kaunakakai, HI 96748 ☎808-558-8113 This trail is another very difficult trek; it takes about 12 hours and passes through some muddy rainforest regions. The trailhead is off Route 450 about 15 miles east of Kaunakakai. The trail extends across nearly the entire island from south to north. Dangers include deep mud and wild boar. To hike it, you must obtain permission from Pearl Petro. Send a self-addressed stamped envelope with a letter of nonresponsibility.

KALAUPAPA TRAIL ☎808-567-6171 The Kalaupapa is the easiest and best-maintained trail descending the north *pali*. A trail description is given in the "Kalaupapa" section in this chapter. To hike here you must obtain permission and pay $40 for a mandatory tour of this colony. Bring food and water along for this four-hour tour. Call Damien Tours for permission and information. Reservations required. Closed Sunday.

HALAWA VALLEY TRAIL ☎808-553-5926 One of Molokai's prettiest hikes, this one extends for two miles from the mouth of the valley to the base of **Moaula Falls**. This 250-foot cascade tumbles down a sheer cliff to a cold mountain pool perfect for swimming. **Hipuapua Falls**, a sister cascade just a third of a mile north, shoots 500 feet down the *pali*. The trail can be accessed only through a guided tour. Call Molokai Fish & Dive (808-553-5926) to schedule one.

TRANSPORTATION

AIR

AIRLINES Aloha Island Air, Pacific Wings, Paragon Air and **Mokulele (go! Express)** all fly into Molokai. **Molokai Air Shuttle** (808-567-6847) flies small prop planes.

MOLOKAI AIRPORT When your plane touches down here, you'll realize what a one-canoe island it is you're visiting. There's a snack bar and adjoining lounge, which seem to open and close all day, plus a few car rental and airline offices. It's seven miles to the main town of Kaunakakai. There's no public transportation available. However, shuttle service can be arranged through some of the hotels, and taxis are available.

To fly direct from Honolulu to Kalaupapa, try **IslandAir** (800-652-6541). **Paragon Air** (800-428-1231) also has service to the peninsula.

CAR RENTALS

The existing companies are **Dollar Rent A Car** (808-567-9012, 800-800-4000 from the mainland, 800-367-7006 in Hawaii), **Budget Rent A Car** (808-567-6877, 800-527-7000 from the mainland, 800-527-0700 in Hawaii) and **Island Kine Auto Rentals** (808-553-5242).

JEEP RENTALS

BUDGET RENT A CAR ☎ *808-567-6877, 800-527-7000 (from the mainland), 800-431-3600 (in Hawaii)* Budget rents jeeps, but requires that you drive them only on paved roads! (Be aware that the rental car collision insurance provided by most credit cards does not cover jeeps.)

TOURS

MOLOKAI OFF-ROAD TOURS ☎ *808-553-3369* This off-road tour company will take you to see the Coffees of Hawaii plantation, a macadamia nut farm, St. Joseph's Church and the fishponds. They also arrange mule tours.

KAUAI

Seventy miles northwest of Oahu, across a rough, treacherous channel that long protected against invaders, lies Kauai. If ever an island deserved to be called a jewel of the sea, this "Garden Isle" is the one. Across Kauai's brief 33-mile expanse lies a spectacular and wildly varied landscape.

Along the north shore is the Hanalei Valley, a lush patchwork of tropical agriculture, and the rugged Na Pali Coast, with cliffs almost 4000 feet above the boiling surf. Spanning 14 miles of pristine coastline, the narrow valleys and sheer walls of Na Pali are so impenetrable that a road entirely encircling the island has never been built. Here, among razor-edged spires and flower-choked gorges, the producers of the movie *South Pacific* found their Bali Hai. To the east flows the fabled Wailua River, a sacred area to Hawaiians that today supports a sizable population in the blue-collar towns of Wailua and Kapaa.

Along the south coast stretch the matchless beaches of Poipu, with white sands and an emerald sea that seem drawn from a South Seas vision. It was here in November 1982 that Hurricane Iwa, packing 110-mile-an-hour winds and carrying devastating storm surf, overwhelmed the island. Ironically, it was also this area that sustained some of the most severe damage when Hurricane Iniki struck on September 11, 1992.

The tourist enclave of Poipu gives way to rustic Hanapepe, a former agricultural town now becoming more of an arts community, and Waimea, where in 1778 Captain James Cook became the first Westerner to tread Hawaiian soil. In Kauai's arid southwestern corner, where palm trees surrender to cactus plants, snow-white beaches sweep for miles along Barking Sands and Polihale.

In the island's center, Mount Waialeale rises 5148 feet (Mount Kawaikini, at 5243 feet, is Kauai's tallest peak) to trap a continuous stream of dark-bellied clouds that spill more than 480 inches of rain annually, making this gloomy peak the wettest spot on Earth and creating the headwaters for the richest river system in all Hawaii—the Hanapepe, Hanalei, Wailua and Waimea rivers. Also draining Waialeale is the Alakai Swamp, a wilderness bog that covers 30 square miles of the island's interior. Yet to the west, just a thunderstorm away, lies a barren landscape seemingly borrowed from Arizona and featuring the 2857-foot-deep Waimea Canyon, the "Grand Canyon" of the Pacific.

From Lihue, Kauai's county seat and most important city, Route 50 (Kaumualii Highway) travels to the south while Route 56 (Kuhio Highway) heads along the north shore. Another highway (Route 550) climbs past Waimea Canyon into the mountainous interior.

Papayas, taro and bananas flourish in lush profusion along these roads and marijuana is grown deep in the hills and narrow valleys, but coffee is now the most significant crop. Tourism, however, has overtaken agriculture in the Kauai economy and is vital to the island's 61,000 population.

The decline of the sugar industry has intensified demands to replace agricultural income with tourist dollars. But the Garden Isle still offers hidden beaches and remote valleys to any traveler possessing a native's sensibility. And even though sugar is in retreat, some cane fields are still evident across the island.

A number of years ago, Kauai provided a window on 19th-century life, when sugar was king. Deep-green stalks covered the landscape in every direction, edging from the lip of the ocean to the foot of the mountains. But foreign competition and a waning industry have led to many cane fields being left fallow or converted to asparagus, papaya and various truck crops and gentlemen's estates.

Nevertheless, one sugar mill is still redolent with the cloyingly sweet smell of cane, and on the westside mammoth cane trucks, sugar stalks protruding like bristles from a wild boar, continue to charge down dusty roads. Depending on the phase of the growing cycle, visitors pass fields crowded with mature cane, tall as Midwest corn, or deep-red earth planted with rows of seedlings. In the evening, when harvested cane is set afire, black smoke billows from deep within the fields.

Historically, Kauai is Hawaii's premier island—the first to be created geologically and the first "discovered" by white men. It was here that Madame Pele, goddess of volcanos, initially tried to make her home. Perhaps because of the island's moist, tropical climate, she failed to find a place dry enough to start her fire and left in frustration for the islands to the southeast.

Formed by a single volcano that became extinct about five million years ago, Kauai is believed by some anthropologists to be the original Hawaiian island populated by Polynesians. After Captain Cook arrived in 1778, explorers continued to visit the island periodically. Ten years later, settlers began to arrive, and in 1820 the first missionaries landed in the company of Prince George, son of Kauai's King Kaumualii. By 1835, the Koloa sugar plantation was founded, becoming the first successful sugar mill on Kauai.

Kauai was the site not only of the original but the anomalous, as well. In 1815, Georg Scheffer, a Prussian adventurer representing Czar Nicholas of Russia, built a fort in Waimea. He soon lost the support of both the Czar and Kauai's King Kaumualii, but left as his legacy the stone ruins of Russia's imperialist effort.

Kauai was the only island not conquered by Kamehameha the Great when he established the Hawaiian kingdom. Thwarted twice in his attempts to land an attack force—once in 1796 when high seas prevented an invasion from Oahu and again in 1803 when his battle-ready army was suddenly ravaged by disease—he finally won over Kaumualii by diplomacy in 1810.

But Kauai's most fascinating history is told by mythmakers recounting tales of the *Menehune*, the Hobbits of the Pacific. These miniature forest people labored like giants to create awesome structures. Mysterious ruins such as the Menehune Fishpond outside Lihue reputedly date back before the Polynesians and are attributed by the mythically inclined to an earlier, unknown race. Supernaturally strong and very industrious, the *Menehune* worked only at night, completing each project by dawn or else leaving it forever unfinished. Several times they made so much noise in their strenuous laboring that they frightened birds as far away as Oahu.

They were a merry, gentle people with ugly red faces and big eyes set beneath long eyebrows. Two to three feet tall, each practiced a trade in which he was a master. They inhabited caves, hollow logs and banana-leaf huts, and eventually grew to a population of 50,000 adults.

Some say the *Menehune* came from the lost continent of Mu, which stretched across Polynesia to Fiji before it was swallowed by floods. Where they finally traveled to is less certain. After the Polynesians settled Kauai, the *Menehune* king, concerned that his people were intermarrying with an alien race, ordered the *Menehune* to leave the island. But many, unwilling to depart so luxurious a home, hid in the forests. There, near hiking trails and remote campsites, you may see them even today.

LIHUE AREA

Although Lihue is a rather dreary little town of 5700, visitors will likely pass through this tiny city several times because it's so centrally located. This is where the island's two highways converge—Kuhio heading north and Kaumualii going south. Here you'll find Kauai's airport and helicopter facilities, Nawiliwili Harbor and its commodity barges and cruise ships, government offices that issue camping and hiking permits, fast-food joints, industrial parks and big box retailers, and the island's largest shopping mall, Kukui Grove Center. In short, it's the civic and commercial center of the island.

But that doesn't mean the area is devoid of charm. The beautiful Haupu Ridge dominates the landscape to the south while the rambling peaks of Kalepa Ridge loom in the interior, and the Huleia River, which feeds the legendary Menehune (Alekoko) Fishpond, is one of the island's prettiest. And for those seeking convenience, or lacking transportation, Lihue is an excellent choice for home base.

SIGHTS

KAUAI MUSEUM

✉*4428 Rice Street, Lihue* ✆*808-245-6931* 📠*808-245-6864* ✑*www.kauai museum.org, museum@kauaimuseum.org* Among the attractions you will find in Lihue is this museum, a two-building complex rich in Hawaiiana. It is a prime spot to learn about the history, culture and natural history of the island. The main building focuses on Hawaiian heritage with its displays of feather leis, Hawaiian quilts, *koa* furniture and ancient calabashes. In the adjacent exhibition, 19th-century plantation life is revealed in a collection of old photographs, shot by W. J. Senda, a Japanese immigrant. Closed Sunday. Admission.

GROVE FARM HOMESTEAD MUSEUM ✉*Hawiliwili Road* ✆*808-245-3202*
📠*808-245-7988* ✑*www.grovefarm.net* Providing a wide window on Kauai's sugar-cane heritage is this beautifully preserved 80-acre homestead. Acquired in 1864 by the son of missionaries, the plantation is like a living museum with the main house, farm office, workers' homes and private cottages still intact. Surrounding these tinroof buildings are banana patches, gardens and pastures. Two-hour guided tours of this fascinating facility are available (Monday, Wednesday and Thursday at 10 a.m. and 1 p.m.) by reservation.

NAWILIWILI HARBOR An interesting side trip from Lihue is down Rice Street to this busy harbor. A deep-water port, with its cruise ships and cargo vessels, it is the island's major seaport. On December 31, 1941, it was shelled by the Japanese during World War II but sustained little damage. Nearby **Kalapaki Beach** is one of Kauai's most popular strands, both because of its proximity to Lihue and its pretty white sands.

KAUAI MARRIOTT RESORT & BEACH CLUB ✉*3610 Rice Street, Lihue*
✆*808-245-5050, 800-220-2925* 📠*808-245-5049* ✑*www.marriott.com/lihhi* Fronting Kalapaki Beach is this Marriott resort. Some believe that Mother Nature, in the form of Hurricane Iniki, wreaked havoc on its previous incarnation, the Westin Kauai, because it was so un-Hawaiian in nature—it looked like a Las Vegas version of Rome. Today its lush gardens, massive swimming pool (complete with waterfalls)—one of the

KAPAIA STITCHERY
PAGE 436

Hawaiian fabrics, aloha shirts, and quilts designed and sewn by local women

DUKE'S CANOE CLUB
PAGE 434

Great food, next to the beach, Hawaiian music playing and surfing decor dedicated to the granddaddy of surfing, Duke Kahanamoku

NININI BEACH
PAGE 438

Pocket sunbathing beach with numerous springs that bubble out of the lava and percolate up into the sand around you

ALEKOKO FISHPOND
PAGE 429

Boulder-lined, 900-foot-long pond built before the arrival of the Polynesians by the mythical leprechaun-like *Menehune*

largest in the state—and an extensive art collection spread throughout the public spaces warrant a look and see. If nothing else, a stroll along the granite pathway along the white-sand beach is worth the detour.

ALEKOKO (OR MENEHUNE) FISHPOND

✉️*Take Rice Street to Nawiliwili, then right on Route 58, a quick left on Niumalu Road and finally right on Hulemalu Road.* From Nawiliwili Harbor, you can continue on to this 900-foot-long pond. Spread across a valley floor and backdropped by the Hoary Head Mountain Range, it dates back well before the Polynesians. Or so the mythmakers would like you to believe. Legend has it that a line of leprechaun-like *Menehune* 25 miles long passed rocks from hand to hand and built the pond in a single night. Their only request of the prince and princess for whom they built the structure was that these two mortals not watch them while they worked. When the *Menehune* discovered that curiosity had overcome the two, who were watching the midget workers by the light of the moon, the *Menehune* turned them into the pillars of stone you see on the mountainside above the fishpond.

HULEIA NATIONAL
WILDLIFE REFUGE

☎*808-828-1413* Visible from the vista overlooking the Menehune Fishpond is this wildlife refuge, a 238-acre preserve that rises from the river basin up the wooded slopes of Huleia Valley. This estuary, which was the setting for scenes in *Raiders of the Lost Ark*, is home to 31 bird species including four different endangered species of waterbirds—the Hawaiian stilt, Hawaiian duck, Hawaiian gallinule and Hawaiian coot—as well as Hawaiian medicinal plants and wild fruit.

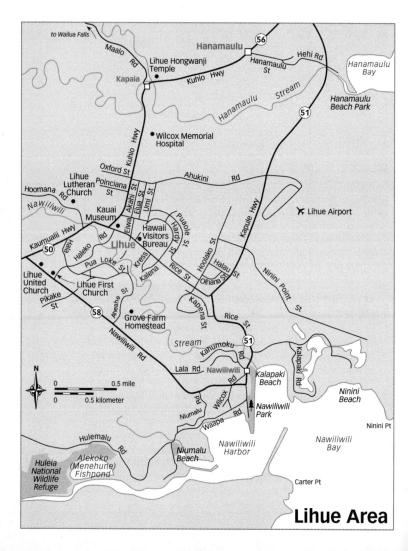

Lihue Area

KAPAIA A short distance from Lihue, Kuhio Highway (Route 56), the main road to Kauai's north shore, descends into the rustic village of Kapaia. Classic plantation-style structures and a gulch choked with banana plants mark this valley. On the right, **Lihue Hongwanji Temple**, one of the island's oldest, smiles from beneath a modern-day facelift.

WAILUA FALLS Off Kuhio Highway, Maalo Road threads through three miles of fields to these twin cascades. They tumble 80 feet into a heavenly pool fringed with *hala* trees. An easily accessible pool lies just a couple hundred yards past the falls.

HANAMAULU Follow Kuhio Highway and you'll arrive in this old plantation town where falsefront stores and tinroof houses line the roadway. If you follow Hanamaulu Road to Hehi Road you'll come to **Hanamaulu Beach Park**. Shaded by coconut palms and ironwood trees, it's a lovely place to picnic. (See "Beaches & Parks" below.)

KILOHANA ✉3-2087 Kuamualii Highway, Lihue ✆808-245-5608 ✆808-245-7818 ✎www.kilohanakauai.com, kilohana@hawaii.net Head a mile and a half southwest from Lihue on Kaumualii Highway (Route 50) to Kilohana for a view of the luxurious side of island life. This 16,000-square-foot Tudor mansion was home to the plantation that once covered these grounds. Today, the 1935 house serves as a center for arts-and-crafts shops and museum displays, and the 35 surrounding acres are devoted to a re-creation of traditional plantation life. Wander down the "coral path" and you'll pass a tropical garden and a succession of corrugated-roof houses. Papaya, banana and avocado trees line the route and roosters crow in the distance. Carriages pulled by Clydesdales tour the grounds and wagon tours lead out into the fields behind the house. There are also weekly luaus.

Train buffs will be drawn to Kilohana's **Kauai Plantation Railway** tours (www.kauaiplantationrailway.com), offered on a narrow gauge railroad, with locomotives that date back to plantation days. Rides are offered on the hour between 8 a.m. and 2 p.m. daily, and again at 5 and 6 p.m. between April and August. A number of vendors display their wares to help folks pass the time while waiting for the train. Admission.

LODGING

If you are in search of budget-priced lodging facilities, there are few places in all Hawaii as inviting as Lihue. And being located near the airport or a block or two from "downtown" Lihue is convenient for those folks without wheels.

TIP TOP MOTEL
$ 30 ROOMS ✉3173 Akahi Street, Lihue ✆808-245-2333 ✆808-246-8988
Accommodations are basic here with tile floors, stall showers and air conditioning. The sheer size of this two-story, two-building complex makes it impersonal by Kauai standards, but I found the management to be very warm. You'll have to eat meals in the adjoining restaurant or elsewhere, since none of the rooms have kitchenettes.

MOTEL LANI

$ 8 ROOMS   ✉4240 Rice Street, Lihue   ☎808-245-2965

Located three blocks from the Rice Shopping Center, this motel has small rooms facing a small patio where guests can lounge about in lawn chairs. The units are clean and comfortable, though sparsely furnished. About half are air-conditioned; all have fans and refrigerators. This place has a noisy lobby (with a television) just off busy Rice Street.

KAUAI PALMS HOTEL

$$ 28 ROOMS   ✉2931 Kalena Street, Lihue   ☎808-246-0908
🖳www.kauaipalmshotel.com, info@kauaipalmshotel.com

If you're looking for a modest room in downtown Lihue for well under $100, Kauai Palms delivers handily. This property has been spruced up by a new owner to include wi-fi, flat screen TVs, refrigerators and new furnishings in each of the units. There's no air conditioning, but the trade winds keep things cool.

KAUAI INN ——————— hidden

$$ 48 ROOMS   ✉2430 Hulemalu Road, Lihue   ☎808-245-9000,
800-808-2330   🖳808-245-3004   🖳www.kauai-inn.com, info@kauai-inn.com

Over 100 years old (and the first hotel on the island), this inn was extensively renovated at the end of the millennium, resulting in a comfortable hotel with remnants of old Hawaii. Convenient to the airport, it sits on three acres near the Hapu Mountains and Huleia River, with a pool and laundry facilities. All guest rooms have a refrigerator and microwave.

GARDEN ISLAND INN

$$–$$$ 21 ROOMS   ✉3445 Wilcox Road, Lihue   ☎808-245-7227, 800-648-0154
🖳808-245-7603   🖳www.gardenislandinn.com, info@gardenislandinn.com

Situated across the street from Nawiliwili Park is this tropical caravansary. You'll find it near the corner of Waapa Road and Wilcox Road, a short walk from Kalapaki Beach. Each room is light and airy with comfortable furnishings, fresh flowers, attractive appointments, air conditioning and DVD players—movies filmed in Hawaii are available for free. You'll hear occasional noise from passing trucks and planes. Children are welcome, and several of the large rooms are sufficiently spacious for families. All of the fully equipped units have refrigerators, wet bars and microwave ovens. Beach gear, including boogieboards, is loaned free to guests, as are golf clubs. The grounds are trimly landscaped and highlighted by a koi pond in which several dozen carp flash their colors.

KAUAI MARRIOTT RESORT & BEACH CLUB

$$$$ 356 ROOMS   ✉3610 Rice Street, Lihue   ☎808-245-5050, 800-872-6626
🖳808-245-5049   🖳www.marriott.com/lihhi, kauai@marriott.com

Fronting a quarter-mile of white sandy beach, one of the island's loveliest, the Kauai Marriott is the Lihue area's premier resting spot. The 124-room hotel and 232-room timeshare property are a stone's throw from the airport and Lihue. Most rooms, appointed in island-style decor featuring Hawaiian tropical floral designs, offer views of the ocean and come with a lanai. A beach promenade of granite tile leads from one end of the beach to the other. For those not interested in swimming in the ocean, the resort sports the largest swimming pool in the islands, replete with waterfalls. A myriad of water sports is available to guests. Restaurants and a fitness center round out the amenities.

CONDOS

BANYAN HARBOR RESORT

148 UNITS ✉️ *3411 Wilcox Road, Lihue* 📞 *808-245-7333, 800-422-6926*
📠 *808-246-3687* 🖥️ *www.vacation-kauai.com, reservations@banyanharbor.net*

A collection of woodframe buildings across a busy street from Nawiliwili Harbor, this resort has condos with ocean and garden views; one-bedroom units are $125 per night while two-bedroom units are $155 per night. Each unit has a full kitchen and laundry facilities. Most of the units here are leased by the month, but a handful rent by the night. Like many condo projects, the units here are all individually owned, and the décor and upkeep varies as a result. Before giving a deposit, you may want to inquire about your options if you should arrive and find you are dissatisfied with your choice. Minimum two-night stay required.

DINING

For good food at modest prices, Lihue is a prime spot. This is the center of most island business so it contains numerous restaurants that cater largely to local folks.

HAMURA SAIMIN _____

$ LOCAL-STYLE ✉️ *2956 Kress Street, Lihue* 📞 *808-245-3271*

You're liable to see lots of local faces lining the curving counter here. When I ate there the place was packed. I had the *"saimin special,"* a combination of noodles, wontons, eggs, meat, onions, vegetables and fish cake in a delicious broth.

OKI DINER _____

$ DINER/LOCAL-STYLE ✉️ *3125 Kuhio Highway, Lihue* 📞 *808-245-5899*

A small and spare eatery, this is a favorite place for locals to dine on ramen, wonton soup and various other Asian dishes.

RESTAURANT KIIBO

$$ JAPANESE ✉️ *2991 Umi Street, Lihue* 📞 *808-245-2650*

Want to go Japanese? Try this contemporary-style restaurant with a tatami room. You'll find the menu filled with yakitori, tempura and tofu dishes, as well as sushi and sashimi. Closed Sunday.

LIHUE BARBECUE INN

$$–$$$ PACIFIC RIM/AMERICAN   ✉*2982 Kress Street, Lihue*
📞*808-245-2921*

A local institution since 1939, this inn offers Asian dishes in addition to all-American meals. The lunch menu includes salads, soups, sandwiches, hamburgers and a daily special that often features teriyaki and Pacific Rim–influenced dishes; at dinner, there's steak, shrimp tempura and scampi. Closed Sunday.

TIP TOP CAFÉ AND BAKERY

$ LOCAL-STYLE   ✉*3173 Akahi Street, Lihue*   📞*808-245-2333*   ✆*808-246-8988*

This café and bakery is a favorite among tourists. Visitors can take their pick from any in a succession of booths in this large and impersonal eatery. Breakfasts are inexpensive—the macadamia-nut pancakes are delicious. Lunch entrées, however, are not very imaginative and have received negative reviews from readers. The well-known bakery serves macadamia-nut cookies, the house specialty. No dinner. Closed Monday.

DANI'S RESTAURANT

$ HAWAIIAN   ✉*4201 Rice Street*   📞*808-245-4991*

A good Lihue meal stop is Dani's, where you can pick up the usual eggs and rice, or authentic Hawaiian food at reasonable prices. It's a bustling coffee shop kind of place that serves breakfast and lunch daily, except Sundays. No credit cards.

DUKE'S CANOE CLUB

$$–$$$$ PACIFIC RIM/LOCAL-STYLE   ✉*Kauai Marriott Resort & Beach Club, Lihue*   📞*808-246-9599*   ✆*808-246-1047*   ✎*www.hulapie.com*

Just a coconut's throw from a sandy beach, Duke's Canoe Club is one of the best spots for an island meal. Besides the fresh fish, Huli Huli chicken, grill items and celebrated salad bar, this open-air restaurant has surfboards, photos and memorabilia commemorating the granddaddy of surfing, Duke Kahanamoku. Roaming musicians entertain nightly.

CAFÉ PORTOFINO

$$$–$$$$ ITALIAN   ✉*Kauai Marriott Resort & Beach Club, Lihue*   📞*808-245-2121*

The menu here features several pasta dishes as well as house specialties like calamari, scampi, eggplant parmigiana and sautéed rabbit. Dinner only.

KALENA FISH MARKET

$ PLATE LUNCHES   ✉*2985 Kalena Street (off Rice Street), Lihue*
📞*808-246-6629*   ✆*808-246-2174*

Stop here for the best plate lunch in Lihue. Fish and meat specials, like breaded mahi, Korean-style barbecue spare ribs and local foods like *laulau* and *kalua* pig with cabbage, change daily. You can choose from a wide array of side dishes: macaroni salad, marinated bean sprouts and *kim chee*. It's clean and modern with a few tables.

GARDEN ISLAND BBQ

$ CHINESE/BARBECUE ✉*4252 Rice Street, Lihue* 📞*808-245-8868*

Whatever the time of day or night, this place is generally packed with customers, nearly all of them locals. The reason? Great food, ample portions, three pages of menu choices that are the same for lunch and dinner, super casual setting and low prices. The menu is predominantly Chinese and the barbecue is more local or Korean-style than Texas, but you can also get burgers, sandwiches and plate lunches. Closed Sunday.

JJ'S BROILER

$$$–$$$$ STEAK/SEAFOOD ✉*3416 Rice Street, Nawiliwili* 📞*808-246-4422* 📠*808-245-7019* ✍*www.jjsbroiler.com, jjsbroiler@hotmail.com*

This is a family-style eatery with standard steak dishes, seafood platters and a salad bar. The waterfront location overlooks Kalapaki Beach and has a sunny Southern California ambience.

THE BEACH HUT

$ AMERICAN ✉*3474 Rice Street, Nawiliwili* 📞*808-246-6330*

Located in Nawiliwili is this laid-back spot offering a full breakfast menu; for lunch and dinner, there are hamburgers, sandwiches and salads. Order at the window and dine upstairs on a deck overlooking the water.

ARA'S SAKANA-YA FISH HOUSE

$ PLATE LUNCHES/DELI ✉*Hanamaulu Plaza at Kuhio Highway and Hanamaulu Road, Hanamaulu* 📞*808-245-1707*

At Ara's you can kill two birds with one stone. Their deli has good plate lunches, sushi and fresh fish, but the best part is you can take your food to the laundromat next door and eat while you wash. Lunch and take-out only.

HANAMAULU CAFÉ

$$ JAPANESE/CHINESE ✉*Kuhio Highway, Hanamaulu* 📞*808-245-2511* 📠*808-245-2497*

If it's atmosphere and a taste of the Orient you're after, reserve a tea room at the Hanamaulu's. My favorite is the garden room overlooking a rock-bound pond filled with carp. Lunch and dinner are the same here, with an excellent selection of Japanese and Chinese dishes. There's also a sushi bar at night. Children's portions are available. Closed Monday.

GAYLORD'S

$$$–$$$$ INTERNATIONAL ✉*At Kilohana on Kaumualii Highway, one-and-one-half miles southwest of Lihue* 📞*808-245-9593* 📠*808-246-1087* ✍*www.gaylordskauai.com, gaylords@hawaiian.net*

Take a plantation manor, add a flowering garden, and you have the setting for Gaylord's. Elevating patio dining to a high art, this alfresco restaurant looks out on the spacious lawns and spreading trees of Kilohana plantation. The menu features fresh island fish, pasta, farm-raised venison, baby back ribs, slow-roasted prime rib and chicken Kauai in addition to exotic specials on Monday and a well-rounded wine list. A rare combination of Old World elegance and tropical ambience; lunch, dinner and Sunday brunch served. Reservations requested.

SHOPPING

SUNSHINE MARKET

✉️*Kapule Highway, Lihue* Don't miss this market every Friday afternoon in the parking lot of the town stadium. Local folks turn out to sell homegrown produce, "talk story," and generally have a good time. It's a great place to buy island fruits and vegetables at bargain prices, and an even better spot to meet Kauai's farmers. It starts at 3 p.m., but get there a little early—before the best produce has disappeared.

KAPAIA STITCHERY

✉️*Kuhio Highway, just north of Lihue* 📞*808-245-2281* 📠*808-245-1772* ✉️*kapaiastitchery@hawaiiantel.net* Half the items are designed and sewn by local women here. There's an array of T-shirts, aloha shirts, Hawaiian quilting pillow kits and patterns, plus stunning patchwork quilts. This is an excellent place to buy Hawaiian fabrics and hand-dyed batiks from Bali. Closed Sunday.

KUKUI GROVE CENTER ✉️*3-2600 Kaumualii Highway, Lihue* 📞*808-245-7784* ✉️*www.kukuigrovecenter.com* This ultramodern complex is the island's largest shopping mall. Here are department stores, bookshops, specialty stores and other establishments. Though lacking the intimacy of Kauai's independent handicraft outlets, the center provides such a concentration of goods that it's hard to bypass.

KAUAI MUSEUM SHOP

✉️*4428 Rice Street, Lihue* 📞*808-245-6931* Stop in at this shop if you're interested in taking home some Niihau shell leis, local crafts or books. They have a nice selection. Closed Sunday.

KAUAI FRUIT & FLOWER COMPANY ✉️*3-4684 Kuhio Highway, Lihue* 📞*808-245-1814, 800-943-3108* ✉️*www.kauaifruit.com* This tropical shop can put together custom-made baskets of coffee, macadamia nuts, papaya salsa, coconut syrup, fresh bread, dried fruit, etc. They make a great gift for anyone you left at home. The store also sells and ships pineapples and papayas. Closed Sunday.

KILOHANA ✉️*Kaumualii Highway, one and one half miles southwest of Lihue* 📞*808-245-5608* ✉️*www.kilohanakauai.com* This is one of Hawaii's most beautiful complexes to shop. Set in a grand sugar plantation house, it rests amid acres of manicured grounds. Many rooms in this museum-cum-mall are furnished in period style to recapture 1930s-era plantation life. The galleries, boutiques and crafts shops are equally enchanting. Here you'll find pillows, hand-blown glassware, Niihau shell leis, pottery and much, much more.

TWO FROGS HUGGING ✉3215 Kuhio Highway, Lihue ✆808-246-8777 ⌨www.twofrogshugging.com, info@twofrogshugging.net Two Frogs Hugging got its campy name from a statue the owners saw that began their foray into imports. Their merchandise consists mainly of intricate, imported wood furniture and stone carvings. Closed Sunday.

NIGHTLIFE

LIHUE CAFÉ ✉2978 Umi Street, Lihue ✆808-245-6471 You'll find a lot of local color at this café. The drinks are cheap, the tourists are few.

ROB'S GOOD TIMES GRILL ✉Rice Shopping Center, Lihue ✆808-246-0311 Rob's is definitely the most happening place in Lihue, with a full food menu, sports bar, pool tables, country line dancing, karaoke and nightly dancing to music mixed by deejays.

KAUAI COMMUNITY PLAYERS ✉Lihue ✆808-245-7700 ⌨www.kauai communityplayers.org, postmaster@kauaicommunityplayers.org Every small town needs its quirky band of players, and Lihue is no exception. The island's only theater troupe is located here. The non-profit has been around since 1971, producing old standbys like Joseph and the Amazing Technicolor Dreamcoat, The Miracle Worker and Sweeney Todd, as well as lesser-known productions.

LIHUE BOWLING CENTER ✉4303 Rice Street, Lihue ✆808-245-5263 You can always head here and knock down a few pins.

BEACHES & PARKS

KALAPAKI BEACH

✉Take Rice Street from Lihue to Nawiliwili Park. Enter from the park.
This wide strand stretches for a quarter-mile in front of the Kauai Marriott hotel. Popular with surfers since ancient Hawaiian times, Kalapaki is situated right on Nawiliwili Bay, an appealing but busy harbor. It is also one of the best swimming beaches on the island since the harbor protects it from heavy shorebreak. Out past the harbor, the Hoary Head mountains rise in the background. Beginner's surfing is best in the center of Nawiliwili Bay, where there is a right slide. More experienced surfers will find good breaks next to the rock wall near the lighthouse, where there's a left slide. There's also good surfing on the right side of the bay. Nicknamed "Hang Ten," these left slide breaks are a good place for nose-riding. Windsurfing is best tried by intermediate-level folks. Snorkeling is so-so at Kalapaki, but anglers should have better luck. Both off the pier and near the

lighthouse are good spots for mullet, big-eyed scad, *papio*, bone-fish and threadfin; sometimes *ulua*, *oama* and red bigeye can be caught here, too. Nawiliwili Park, next to the beach, has a picnic area and restrooms.

NIUMALU BEACH PARK

✉ *Take Rice Street to Nawiliwili, turn right on Route 58, then left on Niumalu Road.*

This tree-lined park is tucked into a corner of Nawiliwili Harbor near a small-boat harbor. With neighbors like this and no swimming facilities, the park's key feature is its proximity to Lihue. It is popular nonetheless with picnickers, and the adjacent Huleia River attracts kayakers, fishermen and crabbers. Facilities include a picnic area, restrooms and showers.

NININI BEACH

✉ *Take the road leading through the Kauai Marriott property in Nawiliwili. Follow this road to the golf course clubhouse. Park and walk across the golf course in a direction several degrees to the right of the lighthouse. The smaller beach can be reached by walking from Running Water Beach toward the lighthouse for about three-tenths of a mile.*

Hidden along a rocky coastline between Nawiliwili Bay and the lighthouse on Ninini Point are two small sand beaches. Lying at the base of a sea cliff, these pocket beaches are separated by a lava rock formation. The smaller beach is about a quarter-mile from Ninini Point and the larger is known as **Running Waters Beach**, named for the numerous springs that bubble out of the lava and percolate up into the sand. Both are excellent for sunbathing but generally not safe for other water activities due to strong currents and undertow; bodysurfers, however, frequent Running Waters Beach. Since both beaches are pretty close to civilization, I don't recommend camping at either one. There are no facilities here.

HANAMAULU BEACH PARK

✉ *Take Kuhio Highway to Hanamaulu, then turn down the road leading to the bay.*

Here's an idyllic park nestled in Hanamaulu Bay and crowded with ironwood and coconut trees. The beach is a narrow corridor of sand at the head of Hanamaulu Bay. The bay is well-protected, but the water is usually murky and of questionable quality so swim at your own risk. I found this a great place for picnicking and shell collecting. Anglers can expect to hook bonefish, mullet and bigeyed scad. A picnic area, restrooms, showers and a playground are some of the facilities here.

⛰ Needles from the ironwood trees make a natural bed at this lovely site. Tent and trailer camping (closed Wednesday); county permit required.

✉ *Located north of Nawiliwili Harbor. Take Waapa Road north until it connects with Rice Street (Route 51). The park is east of the junction.*

🚤 Not the most beautiful setting on the island, this park nevertheless offers a swath of grass and picnic tables as well as access to good surf and fishing grounds. There's also playground equipment for the little ones. Picnic tables, a pavilion and restrooms round out the facilities.

The Forbidden Island—Niihau

There's little doubt that the most hidden place in "hidden Hawaii" is Niihau, Hawaii's westernmost inhabited island. About 160 native Hawaiians live on this privately owned island under conditions similar to those prevailing during the 19th century. Used as a cattle and sheep ranch and closed to the public, it is Hawaii's last unspoiled frontier.

The Robinsons, a Scottish family that came to Hawaii from New Zealand, purchased the island in the 1860s and have protected (some critics say segregated) its inhabitants from the rest of the world ever since. Residents of Niihau are free to leave the island but must ask permission to return, and while the situation does have a company-town aura about it, the Robinsons have historically shown an abiding concern for the people and ecology of Hawaii.

While Niihau measures a mere 70 square miles and rises only 1281 feet above sea level at its highest point, the island lays claim to rich fishing grounds and is famous for its Niihau shell necklaces, fashioned from rare and tiny shells that wash up on the windward shore only a few times a year.

NIIHAU HELICOPTER ✉ *Kaumualii Highway* 📞 *808-335-3500* Until the 1980s, Niihau fully deserved its nickname, "The Forbidden Island." But today outsiders with a sense of adventure (and some extra cash) can climb aboard a Niihau Helicopter flight and tour a part of the island. You'll fly over most of the island, avoiding the village where the population is concentrated, and land on a remote beach for a short hike along the shore. You won't meet any Niihau residents, but you will have an experience that could prove to be your ultimate encounter with "hidden Hawaii."

HOLOHOLO CHARTERS ✉ *Elele* 📞 *800-848-6130* If you'd rather explore the island by sea, HoloHolo Charters offers an interesting option. Leaving from Port Allen and including a continental breakfast, their "Supertour" first stops at the Na Pali Coast to view the natural wonders of that area. They then head to Niihau for a snorkeling visit. A lunch follows. During the meal, the crew discusses the people and history of Niihau.

POIPU AREA

The Poipu area, crown jewel of the southside of Kauai, specializes in beaches—along with a steady stream of sunshine. What you'll find in this warm, dry, white-sand corner of the island is a prime example of everyone's favorite combination—the old and the new. The traditional comes in the form of Koloa Town, site of Hawaii's first successful sugar mill, a 19th-century plantation town that has been splashed with tropical colors. For the modern, you need look only a couple miles down the road to Poipu, a series of scalloped beaches that has become action central for real-estate developers.

Anchoring these enclaves to the east is Puhi Mount, scene of the last volcanic eruption on Kauai. To the north rises Haupu Ridge, a wall of wooded mountains that divides the district from the Huleia Valley and Lihue. Everywhere else you'll find abandoned sugar fields or acres planted with corn. The tiny, old communities of Lawai and Omao comprise the rest of what is known locally as the southside.

Developers are proceeding with plans for extensive new vacation home and resort projects that will span two decades and greatly impact Poipu, Koloa, Omao, Lawai and the Spouting Horn area. Vacationers need to be aware that rock blasting, dust and noise are part of this effort, so it's wise to inquire when making reservations about the proximity of the nearest construction project. In any case, expect traffic delays and generally a lot more commotion in this once quiet region.

SIGHTS

QUEEN VICTORIA'S PROFILE Without doubt, you'll want to drive out from Lihue along Kaumualii Highway (Route 50) to explore the south coast. Along the way, if you possess a Rorschach test imagination, you'll see Queen Victoria's Profile etched in the Hoary Head Range. (Need a helping eye? Watch for the Hawaii Visitors Bureau sign on the side of the highway.)

TREE TUNNEL When you turn south toward Poipu on Maluhia Road (Route 520), you won't need a road sign to find what locals refer to as Tree Tunnel, an arcade of towering eucalyptus trees that forms a shadowy tunnel en route to the timeworn town of **Koloa**. The remains of the original sugar plantation stand in an unassuming pile on the right side of the road as you enter town; a plaque and sculpture near this old chimney commemorates the birth of Hawaii's sugar industry, a business that dominated life in the islands throughout most of the 19th and 20th centuries. A sugar mill continued to operate until 1996 just outside town and Koloa still consists primarily of company-town houses and humble churches surrounded by former sugar cane fields. But the main street was gentrified during the 1980s as tropical-colored paints were added to the old woodframe and falsefront town center.

KOLOA HISTORY CENTER ⊠ *Koloa Road, Koloa* This tiny center, located in the Old Koloa Town mall, provides a brief introduction to the history of the area in the form of artifacts from the old plantation days.

WAITA RESERVOIR A dirt road at the end of Weliweli Road near the sugar mill leads to the largest manmade reservoir in Kauai and on the islands. Covering over 350 acres Waita Reservoir (closed to the public) is built on former marshlands on the eastside of Koloa.

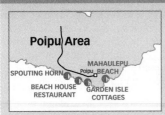

SPOUTING HORN

PAGE 450

A great place to meet local artisans selling their own jewelry creations made from coral, shells and mother-of-pearl

BEACH HOUSE RESTAURANT

PAGE 448

The perfect oceanfront location to catch the sunset while enjoying the island's tastiest Pacific Rim cuisine

GARDEN ISLE COTTAGES OCEANFRONT

PAGE 444

Pretty one-bedroom hideaways located on a small bluff above the best snorkeling spot on the island

MAHAULEPU BEACH

PAGE 452

A tropical corridor of white sand along a reef-protected shoreline—great for snorkeling and surfing

POIPU From Koloa, Poipu Road takes you through fields two miles to the coast and this vacation community. If a one-word association test were applied to Poipu, the word would be "beach." There really is no town here, just a skein of hotels, condominiums and stores built along a series of white-sand beaches. Nevertheless, this is Kauai's premier playground, a sun-soaked realm that promises good weather and good times.

MOIR GARDENS

✉Kiahuna Plantation, 2253 Poipu Road, Poipu ☎808-742-6411 ☎808-742-1698 Near the center of Poipu, tucked into the grounds of Kiahuna Plantation, are these gardens. What was once a labor of love for the Koloa Sugar Plantation manager's wife has grown over the years from a small cactus garden into its present-day incarnation, filled with a variety of tropical plants as well as a broad collection of succulents. If you're staying in Poipu, it's worth strolling through.

SPOUTING HORN ✉End of Lawai Road While civilization has encroached to the very side of the sea, nature continues to display some of its gentle wonders along the colorful reefs and pearly sands. Most remarkable of all is this underwater lava tube with an opening along the shore. Surf crashing through the tube dramatically transforms this blowhole into a miniature Old Faithful. The mournful sounds issuing from Spouting Horn are said to be the plaintive cries of a legendary lizard or *mo'o*. It seems that he was returning from another island where he had been told of the death of his two sisters. Blinded by tears he missed his landing and was swept into the blowhole. Try to time your visit with the high tide when the spumes from Spouting Horn reach their greatest heights. You should look around at this intriguing coastline, which is covered by coral outcroppings and tidepools.

KOLOA LANDING During the 1800s, this was a major port for whalers in the islands and was, until the 20th century, the main port of Kauai. Now it's a major spot for scuba divers.

PRINCE KUHIO PARK
⊠*Lawai Road, Poipu* On Lawai Road, a pretty palm-framed greensward commemorates the life of Prince Kuhio, who died in 1922 and was the last designated heir to the Hawaiian throne. A statue of the prince graces the park, as well as the well-preserved **Hoai Heiau**, the foundation of the prince's home and the remains of an ancient fishpond.

KUKUIULA BAY Beyond Prince Kuhio Park is Kukuiula Bay, a popular spot for fishing, snorkeling and scuba diving. There's an offshore reef and boaters and kayakers often launch their vessels here.

NATIONAL TROPICAL BOTANICAL GARDEN
⊠*Lawai Road, Poipu* ☎*808-742-2623 (reservations)* ⏎*www.ntbg.org* This garden encompasses 300 acres in the Lawai Valley, and within its lush grounds are offered two distinct tours: the Allerton Garden Tour and the McBryde Garden Tour. The Allerton tour ($35 per person) is guided and includes the summer cottage of the late Queen Emma and the former home of Chicago millionaire Robert Allerton. The McBryde tour ($20 per person) is self-guided and explores the scientific garden as well as some historic buildings that were part of the old McBryde sugar plantation tours. Both tours offer a wealth of information about the 10,000 species of plants cultivated in the valley, as well as NTBG's mission to save rare tropical plants from around the world. The NTBG Visitor Center is located across from Spouting Horn.

MAHAULEPU BEACH
For a real "Hidden Hawaii" adventure, follow Poipu Road east past the Hyatt Regency Kauai. The pavement will end and you'll find yourself on an old cane road. Follow it for about two miles. Minor cane roads will intersect the main one—ignore them. When you come to a major cane road (you'll know it by the telephone poles), turn right and follow this road. After about a mile

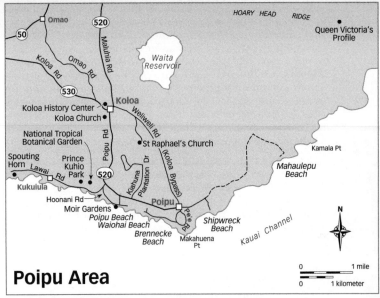

Poipu Area

you'll see roads leading to the beach. There's a guard shack at the turnoff (you're venturing into private property) and you may have to sign a waiver to continue on to this beach—the south shore's hidden strands. In addition to being incredibly beautiful and ripe with potential for outdoor sports, Mahaulepu Beach is important scientifically. Look around for petroglyphs or play in the 100-foot-high sand dunes. (See "Beaches & Parks" below for more information.)

LODGING

ELLIE'S KOLOA HOUSE

$$$$ 1 UNIT   ✉ Koloa   ☎ 800-779-8773

To get away from the construction that is running amok in Poipu, bed down in this sweet property reminiscent of old Hawaii. The gardens come with plumeria, hibiscus, banana, ginger, ti, heliconia, papaya, avocado and an assortment of palms. There's also an outside lanai with a barbeque at this two-bedroom, two-bath facility that rents for a song. Koloa town is a five-minute walk and Poipu Beach is just a mile away. Beach gear, washer-dryer, wi-fi, full kitchen—anything you will need and more is available here. The best feature, however, is the friendliness of the owner, Ellie.

KAHILI MOUNTAIN PARK

$-$$ 6 UNITS   ✉ The park is five miles from Koloa and about one mile off Kaumualii Highway.   ☎ 808-742-9921   📠 808-742-6628   🖥 www.kahilipark.org

One place for people wanting to rough it or to establish a base camp is this park, run by the Seventh Day Adventist Church. Facing Haupu

Ridge and backdropped by Kahili Mountain, this 197-acre domain offers an easy compromise between hoteling and camping. The two-bedroom cabin comes equipped with lanai and private bathroom, plus a funky kitchenette; the other cabins are one-bedroom units. The facilities also include cabinettes that share the park restrooms. Both types of facilities should be reserved several months in advance. Though cooking utensils and bed linens are provided, furnishings are a bit spartan: The floors are uncarpeted and the sole decoration is the surrounding mountains. Thank God for nature. At this rustic resort you can enjoy the swimming pond or hike the nearby trails. (Check their website for restrictions or write to Kahili Mountain Park, P.O. Box 298, Koloa, HI 96756.)

GRAND HYATT KAUAI RESORT & SPA

$$$$ 602 ROOMS   ✉1571 Poipu Road, Koloa   ☎808-742-1234, 800-554-9288
📠808-742-1557   🖰www.grandhyattkauai.com

It would be an elastic stretch of the imagination to call this Grand Hyatt a hidden destination. This *is*, after all, a Hyatt Regency—with over 600 guest rooms, several pools, six restaurants, six lounges and several acres of manmade lagoons. But before this luxury resort was built, the beach on which it sits was one of the great hidden locales on Kauai. Shipwreck Beach is still a magnificent crescent of white sand, and the Hyatt Regency Kauai Resort & Spa, backdropped by deep-green mountains, enjoys some of the seclusion for which Keoneloa Bay was renowned. With its wood-paneled lobby, atrium garden and plush guest rooms, it is one of Kauai's prettier hotels.

GARDEN ISLE COTTAGES OCEANFRONT

$$$$ 2 ROOMS   ✉2658 Puuholo Road, Koloa   ☎808-639-9233,
800-742-6711   📠808-742-1933   🖰www.oceancottages.com,
vacation@oceancottages.com

Located on a small bluff overlooking the ocean these pretty one-bedroom hideaways are decorated with artistic flair: Oil paintings and woven pieces adorn the walls, the furnishings are racattan and the kitchens are modern. The rooms, which are decorated with Asian, Polynesian and Indonesian themes, overlook Koloa Landing, site of the best snorkeling on the island. There is usually a two-night minimum stay. Closed Saturday and Sunday.

KAUAI COVE COTTAGES

$$–$$$ 3 ROOMS   ✉2672 Puuholo Road, Koloa   ☎808-651-0279,
800-624-9945   🖰www.kauaicovecottages.com

Walking proximity to Koloa Landing and Poipu Beach, and reasonable rates, make Kauai Cove a good choice. It's just three self-contained studio homes, each with a patio, tucked into lush landscaping. The managers will lend beach basics.

POIPU PLANTATION RESORT

$$–$$$ 13 ROOMS   ✉1792 Pee Road, Koloa   📞808-742-6757, 800-634-0263
🖥www.poipubeach.com

Offering a mix of B&B and vacation rental accommodations, this resort has three bedrooms, each with private bath and a full breakfast. There is also a wedding suite in a large, restored 1938 plantation-era house. Or you can rent one of nine one- or two-bedroom studios that come with cooking facilities and are placed around the extensively landscaped grounds.

SHERATON KAUAI RESORT

$$$$ 394 ROOMS   ✉2440 Hoonani Road, Poipu   📞808-742-1661, 800-782-9488
📠808-742-9777   🖥www.sheraton-kauai.com

With one of the southside's few truly oceanfront locations, as well as a pool that takes full advantage of the enviable view, this Sheraton is a pleasant, subdued hotel. The rooms, like the resort itself, are totally comfortable and standard Sheraton, but with an understated elegance. The grounds are lushly landscaped, giving the resort a private feel.

MARJORIE'S KAUAI INN

$$$ 3 ROOMS   ✉Lawai   📞808-332-8838, 800-717-8838
🖥www.marjorieskauaiinn.com, marjorie@marjorieskauaiinn.com

Marjorie's overlooks grazing horses in the Lawai Valley, and you can enjoy the view from your private deck. All three spacious guest rooms have a refrigerator, a microwave, a coffee maker and a toaster; you'll receive bread, fruit, juice and coffee on your arrival, and a continental breakfast is served daily. Guests have access to a swimming pool, and you can ask your hostess for use of a barbecue grill, a blender and beach chairs. Marjorie's a good resource for information about local attractions. Adults only.

CONDOS

The best way to shop for value and location among Poipu condos is to contact one of the local rental agencies.

POIPU BEACH RESORT ASSOCIATION

✉2440 Hoonani Road, Koloa   📞808-742-7444, 888-744-0888   📠808-742-7887
🖥www.poipubeach.org, info@poipubeach.org

This agency offers a variety of accommodation options in the South Shore from condos to cottages, many right on the beach or with ocean views. They can also help visitors with planning activities or finding important basics such as libraries, grocery stores and rental services.

GRANTHAM RESORTS

✉3176 Poipu Road, Poipu   📞808-742-2000, 800-325-5701   📠808-742-9093
🖥www.grantham-resorts.com, stay@grantham-resorts.com

Offering vacation homes, condos and resorts, this specialty service has plenty of high-end options featuring pools, gardens and on-site recreational activities. For easier selection, their available properties are arranged by romantic getaways, oceanfront options and group gatherings.

R & R REALTY & RENTALS

✉*1763 Pe'e Road, Poipu* ✆*808-742-7555, 800-367-8022* ✺*808-742-7434*
✎*www.r7r.com, randr@r7r.com*

The R&R stands for exactly what this service provides: rest and relaxation. Along with many rental resort properties, they also sell vacation homes and offer a lot of information about notable sightseeing stops in the Kauai area.

POIPU KAPILI

60 UNITS   ✉*2221 Kapili Road, Koloa* ✆*808-742-6449, 800-443-7714* ✺*808-742-9162*
✎*www.poipukapili.com, aloha@poipukapili.com*

Neatly situated near the oceanfront just a short jaunt to the beach, here you get both sunshine and relaxation. The complex includes a pool and tennis courts set amid lush vegetation. Each condo, uniquely decorated by its owner, offers views (and sounds) of the blue Pacific. One-bedroom condos start at $230.

WHALER'S COVE

24 UNITS   ✉*2640 Puuholo Road, Koloa* ✆*808-742-7571, 800-225-2683*
✺*808-742-1185* ✎*www.whalers-cove.com, stay@whalers-cove.com*

This is a secluded condominium resort that serves up an idyllic shoreline setting. Its roomy, two-bedroom units (which sleep up to six and range from $507 to $656) feature oceanfront lanais that face onto the bright blue Pacific; one-bedroom units run from $349 to $469. Koloa Landing, an excellent snorkeling and shoreline dive spot, is right next door. Each condo has cheery, modern decor. The resort has a pool, a hot tub and the ubiquitous barbecue.

KIAHUNA PLANTATION

333 UNITS   ✉*2253 Poipu Road, Poipu* ✆*808-742-6411, 800-688-7444*
✺*808-742-1698* ✎*www.outrigger.com*

A particularly well-known destination, this 35-acre beachfront spread is an ideal family resting spot. It is a complex of resort condominiums landscaped with lily ponds, lagoon and a spectacular cactus garden. The beach here provides lots of fun for bodysurfers. The units are housed in attractive plantation-style structures, which dot the resort's rolling lawns. In peak season, one-bedroom condos are $265 to $499; two-bedroom units are $405 to $545. Ask for a condo away from the street and parking lot.

POIPU CRATER RESORT

30 UNITS   ✉*Hoohu Road, Poipu* ✆*808-742-7400, 800-367-8020*
✺*808-742-9121* ✎*www.suite-paradise.com, mail@suite-paradise.com*

One of the most unique condos around is found at this resort. Located just 600 yards from the beach, it's also one of the best deals. This entire 30-unit facility rests in the crater of an extinct volcano. The accommodations are contained in attractive woodframe houses; all are two-bedroom condos and rent for $156 to $213 in peak season, depending on length of stay. There's a pool, tennis courts, a sauna and a barbecue area.

POIPU KAI RESORT

180 UNITS ✉1941 Poipu Road, Poipu ☎808-742-7400, 800-367-8020
📠808-742-9121 🖥www.suite-paradise.com, mail@suite-paradise.com

Consisting of a succession of separate buildings spread around a spacious lawn is this resort with seven pools and nine tennis courts plus a restaurant, jacuzzi and barbecues. The entire complex fronts Shipwreck and Brennecke's beaches. Economy cottages start at $97 and one-bedroom condos start at $128, depending on the length of your stay.

POIPU SHORES

39 UNITS ✉1775 Pe'e Road, Poipu ☎808-742-7400, 800-367-8020
🖥www.suite-paradise.com

A small complex right on the ocean with a swimming pool, this place is so close to the water the waves seem poised to break across it. Two-bedroom units start at $261 ($222 off-season).

SUNSET KAHILI CONDOMINIUMS

35 UNITS ✉1763 Pe'e Road, Poipu ☎808-742-7434, 800-827-6478 📠808-742-1559
🖥www.r7r.com, info@r7r.com

At Sunset Kahili, one-bedroom apartments start at $125 and sleep up to four, and two bedrooms house up to six and begin at $225. All units have ocean views. Four-night minimum stay gets a discount; two-week stay required during holiday season.

KUHIO SHORES

75 UNITS ✉5050 Lawai Road, Poipu ☎808-742-7555, 800-367-8022 📠808-742-1559
🖥www.r7r.com, randr@r7r.com

On the shore, but lacking a beach, this property has one-bedroom apartments starting at $225 for one to four people. Lower rates for stays longer than three days, and for weeklong reservations.

DINING

TOMKATS GRILLE

$$ AMERICAN ✉5404 Koloa Road, Koloa ☎808-742-8887

For patio dining stroll down the street to TomKats. Situated in a small interior courtyard, this easy-going restaurant has fresh seafood, as well as sandwiches and chicken fingers for the kids.

PIZZETTA

$$–$$$ ITALIAN ✉5408 Koloa Road, Koloa ☎808-742-8881 📠808-742-2715
🖥www.pizzettarestaurant.com

This area is not known for an abundance of restaurants, so you're lucky to find Pizzetta. Tastefully decorated with Italian scenes and tiles, the full bar will mix you up a drink while you wait for your order. The menu is basic Italian: calzones, mozzarella sticks, etc. But the pizza is particularly good, with its homemade crust and sauce, and reasonably priced. You can eat in, dine on the deck, or take it to go.

KOLOA FISH MARKET

$ PLATE LUNCHES ✉5482 Koloa Road, Koloa ☎808-742-6199
📠808-742-1018

For super fresh sashimi, a variety of fish *poke* and hearty plate lunches, stop in at this fish market. These plate lunches are several steps above the competitors in quality, and the raw fish items are fresh. Lunch only. Closed Sunday.

BEACH HOUSE RESTAURANT

$$$–$$$$ PACIFIC RIM ✉5022 Lawai Road, Koloa ☎808-742-1424
📠808-742-1369 🖥www.the-beach-house.com

The stars, the ocean and the Beach House Restaurant provide a perfect framework for some of Kauai's best Pacific Rim cuisine. Signature items include the "*Ahi* Taster," Kauai asparagus salad, lemongrass-and kaffir lime–crusted scallops, wasabi-crusted snapper and a Hawaiian chocolate *haupia* cake. Not only is the food worth the splurge, the oceanfront location, on the road to Spouting Horn, is an ideal place to catch the sunset. Dinner only.

CASABLANCA AT KIAHUNA

$–$$$$ MEDITERRANEAN ✉2290 Poipu Road, Koloa ☎808-742-2929

Consistently good Mediterranean food can be found at this attractive garden setting restaurant at the Kiahuna Swim and Tennis Club. A full tapas menu, as well as wraps and Moroccan lamb, are served.

PLANTATION GARDENS RESTAURANT

$$$–$$$$ PACIFIC RIM ✉2253 Poipu Road, Koloa ☎808-742-2216,
877-745-2824 📠808-742-1570 🖥www.pgrestaurant.com,
info@pgrestaurant.com

This restored Polynesian-style home tucked away in the densely landscaped grounds of Kiahuna Plantation Resort offers excellent atmosphere. Meals, served inside and on the open-air veranda, have a Pacific Rim influence. Try their signature dish: seafood *laulau*. The menu emphasizes organic, locally grown herbs and vegetables. Dinner only.

TIDEPOOLS

$$$$ SEAFOOD ✉Hyatt Regency Kauai Resort & Spa, 1571 Poipu Road, Koloa
☎808-240-6456 📠808-742-1557 🖥www.kauai-hyatt.com

Without a doubt, this is one of the most imaginative restaurants on the island. The theme is grass-shack Polynesia, with each of the several dining rooms resembling a classic *hale pili*. Set in a quiet lagoon and graced with classic Hawaiian sunsets and ocean breezes, it's a great place to dine. The offerings include charred ahi sashimi and a mixed seafood grill with lobster, scallops, shrimp and fish. Dinner only. Reservations recommended.

KEOKI'S PARADISE

$$–$$$$ STEAK/SEAFOOD ✉ *Poipu Shopping Village, 2360 Kiahuna Plantation Drive, Poipu* ☎ *808-742-7534* 📠 *808-742-7847* 🖥 *www.hulapie.com, keokis@keokishawaii.com*

A beautiful patio-style restaurant centered around a tropical garden and pond, Keoki's is located in Poipu Shopping Village. They feature a steak-and-seafood menu. Some say the seafood is the best you'll get for the price. The setting alone makes it worth a visit.

ROY'S POIPU BAR & GRILL

$$–$$$$ HAWAIIAN/AMERICAN ✉ *Poipu Shopping Village, 2360 Kiahuna Plantation Drive, Poipu* ☎ *808-742-5000* 📠 *808-742-5050*

It seems like everywhere you go in Hawaii these days, Roy Yamaguchi has a restaurant. On Kauai it is this informal dining room with the kitchen behind a glass partition. The menu is a sample of what the staff calls Hawaiian fusion cuisine. You can order steamed fresh fish, hibachi-style salmon or *kiawe*-grilled ribeye steak. Or at least that's what was on the ever-changing menu last time I was in. In any case, it's hard to go wrong. Reservations are strongly recommended. Dinner only.

POIPU TROPICAL BURGERS

$$ AMERICAN ✉ *Poipu Shopping Village, 2360 Kiahuna Plantation Drive, Poipu* ☎ *808-742-1808*

Families will love this spot with its *keiki* meals, casual, open-air setting, low prices and wide range of items. Gourmet burgers, sandwiches, meal-sized salads, fresh fish, steak and pasta make up the menu. Portions are hearty, and it's open for three meals a day.

BRENNECKE'S BEACH BROILER

$$–$$$$ AMERICAN ✉ *2100 Hoone Road, Poipu* ☎ *808-742-7588, 888-384-8810* 📠 *808-742-1321* 🖥 *www.brenneckes.com, bob@brenneckes.com*

Overlooking Poipu Beach is Brennecke's. Downstairs at this two-level dining spot you'll find a budget-priced deli serving sandwiches and shave ice. The upper deck is occupied by an open-air restaurant that serves appetizers, lunch and dinner daily. Dinner selections include fresh fish dishes, steak, chicken, pasta and seafood kebab.

TAQUERIA NORTENOS

$ MEXICAN ✉ *2827 Poipu Road, Poipu*

Huge (and tasty) portions that will last you two meals, or can be shared, are served up at this eatery in the Poipu Plaza. The decor isn't much to write home about, but you can take your Mexican food to go, and with prices like this it's hard to complain. You might want to try the *chalupas* or burritos. For dessert order the *bunuelos*. Closed Wednesday.

SHOPPING

On the way to Poipu, the former plantation town of Koloa supports a cluster of shops as well as a miniature mall. Several clothing stores line Koloa Road. The minimall, called Old Koloa Town (even though it was totally overhauled in the 1980s), houses a string of small jewelry stores, a T-shirt shop and a photo studio.

9 KAUAI POIPU AREA SHOPPING

CHRISTIAN RISO FINE ARTS ✉*5400 Koloa Road, Koloa* ☎*808-742-2555* This quality shop has contemporary Hawaiian paintings, prints and frames.

ISLAND SOAP & CANDLE WORKS ✉*5428 Koloa Road, Koloa* ☎*808-742-1945* Walk into Island Soap & Candle Works and get an education in how to make both. This amazing little shop has soaps made from coconut, guava, plumeria and every other island product imaginable. There are bath gels, botanical hand lotions and, oh yes, candles—dozens of different kinds.

POIPU SHOPPING VILLAGE ✉*2360 Kiahuna Plantation Drive, Koloa* ☎*808-742-2831* This is a resort-style shopping complex with several businesses, including restaurants, a store that sells only designer jewelry, two art galleries, a surf shop and a sundries shop. It's a good spot to stop at before a day at the beach.

GRAND HYATT KAUAI RESORT & SPA ✉*1571 Poipu Road, Koloa* ☎*808-742-1234* You can venture down to this spectacular resort property, which is well worth touring and also offers a variety of sleek shops.

SPOUTING HORN ─────
✉*End of Lawai Road, Poipu* My favorite shopping spot around Poipu has always been at the Spouting Horn. Here, next to the parking lot that serves visitors to the blowhole, local merchants set up tables to sell their wares. You're liable to find coral and *puka* shell necklaces, trident shell trumpets, rare Niihau shell necklaces and some marvelous mother-of-pearl pieces. You are free to barter, of course, though the prices are pretty good to begin with. If you're interested in jewelry and want to meet local artisans, this is an intriguing spot.

NIGHTLIFE

BRENNECKE'S BEACH BROILER ✉*2100 Hoone Road, Poipu* ☎*808-742-7588* To catch a local crowd, head down to Brennecke's. There's no music, but the crowds are young and the views otherworldly.

KEOKI'S PARADISE ─────
✉*2360 Kiahuna Plantation Drive, Poipu* ☎*808-742-7534* Keoki's in Poipu Shopping Village features contemporary Hawaiian music Monday through Friday nights and Sunday during the day. You can sit outdoors in a garden setting and enjoy the sounds. Also in the mall, check out the Polynesian dance show Tuesday and Thursday evenings on the mall's center stage.

THE POINT ✉*Sheraton Kauai Beach Resort, 2440 Hoonani Road, Poipu* ☎*808-742-1661* There's live Hawaiian and light contemporary music here on Wednesday, and dancing on Thursday, Friday and Saturday. The 225-degree view and wavefront location are an even stronger draw. Great at sunset.

STEVENSON'S LIBRARY ✉️*Grand Hyatt Kauai Resort & Spa, 1571 Poipu Road, Poipu* 📞*808-742-1234, 800-633-7313* The Grand Hyatt Kauai Resort & Spa, with its spectacular location on Shipwreck Beach, hosts the area's upscale nightspots. Stevenson's Library is a stately wood-paneled lounge that evokes a sense of colonial-era Polynesia. For a drink with a view of the beach, try the **Tidepools Restaurant**. Hawaiian sunsets and music go hand in hand at **Seaview Terrace**, located in the hotel's lobby.

BEACHES & PARKS

POIPU BEACH AND WAIOHAI BEACH
✉️*Along Poipu Road near the closed Waiohai hotel*

Extending along the main hotel area in Poipu are two adjacent white-sand beaches crowded with visitors. Popular with sunbathers, swimmers and water-sport aficionados, both are protected by a series of offshore reefs. At Poipu Beach there is good surfing for beginners near the beach, for intermediate surfers about 100 yards offshore and for expert surfers about a half-mile out at "First Break." This beach is also popular with windsurfers. Waiohai Beach has an offshore break near the reef known as "Waiohai." There's fishing from the nearby rocks (the beach area is usually crowded). There are lifeguards.

POIPU BEACH PARK
✉️*On Hoone Road in Poipu*

This has got to be one of the loveliest little parks around. There's a well-kept lawn for picnickers and finicky sunbathers, a crescent-shaped beach with a protecting reef and the sunny skies of Poipu. Since the water here is relatively flat, most days it's not good for surfing. However, swimming is excellent, and the entire area has some of the best diving on the island. An offshore sandbar makes for good bodysurfing. Bonefish, rockfish and *papio* are common catches; there's also good spearfishing on the nearby reefs. You'll find a picnic area, restrooms, showers and lifeguards.

SHIPWRECK BEACH
✉️*From the Poipu Beach area, follow Poipu Road east and simply look for the Hyatt Regency Kauai, which borders the beach.*

Back in the 1980s, this was one of the greatest of Kauai's hidden beaches. Then condominiums began crawling along the coast and eventually the Hyatt Regency Kauai was built right on the strand. Today, it's a sandy but rock-studded beach, quite beautiful but bordered by the resort. Swimming is good when the surf is low. This is also an outstanding bodysurfing and windsurfing area (the best spot is at the east end of the beach). Fishing is good from nearby Makawehi Point.

LAWAI BEACH PARK
✉️*Next to the Beach House Restaurant on Lawai Road*

A small white-sand beach, tucked in next to the Beach House Restaurant, is world-renowned for its surfing breaks: "P.K.s," "Centers" and "Acid Drops." Not only are surfers

---

happy, the beach also offers some of the best snorkeling in the Poipu area. The park offers plenty of parking, restrooms, a telephone and a shower.

MAHAULEPU BEACH

✉ *From the Poipu Beach area, follow Poipu Road east past the Hyatt Regency Kauai at Shipwreck Beach. Beyond Shipwreck, the pavement ends and the thoroughfare becomes a cane road. Continue on the main cane road (which is like a dirt road continuation of Poipu Road). Follow this road for about two miles (even when it curves toward the mountains and away from the ocean). Numerous minor cane roads will intersect from the right and left: ignore them. Finally, you will come to a crossroads with a major cane road (along which a line of telephone poles runs). Turn right and follow this road for about a mile (you'll pass a quarry off in the distance to the right), then watch on the right for roads leading to the beach. You will encounter a guard shack at the turnoff where you are required to sign a waiver to continue onto the property. The beach entrance is closed from 7 p.m. to 7:30 a.m.*

If you've come to Kauai seeking that South Seas dream, head out to these lovely strands. Mahaulepu is a tropical corridor of white sand winding for two miles along a reef-protected shoreline and including several strands and pocket beaches. In addition to being incredibly beautiful and ripe with potential for outdoor sports, Mahaulepu is important scientifically. Remains of extinct birds have been found at Mahaulepu Beach, and petroglyphs have been discovered along the shoreline.

Flocks of seabirds inhabit the area, and if that's not enough, the area boasts 100-foot-high sand dunes. There are well-protected sections of beach where you can swim, as well as rocky areas where you can fish. Snorkeling and surfing are also good here. The beach has no facilities.

WAIMEA AREA

The Western world's relationship with Hawaii, a tumultuous affair dating back more than two centuries, began in southwest Kauai when Captain James Cook set anchor at Waimea Bay. Cook landed on the leeward side of the island, a hot, dry expanse rimmed by white-sand beaches and dominated to the interior by Waimea Canyon, the "Grand Canyon of the Pacific."

The climate at the southwestern end of the island is conducive to sugar cane, which is partly why Gay & Robinson is the only plantation to still survive on Kauai. Its fields line the roads, along with Kauai Coffee groves.

The towns here have retained an old-Hawaii feel, even though vacation rentals are now creeping up along the handsome stretch of coastline. Beyond the towns, it's either west to the Pacific Missile Range Facility

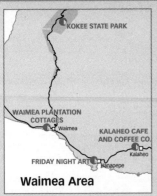

Waimea Area

KOKEE STATE PARK

PAGE 466

Heavily wooded trails high in the mountains above Waimea canyon—a mecca for hikers

WAIMEA PLANTATION COTTAGES

PAGE 458

Charmingly rustic and carefully restored 1920s plantation cottages fronting a salt-and-pepper beach

KALAHEO CAFE AND COFFEE CO.

PAGE 459

A cheery spot popular with locals for friendly service and can't-miss yummy homemade cinnamon rolls

FRIDAY NIGHT ART

PAGE 462

Art demonstrations, poetry readings and musical performances in the artist enclave of Hanapepe

and enough long, broad, thick, sandy beaches to satisfy the most dedicated beach bum, or north to the cool, often misty, forested elevations of Kokee.

Although the westside is a place of many topographic contrasts, when it comes to population and lifestyle, it's still local to da max. The old ways of hunting, fishing and farming prevail here, supported by the expanses of open space running from the mountains to the sea.

SIGHTS

The Coast

KALAHEO This is one of the first plantation towns you'll encounter driving west on Kaumualii Highway (Route 50). A detour up the hillside in Kalaheo, up **Puiilima Road**, will give you a broad overview of the area, as well as a taste of residential life on this part of the island.

KUKUIOLONO PARK

✉*Take a left on Papalina Road, which will lead a mile up to the park.* A lightly visited Japanese garden complete with stone bridge, ornamental pool and florid landscaping is found in this residential community. Take a stroll through this peaceful retreat and you'll

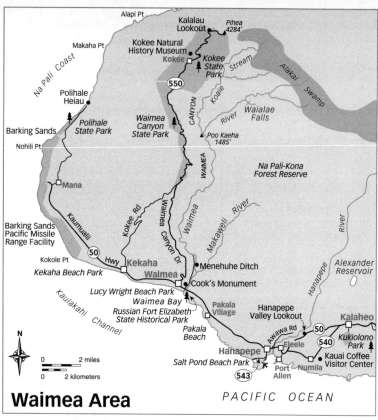

Waimea Area

PACIFIC OCEAN

also enjoy a stunning view that sweeps across a patchwork of fields to the sea.

ELEELE Route 50 continues along to another residential town. From here you can take Route 541 to the community of **Port Allen** and its small boat harbor and shopping center. If you're interested in fishing charters or tour boats, a few operate out of this area.

HANAPEPE VALLEY LOOKOUT Back on Route 50, en route from one tinroof town to the next, you'll pass this lookout, which offers a view of native plant life dramatically set in a gorge ringed by eroded cliffs. Taro patches grow in abundance in this wet and lush valley.

HANAPEPE ⓗidden

Be sure to take the nearby fork into this vintage village complete with wooden sidewalks and weather-beaten storefronts. During the 1924 sugar strike, 16 workers were killed here by police. Even today, the independent spirit of those martyrs pervades this

proud little town. It has become a haven for artists, and galleries
seem to outnumber residents.

AWAWA ROAD For a sense of Hanapepe during the plantation days,
drive out on this road. Precipitous red lava cliffs rim the roadside, while
rickety cottages and intricately tilled fields carpet the valley below.

SALT PONDS On the outskirts of Hanapepe, turn right on Route 543
toward the ocean. Here you'll see ancient salt ponds, which are still
used today. Continue to the end of the road to get to **Salt Pond Beach
Park**, a spot frequented by windsurfers and locals.

KAUAI COFFEE VISITOR CENTER ✉*Route 540, between Kalaheo and Hanapepe* ✆*808-335-0813* 🖷*808-335-3149* 🖎*www.kauaicoffee.com, greensales@ kauai
coffee.com* A short detour off Route 50 from either Kalaheo or Hanapepe
leads to this visitor center. Housed in a former plantation-worker's
home, the center has pictures from the area's sugar-plantation days, as
well as information about contemporary coffee production. A self-
guided walking tour is available. Best of all, they have a small café and
free tastings.

ROBINSON FAMILY ADVENTURES ✉*Near the 19-mile marker on Kaumualii Highway, Waimea* ✆*808-335-2824* 🖎*www.robinsonadventures.com, info@robinson
adventures.com* As Kaumualii Highway winds its way past small communities, you'll see that this is still sugar country. A side trip to one of
Hawaii's few remaining sugar plantations leads to the mill and to Robinson Family Adventures. The road is lined with monkeypod trees and
passes by former plantation-managers' homes, with their manicured
gardens. Even if you don't go on a tour, it's worth seeing this street. The
tour office features a mini-museum, and the tour itself takes in the cane
fields and factories of a classic Hawaiian plantation. (If you take the
tour, you'll need to wear closed-toe shoes and clothes you don't mind
being stained red by the soil.) Reservations required. Admission.

RUSSIAN FORT ELIZABETH STATE HISTORICAL PARK ✉*Just
past the 22-mile marker is a road that takes you to Russian Fort Elizabeth State Historical
Park.* Now just a rubble heap, historically it represents a fruitless attempt
by a maverick adventurer working for a Russian trading company to
gain a foothold in the islands in 1815. Designed in the shape of a six-
pointed star, the original fort bristled with guns and had walls 30 feet
thick. Two other forts were built on the island—one in Princeville and
another in Hanalei. Nothing is left of them.

COOK'S MONUMENT ✉*Just after you cross the Waimea River, on the road to
Lucy Wright Park* Captain James Cook's 1778 "discovery" of Hawaii is com-
memorated with a lava monolith near his landing place in Waimea.
Watch for roadside markers to the monument.

MENEHUNE DITCH

✉*North of Waimea on Menehune Road* Cook was not the only outsider
to assume a role in Waimea's history. It seems that those industrious leprechauns who built the fishpond outside Lihue were

also at work here constructing this ditch. Built with hand-hewn stones in a fashion unfamiliar to the Polynesians, this waterway has long puzzled archaeologists.

WAIMEA In the early 20th century, Waimea was a thriving sugar community. Drive around town and you'll see several structures that have withstood the test of time, like the restored **Waimea Theater** and the **Yamese** and **Masuda** buildings.

You'll pass the town of Kekaha, home of a now-defunct sugar mill and a colony of plantation houses, before arriving at the next stop on this scenic itinerary.

BARKING SANDS AIRFIELD Actually, it's not the airfield but the sands that belong on your itinerary. These lofty sand dunes, among the largest on the island, make a woofing sound when ground underfoot. This, according to scientists, is due to tiny cavities in each grain of sand that cause them to resonate when rubbed together (similar sands are found in Egypt's Sinai Desert, the Gobi Desert of Mongolia and in Saudi Arabia). If you have trouble making the sound, remember what one local wag told me: The hills actually got their name from tourists becoming "dog-tired" after futilely trying to elicit a growl from the mute sand. (Since the beach here at Major's Bay is on a military reservation, call to make sure the facility is open to the public.)

An unmanned, solar-powered aircraft named *Helio* has been built by NASA and AeroVironment and launched from Barking Sands, Kauai. A long, thin flying wing that researchers hope will reach 100,000 feet in altitude, more than three times higher than commercial jets fly, it is to be used as a surrogate satellite or low-cost telecommunications platform. On its first test flight from Barking Sands it soared to 76,000 feet.

PACIFIC MISSILE RANGE FACILITY ☎ 808-335-4229 Near Barking Sands is this important launch area for military and meteorological rockets and the site of periodic war games.

POLIHALE STATE PARK Having made a fool of yourself trying to get sand to bark, continue on past Mana, a deserted town (along a graded dirt road for the last five miles) to the United States' westernmost state park. This very hot, very dry, very beautiful retreat represents the last stretch of a 15-mile-long sand beach, one of the longest in the state, that begins way back in Kekaha. The sand marathon ends at the foot of the Na Pali cliffs, in an area sacred to the Hawaiians. Here the ancients built **Polihale Heiau**, a temple whose ruins remain. This sacred place is where the spirits of the dead made their leap into the spiritual world. And here the road ends, further passage made impossible by the sea cliffs that wrap around Kauai's northwest corner.

The Mountains

WAIMEA CANYON ✉ Take Route 550 or Kokee Road to Route 550. ☎ 808-274-3433 Another candidate in the contest for ultimate adventure—one that is free, doesn't require a helicopter and always lies open to exploration—is Waimea Canyon. Touring the "Grand Canyon of the Pacific" involves a side trip from either the town of Waimea or Kekaha. Waimea Canyon Drive leads from the former and Kokee Road climbs from the latter; they join about halfway up the mountain. For an overview of the entire region, go up along Waimea Canyon Drive, since it hugs the canyon rim and provides the best views, then follow Kokee Road down.

WAIMEA RIVER As the paved road snakes along the side of this 2857-foot-deep canyon, a staggering panorama opens. The red and orange hues of a barren Southwestern landscape are splashed with tropic greens and yellows. Far below, the Waimea River, which carved this ten-mile-long chasm, cuts a sinuous course. Several vista points provide crow's-nest views of the territory, including **Puuhinahina Overlook** at 3500-feet elevation, which offers views of the canyon to the east and Niihau to the west.

KOKEE STATE PARK From Kokee Road, continue deep into Kauai's cool interior before arriving at this state park, a preserve of *koa* trees, with their crescent-shape leaves, and *ohia* trees, with their gray bark and red pompon flowers. You're apt to see a variety of birds here, including the red *apapane*, the yellow-green *amakihi*, the white-tailed tropic bird and maybe the state bird, the *nene*. Wild boar roam the area and trout fishing is a favorite sport in the park. Hiking trails meander through the park. (See "Hiking" at the end of the chapter for more information.) Within this 4345-acre park you'll find a restaurant and cabins.

KOKEE NATURAL HISTORY MUSEUM ✉*Kokee Road, past the State Park headquarters* ☎*808-335-9975* ☏*808-335-6131* ✐*www.kokee.org, information@kokee.org* At this natural history museum is a small display space devoted to the flora, fauna and natural history of the area, as well as an exhibit about Hurricane Iniki. Collections of shells and Hawaiian artifacts are also featured.

KALALAU LOOKOUT It's a short drive onward and upward from Kokee Natural History Museum to this lookout, where Kauai's other face is reflected in knife-edged cliffs and overgrown gorges that drop to the sea 4000 feet below. Another nearby overlook gazes out across the **Alakai Swamp** to **Mount Waialeale**. (Because of cloud cover in the valley, it's best to arrive at the overlook before 10 a.m. or after 4 p.m.) One more spectacular scene along the way, one more reason to bring you back to this magnificent island.

LODGING

Accommodations on Kauai's southwest side include beachside cottages in Waimea and ethereal facilities in Kokee State Park.

The Coast
KALAHEO PLANTATION
$–$$ 6 ROOMS ✉*4579 Puuwai Road, Kalaheo* ☎*808-332-7812* ☏*808-332-7812* ✐*www.kalaheo-plantation.com, celj@hawaiiantel.net*
Nightly, weekly or monthly, this 1926 plantation-style home is a good bargain. Located a couple of miles from the beach, it once belonged to a

district judge. The management polished up the floors, added some new windows and, they won't hesitate to tell you, 500 plants, and opened for business. These are modern suites with either a kitchenette or full kitchen; some have private lanais. You can rent the whole house but you can't wear your shoes inside.

WAIMEA PLANTATION COTTAGES

$$$$ 56 COTTAGES ✉9400 Kaumualii Highway, Waimea ☎808-338-1625
🖷808-338-2338 🖉www.waimeaplantation.com,
info@waimeaplantation.com

Waimea Plantation Cottages is one of the most alluring and secluded facilities on the entire island. Here in a spectacular coconut grove, fronting a salt-and-pepper beach, is a cluster of charmingly rustic 1920s-era plantation cottages. Each has been carefully restored and many are furnished with rattan furniture. These one-, two- and multibedroom houses have full kitchens. Maid service is every third day. Like the rest of the complex, the swimming pool follows the style of an earlier era (most visitors swim here since the offshore waters are usually murky). A new low-key day spa adds to the relaxed atmosphere. The place is a little gem out on Kauai's remote westside.

CLASSIC VACATION COTTAGES

$–$$ 7 ROOMS ✉P.O. Box 901, Kalaheo, HI 96741 ☎808-332-9201
🖷808-332-7645 🖉www.classiccottages.com, clascot@hawaiian.net

Those seeking a neighborhood setting may prefer these seven stand-alone vacation rentals of varying sizes at the end of a residential cul-de-sac in the quiet, hilly town of Kalaheo. They range from a modest studio to an attractive full-sized home that sleeps eight. The larger units have full kitchens, too, making them a bargain for two couples or a family. Of course, the beach isn't nearby, although Kukuiolono hilltop park and golf course aren't far. The communal hot tub is another plus.

KALAHEO INN

$$ 15 ROOMS ✉4444 Papalina Road, Kalaheo ☎808-332-6032, 888-332-6023
🖉www.kalaheoinn.com, ki@hawaiiantel.biz

Tucked away in downtown Kalaheo, or what passes as such, is this modest little inn, which rents a mix of studios and one- to three-bedroom suites. Some have full cooking facilities. This inn is well used, but it's clean and a good locale if you want to explore Kokee.

COCO'S

$$ 1 ROOM ✉P.O. Box 690169, Makaweli ☎808-338-0722, 808-639-1109
🖉www.cocoskauai.com, ian@hawaiian.net

While the accommodations here are clean, spacious and comfortable, with a kitchenette and all the standard amenities, its greatest appeal is its locale: a 12-acre private estate owned by the Robison Family, and within walking distance of the popular Westside surfing beach, Pakala's. A continental breakfast is included.

The Mountains

THE LODGE AT KOKEE

$ 12 UNITS   ✉*Kokee State Park*   ☎*808-335-6061*
🖱*www.thelodgeatkokee.net, info@thelodgeatkokee.net*

Nestled in secluded woods between Waimea Canyon and the Kalalau Lookout are these rustic cabins. Each of the mountain units, varying in size from one large room to two-bedroom complexes, comes with a wood-burning stove, a basic kitchen and rustic furnishings. These wood cabins, 3600 feet above sea level, are a mountaineer's dream. With forest and hiking trails all around, Kokee is ideal for the adventurer. It gets chilly, so bring a jacket or sweater. Reservations are essential.

DINING

Traveling west toward Waimea Canyon and Barking Sands, you'll find the watering places decrease as rapidly as the rainfall. Most restaurants en route are cafés and takeout stands. If you're on a budget, you're in luck; if you're looking for an exclusive, elegant establishment, you'll find slim pickings out Waimea way.

The Coast
BRICK OVEN PIZZA

$–$$ ITALIAN   ✉*2-2555 Kaumualii Highway, Kalaheo*   ☎*808-332-8561*
🖱*808-332-3800*

Family-owned and -operated Brick Oven is commonly touted as having the best pies on the island. But don't expect the Americanized version of the dish. The chefs here specialize in authentic Italian: thin crust brushed with garlic butter and minimal sauce. Red-and-white-checked tablecloths and an amiable staff complete the image. The place is often jammed, so plan ahead if you have hungry kids in tow. Closed Monday and for one week in September.

KALAHEO STEAK HOUSE

$$–$$$ STEAK   ✉*4444 Papalina Road, Kalaheo*   ☎*808-332-9780*

At this steak house you'll step into a comfortable wood-paneled dining room. Pull up a chair, rest your elbows on the table (it's permitted) and choose among sirloin, filet mignon, scampi, Cornish hens and several other appealing entrées. No reservations accepted. Dinner only.

KALAHEO CAFE AND COFFEE CO.

$$ COFFEEHOUSE/DELI   ✉*2-2560 Kaumualii Highway, Kalaheo*   ☎*808-332-5858*   🖱*808-332-5868*   🖱*www.kalaheo.com*

Always bustling, locals arrive here in droves for the omelettes, hearty deli sandwiches and burgers, yummy homemade cinnamon rolls and coffee drinks. With small wooden tables and a tiny retail area, it's a cheery, clean place, with friendly service. Breakfast and lunch daily, no dinner Sunday through Tuesday.

CAMP HOUSE GRILL

$–$$ HAWAIIAN   ✉2-2431 Kaumualii Highway, Kalaheo   ☎808-332-9755
🖥808-332-7052

This is a trim little café with an island-style menu. Favored by nearby residents, they serve *huli huli* chicken and pork ribs, and big, satisfying breakfasts. The homemade pies are a big draw.

TOI'S THAI KITCHEN

$$ THAI   ✉Eleele Shopping Center, 178 Hanapepe Bay, Eleele
☎808-335-3111

A family-run eatery, Toi's serves a lunch and dinner menu consisting primarily of Thai food such as yellow curry chicken and stir-fried eggplant with tofu. Fried chicken and mahimahi are also served. The decor is simple and the food is good. Closed Sunday and Monday.

DA IMU HUT CAFÉ

$ HAWAIIAN   ✉3771 Hanapepe Road, Hanapepe   ☎808-335-0200

Stop here for Hawaiian dishes, *saimin*, fried chicken, teriyaki chicken, fried noodles and hamburgers at 1950s prices. It's not much on looks, but it fills the belly. It's open at unusual hours, so be sure to call ahead.

HANAPEPE CAFE AND ESPRESSO

$$$ ITALIAN/VEGETARIAN   ✉3830 Hanapepe Road, Hanapepe   ☎808-335-5011

Gourmet vegetarian with an Italian flair is the way they describe the food at Hanapepe's. Every Friday night you'll find them preparing such dinner entrées as eggplant lasagna, pasta primavera with portobello mushrooms or marinara dishes made with locally grown produce. They're also open for a more casual lunch Monday through Friday. That's when you can stop by for a caesar salad, a "healthnut sandwich," pasta specials, garden burgers or baked frittata. Dinner reservations recommended. Closed Saturday and Sunday.

WAIMEA BAKERY & DELI

$ BAKERY/DELI   ✉9875 Waimea Road, Waimea   ☎808-338-1950

Breakfast burritos, melts and deli sandwiches, fish plates and other specials are found at this roadside eatery that also prepares an especially good taro-teriyaki burger. Their smoothies, milk shakes, tropical fruit turnovers, Hawaiian sweetbread and other baked goodies add to the appeal. Closed Tuesday.

WAIMEA BREWING COMPANY

$$–$$$ AMERICAN   ✉*9400 Kaumualii Highway, Waimea* ✆*808-338-1625*
✆*808-338-2338* 🖱*www.waimea-plantation.com*

Located at Waimea Plantation Cottages, this is one of those places you go to for the novelty value as much as the refreshment. Served alongside the beer are sandwiches and burgers, pasta dishes, grilled meats, chicken and fresh fish. There's relaxed, plantation-style decor inside, with a delightful, broad lanai for outdoor dining.

PACIFIC PIZZA AND DELI

$–$$ PIZZA/DELI   ✉*Wrangler Restaurant Building, 9852 Kaumualii Road, Waimea*
✆*808-338-1020*

At this spot you can certainly order a typical cheese pie, but they also offer more exotic versions such as Thai or Mexican pizza. Deli sandwiches, wraps and coffee drinks are available, too. Closed Sunday.

WRANGLERS STEAKHOUSE

$$–$$$ STEAK   ✉*9852 Kaumualii Highway, Waimea* ✆*808-338-1218*
✆*808-338-1266*

Steaks, naturally, are the order of the day at Wranglers. Here guests can choose to take their meals outside or indoors in a rustic dining room. Hardwood floors and galvanized awnings contribute to the Western feel, as do the old wagon and wooden horse. The menu features classic surf and turf dishes. You might want to take a peek at the *paniolo* artifacts in their small museum. No lunch on Saturday. Closed Sunday.

The Mountains
THE LODGE AT KOKEE

$ DELI/LOCAL-STYLE   ✉*Kokee State Park* ✆*808-335-6061* ✆*808-335-5431*

When you're up in the heights above Waimea Canyon you'll be mighty glad to discover this restaurant in remote Kokee State Park. From the dining room of this homey hideaway, you can gaze out at the surrounding forest. The emphasis here is on fresh, healthy dishes and local specialties like *lilikoi* pie. For breakfast try the cornbread, and for lunch choose from soups, sandwiches and salads.

SHOPPING

RED DIRT HAWAII ✉*4350 Waialo Road, Eleele* ✆*800-717-3478* ✆*808-335-3478*
🖱*www.dirtshirt.com, onlinesales@dirtshirt.com* Head up to Eleele off of Route 50 near Kalaheo and you'll discover the home of the "original Red Dirt shirt." Made with stains from the iron-rich soil of Kauai, these T-shirts are a cottage industry with workers all over the island coloring them. If your shirt starts fading, don't worry—just roll it in the dirt or wash it with mud and it will look like new again!

Hanapepe, a turn-of-the-20th-century town with a falsefront main street, has developed into an arts center.

8 BELLS GALLERY

✉️*4510 Hana Road, Hanapepe* 📞*808-335-0550* This gallery displays a range of mediums by local artists. They feature oil, sculpture, watercolor and limited-edition prints, and are known for their excellent framing with Hawaiian wood. Closed Sunday.

ARIUS HOPMAN GALLERY ✉️*3840-C Hanapepe Road, Hanapepe* 📞*808-335-0227* Well-known local watercolorist Arius Hopman is spotlighted at this eponymous gallery.

DAWN M. TRAINA GALLERY ✉️*3840-B Hanapepe Road, Hanapepe* 📞*808-335-3993* The paintings, drawings and prints of native Hawaiian people featured here are created by the store's namesake. Closed Sunday and occasionally closed Saturday and Monday (call ahead).

KAUAI FINE ARTS ✉️*3905 Hanapepe Road, Hanapepe* 📞*808-335-3778* 🖱️*www.brunias.com* Hanapepe is also the home of this singular gallery housing an outstanding collection of antique maps and prints. Open weekends by appointment only.

GIORGIO'S GALLERY ✉️*3871 Hanapepe Road, Hanapepe* 📞*808-335-3949* Consider a tropical oil painting or one of the sculptures at Giorgio's. Closed Sunday.

COLLECTIBLES & FINE JUNQUE ✉️*9821 Kaumualii Highway, Waimea* 📞*808-338-9855* This shop has an amazing collection of glassware, aloha shirts, dolls and old bottles. It's a good place to pick up antiques or knickknacks. Closed Friday through Sunday.

NIGHTLIFE

FRIDAY ART NIGHT

Every week Hanapepe hosts "Friday Art Night," showcasing local artists in the numerous galleries in town. From 6 to 9 p.m. most galleries in this artist enclave keep their doors open, offering refreshments, a chance to talk story with the artists, and frequent musical performances. Art demonstrations, poetry readings and other performances can be found along the street.

HANAPEPE CAFE AND ESPRESSO

✉️*3830 Hanapepe Road, Hanapepe* 📞*808-335-5011* This place is a bit of an anomaly, with gourmet vegetarian food that would seem more at home in California than in this tiny town. On Friday night (the only evening they are open) the place is packed, with local entertainers performing Hawaiian slack-key guitar. There's no bar, but you can sit and have an espresso and dessert.

The Coast
SALT POND BEACH PARK

✉ *Take Kaumualii Highway to Hanapepe. Turn onto Route 543 and follow it to the end.*

A pretty, crescent-shaped beach with a protecting reef and numerous coconut trees, this park is very popular with locals and may be crowded and noisy on weekends. It's a good place to collect shells, though. The road leading to the park passes salt ponds that date back hundreds of years and are still used today to evaporate sea water and produce salt. Swimming is good in this well-protected area. Snorkeling is fair and there is diving near rocks and along the offshore reef. For surfing, there's a shore break by the mouth of the Hanapepe River nearby in Port Allen. Sandy and shallow with small waves, this area is safe for beginners. There are left and right slides. Along the outer harbor edge near Port Allen Airport runway there are summer breaks, for experienced surfers only, which involve climbing down a rocky shoreline. At Salt Pond there are occasional summer breaks (left and right slides) requiring a long paddle out. This is also a very popular windsurfing area. Rockfish and mullet are the most common catches here. Facilities include a picnic area, restrooms, showers and lifeguards.

▲ There's a grassy area near the beach for tent camping; a county permit is required.

PAKALA BEACH

hidden

✉ *Located along Kaumualii Highway near the 21-mile marker (two miles east of Waimea) you'll see a concrete bridge crossing Aakukui stream with the name "Aakukui" chiseled in the cement. Go through the gate just below the bridge and follow the well-worn path a few hundred yards to the beach.*

This long narrow ribbon of sand is bounded by trees and set in perfectly lush surroundings. Surfers will probably be the only other people around. They may come out of the water long enough to watch the spectacular sunsets with you and to tell you of the fabled summer waves that reach heights of 10 to 12 feet. If this book were rating beaches by the star system, Pakala Beach would deserve a constellation. When the surf is low it's a good place to swim. You can also snorkel along the reef. This is one of Hawaii's top summer surfing spots. The incredibly long walls that form along a wide shallow reef allow you to hang ten seemingly forever. Hence the nickname for these breaks—"Infinity." The one drawback: It's a long paddle out. Fishing is good from the rock outcropping off to the left. There are no facilities here.

LUCY WRIGHT BEACH PARK

✉ *In Waimea*

This five-acre park at the Waimea River mouth is popular with locals and therefore sometimes a little crowded. Despite a sandy beach, the park is not as appealing as others nearby: The water is often murky from cane field spillage. If you're in need of a campground you

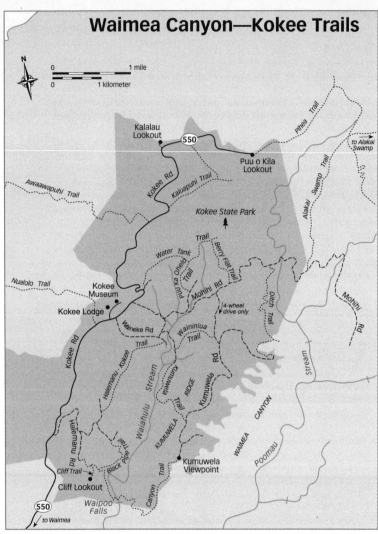

Waimea Canyon—Kokee Trails

might stop here, otherwise, I don't recommend the park. Swimming is fair, unless the water is muddy. Surfing varies from small breaks for beginners to extremely long walls that build four different breaks and is best near the river mouth. There's a left slide. In Waimea Bay, there are parrotfish, red goatfish, squirrelfish, *papio*, bonefish, bigeyed scad and threadfin. You can also fish from the pier a few hundred feet west of the park. Facilities include a picnic area, restrooms and showers.

▲ Tent camping only. County permit required.

KEKAHA BEACH

✉*Kaumualii Highway*

🏄 🤿 This narrow beach parallels Kaumualii Highway for several miles along the eastern edge of Kekaha. Although close to the highway, the lovely white strand offers some marvelous picnic spots, but the rough surf and powerful currents make swimming dangerous. There are many surfing spots along here; the foremost, called "Davidson's," lies off Oomano Point.

KEKAHA BEACH PARK

✉ *On Kaumualii Highway in Kekaha*

Set on a beautiful ribbon of sand, this 20-acre park is a great place to kick back, picnic and catch the sun setting over the island of Niihau. Swimming is good when surf is down; otherwise it can be dangerous. For surfers, immediately west of the park are several breaks, including "Inters" (near Kaumualii Highway and Akialoa Street) and "First Ditch" and "Second Ditch," located in front of two drainage ditches. Anglers try for threadfin. There are picnic facilities and restrooms.

KOKOLE POINT

✉ *Take the road that leads off Kaumualii Highway one mile west of Kekaha (there's a sign directing traffic to the dump). Follow any of the dirt roads in as far as possible. These will lead either to the dump or to a nearby landing strip. Walk the last three-tenths of a mile to the beach.*

Out by an old landing strip/drag strip, a local dump and a rifle range, there is a wide sandy beach that stretches forever and offers unofficial camping and outrageous sunsets. Fishermen, joggers and beachcombers love the place, but those who hold it nearest their hearts are surfers. The breaks here go by such names as "Rifle Range," "Targets" and "Whispering Sands." Currents and high surf usually make swimming unadvisable. However, fishing is good. There are no facilities.

BARKING SANDS

✉ *Take Kaumualii Highway several miles past Kekaha, then watch for signs to the Pacific Missile Range Facility.* ☎ *808-335-4229*

The military installation at Major's Bay is bounded by very wide beaches that extend for miles. You'll see the Barking Sands dunes and magnificent sunsets and get some of the best views of Niihau anywhere on Kauai. The weather is hot and dry here: a great place to get thoroughly baked, but beware of sunburns. The Pacific Missile Range Facility is located here, and the area is sometimes used for war games, so these beaches are sometimes closed. Swimming is good, but exercise caution. The coral reefs make for good snorkeling. **Major's Bay** is an excellent surfing spot with both summer and winter breaks. Other breaks include "Rockets" near the rocket launch pad, "Kinkini" at the south end of the airfield runway, and "Family Housing" just offshore from the base housing facility. Windsurfers also frequent Major's Bay and "Kinkini." A particularly good fishing spot is around Nohili Point; the most common catches are bonefish, threadfin and *ulua*. There are no facilities. Due to heightened security measures, obtaining access to the beach can be complicated. Upon arrival in Hawaii, those wishing to visit must contact the local naval center, where they will be asked to complete a clearance form. The completed form must be taken to the Lihui Police Department for a criminal background check. A photo I.D. pass will be issued, though the entire process takes a week. Call ahead for public hours.

POLIHALE STATE PARK

✉ *Take Kaumualii Highway until it ends, then follow the signs along dirt roads for about five miles.*

🏊 🏄 🚿 This 300-foot-wide beach blankets the coast for over two miles along Kauai's west end. The United States' westernmost state park, Polihale is worth visiting—just to see the endless white-sand expanse. It borders the sea cliffs of the Na Pali Coast, covering 138 acres. The hot, dry weather is excellent for sunbathing and prime for burning, so load up on sunscreen. You might even want to bring an umbrella or other form of shade. The afternoons bring great sunsets. This park has magnificent mountain surroundings: Niihau looms in the distance. Swimming is for experts only. The safest swimming is at **Queen's Pond**, an area that, depending on the year's weather conditions, floods and creates a protected lagoon along the beachfront near the middle of the park. Surfing is okay; there's a shore break with left and right slides. There's good windsurfing off Queen's Pond. This beach is also especially great for shell collecting. Bonefish, threadfin and *ulua* are the most common game fish. Facilities include a picnic area, restrooms and showers.

▲ You can pitch a tent on the beach under a star-crowded sky, or find a shady tree (though they are rare in these parts) for protection against the blazing sun. This is a wonderful place to camp for a day or two. After that, the barren landscape becomes tiresome and monotonous. Tent camping allowed. A state permit is required.

The Mountains

KOKEE STATE PARK

✉ *Take Kaumualii Highway to Waimea, then pick up Waimea Canyon Drive from Waimea or Kokee Road from Kekaha. They eventually join and lead about 15 miles up to the park.* ☎ *808-335-9975* 📠 *808-335-6131*
💻 *www.kokee.org, kokeemuseum@earthlink.net*

🚶 🚿 This spectacular park, high in the mountains above Waimea Canyon, is a mecca for hikers, campers and other outdoor enthusiasts. Sprawling across 4345 heavily wooded acres, this rugged country offers a unique perspective on the Garden Isle. In the rivers there's excellent freshwater angling for rainbow trout during August and September; a state license is required, though. Kokee has everything but a grocery store, so come well-stocked or plan to eat at the lodge restaurant (breakfast and lunch only; 808-335-6061). There is seasonal plum picking, and pig, goat and deer hunting is allowed in the public hunting and fishing areas. The lodge (808-335-6061) also has a museum and gift shop. Nearby are cabins, restrooms, showers, a picnic area and hiking trails.

▲ An area at the north end of the park has been allocated for tent camping. There are also several wilderness camps along the hiking trails. A state permit is required for nonwilderness camping.

WAILUA–KAPAA AREA

If Lihue is the commercial center of Kauai, Wailua is the cultural heart of the island. Here along the Wailua River, the only navigable river in Hawaii, the *alii* built *heiau* and perpetuated their princely lines. There are broad surfing beaches here as well as cascades and grottos up along the Wailua River. What attracted Hawaiian royalty to Kauai's east coast was the weather along this windward shore, cooler in the summer than the baking sands of Poipu but not as moist as the tropical rainforests to the north. The Hawaiian nobility added fishponds and coconut groves to these natural features and forbade commoners from entering their domain. The oral tradition they handed down tells of a Tahitian holy man named Puna, one of the first Polynesians to arrive in Hawaii, who chose this sacred spot to live. Other legends recount the lost tribe of Mu, a pre-Polynesian people, dwarfish and cruel, who inhabited caves far up the Wailua River.

Although developed as a resort area before Princeville and Poipu, this region was long a low-key destination. But a new resort in Waipouli, and plans for three more, are causing concerns about overdevelopment, especially since roads have not been upgraded to handle the increased traffic. To ease the congestion through Kapaa, the Kapaa Bypass Road was built. Pick it up just before the Coconut Plantation in Wailua. It takes you to the north side of Kapaa, cutting through fields behind town.

SIGHTS

LYDGATE PARK

⊠*Kuhio Highway, Wailua* At the confluence of the Wailua River and the ocean is this center of sacred Kauai. The *alii* established the rocky remains of the **Hauola Place of Refuge** on this site. Here *kapu* breakers under sentence of death could flee; once inside its perimeter, their crimes were absolved. A stone retaining wall also marks the ancient **Hikina a ka la Heiau**. The **petroglyphs** etched in the rocks at the mouth of the river can be seen at low tide. Near the entrance to the marina you'll find the **Malae Heiau**. It is easy to see why this area was sacred to ancient Hawaiians—the serenity is palpable, the beauty extraordinary.

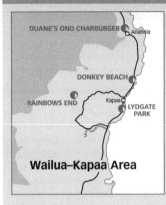

Wailua–Kapaa Area

DUANE'S ONO CHAR-BURGER

PAGE 476

Awesome burgers with an array of toppings, including pineapple—the teriyaki burger is an island favorite

DONKEY BEACH

PAGE 480

Broad, curving gem favored by locals as a hideaway and nude beach

RAINBOWS END

PAGE 472

A classic restored plantation cottage with cozy country decor, mahogany inlaid floors and fresh fruit from the orchard

LYDGATE PARK

PAGE 467

Ancient oceanfront center of sacred Kauai, where the serenity is palpable, the beauty extraordinary

FERN GROTTO ☏ 808-821-6895 🖷 808-822-4520 ✐ www.smithskauai.com, smiths@aloha.net The marina adjacent to Lydgate Park is the departure point for boat trips up the Wailua River to this grotto. The scenery along the way is magnificent as you pass along a tropical riverfront that is luxuriously overgrown. The grotto itself is a 40-foot cavern draped with feathery ferns, a place so beautiful and romantic that many people choose to marry here. Traditional Hawaiian musicians take advantage of the grotto's natural acoustics. Unfortunately, the boat ride is one of the most cloyingly commercial experiences in Hawaii, a 20-minute voyage during which you are crowded together with legions of tourists and led in chants by a narrator with an amplifier. Admission.

For those not interested in joining in on this tourist institution, you can rent a kayak and paddle yourself upriver to the grotto (legally, however, you cannot dock at the grotto).

COCO PALMS Movie buffs should take note when passing along Route 56. The large abandoned complex surrounded by a beautiful stand of palm trees is the Coco Palms. This resort, the first constructed on Kauai, was built around a coconut grove planted in the 1800s by a German immigrant; the area around the resort was home to Kauai's Queen Kapule in the mid-1800s. The final 20 minutes of *Blue Hawaii*, Elvis' last movie, were filmed here. Some scenes from *South Pacific* and *Miss Sadie Thompson* were also filmed here, and for "Fantasy Island" viewers, this is where Tatoo goes zipping by in his jeep. In fact, Hollywood was drawn to this location numerous times. However, it has stood empty since September 1992, when Hurricane Iniki ravaged the resort. Renovation plans are in the works, but continue to be delayed due to disagreements between developers and the court.

HOLO-HOLO-KU HEIAU

⊠*Kuamoo Road (Route 580)* Take a detour onto Route 580, which courses through Kauai's most historic region, the domain of ancient Hawaiian royalty. Watch for Hawaii Visitors Bureau signs pointing out the Holo-Holo-Ku Heiau, one of the oldest temples on the island, a place where human sacrifices were performed. A short distance uphill, you'll find a small but interesting **Japanese cemetery**. Ironically, this is also the site of **Pohaku-Ho-o-Hanau**, a sacred spot where royal women came to give birth.

POLIAHU HEIAU

Up Route 580, the lush Wailua Valley opens to view. On the left along the hilltop rest the rocky remains of this temple, purportedly used by Kauai's King Kaumualii. A short path leads down to the **Bell Stone**, which resounded when struck with a rock, loudly signaling the birth of royal infants. All these places, vital to Hawaii's past, were located along the old King's Highway, a sacred thoroughfare used only by island rulers.

OPAEKAA FALLS For vivid mountain scenery, continue on Route 580 past these 40-foot cascades (a parking area along the highway brings you to a great viewpoint). The road then proceeds past **Wailua Homesteads**, what used to be a ranch and farm region filled with fruit orchards, pastures and vegetable fields but is now rapidly becoming residential.

KAMOKILA HAWAIIAN VILLAGE ⊠*6060 Kuamoo Road, off Route 580, just past the Wailua Bridge across from Opaekaa Falls* ☎*808-823-0559* This re-created Hawaiian village is so isolated, it appears to have been carved out of the surrounding tropical labyrinth. It evokes authentic early Hawaii with food- and craft-making demonstrations. Self-guided tours will take you through the paces of ancient Hawaiian life, including an assembly hall, birthing house, chief's quarters, cooking pit and athletic ground. It's also the site of a decidedly contemporary obsession: movie making. *Outbreak*, starring Dustin Hoffman and Morgan Freeman, for example, was filmed here. Closed Sunday. Admission.

SAIVA SIDDHANTA CHURCH

⊠*About four miles up Kuamoo Road (Route 580) at 107 Kaholalele Road* ☎*808-822-3012 ext. 411 (tour information)* ✐*www.gurudeva.org, iraivan@hindu.org*
A detour off of Route 580 takes you to this Hindu monastery, a unique cultural experience in Kauai. The Kadavul Hindu Temple

is open mornings between 9 a.m. and noon, and tours are offered weekly. Currently, the Iraivan Temple—the first all-stone, hand-carved, granite Agamic temple ever built in the West—is under construction there.

KEAHUA FORESTRY ARBORETUM Route 580 ends at this arboretum, where hiking trails wind through groves of painted gum trees. The adjoining state forest climbs all the way to one of Kauai's tallest peaks **Mount Waialeale** (5208 feet), although no trails lead there. The mountain has an annual rainfall of more than 400 inches.

KAPAA Back on Route 56, as the road dips down into Kapaa, you'll be passing from one Hawaiian era to another. The largest of Kauai's towns—population wise—Kapaa has a real local feel to it. At one time it was a center for rice cultivation. Later came sugar and pineapple. Now this 19th-century town, with its falsefront stores and second-story balconies, is home to everyday folks. This is where the local plumber, carpenter and fisherman live. The population is Japanese, Hawaiian, Caucasian, Filipino and Chinese. They reside in small plantation houses and attend the local churches that dot the surrounding countryside.

HAWAII MOVIE TOURS ✉*Kapaa* ✆*808-822-1192, 800-628-8432* 📠*808-822-1608* ⌨*www.hawaiimovietour.com, tourguy@hawaiian.net* You may notice that parts of Kauai are familiar to you. Are you on the set of *Gilligan's Island*? Isn't that Bali Hai from *South Pacific*? Kauai's beauty and tropical ambience have provided numerous backdrops for blockbuster movies and television shows. The Wailua Rainforest still sports the support for the *Jurassic Park* gates, and the Coco Palms Resort, abandoned after Hurricane Iniki in 1992, awaits Elvis' return to *Blue Hawaii*. This tour company takes you to some of these sites while you watch the featured scenes in your "theater on wheels." (If you want to take home the scenes, purchase *The Kauai Movie Book* by Chris Cook.)

COCONUT MARKETPLACE In its northerly course between Wailua and Kapaa, Kuhio Highway (Route 56) passes this marketplace with its sprawling shopping mall and grove of royal palm trees.

SLEEPING GIANT From Kapaa, there's an excellent view of this recumbent figure naturally hewn out of the nearby mountain range.

KEALIA BEACH Follow Route 56 and you'll arrive at this curving ribbon of sand. Across the road are a store and post office. The clapboard buildings represent in its entirety the tiny town of **Kealia**. From Kealia, the Kuhio Highway climbs and turns slightly inland through former sugar cane fields and continues through the town of **Anahola**, a small Hawaiian homestead settlement.

LODGING

ROSEWOOD
$–$$$$ 26 UNITS   ✉*872 Kamalu Road, Wailua* ✆*808-822-5216* 📠*808-822-5478*
⌨*www.rosewoodkauai.com, rosewood@aloha.net*
Exuding cheerfulness, charm and high standards, this Wailua Homesteads bed and breakfast is a reliable choice. Units include a three bed-

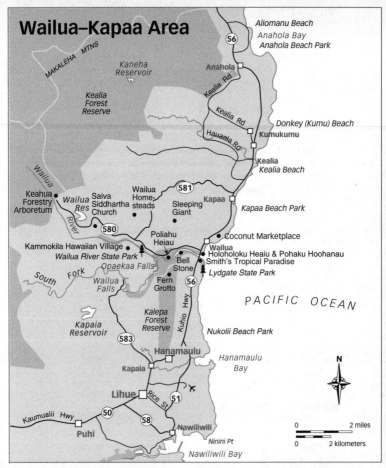

Wailua–Kapaa Area

room home, a Victorian cottage, rooms in the main house and a se-cluded thatched cottage. A bunkhouse, which has private sleeping lofts and shared toilets and showers, is a super budget option. Hardwood floors, color-washed walls, quality linens, nice landscaping with old shade trees and a lily pond, along with delightful outdoor showers, are just a few of the highlights. All room options come with kitchens or kitchenettes. There's also a common room with internet access. A breakfast basket comes with the more expensive units, or daily break-fast is served in the main house for an extra charge. Rosewood is set in a rural area, with mountain views and sheep grazing across the road, but there is some traffic noise. Not totally secluded, it's located three miles from the east side beaches and restaurants.

KAUAI SANDS HOTEL

$$ 200 ROOMS ✉ 420 Papaloa Road near the Coconut Marketplace, Wailua
📞 808-822-4951, 800-560-5553 📠 808-822-0978 🖱 www.kauaisandshotel.com

This hotel is a bargain. You'll find a relaxed and spacious lobby, a restaurant, two pools, a well-tended lawn, carpeting, a lanai, imaginative decor and a touch of Hawaiiana. Ask about discounts.

RAINBOWS END

$$$ 1 ROOM   ✉6470 Kipapa Road, Kapaa   ☎808-823-0066
📠808-823-0071 🖱www.rainbowsendkauai.com,
info@rainbowsendkauai.com

A classic restored plantation cottage, this spot has romance written all over it. Set in a secluded rural area near the hosts' home, it has special features like floors with inlaid mahogany, cozy country-decor furnishings, extra thick towels, a clawfoot whirlpool tub and an enclosed outdoor shower. It's a one-bedroom place with a kitchenette, as well as a futon in the living room for extra guests. Amenities include cable TV, VCR, videos, books, beach equipment and good information about nearby trails and activities. Breakfasts include fruit grown on-site. Gay-friendly.

HOTEL CORAL REEF

$$–$$$ 21 ROOMS   ✉1516 Kuhio Highway, Kapaa   ☎808-822-4481, 800-843-4659
📠808-822-7705 🖱www.hotelcoralreefresort.com, hotelcoralreef@hawaiilink.net

To get any closer to the water than this, you'd have to pitch a tent in the sand. Located on Kuhio Highway in Kapaa, it's within strolling distance of markets and restaurants and is a good choice for the wanderer without wheels. A floral garden leads out to a comfortable strip of sand next to Kapaa Beach Park. In this beachfront building you can enjoy a touch of wood paneling, soft beds, refrigerator and a delightful seascape just beyond those sliding glass doors. A second building offers rooms with jacuzzi tubs and ocean views.

KAUAI INTERNATIONAL HOSTEL

$ 30 BEDS   ✉4532 Lehua Street, Kapaa   ☎808-823-6142

Both dormitory and private rooms at low prices are available here. Facilities, as you might expect, are simple, but they are clean. There's a garden with a waterfall; guests share a television room, a kitchen, a washer-dryer and a pool table. Like hostels everywhere, it's a good deal for the dollar.

Gay Lodging
MOHALA KE OLA

$$ 4 ROOMS   ✉5663 Ohelo Road, Kapaa   ☎808-823-6398, 888-465-2824
🖱www.waterfallbnb.com, kauaibb@aloha.net

There are four comfortable, airy guest rooms at this gay-friendly bed and breakfast. It's situated near the river from Opaekaa Falls and offers grand views of Mount Waialeale and Secret Falls. Relax with acupuncture, massage, yoga or even crystal healing. Amenities include a pool and jacuzzi; continental breakfast served on the deck.

MAHINA KAI OCEAN VILLA

$$$$ 4 UNITS   ✉4933 Aliomanu Road, Anahola   ☎808-822-9451, 800-337-1134
🖱www.mahinakai.com, reservations@mahinakai.com

Looking like it has been lifted straight out of the Japanese countryside,

Mahina Kai has a Japanese garden and teahouse to match. Three suites, one of which is completely detached, and one single guest room are fitted with kimono quilts and shoji screen doors and share a kitchen; another cottage includes a kitchenette. There's an indoor pond and a pool as well as an ocean view from this two-acre property.

CONDOS

KAHA LANI

35 UNITS ✉4460 Nehe Road, Wailua ☎808-822-9331, 800-367-5004 📠808-822-2828

This isn't a place you'd find unless you were looking for it, making these isolated condominiums, perfect for a quiet retreat. Families will also enjoy the property's proximity to Lydgate State Park, with its child-designed Kamalani playground and protected *keiki* pools along the water. The comfy condos have well-equipped kitchens, and most are demurely decorated in a muted tropical theme. (They are individually owned, so the decor varies.) One-bedroom units start at $250; two bedrooms start at $325.

WAILUA BAY VIEW

3 UNITS ✉4379 Rice Street, Kapaa ☎808-245-4711, 800-767-4707 📠808-245-8115 🖥www.prosserrealty.net, holiday@prosserrealty.net

All of the apartments here are one bedroom and include ocean views. Sleek and tropical, they run $125 for up to four people; three-night minimum stay.

KAPAA SANDS RESORT

21 UNITS ✉380 Papaloa Road, Kapaa ☎808-822-4901, 800-222-4901 📠808-822-1556 🖥www.kapaasands.com, info@kapaasands.com

Studio apartments at Kapaa Sands are $120 single or double, $150 for an oceanfront unit. Two-bedroom apartments, $170 (one to four people); $185 for an oceanfront location.

KAUAI COAST RESORT

108 UNITS ✉520 Aleka Loop, Kapaa ☎808-822-3441, 877-977-4355 📠808-822-0843 🖥www.kauaicoastresort.com

Located behind the Coconut Marketplace, this resort is popular with swimmers and shoppers alike. You'll find a pool, a spa, a fitness center and tennis courts amid the central grounds, plus a windswept lobby with adjoining restaurant. For pleasant surroundings near the center of the action, it's definitely among the area's top choices. All the condominiums are air-conditioned and include TVs, full kitchens, washer-dryers and lanais. Studios start at $195; one-bedroom units start at $255 per night; and two-bedroom units start at $330. The decor is quite tasteful, and the rates, considering the amenities, are reasonable.

MOKIHANA OF KAUAI

80 UNITS ✉796 Kuhio Highway, Kapaa ☎808-822-3971 📠808-822-7387

This simple establishment has studio apartments that run $85 single or double. These units are supplied with a hotplate and small refrigerator.

KAUAI KAILANI

57 UNITS ✉856 Kuhio Highway, Kapaa ☎808-822-3391 📠808-822-7387

Featuring two-bedroom apartments, at this property the prices are $90

474

for up to four people; $7.50 for each extra person. This offers a lot of square footage for the money, but there's one catch—reservations are difficult to obtain and should be made a year in advance. Three-night minimum (loosely enforced).

DINING

KOREAN BBQ

$ KOREAN-BARBECUE ✉4-356 Kuhio Highway (Kinipopo Shopping Village), Wailua ✆808-823-6744

Never mind the stark setting of fluorescent lighting and booths with formica-topped tables, the food here is good, plentiful and cheap. Of course, they offer a variety of Korean dishes such as fish *jun*, barbecue chicken or beef, cold noodles with mixed veggies and soups. You can substitute tofu for many of the meat dishes. Eat in or take-out.

RESTAURANT KINTARO

$$$ JAPANESE ✉4-370 Kuhio Highway, Wailua ✆808-822-3341 ✎808-822-2153

Antique Japanese screens set the theme at Kintaro's, where you can dine at the sushi bar or enjoy *teppanyaki*-style cooking. If you decide on the latter, choose between filet mignon, shrimp, scallops, steak teriyaki or oysters sautéed with olive oil. They also prepare traditional tempura and yakitori dinners as well as *yosenabe* (Japanese bouillabaisse). Closed Sunday.

COCONUT MARKETPLACE

$ INTERNATIONAL ✉4-484 Kuhio Highway, Wailua

There are short-order stands galore at this marketplace. **Harley's Tropical Barbecue** (808-822-2505) delivers what its name promises. The **Fish Hut** (808-821-0033) lives up to its name. You'll never guess what they serve at **Aloha Kauai Pizza** (808-822-4511). Any time from early morning until 8 or 9 p.m., several of these stands will be open. An interesting way to dine here is by going from one to the next, nibbling small portions along the way.

EGGBERT'S

$$ AMERICAN ✉Coconut Marketplace, 4-484 Kuhio Highway, Wailua ✆808-822-3787 ✎808-822-2012

A favorite breakfast institution, Eggbert's is a perfect place for people watching. Try the hotcakes with coconut syrup, or the sour-cream-and-chives omelette. Lunch offerings are mainly sandwiches and salads, while dinner choices include steak, meatloaf, pork and chicken; the stir-fry is a good vegetarian option. No dinner on Sunday.

WAIPOULI DELI & RESTAURANT

$ LOCAL-STYLE ✉Waipouli Town Center, 4-771 Kuhio Highway, Kapaa ✆808-822-9311

If cost is a consideration, stop by this deli & restaurant, located next to Blockbuster and behind McDonald's, for super-cheap and decent local-style food. The stark decor is a bit gritty and uninspired, but you can fill up on *saimin*, various fried meats, eggs and rice without running up a large tab. Closed Monday.

PAPAYA'S NATURAL FOODS

$ VEGETARIAN/DELI ✉Kauai Village Shopping Center, 4-831 Kuhio Highway, Kapaa
📞808-823-0191 📠808-823-0756

For a light, healthful meal, you can duck into Papaya's. This takeout counter with outdoor tables has sandwiches and salads. Papaya's also caters to vegetarians and vegans. Closed Sunday.

KING AND I

$$ THAI ✉4-901 Kuhio Highway (Waipouli Plaza), Kapaa 📞808-822-1642

Thai restaurants have mushroomed in Kapaa, but this old-timer is still a good bet. The small, pink dining room is decorated with ornate Thai art and cascading orchids. The food is reliably good, with lots of vegetarian choices. Try the garlic eggplant, pungent green papaya salad, *pad thai* noodles and curries. Black rice pudding is a must for dessert.

KAUAI PASTA

$–$$ ITALIAN ✉4-939B Kuhio Highway, Kapaa 📞808-822-7447

A solid choice is this pasta restaurant, which serves a variety of well-made pastas, along with salads, crab cakes and other fresh fish specials. The fresh bread is excellent for sopping up all the good sauces. It's run by a former Roy's chef, and he knows his way around the kitchen. Open for dinner nightly except Mondays.

THE BULL SHED

$$–$$$ STEAK/SEAFOOD ✉796 Kuhio Highway, Kapaa 📞808-822-3791
📠808-822-4041

It's beef, beef and beef here. We're talking about prime rib, beef kebab, top sirloin, garlic tenderloin and teriyaki steak. All this in a casual restaurant that's so close to the surf your feet feel wet. Speaking of surf, they also serve lobster, broiled shrimp, Alaskan king crab and fresh fish. Dinner only.

KOUNTRY KITCHEN

$ AMERICAN ✉1485 Kuhio Highway, Kapaa 📞808-822-3511

When nothing will do but a hearty, old-fashioned breakfast, this restaurant delivers the goods. Booths line the place, which strives for an old-fashioned coffee shop look, and it's been around long enough to carry it off. Lunch is sandwiches, burgers, salads and other simple fare. Breakfast and lunch only.

NORBERTO'S EL CAFÉ

$$ MEXICAN ✉4-1373 Kuhio Highway, Kapaa 📞808-822-3362

In the center of Kapaa and known to Mexican food aficionados for miles around, Norberto's draws a hungry crowd of young locals for dinner. The owners raise a lot of their own vegetables, and they serve monstrous portions. If you're not hungry, order à la carte or one of the smaller dinners. If you are, choose from a solid menu ranging from enchiladas (including Hawaiian taro-leaf enchiladas) to burritos to chiles rellenos. Children's portions are available and all meals can be converted to cater to vegetarians. Definitely worth checking out. Dinner only. Closed Sunday.

ONO FAMILY RESTAURANT

$ LOCAL-STYLE   ✉1292 Kuhio Highway, Kapaa   ☎808-822-1710
🕿808-823-8784

This breakfast jewel offers a more exotic take on the day's main meal. Fried rice with *kim chee* omelettes are balanced by simpler selections. Lunch centers around sandwiches (cod, egg salad) and burgers (bacon, chili); stir-fry is also on the menu. Their coconut syrup and pineapple/papaya jam can be bought here, too.

MERMAID'S CAFÉ

$$ INTERNATIONAL/VEGETARIAN   ✉4-1384 Kuhio Highway, Kapaa   ☎808-821-2026

The local crowds attest to the quality and value here. Serving lunch and dinner, this tiny place offers vegan and vegetarian choices as well as wraps, burritos, and chicken satay and curry plates. The menu favorite, an *ahi nori* wrap, contains local tuna.

OLYMPIC CAFÉ

$$–$$$ AMERICAN   ✉4-1354 Kuhio Highway, Kapaa   ☎808-822-5825

Portions are hearty at this café, which looks down on the main Kapaa drag, making it a great place to people watch. The food is high-quality and well-prepared: tasty egg dishes, omelettes and pancakes for breakfast; a choice of big salads, sandwiches and burgers for lunch. Or try one of the Mexican entrées, like burritos. Juices, coffee drinks and drinks from the full bar soothe parched throats. The open-air dining room is casual and has views of the ocean and mountains.

DUANE'S ONO CHAR-BURGER

$ AMERICAN   ✉4-4350 Kuhio Highway, Anahola   ☎808-822-9181

Some of the best hamburgers on the island are found at this eatery, a wood-planked burger stand next to the Anahola Post Office. Cheddar, mushrooms, bleu cheese and pineapple are some of the toppings heaped onto the thick patties. The juicy teriyaki burger is an island favorite. Don't feel like ground beef? You can also opt for a veggie burger, broiled chicken or fried fish. To round off your meal, order a fruit shake and a side of crispy fries.

SHOPPING

TIN CAN MAILMAN   ✉4-356 Kuhio Highway, Wailua   ☎808-822-3009   In the
Kinipopo Shopping Village, this store specializes in new, used and rare books, particularly Pacific Island titles. It is also rich in stamps, maps, tapa cloth and botanical prints. Closed Sunday.

BAMBULEI ✉ *4-369D Kuhio Highway, Wailua* ☏ *808-823-8641* For campy antiques, "tropical wear" plus new and vintage clothing, try this shop, hidden behind the Wailua Shopping Plaza. If Hawaiiana from the 1950s appeals to you, this is the place for a little treasure hunting. Be careful: Two cottages filled to the rim with funky knickknacks may make you forget the beach.

COCONUT MARKETPLACE ✉ *4-484 Kuhio Highway, Wailua* ☏ *808-822-3641* ⌨ *www.coconutmarketplace.com* Here is a theme mall that consists of wooden stores designed to resemble little plantation houses. For decor you'll find the pipes, valves, gears and waterwheels characteristic of every tropical plantation. This is a good place for clothing, curios, jewelry, toys, Asian imports and T-shirts. If you don't want to buy, you can always browse or have a snack at the many short-order stands here.

Two galleries within the Marketplace are worthy of note. **Kaleidoscope Galleries of the Pacific** (808-822-3636) features locally and internationally known artists. Focusing on Hawaiian seascapes and landscapes, the gallery offers work by Roy Tabora. Also consider **Ship Store Galleries** and its maritime theme (808-822-7758), which highlights an eclectic group of artists. **Overboard** (808-822-1777), also in the Coconut Marketplace, has aloha shirts and other Hawaiian wear.

KAUAI VILLAGE SHOPPING CENTER This multi-store complex in the center of Kapaa is another of Kauai's shopping destinations. Anchored by a grocery store, it features a string of small shops.

HULA GIRL ✉ *4-1340 Kuhio Highway, Kapaa* ☏ *808-822-1950* With clothing and gifts for the entire family, the focus here is Hawaiiana, with a great selection of bowls, books and prints.

ISLAND HEMP & COTTON ✉ *4-1373 Kuhio Highway, Kapaa* ☏ *808-821-0225* Talk about unusual. This store specializes in things made from the "evil" weed. There's an attractive line of women's clothing here, not to mention soap, paper, and body lotion, all fabricated from hemp.

KELA'S GLASS GALLERY ✉ *4-1354 Kuhio Highway, Kapaa* ☏ *808-822-4527* This gallery offers an exquisite and colorful collection of handmade glass vases, bowls, plates and art pieces. They're happy to wrap up your fragile purchase for a safe journey home.

NIGHTLIFE

TRADEWINDS ✉ *Coconut Marketplace, Wailua* ☏ *808-822-1621* If it's karaoke you want, check out this spot, where it's offered nightly except Wednesday, Friday and Saturday, when a deejay takes over the dancefloor at this South Seas–style bar.

LIZARD LOUNGE ✉ *Waipouli Town Center, 4-771 Kuhio Highway, Kapaa* ☏ *808-821-2205* If your image of the perfect paradise vacation includes tropical drinks, you're in for a treat here. The place is on the funky side but the drinks are delicious and the mood festive. You can play darts, watch the game and gnaw on buffalo wings while you sip one of thirty beers.

BEACHES & PARKS

NUKOLII BEACH PARK

✉ *At the end of Kauai Beach Drive. To reach the more secluded sections, go north from Lihue on Kuhio Highway and take a right onto the road that runs along the southern end of the Wailua Golf Course. This paved road rapidly becomes a dirt strip studded with potholes. Driving slowly, proceed a quarter-mile, then take the first left turn. It's another quarter-mile to the beach; when the road forks, take either branch.*

Located adjacent to the Hilton Kauai Beach Resort, this is a long narrow strand with a shallow bottom. From the park, the beach extends for several miles all the way to Lydgate Park in Wailua. One of the island's prettiest beaches, it provides an opportunity to use the park facilities or to escape to more secluded sections (adjacent to Wailua Golf Course). If you seek seclusion, just start hiking farther north along the shore. You'll find places galore for water sports. Swimming is good in well-protected and shallow waters. Snorkelers will be content swimming among reefs and there are good surf breaks on the shallow reef at "Graveyards." Fishing is best near the reefs.

LYDGATE BEACH AND LYDGATE PARK

✉ *From Kuhio Highway, turn toward the beach at Leho Drive, the road just south of the Wailua River.*

The awesome ironwood grove and long stretches of rugged coastline make this one of Kauai's loveliest parks. Near the Wailua River, it is also one of the most popular. The Hauola Place of Refuge and other sacred sites are located within the state park. (See page 132 for more information.) Two large lava pools, one perfect for kids and the other protecting swimmers and snorkelers, make it a great place to spend the day. Surfers must take a long paddle out to breaks off the mouth of Wailua River. There's a right slide. This park is also favored by windsurfers. *Ulua* is the most common catch. You'll find a picnic area, showers, restrooms, a playground and lifeguards. With kids in tow, Kamalani Playground in Lydgate Park offers a distracting alternative to making sandcastles.

WAILUA RIVER STATE PARK

✉ *Take Route 56 to Kuamoo Road (Route 580).*

Home to the famous Fern Grotto, this small park features sacred historic sites and breathtaking views of river and mountains. It also has a marina and is the launching point for motorized and kayaking tours up the famous river, which is billed as the only truly navigable waterway on the island. In addition, waterskiing is allowed and canoe clubs practice here. There are lots of shady areas and picnic tables. Although the park is public, boat companies pay to maintain the landing at Fern Grotto upriver, which is technically off-limits to kayakers. Restrooms are available here.

WAILUA BEACH

This beach, near the Coco Palms Resort, is easily accessed only when traveling north on Kuhio Highway.

One of east Kauai's nicest and most accessible stretches of broad sand, this beach is perfect for sunbathing and beachwalking. Conditions can be treacherous for swimming, however, because the frequently blowing trade winds often create rough waters and the Wailua River empties into the ocean here. In rainy weather, the river often creates a strong current at the south end of the beach. Boogie-boarders challenge the waves here, and a hot surf break known as "Horner's" is found at the northern end of the beach. Children gravitate toward the river area. A lifeguard is on limited duty but there are minimal facilities. The best parking is near the Wailua Bridge.

WAIPOULI BEACH

The beach can be accessed at a number of points behind Coconut Marketplace and along the shoreline road that runs parallel to Kuhio Highway, a few blocks makai (toward the ocean).

The longest, narrowest strip of sand on the eastside begins behind the Coconut Marketplace shopping center and ends about two miles down the road at Waikaea Canal in Kapaa. Even though many condos and resorts border this beach, it isn't that crowded and it's easy to find lots of hidden coves. Monk seals, one of two species of tropical seals left, sometimes snooze in the sand here; don't disturb their naps! The ocean in this area is usually rough, and most of the coastline is either beachrock or reef. Swimming is not recommended. Fishermen are common here, pole fishing or hunting octopus in the sand. About midway along this stretch is a protected shallow section in the reef known as "Baby Beach," because many families come here with small children. No facilities except at the boat-launching area near the canal, where you'll find restrooms and pavilions, and often some hard-drinking locals just hanging out. There's a nice trail for getting your exercise biking or walking along Waipouli Beach.

KAPAA BEACH PARK

A block from Kuhio Highway, Kapaa

While it sports an attractive little beach, this 15-acre facility doesn't measure up to its neighbors. Located a block from the highway as the road passes through central Kapaa, the park is flanked by ramshackle houses and a local playing field. The area has a picnic area with barbecue pits and restrooms. Swimming and fishing are only fair, but there is good squidding and torchfishing.

KEALIA BEACH

On Kuhio Highway, Kealia

This strand is one of those neighbors that makes Kapaa Beach the pimply kid next door: It's a wide, magnificent beach curving for about a half-mile along Kuhio Highway. The swimming is good, but requires caution. Lifeguards are on duty daily. Surfing and bodysurfing can be found at the north end of the beach. Fish here for *papio*, threadfin and *ulua*. There are no facilities.

DONKEY BEACH OR KUMU BEACH

✉ *Follow Kuhio Highway north from Kealia. At the 11-mile marker the road begins to climb slowly, then descends. At the end of the descent, just before 12-mile marker, there is a parking area and a path to the beach.*

This broad, curving beach is flanked by a grassy meadow and towering ironwoods. Favored as a hideaway and nude beach by locals, it's a gem that should not be overlooked. Also note that the two-mile stretch from here north to Anahola is lined by low sea cliffs that open onto at least four pocket beaches. This entire area is popular with beachcombers, who sometimes find hand-blown Japanese glass fishing balls. Swimmers, take care: Currents here can be treacherous and the nearest lifeguard is a world away. Surfers get their kicks at Donkey Beach, or try "14 Crack" just north of the beach. Anglers frequent this beach for pole-fishing and throw-netting. There are no facilities here.

Unofficial camping is common.

ANAHOLA BEACH PARK

✉ *Turn onto Anahola Road from Kuhio Highway in Anahola; follow it three-quarters of a mile, then turn onto a dirt road that forks left to the beach.*

A slender ribbon of sand curves along windswept Anahola Bay. At the south end, guarded by ironwood trees, lies this pretty little park. Very popular with neighborhood residents, this is a prime beachcombing spot where you may find Japanese glass fishing balls. There is a protecting reef here; but as elsewhere, use caution swimming because of the strong currents. Snorkeling is good behind the reef. Surfers have a long paddle out to summer and winter breaks along the reef (left and right slides). There is a break called "Unreals" offshore from the old landing. This is also a popular bodysurfing beach. There's good torchfishing for lobsters, and anglers often catch *papio*, rudderfish, *ulua*, threadfin, bonefish and big-eyed scad. Facilities include a picnic area, restrooms, showers and limited lifeguard duty.

You can pitch a tent on the grassy area near the beach; county permit required.

ALIOMANU BEACH

✉ *Turn off Kuhio Highway onto Aliomanu Road just past Anahola.*

On the far side of Anahola Bay, separated from the park by the Anahola River, lies another sandy beach. Shady ironwood trees and roadside houses dot this area, which is a favorite among locals. What makes Aliomanu particularly popular is the offshore reef, one of Kauai's longest and widest fringing reefs. This is an excellent area for gathering edible seaweed. Swimming is fairly safe in summer, but use caution the rest of the year. Local residents spear octopus and go torchfishing here.

NORTH SHORE

It is no accident that when it came time to choose a location for Bali Hai, the producers of *South Pacific* ended their search on the North Shore of Kauai. The most beautiful place in Hawaii, indeed one of the prettiest places on earth, this 30-mile stretch of lace-white surf and emerald-green mountains became Hollywood's version of paradise.

Backdropping this thin line of civilization is the Na Pali Coast. Here, sharp sea cliffs vault thousands of feet from the ocean, silver waterfalls streaming along their fluted surfaces. There are pocket beaches ringed by menacing rock formations and long, wide strands as inviting as a warm tub.

The North Shore is wet and tropical, drawing enough precipitation to dampen the enthusiasm of many tourists. It is suited for travelers who don't mind a little rain on their parade if it carries with it rainbows and seabirds and a touch of magic in the air.

SIGHTS

KILAUEA The natural place to start a tour of the North Shore is this former sugar town with a cluster of stores and a couple of noteworthy churches. The cottages that once housed plantation workers are freshly painted and decorated with flowering gardens and the place possesses an air of humble well-being.

CHRIST MEMORIAL EPISCOPAL CHURCH ⊠*Kilauea Road, Kilauea* This is an ideal spot for reflection. The beautiful building was conse-crated in 1941. It's built out of lava stone and has stained-glass win-dows imported from England.

ST. SYLVESTER'S ROMAN CATHOLIC CHURCH ⊠*Kilauea Road, Kilauea* ☎*808-822-7900* ☏*808-822-3014* A chance for history cum medita-tion is this church, an octagonal building containing works by Jean Charlot, a local artist. The church was constructed, in part, to illustrate the importance of art to the Catholic religion.

KILAUEA POINT NATIONAL WILDLIFE REFUGE

⊠*End of Kilauea Road, Kilauea* ☎*808-828-1413* ☏*808-828-6634* ⊘*www.kilaueapoint.org* Along the North Shore, humankind is a bit player in the natural drama being presented here. To take in that scene, you need venture no farther than Kilauea Point. Here, a lofty peninsula that falls away into precipitous rockfaces, you'll have the same bird's-eye view of the spectacular coastline as the boo-bies, tropicbirds, albatrosses and frigatebirds. As you stand along this lonely point, gazing upon the ocean and along the cliffs, birds—graceful, sleek, exotic ones—swarm like bees. A vi-tal rookery, the refuge is also frequented by Hawaiian monk seals and green turtles, as well as occasional whales and dolphins. Off-shore is **Moku Aeae Island**, a state bird preserve. Admission.

KILAUEA LIGHTHOUSE Counterpoint to this natural pageant is the lighthouse, a 52-foot-high beacon built in 1913 that bears the world's largest clamshell-shaped lens. Capable of casting its light almost 100 miles, it is the first sign of land seen by mariners venturing east from Asia. This old lighthouse, now replaced by a more modern beacon, sits on the northernmost point of Kauai. People gather at the point for interpretive talks of the bird life and natural history of the region.

KALIHIWAI BAY Along Route 56 you'll see this bay. There's another (ho-hum) beautiful beach here, surrounded by ironwood trees. A sweeping but shallow lagoon has been formed by the Kalihiwai River. (See "Beaches & Parks" below for directions to Kalihiwai Beach.)

PRINCEVILLE Civilization stakes its claim once again at this one-time plantation named by R. C. Wyllie in honor of the son of Kamehameha IV and Queen Emma. This 11,000-acre planned resort community combines private homes, condominiums and the elegant Princeville Resort. Set along a luxurious plateau with scintillating views of the Na Pali Coast, it is a tastefully designed complex complete with golf courses and acres of open space.

QUEEN'S BATH ⊠*In Princeville, near the Pali Ke Kua condominium parking lot. There is a sign pointing to the trail.* The adventurous might want to make the trek down here to this large lava tidepool at the end of a slippery trail that is closed during winter due to especially hazardous conditions. If you do go, exercise extreme caution as this spot has been the scene of numerous drownings.

HANALEI VALLEY LOOKOUT Past Princeville, the road opens onto a vista point that transcends prose with its beauty. Below you spreads a patchwork of tropical vegetation, fields of broad-leafed taro that have been cultivated for over 1200 years. This green carpet, swaying and shimmering along the valley floor, is cut by the thin silver band of the Hanalei River. Framing this scene, as though a higher power had painted the entire tableau, are deep-green cliffs, fluted and sharp, that rise 3500 feet from the tilled fields.

HANALEI RIVER Designated one of fourteen American Heritage Rivers, the Hanalei receives federal monies to help preserve the 15-mile waterway. The river is one of the largest in the state, and considered among the most pristine in Hawaii. Together with its estuarine bay it is considered "outstanding in Hawaii and in the Pacific for the abundance and quality of natural, cultural and scenic resources."

HANALEI In town, a combination of plantation-style buildings, dramatic mountain views and curving beaches creates a mystique that can only be described in a single word—Hanalei. It makes you wonder if heaven, in fact, is built of clapboard. The town is little more than a string of woodframe bungalows and falsefront stores lining the main road. On one side a half-moon bay, rimmed with white sand, curves out in two directions. Behind the town the *pali*, those awesome cliffs that fluctuate between dream and reality in the focus of the mind, form a frontier between Hanalei and the rest of the world.

North Shore

KILAUEA POINT NATIONAL REFUGE

CAMP NAUE

560

Haena

Hanalei

Kilauea

56

TAHITI NUI RESTAURANT

HANALEI TARO & JUICE CO.

KILAUEA POINT NATIONAL WILDLIFE REFUGE

PAGE 481

Lofty peninsula with a bird's-eye view of spectacular coastal cliffs where boobies and albatrosses soar above and monk seals and dolphins swim below

CAMP NAUE

PAGE 488

Camping in paradise! For a few dollars, sleep on the beach in one of the most beautiful spots on Earth

HANALEI TARO & JUICE CO.

PAGE 490

Fruit smoothies, sandwiches and dessert treats—all made from taro grown at the owner's nearby farm

TAHITI NUI RESTAURANT

PAGE 493

Classic, thatched-canopy tiki bar that serves up tropical drinks amid Pacific Island carvings and live Hawaiian music

HANALEI PIER On the National Register of Historic Places, this pier was constructed in 1892. Although it has since been reinforced with concrete, it still adds a touch more romance to the already unreal seascape.

WAIOLI HULIA CHURCH ⌂ *Kuhio Highway, Hanalei* ☏ *808-826-6253* ✆ *808-826-9625* That little green-and-white church along the highway is the Waioli Hulia Church, part of the Waioli Mission, built in 1912. If you get a chance to go in, take a look at the beautiful stained-glass windows.

WAIOLI MISSION HOUSE ⌂ *Kuhio Highway, Hanalei* ☏ *808-245-3202* ✆ *808-245-7988* It's almost superfluous that this house, built in 1836, provides glimpses of a bygone era: The entire town seems a reflection of its former self. But this one-time home of Abner and Lucy Wilcox, missionaries from New England, extends a special invitation to step back into the 19th century. A small but stately house, clapboard in design with a second-story lanai, it sits amid palm and *hala* trees on a broad lawn. The rooms look undisturbed since the days when the Wilcoxes

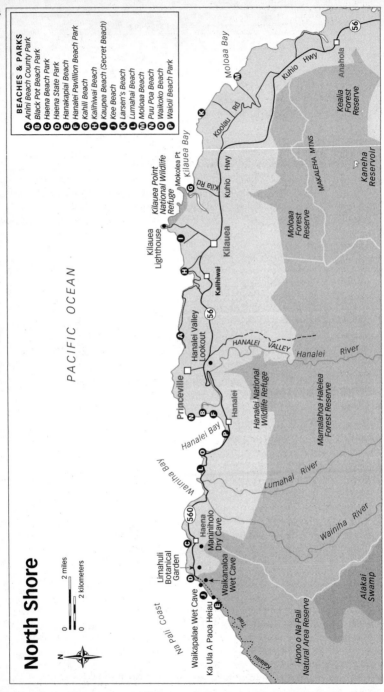

North Shore

BEACHES & PARKS

- Ⓐ Anini Beach County Park
- Ⓑ Black Pot Beach Park
- Ⓒ Haena Beach Park
- Ⓓ Haena State Park
- Ⓔ Hanakapiai Beach
- Ⓕ Hanalei Pavillion Beach Park
- Ⓖ Kahili Beach
- Ⓗ Kalihiwai Beach
- Ⓘ Kaupea Beach (Secret Beach)
- Ⓙ Kee Beach
- Ⓚ Larsen's Beach
- Ⓛ Lumahai Beach
- Ⓜ Moloaa Beach
- Ⓝ Puu Poa Beach
- Ⓞ Waikoko Beach
- Ⓟ Waioli Beach Park

PACIFIC OCEAN

Moloaa Bay

Anahola

Kuhio Hwy

Koolau Rd

Kealia Forest Reserve

Kaneha Reservoir

MAKALEHA MTNS

Kilauea Bay

Mokolea Pt

Kila Rd

Kuhio Hwy

Kilauea Point National Wildlife Refuge

Kilauea Lighthouse

Kilauea

Moloaa Forest Reserve

Kalihiwai

Hanalei Valley Lookout

HANALEI VALLEY

Hanalei River

Hanalei National Wildlife Refuge

Mamalahoa Halelea Forest Reserve

Princeville

Hanalei

Hanalei Bay

Waioli Bay

Lumahai River

Haena Maniniholo Dry Cave

Wainiha River

Limahuli Botanical Garden

Waikapalae Wet Cave

Ka Ula A Paoa Heiau

Waikanaloa Wet Cave

Na Pali Coast

Alakai Swamp

Hono o Na Pali Natural Area Reserve

Kalalau Trail

N

0   2 miles

0   2 kilometers

prayed and proselytized. The china rests in the cupboard and an old rocker sits in one room while the canopied bed and cradle still occupy a bedroom. The walls are decorated with photos of Abner and Lucy Wilcox and knickknacks from their era are scattered about the entire house. Guided tours are led Tuesday, Thursday and Saturday between 9 a.m. and 3 p.m.

HANALEI NATIONAL WILDLIFE REFUGE

✉ *To get a close-up version of this panorama, turn left onto Ohiki Road near the old bridge at the bottom of the hill. It will lead you back several eras to a region of terraced fields and simple homesteads. There is no parking or facilities.* Taro patches and wetlands comprise this 917-acre refuge, home to the Hawaiian duck, Hawaiian stilt, the Hawaiian coot and the Hawaiian moorhen, all of which are endangered. For wildlife protection, humans are not allowed inside.

LUMAHAI BEACH ✉ *Off Kuhio Highway about five miles west of Hanalei* The road winds on from Hanalei past single-lane bridges and overgrown villages. The air seems moister and the real world more distant as you pass this sandy scimitar where Mitzi Gaynor vowed to "wash that man right out of my hair" in the 1957 movie *South Pacific.*

MANINIHOLO DRY CAVE ✉ *Mauka of Haena State Park* Several caves along this route were created eons ago when this entire area was underwater. This is the first one which geologists claim is a lava tube but which legend insists was created by *Menehune.* The **Waikapalae** and **Waikanaloa Wet Caves,** farther north along the highway, are said to be the work of Pele, the Hawaiian goddess of volcanos, who sought fire in the earth but discovered only water.

LIMAHULI BOTANICAL GARDEN

✉ *Kuhio Highway, .5 mile past mile marker 9* ☎ *808-826-1053* 🖰 *www.ntbg. org* A loop trail three-quarters of a mile long winds through these botanical gardens. Devoted to conservation of native and Polynesian-introduced plants, the valley is rich in history and contains several archeological sites. A path winds through ancient terraces with Hawaiian taro, into a forest being restored with many endangered Hawaiian plants, and out to ocean and mountain views. The Limahuli Stream meanders through the property and is home to a number of indigenous aquatic species. Self-guided and guided tours are available; reservations required for guided tours. Closed Sunday and Monday. Admission.

KEE BEACH ✉ *At the end of Route 56* The cinematic appears once more at this lovely strand with protecting reef that was used to film some of the torrid love scenes in "The Thorn Birds." It was just east of Kee Beach that the 1960s encampment, dubbed Taylor Camp after actress Elizabeth Taylor's brother, who owned a piece of the land, was located. Now it's over-"occupied" by daytrippers who flock to the beach park. This is the end of the road, beyond which the fabled Kalalau Trail winds along the Na Pali Coast.

KA ULU A PAOA HEIAU

✉ *Follow the path on the top of the stone wall just above Kee Beach. About ten yards past the end of the beach, take the left fork in the path. Another 20 yards and you will be on the platform.* Just above Kee Beach at the far west end of the strand rises this grass-covered terrace. It was also the site of a hula platform and ceremonial hall; Hawaii's greatest hula masters once taught here. According to legend, the volcano goddess Pele departed Kauai from here, settling on the Big Island, where she still lives. As with all Hawaiian sacred spots, it is inappropriate to sunbathe, picnic, get married, leave offerings,

Na Pali Coast

With sea cliffs sculpted by wind and rain that seem to reach to the stars, towering over lush mountain valleys—this is hidden Kauai. There are various ways to explore this misty and mystical region. Numerous outfitters offer catamaran, sailboat or zodiac rafting trips along the coast. Kayakers can cruise the coastline in a group tour or on their own. Helicopters fly deep into the valleys, swooping like birds, brushing up against waterfalls and adze-like cliffs. Or you can hike along an ancient Hawaiian trail 12 miles to Kalalau Valley. (See "Hiking Kalalau" later in this chapter) Anyway you can, do it. This is truly one of the most magnificent spots on earth.

HANAKAPIAI BEACH For those wanting just a taste of the coastline, there's a two-mile hike to this beach. It's an arduous trek climbing up some 800 feet, hugging cliffs along a narrow trail, crossing streams, and walking in mud. But the reward at the end is a spectacular valley with a picture-perfect white-sand beach. (The current can be tricky here; use caution when swimming.) Two more miles inland on a rough and often slippery trail are **Hanakoa Falls**, which feed a large swimming pond.

HONO O NA PALI NATURAL AREA RESERVE Tucked into this verdant area is Hono o Na Pali. This was a major taro-growing region in ancient times, with remnants of terraced hills still clearly visible. Wild fruit and coffee plants thrive in the rain-soaked valleys and on surrounding cliffs.

KALALAU BEACH If you're on foot, it's another five and a half miles from Hono O Na Pali to this beach and the once-thriving **Kalalau Valley**. Two miles wide and three miles deep, studded with guava and mango trees, it was not so very long ago, in the early 1900s, that a community populated this area. Now, hikers and kayakers, who need permits to visit, seek out the freshwater pools and pristine beach. For the less adventurous, the valley can be viewed from the Kalalau Lookout at Waimea Canyon.

A note of caution: If you do venture along the coast in a kayak or on foot, remember that this coastline is wild and unpredictable. Even experienced adventurers have needed to be rescued here.

move stones or do much of anything else here, except walk around the perimeter of the structure.

NORTH COUNTRY FARMS

$–$$ 2 ROOMS ✉Kahili Makai Street, Kilauea ☎808-828-1513
📠808-828-0805 🖥www.northcountryfarms.com, ncfarms@aloha.net

Farm life, North Shore Kauai–style, is the experience at this small organic family farm with two separate cottages (one of which can accommodate up to six people) that are run like a bed and breakfast. The setting is pleasant and quiet, amid fields and orchards, with mountain views, and owner Lee Roversi strives to use and serve natural products. The cottages are clean, simple and comfortable, with an instant homey feel that families, couples or those planning a longer stay would appreciate. Each sleeps at least four comfortably, with no cleaning fee, making this a real bargain for the $130 per night price. Both have a TV/VCR (one with cable), but plenty of books, puzzles, games and toys will keep you occupied, if that's what you prefer.

PRINCEVILLE RESORT

$$$$ 252 ROOMS ✉Princeville ☎808-826-9644, 800-325-3589 📠808-826-1166
🖥www.luxurycollection.com

The North Shore's premier resting place is this clifftop roost. Situated on a point and sporting one of the best views this side of paradise, it's decorated in European style with a large touch of Hawaiiana. The hotel rises above a white-sand beach and features several restaurants as well as a pool and jacuzzi. Trimmed in gold plating and marble, this is a concierge-and-doorman resort long on service.

HANALEI BAY RESORT

$$$$ 134 ROOMS ✉5380 Honoiki Road, Princeville ☎808-826-6522, 800-827-4427
📠808-826-6680 🖥www.hanaleibaykauai.com

Spectacularly perched on a hillside overlooking the coastline, this resort provides full vacation facilities. The 22-acre property, which descends to a beach, contains a restaurant, lounge, tennis courts and two spacious swimming pools. The guest rooms are located in three-story buildings dotted around the grounds; some include kitchens. Be forewarned: We have had complaints that the facilities do not warrant the price tag.

MANA YOGA

$$ 2 ROOMS ✉Ahonui Place, Princeville ☎808-826-9230, 808-652-3823
🖥www.kauainorthshorevacationrentals.com, manayoga@yahoo.com

Here is a great little vacation hideaway in a rural North Shore area that has stunning mountain and waterfall views. It's on a five-acre farm, and there are two units in the downstairs portion of the Edwards' family home. But not to worry—there's plenty of privacy, with your own lanai, entrance, kitchen and bath. It has two bedrooms and easily sleeps four people. Yoga classes, private and public, are provided by the owner, who is also a masseuse. Three-night minimum stay.

CAMP NAUE

$ 50 BEDS   ⊠Off Kuhio Highway, Haena   ☎808-246-9090

At the YMCA's beachfront camp, there are dormitory accommodations in bunkhouses. Bring your own bedding. There is also an adjacent area for camping. Reservations can only be made for large groups; otherwise, it is on a first-come, first-served basis. Calls will only be returned if they're local or if the campsite can call collect.

CONDOS

HANALEI VACATIONS

⊠P.O. Box 223206, Princeville, HI 96722   ☎808-826-7288, 800-487-9833
📠808-826-7280   🖥www.800hawaii.com, rentals@aloha.net

For information on other condominiums, as well as cottages and houses, and to learn where the best deals are available during any particular time, check with this company. You can also browse (virtually) through every one of their properties at their website.

THE CLIFFS AT PRINCEVILLE

130 UNITS   ⊠Kauai Coast Resort, 520 Aleka Loop Suite 12, Kapaa   ☎808-826-6219, 800-367-8024   📠808-826-2140   🖥cliffs-princeville.com

Adjacent to the championship Princeville Golf Course, this condominium complex sits on a spectacular bluff overlooking the ocean. Amenities include a pool, a spa and sauna, tennis courts, a putting green, a barbecue area and fully equipped kitchens. Prices range between $180 and $250.

PAHIO AT KAEO KAI

84 UNITS   ⊠3970 Wyllie Road, Princeville   ☎808-826-6549   📠808-826-6715
🖥www.pahio.com

Set in lush surroundings, these spacious condominiums come with modern kitchens, washer-dryers, two bathrooms and lanais perfect for lounging. On the grounds you'll find two swimming pools, a spa and tennis courts. Prices begin at $300.

PALI KE KUA

96 UNITS   ⊠Princeville Vacations, P.O. Box 223552, Princeville, Hawaii 96722
☎808-826-9394   📠808-826-4159   🖥www.princeville-vacations.com

The starring feature at this condominium complex is the ocean view; all units sit atop a bluff looking out over the Pacific. One- and two-bedroom units are available and start around $170.

SEALODGE

90 UNITS ✉Princeville ☎808-826-6751

Although the Princeville Resort area is awash with condos, they're generally pretty bland. Tucked away on a quiet side street, this is the exception. The privacy and setting make these condos distinct. One-bedroom units are $140 per night, while two-bedroom apartments run $160. A pool, barbecue area, and plenty of parking round out the special features.

HANALEI COLONY RESORT

48 UNITS ✉Kuhio Highway, Hanalei ☎808-826-6235, 800-628-3004 ᚛808-826-9893
✐www.hcr.com, aloha@hcr.com

This is the only beachfront condominium complex on the North Shore. It's a five-acre lowrise complex with the ocean as your only distraction (no TVs or phones). All are two-bedroom condos, most with two bathrooms, all with fully equipped kitchens and private lanais. Each unit is stylishly furnished with Hawaiian-style decor. In summer they run a special program for families. The Hanalei Day Spa (treatments, yoga classes), Mediterranean Gourmet Restaurant (lunch and dinner) and Napili Art Gallery and Coffee House are recent additions. Check their website for more information. Two-bedroom condos run $195 to $385.

DINING

LIGHTHOUSE BISTRO

$$–$$$ PAN-ASIAN ✉Kong Lung Center, Lighthouse Road, Kilauea ☎808-828-0480
᚛808-828-0481 ✐www.lighthousebistro.com, finedining@lighthousebistro.com

In the historic Kong Lung Center in the little town of Kilauea, the Lighthouse offers bistro-style fare with European and Asian influences in an open-air setting. This translates into shrimp parmesan; blackened, broiled or sautéed fresh fish with various sauces, like Thai mango sesame; chicken and steak. Lunch is sandwiches, pasta and salads. Full bar and good wine list.

PAU HANA PIZZA

$$–$$$ PIZZA ✉Kong Lung Center, Lighthouse Road, Kilauea ☎808-828-2020

If you'd simply like a pizza, the little town of Kilauea offers up this combination kitchen and bakery that cooks up some delicious pies.

KILAUEA FISH MARKET

$–$$ SEAFOOD ✉Kilauea Lighthouse Road, Kilauea ☎808-828-6244

If you're in the mood for fish, head to the fish market, where you can pick up fresh island fish served grilled with a variety of sauces, over salads, in stir-fries and in hefty, two-handed wraps. Service is slow, but it's a pleasant enough place to wait, with outdoor tables for eating.

PARADISE BAR & GRILL

$$ SEAFOOD/AMERICAN ✉Princeville Market, Princeville ☎808-826-1775

In the Princeville market you'll find this informal restaurant. It serves sandwiches at lunch and steak and seafood every evening.

LA CASCATA

$$$$ ITALIAN/MEDITERRANEAN   ✉*Princeville*   ☎*808-826-9644*   📠*808-826-1166*

The prize for prettiest dining room on the North Shore goes to the Princeville Resort's signature restaurant. That is not even taking into account the edenic views of the Na Pali Coast or the soft breezes wafting in from the ocean. All we're counting is the tilework, the murals and the Mediterranean pastel colors. The bill of fare is mostly Italian-influenced Mediterranean. Dinner only.

BALI HAI RESTAURANT

$$$-$$$$ PACIFIC RIM   ✉*Hanalei Bay Resort, 5380 Honoiki Road,*
Princeville   ☎*808-826-6522*   📠*808-826-6680*   🖱*www.hanaleibayresort.com*

Any restaurant critic in the world would immediately award five stars to the view at Bali Hai. Perched on a deck high above Hanalei Bay, it overlooks a broad sweep of mountains and sea. The menu features classic island fare, ranging from fresh catches to steak to pasta. Reservations are recommended. Closed Monday and Tuesday.

As beautiful and popular as Hanalei happens to be, the area possesses only a few low-priced facilities. If you've ever tried to find a place to stay here, you know how tight things can be. And the budget restaurant situation is not a whole lot better.

HANALEI WAKE-UP CAFÉ

$ DINER   ✉*Aku Road, Hanalei*   ☎*808-826-5551*

This is a low-key eatery with omelettes and other egg dishes in the morning. There's a small dining room with a deck. Breakfast only.

POSTCARDS

$$-$$$ INTERNATIONAL   ✉*5075-A Kuhio Highway, Hanalei*   ☎*808-826-1191*

A fun, gourmet semi-vegetarian restaurant is tucked into an old plantation cottage on the outskirts of town. The dinner menu here features lots of organic produce and is short and simple: fresh fish specials, pasta with veggies or seafood, Cajun crusted *ahi* with chipotle sauce, phyllo wraps with veggies and taro fritters. Smoothies, juices and salads, too. Service can be sketchy, but then, it *is* Hanalei. Dinner only.

HANALEI TARO & JUICE CO.

$ LOCAL-STYLE   ✉*5-5070 Kuhio Highway, Hanalei*   ☎*808-826-1059*

Owned by a couple who farm taro just down the road, this roadside cart lays to rest the notion that taro equals sour poi. With a couple of covered picnic tables out front, they sell fruit smoothies, sandwiches and dessert treats, all made from the wholesome, starchy vegetable that was a mainstay of Hawaiian diets. They bake their own taro *mochi*. Lunch only. Closed Sunday.

$$–$$$ PACIFIC RIM   ✉5-5161 Kuhio Highway, Hanalei   ☏808-826-2524
📞808-826-6007   ⌨www.hanaleigourmet.com

The atmosphere here is laidback and local. To fit this feeling, the menu is solid but unpretentious. There are numerous salads, including a chicken salad boat. The sandwich selection features a shrimp sandwich and a special concoction with eggplant and red peppers. Following this seafood and vegetable theme are the dinner entrées, which change nightly. The bar scene is lively, there's live entertainment at least five nights a week and the kitchen prepares good food at favorable prices.

BAR ACUDA

$$$–$$$$ MEDITERRANEAN   ✉Hanalei Center   ☏808-826-7081

If you're looking for truly outstanding cuisine, the tapas bar with the clever name—Bar Acuda—is your choice. The small servings, which are designed to be purchased in quantity and shared, are creative, fresh, original and top notch, and the menu changes weekly. You can dine inside, or on the cool, shady porch, and the service is excellent. Closed Sunday and Monday.

VILLAGE SNACK AND BAKERY

$ DELI/BAKERY   ✉Ching Young Village, Kuhio Highway, Hanalei   ☏808-826-6841

There are several luncheonettes in the Ching Young Village, including this one, which serves standard lunch fare.

SUSHI BLUES GRILL

$$$ SEAFOOD/SUSHI   ✉Ching Young Village, Kuhio Highway, Hanalei
☏808-826-9701   ⌨www.sushiandblues.com

This Hanalei hotspot, combines industrial decor with live entertainment every night. The menu at the second-floor restaurant/club includes sizzling seafood stir-fry, coconut shrimp, linguine and scallops, and of course a host of sushi selections. Dinner only.

POLYNESIAN CAFÉ

$–$$ INTERNATIONAL   ✉Ching Young Village, Kuhio Highway, Hanalei
☏808-826-1999

Hearty Mexican meals like fajitas and enchiladas, as well as quiche, veggie burgers, salads, wraps and more, are prepared well here. Coffee drinks, ice cream smoothies and yummy baked goods baked on-site add to the appeal, along with a cheerful staff.

BUBBA'S

$ DINER   ✉5-5161 Kuhio Highway, Hanalei   ☏808-826-7839

Forget all this nonsense about good health and low cholesterol, step up to the window at Bubba's and order a hot dog or a "Big Bubba" (a half-pound hamburger with three patties).

TROPICAL TACO _____

$ MEXICAN   ✉5088 Kuhio Highway, Hanalei   ☏808-635-8226

On the road since 1978 was this van cum taco stand that is now dispensing its mouth-watering fish tacos from a permanent location. Dine inside or on the deck, where you can do some serious people watching. Closed Sunday.

CALYPSO ISLAND BAR AND GRILL

$$–$$$ AMERICAN ✉ *5-5256 Kuhio Highway, Hanalei* ☎ *808-826-9700*

With woven *lauhala* walls, bamboo bar and outrigger canoe, this eatery certainly looks the part. It's airy and informal—a great spot to relax. When you're ready to order, you'll find an eclectic menu. The central focus is pasta: linguine and clams with toasted pine nuts, shrimp pasta and an all-you-can-eat spaghetti dish. But they also have steak, baby back ribs and fresh seafood.

TAHITI NUI RESTAURANT

$$ AMERICAN ✉ *5-5134 Kuhio Highway, in the center of Hanalei* ☎ *808-826-6277*

In business for over 50 years, the aloha spirit continues here though the menu has changed. Now they feature steak, fresh fish, calamari, scampi, pasta and chicken dishes. And check out the bamboo-fringed lanai, or the lounge decorated with Pacific Island carvings and overhung with a thatch canopy.

HANALEI DOLPHIN RESTAURANT AND FISH MARKET

$$$–$$$$ SEAFOOD ✉ *5-5016 Kuhio Highway, Hanalei* ☎ *808-826-6113*
📠 *808-826-6699* 🖱 *www.hanaleidolphin.com*

From the porthole windows to the Japanese fishing balls, the Hanalei Dolphin presents an interesting aquatic decor. Built smack on the bank of the Hanalei River, this eatery offers a surf-and-turf menu that includes fresh fish, shrimp dishes and New York steak. The restaurant, which is highly recommended, does not take reservations. The fish market at the back of the restaurant offers many of the same fish found on the menu to take home and cook yourself.

SHOPPING

KONG LUNG CO. ✉ *Kilauea Lighthouse Road, Kilauea* ☎ *808-828-1822* This shop carries a marvelous assortment of Pacific and Asian treasures in addition to a good selection of Hawaiian books. Don't miss it.

PRINCEVILLE SHOPPING CENTER ✉ *Off Kuhio Highway, Princeville* ☎ *808-826-9497* This is the closest you will come to a shopping mall on the North Shore. It features a cluster of shops that represents the area's prime spot for window browsers. Kids define heaven as **Magic Dragon Toyland and Supply** (808-826-9144) which specializes in unique toys and games and a variety of fine art supplies—fun for the whole family.

CHING YOUNG VILLAGE ✉ *Kuhio Highway, Hanalei* 🖱 *www.chingyoung village.com* Hanalei's small shopping mall contains a variety store, clothing shops and several other outlets. There's a **Hot Rocket** (808-826-7776) here for beachwear and **On the Road to Hanalei** (808-826-7360) for tapa cloth, woodcarvings, jewelry, quilts and other locally and globally fashioned craft items. **Pedal 'N Paddle** (808-826-9069) provides any equipment you may need for a variety of outdoor activities, from kayaking to camping. The shopping center also has **Blue Kauai Tattoos** (808-826-0114), for obvious reasons.

HANALEI CENTER ✉Kuhio Highway, Hanalei ✆808-826-7677 Made up of seven buildings, six of which are restored historical structures including the Old Hanalei School Building, here you'll find shops, restaurants, a health clinic, a yoga studio, and more.

OLA'S HANALEI ✉Off Kuhio Highway, next to Hanalei Dolphin Restaurant, Hanalei ✆808-826-6937 This store showcases the work of over 100 craftspeople from Hawaii and the mainland.

KAI KANE ✉5-5088 Kuhio Highway, Hanalei ✆808-826-5594 This is an attractively decorated shop featuring original fashions of their own design. It's a great place to shop for aloha wear.

YELLOWFISH TRADING COMPANY ✉Hanalei Center, Kuhio Highway, Hanalei ✆808-826-1227 Here you'll find a marvelous collection of antiques and Hawaiian collectibles.

NIGHTLIFE

LIVING ROOM BAR ✉Princeville Resort, Princeville ✆808-826-9644 In all the world there are few entertainment spots with a view as grand as the Living Room Bar. Overlooking Hanalei Bay, it also features a singer and pianist playing standards and contemporary music nightly.

HAPPY TALK LOUNGE ✉5380 Honoiki Road, Princeville ✆808-826-6522 At Hanalei Bay Resort's lounge, you can enjoy the views of Hanalei Bay and relax with contemporary Hawaiian music on Tuesday and jazz on Sunday.

TAHITI NUI RESTAURANT
✉5-5134 Kuhio Highway, Hanalei ✆808-826-6277 For a tropical drink amid a tropical setting, place your order at "da Nui," the oldest bar in Hawaii. Sit back and enjoy the atmosphere. Live Hawaiian music most nights.

HANALEI DOLPHIN RESTAURANT ✉Kuhio Highway, Hanalei ✆808-826-6113 Try the Hanalei Dolphin, which serves appetizers and cocktails until 9 p.m. and features a full-service bar.

HANALEI GOURMET ✉5-5161 Kuhio Highway, Hanalei ✆808-826-2524 Here you'll find live performances by local artists Wednesday and Friday evenings and Sunday afternoons. Call to see if any extra shows have been scheduled.

SUSHI BLUES GRILL ✉Ching Young Village, Hanalei ✆808-826-9701 There's music seven nights a week at the Sushi Blues Grill. One night there's karaoke, another night there's dancing, and the rest of the time they have jazz and blues. Occasional cover on Friday and Saturday.

BEACHES & PARKS

MOLOAA BEACH

✉ *Take Koolau Road where it branches off Kuhio Highway near the 16-mile marker. Go one and three tenths miles, then turn onto Moloaa Road. Follow this to the end. All roads are paved.*

Nestled in Moloaa Bay, a small inlet surrounded by rolling hills, this beach is relatively secluded, though there are homes nearby. A meandering stream divides the beach into two strands. You'll see a coral reef shadowing the shore. There is good beachcombing at the west end of the strand. Swim with caution. Snorkeling and fishing are good, as is lobster diving. There are no facilities.

LARSEN'S BEACH _____

✉ *It's hard to get to, but more than worth it when you arrive. Take Koolau Road as it branches off Kuhio Highway near the 16-mile marker. Go two and a half miles to a cane road on the right, which switches back in the opposite direction. Get on this road, then take an immediate left onto another dirt road (lined on either side with barbed wire). Don't let the fences scare you—this is a public right of way. Follow it a mile to the end. Hike through the gate and down the road. This leads a half-mile down to the beach, which is on your left. (There is also an access road from Koolau Road that is located one and a fifth miles from the intersection of Koolau Road and Kuhio Highway.)*

This narrow, sandy beach extends seemingly forever through a very secluded area. Rolling hills, covered with small trees and scrub, rim the strand. Glass fishing balls and other collectibles wash ashore regularly, making this a prime beachcombing spot. A protecting reef provides excellent swimming and snorkeling. It is also very popular for seaweed gathering and throw-netting. There are also good fishing spots. Surf is sometimes dangerous here, so exercise caution. There are no facilities.

KAHILI BEACH _____

✉ *From Kuhio Highway, about two miles south of Kilauea town, head east on Wailapa Road for about three-quarters of a mile. Look to your left for the white post that marks the dirt beach access road. Take this road about one mile to the beach; it's rough, but passable, although it can be very muddy during wet weather.*

Tucked away in Kilauea Bay, this beach is bordered by tree-covered hills and a rock quarry. It's a lovely, semi-secluded spot with a lagoon that represents one of Hawaii's most pristine estuaries. Kahili is also a prime beachcombing spot. For a spectacular view of windswept cliffs, follow the short quarry road that climbs steeply from the parking area. Swimming is good when the sea is calm. The favorite surf break is "Rock Quarry," located offshore from the stream. Fishing is rewarding, and the reef at the east end of the beach is also a favored net-throwing spot. There are no facilities.

▲ Unofficial camping. *Note:* The U.S. Fish and Wildlife Service recently acquired ownership of the wetlands around the Kilauea River; an enforcement officer patrols the entire beach for campers and illegal fishing activities.

KAUAPEA BEACH OR SECRET BEACH

✉ *The beach can be seen from Kilauea Lighthouse, but getting there is another matter. From Kuhio Highway just west of Kilauea, turn onto Kalihiwai Road (be sure to get on the eastern section of Kalihiwai Road, near Banana Joe's Tropical Fruit Farm). The road immediately curves to the left; go right onto the first dirt road; proceed three-tenths mile to a parking lot; from here follow the fenceline down into a ravine to Kauapea Beach.*

Inaccessibility means seclusion along this hidden strand. Ideal for birdwatching, swimming and unofficial camping, this half-mile-long beach lies just below Kilauea Lighthouse. Very wide and extremely beautiful, it is popular with nudists and adventurers alike. No facilities spoil this hideaway. Note that this place is notorious for car break-ins, so leave nothing in your vehicle.

▲ Unofficial camping.

KALIHIWAI BEACH

✉ *Take heed—there are two Kalihiwai Roads branching off Kuhio Highway between Kilauea and Kalihiwai. (The washed-out bridge once connected them.) Take the one closest to Lihue. This paved road leads a short distance directly to the beach.*

Bounded by sheer rock wall on one side and a rolling green hill on the other, this semi-secluded beach is crowded with ironwood trees. Behind the ironwoods, the Kalihiwai River has created a large, shallow lagoon across which stretches the skeleton of a bridge, a last grim relic of the devastating 1946 tidal wave. "Kalihiwai" is one of the top expert winter surfing breaks on the North Shore. It's also popular for bodysurfing. Swimmers should exercise caution. Bonefish and threadfin are the most common catches. This is also a great spot for surround-netting of *akule*. No facilities.

ANINI COUNTY BEACH PARK

✉ *Between Kilauea and Hanalei, turn off Kuhio Highway onto the second Kalihiwai Road (the one farthest from Lihue, on the Hanalei side of the Kalihiwai River). Then take Anini Road to the beach.*

Here a grass-covered park fronts a narrow ribbon of sand, while a protecting reef parallels the beach 200 yards offshore. I thought this an ideal place for kids: The ocean is glass smooth and the beachcombing is excellent. As a result, it's very popular and sometimes crowded. Swimming is excellent and very safe. Snorkeling is also topnotch. Surfers' note: There are winter breaks on very shallow reef (left and right slides). This is also a very popular windsurfing site for beginners. The beach has the only boat launch on this side of the island, and anglers take advantage of it to catch bonefish, *papio* and *ulua*. People also torchfish, throw-net, spear octopus and harvest seaweed at Anini. Facilities include a picnic area, restrooms and a shower.

⚑ Pleasant, but lacks privacy. A county permit is required. Tent camping only.

PRINCEVILLE BEACHES

✉ *To reach Sealodge Beach, turn right from Kuhio Highway onto Kahaku Road and into the Princeville complex. Turn right on Kamehameha Road and follow it to the Sealodge condos. Access to Hideaways is located between Puu Poa condos and the Princeville Resort near the end of Kahaku Road.*

There are three beaches directly below the plateau on which the Princeville Resort complex rests. The most popular is **Puu Poa Beach**, a long and wide strand located next to the Princeville Resort and reached through the hotel. It offers good swimming and easy access to the hotel's (expensive) facilities but is often crowded. The other two are pocket beaches. **Sealodge Beach**, reached via a right of way behind Unit A of the Sealodge condominium, is a white-sand beach backdropped by cliffs. Offshore is a surfing break called "Little Grass Shacks." **Hideaways** consists of two mirror-image beaches, one below Pali Ke Kua condos and the other below Puu Poa condos. They are both good spots for swimming and snorkeling and feature a well-known surf break.

HANALEI BAY BEACHES

✉ *In Hanalei just off Kuhio Highway*

A sandy, horseshoe-shaped strip of sand curves the full length of Hanalei Bay. Along this two-mile strand there are four beach parks. **Black Pot Beach Park**, a local gathering place, lies at the eastern end of the bay and is bounded on one side by the Hanalei River and on the other by a 300-foot-long pier (Hanalei Landing). With showers and lifeguard facilities available to beachgoers, it is very popular with watersport enthusiasts of all stripes—swimmers, surfers, bodysurfers, windsurfers, kayakers and anglers. It is located at the eastern end of Weke Road. **Hanalei Pavilion Beach Park**, located along Weke Road between Pilikoa and Aku roads, is a favorite picnic spot. **Waioli Beach Park**, a small facility set in an ironwood grove, is situated near the center of the half-moon-shaped bay. It can be reached from the end of either Hee Road or Amaama Road. Black Pot Beach Park, Hanalei Pavilion Beach Park and Waioli Beach Park all have lifeguards on duty. **Waikoko Beach** is a slender strand paralleled by a shallow reef. Popular with families who come here to swim and snorkel, it lies along Kuhio Highway on the western side of the bay.

There are three major surf breaks here. "Impossible" breaks require a long paddle out from the pier; right slide. "Pine Tree" breaks, off Waioli Beach Park, are in the center of the bay. "Waikoko" breaks are on the shallow reef along the western side of the bay. All are winter breaks. Surfing in Hanalei is serious business, so be careful. Early morning and late afternoon are the best surfing times. The bay is also a popular bodysurfing area. Fish for squirrelfish, rockfish, red bigeye, *oama*, big-eyed scad, *ulua* and *papio*. There is crabbing off Hanalei Landing pier. All beaches have picnic areas, restrooms and marvelous ocean and mountain views.

▲ Tent camping permitted on weekends and holidays at Black Pot Beach Park only. A county permit is required.

LUMAHAI BEACH

✉ *Watch for a vista point near the 5-mile marker on Kuhio Highway. From here, a crooked footpath leads to the beach. The beach can more easily be accessed about a mile down the road, at the Lumahai River bridge. Do not swim at the river mouth because of strong currents.*

Many people know this strand as the Nurse's Beach in the movie *South Pacific*. Snuggled in a cove and surrounded by lush green hills, Lumahai extends for three-fourths of a mile. With white sand against black lava, it's a particularly pretty spot. Swim only when the sea is very calm and exercise extreme caution. During the winter months, it's one of the most treacherous spots on the island. You can try for *papio* and *ulua*. There are no facilities.

TUNNELS (MAKUA) BEACH AND OTHER HAENA BEACHES

✉ *These beaches are located along Kuhio Highway near Wainiha Bay and Kepuhi Point. Tunnels is two-fifths mile east of Maniniholo Dry Cave.*

There are beach access roads all along Kuhio Highway near Haena. Taking any of these dirt roads will shortly lead you to secluded strands. Most popular of all is "Tunnels," a sandy beach with a great offshore reef. According to divers, the name "Tunnels" derives from the underwater arches and tunnels in the reef; but surfers claim it's from the perfect tunnel-shaped waves. Windsurfers consider this one of the best sites on Kauai. You'll also find swimmers, snorkelers, sunbathers and beachcombers here. Kepuhi Point is one of the best fishing spots on the North Shore; Tunnels attracts fishermen with nets and poles. There are no facilities here.

HAENA BEACH PARK
✉ *On Kuhio Highway five miles west of Hanalei*

This grassy park, bounded by the sea on one side and a sheer lava cliff on the other, is right across the street from Maniniholo Dry Cave. It's very popular with young folks and provides good opportunities for beachcombing. There are very strong ocean currents here, which make swimming impossible in winter but fine in summer. Surfing "Cannon's" breaks on a shallow reef in front of Maniniholo Dry Cave is for experts only (right slide). There is excellent surfcasting and torchfishing for red bigeye, squirrelfish, *papio* and *ulua*. Cardinal fish are sometimes caught on the reef at low tide during the full moon. A picnic area, restrooms and a shower are the facilities here.

⛰ It's an attractive campground, sometimes crowded, open to both tents and trailers, and requiring a county permit. There is also camping nearby at the YMCA's **Camp Naue** (808-246-9090).

HAENA STATE PARK AND KEE BEACH
✉*At the end of Kuhio Highway*

🚤 🦞 ⛱ ⛵ At the end of Kuhio Highway, where the Kalalau trail begins, 65.7-acre Haena State Park encompasses a long stretch of white sand, with Kee Beach at its western end. This reef-shrouded beach is one of the most popular on the North Shore. When the surf is gentle, swimming is superb. At such times, this is one of the best snorkeling beaches for beginners, with its protective coral reef brilliantly colored and crowded with tropical fish. In addition, there are 4000-year-old sea caves to explore. The Haena shoreline is also one of the island's best shelling beaches. Surfing is good at "Cannons" and "Bobo's" breaks. This is also a prime windsurfing area. There is good fishing along the reef. There are restrooms and showers.

OUTDOOR ADVENTURES
CAMPING

To visit Kauai without enjoying at least one camping trip is to miss a splendid opportunity. This lovely isle is dotted with county and state parks that feature ideal locations and complete facilities. There are also many hidden beaches where unofficial camping is common.

COUNTY PARKS ✉*4444 Rice Street, Suite 330, Lihue* 📞*808-241-4463* 📠*808-241-4497* Camping at county parks requires a permit. These are issued for seven days. You are allowed to camp a total of 60 days per year at all county parks. Permits cost $3 per person per night; children under 18 are free. Permits can be obtained weekdays at the Division of Parks and Recreation and at the Kilauea, Hauepepe, Kapaa and Kalaheo neighborhood centers on Wednesday mornings, except holidays.

STATE PARK ✉*3060 Eiwa Street #306, Lihue, HI 96766* 📞*808-274-3444* State park permit fees vary by location. They allow camping five consecutive days at each park, and should be requested at least one month in advance for winter, at least a year in advance for summer reservations. These permits are issued by the Department of Land and Natural Resources.

FOREST RESERVES ✉*3060 Eiwa Street, Room 306, Lihue, HI 96766* 📞*808-274-3433* The State Division of Forestry maintains camping areas in the forest reserves. Currently, these are free (but call the Division of Forestry to see about new fees); permits are available at the State Division of Forestry. Camping is limited at each site, and there's a four-night maximum at the Kukui Trail campsites near Waimea Canyon and a three-night limit at the Sugi Grove and Kawaikoi sites in the rainforest area at the top of Waimea Canyon.

Camping elsewhere on the island is officially prohibited. While local people and visitors do sometimes camp on hidden beaches anyway, the authorities crack down on this regularly. By the way, an extra effort should be made to keep these areas clean. One of the best suggestions I've ever heard is to leave your campsite cleaner than when you arrived.

Rainfall is much heavier along the North Shore than along the south coast, but be prepared for showers anywhere. The Kokee area gets chilly, so pack accordingly. And remember, boil or chemically treat all water from Kauai's streams. Water from some of these streams can cause dysentery and leptospirosis, a serious illness with flu-like symptoms, and none of the waterways are certified safe by the Health Department.

FISHING

Both saltwater and freshwater fishing opportunities make Kauai popular with anglers. Intriguing possibilities include overnight adventures off the Niihau coast, fishing for giant tuna and marlin. Keep a sharp eye out on your trip and you may spot spinner dolphins or breaching whales along the way. For deep-sea fishing you'll have to charter a boat, and freshwater angling requires a license, which can be obtained at sportfishing stores.

DIVISION OF AQUATIC RESOURCES ✉ *3060 Eiwa Street, Room 306, Lihue, HI 96766* ☎ *808-274-3344* ✆ *808-274-3448* For information on seasons, licenses and official regulations, check with this agency, which is part of the State Department of Land and Natural Resources.

C-LURE FISHING ✉ *Nawiliwili Harbor, Lihue* ☎ *808-822-5963* This company provides everything you need to fish for marlin, *ahi*, *ono* and *aku* on Kauai's south and east coasts. The new 41-foot boat accommodates up to six people; four-, six- and eight-hour charters are also available.

SNORKELING & SCUBA DIVING

The Garden Isle offers snorkeling and scuba opportunities at such spots as Haena Beach, Tunnels Beach, Moloaa and Koloa Landing. In the Poipu area, Koloa Landing has a number of green sea turtles in its midst and is mainly for experienced snorkelers. The beach in front of Lawai Beach Resort is another popular spot for snorkelers. Even if you have your own equipment, it's a good idea to stop by one of the local dive shops to pick up a map, as well as advice on local conditions.

SNUBA TOURS OF KAUAI ☎ *808-823-8912* ✎ *www.snubakauai.com, snuba@ snubakauai.com* Snuba is for those who want to take snorkeling a step further but may not be quite ready for scuba diving. It's a shallow-water dive system that allows underwater breathing. Groups of up to eight participants are taken out with a guide. They can dive up to 20 feet. Snuba Tours of Kauai leaves from Lawai Beach in Poipu. The personalized instruction extends to the underwater tour; all equipment (and fish food) is provided. No dives on weekends.

Lihue Area

KAUAI BEACH BOYS ✉ *Kalapaki Beach, Lihue* 📞 *808-245-9662, 888-245-1707*
📠 *808-246-9661* 🖥 *www.kauaifun.com* Certified dives, introductory dives and certification classes are available from these "boys." They'll also give you snorkeling tips and a site map when you rent snorkel gear.

Poipu Area

FATHOM FIVE DIVERS ✉ *Poipu Road, Koloa* 📞 *808-742-6991* 🖥 *www.fathom five.com* To familiarize yourself with the area's treasures you may want to begin with a group tour. This outfit rents diving and snorkeling equipment and takes groups, limited to a maximum of six people to ensure personal attention, to hot spots such as Sheraton Caverns and Brennecke's Ledge. Divers often spot fish unique to Kauai such as bandit angel fish, long-nosed hawkfish and boarfish. Half-day dives leave every morning and afternoon.

SEASPORT DIVERS ✉ *2827 Poipu Road, Poipu* 📞 *808-742-9303* 🖥 *www.sea sportdivers.com* Here you can rent snorkeling and scuba equipment. They also offer lessons, tours, and day and night dives.

Wailua–Kapaa Area

SNORKEL BOB'S KAUAI ✉ *4-734 Kuhio Highway, Kapaa* 📞 *808-823-9433* 🖥 *www.snorkelbob.com* Snorkel Bob's rents snorkeling equipment returnable at branches on all the other islands. The shop puts together a tip sheet of the best current snorkel spots (factoring in the weather, tides and so forth).

North Shore

HANALEI SURF COMPANY ✉ *5-5161 Kuhio Highway, Hanalei* 📞 *808-826-9000* 🖥 *www.hanaleisurf.com* This is a good place for snorkeling rentals. Also, check out their supply of boogieboards, wet suits and surfboards.

PEDAL 'N PADDLE ✉ *Ching Young Village, Hanalei* 📞 *808-826-9069* Here you'll find snorkels, masks and fins as well as single and double kayaks for rent.

SURFING & WINDSURFING

Kauai surfers can lead you to such breaks as "Tunnels," "Donkey Beach," "Pakala," "P.K.s," "Centers" or "Acid Drops." You might want to consult with a local surf shop or the internet about what the swells look like that day and which locales are appropriate for your skill level (some are mellow, some are awesome). Surfing on Kauai means summer breaks in the south and winter breaks in the north. For windsurfers, Anini Beach is a good place to start; Kalapaki Beach offers a more challenging ride; and for you advanced windsurfers, "Tunnels" is a spectacular place to jibe and plane.

Poipu Area

PROGRESSIVE EXPRESSIONS ✉ *5420 Koloa Road, Koloa* 📞 *808-742-6041* Surfers head for the Poipu coastline. Progressive Expressions not only sells and rents surfboards, they make their own. Bodyboards and swim fins are also available.

NUKAUMOI BEACH AND SURF CENTER ✉Next to Brennecke's Beach Broiler, Poipu ☏808-742-8019 Surfing champion Margo Oberg's surf center offers beginner's surfing lessons on Poipu Beach. Boogieboards, snorkel gear and accessories are for rent.

KAUAI SURF SCHOOL ✉Poipu ☏808-332-7411 ✐www.kauaisurfschool.com If you're new to surfing, or just want a refresher course, sign up for a lesson here. They give two-hour private and group lessons, mainly aimed at beginners, although intermediate and advanced classes are also available. Groups are limited to four per instructor so that everyone receives personalized instruction.

Wailua–Kapaa Area
KAUAI WATER SKI, SURF AND KAYAK COMPANY ✉4-356 Kuhio Highway, Wailua ☏808-822-3574 Here they rent surfboards and offer all levels of lessons, usually conducted on Wailua Beach.

North Shore
HANALEI SURF COMPANY ✉5-5161 Kuhio Highway, Hanalei ☏808-826-9000 ✐www.hanaleisurf.com Both fiberglass and soft surfboards, boogieboards and swim fins can be rented here.

WINDSURF KAUAI ☏808-828-6838 Rentals and beginner-to-expert windsurfing lessons are offered at this outfit. The North Shore's Anini Beach, with its reef-protected lagoon, is often the setting for the lessons.

BOAT TOURS

The trade winds ensure excellent sailing in Kauai waters. From a catamaran trip along the southern shore to a thrilling trip along the rugged Na Pali Coast, these waters are ideal for cruising. Many of the cruises stop at isolated beaches and also offer excellent snorkeling opportunities.

Lihue Area
KAUAI BEACH BOYS ✉Kalapaki Beach, Lihue ☏808-245-9662, 888-245-1707 ✆808-246-9661 ✐www.kauaifun.com Here you'll find sailboat rentals. With exclusive boating rights to Kalapaki Bay, they conduct one-hour rides of the area; personalized tours will take you to remote destinations of your choice. All levels of sailing lessons are offered.

Waimea Area
CAPTAIN ANDY'S SAILING ADVENTURES ✉Port Allen ☏808-335-6833 For south coast sailing tours on the 55-foot-long *Spirit of Kauai* or the *Akialoa* catamaran, weigh anchor with Captain Andy's. Along the way, you may spot humpback whales or giant green sea turtles. Sunset sails are among the intriguing possibilities.

HOLOHOLO CHARTERS ✉Port Allen Boat Harbor ☏808-335-0815, 800-848-6130 ✐www.sail-kauai.com This charter service runs 7.5-hour snorkel sails to the Na Pali Coast. 3.5-hour sunset sails are also available.

NA PALI RIDERS ✉P.O. Box 1082, Kalaheo, HI 96741 ☎808-742-6331 ✐www. napaliriders.com Na Pali Riders has a rafting trip that explores the entire Na Pali Coast including the sea caves, and offers snorkeling at the Nualolo Kai reef. Lunch and equipment included.

LIKO KAUAI CRUISES ✉9875 Waimea Road, Waimea 888-732-5456 ✐www. liko-kauai.com This top-notch, family-run operation offers snorkeling, whale watching and sunset tours on a 49-foot power catamaran. The captain is Liko Hookano, a Kauai-born Hawaiian who knows the Na Pali Coast like his own backyard, which it is.

CAPTAIN ANDY'S ✉Port Allen ☎808-335-2719, 800-535-0830 ✐www.napali. com, fun@capt-andys.com Here you can take rafting expeditions along the Na Pali Coast. Five-and-a-half-hour trips include visits to sea caves, beautiful reefs and an ancient fishing village. All trips include some snorkeling, and equipment is provided. Sunset cruises are offered in the summertime, while whale watching along the north shore in the winter months is also featured.

KAUAI SEA TOURS ✉Port Allen ☎808-335-5309, 800-733-7997 ✐www.kauai seatours.net, seatour@aloha.net See the Na Pali Coast on zodiac and catamaran tours. Full-day snorkeling tours take you to a landing on a secluded beach for first-rate snorkeling during the summer, while winter and spring whale-watching tours are led by naturalists. Or choose the sunset dinner cruise (with or without snorkeling).

NA PALI EXPLORER ✉9935 Kaumualii Highway, Waimea ☎808-338-9999, 877-335-9909 ℻808-338-0742 ✐www.napali-explorer.com Expect more than a cruise along the extraordinary Kauai coastline when you board the Explorer. In addition to providing descriptions of flora, fauna and Hawaiian culture that make the experience educational, the crew is always on the lookout for dolphins and sea turtles. They'll take you snorkeling amid the region's colorful coral reefs. You can't miss with one of their trips. These five-hour expeditions run year-round; snorkeling gear, light snacks and deli-style lunch are provided.

KAYAKING

Kayaking is one of Kauai's fastest growing water sports. And why not? Choose from verdant river valleys or, if you like, go down to the sea again.

Lihue

ISLAND ADVENTURES ✉Nawiliwili Small Boat Harbor, Lihue ☎808-245-9662 ℻808-246-9661 ✐www.kauaifun.com, info@kauaifun.com Board your kayak and head down the Huleia River, home to the legendary Menehune Fishpond. This eco-friendly kayaking company, escorts you to the heart of the Huleia National Wildlife Refuge. A short hike brings you to two waterfalls. A picnic lunch overlooking Huleia Valley wraps up the day. A very enjoyable, laidback Hawaiian adventure.

KAUAI BEACH BOYS ✉Kalapaki Beach, Lihue ☎808-245-9662, 888-245-1707 ℻808-246-9661 ✐www.kauaifun.com Single or double kayaks are available here, along with paddle and boogie boards. They also provide outrigger canoe rides.

Poipu Area

OUTFITTERS KAUAI ✉2827-A Poipu Road, Koloa ✆808-742-9667, 888-742-9887 ☎808-742-8842 🖥www.outfitterskauai.com, info@outfitterskauai.com Here they offer paddling around Poipu during the winter months, and North Shore trips in the summer. Bring your snorkel gear along, as there will be time to explore underwater as well.

Wailua–Kapaa Area

KAYAK KAUAI ✉Kapaa and Hanalei ✆808-826-9844, 800-437-3507 ☎808-826-7378 🖥www.kayakkauai.com, info@kayakkauai.com Kayak Kauai rents kayaks and runs snorkel trips. They also sponsor river tours of waterfalls on the Wailua River, as well as all-day tours of the Na Pali Coast from May to September. That trip includes a lunch break at the ruins of an ancient Hawaiian fishing village.

KAYAK WAILUA ✆808-822-3388 🖥www.kayakwailua.com, kayak@kayakwailua.com Here you can take guided adventures: they'll supply equipment and guide you two and a half miles up Wailua River. At Kamokila Hawaiian village along the way, you can secure your boats and continue on foot where you'll discover canyons, waterfalls, and a swimming hole where ancient Hawaiian kings and high chiefs once bathed. Closed on Sunday.

North Shore

KAYAK HANALEI ✉Ching Yong Shopping Center, Kuhio Highway, Hanalei ✆808-826-1881 🖥www.kayakhanalei.com, a1kayak@aloha.net Take a relaxing tour of the river, stopping to snorkel, eat and laze. Or, if you prefer, they'll introduce you to the rich history of Kauai on a narrated tour. All equipment is provided.

PRINCEVILLE RANCH ADVENTURES ✉Princeville ✆808-826-7669, 888-955-7669 🖥www.adventureskauai.com Here you'll find kayaking, as well as other outdoor activities. Children over five are welcome.

WATERSKIING

If you've ever wondered what it feels like to waterski through paradise, why not head for the town of Wailua. The serene Wailua River is the perfect place to glide through verdant canyons graced by waterfalls. You can practice your slalom technique, try out a pair of trick skis or enjoy yourself on the hydroslide.

KAUAI WATERSKI AND SURF COMPANY ✉4-356 Kuhio Highway, Wailua ✆808-822-3574 🖥surfski@aloha.net Here they offer trips for intermediate to advanced waterskiers. Hot doggers will want to try out the competition slalom course; hour-long runs or more can be arranged.

HANG GLIDING

BIRDS IN PARADISE ✆808-822-5309 🖥www.birdsinparadise.com, birds@birdsinparadise.com What better way to see Kauai than to soar on high with the birds? Okay, so you don't have wings. How about trying a motorized hang glider, accompanied by a certified flight instructor? Be assured, you'll get a briefing on the basics of flying in a "weight-shift aircraft," and you will always be in communication with the pilot through an intercom on your helmet.

RIDING STABLES

From scenic coastal trail rides to journeys up North Shore valleys, Kauai is an equestrian's delight.

CJM COUNTRY STABLES ✉*At the end of Poipu Road* ☎*808-742-6096* *808-742-6015* In the Poipu area, try these stables. Possibilities include two-hour rides along the south shore to Mahaulepu and Haupu beaches. They also offer three-hour rides and cover some of the best beaches in the Poipu area. You may be tempted to return later on foot to explore these hidden spots. (No rides on Sunday.)

PRINCEVILLE RANCH STABLES ✉*Kuhio Highway, Princeville* ☎*808-826-6777* *www.princevilleranch.com* In the Hanalei area, contact these stables for three- or four-hour picnic rides to waterfalls (includes a moderately strenuous hike), as well as 90-minute country rides to the bluff overlooking Anini Reef. Closed Sunday.

GOLF

Some of the best golfing in Hawaii is found on the Garden Isle. In addition to outstanding resort courses at Princeville, the Kauai Marriott and the Hyatt Regency Kauai, you can enjoy several excellent public courses. Beautifully situated with dramatic ocean and mountain backdrops, all of these links will make your game a pleasure.

Lihue Area
KIELE COURSE AND THE MOKIHANA COURSE ✉*Adjacent to the Kauai Marriott, Nawiliwili* ☎*808-241-6000, 800-634-6400* Both created by Jack Nicklaus, these are two of the island's best-known golfing spots. Both courses have 18 holes, full equipment rental, spectacular ocean views, and guava and mango forests.

Poipu Area
POIPU BAY RESORT GOLF COURSE ✉*2250 Ainako Street, Koloa* ☎*808-858-6300* Next door to the Hyatt Regency Kauai is this Robert Trent Jones Jr.–designed, 18-hole course. Full equipment rental is available at this course that was specifically designed to provide an ocean view from each hole.

Waimea Area
KUKUIOLONO GOLF COURSE ✉*854 Puu Road, Kalaheo* ☎*808-332-9151* On the south side of the island, this semiprivate course in Kalaheo is also popular. It's a nine-hole course that offers views of the ocean and the Kalaheo mountains.

Wailua–Kapaa Area

WAILUA GOLF COURSE ✉Wailua ☎808-241-6666 The golfing public is well served at this 18-hole, oceanfront golf course, and the low green fees make this course a best buy.

North Shore

PRINCEVILLE MAKAI GOLF COURSE ✉Princeville ☎808-826-3580 Designed by Robert Trent Jones is this 27-hole course. Full equipment rental is available and the scenery is beautiful.

PRINCEVILLE GOLF CLUB ✉428 Kuhio Highway, Princeville ☎808-826-5000 A demanding 18-hole course next door to the Princeville Makai, this club also has a driving range to help sharpen your skills.

BIKING

There are no bikeways on Kauai and most roads have very narrow shoulders, but the Garden Isle is still the most popular island in the chain for bicycling. Roads are good and, except for the steep 20-mile climb along Waimea Canyon, the terrain is either flat or gently rolling. The spectacular scenery and network of public parks make this a cyclist's dream.

One local spot for biking is along **Route 56**. This is a narrow road with one-lane bridges that keep tour buses and large trucks out of the area, though car traffic can be quite heavy.

POWERLINE TRAIL ✉To get to the trailhead, turn inland at the corner of Princeville stables and continue beyond the row of houses. For hearty mountain bikers, this trail (15 miles) is an arduous but rewarding challenge. It follows a powerline that connects the North Shore with the east side of Kauai. The trail takes you into the interior of the island, offering views of Mt. Waialeale, one of the wettest spots on earth. Be sure to bring a U.S. Survey map (available at local camping stores), water and food with you. This journey is for experienced mountain bikers who are in the best of shape.

Bike Rentals

OUTFITTERS KAUAI ✉2827-A Poipu Road, Poipu ☎808-742-9667 ⌨www.out fitterskauai.com Here they rent hybrid, full-suspension and road bikes as well as children's mountain bikes and baby seats.

PEDAL 'N PADDLE ✉Ching Young Village ☎808-826-9069 In Hanalei, come here to rent beach cruisers. Popular destinations from here include Princeville and the lagoon at Kee Beach.

Bike Repairs

BICYCLE JOHN'S ✉3215 Kuhio Highway, Lihue ☎808-245-7579 In Lihue, John's offers a full-service sales and repair shop. Closed Sunday.

OUTFITTERS KAUAI ✉*Poipu Plaza, 2827A Poipu Road, Poipu* ☎*808-742-9667,*
888-742-9887 ✐*www.outfitterskauai.com, info@outfitterskauai.com* Here you can
take an afternoon bike tour that stops along the way for photo ops and
interesting lectures on the history and folklore of the area. The best part
is that they'll bring you up the hill in a van.

HIKING

Hiking is among the finest, and certainly least expensive, ways of touring the Garden Isle. Kauai's trails are concentrated in the Na Pali Coast
and Waimea Canyon–Kokee regions, with a few others near the Wailua
River. Most are well maintained and carefully charted. For further information, contact the **State Department of Land and Natural
Resources** (808-274-3433; www.hawaiitrails.org).

All distances listed for hiking trails are one way unless otherwise noted.

KAUAI NATURE TOURS ✉*Koloa* ☎*808-742-8305, 888-233-8365* ✐*www.*
kauainaturetours.com, teok@aloha.net This is a company that encourages "effective co-existence of earth's environment and its human inhabitants." To this end, all tours are led by local scientists and provide a detailed look into the natural wonders of Hawaii. The "Waimea Canyon
Explorer" tour explores Kauai's geologic past. The "Mahaulepu Coast"
hike shows you Kauai's limestone ledges and discusses the history of
the coastline. This is a perfect way to learn to "take only pictures, leave
only footprints."

Wailua River

While none of these hikes actually follow the Wailua, all begin near
Route 580, which parallels the river.

Nounou Mountain Trail—East Side (1.75 miles) begins off Haleilio Road
at the parking lot in the Wailua Houselots and climbs 1250 feet to the
Sleeping Giant's head at Mount Nounou summit. This trail is strenuous.

Nounou Mountain Trail—West Side (1.5 miles) begins off Route 581
and ascends with moderate difficulty 1000 feet to join the East Side trail.

Keahua Arboretum Trail (0.5 mile) begins two miles past the
University of Hawaii Wailua Experiment Station on Route 580. This
easy nature trail is lined with foreign plants.

Kuilau Ridge Trail (2.1 miles) begins on Route 580 near the Keahua
Arboretum. This moderate, scenic hike goes past several vista points
and picnic areas.

Waimea Canyon-Kokee

Kokee State Park has about 45 miles of hiking trails through rugged,
beautiful country. Along the mountain paths listed here, you'll discover
some of the finest hiking in all Hawaii.

Alakai Swamp Trail (3.5 miles) passes through bogs and scrub rainforests to the Kilohana Lookout. This moderate once-muddy trail is

now partially covered with boardwalks. It begins off Mohihi (Camp 10) Road, but is also accessible by the Pihea Trail.

Awaawapuhi Trail (3.1 miles) starts on Route 550 midway between Kokee Museum and Kalalau Lookout. This physically challenging trail leads through a forest to a vista at 2500-feet elevation that overlooks sheer cliffs and the ocean. The trail then connects with Nualolo Trail for a 13-mile loop.

Berry Flat Trail (0.6 mile) and **Puu Ka Ohelo Trail** (0.5 mile) combine off Mohihi (Camp 10) Road to form an easy loop that passes an interesting assortment of trees, including California redwood, *ohia*, *sugi* pine and *koa*.

Black Pipe Trail (0.5 mile) links Canyon Trail with Halemanu Road. It follows a cliff past stands of the rare *iliau* plant, a relative of Maui's famous silversword.

Canyon Trail (1.4 miles) forks off Cliff Trail and follows a relatively easy path around Waimea Canyon's northern rim to a vista sweeping down the canyon to the sea.

Cliff Trail (0.1 mile) begins at the end of the right fork of Halemanu Road and offers a pleasant walk to a viewpoint above Waimea Canyon. Feral goats are often spotted.

Ditch Trail (3.5 miles) runs from Mohihi Road at one end to Waininiua Road at the other. It's a moderate trail with spectacular views of forest areas and the Poomau River.

Halemanu-Kokee Trail (1.2 miles) sets out from the old ranger station. Birdwatchers should especially enjoy this easy jaunt.

Iliau Nature Loop (0.3 mile roundtrip) starts along Route 550 on a short course past 20 local plant species, including the *iliau*, endemic only to the Garden Isle. This easy trail offers good views of both Waimea Canyon and Waialae Falls.

Kalupuhi Trail (2.0 miles) begins at Route 550 en route to a plum grove. The plums are in season every other year. In a good year, you can enjoy both plums and a pleasant hike.

Kawaikoi Stream Trail (1.8 miles roundtrip), an easy loop trail, starts on Mohihi (Camp 10) Road across from Sugi Grove and follows near the stream through a manmade forest.

Koaie Canyon Trail (3 miles) branches off the Waimea Canyon trail near Poo Kaeha. It's a moderate hike that crosses the Waimea River and passes ancient terraces and rock walls en route to Lonomea camp, a wilderness campsite. Here you'll find a shelter and a stream chock-full of swimming holes.

Kumuwela Trail (1 mile) begins off Mohihi (Camp 10) Road and passes through a fern-choked gulch. Good for birdwatchers.

Nature Trail (0.1 mile) begins behind the Kokee Museum and passes through a *koa* forest.

Nualolo Trail (3.8 miles) starts near Park Headquarters. Along the strenuous path you'll be able to see Nualolo Valley on the Na Pali Coast.

Pihea Trail (3.8 miles) offers excellent views of Kalalau Valley and the Alakai Swamp. This moderate trail also features a variety of birds and plant life. It begins at Puuokila Lookout.

Poomau Canyon Lookout Trail (0.3 mile) heads through a stand of Japanese *sugi* trees and a native rainforest. It begins from Mohihi (Camp 10) Road and ends at a vista overlooking Poomau and Waimea Canyons.

Waimea Canyon Trail (11.5 miles) can be reached from the Kukui Trail. Its very challenging path follows the Waimea River through the center of the canyon.

Waininiua Trail (0.6 mile) leads from the unpaved Kumuwela Road through a forest where ginger grows.

North Shore
The Powerline Trail (11.2 miles) is a strenuous hike through Kauai's interior. Beginning in Princeville, it follows the Hanalei River, offering views of countless waterfalls and Mt. Waialeale, ending on the east side of the island near Kapaa. If you're feeling less adventurous, hike in a few miles and enjoy the waterfalls and lush vegetation before turning back the way you came. To get to the trailhead, turn inland at the corner of Princeville stables and continue beyond the row of houses.

Kauai's premier hiking trail is, of course, the **Kalalau Trail**. It's one of the finest treks in all the islands and follows an 11-mile trail along the rugged Na Pali Coast. Streams and mountain pools along the path provide refreshing swimming holes. Wild orchids, guavas, kukui nuts, mangos and mountain apples grow in abundance. (You will need a permit to camp along this trail.) See page 486 for more information.

TRANSPORTATION

AIR

LIHUE AIRPORT ☎ *808-246-1400* Visiting Kauai means flying to this centrally located airport. United Airlines offers direct service from Los Angeles and San Francisco and American Airlines offers a non-stop, daily flight from Los Angeles. SunTrips offers a charter from Oakland International Airport (OAK) once a week.

Otherwise you need to fly to Honolulu (see Chapter One, Transportation) and take either Aloha Airlines, Hawaiian, go! or Island Air. **Princeville Airport** is on the North Shore and just 10 minutes from Hanalei but is only accessible by private plane.

Lihue Airport has a restaurant, a cocktail lounge, lockers, a newsstand, a gift shop and a flower shop. What you won't find are buses, far more useful to most travelers than cocktails and flowers. Transportation (it's two miles into town) requires reserving a seat on a shuttle, renting a car, hailing a cab, hitching or hoofing. Cabs generally charge about $6 to Lihue.

CAR RENTALS

Aross the street from the terminal at Lihue Airport you'll find a series of booths containing car-rental firms. These include **Alamo Rent A Car** (808-246-0645, 800-327-9633), **Avis Rent A Car** (808-245-3512, 800-331-1212), **Budget Rent A Car** (808-245-9031), **Dollar Rent A Car** (800-800-4000) and **National Car Rental** (808-245-5636, 800-227-7368).

JEEP RENTALS

BUDGET RENT A CAR ✉Lihue Airport ✆800-527-0700 Here you can rent four-wheel drives. However, most Kauai roads, including cane roads, are accessible by car so you probably won't need a jeep.

PUBLIC TRANSIT

KAUAI BUS ✆808-241-6410 This shuttle travels between Lihue and Hanalei seven times a day from 6:45 a.m. to 6 p.m. It stops at about a dozen places, including two major shopping centers.

JEEP TOURS

ALOHA KAUAI TOURS ✆800-452-1113 ✎www.alohakauaitours.com Take a half-day, off-road four-wheel-drive tours into the mountains of Kokee State Park and other areas of the island. Bring comfortable walking shoes and binoculars, as the tours often include a hike.

AERIAL TOURS

Whether you choose a whirlybird's-eye view from a helicopter or prefer the serenity of a glider, aerial sightseeing is one of Kauai's great thrills. From simple flyovers to thrilling acrobatic flights, you'll gain a unique perspective on the island's canyons and rainforests, hidden beaches and tropical retreats.

ISLAND HELICOPTERS ✉Lihue Airport ✆808-245-8588, 800-829-5999 Here they offer a one-hour tour of all the major scenic areas of the island, from the Na Pali Coast to the Mount Waialeale Crater.

HELI USA ✆808-826-6591, 866-936-1234 ✎www.heliusa.com Based in Princeville Airport, these tours feature unique glimpses of scenic treasures like Waialeale, the Na Pali Coast and Waimea Canyon.

TROPICAL BIPLANES ✉Lihue Airport ✆808-246-9123 If you want an airplane tour, here they will take you up in a bi-plane for a thrilling tour of the island.

NIIHAU HELICOPTERS ✉Kaumualii Highway ✆808-335-3500, 877-441-3500 Niihau specializes in trips to the Forbidden Isle. Bring your own snorkeling equipment because the twin-engine helicopter will land on one of the island's remote beaches, ideal for exploring its pristine underwater environment. Book tours at least a week in advance. Closed Sunday.

INDEX

Abbreviations used for island names are (H) Hawaii, (K) Kauai, (L) Lanai, (M) Maui, (Mo) Molokai and (Oa) Oahu.

INDEX

HOSTELS

LODGING SERVICES

DINING INDEX

h DINING INDEX

530 HIDDEN GUIDES

Adventure travel or a relaxing vacation?—"Hidden" guidebooks are the only travel books in the business to provide detailed information on both. Aimed at environmentally aware travelers, our motto is "Where Vacations Meet Adventures." These books combine details on unique hotels, restaurants and sightseeing with information on camping, sports and hiking for the outdoor enthusiast.

PARADISE FAMILY GUIDES

Ideal for families traveling with kids of any age—toddlers to teenagers—Paradise Family Guides offer a blend of travel information unlike any other guides to the Hawaiian islands. With vacation ideas and tropical adventures that are sure to satisfy both action-hungry youngsters and relaxation-seeking parents, these guides meet the specific needs of each and every family member.

Ulysses Press books are available at bookstores everywhere. If any of the following titles are unavailable at your local bookstore, ask the bookseller to order them.

You can also order books directly from Ulysses Press
P.O. Box 3440, Berkeley, CA 94703
800-377-2542 or 510-601-8301
fax: 510-601-8307
www.ulyssespress.com
e-mail: ulysses@ulyssespress.com

HIDDEN GUIDEBOOKS

____ Hidden Arizona, $18.95
____ Hidden Bahamas, $14.95
____ Hidden Baja, $15.95
____ Hidden Belize, $15.95
____ Hidden Big Island of Hawaii, $14.95
____ Hidden Boston & Cape Cod, $14.95
____ Hidden British Columbia, $18.95
____ Hidden Cancún & the Yucatán, $16.95
____ Hidden Carolinas, $17.95
____ Hidden Coast of California, $19.95
____ Hidden Colorado, $15.95
____ Hidden Disneyland, $13.95
____ Hidden Florida, $19.95
____ Hidden Florida Keys & Everglades, $15.95
____ Hidden Georgia, $16.95
____ Hidden Guatemala, $16.95
____ Hidden Hawaii, $19.95
____ Hidden Idaho, $14.95
____ Hidden Kauai, $13.95
____ Hidden Los Angeles, $15.95
____ Hidden Maui, $14.95

____ Hidden Miami, $14.95
____ Hidden Montana, $15.95
____ Hidden New England, $19.95
____ Hidden New Mexico, $15.95
____ Hidden New Orleans, $14.95
____ Hidden Oahu, $14.95
____ Hidden Oregon, $15.95
____ Hidden Pacific Northwest, $19.95
____ Hidden San Diego, $14.95
____ Hidden Salt Lake City, $14.95
____ Hidden San Francisco & Northern California, $19.95
____ Hidden Seattle, $14.95
____ Hidden Southern California, $19.95
____ Hidden Southwest, $19.95
____ Hidden Tahiti, $18.95
____ Hidden Tennessee, $16.95
____ Hidden Utah, $16.95
____ Hidden Walt Disney World, $13.95
____ Hidden Washington, $15.95
____ Hidden Wine Country, $14.95
____ Hidden Wyoming, $15.95

PARADISE FAMILY GUIDES

____ Paradise Family Guides: Kaua'i, $16.95
____ Paradise Family Guides: Maui, $16.95

____ Paradise Family Guides: Big Island of Hawai'i, $16.95

Mark the book(s) you're ordering and enter the total cost here ⇨ [   ]

California residents add 8.25% sales tax here ⇨ [   ]

Shipping, check box for your preferred method and enter cost here ⇨ [   ]

❑ Book Rate   FREE! FREE! FREE!

❑ Priority Mail/UPS Ground   cost of postage

❑ UPS Overnight or 2-Day Air   cost of postage

[   ]

Billing, enter total amount due here and check method of payment ⇨

❑ Check   ❑ Money Order

❑ Visa/MasterCard _____ Exp. Date_____

Name_____ Phone _____
Address_____
City_____ State_____ Zip _____

MONEY-BACK GUARANTEE ON DIRECT ORDERS PLACED THROUGH ULYSSES PRESS.

ABOUT THE AUTHOR

RAY RIEGERT is the author of eight travel books, including *Hidden San Francisco & Northern California*. His most popular work, *Hidden Hawaii*, won the coveted Lowell Thomas Travel Journalism Award for Best Guidebook as well a similar award from the Hawaii Visitors Bureau. In addition to his role as publisher of Ulysses Press, he has written for the *Chicago Tribune, Saturday Evening Post, San Francisco Chronicle* and *Travel & Leisure*. A member of the Society of American Travel Writers, he lives in the San Francisco Bay area with his wife, co-publisher Leslie Henriques.

ABOUT THE PHOTOGRAPHER

ROBERT HOLMES, born in England, first visited the U.S. in 1976 at the invitation of Ansel Adams. Since moving to the United States to live in 1979, his photographs have appeared in virtually every major travel magazine including *National Geographic, GEO, Islands* and *Travel & Leisure*. In addition to his magazine credits, he has illustrated 40 books and authored 4. He is the first photographer to have twice received the Travel Photographer of the Year award. He lives in Mill Valley, California, with his two daughters.